The Ordeal of Otto Otepka

WILLIAM J. GILL

THE ORDEAL OF
OTTO OTEPKA

ARLINGTON HOUSE   NEW ROCHELLE, N. Y.

For Brian and Christopher

Contents

BOOK I

BOOK II

BOOK III

CONTENTS

Preface

THE CASE OF OTTO OTEPKA IS WITHOUT PARALLEL IN AMERICAN HIStory. Echoes of the Billy Mitchell trial haunt the record, and indeed there is a disquieting resemblance between General Mitchell's futile effort to alert the nation to impending danger before World War II and Otepka's muted warnings in the 1960s. Mitchell, however, was never placed under criminal charges and certainly no one ever accused him of violating the Espionage Act.

One must flash back to the *fin de siècle* in France and the ordeal of Alfred Dreyfus to find an affair even roughly comparable in any of the Western democracies. A few columnists have, in fact, fleetingly drawn this analogy between Otepka and Dreyfus. Yet despite striking similarities in what these two men were subjected to by the ruling elite of their respective governments, there remain essential differences between both the historical setting and the separate circumstances which confronted each of them.

Of the two, the Otepka case is easily the more fateful for the ultimate destiny of man. There were very ugly implications in *l'affaire Dreyfus*. But except in the context of the old behavioral problem of man's ancient inhumanity to man, the Dreyfus case did not encompass the central question of man's ultimate survival on this planet. The Otepka case does.

When Captain Dreyfus, an artillery officer on the French General Staff, was convicted, and later exonerated, of selling military secrets to Imperial Germany, the Curies were still pondering the mysterious properties of radium in their rudimentary Paris laboratory. By 1963 when Otto Otepka, once the working chief of the Department of State's personnel security program, was cast into exile and threatened with prosecution under the Espionage Act, the mysteries of radioactivity had long since been solved.

Latter day disciples of the Curies had brought forth The Bomb, which in turn spawned a frightening family of ever more sophisticated and terrifying nuclear devices for mass destruction. Both Otepka and the men who worked so diligently for his removal from the State Department lived oppressively under the mushrooming shadow of Armageddon. By

1

PREFACE

comparison, the Curie-Dreyfus era, whatever it portended for future scientific development and human misbehavior, was an age of civilized innocence.

Nonetheless, the similarities persist. Both Otepka and Dreyfus were singled out for special treatment by their governments. Both were to be transfigured into lasting object lessons that would strike fear into the souls of men who were not in total agreement with the people who ran those governments. Both were framed on false charges. Both were innocent. Both struggled tenaciously against injustice. Both suffered indignities that would have broken most men. Both withstood their ordeals admirably—Dreyfus with fierce and passionate protest, Otepka with quiet stoicism and unshakeable determination.

There the analogy ends.

The Dreyfus case was fought out on an open stage with the full bright glare of publicity feverishly driving it into the dimmest recesses of the public conscience. The press of the world, stirred by Emile Zola and Anatole France, rallied to the Captain's defense. For five years, from Dreyfus' arrest in the autumn of 1894 to his ultimate exoneration at the second court martial at Rennes in the summer of 1899, the issue of his innocence or guilt was paraded before the inhabitants of six continents.

Reporter William Harding of the Associated Press did not exaggerate when he wrote: "The name of this Franco-Hebrew captain has been spoken, and his fate discussed by the trappers of the Yenisei, by the Peruvian silver miners, by the alcaldes of Guatemala, by the priests of Tibet, and by the gamblers of Monte Carlo."[1] The Dreyfus case was, in short, a *cause célèbre*—one which school children still review in their history texts today.

By contrast, the ordeal of Otto Otepka was unfolded behind the heavy black velvet curtain of managed news. Only occasionally has the curtain parted to permit a passing glimpse of the man. It has never been kept open long enough for the press or the public to view the vital issues involved.

No Zola or Clemenceau or Leon Blum has rushed to Otepka's defense. Only a handful of newsmen among the hundreds in the Washington press corps even troubled to determine what the Otepka case was all about. Regrettably, the rest failed to follow their lead in digging beneath the surface.

This is all the more odd when one reflects on the *dramatis personae*. Virtually every major figure who played a heavy role in formulating

United States foreign policy in the 1960's was involved in one way or another with the Otepka business—Presidents Kennedy and Johnson, Dean Rusk, Robert Kennedy, Walt Whitman Rostow, George Ball, Nicholas Katzenbach, Harlan Cleveland. Name them, and there they are.

At times it was difficult to discern the depth or extent of their involvement. The news had been managed well, and on that count the press can plead ignorance. But there *were* ways of getting behind the executive branch's coverup curtain, as Clark Mollenhoff, Willard Edwards, David Sentner, Edward O'Brien and the handful of other reporters demonstrated and as a few columnists like Henry J. Taylor, Richard Wilson, Holmes Alexander, Paul Scott and Edith Kermit Roosevelt also proved.

Mollenhoff, the Pulitzer Prize-winning correspondent of the Cowles newspapers in Minneapolis and Des Moines, stated the case bluntly in an article for the *Nieman Reports,* published by Harvard's Nieman Fellowship alumni council.

"More outrageous than the State Department's action has been the press performance," Mollenhoff observed. "The Otepka case involved the effectiveness of the whole (State) Department security program. It involves the question of the integrity of many high level officials in a Department entrusted with vital foreign policy decisions. Yet, with only a few exceptions, the press has ignored this major investigation or has given it coverage warped by State Department distortions."[2]

Between November 1961 when Otepka first testified in secret session before the Senate Internal Security Subcommittee and the fall of 1968 when the Civil Service Commission again upheld Secretary of State Rusk's final decision, only one mass circulation magazine had printed a major article on Otepka—from which, incidentally, the title of this book is taken.[3] That story, which this author initiated, was published by the *Reader's Digest* in August 1965. The State Department's reaction was typical of its entire handling of the Otepka matter. It responded to all inquiries with a form letter claiming that Otepka was under "criminal charges." To the average recipient of the letter, this hinted darkly of something tantamount to treason. Crimes within the Department of State are inevitably assigned such a connotation by the public.

Dean Rusk knew better, of course. So did a whole regiment of his subordinates. They were fully aware that the ten "criminal charges" the department had lodged against Otepka in September 1963 had no more substance than an ephemeral dream concocted in an opium pipe. These charges sprang, in point of fact, from the deliberate frame-up of Otepka many of these same department officials had participated in or countenanced.

Unfortunately, the Otepka case focused from the outset on his cooperation with the Senate Internal Security Subcommittee. Even those few reporters who attempted to bring the business under closer public scrutiny almost invariably presented it in the framework of the traditional struggle between the executive and legislative branches of the United States government. Involved was the right of Congress to know what is going on in the federal bureaucracy, and the corresponding right of federal employees truthfully to inform the elected representatives of the people about what goes on.

Otto Otepka does stand as a symbol of that issue, and no citizen should lightly minimize its importance. There is, however, a second, and far more urgent, aspect of the Otepka affair which this book strives to bring into focus. At stake here is the survival not only of representative government but of the nation itself and, if we are to believe former Secretary of Defense Robert McNamara, the very lives of upwards of 140 million Americans.

This issue centers on two divergent and perhaps irreconcilable views on how best to prevent a nuclear holocaust. The one holds that the United States can avoid this terrifying disaster only by maintaining superiority in strategic weapons. The other believes, to use McNamara's word, that nuclear war is "unthinkable" and, ergo, America must lead the way towards general and complete disarmament with a vaguely defined world government presiding over the millennium of peace that is certain to follow.

Otto Otepka was caught in the withering crossfire exchanged by these two camps in their running—and still unresolved—battle. He came to the State Department, and rose to working chief of its worldwide personnel security system, during the Eisenhower years. Slowly, oft-times painfully, Otepka and his men in SY built a security-screening defense against fresh infiltration of the Department. The defense did not always work, as Richard Nixon openly acknowledged in 1968. But pro-Communist influences gradually waned, though even Otepka would not claim that they disappeared entirely, as the record of Fidel Castro's coup in Cuba with State Department connivance clearly shows.

For Otepka, and for the nation John F. Kennedy's ascension to the White House marked the end of an era. The embattled band that believed the key to world peace lay in maintaining America's strategic defenses was driven wholesale from the councils of government. Another group took over, a group dedicated, sometimes fanatically dedicated, to the unproved proposition that the Communist system was changing and, thus, America could risk taking a whole series of bold steps towards "peace."

A goodly number of the incoming New Frontiersmen harbored a deep-seated hatred of any and all measures designed to protect the government from subversion. It is not unfair to say that a large and very influential segment of them simply did not believe in subversion at all. They refused to countenance the possibility of espionage agents or Communist sympathizers worming their way into policy-making positions in the United States government.

In view of the well-publicized success of subversive operations in this and other countries, this prevalent syndrome seems to defy accurate diagnosis. Somehow, the disbelievers seem to say, the United States is immune to infiltration and impervious to espionage. Then how do they explain the Perlo Ring? The Alger Hiss case? The Rosenbergs? Or Martin and Mitchell, who mixed spying with homosexuality before they flitted from the National Security Agency to the Soviet Union in 1960?

Strange to say, they do not even attempt an answer. They simply ignore the questions raised by the overwhelming evidence—and, like the three little monkeys, swiftly clap their hands over their eyes, ears and mouths. They were, however, quick to remove their hands, quick to see, hear and speak evil, quick to denounce or denigrate the Otto Otepkas who strove to protect the national security, no matter how balanced and humane the Otepkas were in their approach to this sensitive problem.

The motivation of these people is often, though not always, difficult to fathom. It was a matter of conditioning more than conspiracy. From childhood they had been taught that all evil is relative and, that being the case, one should be tolerant of it, learn to live with it, convert it where possible. Communism was said to have a great deal of good in it, and everyone knew that capitalism contained much that was bad. If the good features of both systems could be merged it would be possible to evolve a new system that would be more responsive to human needs.

One should not completely discount the element of conspiracy, however. To deny that it exists is to blind oneself to the transcendent reality of our century—the fact that communism is a criminal conspiracy against all people and all nations, including Russia. It is suicidal to ignore the lesson of the Alger Hisses, the Rosenbergs, the Klaus Fuchs, the Kim

Philbys. It is pure folly to refuse to believe that many others like them may still be at work, unknown and undetected. It is impossible to disown the facts in the Otepka case. "How can anyone fail to see that there was a conspiracy here?" asks Otepka wearily, and logic cannot refute him.

The nagging question of motivation arises again, and the identity of the conspirators. The reader will meet them in this book and it will quickly be seen that their motives, although frequently impossible to perceive, were multiple. They fall, however, into several broad groups.

For the first of these groups their seething hatred of all loyalty programs was often a purely defensive mechanism: many of them knew that under the "reasonable doubt" strictures of Eisenhower's Executive Order 10450 they could never hope to win security clearance for the high government positions after which they hankered. They had grown up in the popular front period of the 1930s and '40s and a veritable brigade of them had joyfully joined Communist fronts. Some had carried on hot flirtations with the Party itself or with the Young Communist League. No doubt most of them later regretted their early indiscretions. But they knew there were black marks in their security files, and the only way they could erase them was to change the country's stupidly suspicious attitude towards security per se.

This group, the self-serving enemies of security, provides only part of the answer to the symbolic riddle of the Otepka case. There are many others high in the State Department with virtually impeccable security records who had little to fear from Otepka's Office of Security but who eagerly joined the pack bent on hounding him and his team out of Foggy Bottom. Some of these, like Otepka's boss, John Francis Reilly, were bureaucratic opportunists, determined to please their own bosses and advance their own careers, whatever the cost. This particular gang probably constituted a majority of the pack. They were pliable material, to be manipulated and molded at will by the basically frightened, self-defensive foes of security—and by a third and far more powerful faction.

Sophisticated, articulate, worldly in a new sense of the word, the members of this third group thought of themselves as the apostles of a modern philosophy that seeks to create a new world order. A surprising number of them were Rhodes scholars in their youth. No doubt many first received The Word over tepid tea from an Oxford or Cambridge don pompously puffing knowledge at them through the smoke of a briar pipe, or in the peace debates that echoed interminably in those great universities during the Thirities.

Dame Rebecca West in her brilliant 1964 book, *The New Meaning of Treason*, describes the British classmates of the American apostles in deep and searching detail. A sentence or two will suffice to give the flavor of her indictment:

"Of the other virtues, patriotism, it is to be remarked, was the first to get its dismissal. It was naive for a man to feel any conviction that his own country was the best, or even as good as any other country. . . ."[4]

From this basic tenet, it is not such a very long step to a vision of the world in which nations cease to exist. Hence, former Rhodes scholar Dean Rusk could declare national sovereignty outmoded when he spoke as the U.S. Secretary of State in Brussels in May of 1964, and former Rhodes scholar Walt Whitman Rostow, President Johnson's top advisor on national security matters, could openly call for "an end of nationhood."

When they say these things, the American people can be forgiven if they do not understand. The concept of a nationless world must seem as unrelated to present-day reality as the revelations of the Puritan divines appeared to the Indian tribes on the Massachusetts frontier in the 17th century. But if Americans value their country, their freedom, and perhaps their lives, they would do well to make at least an effort to find out what the Rusks and Rostows mean.

Otto Otepka found out too late what they meant, though in Rostow's case, at least, he thought he had a pretty good idea. For one thing, Otepka discovered, they meant that a necessary first step towards the realization of their cherished new world order was the destruction of a workable internal security system within the Department of State.

In the 1960's the Rusks and the Rostows, and even a supposedly pragmatic Texas politician like Lyndon Johnson, believed the goal of global government was at last within man's grasp. The age-old dream of mankind would be realized in our lifetime. *Pacem in terris.* Peace on earth. Pax. Otto Otepka was among the first to find that the dream did not embrace the concomitant clause, good will towards men. To some men, yes. But not to all men, and most certainly not to him, nor to the seven other security officers purged with him, nor to many more who sought to protect their country against subversion.

Everett McKinley Dirksen, who as a member of the Senate Internal Security Subcommittee sat in on enough of the interminable hearings in the Otepka case to take the measure of the man—and of the central issue—summed it all up succinctly. In the Minority Leader's office on the main floor of the Capitol of a wintry afternoon in 1967, this writer asked him what he thought was the main motivation for the State Department going to such pains to rid itself of Otepka.

"Why," replied Senator Dirksen in that incomparable throaty voice, "it is perfectly obvious what their motivation was. The ultra-Leftists in the Department of State saw Otepka as an obstacle to their plans. They *had* to remove him—and they did."

In this book, I intend to show not only how these people went about removing Otto Otepka, but also what their plans were and why they believed Otepka stood in their way.

At certain critical junctures of history, it is sometimes given to one man to stand and hold back onrushing and seemingly irresistible forces. Thus it was with Horatius when he took his stand on the bridge over the Tiber, and with the little Dutch boy who planted his thumb in the dike on the Zuider Zee, and with Cortez when he led his bleeding little band against the Aztec hordes on the Plain of Otumba after the crushing defeat of the Noche Triste.

Whether Otto Otepka will assume such heroic proportions in the history books of the future depends largely on who will be writing history in the centuries ahead. If the forces he stands against should win through, he will be cast in the role of a very minor villain, or ignored entirely. If the remnant he represents should somehow turn the tide, he may fare better.

A quiet, modest man, Otepka has never, I'm sure, thought of himself as a potentially historic figure. But if all the implications of his long and complex case are ever grasped by the American people, he may yet go down as the man who stood, unbudging and immovable, at the confluence of the labyrinthian maze on Foggy Bottom, and by so standing forced the people to *think*, before it was too late for them to act.

WILLIAM J. GILL
Washington, D.C., 1969

BOOK ONE

CHAPTER I

The First Encounter

A FEW MINUTES BEFORE SEVEN O'CLOCK OF A SHROUDED WINTER EVEning in late December 1960, a large, powerfully built, dark-haired man walked quietly through the maze of antiseptic corridors in the new State Department Building a few blocks from the Lincoln Memorial. His destination was a suite of offices tucked inobtrusively away in a far corner on the first floor, a suite but recently occupied by the incoming Secretary of State, Dean Rusk.

The building, a low-lying complex of mundane and uninspiring look-alike structures, was still in various stages of construction. In the just completed wing off C Street where the Secretary-designate's temporary office lay, the corridors had been cleared of scaffolding and the marble floors, waxed to a high sheen, were inclined to be slippery. With unhurried steps, taking care not to lose his footing on the shining marble, the large man made his way to Rusk's office. Promptly at 7:00 he arrived at the door and passed inside.

Two people were sitting in the reception room. One was a woman secretary; the other a security man assigned to the "protective detail," a diplomatic euphemism for bodyguard. The woman, middle-aged and quietly alert, had grown gray in the service of successive high-ranking

officials of the Department. She looked up from her desk when the door
opened and greeted the visitor with habitual ... hed cordiality.

"Mr. Otepka," she smiled with exactly the right touch of professional
warmth, "won't you have a seat for just a moment? Mr. Rusk will be right
with you."

Otto Otepka thanked her and took a chair. Beaming broadly, the
security man rose and moved closer to chat. Otepka, as Deputy Director
of the Office of Security (SY), was technically the bodyguard's boss.
Traditionally, the Director of SY was a transient Foreign Service Officer,
spending a few unhappy years in a strange and unfamiliar area that most
FSO's regard as menacing and odious.

Since April 1957 Deputy Director Otepka, whose job came under Civil
Service to protect it from the vagaries of the spoils system, had for all
practical purposes run SY. Almost everyone in the higher echelons
agreed that he ran it exceedingly well. In 1958 John Foster Dulles had
bestowed on Otepka the State Department's coveted Meritorious Service Award. Both before and after this, a veritable parade of undersecre-
taries and other ranking officers had heaped praise and commendations
on him for his dedication, discretion, and outstanding performance.

It was, perhaps, a singular mark of his importance to the department
that the new Secretary had summoned him to a conference during this
hectic transition period between the Eisenhower and Kennedy Administrations. Late that same afternoon, the current Director of SY, William
O. Boswell, informed Otepka that Dean Rusk wanted to meet with him.
The appointment was set for 7:00. Otepka was to go alone, but there was
no hint as to what the meeting would be about.

Otepka, with the sure instinct gained from nearly a quarter-century of
federal service, privately made a well-educated and, as it turned out,
accurate guess. He sensed the meeting would pertain to the delicate
matter of obtaining security clearances for the small army of new officials
then getting set to move into the State Department right after the inauguration of John Fitzgerald Kennedy.

Foreign policy, the critical domain of the Department of State, was
necessarily *the* top priority problem for Mr. Kennedy, as indeed it must
be for any President in this age of nuclear weaponry. Who would make
and implement that policy was therefore a subject of almost overriding
interest to him and to his Secretary of State.

The law, however, required that people in policy-making positions at
State be cleared for access to the classified information they must have

in order to carry on their jobs, or for that matter, even to get and hold those jobs. Under the law, Otepka's Office of Security was charged with handling all such clearances.

Over the years, Otepka had inevitably stepped on many high-placed toes. The New York *Times*, when Otepka later emerged from the anonymity he then enjoyed, accurately assessed the dangers inherent in his position: "He has," said the *Times*, "probably passed at least preliminary judgment on the security pedigrees of more ranking Government officials than any other person in Washington."[1]

Assuredly, this job would have been a heavy responsibility for any American. Ideally, it required a person embodying the courage of a David, the strength of Samson, the wisdom of Solomon, and patience of Job. Otepka, undoubtedly, would laugh at the thought that any one man could come close to fitting this description. But if the responsibilities of his position weighed him down, it did not show in those waning days of 1960.

Waiting in Dean Rusk's reception room that December evening, Otepka appeared under no noticeable strain. Effortlessly, he made small talk with the bodyguard and the woman secretary. But this interlude lasted no more than five minutes.

A soft buzzer whispered on the woman's desk. She picked up the telephone and murmured a hushed reply to an inquiry. Then, with elaborate courtesy, she ushered Otepka into the spacious and tastefully furnished inner office.

Dean Rusk, wearing the shy little half-smile that was to become so familiar to the nation in the years ahead, rose behind his broad desk and extended his hand. Otepka grasped it, returning the smile and spoken amenities, remembering to congratulate the new Secretary on his appointment.

There were certain physical similarities shared by these two dissimilar men, though one could not say they actually resembled each other. Both were tall and heavy set, with the slow, deliberate movements and gently subdued manners of so many large men. Rusk, then 51 and six years Otepka's senior, retained only a thin fringe of fast-graying hair around the sides of his otherwise bald head, whereas Otepka had very thick, entirely black wavy hair. Rusk's complexion was sallow to the point of pallidity; Otepka's dark, almost swarthy. Rusk's big frame appeared somewhat flabby under his loose-fitting blue suit; Otepka's build, despite a very slight tendency to portliness, was obviously hard and muscular.

This was the first time Rusk and Otepka had met, though they were not by any means unfamiliar with each other. Rusk had kept in close touch with the State Department during the years of exile at the Rockefeller Foundation following his resignation as Assistant Secretary at the end of 1951. The area of Otepka's professional activities had continued to be one of his prime concerns.

Otepka, for his part, was completely conversant with Dean Rusk's background, though the Secretary of State-to-be had been an obscure, virtually unknown figure to the public when the President-elect announced his appointment from the steps of the Kennedy home in Georgetown on December 12. Having studied Rusk's personal security file with characteristic care, Otepka, with only a glimmer of misgiving, had approved clearance a few days before.

That clearance would pave the way for Rusk's confirmation as Secretary by the Senate Foreign Relations Committee and the full Senate. Indeed, without it, neither Rusk nor any of the State Department's other new high officials could hope to receive the necessary Senatorial blessing.

After the hasty amenities, Rusk politely gestured Otepka to a comfortable chair drawn up in front of his desk. With but the faintest flicker of the shy smile, he informed the security chief that they would have to "wait for Robert Kennedy." The newly named Attorney General was, Rusk said, coming over from the Justice Department to talk with them.

Rusk glanced laconically at his watch, excused himself with the remark that he had to "get some work done," and turned to the papers on top of his desk. Otepka, lacking anything useful to do, crossed his legs and stared reflectively at his shoe.

Minutes dragged by. Rusk frowned occasionally at his watch, once or twice directing a quizzical look at his guest. Soon it was 7:30.

Masking his impatience, Rusk picked up the phone and placed a call to Justice. He was told that Bobby had left a good half-hour ago. He relayed this information to Otepka, wondering aloud what had happened to Mr. Kennedy.

Fifteen minutes later Bobby bustled in, his face contorted between a smile and a scowl. The expensively tailored suit was crumpled and visibly soiled. His tousled blonde hair, trimmed somewhat shorter in those days but cut long nonetheless, tumbled in studied disarray over the forehead almost to his eyes.

"I got lost in the corridors," Bobby confessed with some heat. It was not an apology. Since long before his brother was elected President of the

United States, Robert Francis Kennedy had seldom, if ever, been known to apologize for anything.

He shook hands with Rusk and Otepka. It was the practiced half-clasp of the politician who has arrived, a reflex action devoid of meaning.

Rusk came out from behind his big desk. He carried a single fat security file adroitly fished from a side drawer. With a nod and a murmured invitation he indicated a long varnished conference table in the center of the dimly lit office. Rusk took the chair at the head of the table. Kennedy sat at his left, Otepka on his right.

When all three were seated, Rusk asked a few preliminary questions about security regulations. Then he tapped the bulging folder he had laid on the table and drove straight to the point. The security file contained summaries of background information on a man—Rusk mentioned his name—whom the new Administration wanted to place in an important position in the Department of State. Rusk said he had gone over the file. Mr. Kennedy had been through it. Now they wanted Otepka's evaluation, his recollection of what had been done in the past and why. "What kind of security problem would be encountered?" was the way Rusk phrased it. Unasked, but implicit, were the questions: Why had you denied this man a security clearance in 1955 and again in 1957? What are the chances of your giving him a clearance now? What do you know that we don't know?

Otepka remembered the case well. Five years before, the individual in question had been nominated for an advisory post. He was to have served as a State Department consultant, and probable chairman, on the so-called Quantico Panel which was to help the OCB reshape America's psychological strategy in the Cold War. This panel was slated to serve as a sort of dispassionate alter ego to the super-sensitive Operations Coordinating Board of the President's top-level National Security Council. For some unexplained reason, the Quantico Panel was being put together on an urgent, high-priority basis. Clearances for the half-dozen State Department consultant members, all of whom had to meet the strict standards of the U.S. Intelligence Board, were demanded literally overnight.*

On that particular evening in 1955, Otepka was scheduled to go bowl-

* There are many different type security clearances issued by various government departments. The standards for each vary, depending on the sensitivity of the information needed to fulfill the functions of a particular position. The U.S. Intelligence Board, which assesses a broad variety of top-secret data critical to the national security, is comprised of high-level representatives of ten government agencies, including the Defense (military) Intelligence arms, CIA, State, NSA, and the Atomic Energy Commission.

ing with his State Department team at the Lafayette Alleys on 15th and I Streets. But about 5:30 p.m., as he was preparing to leave the office, he was notified that the Office of Security's Evaluations Division, which he then headed, would have to work on the Quantico Panel nominations. He called in two of his men and they split up the cases among them. Otepka personally took on the case of the man about whom Rusk and Kennedy were now inquiring.

Otepka recalled that telephone calls were made to the FBI, CIA, and the military intelligence agencies requesting them to send him forthwith every scrap of information they had on the man. CIA insisted their file was to be "for your eyes only." They dispatched one of their top officials to hand-carry it to the State Department. He sat with Otepka for several hours, never letting the file out of his sight while Otepka studied it.

By the time Otepka pulled in all the information from the other agencies, completed writing his report and reviewing the evaluations on the other Quantico nominees, it was 4:30 a.m. He deposited the end products on the desk of Robert Cartwright, then Deputy Administrator of the Bureau of Security and Consular Affairs. Cartwright relayed Otepka's findings to Undersecretary of State Herbert Hoover, Jr. first thing in the morning. Hoover was chief of the Operations Coordinating Board and the man who would have to accept or reject SY's evaluations.

Otepka is known throughout the Intelligence community for his prodigious and precise memory. From his findings of that long night in 1955, he now raised the following points with Dean Rusk and Robert Kennedy:

• The man they were inquiring about had a long history of close association with a number of individuals who were known to be members of the Communist Party. Several of these people had been identified as active Soviet espionage agents.

• Two of the man's aunts were definitely identified, by reliable informants and undercover agents, as members of the Communist Party in the late 1940's. So far as Otepka knew they were still members in 1955. The aunts were by no means remote relatives. They had been intimately close to the man's family, and the family had never repudiated them.

• The man's father, a native of Russia, had been an active Socialist revolutionary in his homeland just before the Socialists split into the Bolshevik and Menshevik factions. He had continued, ostensibly, as a Socialist activist after migrating to the United States in 1905, the year of the abortive Leftist revolt in Russia.

• CIA had deftly dropped this individual from a sensitive contract with a private organization and CIA was not, even then, known to have any great aversion for innocent Liberals.

• Air Force Intelligence, which had investigated him thoroughly in connection with another contract he was to have been involved in for the Air Force, flatly declared the man a security risk—a term not used lightly anywhere in the Intelligence community.*

At this point, Bobby Kennedy exploded. "Those Air Force guys are a bunch of jerks," he growled. "They're nuts!" Angrily, he shifted in his chair and glared at the polished table top.

Dean Rusk seemed momentarily taken aback by this outburst. But his considerable aplomb did not desert him. Quietly, with a polite lifting of his brows, he asked whether Otepka thought the man was a Communist.

Otepka's reply was typically cautious. He had seen too many men fall into *that* trap. He said he had no indisputable proof that the man was a member of the Communist Party, and he had made no such finding in 1955. He had recommended against granting a clearance because of the obviously serious character of the information in the file, and because of the highly sensitive nature of the position the individual had been nominated for with the National Security Council.

Undersecretary Hoover, Otepka pointed out, had fully upheld his findings. He refrained from mentioning that Hoover had given him a private commendation for this particular piece of work and had thanked him in a memorandum sent through his immediate superiors. But he did emphasize the fact that he had been upheld a second time when he rejected clearance for the same individual in 1957, when yet another attempt had been made to appoint him as a State Department consultant.

Rusk inquired as to "what would be required now" to obtain a clearance for the man. Otepka made it politely plain that he would have to insist on a current, full field investigation by the FBI to bring the file up to date.

Then, too, there was Executive Order 10450.

Otepka did not feel he had to spell out the strictures of E.O. 10450 for men who were to fill Cabinet posts as Secretary of State and Attorney General. Everyone in or close to government knew the implications of that historic Presidential order imposed by Dwight D. Eisenhower.

In the wake of the shocking disclosures of Communist penetration and

* These items of information came from two sources, neither of them ever connected with the State Department, who had access to this man's security files in other agencies. Confronted with this list, Otepka refused to deny that they were among the things he discussed with Rusk and Kennedy on the case.

Soviet espionage within the government during the Roosevelt-Truman Administrations, President Eisenhower had valiantly sought to bar the door to future subversion. Soon after taking office in 1953, he issued Executive Order 10450 to reinforce the intent of the McCarran Act and other similar legislation passed by Congress.

Under 10450 it became mandatory that whenever there was "reasonable doubt" in personnel security cases, that doubt must be resolved in favor of the country, its people and their government. No longer could a Cabinet official or his subordinates give an individual the benefit of doubts concerning his past activities. It underlined the ancient tenet that government service, in appointive positions at least, is a privilege to be granted on the basis of past conduct and performance, and not an inalienable right open to anyone, including citizens who have demonstrated by word and action that they are not in favor of America's form of government.

The Executive Order applied not only to loyalty cases. It applied equally to questions of "suitability" for government office. This might involve anything from innocent absentmindedness which could cause the loss of classified documents to habitual drunkenness, homosexuality or other blackmailable conduct.

Moreover, E.O. 10450 would carry the force of law in succeeding administrations unless, of course, the Supreme Court declared it unconstitutional or it was specifically countermanded by a new Executive Order or laws passed by Congress.

Obviously, the case Otepka had just outlined for Rusk and Kennedy could never pass the acid test of 10450—no matter what might be the result of new FBI investigations filling in activities of the last four or five years. Rusk knew this, probably with more certainty than the young man who would soon take over as Attorney General. After hearing out Otepka, he adroitly changed the subject to the broader question of security clearances in general.

There would be dozens of "Presidential appointees" clambering aboard at State after Inauguration Day, less than a month away. The Secretary, of course, had an intimate interest in expediting the changeover. Robert Kennedy's interest was at least equal to Rusk's. It was already well known around Washington that Bobby was in charge of patronage for the onrushing New Frontier and this meeting confirmed that fact.

Otepka understood their problem, or thought that he did. The toughest part of it would be to get all their appointees approved by the Senate, which had been known to kick up its heels on occasion. The recent election had not greatly changed the complexion of that august body, and only last summer, during the special session held after Jack Kennedy's nomination at that wondrous Los Angeles convention, the Senate and the House both had demonstrated their skepticism. The Democrat-controlled Congress had refused to pass even one of the seven major bills Senator Kennedy had tried to push through in an effort to build a record of achievement for the coming campaign.

There were at least a few members of the Senate Foreign Relations Committee, which had to pass on appointments to policy posts in the State Department, who might cause trouble. In answer to a question from Rusk, Otepka emphasized that the Department had a long-standing agreement with the Senate committee which his Office of Security would have to observe. The agreement called for SY to obtain a comprehensive FBI field investigation on each appointee. The investigation had to be made within one year preceding the date of the appointment.

Unlike the more cursory "national agency" checks which sufficed for personnel in less sensitive government departments, these full field investigations of prospective State Department officials often took time. It was not unusual for the FBI to spend six months, or even a year, on a single case. The agents frequently had to run down tenuous leads to dig out facts on an individual which might bring unresolved information into better focus. Unfortunately, there were no short cuts in this kind of work.

Otepka told Rusk and Kennedy he could see no way around the Senate's requirement, which the Foreign Relations Committee and SY had faithfully enforced since the original agreement was made in 1954. Then he detailed some of the other established procedures and regulations governing security clearances in State.

At last, Kennedy shifted uncomfortably in his chair and Dean Rusk picked up his cue. He rose rather abruptly and said: "Thank you very much. That will be all."

Bobby got up too. This time he did not attempt a smile when Otepka shook his hand. His veiled blue eyes made no effort to meet those of the security chief. He seemed to be staring beyond Otepka into the cloudy gray mists of the future.

Rusk's farewell was more cordial, if somewhat peremptory, and Otepka departed with a vague uneasiness. Kennedy stayed behind with Rusk.

Otepka was not the type of man who wasted time or anguish on post-mortems. He was usually content to tuck an incident away in his encyclopedic memory bank, close the door, and move on to the next job. But there were certain things about this particular meeting that he continued to reflect on from time to time as the thousand days of the New Frontier wore on. He reflected on them even more as the Johnson Administration bounced from one foreign policy failure to the next—from frustration in Vietnam to the slow crumbling of NATO; from the withering of U.S. influence in the Mideast to the consolidation of Russia's power in Cuba; from "building bridges" to the Soviet Bloc to granting the USSR a dangerous "parity" in nuclear weapons.

Bobby Kennedy's angry response when he had ticked off the Air Force Intelligence findings on the man they questioned him about troubled Otepka particularly. The new Attorney General's reaction was so patently emotional that Otepka reluctantly concluded that it was symptomatic of a conditioned reflex. His words—"Those Air Force guys are a bunch of jerks. They're nuts!"—stuck in Otepka's mind.

Before many months had passed, Otepka came to see that Bobby's irritable remark foreshadowed the Kennedy-Johnson Administration's whole philosophy on, and approach to, internal security programs, not only in the State Department but in all government agencies.

At the outset, however, Otepka was not surprised when Secretary Rusk failed to appoint the man he and Kennedy had been so curious about to the Department of State. Otepka had made it implicitly plain that he would refuse to issue a clearance in this case. Rusk could have overruled him, of course. But in so doing the Secretary would have tipped his hand before he was ready to move on a broader solution to the whole irksome problem of security.

Instead, the man in question was named to John Kennedy's personal staff at the White House with the impressive title, Deputy Special Assistant to the President for National Security Affairs. His influence, if we are to credit such New Frontiersmen as Arthur Schlesinger, Jr., was even more pregnant than his title.

In November 1961, with the "Otepka problem" apparently under control, President Kennedy dispatched him to the State Department with orders to "catch hold" of the "long-range planning." State was forced to honor his White House clearance, and as Chairman of the Department's powerful Policy Planning Council he helped, says Schlesinger, to "shape policy on a dozen fronts."[2]

He remained at State, where he "caught hold" very well indeed, until another President, Lyndon Baines Johnson, summoned him back to the White House in April 1966. This time he was *the* top Presidential advisor on all national security matters, playing a major role in charting the increasing troop buildups in the Vietnam War. By so doing he won the reputation in Administration and military circles as "a real hard-liner."

In 1967 he was described in an adulatory article in *Business Week* magazine as "the principal conduit and point of contact between Johnson and the vast bureaucracies of State, Defense, the Central Intelligence Agency, and other operating agencies as they become involved in foreign affairs."

"This," the article said, "gives him essentially three roles:

"Bringing to the President's attention those issues ripe for decision.

"Advising what the decision should be.

"Seeing that the decision is implemented—whether it went his way or not."[3]

In addition, he headed up the staff of the National Security Council, to which, a decade earlier, he had been denied a security clearance in merely a consultant-advisory role.

Lyndon Johnson summed up this man's position succinctly in 1967: "He has," said the President, "the most important job in the White House, aside from the President."[4]

The man was, of course, Walt Whitman Rostow.

CHAPTER **II**

Otepka

THE VAGUE UNEASINESS THAT NAGGED OTTO OTEPKA AFTER HIS MEET-
ing with Robert Kennedy and Dean Rusk is seen in retrospect as a mild
and moderate reaction to an experience which would have badly jolted
most men in the federal security service. Otepka, however, had always
been an exceedingly careful man.

The New York *Times* once summed up both the man and his profession in a quote from an anonymous former associate in the Department
of State: "Some people in his line of work tend to be a little electric.
When they speak, pinwheels go around. They are zealots—a little weird,
a little frightening. But this man is calm, deliberate, articulate and cautious. He goes by the book."[1]

Over the years, Otepka had rigorously trained himself to refrain from
judging people until all the evidence was in, properly digested, and
meticulously evaluated. Characteristically, he deferred making a private
judgment of the incoming Attorney General and Secretary of State on
the basis of this one disquieting encounter.

It was not until many months later that he discerned the real purpose
of that evening conference in Dean Rusk's office. Slowly, reluctantly, he
came to see that the aim was not so much to explore the possibility of
obtaining a security clearance for Walt W. Rostow. That was secondary.

The primary purpose was to give Rusk and Kennedy an opportunity to evaluate Otto Otepka.

The chances are their evaluation was faulty. But having made it, having determined the security chief's attitude with this single critical test, having weighed whether he would be a stumbling block or merely a minor irritant, they could then proceed with their plans for repopulating the State Department.

Undoubtedly, Rusk and Kennedy were confident they could improvise a way to handle the special problem Otepka presented. There is more than one way to skin the protective covering that allegedly shields Civil Service employees from the ravages of the spoils system. Between them, the Secretary of State and the Attorney General could certainly devise some painless surgery that would strip Otepka of his authority without embarrassment to the new Administration.

Meanwhile, the decision to place Dr. Rostow in the White House instead of in the State Department clearly indicates Rusk and Kennedy elected for a cautious, gradualist approach to a question potentially loaded with dangerous political fallout. The public still had the annoying habit then of seeing internal security problems through a narrow and thoroughly emotional prism. It would be best not to arouse the citizenry at a time when the new President, so recently elected by something less than a clear majority, needed the public's confidence to "get the country moving again."

Nonetheless, it was apparent to Otepka, even then, that both Rusk and Kennedy displayed serious symptoms of that peculiar blindness on internal security that afflicts so much of the body politic in the United States. It is an affliction that has been endemic in government for several generations. Otepka was not at all surprised to discover it at such high official levels. He had found it there before. He fully expected to find it there again.

All through the Eisenhower years, Otepka had patiently treated the security blind spots acquired by his superiors in the Department of State. Invariably, his prescription was a healthy dose of facts—as many facts as he and his overworked team in the Office of Security could marshal and present in lucid order.

This did not always effect the desired cure. But under Ike and his Secretaries of State, Foster Dulles and Christian Herter, it kept the epidemic under some control and prevented it from proving immediately fatal to representative government.

Now, however, Otepka sensed that he was confronted with a more virulent strain of security blindness, one that defied immediate diagnosis. He was well aware of Dean Rusk's attitude. This was a matter of private and public record dating back many years to Rusk's prior tenure at State and, before that, to his service in the old War Department and his stint in Army Intelligence. Gingerly, Otepka had weighed the new Secretary's old actions and statements before he signed the clearance needed for Rusk's confirmation by the Senate. On the record Rusk's affliction seemed to be in the traditional mold, and Otepka may have deluded himself that, given time, he could doctor the Secretary back to reality.

It was not Dean Rusk's attitude that greatly troubled Otepka then. It was Bobby Kennedy's reflex reaction. A man in government, especially one who was to occupy the powerful post of Attorney General of the United States, does not lightly—even angrily—dismiss a report and evaluation prepared by thoroughly experienced military Intelligence officers, particularly when they are supported by evidence from other security agencies, including the FBI and CIA.

The head of the Justice Department, which is charged with the prosecution of all cases of espionage and subversion, may question the Intelligence community's findings, as indeed he should. But summarily to judge the Air Force Intelligence men as "jerks" and then vernacularly pronounce them insane, betrayed a degree of imprudence and impetuosity that mightily puzzled Otepka.

For the moment, Otepka was willing to chalk up Bobby's knee-jerk response to his youth. (He didn't know it, but not long before, Jack Kennedy had described his brother as "young and very hotheaded.") Yet the nagging uneasiness persisted.

That Otepka was soon bound to find himself on a collision course with the young Attorney General, the Secretary of State, and the White House itself should have been apparent to anyone who really knew Otepka. Curiously, few people, even among his close friends, really did.

To his superiors in the State Department, Otepka was a thorough, conscientious, and painstakingly careful security officer. One later described him as "a helluva good cop." The Intelligence community knew he was that—and more. Few men had such a firm grasp of the intricate maneuverings of the Communist conspiracy. Fewer still had what many Intelligence experts called "Otepka's encyclopedic knowledge" of the Soviet Union's too often successful attempts to penetrate the United States government.

This is not to say that he did not, like any human being, have his weak spots. He was, after all, a member of the bureaucracy and he had learned that on occasion you had to roll with the punches. When he was over-ruled on security cases by those above him, he had to accept the decision with equanimity. It was either that or quit. And, much like J. Edgar Hoover and myriad other government servants, Otepka rationalized that it was better to acquiesce and stay to fight yet another day.

"I often think," he said in a reflective mood in 1968, "that they all thought I was pretty easygoing. After all, you have to get along with the people you are associated with and work for and there was no point in losing your temper every time a dispute arose. If you did," he smiled, "in the State Department you could be fighting all the time. You would never have gotten any work done."

Certainly, neither Bobby Kennedy nor Dean Rusk could have con-ceived of his becoming the source of a seemingly unending behind-the-scenes crisis. If they bothered to study his background, which they probably did not, except, perhaps, in the most cursory way, Kennedy and Rusk would not have been impressed. There was nothing there, on the surface at least, that really assessed Otepka's true strength. In a sense, however, his whole life had been a preparation for the trials that beset him—and his country—in those incendiary years, 1961 through 1968.

Otto Fred Otepka was born in his family's home on the southwest side of Chicago on May 6, 1915. An astrologist would doubtless read some-thing into this, since his birth coincided with the ascendancy of the sign of Taurus, which is said to bestow unusual tenacity and determination on its children. Otepka, however, came by these qualities in other ways, principally by the example set for him by his parents.

Otepka's father and mother were both born in Bzenec, Moravia, now a part of Communist Czechoslovakia, but then a province of the Austro-Hungarian Empire. His father, Ferdinand Otepka, oppressed by condi-tions in Moravia and sensing the imminence of the suicidal war that was soon to embrace Europe in a death grip, came to America as an immi-grant in mid-April 1912. The ship he sailed on missed the hidden icebergs floating loose in the North Atlantic that spring, but another liner, the *Titanic*, did not. The elder Otepka's ship circled about to pick up survi-vors and was several days behind schedule when it sailed into New York harbor and past the Statue of Liberty.

Like so many immigrants before him, Ferdinand Otepka was proc-essed through Ellis Island. After the required three-day quarantine, he took a train for St. Louis, where he worked briefly, and moved from there to Chicago. Trained in Moravia as a blacksmith, the husky 27-year-old Otepka had little difficulty finding a job. The automobile had not yet supplanted the horse, even in the cities. On Chicago's West Side he readily found a chance to work at his trade in the forge of a wagonmaker, Peter Schuttler.

Carefully saving his money, Ferdinand Otepka was able to send for his young bride, Johanna, who had stayed behind in Moravia while he got his start in the New World. Proudly, he brought her to the freshly painted house he had rented in the 2600 block of South Lawndale Avenue. Johanna was delighted with it, and with America. Neither she nor her husband ever seriously thought of returning to live in Central Europe. Two years after her arrival, the first of their two sons was born. They named him Otto.

When Otto was two, his father had saved enough to buy his own home. It was at 3225 South Hamlin Avenue, not far from their first home on Lawndale and still well within the district that the immigrants had dubbed *Ceska Kalifornie* (Czech California). It was a modest home, in a neighborhood of modest homes. But the houses were all well kept. In front, each one had a small but tidy lawn, most with flower gardens; in back, almost every house had a second garden for vegetables and, behind some, room for chickens and geese.

Ceska Kalifornie was not all Czech and Moravian. There was an abundance of Poles, Slovaks, some Germans, a sprinkling of Hungarians and other nationalities. People from countries that had been intermittently at war for a thousand years discovered they could get along quite well with one another in America. They were all hard-working, thrifty folk, and although they naturally gravitated to their own national groups, mainly because of the common language, they respected and scrupulously observed the rights of their neighbors. Otto Otepka and his younger brother, Rudy, belonged to the neighborhood *Sokol,* and from the time he was eight on through his teens, Otto took part in the annual gymnastic exhibitions at the *Sokol* Hall on 26th and Lawndale.

On Sundays in the summertime, the family frequently went on picnics to Pilsen Park, a sprawling garden owned by a local brewery. Sometimes, Otto would visit his father at the forge where he worked. This meant taking an adventurous tram ride through the Loop to Chicago's near North Side. The wagonmaker had gone out of business after World War I and Ferdinand Otepka was now a blacksmith at the Cherney Teamster

Company on East Illinois Street near the new Tribune Tower. Otto would sit by the hour and watch him shoe the big dray horses that remained in service into the late 1920's.

At the Gary Elementary School, where he went through all eight grades with ease, Otto was the champion speller in every grade and he won several awards for essays on citizenship. After school, at the *Sokol,* he studied the Czech language and history. His parents still used the old country tongue at home, though their sons spoke English without a trace of accent.

A thin, spindly youngster growing up, Otto played outfield on the neighborhood baseball team and, like virtually all the other boys in the Lawndale district, was an avid fan of the Chicago Cubs. Occasionally, he went to the Cub games at Wrigley Field with the Chicago Boys Club. One of his biggest thrills was when the Cubs won the National League pennant in 1929, the year he graduated from Gary School. He stayed "glued to the radio" all during the World Series that fall, and felt crushed when the Cubs lost to Connie Mack's mighty Athletics.

Another event he vividly recalls occurred in February 1933. Mayor Anton J. Cermak of Chicago, a product of *Ceska Kalifornie* and the neighborhood hero, was fatally wounded in an assassination attempt on President-elect Franklin D. Roosevelt in Miami, Florida. The assassin was an anarchist named Joseph Zangara.

The Otepkas, like an overwhelming majority of their neighbors, were Democrats, and though they were not active in politics, the truly extremist philosophies of that day—Fascism, Nazism and Communism—were anathema. Ferdinand Otepka regarded the new "isms" with deep suspicion. He felt strongly that they were all just another guise for the absolutism he had left Europe to escape. Despite the Depression, he staunchly maintained that the United States enjoyed the greatest form of government ever devised by man.

In the fall of 1929, Otto Otepka entered Harrison Technical High School, which also offered a solid academic curriculum. Otto took the college preparatory course, majoring in science. His mother and father saved for years to send him to college. But by the time Otto graduated from Harrison in 1933, his father had long since lost his blacksmith's job to technology and the Depression. The family savings were almost gone and college was out of the question.

In high school, and even back in grade school, Otto had worked to augment the family income. He delivered newspapers over an expanding route—the Chicago *Tribune* on Sundays and the *Herald-Examiner* during the week. He built his route into quite a profitable venture and at 15 turned it over to his brother Rudy, four years his junior. For Rudy Otepka it was the start of a tremendously successful career in the printing business.

Otto then went to work delivering milk for a dairy, getting up at 4 a.m. each morning to cover his route in time to attend his high school classes from noon until 5:30 p.m. Upon graduation, he got a job distributing advertising circulars. There was no time for sports in those years, and little for any kind of recreation. Fortunately, Otto Otepka was more interested in his studies anyway and he never felt the loss.

Jobs were getting more scarce for young men in spite of Franklin Roosevelt's New Deal, and in 1934 Otepka joined the Civilian Conservation Corps. He spent a year at Camp Salt Creek, west of Chicago, and was disappointed that he wasn't shipped off to California with a group of his friends.

Towards the end of 1935 he left the CCC, hoping to get a job to help his family more and determined to save enough for college. The only thing he could find was a job in a bottling plant at the National Recovery Administration (NRA) rate of 31 cents an hour. He had to labor 71 hours a week to earn $22. The future looked bleak, and though often discouraged, he doesn't recall ever succumbing to despair. Then, in June 1936, he received a letter that was eventually to start him on a career and carry him to the top of a new and strange profession that was not then known in the United States.

Otepka had taken several Civil Service examinations before he joined the CCC. He had scored high in each try, but it was not until that June that the government finally called him. He was offered a job as a messenger with the Farm Credit Administration in Washington at $1,080 a year. At last, he had the opportunity to continue his education, if only part-time. He left Chicago and started work at the FCA on July 1.

Studying at night and working days, Otepka rose steadily through the Civil Service ranks. In June 1942 he received his law degree from Columbus University, now incorporated with Catholic University of America.

It was during this same period that Otepka made perhaps the most fortunate discovery of his life. Right next door to the apartment he had occupied in Washington he found a young schoolteacher named Edith Simon. The daughter of an old Maryland family, Miss Simon had come to Washington to complete her education and to teach. Otepka first observed her sitting on a porch swing correcting school papers. He wangled an introduction from his landlady, started dating Edith Simon, and upon his graduation from law school they married.

The following month Otepka left the Bureau of Internal Revenue, where he had worked the previous three years, and joined the Civil Service Commission as an investigator. For the next sixteen months he was stationed in New York, assigned principally to loyalty cases. At that time, the commission was mainly on the alert for Fascists and Nazis, but inevitably his work was also involved with Communists. He noted certain similarities in all three of these groups and he began a study of totalitarian movements generally.

In October 1943 Otepka entered the Navy as a personnel classification specialist. His duties primarily centered on interviewing and placing Navy recruits in jobs and training schools where the best use could be made of their civilian skills and aptitudes.

Honorably discharged from the Navy in March 1946, Otepka resumed his duties in the Investigations Division of the Civil Service Commission in New York. The massive infiltration of government agencies by Communists during World War II, when the doors had been opened wide to them because the Soviet Union was formally an ally of the United States, was already causing severe problems. But in the immediate postwar period there was as yet no official policy with regard to these people. On the contrary, more were being brought into government every day through the good offices of their comrades who were already on board.

Otepka and the other Civil Service investigators spent a good deal of their time in 1946 and 1947 trying to weed out Fascist and Nazi spies and sympathizers. Although these subversives had been deprived of their international power bases by the Allied victories over Germany and Italy, they were still regarded as the major threat. Public attention was focused on the Nuremberg Trials, the hanging of the traitorous "Lord Haw-Haw" (William Joyce) in England, the blithe confessions of "Tokyo Rose," and the housing, automobile, and other shortages in the United States.

Lost somewhere in all this was the significance of the tentative, but ominous, moves made by the secretive men in the Kremlin on the vast Eurasian chessboard. The conferences at Teheran and Yalta had already put most of East-Central Europe in Stalin's hip pocket and provided him with an important bridgehead in Manchuria as well. Now, the confusion and apparent weakness of the West's will encouraged him to consolidate his diplomatic conquests and reach for more.

Stalin's overt aggression was augmented by covert espionage agents and armies of open Communist sympathizers in every Western country. Let it be said that Moscow did not always have to demand formal baptism of its converts in the West. It found there thousands, perhaps millions, of ready-made dupes who had long embraced some more diluted form of the secular religion of Marxism, whether they called it by its name or not.

In these people, the Kremlin had discovered a growing sect that shared communism's goal of a new world order. Frequently, they made ideal espionage agents and policy saboteurs because they were the more difficult to identify. If caught, they could always plead that they knew not what they did, and in truth many of them did not, though some knew very well, of course. The results, however, for the governments and societies they were subverting, would ultimately be the same.

Otto Otepka did not fully grasp this essential element, but that should not be held against him. There are many, in positions of much greater authority than he ever held, who at this late date have not grasped it yet. As an investigator for the Civil Service Commission, Otepka was forced to deal only with identifiable, finite facts. This was difficult enough, for many of the facts he uncovered on applicants for federal jobs, and on those being considered for promotion, did not, in 1946-47, appear on the surface to be very significant.

The Popular Front period of the 1930's and '40's had given rise to a numerous and bewildering array of Communist fronts. Very often they were not even started by Communists at all. Even after Communists, sometimes only a tiny minority of the total membership, wormed their way in and won control, the fronts maintained respectable facades.

There was no Attorney General's list of subversive organizations to guide Otepka and his fellow investigators. The steam had long since gone out of the old Dies Committee. Other Congressional committees were just beginning their first tentative investigations of subversion. The hearings were invariably held behind closed doors and the committees had not yet begun to cite organizations as subversive.

Gradually, however, Otepka and others began to detect certain patterns of membership in these fronts. A perfectly innocent person might belong to one, or even several. But when a subject joined a number of organizations formed for ostensibly unrelated purposes, he was worth looking into more closely. Often, but not always, this led to his being traced to an association with the Communist Party or with known members of the Party.

By the spring of 1947, Otepka's pioneer work in this shadowy realm won him recognition with the Civil Service Commission. He was transferred to Washington to work almost exclusively on what were just beginning to be called "loyalty cases." In December of the same year he was appointed by the commission as Technical Advisor on Loyalty in the Central Office Investigations Division.

Otepka's new job carried broad responsibilities. He and his staff were charged with reviewing all loyalty cases involving Civil Service employees and applicants. They also had to prepare comprehensive analyses, tantamount to legal briefs, to justify the referral of these cases to the FBI for investigation under the new Federal Employees Loyalty Program established by President Truman. On top of that, Otepka's office was responsible for collecting, evaluating and disseminating information on all types of subversive activities to all government departments and agencies.

The staff Otepka supervised for the next five-and-a-half years averaged several score people. He could easily have used two or three times that many to keep up with the mounting work load after the formidable dam, built within government to keep information on subversion from flowing to the public, finally broke in the summer of 1948. Beginning July 31, of that year, the nation was sent into a state of semi-shock by the amazing disclosures of Whittaker Chambers and Elizabeth Bentley before the House Committee on Un-American Activities.

The revelations of these two former Communist espionage couriers was so startling that most Americans could not bring themselves to believe them. Otto Otepka, however, knew they told the truth. His investigations had already turned up many of the people Chambers and Miss Bentley identified as Soviet agents, though he had often lacked positive proof. Moreover, he had long ago heard that a Communist defector had given the names of a score or more of these agents to a high-ranking State Department official. The defector, of course, was Chambers.

At the behest of editor Isaac Don Levine, and in his presence, Chambers had provided Assistant Secretary Adolf A. Berle with the names and Communist connections of Lee Pressman, Nathan Witt, Harold Ware, John Abt, Charles Kramer (alias Krivitsky), Henry Hill Collins, Vincent Reno, Lawrence Duggan, Henry Julian Wadleigh, Lauchlin Currie, Virginius Frank Coe, Alexander Trachtenberg, David Weintraub, and a dozen more, including, at the very end, Donald and Alger Hiss. Chambers did this at Berle's home in Washington on the night of September 2, 1939. No action was ever taken on this information. In *Witness*, a book which still stands as the greatest classic on communism in the United States, Whittaker Chambers told why:

"Weeks passed into months. I went about my work at *Time.* Then, one day, I am no longer certain just when, I met a dejected Levine. Adolf Berle, said Levine, had taken my information to the President (Roosevelt) at once. The President had laughed. When Berle was insistent, he had been told in words which it is necessary to paraphrase, to "go jump in a lake."[2]

The last laugh, of course, was not on Adolf Berle, Whittaker Chambers, or Isaac Don Levine. It was on America—for relaxing the vigilance its very first President had warned was the price of liberty.

Nine long years went by, years in which Alger Hiss rose to a position of considerable influence in the Department of State. With Harry Dexter White he helped organize the Bretton Woods Conference, where the seeds for the United Nations were first planted and where the international monetary system under which the world still operates took shape. At Yalta, Hiss sat at the right hand of President Roosevelt and helped deliver Eastern Europe into Soviet bondage. In 1945 he served as Secretary General of the founding meeting of the U.N. in San Francisco, helped draft the U.N. charter, and subsequently recruited dozens of American Communists for the U.N. staff.

Although Hiss' espionage activities were repeatedly reported to the FBI and other Intelligence agencies, he might never have been publicly unmasked if it had not been for an unknown Roman Catholic priest, the Reverend John Cronin. Father Cronin heard about Hiss through friends in the FBI and he passed the word along to two Congressmen he knew—Charles Kersten of Wisconsin and Richard Nixon of California. Soon these two were joined by Karl Mundt of South Dakota, acting chairman of the House Committee on Un-American Activities, and others in the Congress who were growing more and more curious about Communist infiltration of the federal government. On the morning of August 3, 1948, Whittaker Chambers was summoned to testify before the House Committee. When he identified Alger Hiss as a Soviet agent, he was pilloried from coast to coast. In much of the press, Chambers became the villain and Hiss the hero.

Thanks in large measure to the persistence of one Congressman, Richard Nixon, those roles were slowly, painfully reversed, though never entirely. To this day the feeling still persists in many quarters that Chambers was some kind of vindictive psychopath. Yet Alger Hiss was indicted, tried twice, finally convicted and imprisoned for perjury on

Chambers' proven testimony. When it was all over, Congressman Nixon rose on the floor of the House on January 26, 1950, and reviewed the whole unsettling drama.

"The great lesson which should be learned from the Alger Hiss case," said Nixon, "is that we are not just dealing with espionage agents who get thirty pieces of silver to obtain the blueprint of a new weapon—the Communists do that, too—but this is a far more sinister type of activity, because it permits the enemy to guide and shape our policy; it disarms and dooms our diplomats to defeat in advance before they go to conferences; traitors in the high councils of our own Government make sure that the deck is stacked on the Soviet side of the diplomatic table."

It was a lesson, alas, that America soon forgot.

CHAPTER III

'It Can't Happen Here'

DESPITE HIS WIDE AND GROWING KNOWLEDGE OF COMMUNIST SUBVER-sion, Otepka was nonetheless shocked to learn, in 1948, that the State Department had for seven years been sitting on the information Adolf Berle gave to President Roosevelt in 1939. Moreover, the FBI got the same information directly from Whittaker Chambers, with Berle's per-mission, two years after Berle carried it to the White House.

The only difference in the lists Chambers provided Berle and the FBI was that he added two more names when the Bureau's agents interviewed him. The two new people were Harry Dexter White and George Silver-man. Chambers had not mentioned them to Berle because, in 1939, he "still hoped that I had broken them away from the Communist Party".[1] That hope had long since proved forlorn.

During the intervening years, from the time the FBI acquired the names until 1948 when Congressmen Richard Nixon and Karl Mundt caused the youthful House Committee on Un-American Activities to break loose the sorry story of subversion, Alger Hiss was not the only one identified by Chambers who had risen to a position of great responsi-bility within the United States government.* Alger's brother, Donald

* Allen Dulles, former CIA chief, gave this conservative estimate: "The Soviet had over 40 high-level agents in various Washington departments and agencies during World War II. At least this many were uncovered; we don't know how many remained undetected."

34

Hiss, held an important job in the Legal Advisor's Office of the State Department. Lauchlin Currie became an administrative assistant to President Roosevelt. Frank Coe moved in and out of various sensitive posts, among others, assistant chief of the Foreign Economic Administration. Coe's brother, Charles (alias Bob Digby), was in the Office of War Information.

John Abt was special assistant to the Attorney General. Lawrence Duggan became head of the Bureau of Inter-American Affairs at State. Julian Wadleigh shifted from a key State Department job to the U.N. Relief and Rehabilitation Agency (UNRRA) where he found compatible company. Charles Kramer (Krivitsky) was on the National Labor Relations Board and had served several senators and Senate committees. Henry Hill Collins also worked on Capitol Hill, and in State's Displaced Persons program, which the Soviet was much interested in controlling.

Harry Dexter White rose to Assistant Secretary of the Treasury, from whence, among many other things, he effectively sabotaged the United States aid program to Nationalist China. Vincent Reno was still at the Aberdeen Proving Grounds, where new United States weapons are tested, when Chambers identified him publicly in 1948. David Weintraub had worked for Presidential assistant Harry Hopkins and, in UNRRA, for Herbert H. Lehman, in addition to holding a key post in the State Department.

This was, however, only a small part of the total picture. Elizabeth Bentley, who independently named many of these same people, added more new pieces to the puzzle. Among others, she identified Michael Greenberg as a member of an espionage ring within the Foreign Economic Administration; Maurice Halperin, a Soviet spy who was chief of the OSS Latin American division; Nathan Gregory Silvermaster, who headed a Communist spy cell in both the Labor and Treasury Departments; Victor Perlo, who was in charge of airplane production on the War Production Board and William Remington, also employed by the WPB while carrying out espionage assignments for the Soviets.

How many others these people brought into government can, even now, only be guessed. But for Otto Otepka and his fellow security officers it became "significant information" when these and other names popped up as references on job application forms submitted prior to 1948. It was *not*, however, considered sufficient evidence to warrant firing under Truman's loyalty program. Thus, many officials first helped into federal service by Hiss, Perlo, Silvermaster, et al. *are still there.* But they have risen to positions of much greater influence today.

While in the Civil Service Commission, Otepka became particularly interested in the Department of State. Although the Foreign Service Act removed many of State's employees from his jurisdiction, many more still came under Civil Service.

Otepka learned that as early as 1945, Secretary of State Edward R. Stettinius, Jr. was deeply troubled by some of the people he found around him. Stettinius called in the FBI and asked for an investigation of his Department.

The probe had hardly begun when the OSS, acting independently, conducted a midnight search, on Manhattan's lower Fifth Avenue, of the offices of *Amerasia*, a Left-wing magazine peddling the pro-Mao, anti-Chiang line. The OSS found there no less than 1,700 documents stolen from United States government files. Most were confidential; many were slugged "Top Secret." One was marked "A Bomb." Although the papers had originated in a number of government agencies, including OSS and the other Intelligence services, *they all bore the seal of the Department of State.* The OSS agents quickly made photo copies of selected documents and departed, so they could mount a surveillance of *Amerasia* without being detected.

Within twenty-four hours after this raid, William J. Donovan, the head of OSS, took a few of the more sensitive *Amerasia* photocopies to the Washington apartment of Secretary Stettinius. As Stettinius looked through the documents, at one point he turned to Assistant Secretary of State Julius Holmes, and exclaimed:

"Good God, Julius! If we can get to the bottom of this we will stop a lot of things that have been plaguing us."

That was in March. In June, Edward Stettinius was replaced as Secretary of State by James F. Byrnes, a Senator who knew quite a bit about a lot of things, but very little about the Department of State.

On June 6, 1945, three weeks before Stettinius stepped out, the FBI made six arrests in the *Amerasia* case. Charged, originally, with violation of the Espionage Act were John Stewart Service, a State Department official recently returned from China; Emmanuel Larsen, another State Department employee; Philip Jaffe, a native of Russia and editor of *Amerasia*; Kate Mitchell, Jaffe's co-editor and a former staff member of the Institute of Pacific Relations; Lieutenant Andrew Roth, then on active duty with Naval Intelligence; and Mark Julius Gayn, a free-lance writer born in Manchuria of Russian parents, educated in the Soviet

Union and at the Columbia School of Journalism, and employed since 1934 as a reporter in China and America.

Service, who later became one of the heaviest crosses Otto Otepka had to bear at the State Department, was suspended immediately. (He had just received a double promotion while under investigation.) But after a vicious press campaign of vilification against Acting Secretary of State Joseph Grew, who announced the arrests, a Washington Grand Jury refused to indict Service, Gayn and Kate Mitchell; a federal judge arbitrarily quashed the indictments against the other three, including Jaffe, who had previously agreed to plead guilty.

Secretary Byrnes wrote Service a personal letter congratulating him on his courtroom victory. The young "old China hand" was then reinstated, with back pay, and assigned as political advisor to General MacArthur's staff in Tokyo. MacArthur refused to accept him and he was shipped off temporarily to New Zealand, later returning to Washington where his trail subsequently crossed Otepka's.

Meanwhile, the FBI had completed its survey of the State Department and had recommended that a professional security officer be appointed to supervise personnel and physical security within the Department. Amazingly, the Department had never had a security man who officially functioned in this capacity. But five days before he departed State, Stettinius named Robert L. Bannerman to this new and critical position. Bannerman was placed under Frederick B. Lyon, Director of the Office of Controls.

Previously, whatever investigative functions existed were handled by the Department's Chief Special Agent. His confidential reports on questionable employees were reviewed by people in the Personnel Division who had no experience at all in evaluating security information. As Otepka was to discover, these procedures were about as effective in straining out security risks as a sieve with very large holes.

Bannerman did his best to plug those holes but it was a losing fight from the start. He had been with the State Department for eleven years, mostly in Intelligence, and he knew where some, though by no means all, of the holes were. At the outset, he took over the personnel review work and the evaluation of security data. However, Bannerman had no authority to make final decisions. All he could do, as Otepka did for years after him, was to make recommendations to those higher up, at the Assistant Secretary level and above.

Five days after Bannerman became Security Officer, Jimmy Byrnes was appointed Secretary of State. Over Bannerman, Byrnes placed Donald Russell as Assistant Secretary for Administration. Russell in turn named J. Anthony Panuch, a New York lawyer, as his deputy. Panuch was, in effect, Bannerman's boss.

The new Office of Security (SY), as it later came to be known, barely got started when in October 1945 President Truman merged five wartime agencies with the State Department—OSS, the Office of War Information (OWI), the Foreign Economic Administration, the Office of Inter-American Affairs, and the Office of the Army-Navy Liquidation Commissioner. This added 12,797 more employees, including several hundred aliens, to State's rolls, very nearly doubling the Department's staff.

Anthony Panuch later told a Congressional committee that the really big Communist infiltration of the State Department could be traced directly to this massive merger. Louis Budenz, former managing editor of the *Daily Worker*, testified after he left the Communist Party that literally *thousands* of Communists moved into government posts before, during and immediately after World War II. It is well known that many worked their way into the wartime agencies, and through them, into State.

For most of those who were in OSS, the State Department was merely a temporary way stop en route to CIA, which was created later as an autonomous agency. The same was true of the OWI crowd, which was to move on into the Voice of America. But many from both of these agencies, and from the other three involved in the merger, stuck with State. They were still there when Otepka came to SY in 1953 and many are still there today.

After the merger, Congress began to evince concern over the mysterious security situation in the Department of State. In 1946 Secretary Byrnes was asked by the Senate Appropriations Committee why he didn't do something about it. Byrnes replied that his hands were tied by the intricate Civil Service proceedings required to effect dismissals.

Senator Pat McCarran, an old-line Democrat from Nevada, suggested a way out of this dilemma. Accordingly, the "McCarran Rider" was tacked on to the State Department Appropriation Bill for fiscal 1947, and for several years thereafter. It gave the Secretary of State, "in his absolute discretion," the power to fire any official or employee "whenever he shall deem . . . necessary or advisable in the interests of the United States."

Over the next two years, a grand total of two State Department employees actually were fired under the McCarran Rider though it did force the resignation of some others.* Byrnes and his successor, George Marshall, made repeated promises to Congress that they would "clean house." The promises were never kept.

Despite Harry Truman's charges that the Republican-controlled 80th Congress played politics with the security issue, the evidence is overwhelming that the Congress bent over backwards to give the State Department every chance to clean up the mess itself long before the public got wind of it. Senator Styles Bridges of New Hampshire, later maligned almost as much as Joe McCarthy, insisted that the problem was so serious that it would destroy public confidence in the government if it ever got out.

On June 10, 1947—more than a year before Chambers testified before the House committee—Bridges and Senator Joseph H. Ball of Minnesota met privately with Secretary Marshall and presented him with a long list of the more serious security risks at State. At first, Marshall refused to believe the charges. Later, he dismissed ten (out of 64) from the Bridges-Ball list.

Seven of these ten officials promptly retained the Washington law firm of Arnold, Fortas and Porter to fight their dismissals.** The press laid down a withering barrage against the State Department (one reporter won a Pulitzer Prize for his stories***) and George Marshall quickly wilted. He accepted the law firm's demand that the seven be permitted to resign "without prejudice," although a week earlier Marshall had hinted that "some" of them were not just risks, but spies for "foreign powers."

This skirmish took place in 1947, nearly three years before Joseph McCarthy made his debut on the national stage with his sensational charges of security risks in high places. A careful study of the record of those intervening years would convince all but the most fanatical Leftists that the patience of Congress had been sorely tried. It was only after two-and-a-half years of unbelievable stalling, alibiing, and pussyfooting by the State Department that Congress finally broke the issue of subversion into the open.

One of the things that triggered the Congress' decision was the Truman Executive Order, No. 9835. Issued in 1947, ostensibly to set up a

* One of the officials fired was Carl Aldo Marzani who was operating a Communist Party publishing house in the late 1960's.
** Arnold, Fortas and Porter were Thurman Arnold, former Justice of the U.S. Court of Appeals; Abe Fortas, appointed by President Lyndon Johnson in 1966 to the U.S. Supreme Court, and Paul Porter, former Administrator of the OPA.
***Bert Andrews, Chief of the Washington Bureau of the *New York Herald Tribune.*

new "loyalty" program, it also was aimed at plugging up the increasing "leaks" on subversion from within the State Department. This order was reinforced by the President on March 13, 1948, on the eve of the Congressional hearings on Alger Hiss, et al. The 1948 directive, which years later formed the basis for the charges against Otepka, forbids federal employees to divulge information on government policy and personnel to anyone outside the executive branch, including the Congress.

With the door slammed firmly in its face, Congress reacted in the only way it could. It began looking elsewhere for information on subversion, mainly from Communist defectors like Chambers, Budenz and Miss Bentley. And at long last it decided to make the public aware of at least some of the security risks within the government.

Influential segments of the press turned this around, and made of it a holy war for civil liberties, charging that Congress was violating the rights of individuals. It should have been apparent, but it wasn't, that the overwhelming majority of the populace had some rights too, among them the right to be protected against betrayal. But by indiscriminate use of the twisted logic that still rules the minds of men, Congress was made into the villain, and the Communists were somehow transformed into innocent victims of a "witchhunt."

The whole issue of subversion soon became a privileged sanctuary that respectable politicians in both parties dared not touch. As early as 1948, Thomas E. Dewey was constrained from injecting it too strongly into his campaign. His powder-puff approach to this, and other issues, resulted in his defeat by Harry Truman, who projected the image of a tough fighter, championing the rights of the "little guy" so oppressed by the "special interests" of the capitalist barons.

It was the McCarthy era, however, that forever removed subversion from the list of palatable political issues in America. No doubt Senator McCarthy's free-swinging approach to the problem offended thousands of citizens, among them Otto Otepka and this writer. Yet today many of these same people have grudgingly come to understand that even if McCarthy had elected for a completely different approach—careful, cautious, restrained, in short all the things Joe McCarthy admittedly was not—his ultimate fate would not have been markedly different from what it was. It may have taken his opponents a bit longer to get him, but in the end they would have had his head just the same.

One is tempted to speculate that if no Joe McCarthy had ever existed whether the Left would not have felt compelled to invent him. The Left badly needed a Devil just then. Not only the Communists had been sorely wounded by earlier thrusts of Congressional committees; the whole Liberal community had suffered painfully. Virtually all of the people identified as Soviet spies had been fully accepted for years as bona fide Liberals. The non-Communist Left could not bring itself to believe that so many of its blood brothers were really Russianized wolves in sheep's clothing. To do so would have been tantamount to pointing an accusing finger at themselves. For the Liberals knew that a good many of the policies they had embraced, and implemented in government, had originated with the very people who now stood accused as espionage agents for a foreign power.

The Left, united more firmly than in its popular front heyday, reacted against McCarthyism with an outburst of emotionalism unprecedented in this country. "Contortions of such severity have not been observed since the St. Vitus dance epidemics of the Middle Ages," writer Willi Schlamm noted in remarking on the virulent surge of anti-McCarthyism that swept reason from the minds of even the best-intentioned men.[2]

After McCarthy, anti-communism was dead, not only as a political issue, but as the subject for any meaningful intellectual exploration. In fact, communism itself seemed to expire, at least as an internal threat. Not even the bitter lesson of the Hungarian Revolution, nor Fidel Castro's take-over of Cuba, could revive it for long.

Over and over again Americans were told, mostly by subtle inference, that it simply could not happen here. The public was lulled into a sense of complacency by repeated assurances that the FBI was watching over all spies and subversives. It was felt that no espionage agent could escape the nets thrown out by the super-efficient Bureau.* The overworked agents in the FBI knew better, of course. But they were condemned to eternal silence. Only J. Edgar Hoover could really speak for the Bureau. Unhappily, as the years went on fewer and fewer people paid any attention at all to Mr. Hoover. As his audience shrank, so did his influence.

Very early in the Kennedy Administration, Director Hoover discovered just how much weight his word would carry in the future. Upon learning that Adam Yarmolinsky was scheduled for appointment to a very key position in the Department of Defense, Hoover made one of his rare sallies outside established official channels and sent a resumé of Yarmolinsky's FBI file to the White House. The young lawyer was the

* In spite of numerous explanations by the FBI, the public has never grasped the salient fact that the Bureau has no control whatever over personnel policies in other government departments and agencies. It has a purely *investigative* function. The FBI cannot recommend against the employment of any individual, even if it has hard evidence that he is a spy. All it can do is pass on the results of its investigations to people in the security offices of the various departments and hope for the best.

son of a Russian-born minor literary figure, Avram Yarmolinsky, and Babette Deutsch, both notorious champions of Communist causes for many years. Reliable reports placed their son in the Young Communist League at Harvard. Adam denied he had ever been a member, though he cheerfully conceded that "they [the Young Communists] believed, and I was inclined to believe, that a so-called Communist government was a desirable end."

There was much more of the same in Yarmolinsky's file, a good deal of it of far more recent vintage. In the mid-1950's, for instance, he had masterminded an all-out assault on the internal security system via a study subsidized by his employer, the Ford Foundation-financed Fund for the Republic. But the White House ignored J. Edgar Hoover and placed the bristling little legal intellectual in the Defense Department. His qualifications for any post in DOD were nil, but he became, in effect, Robert Strange McNamara's civilian chief-of-staff, ably implementing the policies concocted by Walt W. Rostow and his friends in the White House and at State.

The reason for Yarmolinsky's Svengali-like hold on McNamara for years remained one of Washington's most puzzling mysteries. Then Arthur Schlesinger, the ubiquitous gossip of the New Frontier, hinted that McNamara probably owed his job to, of all people, Adam Yarmolinsky! It seems that right after the 1960 election, Yarmolinsky was an important member of the small group working under the Kennedy brother-in-law, Sargent Shriver, on the recruiting of Cabinet members and other officials for the incoming Administration. McNamara, a nominal Republican and president of the Ford Motor Company, was not even in the picture for consideration to any post. But Yarmolinsky apparently put him there.

Overnight, Robert McNamara was unveiled as a thoroughly acceptable Liberal. It was learned that after his graduation from the University of California at Berkeley, he had moved on to Harvard Business School where he won fame, of a sort, by becoming one of two members of the faculty (out of one hundred) who backed Franklin Roosevelt against Wendell Willkie in 1940.* More recently McNamara had exhibited sympathy for such organizations as the American Civil Liberties Union. Moreover, he had voted for Jack Kennedy for President and put up some money for the Kennedy campaign.

"Kennedy knew none of these last facts, however," Schlesinger tells us. "But Shriver reported that one of his associates in the talent search,

---

* The other one was Eugene Zuckert, who became Secretary of the Air Force under McNamara in the early 1960's.

Adam Yarmolinsky, had met McNamara and had the highest opinion of him."[3] That, and later recommendations from John Kenneth Galbraith and others, clinched the job for McNamara. Actually, he was given his choice of Treasury or Defense, but under Yarmolinsky's wise tutelage he picked the Pentagon, and carried Adam piggyback in with him to rule the military establishment with, as one wag put it, Yarmolinsky's velvet fist in McNamara's iron glove.

Raymond Loughton, Otepka's counterpart at the Pentagon, strongly objected to Yarmolinsky's clearance. Six months later Loughton left Defense and joined Otepka on a "special project" at State.

The appointment of an Adam Yarmolinsky to the Defense Department would, under normal circumstances, raise storm signals throughout the security-intelligence community. In early 1961, however, it passed almost unnoticed. For the security professionals, and particularly Otto Otepka, found that the storm was already upon them. They were being inundated with the appointments of so many Yarmolinskys that one more caused hardly anything but a resigned shrug.

CHAPTER **IV**

The Man in SY

IN 1967, WHEN THERE WAS HARDLY A VOICE LEFT, IN OR OUT OF CON-
gress, that dared mention the *verboten* issue of subversion, Otto Otepka
was "tried" by the State Department under the archaic Truman directive,
issued twenty years earlier to protect a President from political embarrassment and a Soviet spy from public disclosure. The deep and far-
reaching damage done by that order can never be fully calculated. For
twenty years it had effectively shielded countless security risks within the
government as well as all manner of political chicanery and corruption.

Incredibly, the Congress, which was the principal target and remains
the chief victim of the Truman directive, has permitted it to stand without serious challenge. Each time an attempt has been made to strip off
the executive branch's iron muzzle with new legislation, the Congress has
sidestepped the issue. In 1951, for example, a bill was introduced by then
Senator Richard M. Nixon. It provided for a $5,000 fine and up to five
years imprisonment for any government official who demoted, dismissed,
or otherwise disciplined a subordinate because of truthful testimony
before a Congressional committee.[1] The Nixon bill was permitted to die,
just as a similar measure which arose directly from the Otepka case was
allowed to expire in 1968.

Thus, each year the lawmakers of both parties tacitly agree, when they vote on the appropriations bills for the Department of State and other sensitive agencies, that they are willing to put up the taxpayers' money to pay the salaries of people they are forbidden to know anything about. In effect, Congress has elected to play a dangerous game of blind man's bluff on Capitol Hill while running grave risks with the national security.

In fairness, it should be pointed out that in most cases the senators and congressmen have no other alternative. With the object lesson of Senator Joseph McCarthy indelibly stamped in their minds, they realize that any attempt to force the issue and demand information from the personnel security files of the executive branch would brand them as McCarthyites, which is to say they would be considered by their colleagues and constituents as never again worthy of serious consideration, either in the Congress or at the polls.

Fortunately for Otepka, he was still an anonymous official in the Civil Service Commission when the great storms generated by the early Congressional investigations into subversion swept the country from its intellectual moorings. If he had been in the Department of State, he undoubtedly would have been taken out of the game a decade or more before he was finally removed. The Department was, even then, a treacherous swamp for any official conscientiously bent on protecting the government against infiltration.

On July 15, 1948, for example, Robert Alexander, then Assistant Chief of the Visa Division, testified before the Senate Judiciary Committee that numerous aliens working at the United Nations in New York were exceedingly doubtful security risks.[2] Alexander was promptly suspended, and a State Department commission issued a press release professing that it was "shocked by the manner in which these serious charges were made."[3]

At the time, Dean Rusk was Director of State's Office of U.N. Affairs. Since his domain was threatened, Rusk did not hesitate to help the handpicked commission publicly smear Alexander for giving "irresponsible testimony" which "embarrassed the United Nations."

A few months later, Valentin Gubitchev, a Soviet engineer employed by the U.N., was arrested with Judith Coplon, a Justice Department "G-girl" who seasoned her amours with espionage. Both were convicted and the public has long since lost count of the other spies working out of the great glass tower below the East River's Hell's Gate.

Ironically, Robert Alexander was branded as "irresponsible" at the very time the State Department was pleading with the country to give Alger Hiss a "fair chance." Assistant Secretary of State Edward Miller organized a defense fund for Hiss while Alexander was placed under charges by the Department. Alexander demanded an open hearing and the charges were dropped, but he was still reprimanded. His career, of course, was ruined and he has since died.

In January 1949 the Senate confirmed Dean Gooderham Acheson as Secretary of State, although he had staunchly defended his friend, Alger Hiss. A year later, *after* Hiss was convicted, Acheson, having served as a character witness for Hiss at his trial, haughtily issued his famous pronouncement: "I do not intend to turn my back on Alger Hiss."[4]

In the 1960's, with Alger's brother, Donald Hiss, still employed by Dean Acheson's law firm, Acheson became an advisor to President Kennedy and won a reputation as a "hawk" in Administration circles. His son-in-law, William P. Bundy, brother of Presidential assistant McGeorge Bundy, had Dean Rusk's old job as Assistant Secretary for Far Eastern Affairs and was also deemed "hawkish" on Vietnam and other matters.

On June 27, 1950, America was plunged into the Korean War, which Acheson practically invited by announcing that South Korea was *not* a vital sphere of the United States. As it became apparent that this was to be America's first winless war, the people slowly awakened to the fact that something was rotten in Washington. Dwight D. Eisenhower was elected in 1952 running on a Republican platform pledged to clean up the mess and do something about Korea. Explicit in the GOP campaign was the promise that a thorough housecleaning of the State Department would be forthcoming.

With a nudge from Styles Bridges, Secretary of State John Foster Dulles brought in R.W. Scott McLeod, a former FBI man, to tackle the Department's formidable security problem. Years later, McLeod told the Senate Internal Security Subcommittee: "If I did not do anything else down there [at State], I did get the man I think is the best [security] evaluator in the government today. His name is Otto Otepka."[5]

Becoming a security evaluator at State was for Otepka the equivalent of a demotion, at least insofar as his personal area of responsibility was concerned. At the Civil Service Commission he pretty much ran his own show and had a large staff under him. At State he would be, in the beginning at least, just another cog in a security machine that had not yet begun to operate.

Moreover, Otepka realized he would be giving up a safe sinecure that offered steady advancement to plunge into dangerous shoals that had already washed out a number of good security officers, or eroded their will to the point where they had become mere hangers-on riding the government payroll. But Scott McLeod was persuasive. He convinced Otepka that great changes were in the offing at the State Department. The McCarran Act, which greatly strengthened the government security program, had gone into effect in 1950, and Executive Order 10450 would strengthen the program even more.

Otepka was aware, of course, that State was where the real action was. Unless the security situation could be corrected in the department which shaped and guided United States foreign policy, there was little hope America could change the dangerous course it had been following for so many years. Otepka decided his personal risks were overshadowed by more important considerations, and on June 15, 1953, after setting his house in order at the Civil Service Commission, he transferred to the Department of State.

McLeod and Otepka found the haphazard security setup at State in chaos. As McLeod later testified, "There were more files outside the file room than there were inside the file room, and in many cases of em- ployees that had been on the rolls for years, there was no security file whatever."[6] Equally serious, Otepka discovered that many of the files had been systematically rifled and all derogatory information, especially on certain high-ranking Department officials, had vanished.

Working day and night, Otepka gradually helped McLeod and his new Bureau of Security and Consular Affairs bring a semblance of order out of the chaos. McLeod established a system whereby every official who passed on a security case had to initial the file. Amazingly, this had never been done before and no one knew who was responsible for clearing people suspected as security risks.

McLeod also believed "security should be a continuing process; that every time a man was promoted or transferred, the Security Office should bring his file up to date and should assure themselves that he still met the requirements of the order [10450]."[7] Otepka was placed in unofficial charge of the staggering job of reviewing the background and files of the State Department's 11,000 employees. In the process, he weeded out a substantial number of security and suitability risks.* Many of them re- signed rather than face dismissal charges. As time went on, however, Otepka's job became more difficult.

Foster Dulles was in favor of establishing a sound security program at

---

* McLeod placed the figure at "around 300" in February 1954. All told, the State Depart- ment and other sensitive federal agencies unloaded some 3,900 employees in 1953-54. However, many simply shifted to other, non-sensitive agencies, and in 1961 not a few returned to their old departments.

State, but he had the lawyer's proclivity for insisting that all the intricate legal procedures be followed even after Eisenhower armed him with E.O. 10450. Any employee charged on security or suitability grounds could appeal. This entailed a long drawn-out hearing and the right to confront his accusers face-to-face. Since a good deal of the information on which charges were based came from undercover agents of the FBI and other Intelligence agencies, confrontation was, more often than not, impossible.

The Intelligence community has to protect its sources. This is not merely a matter of maintaining the effectiveness of underground operatives. Sometimes it is literally a matter of life or death.

The lawyer's essentially superficial view of this hard, brutal world of espionage, which in recent years has been much mocked by novelists and movie makers, is still attuned to a more leisurely century when Blackstone was setting down the rules of English common law. Today, as a British white paper on the Burgess-McLean affair points out, no government can hope to protect itself against Communist agents if it considers government employment an inalienable right and stands on legal ceremony in attempting to dismiss suspected security risks.

Scott McLeod conceded, however, that "about half the time"—and possibly as much as 75 percent of the time—he was overruled when his office recommended dismissals. "Relatively few cases were actually processed to the hearing stage," he admitted.[8]

In spite of these setbacks, McLeod and Otepka patiently ploughed ahead. They and their associates in SY were pioneering a fresh new field, barely explored, as yet largely uncharted, fraught with unseen dangers. They were not surprised to find themselves under attack, both from within and without the Department of State. More often than not, these attacks were spearheaded by Liberals and Socialists rather than by known Communists.

Nikita Khrushchev, a refreshingly frank man when he wasn't gulling timid visitors from the United States, once said: "We cannot expect Americans to jump from capitalism to Communism. But we can assist their elected leaders in giving Americans small doses of socialism, until they suddenly awake to find they have Communism!"

Yet the FBI, the CIA, and all the other Intelligence agencies persist in making a clear distinction between disloyal Communists and loyal Socialists. Not that this distinction shouldn't be made. It should, of course. But not quite in the way the Intelligence community makes it, for it misses two vital points: (1) that socialism, by its very nature, is *international,* not national, at heart, and (2) that the Soviets have long preferred to use Socialists, rather than Communist Party members, for varying shades of espionage activity.* The failure of the Intelligence community to recognize these salient points has removed virtually all Socialists from its limited line of vision, and seriously undermines the national security.

Otto Otepka, with the benefit of hindsight and his own bitter experience, came to this recognition reluctantly, after years of observing subversion in government. By then it was too late for him to do anything about it, though it is unlikely that he ever could have corrected it. *That* would have taken a policy decision from the White House; and if Dwight Eisenhower's White House never made it, simply because it never understood the nature of socialism, one could hardly expect Lyndon Johnson's White House to make it.

At any event, McLeod and Otepka had difficulty enough trying to ferret out bona fide Communists without dissipating their energies on the larger problem of socialism. In addition, they were saddled with the burden of establishing what was essentially a brand new profession within the State Department. There were precious few qualified security evaluators in all the government, and it largely fell to Otepka to formulate the guidelines both for the job and the kind of individual who should fill it.

As the New York *Times* very accurately put it, Otepka helped write "the book" for the whole security community.[9] Even the *Times* might once have been willing to concede that it was an eminently fair and reliable roadmap to sound security.

Going by the book, Otepka soon found himself engaged in a behind-the-scenes struggle with that "most powerful man in America," Senator Joe McCarthy. In 1953 the Senator put the heat on the State Department to fire one Wolf Ladejinsky, a Department agricultural expert then stationed in the Far East. Ladejinsky had once been employed by Amtorg, the Soviet trade agency in the United States, and that was enough for McCarthy.

On the surface, McCarthy had a good case. Amtorg was well known

* For example, the Democratic Alliance, a Danish student group, infiltrated various Leftist organizations and managed to get seven of its members to the "Baltic Sea Week" youth festival at Rostock, East Germany in July 1964. The Communists made an all-out effort to recruit espionage agents from the West at this festival. However, no attempt was made to recruit the two Alliance members posing as Communists, while every enticement was used to get the five "Socialists" into a spy apparat. "From our documentation it can be said," reported the Alliance, "that the East German intelligence agencies prefer Socialists and others in the Free World for their [espionage] work, rather than fanatic known members of the Free World Communist parties."

as one of the leading conduits for Soviet espionage activities. Under the "reasonable doubt" clause of E.O. 10450, Ladejinsky could easily have been dismissed. But Otepka had made a careful study of Amtorg years before and he had come to the conclusion that during the 1930's and 1940's the Soviets had hired a number of loyal American citizens in Amtorg to help them establish a respectable trade front. In his view, Wolf Ladejinsky was one.

Scott McLeod, who at first was inclined to agree with McCarthy, was swung around by Otepka's analysis of Amtorg and by his thorough evaluation of Ladejinsky's background. But McCarthy was adamant. He insisted Ladejinsky be fired at once. Word of his clash with the Republican-controlled State Department soon got out to the press. In the end, Otepka won out. Ladejinsky was kept on and McCarthy had seriously undercut his influence with the Administration.

There is a curious irony in the fact that Clark Mollenhoff, who has picked up virtually every major journalism award extant, won three of them (Heywood Brown, Raymond Clapper, and Sigma Delta Chi Golden Quill Award) for his stories on the Ladejinsky Case. Mollenhoff did not know Otepka then, and, in fact, knew nothing of Otepka's role in the case. But when Mollenhoff did get to know him, a decade later, he came to understand how Otepka's ingrained sense of fair play would never permit him to knuckle under to powerful forces.

The Ladejinsky affair was only one instance in which Otepka was in disagreement with McCarthy, and more important for him, with Scott McLeod. But McLeod always listened attentively to Otepka's quiet argument, and more often than not went along with his recommendations. Nonetheless, both in and out of the State Department, McLeod was fast earning a reputation as being something of a bull in the china shop. He was under constant attack from the press and there was a steady stream of mysterious news leaks from within the Department that kept McLeod in hot water.

One case that had McLeod stewing on the Fourth Estate's civil liberties burners was handled, as were many others, by his anonymous evaluator, Otepka. This one concerned the old pro-Mao China cabal, and specifically John Paton Davies. Among many other things, it had at long last come to light, through the Institute of Pacific Relations hearings and Intelligence sources, that Davies had knowingly delivered confidential and secret government documents to Communist agents to help put the skids under America's ally, Nationalist China.

Otepka's findings in the Davies case went up to an independent

Security Hearing Board, which voted 5-0 for Davies' dismissal as a security risk. Secretary Dulles upheld Otepka's findings, and the board's vote, and Davies was fired* despite an anguished outcry from that influential segment of the press whose reaction in such cases can always be predicted.

The Davies case earned Otepka the everlasting enmity of that part of the Foreign Service Corps which considers its ranks sacrosanct against any disciplinary action, no matter how serious the offense. However, McLeod bore the brunt of the public attack and was widely denounced, for this and other transgressions, as a McCarthyite witchhunter, first class.

That Scotty McLeod was not deserving of this rough treatment is evidenced, in part, by his high regard for his eminently fair-minded and invariably cautious evaluator. On April 25, 1954, he promoted Otepka to Chief of the Division of Evaluations, the critical nerve center of the whole Office of Security.

Otepka was now on the spot. Logically, he should have become the target for every security-hating malcontent in the Department of State, and to some degree he was. But he also won the grudging admiration of many, even in the Foreign Service Corps, who recognized and appreciated, as one of them wrote him from Geneva, "those qualities of judgment, fairness, and calm appraisal which you have always demonstrated."[10]

The beginning of the second Eisenhower term brought some changes, and security clearances had to be issued for new Presidential appointees. Otepka's Evaluations Division took on the job, and when it was done he was commended, through E. Tomlin Bailey, the Foreign Service officer who then occupied the post of Director of SY, "for the expeditious handling of many of these delicate cases on very limited notice."[11]

President Eisenhower's last term also caused some shuffling in the Bureau of Security and Consular Affairs. Scott McLeod had become a bit too hot to handle and he was shunted off to the United States embassy in Dublin. Senator John Fitzgerald Kennedy opposed his nomination as ambassador, probably to score a few more brownie points with the Liberals, but McLeod was confirmed.

Theodore Sorensen claims Kennedy told him at the time, "I sympathize with their wanting to get rid of McLeod, but why pick on poor old Ireland."[12] But as Sorensen also informs us, he sometimes "invented"

---

* Davies received a security clearance and returned to government service as a $75-a-day consultant on disarmament in January 1969.

appropriate quotes for Kennedy to use, attributing them to "one of our founding fathers."[13] So perhaps he invented Kennedy's comment on McLeod too.

Before McLeod departed for Ireland, Otepka completed a prodigious task that SY had been working on for nearly four years. It was a by-product of the extensive security review of all Department personnel begun in 1953. During this review, SY had flagged the staggering total of 1,943 cases on whom some form of derogatory information existed. This represented nearly 20 per cent of the State Department's total complement.

Otepka later disclosed that out of these 1,943, "722 of the persons left the Department for various reasons, *but mostly by transfer to other agencies, before a final security determination was made.*"[14] That left 1,221 on State's payroll. From these, Otepka selected 858 individuals as well worth keeping an eye on. This list he sent to McLeod in December 1955.

Not all these 858 were security cases, per se. Some were habitual drunks. Some were homosexuals. Others had made false statements on applications and elsewhere. Still others had known mental illnesses. But there *were* on this list a fair number who had been reported by the FBI and other agencies as members of the Communist Party or the Young Communist League, or of the multiple front organizations. Some had knowingly associated with espionage agents.

McLeod's staff took Otepka's list and winnowed it down from 858 to 258 which they pronounced "serious," particularly in light of the positions the 258 then held. Approximately 150 were in high-level posts where they could in one way or another influence the formulation of United States foreign policy. And fully half of these 258 serious cases were officials in either crucial Intelligence assignments or serving on top-secret committees reaching all the way up and into the National Security Council.

This became known as the "McLeod List." During the Otepka Hearings before the Senate Internal Security Subcommittee in the mid-1960's, the State Department at first denied the list ever existed; later admitted it did exist; then washed it out in strong detergent, Foggy Bottom brand, claiming that the list consisted mainly of cases of "mistaken identity."[15]

McLeod's office instructed Otepka to keep a separate set of files on these 258 questionable cases and earmark them "for special attention and reinvestigation systematically when these individuals came up for promotion or reassignment."[16] McLeod's concern, equally shared by Otepka, was that these people would keep moving on up the promotion ladder and ultimately do far more damage than they may have wrought already.

In June 1956 McLeod passed the list along to Undersecretary Loy Henderson. He reminded Henderson that four separate Soviet Intelligence rings had been known to be operating within the government during the 1940's, but only three had been identified.* The fourth must be presumed to be still in existence.

Whittaker Chambers, who worked for two of these Soviet apparats, tells us that shortly before he left the Communist underground, his espionage "control," one Colonel Bykov, informed him that Moscow wanted Chambers to establish "an entirely new apparatus within the American Government. It was to be made up of men as highly placed as I could recruit. But it was to be wholly a reserve apparatus. Its members were not to engage in active espionage. They were to become active only . . . when the other apparatuses might be disabled or destroyed."[17]

Chambers broke with communism before he could carry out this assignment, but it is a reasonable assumption that it *was* carried out by other agents. If so, it has now been operating for some thirty years, with younger recruits added as each new generation comes to maturity. How many separate and distinct apparats have been formed in addition to this one is impossible to estimate, but only a fool would say there have been no more.

McLeod, whatever his faults, was no fool, though the press did its damndest to paint him as one. Entirely apart from the list he sent up to Loy Henderson, he said he recognized very well that the Department could be harboring a "sleeper," an agent about whom there was absolutely no unfavorable information at all. This, of course, is the ideal agent, and there have been many such in recent history. Colonel Stig Wennerstroem, the former Swedish Air Force attaché in Washington, is but one. For five years Wennerstroem operated right under the noses of the FBI and CIA, passing United States defense secrets to Soviet Embassy contacts, earning the secret rank of General in the Soviet Army before he was caught in 1963.

SY could do little about "sleepers," and after January 1961 Otepka found that he would not be permitted to do anything further about the

---

* Most security people hold that two were identified. McLeod apparently subdivided one of the rings.

258 individuals on McLeod's list either. Many of them are still in the Department of State, only, as McLeod feared, they have moved steadily upward.

After McLeod left for Ireland, Otepka was appointed Deputy Director of the Office of Security. The appointment went into effect April 7, 1957, and for the next four years he was, in everything but name, the working chief of State's far-flung personnel security system.

Otepka's new duties, which encompassed all aspects of the State Department's revamped security program, did not prevent him from keeping a weather eye on his old Evaluations Division. He knew that was the heart and soul of the whole security system at State and he had no intention of letting it lapse back into the doldrums in which it had become so hopelessly mired before his arrival.

However, Otepka did not anticipate that he would continue to be burdened with the tedious and time-consuming job of evaluating cases himself. Yet the widespread reputation he had won for fairness and objectivity made that inevitable. In June 1957, for example, his superiors dumped another tough evaluation job in his lap with instructions to handle it himself. It was the case of John Stewart Service.

The Service problem had been bouncing around the State Department for a dozen years, since the FBI had arrested the then young "China expert" in 1945. Following the curious quashing of his indictment and his triumphant return to the Department (he had never actually been removed from the payroll), Service was cleared several times by various departmental boards, including one which boasted such distinguished members as Dean Acheson and Nelson Rockefeller. (The transcript of *that* particular proceeding had vanished without a trace by 1957.)

In 1951, the Civil Service Commission bluntly told the State Department that it was "stretching the mantle of charity too far" for Mr. Service and ordered the Department to get rid of him. Reluctantly, State dismissed its wayward China hand. But in 1952 he filed suit in Federal Court and on June 17, 1957, the Supreme Court handed down its decision in the case of Service vs. Dulles.

In one of those weird rulings that have greatly undermined the Government's security program during the past decade, the Supreme Court ruled in favor of John Stewart Service on a technicality that strained to put the proverbial camel through the eye of the needle. The Court said the State Department had failed to afford Service a hearing under the McCarran Rider, which was in effect from 1947 to 1953, and therefore the Department had to take him back. This, despite the fact that Service had been granted a full and fair hearing under the Truman loyalty order which superseded the McCarran Rider! Under the ruling, the Department had to reinstate Service in grade, with some $60,000 in back pay—plus interest.

When Otepka interrogated Service in 1957, the Director of SY, E. Tomlin Bailey, decided to sit in. Service himself was reasonably frank and open about his part in the *Amerasia* affair. He admitted delivering eighteen classified State Department documents to Philip Jaffe, but he insisted he knew Jaffe only as a "magazine editor," and was not aware of Jaffe's Communist connections, though he began to suspect something of the kind about six weeks before his arrest. (This hardly explains why Service gave Jaffe Chiang's troop dispositions and other military plans, or why Jaffe, as a "magazine editor," should have been so interested in such details.)

Service said his only motive in handing the documents to Jaffe was to discredit Ambassador Pat Hurley, who had tossed him out of China early in 1945. (Hurley took this action after Intelligence reported Service had transmitted a secret document to an agent of Mao Tse-tung.) Service couldn't understand why he should have been fired for merely trying to get Ambassador Hurley fired, though he conceded, reluctantly, that under the State Department's present regulations, namely E.O. 10450, he wouldn't have a legal leg to stand on.

Throughout Otepka's interrogation of John Service, Tomlin Bailey frequently broke in with the gentle enjoiner, "Now, Jack, you don't really mean that." But Service took him aback several times by saying, yes he did mean it.

Afterwards, Otepka turned out one of his typically thorough evaluations of the case. He concluded that Service was not a Communist, but in view of all the evidence he recommended that action be taken against him under the Foreign Service Act, which provided an easier route for dropping people for misconduct than the terribly involved hearing system. His evaluations also disclosed serious irregularities in the previous handling of the case, including a coverup of the *Amerasia* scandal.

Bailey promptly overruled Otepka and recommended that Service be given a clearance without any further proceedings. Roderic O'Connor, who had replaced McLeod as Administrator of the Bureau of Security & Consular Affairs, then overruled Bailey. But O'Connor was in turn overruled himself by Loy Henderson, a career Foreign Service officer, and Service was dispatched to Liverpool as Consul General. He remained there until 1960, enjoying normal promotions until he retired, on a comfortable pension, with the rank of Foreign Service Officer Class 2. Typically, he found a safe harbor in Academe. Upon leaving State, his friends had a berth waiting for him at the Center for Chinese Studies in Berkeley.

When the Foreign Service Corps learned what Otepka had tried to do to their old comrade in arms, John Stewart Service, they ticked off yet another black mark against his name.

The Corps was further chagrined when, in April 1958, Secretary Dulles bestowed on Otepka the Department's coveted Meritorious Service Award. Unfortunately, Dulles' cancer, which had for some time been eating his life away, was getting more severe in the spring of 1958 and he was unable to be on hand when Otepka received the citation during a ceremony in the State Department auditorium. The award, signed by Dulles, read in part:

"For meritorious service, loyalty and devotion to duty. . . outstanding display of sound judgment, creative work and unusual responsibilities, [Otto Otepka] has reflected great credit on himself and the Department and has served as an incentive to his colleagues."

In recommending Otepka for the award, E. Tomlin Bailey noted: "The improved relationships which the Department has enjoyed with the Congress on matters relating to personnel security during the past year or two are due in no small part to the outstanding staff work done by Mr. Otepka."

This era, however, was fast drawing to its close. It went out, not with a whimper, but a bang—of sorts—in the Presidential election of 1960. By then the stage was already set for Otto Otepka's fall from grace. Dean Rusk and Bobby Kennedy were waiting in the wings, ready to play their parts, and they were haphazardly rehearsing a host of spear-carriers to administer the final coup.

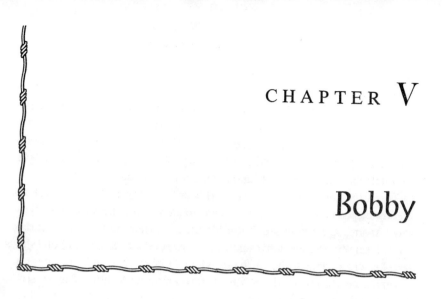

CHAPTER V

Bobby

THE SHADOWY ROLE OF ROBERT F. KENNEDY IN THE PURGE OF OTTO
Otepka and his associates from the State Department's Office of Security
did not come into view until Otepka's departmental hearing in June
1967. Nonetheless, the quiet man in SY felt Bobby's hand stealthily
reaching into the sensitive affairs of his office as early as December 1960.
Kennedy's concern for the career of Walt W. Rostow was but one case
in point.

The new Attorney General's unique position, forged by ties of blood
with the President, enhanced his power tremendously and set him quite
apart from the ordinary run of Cabinet members and White House advisors. Placed in overall charge of patronage for the new Administration,
he naturally took a personal interest in the appointments being made
through all departments of the government. But there was none in which
he evinced a deeper interest than the Department of State. Inevitably,
this brought Bobby into conflict with Otepka, the man who policed that
realm.

Jack Kennedy had been led to believe that his forte was foreign affairs.
Moreover, he rightly sensed that the future of the nation, and of the
world, would be decided largely in that exotic arena. His concern for
domestic issues, even the potentially explosive issue of civil rights, was

peripheral. He intended to stake out his claim on history in the volatile field of foreign policy where war and peace, security or annihilation, hung in the balance. Bobby Kennedy, finely attuned to his brother's thought and desire, could hardly avoid embroiling himself in the same treacherous caldron.

Not long after their meeting with Otepka towards the end of 1960, Kennedy and Rusk happily found a temporary expedient which removed the security chief for a time from the critical day-to-day business of issuing clearances. They did not have to invent it. The expedient was ready-made, as we shall see. But it took the pressure off them during the crucial early period when they were repopulating and reshaping the Department of State.

Otepka, of course, had no way of foreseeing that within a very few years Robert Francis Kennedy would be propelled from the unenviable position of vague villain of the Liberals to the lofty perch of doyen of the New Left, publicly advocating such dubious measures as the shipping of American blood plasma to the Communist forces in North Vietnam. If, however, he had studied Bobby's background more carefully then, he may possibly have detected a few clues that might have better explained the intemperate outburst during their meeting with Dean Rusk and perhaps have raised a few warning signals for the future.

On the surface, though, the bare bones of Bobby's career up to 1960 reveal very little that would suggest that as Attorney General he would be in any way "soft" on internal security matters. In fact, the main reason the Left openly distrusted him in those days was his past association with Senator Joseph McCarthy.

Add to that Bobby's outrageously capitalist family background. Sprinkle it with the stardust that seems to protect sons of Erin from Marxism. Then mix in the undeniable fact that Kennedy was a devout Roman Catholic, at a time when Catholicism was still considered synonomous with inflexible anti-communism. The inescapable conclusion, in 1960 at least, was that Robert Kennedy was bound to be rough on Reds.

Few Americans, Otto Otepka not excepted, could have had any inkling on Inauguration Day 1961 that the Kennedys would soon become the world leaders of the burgeoning movement to achieve a détente with communism. Throughout the 1960 campaign, and rather emphatically in his ringing inaugural address, John Fitzgerald Kennedy seemed to promise renewed strength in the White House, most particularly within the twin realms of foreign affairs and the national defense. America, under the Kennedys, appeared destined for an era of vigorous action to roll back the rising tide of Soviet imperialism.

Politically, Jack Kennedy seemed to owe little to that rather large segment of the Left that traditionally denounces any and all efforts to weed Communists or persistent sympathizers out of government. At the Democratic convention in Los Angeles most of the Left had fought bitterly for Adlai Stevenson's third nomination.

Jack Kennedy had drawn his strength from the big city bosses, the more conservative labor elements, and, quite substantially, from the South. Certainly, none of these blocs longed for a revival of the Rooseveltian Popular Front days when platoons of Alger Hisses were strategically deployed throughout the federal bureaucracy.

Bobby Kennedy, even more than his witty and lighthearted brother, conveyed the impression that aggressive measures against communism, both within and without, were in the offing. Managing Jack's campaign for the nomination and then for the election, he had built a formidable reputation for toughness. Liberal author Gore Vidal once described Bobby as "a dangerous, ruthless man." Although Vidal's estimates of people are notoriously colored by his own peculiar outlook on life, there is no denying that Bobby Kennedy prided himself on being tough.

As a little boy, Bobby stammered—some say he had a serious speech impediment—and he was shifted about among tutors and private schools in an effort to correct his speech, or at least make it intelligible. What he lacked in scholastic achievement, he tried hard to make up in sports. And although he never excelled as an athlete, he was known as a rough competitor.

Like Otto Otepka, Bobby Kennedy served as an enlisted man in the Navy during World War II. After the war, when he reentered Harvard, the Cambridge campus was a beehive of Leftist activity. There is no evidence that Bobby, who was bearing down on football, ever partook of the heady intellectual wine that poured so freely around Harvard Yard. (He was a teetotaler then, in every respect.) But he may have whiffed the intoxicating fumes that were so much in the Cambridge air. If so, it does not seem they intoxicated him, though it is possible he may have decided the stuff was really innocuous and not something that would do lasting harm to those who were on that kick.

At Harvard, in sum, Bobby studiously ignored the Left. In that time he certainly shared his family's antipathy to Leftists on both religious and political grounds. He appeared to inherit, to an even greater degree than

Jack, their father's deep-seated dislike of Liberals generally. And Communists ranked even higher in the populous pantheon of the Kennedys' pet hates.

It is inconceivable that Bobby was at all critical of his brother when, as a young Congressman, Jack opened up on the late President Roosevelt for the Yalta "sellout" of Poland and other Eastern European nations. It is equally inconceivable that Bobby registered any complaint when Jack lit out after President Truman and General George C. Marshall for having "frittered away" China.

In these attacks, Congressman Kennedy pulled no punches. He specifically named those two favorite targets of Senator McCarthy, Owen Lattimore and John K. Fairbank, claiming that they had contributed heavily to the tragic loss of China to the Communists.

It was, of course, no secret that Joe McCarthy was very close to the Kennedys. At the height of his Red-baiting career, the junior Senator from Wisconsin was spending pleasant summer weekends at the Kennedy compound on Cape Cod. McCarthy had a romantic eye on at least one of the Kennedy girls and dated Patricia before actor Peter Lawford won her hand. In 1952, when Jack was running for the Senate seat of Henry Cabot Lodge, Father Joe made a substantial contribution to McCarthy's own senatorial campaign in Wisconsin. By way of reciprocating, McCarthy pointedly refused to campaign for fellow-Republican Lodge in Massachusetts.

Congressman Kennedy, with brother Bobby as his campaign manager, weathered the Eisenhower landslide of that year and sailed into the Senate with a safe 70,000-vote plurality. The tacit support of Joe McCarthy, and the open endorsement of publisher John Fox's pro-McCarthy, anti-Communist Boston *Post* certainly helped Jack win through to victory.

There were thousands of wavering Democrats in Irish South Boston and Dorchester alone to whom the *Post* was a modern version of the Douay Bible. Equally important, to these same voters Joe McCarthy was the 1952 reincarnation of Saint Patrick, as intent on sweeping Communists from America's government as the good saint had been in driving the snakes out of Ireland.

Bobby, nervously pacing the floor of the Kennedy campaign headquarters in Boston, was acutely aware of the vote-getting magnetism of the anti-Communist issue then. In fact, soon after the election he joined Joe McCarthy's Senate committee. Perhaps he merely hoped that some of the power generated by "the most powerful man in America" would rub off on him. But for the record, Bobby says he "went to the committee because I felt the investigation of Communism was an important domestic issue."

At 26, Robert Kennedy lacked the political polish he later acquired. He quickly found himself upstaged on the McCarthy Committee by a brash young lawyer, Roy Cohn. Cohn and Kennedy took an instant dislike to each other and Cohn admits they once came to blows.

At first, Bobby was indisputably a member of Joe McCarthy's personal team. Though still a Democrat, he could in good conscience work for a Republican senator in those ancient times. Anti-communism was still pretty much bipartisan early in 1953.

Within a year, however, Bobby turned on McCarthy. The Senator's vaunting popularity had slipped precipitously. By July 1953 the three Democrat members of McCarthy's Permanent Investigations Subcommittee of the Government Operations Committee had resigned. Senators Henry M. (Scoop) Jackson, John L. McClellan and Stuart Symington gave as their reason Chairman McCarthy's "one-man rule" in making staff appointments. It was an odd excuse. Virtually all committee chairmen in the Congress control their staff appointments.

Three weeks after the Democrat boycott began, Robert Kennedy submitted his resignation to "enter the private practice of law." With regret, McCarthy accepted it, saying that Bobby had been "a great credit to the committee and had done a tremendous job."

If Bobby Kennedy practiced law anywhere, it is still a well-kept secret, though he did join the staff of the Hoover Commission for six months. Later, he conceded that his reason for leaving the McCarthy committee was more Cohn than McCarthy.

When the Democrats returned to the committee for the televised "McCarthy vs. the Army" hearings, Bobby came back with them. He could be observed, day after day, seated behind Arkansas' Senator McClellan, scribbling questions for the Democrats to use in baiting McCarthy.

There was, however, no evidence that Bobby had as yet changed his views about the necessity of cleansing the country of subversives. Once the Democrats regained control of the Senate in the 1954 elections, Bobby, as majority counsel of the Government Operations committee, drew up a report that the most exercised anti-Communist could wholeheartedly endorse. If issued before the censure of McCarthy, it would have vindicated the Wisconsin Senator in the feud with the Army that brought about his fall.

Kennedy's report, approved by the committee's Democrat members, stated that the "repeated warnings" of the FBI about Communist penetration into the Army radar laboratories at Fort Monmouth, New Jersey, had been sadly "neglected."

"As a result," the report said, "individuals with subversive backgrounds . . . were permitted to remain as employees in highly sensitive installations doing work of a classified nature. . . . It was only after our investigation had commenced [Kennedy did not mention that McCarthy had 'commenced' it] that 35 individuals were suspended on security grounds from Fort Monmouth. . . .

"A total of 126 witnesses were heard in executive hearings. Forty-one of these invoked the protection of the Fifth Amendment when interrogated about subversive activities.

"The Rosenberg spy ring successfully penetrated the Army Signal Corps and related private commercial establishments. This espionage ring took and obtained secrets from the Army Signal Corps and transmitted them to the Soviet Union. . . . The Rosenberg ring, may, on the basis of available evidence, still be operating."[1]

One wonders if the young man who authored these incendiary paragraphs might not have been prone to look under his bed before retiring to see how many Communists were hiding there each night. But a half-dozen years can be an eternity in the span of a politician's life, and by 1960 Robert Kennedy was apparently sleeping soundly without benefit of seeking Reds under beds.

A lengthy book could be written about how, why and when the Kennedys changed their attitude about the necessity for strong internal security safeguards. If Otto Otepka had been looking, which he was not, he would have noticed the Kennedys executing an adroit about-face on this issue right after the 1956 Democratic National Convention.

Jack Kennedy, with strong backing from the South, came within an eyelash of copping the vice presidential nomination in Chicago that year. Too late, he learned where the real power resides in the Democratic Party. When Hubert Humphrey, after one of those emotional weeping sessions Democrats seem so fond of, threw his labor and Liberal delegates to Estes Kefauver, Jack Kennedy's youthful dream of glory was washed away in the torrent of tears.

From 1956 onward the Kennedys quietly concentrated on infiltrating the Left, especially the Ivy League intellectuals whose influence appeared to extend everywhere. That they succeeded in doing this without disturbing their Southern supporters or alienating their traditional ballot backyard, the Irish Catholic voters in the big cities, is a testimony to their political finesse. Indeed, this feat should forever stand among the most amazing balancing acts in the history of American politics.

To grasp how smartly this was carried off, one needs to be reminded of how far out on the "extremist right" the Kennedys once were. In 1950 young Congressman Kennedy could rashly tell a Harvard audience that he "rather respects" Joe McCarthy; that he thought McCarthy "may have something"; that he was personally delighted with Richard Nixon's defeat of Helen Gahagan Douglas in the recent acrimonious California Senate race marked by charges of Mrs. Douglas' affection for Communists; and that he did not have much use for Secretary of State Dean Acheson, or, indeed, for the Truman Administration in general. Although he didn't mention it, Kennedy had actually gone so far as to make a financial contribution to Nixon's campaign against Mrs. Douglas.

Arthur M. Schlesinger, Jr., the historian of the Kennedy Administration, could later write (one hopes with tongue in cheek) that "Kennedy never gave the slightest support to McCarthyism." The truth is that Kennedy, in the days before he made the history that would have to be thoroughly rewritten, would have smiled at Schlesinger's silly claim.

Even during his early years in the Senate, Kennedy had no hesitancy about telling reporters he thought Liberals were "obnoxious goofs." In 1953 the *Saturday Evening Post* carried a story on "The Senate's Gay Young Bachelor" which had him taking broad swipes at the Liberal Left. "I never joined the Americans for Democratic Action or the American Veterans Committee," Senator Kennedy said. Then, with refreshing candor, he added: "I'm not comfortable with those people."[2]

After the 1956 convention, however, such heresies were silently consigned to the crowded limbo of discarded political positions. To be sure, Robert Kennedy made one final obeisance to the erstwhile idol of anticommunism when he journeyed to Appleton, Wisconsin, on May 7, 1957, to attend the funeral of Senator McCarthy. But that was the last of the once ardent Kennedy flirtation with McCarthyism.

By the time of McCarthy's death the Kennedys' secret love affair with the intellectual Left was heating up to a passionate pitch. A tentative flirtation had begun, almost accidentally, as early as 1953 when Theodore Sorensen signed on as a legislative assistant to the junior Senator from Massachusetts. A second generation Liberal and pacifist, Sorensen had been a conscientious objector during World War II and had escaped service in the Korean War when he was reclassified 4-F.

It is doubtful that Jack Kennedy was looking ahead to bigger things when he hired Sorensen at the outset of his career in the Senate. He probably saw in the young Liberal attorney merely a man who might be helpful in getting a job done. He waived his objection to Liberals in this case on purely pragmatic grounds. Ideology could not have entered into it.

Sorensen, however, turned out to be a happy accident for Kennedy. Through dint of hard work, he gradually won the young Senator's confidence. When Jack Kennedy underwent surgery for a chronic back ailment and was hospitalized for a long period in 1954, it was Sorensen who helped him write his best-selling book, *Profiles in Courage*. And when Jack began making his preliminary moves toward the White House early in 1957, it was Sorensen who helped attract the Liberal intellectuals to his banner.

For Jack Kennedy, Liberal support was a compelling must. No man can hope to win the Democratic Party's nomination without it. The 1956 convention had taught him that the Liberals have the veto power over any candidate. And in 1957 Kennedy still had a long way to go to convince the Liberals that they should not exercise their veto over him a second time.

Kennedy also knew the Left has a long memory. Mrs. Roosevelt, whom Schlesinger called the "conscience of the Liberal community,"[3] was constantly reminding her followers that Kennedy was "soft on McCarthyism." Brother Bobby's association with the McCarthy Committee, although partially atoned for by Bobby's role in the Army-McCarthy battle, still rankled the doctrinaire Liberals. On the Left, John F. Kennedy had a good deal to overcome.

Ted Sorensen helped get his boss over the initial hurdles. And two certified Harvard Liberals, historian Schlesinger and economist John Kenneth Galbraith, played vital roles in Cambridge as Kennedy's twin John the Baptists. "We found ourselves," says Schlesinger, "as we saw more of him, bound to him by increasingly strong ties of affection and respect."[4]

By then, as Schlesinger freely admits, "Kennedy himself was now prepared to go some distance to propitiate the Liberals. After 1956 he made a special effort with issues in the civil liberties field, such as getting rid of the loyalty oath in the National Defense Education Act, and he counted on the strong liberalism of his senatorial record to overcome doubts."[5]

Schlesinger and his Cambridge neighbor Galbraith got Seymour Harris, another Harvard economist, into the Kennedy act. Others followed in increasing numbers.

A turning point in Jack Kennedy's wooing of the Left came in June 1959. The night of the Harvard commencement, Schlesinger arranged a dinner in a private room upstairs at Boston's fine old Locke-Ober's restaurant. On hand to dine with Senator Kennedy were Adlai Stevenson's staunch ally, Thomas K. Finletter and his wife; the Galbraiths; the Schlesingers; McGeorge Bundy, a nominal Republican who was Dean of the Faculty at Harvard; and several other members of the Cambridge intelligentsia.

The principal purpose of this dinner meeting, according to Schlesinger, was to give Kennedy a chance to convert Finletter, who had been Secretary of the Air Force under President Truman and was now a leader of the Reform Democrats in New York. "It seemed useful," says Schlesinger, "not only to broaden Kennedy's New York base but to dispel the suspicions of him entertained by the Liberal group in New York City, so important both as a source of funds and as a shaper of opinion."[6] The device the Liberals used to test Kennedy would, in later years, interest Otto Otepka.

"What stands out from the evening," Schlesinger later wrote, "was a discussion of the confirmation of Lewis Strauss, whose name President Eisenhower had recently submitted to the Senate as Secretary of Commerce. It was politically essential for Kennedy, as a Liberal Democratic presidential aspirant, to vote against Strauss. But, *though he had no use for him*, he had a belief, with which I sympathized, that any President was entitled to considerable discretion in naming his cabinet."[7] (Emphasis added)

Kennedy was "looking for a respectable reason to oppose Strauss," according to Schlesinger. And McGeorge Bundy, who, with Walt Rostow, was to become one of JFK's two top advisors on national security matters, provided the desired rationale when he "suddenly spoke up for rejection." As Schlesinger so cogently phrases it, "The backing of Harvard's Dean of the Faculty may have somewhat reassured Kennedy, who voted against Strauss a few days later." Finletter was appeased, and he "thereafter succeeded to some degree in tempering the anti-Kennedy reflexes of the New York reformers."[8]

There is, however, much to this story that historian Schlesinger has omitted, principally the *reason* why the Liberals were so virulently opposed to the confirmation of Lewis Strauss.

Probably no man nominated for the post of Secretary of Commerce in this century was better qualified for that job than Admiral Strauss. A self-made millionaire by his early twenties, Strauss became a close associate of Herbert Hoover in feeding the starving people of Europe after World War I. His credentials, both as a businessman and as a humanitarian, were impeccable. His economic vision had been proved repeatedly with investments that helped launch new industries and companies, among them Polaroid Camera. His grasp of the great potential of the peaceful uses for atomic energy seems now to smack of uncanny prescience. Years before the Manhattan Project produced the world's first atomic bomb, Lewis Strauss had invested in atomic research. Later, he became a member of the Advisory Committee of the Atomic Energy Commission, and, under Eisenhower, chairman of the AEC itself.

It was this latter post that led to Strauss' downfall with the Left. Under him, the AEC lifted the security clearance of Robert Oppenheimer, former director of the Los Alamos laboratories. As head of the AEC's Advisory Committee, Oppenheimer had deliberately delayed America's development of a hydrogen bomb against the protests of Dr. Edward Teller and other scientists.

Oppenheimer, who had lied repeatedly about his close associations with known Communists, including the notorious Soviet agent, Steve Nelson, became the leading martyr of the Left. And Strauss, because he had withstood unbelievable pressure in upholding the revocation of Oppenheimer's clearance, became the foremost candidate for the role of a modern Pontius Pilate. Cast as Herod in this internal security drama was a brilliant Washington attorney, Roger Robb, who prosecuted the AEC's case against Oppenheimer. A decade later Robb was to become the counsel for Otto Otepka.

When Arthur Schlesinger says Jack Kennedy "had no use for" Lewis Strauss, he is, however, not being entirely forthright. The night Admiral Strauss received word that the Senate had voted, 49-to-46, against his confirmation as Secretary of Commerce, he had a book on his desk. With a wry smile, he opened it and read the handwritten inscription on the flyleaf: *"To a man of courage and distinction."* The inscription was in Jack Kennedy's hand. The book was Kennedy's own *Profiles in Courage.*

By the fall of 1959, when the Kennedys polished their final plans for Jack's campaign for the Democratic presidential nomination, the Senator had built quite a formidable stable of certified Liberals. Working for him as full- or part-time speech writers and policy advisors, in addition to Sorensen, Schlesinger, Galbraith, Seymour Harris and McGeorge

Bundy, were a score of others, mostly drawn from academic circles. They included Abram Chayes, Archibald Cox, Richard Goodwin, Paul Freund, Mark DeWolfe Howe, Max Millikan, and Walt W. Rostow. From outside the academy came labor union attorney Arthur J. Goldberg, journalist Joseph Alsop, pollster Louis Harris, pianist-newsman Pierre Salinger, foundation executive Adam Yarmolinsky.

More flocked to the Kennedy colors following his primary victories in Wisconsin and West Virginia. Among them was Joseph L. Rauh, Jr., alter ego of the ADA who persuaded Hubert Humphrey to withdraw after West Virginia.

The annealing process was complete. John F. Kennedy, by attempting to infiltrate the Left, had, like Franklin Roosevelt before him, taken on the Left's coating and coloration. Bobby, worshipping his older brother, had immersed his mind and soul in the same intellectual caldron.

Again like FDR, both Jack and Bobby probably were confident they could control the more *outré* elements in their new misalliance. "We are a young group and we're going to take over America," Bobby announced to a state caucus at the Los Angeles convention.[9]

But, as Otto Otepka could have told him, no American takes over the Left.

CHAPTER VI

Rusk

FOR SEVERAL YEARS IN THE EARLY 1960's, SENATORS, CONGRESSMEN A handful of newsmen and a small but growing number of informed observers hinted darkly that Otto Otepka's difficulties with the Department of State were being directed from quarters "high up in the Kennedy-Johnson Administration." Bobby Kennedy's name was mentioned frequently. But when Bobby left the executive branch for the Senate, Otepka's ordeal continued. Obviously, Bobby could not have been alone.

It was May 1965 before the persistent reports of another Cabinet member's deep involvement in the affair were finally and firmly confirmed. In that month, the Senate Internal Security Subcommittee was informed that the man principally responsible for the handling of the Otepka matter was none other than the Secretary of State, Dean Rusk.

The informant, oddly enough, was the State Department official virtually everyone in Washington had zeroed in on as the man who was pulling the day-to-day strings in the case—William J. Crockett, Deputy Undersecretary of State for Administration.

According to reporter Clark Mollenhoff, Crockett blew the whistle on his boss as early as August 1964 "in order to clear his own record for promotion to a Foreign Service rank as career minister."[1] Just for good measure, Crockett also put the finger on Undersecretary of State George

Ball, naming him as a co-author of the campaign to purge Otepka.

Actually, there had been other prior indications of Dean Rusk's intimate role in the Otepka affair. Indeed, as early as December 24, 1963, Rusk openly admitted that he had been personally responsible for the management of the case. But, the Secretary insisted, he got into it only *after* October 5 of that year.[2]

This timing was important. By October 5, 1963, Otepka was already under "criminal" charges and thus Dean Rusk absolved himself of any complicity in the purge and its more sinister implications.

However, several months after Deputy Undersecretary William Crockett's startling 1965 disclosure, it came to light that Rusk had himself admitted, nearly two years earlier, that he had *personally ordered* "a thorough investigation" of the Otepka matter some months *before* the State Department preferred charges.

The occasion for this revelation was the belated release, in mid-August 1965, of Rusk's statement to, and cross-examination by, the Senate Internal Security Subcommittee. Rusk had appeared before the Subcommittee, in answer to an urgent summons, on October 21, 1963, at a time when the Otepka case threatened to explode into the most damaging State Department scandal since Alger Hiss.

In the presence of seven of the subcommittee's nine members—Senators Dirksen, Dodd, Ervin, Hruska, Keating, McClellan and Scott—the Secretary of State said:

"During the past summer [of 1963], evidence came to my attention concerning alleged activities of Mr. Otepka. This evidence, if true, seemed to me *on its face to present some serious questions of security in the Department.* [Otepka was accused of delivering information to the Senate subcommittee itself.]

"I asked the appropriate officers to make a thorough investigation of all the evidence and to analyze the questions of law involved. I directed them to prefer [sic] charges only if they were satisfied that there was evidence and basis in law sufficient to warrant such action.

"*I abstained from further participation in the matter because I will make the ultimate departmental decision as the President [Kennedy] mentioned in his last press conference. And as he also indicated in his press conference, the President himself will review the matter.*"[3]

This statement not only proves that Rusk was very much a part of the Otepka business *before* October 5, 1963, as he later claimed; it shows that at the very time he was delivering his alibi to the Senate subcommittee he had *already* failed to "abstain from further participation in the matter" following his summer action. Nor did he keep his pledge to "abstain" *after* his appearance before the Subcommittee.

There is a small mountain of evidence, on and off the official record, to substantiate Dean Rusk's deep involvement right on through 1968. It will suffice to cite but one small piece here. On May 4, 1965, when the beleaguered Mr. Crockett found himself cornered, he was questioned by J.G. Sourwine, Chief Counsel of the Senate subcommittee, before Senators Tom Dodd and Birch Bayh. Crockett was under oath, and though that had not troubled him greatly in the past, his contradictions were catching up with him. This time he decided to tell the unvarnished truth:

SOURWINE: Sir, it has been reported to the committee that you have stated that the Secretary of State considers the Otepka case as "his case." Is that correct?

CROCKETT: Yes; that is correct, in the sense that he has a deep personal interest in it. . . .

SOURWINE: Would you say the Secretary is substantially in charge of the Otepka case?

CROCKETT: Yes, sir; insofar as its final determination is concerned.[4]

Crockett then hedged just a bit by loading some of the responsibility on the State Department's legal advisors. But the damage was done. He had squealed on his boss. By the following year William J. Crockett had departed the Department, where he had labored fifteen years, for the more peaceful precincts of private life.

One of the Senators who sat in on Dean Rusk's performance before the Internal Security Subcommittee in 1963 was later moved to remark: "The man's like quicksilver. You try to put your finger on him here—and suddenly he's over there."[5]

The Senator is not the only one who has been baffled by Dean Rusk's quicksilver style. The truth is that he has been an enigma to the Washington press and diplomatic corps for twenty years. Moreover, he was just as much of an enigma to the man who appointed him to the Cabinet, John F. Kennedy; and, for that matter, to Otto Otepka, who may have known as much about Rusk as any individual in Washington.

David Dean Rusk began life in obscurity, and for the first forty years of his life he chose to remain an essentially faceless man, although chance, intellect and hard work had early thrust him into the center of momentous world events.

In later years, Rusk was fond of recalling his humble beginnings on a small tenant cotton farm in Cherokee County, Georgia. "I am myself a son of Appalachia," the Secretary of State told an audience at the opening of an exhibit of Appalachian handicrafts in Helsinki in the summer of 1966.[6]

When Dean was four, his father, a circuit-riding Presbyterian minister, found his soft voice unequal to the demands of his profession. He was forced to surrender his pulpit, and the rented farm. It was 1913 when the family moved to Atlanta, where the elder Rusk got a job as a postman to support his wife and five children. To help out, Dean started work at age eight in a neighborhood grocery. In his teens he became high school correspondent for the *Atlanta Journal*, earning the truly handsome sum of $40 a month.

Religion and education were the central forces in the Rusk family life. The former remained the passion of his Calvinist father long after the Reverend Mr. Rusk gave up the ministry; the latter derived mainly from his mother, who had once been a schoolteacher.

Always prone to looking far into the future, Dean Rusk claims that at age twelve he drew up a master plan for his next dozen years. The prospectus charted his course through high school, two years of work to earn money for college, four years at Davidson College in North Carolina, and finally a Rhodes scholarship to attend Oxford University in England for three years.[7]

Unbelievably, it all came to pass. When he graduated, with honors, from Atlanta's Boys High, he worked two years as a law clerk. This gave him enough money to enter Davidson (which his father had attended) and he continued to pay his way by working as a waiter and bank clerk. Somehow, he found time to play on the college basketball team and to serve in the R.O.T.C. His high scholastic standing, evidenced by a Phi Beta Kappa key, won him the Rhodes scholarship as planned, and in 1931 he went off to Oxford.

England, and especially Oxford, was in ferment. The Great Depression, following as it did in the wake of the widespread despair caused by World War I, seemed the final death knell of the capitalist system. Socialism and its first cousin, pacifism, were the prevalent philosophies of the day.

Actually, England had been edging towards socialism for decades. The Fabian Society, led by a mystically pragmatic band of London literati, had been inching the British Empire down the road to dismemberment and collectivism since the 1880's. Goaded by the sharp satirical wit of George Bernard Shaw, guided by the grand strategies and niggling tactics of Beatrice and Sydney Webb, intermittently inspired by the dreams of H.G. Wells, the Fabians conjured, a half-century and more before Lyndon Johnson, a many-splendored vision of the Great Society.

Ludicrous as it may seem to us now, *The Great Society* was actually the title of a book published in 1914 by the leading Fabian theorist, Graham Wallas. Otto Otepka, discovering the existence of this volume shortly after the 1964 election, could not suppress a knowing smile when he read the titles of the last three chapters—"The Organisation of Thought," "The Organisation of Will," and, finally, "The Organisation of Happiness." The preface takes the form of a letter from Fabian Wallas to America's wonderful Walter Lippmann, acknowledging Lippmann's inspiration of *The Great Society.*

The Fabians, of course, had much in common with all the other socialist sects, and they welcomed all manner of exotic personages into their fold. Nicolai Lenin was one of them, before he broke with the Fabians on the issue of non-violence: the Fabians preferred it; Lenin obviously did not.

Dame Rebecca West has written eloquently on the milieu in which young Dean Rusk found himself at Oxford in 1931:

Not only were they taught to think of themselves as living in a miserable capitalist world when in actual fact they and most of their neighbors were not miserable at all; they were also taught to think of their parents and themselves as a courageous minority who were attacking the impregnable fortress of capitalism against fearful odds, and this also was not true. . . .

It is obvious that such minds, at once fantasy bound and literal, will turn happily to communism. It is on the left, where they learned in their infancy salvation lay. It has a materialistic basis, and one of its first claims is that it transcends the claims of patriotism, which . . . gives it the authority of a fulfillment of the prophets.[9]

This kind of thinking, as much a part of the Oxford atmosphere in the 1930's as it is at Berkeley and Columbia today, must have puzzled young Rhodes scholar Rusk. One may conjecture that his Calvinist background and R.O.T.C. training resisted it strongly. Nonetheless, it was everywhere about him, like an all-enveloping cloud.

The courses Rusk took—in international law and political science, particularly—were impregnated with Fabian theories, and stronger stuff. He could not escape the "advanced social thinkers" at Oxford, and some wise old dons may have helped him rationalize the new secular religion as merely a worldly manifestation of his inherited Calvinism.

In his application for a Rhodes scholarship, Rusk stated that his main goal at Oxford "would be the study of ways to achieve world peace."[10]

In his final year, he had advanced sufficiently far towards that goal to win the coveted Cecil Peace Prize.

Rusk wrote his prize-winning paper, competing against students from all England's universities, while pursuing his studies in Berlin. The 100-pounds sterling he collected helped pay his expenses at Oxford and cover his Continental interlude.

Berlin in 1933 must also have left its mark on Dean Rusk. This was the year Adolph Hitler came to power as Chancellor of the Third Reich and the year the Reichstag was gutted by fire. Violence was rampant in Germany as the Nazis and Communists fought for power. Whether Rusk took any part at all in this struggle is unknown. Chances are he was merely a silent observer. But the record is equally silent on the impression Germany's death struggle made on him.

Rusk picked up his B.S. degree from Saint John's College, Oxford, in 1933, took his M.A. the following year, and headed back to the United States. He had a job lined up to teach political science at Mills College, a Liberal educational emporium for girls in Oakland, California. The job paid $2,000 a year and Rusk says he was "glad to get it."

The next six years were busy and apparently happy ones for Rusk, though the war clouds gathering over Europe and the Orient must have caused him some uneasiness. In addition to his teaching chores at Mills, he continued his studies in international law at the University of California in Berkeley, just next door to Oakland. He also resumed his R.O.T.C. training, probably with an eye to the threatening clouds, east and west.

Rusk rose to become Dean of the Faculty at Mills, which prompted the girl students playfully to dub him "Dean-Dean." One of them, Virginia Foisie, daughter of a well-to-do Seattle family, was of a more serious bent and Rusk took her on as a research assistant. Research ripened into romance and on June 19, 1937, they were married in Seattle.

The war, having broken out in Europe in the summer of 1939, shattered the pattern of the Rusks' placid academic life. Two months after their first son was born in 1940, Rusk was called to active duty by the Army as a captain in the 3rd Infantry Division. Not long before Pearl Harbor, a number of his fellow officers were dispatched to the Philippines where they fought through Corregidor, suffered the death march from Bataan, and endured nearly four years in Japanese prison camps.

Fate was kinder to Dean Rusk. About this same time, he was plucked out of the 3rd Division and ordered to Washington. He was assigned to G-2 (Army Intelligence) in the British Empire Section. Ostensibly, he got the job because a classification punch card called his Oxford studies to the attention of the Army's personnel people.[11]

Rusk's wartime rise was quietly spectacular. He soon became chief of G-2's British Empire Section, but instead of focusing on Europe, as his experience and education pointed him, he became intricately involved in the Far East. By 1943 he was a lieutenant colonel on the staff of General Joseph Stilwell, commander of the China-Burma-India theater. The following year he became Deputy Chief of Staff for the entire CBI.

In the CBI, Rusk was thrown into close contact with a group of young State Department foreign service officers busily engaged in reshaping United States policy on China. Since he concedes that his duties were more diplomatic than military, Rusk could hardly avoid this group. It included John Stewart Service, John Paton Davies, John K. Emmerson and others later identified as a part of the cabal which cut the ground out from under Chiang Kai-shek while selling Mao Tse-tung to the American government and public as an "agrarian reformer."

In Chungking at the time was Owen Lattimore, sent there as President Roosevelt's personal representative to Chiang. According to one American Intelligence officer who was there, Lattimore devoted considerable effort to convincing General Stilwell that the men he should draw on for political advice were Service, Davies, Emmerson—and Dean Rusk.

Rusk was on Stilwell's staff when "Vinegar Joe" clashed head-on with Chiang over a plan to provide one million Chinese Communists with American arms and place them under Stilwell's own personal command. Moreover, Rusk was reliably reported to be the chief architect of this plan. But Chiang, who had troubles enough trying to hold what was left of Nationalist China against the Japanese, steadfastly opposed the scheme.*

Stilwell and the State Department cabal in Chungking and Washington exerted tremendous pressure on Chiang through President Roosevelt and General George C. Marshall, but the Generalissimo stoically stood his ground. In the end, Roosevelt was forced to recall Stilwell though his Deputy Chief of Staff stayed on, confining his activities largely to India, which was now split off from the China command.

Stilwell's successor in China, General Albert C. Wedemeyer, and the U.S. Ambassador to Chungking, Patrick J. Hurley, strove valiantly to

---

* Columnist Joseph Alsop, who traveled to China with Vice President Henry Wallace, testified before the McCarran Committee on October 18, 1951, that "General Stilwell was strongly gripped with certain attitudes highly favorable to the Chinese Communist cause. . . . he was not only hostile to the Generalissimo [Chiang], but very friendly to the Communists."

heal the breach between China and America. But the Davies-Service-Emmerson cabal fanatically persisted in their efforts to open it yet wider. In Washington they were aided and abetted by John Carter Vincent, chief of the State Department's China desk, working hand in glove with the Institute of Pacific Relations branch of the cabal, including Owen Lattimore and John K. Fairbank.

Dean Rusk, if we are to credit his later position on Mao, was strongly influenced by these people. Subsequently, this group was widely condemned, even by a young congressman named John Kennedy, for having delivered China and its teeming millions to communism. The blood of countless innocent Chinese, among them some millions of women and children, will forever stain their hands.*

Whether Colonel Rusk was an active, working member of the cabal is open to question. He has frequently been accused of being one of the principal designers of America's disastrous China policy. Among many other things, he has been identified as (though not conclusively proven to be) one of the authors of the infamous 1949 White Paper on China that paved the way for Mao Tse-tung's final victory. (It was said to be largely authored by Charles Yost, whom President Nixon named U.S. Ambassador to the U.N., though Phillip Jessup and others had a hand in its writing.) Moreover, Rusk's public statements even *after* China's fall strongly indicate he was at the very least in sympathy with the cabal's disastrous views.

In the personnel security file Otto Otepka examined in December 1960, all this fell under the heading of circumstantial, not substantive, evidence. Otepka's departmental guidelines were quite narrow. Before an individual could be denied a security clearance, the evidence had to show close and continuing association with known Communists, membership in the Communist Party or in a number of critical fronts, or serious "suitability" deficiencies.

Thus, even if Dean Rusk had singlehandedly shaped our China policy in the 1940's, Otepka could not have recommended against his clearance. The only really black mark on Rusk's *security* record was, as we shall see, his relationship with the Institute of Pacific Relations. However, Otepka learned later that there were other black marks against Rusk which did not show in the Department security file.

Rusk ended his Far Eastern tour of duty in 1945 and returned to

* *Time*, in its issue of March 3, 1956, estimated that 20 million Chinese had been systematically liquidated by the Communists. Another 23 million were reported in slave labor camps. How many have died since is unknown, though estimates run as high as 40 million for the years 1949 through 1967.

Washington where he became Assistant Chief in the Operations Division of the War Department General Staff. Even in wartime, non-West Point reserve officers were rarely assigned to the General Staff. But Colonel Rusk had acquired a powerful patron in the person of General Marshall, who was not himself a West Pointer, and tradition bowed before the desires of the U.S. Army's Chief of Staff.

In the Pentagon, Rusk made other influential friends. Among them was the soon-to-be Secretary of War, Robert Patterson, and John McCloy. The Patterson-McCloy group maintained close liaison with the State Department, which indeed was their duty, and when Colonel Rusk was discharged from the Army in February 1946 there was a berth waiting for him at State. He became Assistant Chief of the Division of International Security Affairs.

Rusk's initial stint at State did not last long, however. In May 1946, Rusk says that "Secretary of War Patterson asked me to return to the Pentagon as his special assistant, where my duties involved matters of joint foreign policy of military significance and close working arrangements with the Department of State."

Ten months later Rusk bounced back to State, this time at the personal behest of General Marshall, who had become Secretary of State following his hapless year-long 1946 mission in China. Marshall named Rusk Director of the Office of Special Political Affairs, a post just vacated by Alger Hiss. It was in this job that Dean Rusk received his real baptism in the shadowy realm that later was to bring on his long struggle with Otto Otepka.

CHAPTER VII

The Buddha

ONE MAJOR AND IMMEDIATE CONTRIBUTING FACTOR IN OTTO OTEPKA'S ouster from SY in 1963 was his exposure of the State Department's effort to reinstitute the practice of permitting the United Nations to hire American citizens without prior investigation and screening by U.S. security agencies. This practice had first been put into effect by Alger Hiss in 1945. It was later revoked.

When Dean Rusk succeeded Hiss at the State Department he found that his new job encompassed the whole widening world of America's participation in the U.N. In fact, Rusk's title was soon changed to Director, Office of United Nations Affairs.

Voluminous testimony before Congressional committees and a New York Federal Grand Jury later disclosed that under Alger Hiss this State Department office helped place dozens of American Communists and fellow travelers in U.N. jobs.

What the Grand Jury branded as "massive infiltration" of the U.N. by these native Communists continued uninterrupted during Dean Rusk's tenure. There is no evidence that he ever bestirred himself to correct the loose security practices established by Hiss which permitted the infiltration. On the contrary, he quietly acquiesced in maintaining them.

(On December 16, 1952, Carlisle H. Humelsine, then Deputy Undersecretary of State in charge of security, was questioned by Counsel Sourwine before the Senate Internal Security Subcommittee. Sourwine asked Humelsine:

"Is it the gist of your testimony that while Mr. Dean Rusk was in charge of U.N. affairs, not only was no position of the Department in opposition to the employment of American Communists communicated to the U.N., but actually there was no such official position of the Department, so far as you know?

Humelsine replied with a flat and unqualified *"Yes."*[1]

Moreover, Humelsine made it plain that although there was no "official position" there was very definitely an unofficial policy which *encouraged* the U.N. to hire American Communists. At the end of the hearings, the Senate Subcommittee found that during the Hiss and Rusk reigns "there was no safeguard whatsoever . . . against employment by the United Nations of United States citizens who were disloyal to their country, or who were actively engaged in espionage.")

More important historically is the equally ambiguous role Rusk played in the final act of the fall of China. There is no doubt that he had Dean Acheson's ear during those agonizing months when the Communist curtain clanged down around the world's most populous country. Others did, too, of course. John Carter Vincent was Assistant Secretary for Far Eastern Affairs. But Rusk also served as an Assistant Secretary of State from February 1949 onward as Mao's forces swept south like locusts until they forced Chiang's withdrawal to Taiwan in December.

China might yet have been saved during those crucial first ten months of Dean Rusk's tenure as Assistant Secretary of State. True, the seeds of dissolution sown by the Service-Davies-Vincent cabal had been further fertilized by Rusk's mentor, George Marshall, from 1946 through 1948.* But the harvest of death had not yet been fully reaped in February 1949.

When Rusk stepped into this job, Chiang still controlled most of the south and west of China. Shanghai held out until the end of May. Canton and the other major cities of the south remained in Nationalist hands through mid-summer. The final blow came, not from Peiping (which Mao had taken in January), but from Washington.

In the first week of August, as the Communists converged on Canton,

---

* Marshall once boasted: "As Chief of Staff I armed thirty-nine anti-Communist [Nationalist Chinese] divisions. Now, with a stroke of the pen, I disarm them." With the collaboration of Harry Dexter White in Treasury, an identified Soviet agent, Marshall refused to release $125 million in arms and aid appropriated by the 80th Congress for the Nationalists. He also tried to force the Kuomintang to form a "coalition government" with the Communists, a move which found its feeble echo in Laos in 1961 when Dean Rusk was Secretary of State.

the State Department released the infamous White Paper which sealed the fate of China, and ultimately, perhaps, the world. As Robert Aura Smith, the New York *Times* editorial writer, put it, "this document was designed to justify President Truman's declaration that we should *'give no further aid and advice'* to Nationalist China."[2] The last slice of ground was cut from under Chiang. Confidence crumbled, and with American aid shut off completely, the Nationalists were forced to prepare for evacuation from the mainland.

The White Paper must certainly have passed through the hands of Dean Rusk, who in 1949 was promoted from Assistant Secretary to Deputy Undersecretary in charge of policy planning and coordination. Whether he approved or disapproved it is one of many secrets buried deep in the State Department's classified files. Although the present Ambassador to the U. N., Charles Yost, alledgedly offered it, credit for the final editing goes to Philip Jessup, later U.S. Ambassador-at-Large. A former chairman of the Institute of Pacific Relations, Jessup was involved with five cited Communist fronts, including the American Russian Institute. In the fall of 1951, despite outraged cries from the press, the Senate refused to confirm Jessup's appointment as Ambassador to the U.N. because of his record on communism.

Whatever Rusk's role in the China tragedy, there can be no doubt that he did not look entirely with disfavor on Mao Tse-tung's rise to power. Speaking before the World Affairs Council at the University of Pennsylvania on January 13, 1950—barely a month after Chiang's government fled to Taiwan—Rusk likened the Communist takeover of China to the American Revolution and stated flatly that Mao and his lieutenents "are not aiming toward dictatorship."[3]

Strangely, Rusk did not find this position inconsistent with the one he was to take six months later when, as Assistant Secretary of State for Far Eastern Affairs, he played *the* decisive part in America's entry into the Korean War. At the historic meeting President Truman held after Communist forces, spearheaded by more than100 Russian tanks, crossed the 38th Parallel into South Korea, it was Dean Rusk who pleaded most persuasively for U.S. intervention.

According to a *Time* story written the same week Rusk met with Otto Otepka and Bobby Kennedy in December 1960, Rusk saw in Korea "a precious opportunity" for the U.S. "to intervene through the United Nations." Truman was apparently hesitant, and there were others at the June 1950 conference who opposed sending in American troops. But, said *Time*, Rusk "bent all his gifts of argument." In the end, "his viewpoint prevailed and the following day, the U.N., under U.S. leadership, embarked on a history-making venture in collective security."[4]

Having persuaded the President to throw American forces into Korea, Rusk then did his level best to make certain they did not emerge victorious. During the MacArthur Hearings, the Senate committee discovered that it was Dean Rusk who vetoed Chiang Kai-shek's offer to send Nationalist troops to Korea. Moreover, it was Rusk, more than any other Truman Administration official, who quietly whittled away General MacArthur's authority.

Rusk was at Wake Island with President Truman on October 15, 1950, when MacArthur warned that the Chinese Communists were massing troops in Manchuria. MacArthur said he did not believe the Chinese would risk "utter destruction" from American air power "capable of destroying, at will, bases of attack and lines of supply north as well as south of the Yalu."[5]

Dean Rusk did not demur. Neither did Averell Harriman, Philip Jessup, Army Secretary Frank Pace, nor the other Truman advisors present. "There was no disagreement from anyone," MacArthur said. No one told him American air power would not be used.

But MacArthur sensed something wrong. "The conference at Wake Island made me realize that a curious, and sinister, change was taking place in Washington," he later wrote. "There was a tendency towards temporizing rather than fighting it through."[6]

MacArthur could not know, of course, that Dean Rusk was very much a part of this change, as subsequent events were to prove, not only in Korea, but in Cuba, Laos, Vietnam and on the life-and-death front of disarmament.

After Wake Island, MacArthur became "even more worried by a series of directives from Washington which were greatly decreasing the potential of my air force. . . . step-by-step my weapons were being taken away from me."[7]

The critical conference of the Korean War was held on November 6, 1950. Three days earlier MacArthur had warned that the Chinese had fifty-six divisions—498,000 men—massed above the Yalu River. He informed Washington that he was ordering Air Force General George E. Stratemeyer to unleash his B-29's against the Yalu bridges.

President Truman at once summoned his advisors to Blair House to ponder MacArthur's order. Left to his own devices, Harry S. Truman probably would have let the order stand. But in his memoirs, *Years of Trial and Hope*, Truman tells why he revoked it:

Assistant Secretary of State Dean Rusk pointed out that we had a commitment with the British not to take action which might involve attacks on the Manchurian side of the river without consultation with them.

Mr. Rusk also mentioned the danger of involving the Soviets, especially in the light of the mutual assistance treaty between Moscow and Peiping.[8]

Once again, Rusk prevailed. Truman told his Joint Chiefs of Staff to convey to MacArthur "what Dean Rusk had set forth." MacArthur was ordered, appropriately in a dispatch signed by Secretary of Defense Marshall, "to postpone all bombing of targets within five miles of the Manchurian border."[9]

MacArthur protested vigorously. Truman relented slightly and gave him permission to bomb "the Korean end of the Yalu bridges." But as Stratemeyer told him, "It cannot be done—Washington must have known it cannot be done." The bends in the river made it impossible to hit one end of the bridges without violating the order authored by Dean Rusk. Nonetheless, the Air Force tried—with tragic results.

Years later, MacArthur still vividly remembered the consequences of the Truman-Rusk directives: "One of those bomber pilots, wounded unto death, the stump of an arm dangling by his side, gasped at me through the bubbles of blood he spat out, 'General, which side are Washington and the United Nations on?' It seared my very soul."[10]

MacArthur was on the verge of asking to be relieved of his command. He stayed only because he feared his army "might become demoralized and destroyed" if he departed.

On November 26, 1950, more than 200,000 Chinese Communists swarmed down across the Yalu and descended on the American forces strung out along a broad line in North Korea. A half-million more were to follow, dealing the United States its worst military defeat in history. Despite this, the Americans and South Koreans, with token help from a handful of other U.N. members, fought the Chinese hordes to a standstill. By March they had regained the initiative.

At this point, Truman decided to ask the Communists for a truce. MacArthur again opposed his President's decision, pointing out that the Chicoms were now on the run. Instead of begging for a truce, he urged that the United States issue an ultimatum to the Communists to leave South Korea or risk destruction.

On April 11, Truman removed MacArthur from all his Far East commands. In 1966, *Look* magazine disclosed that the man who "wrote the message for President Truman when he fired General MacArthur" was Dean Rusk.[11]

America suffered 157,530 casualties in Korea, including 54,246 dead and 103,284 wounded. Three-fifths of these casualties were suffered *after* MacArthur's recall and the start of the two-year truce talks at Panmunjom. Moreover, 944 American prisoners believed to be alive at the war's end were forever abandoned by their government to lives of slavery and torture in China and North Korea.

In 1966, Secretary of State Dean Rusk recalled the Chinese Communists' entry into the Korean War: "I was among those who thought they would not come in. I was wrong."[12]

But, Rusk noted, "This is a job that requires ice water in your veins." He was speaking of his present post, of course; yet the observation seemed to apply equally to his past performances.

In December 1951, Rusk began his long sabbatical from the State Department. He was rewarded for his brilliant record in government with the presidency of the Rockefeller Foundation. Something more than personal financial considerations entered into his decision, however.

Five months before Rusk resigned from State, his close associate, Oliver Edmund Clubb, was suspended as a security risk by unanimous vote of a Loyalty-Security Board. The evidence against Clubb included intimate association with a number of Communist agents, including Agnes Smedley, who defected to Peiping posthumously.*

Dean Rusk had leaned heavily on Clubb for advice and guidance and had promoted him to chief of the China Desk. No doubt Rusk was rather embarrassed that his right-hand man had been deemed a security risk.** But more serious embarrassments were in store for him.

The month after Clubb was declared a security risk, the Senate Internal Security Subcommittee, then as now a painful thorn in the side of the "dedicated" men in the State Department, began its year-long investigation of the Institute of Pacific Relations. By December, when Rusk resigned, it had already accumulated substantial, and incontrovertible, evidence of IPR's many-sided links with the Communist conspiracy. Unfortunately, Dean Rusk had enjoyed a close and continuing relationship with IPR right up through 1950.

* Major General Charles A. Willoughby, MacArthur's intelligence chief, identified Miss Smedley as a member of Richard Sorge's notorious espionage ring but the Army issued what amounted to a retraction. After her death, her will disclosed that she left her estate to Red Chinese leader Chu Teh and requested that her ashes be enshrined in Peiping.
** Secretary of State Dean Acheson personally reversed the unanimous decision of the Loyalty-Security Board on February 11, 1952. Acheson summarily "cleared" Clubb, permitting him to retire from the State Department on pension.

In 1961 when the Senate was considering Rusk's appointment to the Kennedy Cabinet, a question was raised about his past affiliation with IPR. Frederick G. Dutton, later Assistant Secretary of State for Congressional Relations, replied that Rusk's only involvement with the Institute of Pacific Relations was as a subscriber to an IPR magazine "while at college on the West Coast" prior to World War II.

To put it kindly, Dutton was bending the truth. Rusk was actually an elected member of IPR's American Council while at Mills College. He may indeed have dropped his membership during the war. But Rusk would, we hope, be the first to admit that some of his best friends were IPR officers, including its former chairman, Philip Jessup.

Rusk's interest in IPR was professional as well as platonic. In 1950, while he was Assistant Secretary of State for Far Eastern Affairs, Rusk made a strong pitch to both the Rockefeller and Ford Foundations for grants to IPR. The Rockefeller request alone was for nearly $2,000,000. Oddly, Rusk's appeal was made *after* former Communists Whittaker Chambers, Elizabeth Bentley, and Louis Budenz had all named high IPR officials as Soviet agents. Among those identified were Frederick Vanderbilt Field, Israel Epstein, Agnes Smedley, and Anna Louise Strong, several of whom fled the country when they were identified as members of the Russian apparat.

Moreover, the Senate subcommittee hearings showed that Rusk was a favorite official of the IPR hierarchy, the man at State to whom they frequently went for help and support. In the fall of 1950, for example, IPR requested Rusk to pick the American delegates to its world conference in Lucknow, India. Nor was Rusk loath to reciprocate. He demonstrated his confidence in IPR by recommending use of its publications to military Intelligence.[13] When the Senate subcommittee had done with the IPR hearings in June 1952, it had flushed out no less than 46 identified Communists from among the Institute's directors, officers, staff and writers. There were many perfectly responsible citizens in IPR, of course. But the subcommittee had no doubts about who ran the show: "Members of the small core of officials and staff members who controlled IPR were either Communist or pro-Communist."[14]

The subcommittee's report on IPR, unanimously approved by both Democrat and Republican members on July 2,1952, minced no words: "The IPR has been considered by the American Communist Party and by Soviet officials *as an instrument of Communist policy, propaganda and military Intelligence.*"[15]

Several of Dean Rusk's staunch allies and friends were caught in the

Senate's IPR net. He himself had been personally embarrassed. It is little wonder, then, that he should harbor a strong antipathy towards Congressional committees concerned with internal security.

After moving into the Rockefeller Foundation, which he had served as a trustee while still at State, Rusk went out of his way to castigate Congressional investigations. In the mid-1950's he became a sort of neo-hero to the Communist press for his repeated attacks on the "witchhunts" conducted from Capitol Hill. On June 27, 1955, for instance, the *Daily Peoples World*, Communist Party organ on the West Coast, ran a boxed, boldface-type story datelined Los Angeles:

> The Rockefeller Foundation will not bend a knee to Congressional witchhunters and go back on its policy of granting scholarships for study and research into controversial subjects.
>
> That note of defiance was sounded Wednesday by Dr. Dean Rusk, President of the Foundation, in a talk before the Pacific Division of the American Association for the Advancement of Science. . . .

Rusk's sensitivity stemmed in this case from a House committee probe into tax exempt foundations during the summer of 1954. "At that time it was alleged that the Rockefeller Foundation had been infiltrated by Communists, a charge the Foundation vigorously denied," said a United Press dispatch featured in the *Peoples World* of December 13, 1954.

In prior Congressional hearings on foundations, Rusk had been caught in another of his habitual inconsistencies. In December 1952 he testified before a House committee about Rockefeller Foundation grants made to Communist institutions and individuals. However, he failed to mention a number of grants to such institutions as the University of Moscow, the University of Leningrad, and the Soviet Minstry of Public Health, all made in the 1920's and 1930's.

In a subsequent letter of "clarification" to the House committee, Rusk said that when he testified he didn't construe the committee's questions to include individuals and institutions that were *openly* Communist when the grants were made.[16]

However, in his previous testimony Rusk *had* cited recent grants to Communist Yugoslavia for medical research, to the British Communist and scientist, J.B.S. Haldane, and of all things, to the Institute of Pacific Relations!

IPR may have been down in Dean Rusk's black book, but it was not yet out. Its tax exemption was lifted for a time during the 1950's. Later it was reinstated. And in 1959, the old IPR line espousing a reappraisal of U.S. relations with Peiping was dusted off and given another whirl by a Rockefeller Foundation report Rusk allegedly helped write. The report argued that America could not afford to be "cut off" from any nation, and suggested that continuance of the hard line towards Communist China could foment a "color" war more "fearful" than the cold war with the Soviet Union.

Though out of government for nine years, Rusk never really left the fascinating stage of world politics. In directing the affairs of the $250 million Rockefeller Foundation, he found ample room for maneuvering behind the scenes, where he much preferred to operate anyway. He traveled extensively on Foundation business, visiting the capitals of the world and poking into the underdeveloped nations where the Rockefellers poured substantial sums of money.

All in all, these were good years. Rusk, for the first time, had a really capitalist salary and, more important, the prestige that went with his job at the Rockefeller Foundation. His three children, two boys and a girl, were growing up. He had a comfortable home in Westchester and he dabbled a bit in politics. In the 1960 campaign he made a fortunate choice of candidates. In Scarsdale, Dean Rusk formed the local campaign committee for Kennedy-Johnson.

After the election, President-elect Kennedy was hard-pressed to find a suitable Secretary of State. His new-found Liberal friends pushed hard for Adlai Stevenson, but Kennedy ruled Adlai out on the grounds that he had opposed him too strenuously at the Los Angeles convention. Others were considered—Senator J. William Fulbright, Robert Lovett, Chester Bowles, McGeorge Bundy, David Bruce, John McCloy. For one reason or another, all were scratched.

Lovett, who had been associated with Rusk in the old War Department, put forth Dean Rusk's name. Jack Kennedy admitted he knew nothing about him. But Dean Acheson and Chester Bowles backed Lovett's choice, and Kennedy agreed to take a closer look. Someone dredged up an article Rusk had written for *Foreign Affairs* the previous spring. It was entitled "The President," and it stressed the Chief Executive's responsibility "to influence and shape the course of events" in world affairs. Jack Kennedy liked that.

Rusk was meeting with the board of trustees of the Rockefeller Foundation at its restoration of Old Williamsburg in Virginia when he got the call. With him were his old friends—Lovett, Bowles, McCloy, Ralph Bunche. The President-elect asked him to drop by the Kennedy home in Georgetown on December 8.

On the appointed morning, Rusk made his way through the crowd of reporters camped on the Kennedy doorstep. The door opened wide, and Rusk walked in. He and Kennedy had never met before, but they hit it off well. Arthur Schlesinger later wrote that Kennedy was attracted by "the quiet competence of his manner and the apparent solidity of his judgment."[17]

The following day Kennedy offered Rusk the job. On December 12 his appointment as Secretary of State was announced concurrently with the appointment of Chester Bowles as Undersecretary and Adlai Stevenson as Ambassador to the United Nations.

"The State Department bureaucracy is unanimously lyrical about Rusk's appointment," Earl Voss reported in the *Washington Star* a few weeks later. "As one of the midwives at the birth of Israel and a chief engineer in sending American forces to the defense of South Korea, Mr. Rusk obtained a reputation there for coolness under pressure and for 'a mind that operates twice as fast as normal,' as one former associate put it."[18]

Rusk himself was complacent. "Power gravitates to those who take responsibility and are ready to live with their decisions," he told Voss quietly.

There are some Rusk decisions, especially those pertaining to China and Korea, which most Americans might have difficulty living with. But as Dean Rusk prepared to move up to the new seventh floor suite prepared for him that winter at the Department of State, his conscience was apparently serene. Schlesinger correctly observed that the man had the face of an inscrutable "Buddha." Whether he was quietly promoting a rerun of the Korean disaster in Vietnam, or steadfastly plotting the purge of Otto Otepka and his associates from SY, one could never tell what the Secretary of State was thinking.

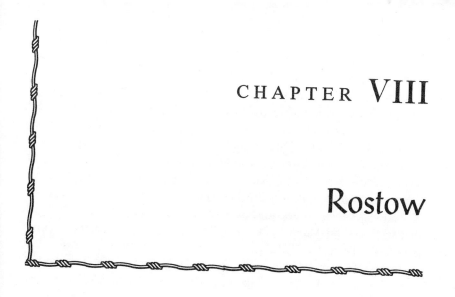

CHAPTER VIII

Rostow

If, in the future, history is written with any regard at all for truth, 1961 may well go down as the most fateful year in the whole dramatic sweep of the American experiment with freedom. All that followed in the realm of the United States' relations with the rest of the world, including our increasingly bloody involvement in the Vietnam War, stems from the policies hatched in Washington during that single twelve-month period.

The people who "saw Otepka as an obstacle to their plans," as Senator Dirksen so cogently phrased it, came galloping into the highest councils of government that year, and though they probably would have galloped roughshod right over Otepka if he had been issuing security clearances then, it made their charge on Foggy Bottom immeasurably easier because he was not. For in 1961 Otepka was bound, Prometheus-like, "to a high-piercing, headlong rock" hard by the lovely Potomac.

The stage was set for the first involuntary exile a month before the 1960 presidential election. In mid-October Otepka was summoned to a meeting with his immediate boss, SY Director William O. Boswell, and John W. Hanes, Jr., the scion of an underwear fortune who had been brought into the State Department by Foster Dulles. For nearly two years Hanes had been Administrator of the Bureau of Security and

Consular Affairs with the rank of Assistant Secretary.

Boswell, the most recent recruit in the passing parade of Foreign Service Officers who nominally headed the Office of Security, had been knocking around various comfortable posts abroad for twenty years when he was drafted as Director of SY in June 1959. He had spent most of World War II in Lisbon and afterwards had served successively in Vienna, Paris, Rome and Milan, in the last two as U.S. Consul General under his friend William J. Crockett. His qualifications for heading up SY, even nominally, were nonexistent but tradition at that time dictated that an FSO should fill the job; Boswell was available, and he moved into the office next to Otepka's.

Once, in an unguarded moment, Boswell told Otepka that he intended to eradicate "the McLeod image" from SY. Otepka, stoical as always, didn't bat an eye, but after that he took care not to give Mr. Boswell too good a view of his strong, broad back; or at least he thought he took care.

Early in the fall of 1960, however, Boswell set a little bee loose in John Hanes' bonnet. During a convivial meeting at the Waldorf-Astoria in New York with two professional SY officers, Elmer Hipsley and Keith O. Lynch, Boswell feigned deep concern about the suspected security risks who were continuing to climb the State Department's promotion ladder. Hanes, who was genuinely concerned about this same problem, rose to the bait. Why not, Boswell suggested, put the best man we have, namely Otepka, to work on a continuing review of high-ranking Department personnel? That way, he maintained, SY could make certain the more questionable characters would not keep moving up.

Real security risks had become increasingly difficult to identify in recent years. This was due in large part to the paucity of new defectors from the American Communist Party. Potential backsliders had seen what happened to Whittaker Chambers and others; they had no desire to suffer similar treatment from a doubting public. The Party had stopped issuing membership cards at the time of the first postwar investigations of communism and, for all practical purposes, it was deep underground.

As the years sped by and the domestic Party strengthened its own internal security while Moscow took tighter control of espionage activities in the U.S., it became virtually impossible to place a suspect definitely within the apparat. Hanes, of course, was aware of these developments, though he could never bring himself squarely to face the possibility of Communist infiltration at State. In his view, the Liberals were the real culprits who sabotaged U.S. foreign policy. Even after nearly eight years in the Department, John Hanes couldn't bring himself to believe that honest-to-goodness Communists found it delightfully convenient to masquerade as Liberals, just as Alger Hiss and all the others had done a decade before.

Yet Hanes sensed the critical need for mounting a permanent watch on the long list of available suspects and he readily fell in with Boswell's plan. When they got back to Washington he and Boswell called in Otepka to announce that he would be in charge of the new project. Otepka had been running an operation almost identical to this for years, and, as a matter of fact, had culled out the old list of 858 names for this very purpose. But he had never been able to obtain approval for a continuing review on a permanent basis by a qualified full-time staff.

John Hanes emphatically stressed the importance of starting this now, and Otepka agreed it was vital. It was absolutely essential, Hanes said, that SY make sure that no employee who had serious derogatory information in his file was then, or would in the future be, assigned to a position where he could make or inflence policy related to the national security. Otepka could start at the very top of the personnel roster and work down from there.

Boswell was equally emphatic. And he suavely indulged in a little flattery by telling Otepka that he was not only the best man for this job, but perhaps the only one who could handle it objectively.

Otepka had a few small reservations, but the Hanes-Boswell request seemed tantamount to an order and he was about to acquiesce. At this point, Boswell sprang a small surprise. Since this all-important task was bound to be a full-time endeavor, he said, Otepka should voluntarily give up his position as Deputy Director of SY. Magnanimously, Boswell offered Otepka the title of "Special Assistant"—to Boswell!

Suddenly realizing that he might be falling into a trap, Otepka demurred. He pointed out that he had spent years earning his job as Deputy Director and, with his intimate knowledge of the Civil Service merit system, he knew it would be a step backward to surrender that job under these circumstances.

Several more conferences followed on what was soon to become known as the "special project," and after the November election Boswell became more insistent that Otepka tackle it at once. Hanes, a Republican, was gone by then and Otepka finally reached a tacit agreement with Boswell that he would take on the project providing he kept his old job too. Boswell then directed Otepka to run a pilot study immediately and submit detailed plans for the project's operation.

The initial trickle of new political appointees to the State Department had started coming in, most of them with a nod from Bobby Kennedy, and as the appointments rose to flood stage in January, Otepka found himself tied ever more tightly to the special project. Boswell breezily assured him that the clearances were being processed strictly according to regulations, but Otepka had grave misgivings. However, every time he tried to pry himself loose to determine what was going on currently, Boswell insisted he get back to work on the great master plan.

Anchored in this fashion, Otepka was forced to stand by while the first great tidal wave of the New Frontier washed in, over and through the Department of State. Early in May, Boswell finally sent Otepka's carefully detailed prospectus up to the Deputy Undersecretary for Administration, Roger Jones, and the project was approved on an on-going basis with the blessing of Dean Rusk.

Much had happened in the meantime, of course, including the tragedy at the Bay of Pigs, which temporarily sent the Kennedy Administration into trauma. But there were other developments that shocked Otto Otepka even more.

Not long after the Inauguration on January 20, he learned that Dr. Walt Whitman Rostow, about whom he had gone into such detail with Rusk and Bobby Kennedy, had been appointed to the White House staff as a special assistant to the President on national security. Steeled as he was, after nearly twenty-five years in government service, to the often irrational behavior of politicians, Otepka nonetheless felt an icy shiver run down his spine.

Actually, it was not necessary to be privy to Rostow's security file, as Otepka was, to share his apprehension. Nor is it necessary even now to question Dr. Rostow's loyalty in order still to wonder why any prudent President would elevate him to such a high position of influence and trust. His writings alone, and they were voluminous prior to 1961, should automatically have eliminated him from the councils of any American government intent on maintaining its sovereignty. For Walt Whitman Rostow may believe in preserving the national identity of some countries, but he has made it repeatedly and abundantly clear that he does *not* believe that the United States has the right to preserve its own "nationhood."

The theme of Rostow's "anti-nationhood" runs not only through virtually all his writings, but through his whole life. Born in New York City on October 7, 1916, Rostow was the second son of Victor Aaron and Lillian Helman Rostow. His father, who claims to have been a Menshevik socialist, immigrated to America from Russia after the 1905 revolution and became a metallurgical chemist. But Victor Rostow did not shed his socialism. On the contrary, he became so enamored of the American brand (which was then virtually indistinguishable from the Russian) that he named two of his three sons after those redoubtable heroes of American socialism, Eugene V. Debs and the "people's poet," Walt Whitman.*

Socialism had a much more open internationalist flavor in that era than it has today. Now that it has seeped into both major political parties and Norman Thomas can boast that the Democrats have enacted almost all the programs he proposed thirty years ago, the global goals are more carefully concealed under the guise of the welfare state. To be sure, President Johnson might speak fuzzily of a "world community" but he did not dare, even in the silly '60's, tell the American people that what this really means is the wholesale surrender of their sovereignty.

In Victor Rostow's day, however, Socialists were more forthright, if not quite so respectable. And World War I, after first giving rise to an aberrant chauvinism in the socialist camp, later lent added impetus to the Socialists' fundamental internationalism. Thus, the sons of Mr. Rostow were conditioned at a tender age to view the world in its wonderful oneness, as yet unachieved but, according to the Socialist messiah, Marx, ultimately inevitable.

When Walt Rostow was still quite small the family moved to Irvington, New Jersey, well within the rapidly expanding New York metropolitan area. When he was ten they moved again, this time to New Haven, Connecticut. After graduation from Hillhouse High School, young Walt automatically entered Yale, where his brother Eugene, four years his senior, had preceded him. Rostow did well at Yale, and when he took his B.A. in 1936, he followed the trail of Dean Rusk and many another bright young man to England, where he attended Oxford on a Rhodes scholarship.**

England had advanced much closer to war by the time Walt Rostow

---

* Although Walt Whitman was probably never an active member of the Socialist Party, he embraced socialism as his philosophy late in life and was deified by the Left. Eugene Debs, who liked to call himself a "Bolshevist" after the Russian Revolution, was convicted in Federal Court on charges of violating the Espionage Act in World War I.
** With his penchant for historical analysis, Walt Rostow may have been intrigued, while a student at Balliol College, by the outdated goals of Cecil Rhodes, the empire builder whose South African diamond mine fortune was financing his education at Oxford. Rhodes, who had been in the habit of laying his hand on a section of the globe and saying, "I want to see all of this red" (for England), had early founded what he called a "secret society" to win the United States back to the British crown and acquire other territories as well. When he died in 1902, Rhodes left a will to establish the scholarship fund under which several thousand young Americans have now studied at Oxford.

arrived at Oxford in 1936 than it had when Dean Rusk left three years earlier. Hitler's legions had reoccupied the demilitarized Rhineland that year; Mussolini had annexed Ethiopia; Spain was in the grip of a bloody civil war. But public attention, in both Great Britain and America, was misfocused as usual, this time on the abdication of King Edward VIII, who gave up his throne for Wallis Warfield Simpson.

Rostow must have immensely enjoyed his sojourn at Oxford in spite of the rising threat of war. For one thing, he found time for side trips to the Continent, where he came in contact with various other "advanced thinkers." Returning to New Haven, Rostow plunged into work on his doctorate at Yale. In 1940, armed with a shining new Ph.D., he began teaching at Columbia as an instructor in economics. Following Pearl Harbor he was commissioned in the OSS and in 1942 shipped off again for England. The story is told that he was aboard a British tanker when it was sunk by a German submarine but was rescued and delivered unscathed to London where he participated in selecting targets for the Allied bombings of Germany.

Rostow spent nearly three years in Britain with OSS, rising to the rank of major. He was awarded the Legion of Merit by the United States and was also decorated with the Honourable Order of the British Empire.

During the next five years, Rostow shifted jobs at least five times, in each instance adding a little more luster to his budding reputation as an advanced internationalist thinker. When OSS was merged with the State Department in 1945, he moved onto State's payroll and became Assistant Chief in the German-Austria economics division, which was in charge of extracting reparations from defeated Germany. From this post, and with a major assist from then U.S. Ambassador to Britain Averell Harriman, Rostow shuttled back to Oxford in 1946 as Harmsworth professor of American history. Having stuck this fine academic feather in his cap, he rode off, after one year, to take another crack at herding Western Europe further into the socialist camp.

For some reason, Rostow's capsule biography in *Who's Who* lists him as "assistant to executive secretary" from 1947 to 1949, of something called the "Economic Commission for Europe." This omits the relevant fact that the commission was a United Nations agency located in Geneva, Switzerland. And more relevant, though there is no reason *Who's Who* should note it, is the fact that the commission's executive secretary, Rostow's immediate boss, was one Gunnar Myrdal.

In 1967 Gunnar Myrdal, a "forward-thinking" Swedish social architect, emerged as principal speaker and patron of the virulently anti-American Vietnam War protest in Stockholm, which followed Bertrand Russell's misbegotten "tribunal" that condemned Lyndon Johnson and the U.S.A. as war criminals. The Stockholm protest hardly bothered to conceal that it was largely organized by Communists, including a large delegation from the Soviet Union. Also active behind the scenes was Myrdal's son, Jan, who surfaced in 1965 as a more or less open Peiping-type Leftist.[1]

Almost as prolific a writer as Rostow, Gunnar Myrdal has turned out a dozen books and scores of tracts over the years, a surprising number of them on what he early called "the Negro problem" in America. It is not too much to say that Myrdal's scholarly rantings helped lay the theoretical groundwork for the discontent that was later escalated to insurrection within the Negro community. Having contributed to this escalation, the Swedish theorist in 1967 advocated that the U.S. spend "trillions of dollars" to de-escalate by eradicating "ghettos."[2] Where America was going to get such a sum at a time when it was struggling to correct its severe balance of payments deficit was, in Myrdal's mind, very simple. All we had to do was surrender to the Communists in Vietnam, end the nuclear arms race with Russia, and halt our space program. That all three of these measures were primary goals of the Soviet Union's plan for America did not, of course, trouble Myrdal, who has long been an open advocate of programs near and dear to the Kremlin's heart.

If Gunnar Myrdal, the premiere Scandinavian critic of the U.S. and apologist for the USSR, felt uncomfortable with Walt Whitman Rostow, later magically transformed into the leading "hawk" of the Johnson Administration, there is no record of it. Indeed, Myrdal felt compatible enough with his assistant to hire his brother, Eugene Debs Rostow, as his replacement when Walt Rostow left the U.N. Commission in 1949.

With the Rostow succession in Geneva thus assured, Walt again bounced back to England. On this trip he became Pitt professor of American history at Cambridge. Clement Attlee's Labor government, which had dismembered the empire and would have totally wrecked the British economy if it had not been for huge transfusions of dollars from America, was still riding high and wide, though it no longer looked quite so handsome to the British people as it did when they forsook Winston Churchill for Mr. Attlee. Yet in spite of the horrendous failures of social-ism evident on every hand, many of Attlee's fellow Fabians were moving deeper and deeper into the mainstream of socialist thought, which they very correctly perceived was flowing from the Moskva rather than the Thames.

A few years later, these people served up a revitalized expression of faith in their floundering socialism. *New Fabian Essays,* warmed-over hash of old Marxism liberally seasoned with modern fears, contained a forward by the Honorable Mr. Attlee commending it "to our comrades not only in this country but overseas."[3]

Although there is no evidence that Rostow was connected with the formulation of this Fabian manifesto, many of the ideas he later expressed in his own books and speeches could have been taken from it verbatim. The British, however, were much less verbose than Rostow and far more forthright and for these reasons it is worth quoting a few samples here.

For instance, the "no win" policy later implemented by Rostow & Company was first spelled out in *New Fabian Essays.* R.H.S. Crossman, a Labor M.P. and member of the Fabian Executive Committee, laid it on the line quite bluntly: "We are members of the Atlantic Alliance. But this does not mean that we are enemies of every Communist revolution. We are opposed to Russian expansion, *but also to an American victory.*"

Just in case anyone missed the point, Crossman reiterated: "If freedom is to survive, it is essential that neither the U.S.A. nor the Soviet Union should win. . . . We must realize that a victory for either side would be a defeat for socialism."

There was yet another line from *New Fabian Essays* that found an echo in the "Rostow Papers" of 1961 and, even more forcefully, in the Reuther Memorandum to Bobby Kennedy which laid down the policy against "extremism." "If we construct an anti-Communist ideology," the credo said, "we shall merely intensify the Cold War and confirm the illusion that the preservation of freedom requires the defeat of Communism."

By the time the Fabian manifesto was issued, Walt Rostow had returned to America, where he was already peddling these and other nostrums for a "peaceful world" of nationless states. With credentials from Yale, Oxford, and Cambridge, he easily found an eminently respectable landing place on the Charles River at the Massachusetts Institute of Technology. Aided by a multi-million dollar "grant" in tax funds engineered by his old OSS comrades now in CIA, Rostow helped launch MIT's Center for International Studies (CENIS), a sort of submarine "think tank" which was soon firing intellectual torpedoes at any and all

U.S. policies that appeared to have a chance of effectively rolling back communism.*

For the next decade, from 1950 until he by-passed Otto Otepka and quietly established himself in the White House, Dr. Rostow used his tank at MIT to pour forth an endless torrent of books, policy papers, "studies," and speeches prophesying the shape of the world to come. He was not alone, of course. The prophets of the brave new world were springing up on every hand through the 1950's. Some working out of MIT were carry-overs from the Old Left, like Harold Isaacs, friend of a number of aging Soviet agents and member of archaic Communist fronts.** More of them adopted Rostow's chameleon strategy, coloring themselves in less readily identifiable hues ranging from pale pink to fuchsia. Most notable among these was Jerome Wiesner, later to emerge as President Kennedy's chief scientific advisor and more recently Provost of MIT.

Compared with all the others, however, Rostow stands like Moses on Mount Sinai, towering above the lilliputian crowd. By accident or design, Rostow's geographical bearings were right on target too. For Sinai in the '50's was Cambridge, Massachusetts, and that is where Walt Rostow, after eight years of wandering in the wasteland of wartime and postwar Europe, at last found his mountain and his pulpit.

The world soon became Rostow's beat. He blossomed forth as an expert on every place and everything. Octopus-like, he embraced the globe, gobbling Communist China for lunch one day, and Africa for breakfast the next. Portraying himself as the perpetual optimist, his omnivorous appetite digested such seemingly diverse subjects as the economics of Latin America and guerrilla warfare, disarmament and the horrid French policy in Indochina.

For recreation, and to keep his waistline within manageable circumference, pudgy Dr. Rostow played tennis. As with everything else, he played hard, and was competent enough to share the honors in doubles in an MIT faculty tournament. Then, too, there was his family. In 1947 he had married Elspeth Vaughan Davies, a Barnard College girl he had met in prewar Geneva, and during these years by the peaceful Charles

* Estimates of CIA's original investment in CENIS range up to $6,000,000. Other funds came from befuddled business-industrial sources who were led to believe they were helping to fight communism.

** Harold Isaacs was identified a number of times in the Senate Internal Security Subcommittee's investigation into the Institute of Pacific Relations. Among other things, he was named a friend of Agnes Smedley, the old China hand who helped the Soviets install Mao Tse-tung in Peiping. Isaacs was also identified as a member of the Shanghai branch of the Society of Friends of the U.S.S.R., a front founded in the early 1930's by Soviet agents in Shanghai.

River their children, Peter and Ann Larner Rostow, were growing up.

None of this, however, diverted Walt Whitman Rostow for long from his many-pronged intellectual tasks. The books began to roll off the presses, and in ten years he gave birth to no less than eight sententious volumes. One of the earliest, written in collaboration with Alfred Levin, was *The Dynamics of Soviet Society*.[4]

Actually a compendium summarizing the findings of a group of CENIS scholars, this abstruse tome followed hard on the heels of Stalin's death and opened beautiful new vistas for brave global thinkers everywhere. It was careful, however, to strike just the right note that would make it acceptable to both the Left and to the Eisenhower Administration. It propounded the theory that the Soviets would never start a war that might destroy their power, but it also appeared to argue for keeping the defenses of the West strong.

A later Rostow book, published about the time Otepka's evaluation barred him from the Quantico Panel of the National Security Council, was a bit more venturesome. In *An American Policy in Asia*, Rostow was especially rough on the French for trying to put down the Vietminh, and equally rough on America for supporting the French. "History," he intoned, "is unlikely to forgive us for serving as banker to a supremely self-defeating French policy in Indonesia."[5]

In another book, Rostow argues that every revolutionary war is prima facie evidence of the failure of social and economic reform—a pronouncement that sadly overlooks the principal cause of revolutions in the twentieth century: Communist propaganda and terrorism, or, in some cases, the reaction *against* impending Communist take-overs, as in Brazil and Indonesia.

Through all of this, Rostow never lost sight of the ultimate goal, first learned at his father's knee. In this same book, *The United States in The World Arena*, he wrote:

> It is a legitimate American national objective to see removed from all nations—including the United States—the right to use substantial military force to pursue their own interests. Since this residual right is the right of national sovereignty and the basis for the existence of an international arena of power, it is, therefore, an American interest to see an end of nationhood as it has been historically defined.[6]

As early as 1955, Rostow was preaching the policy of "convergence" which President Kennedy was to adopt as his own in the 1960's. Since neither the U.S. nor the Soviet Union could hope to defeat the other, ultimately both must "converge"—politically, economically, and, though

Rostow did not say so, obviously morally as well. (This leaves open the rather relevant question of whether the Soviets reject, or America adopts, the KGB tactic of the "knock on *your* door in the middle of the night," but in Rostow's nationless world this is an unimportant detail.)

By 1960, Rostow had "gotten rid of the old-fashioned vocabulary of capitalism vs. communism,"[7] according to an admiring Rudolf Flesch, and had long since moved on to dividing the world into two camps, not East and West, nor even Communist and free, *but North and South*. This theme was to recur again and again throughout Rostow's work and speeches in the 1960's.

Lest the reader think Walt Rostow was trying to resurrect the Old Confederacy, it is best we explain what he means by North and South. The North, which includes the United States, the USSR, and Western Europe, is the industrialized portion of the world which must be forged into a union to uplift the poor benighted nations of the South—in Latin America, Africa, and, though the geography doesn't quite hold, Asia as well.

If this sounds just plain zany, dwell for a moment on the benefits we reap from such a division. For one thing, by getting people to think in terms of North and South, rather than East and West, it becomes obvious that the differences between the Communist world and the tottering free societies of North America and Europe soon will melt away. Then, having converged East and West, the United North can get on with the much more serious business of feeding, clothing and industrializing the impoverished South.

These more *outré* revelations of Dr. Rostow were buried or carefully muted in John F. Kennedy's campaign for the Presidency in 1960. Aiding JFK in quest of votes, he tried a number of more popular tunes on his player piano (Rostow actually does compose pop music, of the variety favored by older hands in Tin Pan Alley), and he is credited with coming up with the slogan, "New Frontier." This alone should have earned him a lasting place in the heart of his candidate. But Rostow is nothing if not prolific, and he added a number of other *bon mots* to Kennedy's vote-getting lexicon, among them the immortal, "Let's get the country moving again!" Until then, most Americans had not realized they were exactly standing still, but there is no doubt that these and other Rostowisms helped move many of them to the polls where they dutifully pulled the proper levers or marked an X in the right box.

It must not be supposed, however, that Rostow's influence in government began with his ascent to the White House on Jack Kennedy's coattails in 1961. Starting with the Truman Administration, after his 1950 return from England, Rostow exerted a continuing, though only spasmodically successful, pressure on U.S. foreign policy.

Otepka succeeded in barring the door to Rostow at the State Department in 1955, but the professor was forever crawling through one of the many other windows into government that Otepka could not slam down. As a matter of fact, he tried slipping into State again in 1957. But Otepka caught his name and for a second time Rostow was quietly denied a State Department security clearance.

Even the Air Force, which had terminated a contract on security grounds because Dr. Rostow was involved in it, continued to let its officers and civilian employees work with the wonderful wizard of MIT. Top-flight Air Force officers were permitted to help Rostow on projects related to the Cold War without ever knowing that Air Force Intelligence had deemed him a security risk.

Most curious of all, however, is the attitude of CIA. Having dropped Rostow from one super-sensitive contract, CIA nonetheless cleared him on "loyalty" grounds and permitted him to work on a number of other CIA projects. It was no secret, even in the 1950's, that the MIT Center for International Studies, where Rostow labored for more than ten years, was (and is) a well-known CIA front. Yet "the Agency," as CIA is euphemistically referred to in Washington, not only tolerated Rostow's presence at its Cambridge annex, but substantially financed him and his visionary disciples.

One explanation for these seeming inconsistencies in security policy is the rigid compartmentalization of giant federal bureaucracies. To update an old saw, which applies very aptly to Washington in the 1960's, the right hand seldom knew what the left was doing, though the left was well informed indeed on the right hand's every move.

Dr. Rostow, still in his early thirties, made his debut in top policy circles in the capital shortly after he arrived at MIT toward the end of the Truman era. Incredibly, he was presented as a "China expert" despite the fact that he had just spent eight years in Europe and had no intimate knowledge of the Far East. A State Department official who sat in on one of Rostow's briefing sessions in 1951 made the mistake of telling his associates that the lecture was "nothing more than the straight Maoist line." The official was never invited to a Rostow briefing again.

During the Eisenhower-Dulles years, adroitly sidestepping Otto Otepka's net at SY, Rostow frequently found an audience in high places. In 1967, a decade after the fact, it was finally disclosed that he was the originator of President Eisenhower's "Open Skies" proposal, which sought to provide for mutual U.S.-Soviet aerial surveillance of military installations.[8]

It was not, however, until 1961 that Walt Rostow finally hit his stride. Rapidly consolidating his position in the White House, he moved brazenly forward on a broad front, scrapping all the old Truman-Eisenhower policies as he went. By the end of the year, with Otepka still moored to the contrived special project, Rostow was ready to shift over to the State Department. Before going, though, he made certain that the United States was committed, once and for all, to a new land war in Asia. In a sense, it was the fulfillment of an old dream, one he had been laboring for a half-dozen years to realize, as Otepka belatedly discovered.

CHAPTER **IX**

The Hawk

A YEAR BEFORE WALT W. ROSTOW WAS FIRST REFUSED A SECURITY clearance on Otto Otepka's recommendation, the ubiquitous oracle of Cambridge played a key role in the partition of Vietnam. Most people suppose that French Indochina was drawn and quartered at the Geneva Conference which resulted in the signing of the ignoble "accords" that consigned twelve million more Asians to Communist slavery on July 21, 1954. But the real decision that carved up this bloody land into a hopelessly divided and virtually indefensible jigsaw puzzle was actually made in Washington three months earlier.

At a top-secret conference in a private dining room on the third floor of the Metropolitan Club in April, Dr. Rostow unveiled his plan for cutting Vietnam into two irreconcilable pieces, neatly flanked by independent Laos and Cambodia. The host for this fateful meeting was C.D. Jackson, President Eisenhower's special assistant on psychological warfare, a title that covered a multitude of important duties. One of Henry Luce's early associates at *Time* and later publisher of *Life*, C.D. was a towering oak of a man who was occasionally bedazzled, like so many Americans, by the intellectual "brilliance" of the Left.

There were a dozen U.S. government officials at the meeting, including three from the State Department. CIA was prominently represented by its Director, Allen Dulles, and two of his top assistants, Richard Bissell and a shadowy figure named Frank Wisner, who later committed suicide. But significantly there were no military men in attendance to ponder what was essentially a military problem.

Dienbienphu was about to fall after a heroic stand and France, beset by the same kind of divisive storms that were to assail America in the following decade, was suing for peace. The United States was reluctant to commit its forces or to step up aid to the French in Vietnam. It agreed, however, to participate in the Geneva negotiations although on the surface it did not become a party to partition. By some sleight of hand MIT's Center for International Studies had been given the task of preparing guidelines for the U.S. delegation journeying to Geneva.

Moscow and Peiping had good reason to halt temporarily the Vietnam conflict that spring. The Soviets were anxious to capitalize on the false hopes raised in the West by the death of Stalin the previous year. They were pushing "peaceful coexistence" and they also wanted to wreck the European Defense Community, which would have consolidated NATO's position. In this latter endeavor they found an ally in Pierre Mendès-France, soon to become Premier of France, and ultimately the Soviets achieved all their goals.

The meeting at the Metropolitan Club in April gave the Russians a formidable start. Max Millikan, the director of MIT's CENIS, introduced Rostow who turned out to be the author of the partition plan. The bespectacled sage then launched into one of his typically sententious briefings. It took him all of forty minutes to read the instructions he had prepared for the American delegation to Geneva, a paper entitled "Démarche for U.S. Policy in Vietnam."

Rostow's tome boiled down to one essential theme—Vietnam should be divided at the 17th Parallel. One of the Intelligence people at the meeting was taken aback. Within the previous week Peiping Radio had begun to stump for splitting Vietnam too—and at the same 17th Parallel. None of the other conferees blinked, however. When Rostow was done there was polite approval all around the table—except for one dissenting voice.

The lone dissenter pointed out that the Vietminh had at least twenty strong guerrilla pockets just below the 17th Parallel, which would certainly simplify the Communist supply problems if they decided to heat up the war after the truce. Rostow's proposed line would also protect the northern flank of the incipient Ho Chi Minh Trail to the South. More-over, the dissenter felt it would be more realistic to establish the demar-cation boundaries closer to General Navarre's fighting line, which was then some eighty miles to the north. In sum, he argued that Rostow was being overly gratuitous in giving away so much real estate.

The dissenter's criticism was met with stony silence and the confer-ence abruptly ended. By tacit consent the Rostow Plan won out, with the result that Ho Chi Minh was handed hundreds of square miles of territory from which, in the 1960's, he launched his devastating attacks on Ameri-can troops in South Vietnam.

Rostow maintained his keen interest in Southeast Asia after moving into the White House. In 1961 he and McGeorge Bundy divided up the crisis areas between them, with Bundy taking Cuba and Berlin and Ro-stow assuming primary responsibility for Laos and Vietnam.[1] According to the 1967 *Business Week* article, "From that point on, Rostow played a key role at every stage of the evaluation of Vietnam policy."

It came as something of a surprise, if not a shock, to his many admirers in the Liberal community when Dr. Rostow, very early in the Kennedy Administration, emerged as a hawk, at least with regard to Vietnam. For years he had been an articulate advocate of reconciliation with the Com-munist bloc, including Red China.

In the spring of 1961, however, Rostow, the man who had so scath-ingly condemned the United States for supporting the French against the Vietminh in Indochina, suddenly executed a smart flip and came down with all his considerable force for sending American troops to Vietnam. Previously, the U.S. had only a handful of "military advisors" in South Vietnam. But now, with the Communist Pathet Lao offensive threatening the whole Mekong Delta, President Kennedy was striving desperately to find a solution that would, as he put it, prevent "an immediate Commu-nist takeover" of Laos and all of Indochina.[2]

On the afternoon of March 20 the President called a meeting of the National Security Council to determine what could be done. According to Schlesinger, the Council "discussed the possibility of moving a small number of American troops into the Mekong valley not to fight the Pathet Lao but to deter them by their presence and provide a bargaining counter for an international conference."[3] It was at this point that Dr. Rostow made his move.

"Walt Rostow argued persuasively for this restricted commitment," says Schlesinger, "but the Joint Chiefs opposed the sending of ground forces to the mainland of Asia. . . . Their recommendation was all or nothing; either go in on a large scale, with 60,000 soldiers, air cover and even nuclear weapons, or else stay out."⁴

Kennedy rejected the advice of the Joint Chiefs, and although he temporarily shelved Rostow's plan as well, it was soon revived. The National Security Council, however, never rose again.* In the meantime, Rostow deftly executed another of his graceful pirouettes and helped draft the plan for the "neutralization" of Laos. This plan was pushed through despite former President Eisenhower's plea to Kennedy, on the day preceding the inauguration, that Laos was the key to the whole military problem in Southeast Asia.

While the Laotian situation was still up in the air, Rostow kept plumping for a U.S. troop commitment in Vietnam. In desperation, he dreamed up the most fantastic plans for getting America into the war. Once, he went so far as to recommend sending ten to fifteen thousand infantry men into the Mekong Delta disguised as "agricultural technicians."

In June 1961 Kennedy "explicitly approved" a Rostow speech warning that America might not only send forces into South Vietnam, but might also carry the war to the Communist North.⁵ It was the first official public indication that the Administration was entertaining serious thoughts of widening the war.

That fall, Rostow finally got his way. When General Maxwell Taylor was brought back as Chairman of the Joint Chiefs, Rostow accompanied him on an inspection tour of South Vietnam. They returned with a persuasive recommendation that a minimum of 10,000 American troops be sent to fight the Viet Cong. Shortly after this, the President despatched the first full units to Vietnam. The United States was irrevocably hooked. The very thing most American military men had warned against for years—getting the U.S. trapped into a bloody ground war in Asia—had come to pass.

By 1968 the United States was spending somewhere between $30 and $40 billion a year on the Vietnam War (depending on which of several sets of figures one studied), and inflation, due in large part to the war, was severely straining the economy. Far more tragic, however, were the casualties. Some 200,000 Americans had been killed or wounded. Nearly

* Schlesinger informs us, on page 210 of *A Thousand Days*, that McGeorge Bundy "slaughtered committees right and left and collapsed what was left of the inherited [from Eisenhower] apparatus into a complex and flexible National Security Council staff [which Rostow headed under President Johnson from 1966 through 1968]. With Walt Rostow as his deputy and Bromley Smith . . . he was shaping a supple instrument to meet the new President's needs."

4,000 U.S. aircraft had been shot down, more than 800 over the Communist North alone. Most of the latter were blasted out of the skies by anti-aircraft guns and SAM missiles which the White House refused to let the Air Force and Navy destroy when these weapons were first being installed by Soviet "technicians."

For years, the State Department cooperated with McNamara's Pentagon in preserving the fiction that the Viet Cong were being principally supplied by Communist China. But by early 1967 this bald fabrication was at last wearing thin and the press began to see through it. "It is the Russians," said *U.S. News & World Report*, "who are furnishing the real sinews for major and prolonged war."[6]

The Soviet Union, now belatedly unmasked as the chief provider of arms to North Vietnam, was reaping a tremendous "profit" on its investment in the war, not only in terms of the far greater sums it was forcing the U.S. to spend, but more important, in American lives.* In addition, the Soviet was enjoying a handsome bonus in the form of damaged U.S. prestige, the crumbling of our traditional alliances, and the gradual isolation of an America miscast in the role of "warmonger." Politically, our country was being torn apart by the longest war in U.S. history, its people divided into recriminatory, and often violent, factions.

Despite the hard evidence of the Soviet's primary role in Vietnam, Rostow was still blithely blaming the war on the Chinese Communists at the end of 1967. "In his eyes," said a *Look* magazine article, "our essential conflict is with an expansive Chinese communism." Yet in this same story Rostow somehow liberated Hanoi from Peiping: "I have no doubt the men in Hanoi cherish their independence," *Look* quoted him as saying. "I do not regard them in any simple way as puppets."

Needless to say, Rostow had long ago severed Ho Chi Minh from Moscow, although Ho is probably the oldest living member of the Comintern and the Soviet's staunchest ally in Asia.

If these intellectual gyrations leave the reader a bit befuddled, they didn't seem to bother Lyndon Baines Johnson, who had brought Rostow back to the White House from State in April 1966 to advise him on the Vietnam War and all other national security matters. "I've never had a man in whom I have more confidence than Walt," the President declared

---

* Official estimates of the Soviet investment in Vietnam vary widely. In his last posture statement to the Congress on February 1, 1968, Defense Secretary McNamara said the "total aid for 1967 may have reached $1 billion." But on May 4, 1968, McNamara told Congress, "It is more than $1 billion . . . I would say they are spending $5 billion more per year." If so, that would bring the total to $6 billion.

in the fall of 1967.[8] Yet by the end of March 1968 Walt Rostow's Vietnam policy, which by its very nature foreclosed any hope of a U.S. victory, had forced Lyndon Johnson to the hard decision to give up the White House.

Rostow had a lot of help in implementing his plans for Vietnam, of course. Dean Rusk, MacArthur's nemesis in the Korean War, was an experienced hand at saddling the military with restrictions that made it impossible for them to win. But Rostow displayed more finesse than Rusk. By advocating increased troop buildups (in early 1965 he was already predicting that 500,000 Americans would be needed in Vietnam), Rostow managed to convince the Joint Chiefs that he was a hawk. It is doubtful that even General William B. Westmoreland knew why he had been deprived of victory before he was recalled from Vietnam in 1968.

Dr. Rostow, the leading "hawk" of the Vietnam War, nevertheless remained an implacable dove on all other issues affecting the national security. Nowhere is the evidence of this better seen than in his evangelistic campaign to defuse America's strategic forces while occasionally rattling the H-bomb to quiet the fears of the military.

Although Rostow's stand on disarmament predated his rise to the White House in 1961, it began to take on more specific shape and substance following his quasi-official visit to Moscow just after the 1960 election. On the last weekend in November that year, Rostow and two dozen others from the United States journeyed to the Soviet Union for the sixth Pugwash Conference of East-West scientists, academicians and miscellaneous advanced thinkers.

The Pugwash Conferences take their name from the site of the first such meeting, held in July 1957 on the estate of Cleveland industrialist Cyrus S. Eaton in Pugwash, Nova Scotia. Eaton, a close friend of Nikita Khrushchev, had been rewarded with the Lenin Peace Prize four months before the 1960 meeting in Moscow.

Most of the giant steps towards disarmament taken by the Kennedy-Johnson Administration, including the 1963 Treaty of Moscow ("Limited" Test Ban Treaty) and the ban on nuclear weapons in space, were germinated in Pugwash conferences in spite of warnings from the Senate Internal Security Subcommittee that the Russian participants, most of them from the Soviet Academy of Science, were either high-ranking Communists or obviously under the control of the Central Committee.

Although Cyrus Eaton put up some of the money for the early Pugwash meetings, the invitations were invariably issued by that sterling old patriarch of "peace," Lord Bertrand Russell. Blissfully ignoring Russell's anti-American stands, the American Academy of Arts and Sciences sponsored the U.S. delegation to the 1960 conference.

In the group accompanying Rostow to Moscow was Dr. Jerome B. Wiesner, director of MIT's electronics research laboratory, leading exponent of dismantling U.S. strategic defenses, and soon to become chief scientific advisor to President Kennedy. Rostow and Wiesner, knowing they were slated to hold high posts in the incoming Administration in Washington, did not let that inhibit them in their avid courtship of the Kremlin. In fact, it added zest to the whole affair.

Among the Soviet leaders whom they admitted talking with in private was Vasily V. Kuznetsov, then Deputy Foreign Minister of the USSR. Rostow later reported that Kuznetsov complained of the "aggressive appearance" of the American bomber and missile bases that then ringed the Soviet Union. The Russian, in effect, accused the U.S. of building a "first-strike" force that could destroy his motherland.

Rostow, only one generation removed from Mother Russia himself, was compassionate and understanding. He says that he replied to Kuznetsov that the U.S. should replace its first-strike force "quickly at whatever expense might be necessary [with] a second-strike capability as well as a highly mobile deterrent against limited war."[9] Thus, in one fell swoop, he gave away America's entire military strategy for the '60's.

Not to be outdone, Dr. Wiesner gratuitously handed the Soviets a couple of other choice tidbits. Even during the Pugwash Conference itself, he held forth at great length on the technology of "hardening" missile sites, giving his Moscow audience much useful information on how they could protect their own missiles against attack.[10] And as if that were not enough, Wiesner went into intimate detail on the Nike-Zeus, then America's most promising anti-missile defense system. He knew quite a good deal about Nike-Zeus too, since he had worked on various phases of its development for the U.S. government. But that did not seem to trouble Wiesner in the slightest. He pledged himself at the Moscow conference to return to Washington and strive for ways to "prohibit the development and deployment of such systems."[11]

Rostow and Wiesner were not making idle promises to the Soviets. They came through on every one. In 1969 the United States still did not have an anti-ballistic missile (ABM) defense, though the Soviets had long since deployed several major ABM systems. Moreover, Rostow's pledge to Kuznetsov to scuttle U.S. first-strike forces in favor of a second-strike defense—i.e., nuclear weapons that would be used only if the United States were hit first—was put into effect almost immediately.

Bustling back from Moscow, Rostow carried an optimistic report to President-elect Kennedy that the door was now open for major moves towards peace. Thomas Ross of the Chicago *Sun-Times* divulged on March 31, 1961, that "striking echoes of Rostow's report" popped up in Kennedy's first defense message to the nation. Indeed, Rostow supplied the major theme. "We are not," said Kennedy, "creating forces for a first-strike against any other nation."

The President meant it, too. One of the first casualties of the Rostow-Wiesner plan was Nike-Zeus, which the Soviets pretended to regard as a first-strike nuclear weapon despite the fact that it could never hit a target in Russia and was designed for purely defensive purposes. The B-70 bomber, the Titan and Atlas ICBMs, the Thor and Jupiter inter-mediate range missiles, Skybolt, Pluto, the Bomarc-A, and other weapons were almost all consigned to the scrap heap.

American taxpayers had spent billions of dollars on these systems, most of which were already operational, but the Soviets found them offensive and they had to go. The Minuteman, an intercontinental missile with a warhead many times smaller than the Atlas or Titan, and therefore an ideal second-strike weapon, was deployed to assuage whatever fears the American public might harbor about Soviet intentions. But as com-pared with the rising Soviet nuclear capability, by the mid-1960's the United States was fast becoming what General Arthur G. Trudeau, for-mer chief of Army Intelligence and later of Research and Development, despairingly called a "nuclear nudist colony."

All of this was accomplished without one single concrete slice of evidence that the Soviets were taking any steps themselves towards disarmament. The United States, under the influence of Rostow, Wiesner, et al., simply waived its previous demands for adequate inspec-tion as a concomitant to disarmament measures.

Not even when the Soviets were so inconsiderate as to break the test ban moratorium in the late summer of 1961 did Rostow and Wiesner veer one inch from their suicidal course. The Soviet tests, several years in preparation while America religiously observed the ban, represented a great leap forward in strategic weaponry. Yet this merely gave Rostow and Wiesner an added excuse to push still harder for a treaty that would freeze American nuclear development while giving the Soviets a free field to perfect their technology and get new weapons into production.

As the Soviet explosions grew increasingly larger, Kennedy realized that the United States had to do something, if only, as he so frankly put it, because of the mounting public pressure. Even the Secretary of Defense, Robert Strange McNamara, who later wilted like an uprooted flower on the whole question of our nuclear preparedness, requested a resumption of U.S. tests. But as late as December 1961, and on into the new year, Wiesner was steadfastly arguing that American tests "are not critical or even very important to our overall military posture."[12]

After weeks of debate, Schlesinger informs us, the President came "to the conclusion that Wiesner was essentially right."[13] Later, Kennedy wavered and was about to issue the order to start the tests. At this point, Prime Minister Harold Macmillan of Britain journeyed to Bermuda, figuratively brandishing Chamberlain's old Munich umbrella, to whip the young President back into line. His eloquent argument against testing stayed Kennedy's unsteady hand once again.

The endless agonizing continued into February when a panel of leading American scientists reported that the Soviets had already made tremendous gains in nuclear weaponry and had developed techniques for mass destruction wholly unknown to the U.S. Among other things, they clearly had the capacity for a 100-megaton bomb—four times more powerful than America's biggest weapon, which, incidentally, has since been retired from our arsenal.

On March 2 Kennedy at long last announced that the United States would resume nuclear tests in the atmosphere—unless the Russians agreed to accept a treaty banning all tests, and came to Geneva to help him forge a major "breakthrough to peace." The Russians, of course, ignored him and on April 25, eight months after the Red nuclear terror began, the U.S. finally got around to starting tests which we now know weren't even in the same league with the Soviets.'

It is difficult, if not impossible, for the average American to understand how any President could procrastinate like this with the lives of every man, woman and child in the country so clearly being placed in jeopardy by an enemy sworn to our destruction. But Otto Otepka understood it very well, because he probably knew more about the people John F. Kennedy had surrounded himself with than any other man in America—not excluding J. Edgar Hoover.

In the State Department, Otepka had access to countless files that the FBI doesn't to this day know exist, whereas the FBI files were almost always made available to him. Moreover, the FBI, as a matter of policy, does not keep a very close watch on overt Socialists. And for years it has been barred from effective surveillance of university campuses where all manner and breed of Leftists have found sanctuary to lay their plans for revolution.

When Jack Kennedy, the King of Camelot, had so much trouble making up his mind on so many vital issues, it came as no surprise to Otepka. He knew, as author Theodore White has so wisely observed, that "the King's ear was held by . . . as visionary a group of thinkers as have ever held the ear of any chief in modern times."[14]

The vision was stated, for once succinctly, by Walt Rostow soon after his return from Moscow in 1960. The ultimate goal, which the Soviets would agree is identical to their own, is, in Rostow's words, "the creation of a world order which can't really stop very short of world law and some form of world government."[15]

Having said this, Rostow really had said everything. Except, of course, who would *control* that world government. But he could not resist the old aching temptation to embellish The Goal with scholarly verbiage. And so he embarked, during his first ten-month tenure at the White House, on a magnificent master plan which from the start was diametrically opposed to the other great plan Boswell had snared Otepka with in the Department of State.

This particular plan was shortly to become known to the world as the "Rostow Papers." However, the world, or at least the American voter, was not permitted to see the actual product. As the New York *Times* noted, the plan was "to remain secret and for the guidance of policy makers only."[16] It leaked out by dribs and drabs anyway—though not all of it—but that comes later and it will have to await another chapter. There are still a few other self-defeating Rostowian "wars" that need to be touched on first, specifically the Bay of Pigs and the Berlin Wall.

Rostow's role in the Bay of Pigs fiasco remained somewhat ambiguous until 1967 when *Life* magazine disclosed that he was "one of the two men assigned by President Kennedy to review the ill-fated invasion plans before the final decision to move."[17] Long before this, however, Otepka knew that Rostow had been in on the White House meetings that led to the dismal defeat and foreclosed all hope of rescuing the trapped Cubans.

Originally planned during the waning months of the Eisenhower Administration, the invasion was Jack Kennedy's first test of strength as President. Surrounded by his visionaries, he vacillated for long weeks on whether to permit the operation at all. Plans were formulated, amended, tentatively canceled, put back into effect, and changed again.

The Cuban brigade, trained in Central America by CIA agents, was initially scheduled to land on the southeast coast of Cuba at the foot of the Escambray Mountains. But the landing site was switched, almost at the last moment, to the Bay of Pigs, a full eighty miles from the mountains through an impassable swamp, and practically at the back door of Havana where Castro had his main force.

All the Cubans later ransomed from Communist prisons agree they were promised large-scale help from the United States, including air cover. Yet only ineffectual token air support materialized. Castro's Soviet-built tanks and artillery cut the invaders to pieces. Those who weren't killed in the swamp were quickly captured.

The President's reaction to the dismal failure of the Bay of Pigs was to find a scapegoat as quickly as possible. CIA was chosen, and the skids greased under its veteran director, Allen Dulles. Yet in the secret recesses of his soul, John Fitzgerald Kennedy knew that he had faltered in his baptism of fire on Pennsylvania Avenue

The Communists, of course, were testing Kennedy, probing for his weak spots, trying to determine how far they could go without getting his Irish up. The Bay of Pigs greatly encouraged them, but even more promising developments were soon to follow.

Early in June the President flew to Vienna to explore the summit of power with Nikita Khrushchev. His three main objectives were to reach a settlement on Laos, somehow to dampen the long-smoldering problem of Berlin, and to see if Khrushchev was interested in taking at least a first step towards disarmament by agreeing to a nuclear test ban treaty.

The Soviet leader was amenable to a coalition government for Laos, naturally. But he was downright threatening when it came to Berlin. He did promise, however, that Russia would not resume nuclear tests in the atmosphere unless the United States did so first. Less than three months later the Soviets broke this pledge, but unfortunately it did not seem to teach the Kennedy Administration anything about the value of Russian promises.

Khrushchev at Vienna, by turns belligerent and patronizingly friendly, treated Jack Kennedy like a schoolboy. And before they parted the old Bolshevik gave him one final examination.

A leading Washington newsman who accompanied the President to Vienna tells how Khrushchev summoned Kennedy to a private meeting on the last day. For a half-hour the bald old Bolshevik heatedly lectured the tall young American, finally shaking his fist under the President's nose.

An hour later a dejected figure with a hat pulled down over his eyes got out of a limousine and walked with bowed head to the Presidential residence. He was not recognized at first, because Jack Kennedy seldom wore a hat. But when he entered the building his entourage was distressed to see that it was indeed the President. He slumped in a chair and his aides, fearing he had taken ill, solicitously surrounded him. When they asked what the trouble was, Kennedy listlessly raised his head.

"Sometimes," he said slowly, "you spend all your life preparing to meet evil. Then, when you come face to face with the Devil, you realize how unprepared you are."

Whatever Khrushchev told Kennedy to shake him so thoroughly may never be entirely known. The newsman, a close friend of Kennedy's, says the President later related that the Russian threatened utterly to destroy the United States, obviously with nuclear weapons. "You may hurt us," Khrushchev reportedly shouted, "but you will never destroy us. And if you try, we will destroy you!"*

Khrushchev tied his threat to the Berlin problem, which steadily worsened during the next two months. By July, more than a thousand refugees a day were streaming into West Berlin from the Communist zone. Senator J. William Fulbright, Chairman of the Senate Foreign Relations Committee, said on a July 30 television program: "I don't understand why the East Germans don't close their border because I think they have a right to close it."

Kennedy was puzzled too. He did not seem to realize that the Soviets were simply waiting for a signal—some sign as to what the United States would do if they sealed off East Berlin. Schlesinger, who may be the world's worst historian but is certainly one of its greatest gossips, tells what happened next:

Early in August the President, strolling with Walt Rostow along the colonnade by the Rose Garden, observed that Khrushchev would have to do something internally to reestablish control over the situation—*and that, if he did, we would not be able to do a thing about it.* Eastern Europe was a vital interest to Khrushchev, and he could not stand by and let it trickle away. *But it was not a vital interest for the United States.*[18] (Emphasis added.)

* This account does not differ greatly from Schlesinger's version of the final official meeting between Kennedy and Khrushchev on page 274 of *A Thousand Days*, though Khrushchev's words, as translated by Schlesinger, were somewhat less belligerent and Kennedy makes no mention of "meeting the Devil."

Not many days later, on August 13, at a few minutes past midnight, Communist police and soldiers closed off most of the crossing points leading into West Berlin. At first, they only threw up roadblocks and barbed-wire barricades. When this brought no response from the American troops on the other side, the Soviets, on August 17, gave the East Germans the green light to begin construction of the Berlin wall.

As 1961 piled one defeat atop another in the critical arena of foreign affairs, President Kennedy became increasingly dissatisfied with the mysterious machinery of the Department of State. In fairness to the Department, it should be noted that Kennedy relied less heavily on it for advice during that first year than any President in modern times. The real decisions on foreign policy were made by his team in the White House. But the team, quarterbacked by Rostow and Bundy, drew support for their more far-out positions from their brethren at State.

Chester Bowles, the Undersecretary of State, was selected as the sacrificial lamb. The firing of Bowles, a man so popular with the Liberal community, was widely interpreted as the President's atonement for the many policy failures. This wasn't quite the case, but it served the purpose.

Bowles was replaced in November 1961 by George W. Ball, a Washington lawyer and close friend of Adlai Stevenson. Ball had been a dedicated but unfailingly cheerful Leftist since his student days at Northwestern and had worked with Walt Rostow in London when Ball was director of the U.S. Strategic Bombing Survey. He came into State as Undersecretary for Economic Affairs early in 1961, while Otepka was still chained to the Special Project.

The Bowles-Ball shuffle was merely one of many changes effected that autumn. A top-to-bottom reorganization of the State Department was ordered by Kennedy with what Schlesinger describes as a fairly massive "blood transfusion from the White House" designed to "revitalize" State.[19] George McGhee, a former Rhodes scholar, stepped into Ball's old job, though his title made him Undersecretary for political rather than economic affairs. Averell Harriman, who Schlesinger says was "always more interested in power than in status," became Assistant Secretary for the Far East. Frederick G. Dutton, Kennedy's Secretary of the Cabinet, shifted over as Assistant Secretary for Congressional Relations, and Richard Goodwin, a 29-year-old product of Harvard, was catapulted into the Deputy Assistant Secretaryship for Inter-American Affairs.

The most important job, as chief of State's Policy Planning Council, went to Walt Whitman Rostow. Upon his departure from the White House, Kennedy explained to Rostow what he was to do: "Over here in the White House we have to play with a very narrow range of choices. We are pretty much restricted to the ideas coming out of the bureaucracy. We can't do long-range planning; it has to be done over there [at State]. I want you to go over there and catch hold of the process at the level where it counts."[20]

Rostow, as we shall see, took the President at his word. He soon stirred the Policy Planning Council, which Alger Hiss had headed in another era, into a buzzing beehive that produced all manner of honey-coated goodies for the New Frontier. Fortunately for him, the State Department had to honor his White House clearance, though Otepka could not have halted his passage from the Rose Garden to Foggy Bottom in any event.

By this time Otepka was himself feeling the lash of the new reorganization. Not content with keeping him on the bench in a makeshift dugout for ten interminable months, his superiors now decided to send him to the showers and, if possible, retire him from the game entirely. Boswell called Otepka in and informed him that the reorganization would abolish twenty-five jobs in the Office of Security and his position as Deputy Director "headed the list."

Whether Dean Rusk, from his discreetly lighted aerie on the seventh floor, had sensed that he had better dispose of Otto Otepka before Walt Rostow and his associates moved over to State is anyone's guess, though a pretty good guess nonetheless. For if Rusk smelled trouble ahead, he was, as it turned out, on exactly the right scent.

BOOK TWO

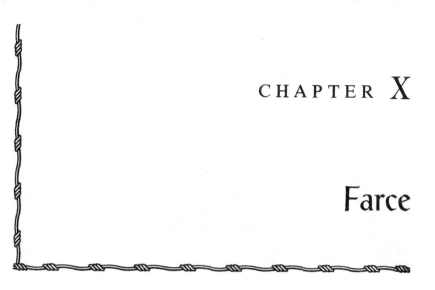

CHAPTER X

Farce

WHAT ARTHUR KROCK, THE VENERABLE WASHINGTON CORRESPOND-
ent of the New York *Times*, was to call "the deceitful and worse State
Department procedures in the Otepka case" first leaked out to the public
in November 1961, just before President Kennedy dispatched Walt W.
Rostow from the White House to take over the long-range planning at
State. In a story datelined November 8, David Sentner, capital bureau
chief of the Hearst Headline Service, broke the news of the impending
"reduction in force" which robbed Otepka of his job as Deputy Director
of the Office of Security.

Sentner accurately predicted that "the security section of the State
Department faces emasculation as the result of a directive aimed at
abolishing the jobs of twenty-five security-trained officials."[1] The story
went on to say that some Democrat members of the Congress were up
in arms over the move. "The decision," wrote Sentner, "was pictured as
gravely affecting national security."

The notices informing the twenty-five affected officials had already
been sent to them by Salvatore A. Bontempo, the recently installed
Administrator of the Bureau of Security and Consular Affairs. Sentner
identified the two principal targets of the housecleaning as "Otto Otepka,
Chief of the State Department's personnel security section, and Elmer

Hipsley, in charge of the Department's physical security matters."

"Bontempo maintained he was merely carrying out the economy order issued by Secretary of State Rusk," the story added. However, Sentner quoted "one high State Department official" as saying: "It is like saving money by getting rid of all the policemen and firemen in the community."

The State Department reacted with righteous indignation. Sentner's story broke in the afternoon editions of the New York *Journal-American* and other Hearst newspapers on Thursday, November 9. A few minutes after 7 p.m. that evening the Department called an "on the record news briefing." Press officer Lincoln White, who later served in the White House as an aide to Lyndon Johnson, presided.

White quoted Otepka's boss, Boswell, as saying: "If I thought the cuts imposed on the Office of Security would endanger the national security, I would resign in protest." Then he added another indignant protest from Herman Pollack, Acting Assistant Secretary of State for Administration:

"The syndicated news report alleged that two veteran security officers would be lost to the Office of Security. This is not so," Pollack said. "There is no intention of separating them from the Office." The press conference then lapsed into that chummy informality so carefully cultivated on Foggy Bottom. "Link," a reporter asked White, "what does this Office do?" White, unwittingly displaying his ignorance of SY's main business, replied:

"Office of Security? It has such functions as physical security here in the Department, physical security of our embassies abroad, security for official visits to this country—things of that nature."[2]

As so often happens with stories out of Washington, the executive branch alibi caught the headlines before the original story had a chance to penetrate the public consciousness. Radio and television carried Lincoln White's quotes from Boswell and Pollack starting with the late evening news programs. And the bulldog editions of the morning papers hit the streets that very night with an Associated Press dispatch highlighting the State Department's denial that the personnel cuts "would gravely affect national security." By the following day the meaning of Dave Sentner's story was smothered under the official disclaimers.

A week later, however, some newspapers which did catch the significance of the "reduction-in-force" revived the issue in editorials. And Henry J. Taylor, United Features columnist and former U.S. Ambassador to Switzerland, set the problem in its true perspective:

The State Department is being rocked by a disgraceful and alarming blow to our Nation's security. Do you remember Alger Hiss? To the utter dismay of officials fighting such subversion and treachery, twenty-five State Department experts in this battle have been dismissed as of December 2 and their whole Bureau of Security and Consular Affairs kicked downstairs to the status of the ribbon counter in Macy's basement. . . . No wonder Khrushchev must sometimes think we are crazy. No wonder his confidence grows and grows.[3]

Taylor called on President Kennedy and Secretary Rusk to correct the situation in SY before it was too late. In a subsequent column, he termed Otepka "a true hero in this [security] work under all administrations for nineteen years" and simultaneously called William O. Boswell's bluff. "If Mr. Boswell understands so shamefully little about organizational requirements and individual competence that he thinks for a single minute this [reduction-in-force] does not endanger national security," said Taylor, "then Mr. Boswell should resign—and the faster the better for the United States."[4] Another small spate of newspaper editorials followed, calling on the President to fire not only Boswell and Bontempo, but Chester Bowles as well. As Undersecretary of State in charge of administration, Bowles was to some degree responsible for the axe falling so heavily on the Office of Security, and so was Bontempo. But the editorial fire missed the true marks, which lay both above Bowles and below Bontempo.

Ironically, Bontempo and Bowles were both pushed out of State while Boswell, the man who had engineered the whole "reduction in force" charade, not only remained but was soon promoted.

While the flap over SY's reorganization was at its short-lived height, Otto Otepka was summoned to appear before the Senate Internal Security Subcommittee for the first time. On November 16, 1961, he testified jointly with Elmer Hipsley and Harris Huston.

Hipsley, a legendary figure in the security community, had been a Secret Service officer for seven years, having once served as personal security man to President Roosevelt and, later, to Harry Truman. He had accompanied FDR on many journeys and was with him at the time of his death in Warm Springs, Georgia. In July 1946, with a pat on the back from Truman, Hipsley moved over to the Department of State as a special agent in security.

He became, in turn, an investigator, evaluator, special assistant to Scott McLeod, and finally, in March 1959, Chief of SY's Physical

Security Division, a post which included supervision of the relentless counter-war against electronic penetration of United States embassies, consulates, and all other Department posts at home and abroad. In September 1959, Hipsley won the gratitude of everyone, from policemen to chiefs of state, for successfully watching over Nikita Khrushchev during his propagandistic tour of the United States.

Harris H. Huston, an Ohioan, Dartmouth graduate, and lawyer, had enjoyed an equally serviceable, if less spectacular, career in government. He had been with the FBI, at State briefly in 1953, in the Pentagon with the Air Force, on Capitol Hill with the House Appropriations Committee for four years, and had returned to the State Department as Acting Administrator of the Bureau of Security and Consular Affairs in the summer of 1957.

This first Senate hearing, in what was shortly to become known as the Otepka Case, was presided over by Senator Dodd. The subcommittee's Chief Counsel, J.G. Sourwine asked the questions. Sitting silently on the sidelines, next to Sourwine, was Benjamin Mandel, the wise old former Communist who more than atoned for his youthful mistakes during his long years as the Senate subcommittee's director of research.

The hearing, like almost all the others that were to follow over the next four years, was conducted in a private hearing room adjoining Suite 2300, the parent Judiciary Committee's chambers in the New Senate Office Building. The room, which is used for executive (secret) sessions, wears an air of disarming informality. However, each witness is solemnly sworn as in court, with the implied threat that any untruths he might be tempted to tell can constitute grounds for legal action against him.

On this mid-November afternoon, at 2:25, Otepka, Hipsley, and Huston were sworn, jointly to save time, and Sourwine opened with the preliminary questions establishing the witnesses' names, occupations and places of residence. A leonine man with wavy white hair, looking more like a Senator than the dandified little Tom Dodd, Sourwine's stentorian voice boomed the opening question:

"Mr. Otepka, have you, within a recent period of weeks, received any notification respecting a change in the status of the job you now hold?"

Otepka replied simply, "Yes; I have," and the first of more than 1,750,000 words of testimony that would be taken by the Senate in his case were noted down by the stenotypist for the official record. Even at the outset, Otepka was obviously reluctant to volunteer any information about the Department or its officials. (Sourwine was later to say, "It is like pulling teeth to get anything out of him.") But under questioning,

Otepka said he had first been told by Boswell, a few weeks earlier, of the abolishment of twenty-five positions in SY. "He notified me that my name headed the list of those positions—he said my name and my position."

More questioning brought out that Otepka did not interpret Boswell's announcement as a notice of dismissal, as the news stories had implied. He seemed confident that his twenty-six years in Civil Service, plus his veterans' preference, would provide adequate protection against firing. "I will have a job somewhere," he said, conceding that it would mean a "diminution in rank."

Sourwine turned to Hipsley, who said he had been told his job "may be in jeopardy," and then went on to Harris Huston. The Department had already succeeded in sidetracking Huston out of Security, though he couched it more diplomatically than that. "I was offered an opportunity to take a post overseas," Huston said, "and so I accepted and they gave me a Foreign Service Reserve rating." He was going to Curacao as Consul General, but he hedged on whether he considered it a promotion. "I guess that is a matter of opinion," Huston replied.*

Returning to Otepka, Sourwine demanded to know more about the so-called reduction-in-force. It took some forty questions for Counsel to wring it out of him that the reorganization would adversely affect the duties of the Office of Security. Otepka refused to admit (probably even to himself then) that it would "substantially endanger the national security," but he finally conceded the State Department would not have "as good security as this country is entitled to."

Otepka was not being evasive. He simply did not want to give his Department a black eye before any punches had actually been thrown to test the new setup, even though Boswell and his other superiors had already dealt him a good hard jab below the belt. He went to considerable lengths in his observance of the bureaucratic equivalent of the Marquis of Queensbury's rules. At times he sounded more like a man who was trying to act as referee between the State Department and the Senate subcommittee than a participant who had just been fouled.

Sourwine led him into a discussion of possible subversives in the Department of State. It took some probing, but Otepka finally replied: "To the best of my knowledge there are no Communists in the Department."

---

* Huston's transfer to the Foreign Service Reserve and an obscure post overseas became a classic pattern for getting rid of knowledgeable security men. They would be permitted to remain in the boondocks for several years, until everyone had forgotten them, before they were retired or "selected out" of the Foreign Service, a far less troublesome expedient than dumping them directly out of the career Civil Service.

"This is beautiful testimony," Sourwine rejoiced. "I think it is helpful to the committee because there are still people that scream that there are Communists in the Department. Of course, that does not mean there are. . . ."

Dodd, knowing what was coming next, quickly interposed, anxious to protect the exposed left flank of his party: "And by the question, it does not mean that we think there are, either."

But Sourwine persisted. Otepka knew what he was driving at: *That does not mean there are no hidden Communists there,* Sourwine wanted to say, but after Dodd rapped his knuckles he phrased it a bit differently: "Now, you are the person able most to help us. . . ."

Otepka was still cautious. He cited the case of George Blake, a British Intelligence Officer recently convicted of spying for the Russians. Blake's own wife apparently had not been aware of his double-agent role. "That," Otepka said, "is probably an outstanding example of a person who is probably a sleeper and about whom there was no information, no ideological background of any kind, who turned out to be a Communist." Then he qualified his previous statement that "there are no Communists in the Department" and made it: *"There are no known Communists."*

"I understand," Sourwine said with real sympathy. "You cannot give a guarantee; you would if you could."

There was a good deal of discussion at the hearing about the number of people affected by the job cuts. Lincoln White, quoting Herman Pollack, had said at the November 9 press conference that "the twenty-five positions involved are part of a force of 273 in the Office of Security in Washington and eighteen other cities throughout the country." In view of the laudable aim, economy, that didn't seem like very much— "roughly ten percent," as White put it, adding that the "Office of Security itself made this determination."

Otepka had never been consulted about the cuts, but he corrected the arithmetic when Sourwine insisted on toting up the score. There were then 248 security personnel, exclusive of clerical employees, Otepka said. (Pollock had apparently added 25 instead of subtracting them!) Out of the 248, 123 were in Washington, the remainder scattered among the domestic field offices. By far the biggest group of positions slated for the meatgrinder—20 in all—came out of the hide of SY's headquarters staff. And that was where they were most needed; especially right then, when the "reorganization" of the State Department, which had been in the works for months, was about to increase SY's workload astronomically.

In fact, men were already being pulled in from the field to help clean up the growing backlog.

Moreover, as the Senate subcommittee said in its report one year later, "the evaluation division in the Office of Security—the key division in the whole personnel security operation—was cut by more than 20 percent." (It was actually a bit more: ten jobs out of a total of thirty-two.) On top of that, the Senate report added, many clerical employees "left that office in disgust because of the disruptions" caused by "Boswell's reorganization."[5]

The subcommittee made it obvious that the State Department wanted Otepka and Hipsley to throw in the sponge too. The special plan drawn· up for them was a masterpiece of bureaucratic duplicity. It must have taken long hours of truly creative thought to devise it.

As the subcommittee report explained it, Otepka, who had seniority, was to "bump" his friend Hipsley out of his job as Chief of Physical Security since Otepka's own job was being abolished. Hipsley would then bump another security officer out of the Evaluations Division. The hope obviously was that Hipsley, having been consigned to a fairly low rank, would start feuding with Otepka or, better yet, both of them would simply resign.

"The prospect of getting rid of Otepka and Hipsley by the above scheme is no specious conclusion," the Senate report emphasized. It then went on to detail Boswell's actions, which make it abundantly plain that the resignations of these two officers are precisely what Boswell had in mind.

The ersatz reorganization sliced up SY like so much delicatessen salami. In lopping off Otepka's job as Deputy Director, it removed all but one of SY's six divisions from his control. Moreover, it hacked off "nearly two-thirds of the authority and responsibilities" Hipsley formerly held, according to the Senate estimate. And just to complete the confusion, Boswell and his friends created no less than three new divisions out of Physical Security, which was itself abolished as a working entity two months later. Physical Security, in case you've lost the thread, was the division Boswell tried to give Otepka in November. In January it no longer existed in its former state.

Not content with this, Boswell and his fellow artists obliterated a substantial part of the Evaluations Division's overall view of the Department of State. They deftly pointed out, to use the words of Boswell's directive of January 2, 1962, "certain recordkeeping functions of SY/E, together with personnel" and shifted them to another branch more amenable to the Seventh Floor's new outlook on the world.

More important, Boswell & Company abolished the crucial Intelligence Reporting Branch of the Evaluations Divisions (SY/E), which gathered in all the reports from the Intelligence community at large, including the FBI and CIA. After reviewing these reports and, where necessary, making copies for its own files, Evaluations had for years served as the distribution point, sending the Intelligence information to the various bureaus in the Department on a "need to know basis." For example, all of the information which poured into State prior to 1959 on Fidel Castro's Communist connections passed through SY/E on its way to the Caribbean desk in the Bureau of Inter-American Affairs. It was not the Evaluations Division's fault that it went no higher and that President Eisenhower was kept in ignorance of Castro's predilections. Even J. Edgar Hoover, who later said the FBI had been feeding the information on Castro to the State Department "for years," reportedly refused to step out of the deep channels of official authority and take the Castro file to the Secretary of State or to the White House.

Eventually, the Intelligence Reporting function of SY was bounced into another office inappropriately called the Intelligence Research Bureau, which was not even under the Bureau of Security and Consular Affairs. Intelligence Research was the nesting place for a good many of the old OSS and other wartime agency transferees who came into the Department in the 1945 merger. Not a few of the people on the McLeod List, and even more on Otepka's larger roster of 858 suspects, were still in this bureau in 1969.

From the point of view of those who reshaped U.S. foreign policy in the 1960's, the bureau must have been the ideal burial ground for information flowing from the FBI, CIA, Defense Intelligence and other agencies. And if the bureau couldn't bury intelligence entirely, it could mold it to fit the views and goals of the hard-working zealots intent upon creating a nationless world.

Otepka's first session with the Senate Internal Security Subcommittee, even shared as it was with Huston and Hipsley, lasted less than an hour. But that was long enough to give Sourwine and Dodd, and later the other Senators, a tantalizing glimpse of what was going on in the Office of Security and the State Department towards the end of Dean Rusk's first year.

The Senators had no desire, however, to embarrass the Kennedy Administration. They kept all the testimony under tight wraps for another year, hoping Rusk would act to correct what was obviously developing into a very dangerous situation. Nothing happened, however, except that the State Department went right ahead with what Dave Sentner called the "emasculation" of SY. On January 2, 1962, Boswell issued a directive outlining the final plans for the reorganization. It went into effect January 15.

Boswell and Rusk threw the Senators a bone, though. They were able to shift the Chief of the Evaluations Division, Emery Adams, into the U.S. Arms Control and Disarmament Agency, a semi-autonomous concoction that camps under State's big circus tent. This made it possible to quiet senatorial fears by placing Otepka in nominal charge of Evaluations, the crucial locus of personnel security. Many of its important functions had been stripped away, and Otepka was further hobbled by a critical shortage of personnel, but at least he had the title, Chief of the Division of Evaluations. His retention of that title was shortly to prove much more troublesome than Boswell and Rusk expected.

The Seventh Floor was delirious with joy when it got hold of the transcript of Otepka's testimony before the Senate subcommittee. Some of the fainter hearts may have feared the worst, but Otepka had refused to blow any whistles on his superiors. Roger W. Jones, the former Chairman of the Civil Service Commission who had been drafted as Deputy Undersecretary of State for Administration, invited Otepka to his office and personally commended the security chief for the way he had handled himself. "You did a magnificent job," Jones rhapsodized. Otepka politely thanked him and went his way.

There were several sequels to the reduction-in-force. After it went into effect in mid-January it was discovered to be a complete farce. No economies were realized. In fact, SY's budget went way up the following year. And although Otepka was short ten positions in Evaluations, no one was actually fired. They played musical chairs within the Office of Security for months and a number of people did quit or accept assignments elsewhere.

Elmer Hipsley, for one, went off to Geneva to look after security for the American mission there. "You just can't fight them," he told this writer after his return and retirement in late 1966. A tall, angular man with effervescent spirits, "Hip," as he was known far and wide to Intelligence people, had rationlized his withdrawal from the battle, and who could blame him? Otepka certainly never did. He was understanding of Hipsley's retreat; it just was not a course he could set for himself.* Loyal members of the Intelligence community are painfully aware of the heavy, unseen toll that has decimated their ranks. They were reminded of it once again the day before Dave Sentner's first story raised the public curtain on the Otepka Case. Scott McLeod, who had come home from Ireland when John Kennedy became President, died on that autumnal Tuesday. It came to light that he had developed a serious heart condition while heading the Bureau of Security and Consular Affairs and the bitter fight over his nomination as Ambassador had not helped his health.

On returning to America, McLeod took a job with the Senate Appropriations Committee. In April 1961 his lucid testimony before the Internal Security Subcommittee gave the lie to the picture that had been painted of him as a frenzied inquisitor. A friend who knew how severely the smear campaign of the 1950's had seared McLeod's soul wrote movingly of his passing:

"Just how much this campaign contributed to his early death [McLeod was 47] can never be known, but it is a fact that he was deeply hurt by it. . . . On November 7, worn down by years of bitter attack, Scott McLeod was felled by a heart attack. One of his closest friends, upon hearing of his death, said, 'Well, they finally got him.' They had, too."[6]

Otepka, saddened by Scotty McLeod's death, hoped that he could avoid the controversies that had brought down his friend. But the fleeting flap over the reduction-in-force farce had barely subsided when he found that once again he was to be the man on the spot. This time he was put there, almost accidentally, by the young man who happened to be President of the United States.

*Elmer Hipsley died in December 1968, in Washington, at the age of 54.

CHAPTER XI

Wieland

THE YOUNG PRESIDENT APPEARED IN A BUOYANT MOOD JUST BEFORE his press conference that Wednesday, January 24, 1962. In Room 1410, across the corridor from a side entrance to the State Department auditorium, he received his last-minute briefings from a handful of trusted aides. There was much in the news that morning, but nothing earthshaking. Dean Rusk had reported from Punta Del Este in Uruguay that he was having trouble getting the Organization of American States to approve the diplomatic and economic sanctions the U.S. had proposed against Castro Cuba. But, Rusk assured him, a compromise was in the making.

The trade pact Cuba had signed with the Soviet Union two weeks ago was all but forgotten, and had never become much of an issue anyway. The Congo was still seething, but the United Nations forces were making slow headway against the stubborn Tshombe. Prince Souvanna Phouma of Laos was having some difficulty getting the rightist Prince Boun Oum to swallow the coalition government the U.S. wanted so badly. In the end, however, President Kennedy was confident Boun Oum would see the light. Either he would, or the United States would have to follow through on its threat to cut off all aid to the loyal Laotian forces attempting to hold the Communist troops at bay.

For once, the horizon appeared clear of crises.

The President and his aides thought they had anticipated all the major questions that might be fired at him in the auditorium. As for the minor ones, those trifling little points reporters for Midwestern and other provincial newspapers insisted upon injecting even when the world seemed to be coming apart, Jack Kennedy could always ad lib. He was good at that. Everyone said so. And if he couldn't think of a suitable reply, he could always fall back on a quip. The reporters loved his quips, so long as they weren't made the butt of his swift and occasionally cutting wit.

Mr. Kennedy no longer felt nervous about press conferences. After a year and four days in office, he had almost come to enjoy them. More important, he had learned to *control* them. He knew all the friendly reporters by sight, and was on intimate terms with many of them. It was a simple matter, really, to ignore the upraised hand of a hostile newsman and recognize an ally in another part of the crowded auditorium. Justifiably, Jack Kennedy felt he was at his best in these simulated give-and-take sessions. Most of the boys played the game his way and they almost always made him look good.

With a hasty glance into the mirror to make certain his tie was straight and one last pass of a comb through his thick brown hair, Jack Kennedy stepped briskly from Room 1410, strode across the narrow corridor and allowed himself to be ushered through the double swinging doors at the side of the auditorium. The stairs to the stage were there on his right when he entered; he permitted himself a smile as he mounted them. The several hundred assembled newsmen were on their feet now and a ripple of respectful applause rose as he walked confidently across the stage to the lectern at the center.

The questions started immediately, pretty much following the anticipated script. Then, quite suddenly, there was a jarring note.

Sarah McClendon, the Washington correspondent for a dozen or so smaller papers in Texas and New England, was on her feet, insistently waving her hand. It was impossible to avoid Sarah sometimes. She was always right *there*, somewhere up front, looking for all the world like a plump, inoffensive grandmother, but asking the damndest questions. Reluctantly, Kennedy recognized her.

"Mr. President," she began in a deceptively soft, matronly voice, "Sir, two well known security risks have recently been put on a task force in the State Department to help reorganize the Office of Security. . . ."

"Well, now," the President bridled, *"who?"* It must have flashed through his mind, *"Who the hell put Sarah up to that?"* But Mrs. McClendon was already replying:

"William Arthur Wieland, a well known man who for over a year the State. . . ."

"You are thinking," Mr. Kennedy interrupted. "Miss McClendon, I think that. . . ." He hesitated again for just a second. "Would you give me the other name?"

"Yes, sir. J. Clayton Miller."

"Right." The President nodded, indicating he knew all about both those cases. "Well, now, I don't . . . I think the term . . . I would say that the term you've used to describe them [security risks] is a very strong term, which I would think you should be prepared to substantiate. I'm familiar with Mr. Miller's record because I happened to look at it the other day. He has been cleared by the State Department. In my opinion the duties which he's now carrying out, he is fit for. And I have done that [from the transcript it isn't clear exactly what he *had* done] after Mr. Rusk and I both looked at the matter, so therefore I cannot accept your description of him."

"Did you look at Mr. William Arthur Wieland too?" Mrs. McClendon persisted.

"Yes," replied the President. "I'm familiar with Mr. Wieland, I'm also familiar with his duties at the present time, and in my opinion Mr. Miller and Mr. Wieland. . . . the duties that they've been assigned to, they can carry out without detriment to the interest of the United States, and, I hope, without detriment to their characters by your question."[1]

Frowning deeply, Mr. Kennedy turned away from Sarah McClendon and quickly pointed at another reporter standing with his hand raised on the opposite side of the room. The subject of Wieland and Miller was precipitately dropped.

As New York *Times* correspondent Anthony Lewis noted in his front page story on the incident next morning, "It was an extraordinary episode for a news conference. Mr. Kennedy had never during his Presidency been so quick and severe in reproving a reporter. His tone and his gestures, even more than his words, made clear his disapproval of the reporter's statement. He interrupted quickly, his finger pointing at her, to demand substantiation."[2] The New York *Herald-Tribune* said the President spoke with "the most chilling anger . . . in low tones with icicles clinging to them."[3]

"Some saw in the President's suggestion that Mrs. McClendon should be prepared to substantiate her charge an implication that she might be subject to suit by the two men," the *Times* claimed. "The State Department's Legal Advisor, Abram J. Chayes, was reported to have given the opinion that Mrs. McClendon's charge was 'defamatory on its face.' "[4]

The matter didn't end there, although the State Department obviously hoped that it would. Newspapers across the country carried the story, describing the encounter in detail. But the radio and television networks—perhaps more sensitive to the Administration's wishes because of their dependence upon Federal Communications Commission licenses—sought an audience with Undersecretary of State George Ball to determine whether they could safely use the story on their news programs that night. Ball told the network representatives he could not guarantee they wouldn't be sued for libel. They would, he said meaningfully, have to consider the legal risks.[5]

To their credit, CBS and ABC defied Ball's implied threat and carried short excerpts on their evening newscasts. NBC, however, eliminated the incident entirely from its programming on the grounds that Mrs. McClendon's "charges are regarded as not legally privileged, or not immune from libel."[6] An NBC spokesman unashamedly proclaimed that "there was no request from the White House that we do this. It was done on our own."[7]

None of the networks, and hardly any newspapers for that matter, made any visible effort to find out what was behind Sarah McClendon's question, or if they did they never let their audiences and readers in on the secret. The newspapers dropped it the next day as other more fresh and seemingly pressing news competed for space and attention. By the weekend it was all ancient history.

If the press corps had scratched just a little beneath the surface of the Kennedy-McClendon clash it might have unearthed some enlightening information. For one thing, it would have discovered that the man in the middle—on the Wieland case at least—was Otto Otepka. Moreover, it would have found out more precisely *why* the State Department was so anxious to be rid of him. Regrettably, only a handful of reporters bestirred themselves and, since Dean Rusk's team kept the facts well hidden, even this handful didn't come close to getting the full story at the time.

Nonetheless, Sarah McClendon had momentarily succeeded in summoning some attention to the sorry security mess on Foggy Bottom. She had plainly touched a very raw nerve, and though she may not have been entirely aware of it herself, she temporarily scared the daylights out of the Department of State.

Within an hour after President Kennedy's press conference, Roger Jones and William Boswell were nervously conferring on what to do. Jones demanded to know the status of Wieland's clearance, which had been up in the air for over a year, ever since the Senate Internal Security Subcommittee had started investigating the dubious role the former chief of the Caribbean desk had played in Fidel Castro's rise to power in Cuba.

Boswell was forced to tell Jones that Wieland's new clearance, needed for promotion to a post abroad, had never been put through. Boswell had tried to get Otepka to clear Wieland the previous September, but Otepka had stubbornly refused. Jones, obviously frightened because the President had stuck his neck out by plainly implying that Wieland had been cleared, now instructed Boswell to order Otepka to issue the clearance. And this time Boswell was to make certain it went through—*at once.*

Immediately after this meeting, Jones called a little press conference of his own. Without batting an eye, he informed the newsmen that both Wieland and Miller had been cleared. "Neither is a security risk, a loyalty risk, a suitability risk, or any other kind of a risk," Jones declared.[8] His voice carried just the right degree of indignation that anyone should have had the temerity to question the security qualifications of two such dedicated patriots.

The lies didn't stop there, however. They went on and on for months. Eventually, Dean Rusk got into the act himself. He told Senator Dodd that he had "cleared" Wieland personally in the summer of 1961—*before* Boswell had tried to get Otepka to issue the clearance.[9] Rusk claimed that he had discussed the matter with President Kennedy at that time, and again early in January 1962. On both occasions, the President agreed with his Secretary of State that no action should be taken against Wieland for his part in the Cuban debacle and for other questionable matters turned up by an exhaustive evaluation of Wieland done by Otepka and his special project team.

If Rusk had really "cleared" Wieland, as Dodd later claimed, certainly Boswell would have told Otepka when the security chief balked at signing the clearance in September. It is inconceivable that Boswell, responsive as he was to the seventh floor's every wish, would have let the matter simply ride for four long months. As Otepka later observed, "The simple, plain, unvarnished fact is that no decision was made until January 1962 after the case blew wide open at the President's press conference."

During his brief whitewashing session with the press on January 24, Roger Jones went all-out to strengthen the President's uncertain hand. After leading the reporters to believe that Wieland had a bona fide clearance, he categorically denied that Wieland had anything to do with the Office of Security as Sarah McClendon had mentioned. Wieland was in the Office of Management straightening out "problems of paperwork flow," Jones insisted. Miller was also working on routine administrative chores in the same office, Jones said, clearly indicating that Miller had nothing to do with SY either.[10]

Jones was, to put it kindly, fudging once again. As he so well knew, J. Clayton Miller had been working on a "management survey" of SY for some months. Moreover, as subsequent testimony before the Senate subcommittee brought out, Miller was the prime mover in shifting the vital Intelligence reporting function from under Otepka into the more amenable Bureau of Intelligence Research. Though it may have been rather harsh to pronounce Miller a security risk, it was certainly well known that he had been an active member of the dubious Institute of Pacific Relations and he had written for *Amerasia*, a publication owned and edited by a Soviet agent.

Curiously, Miller and Wieland shared the same office, even the same file cabinet. And all the while Miller worked on his overhaul of the Office of Security, Wieland was under active investigation by that same office, by the FBI, and by the Senate subcommittee. To assume that Wieland had "absolutely nothing to do with security" during this period, as Roger Jones averred, is naive in the extreme. For as Miller labored at one desk on the intricate problems of the reduction-in-force designed to squeeze Otepka out of SY, Wieland sat nearby smarting under the investigation Otepka was conducting into his affairs. Of course, it may be that Miller and Wieland worked separately under individual "cones of silence," a la Maxwell Smart in the television comedy series. . . .

Originally, Otepka got into the weird matter of William Wieland in the fall of 1960, when SY received a report that Wieland was a Communist. The report was never proved, but Otepka unearthed a good many other interesting facts about him.

When Boswell anchored Otepka to the spurious special project, he also hung the Wieland albatross around his neck. The case became the first significant bit of business tackled by Otepka's special project group. It was also the first time—and the last—that a State Department official had ever been evaluated not only on the basis of his background and associations, but on his performance in the formulation of U.S. foreign policy as well.

At the very outset Otepka found that no real investigation of Wieland had ever been done before despite many warnings and reports on him to the State Department hierarchy. In fact, Wieland had been on the Department payroll for seven long years before even the most cursory check was made of his background in 1948.

Who was William Arthur Wieland? Why did the President of the United States defend him so vigorously? What had he done in the State Department to deserve the special attention of Secretary Rusk?

The Senate subcommittee, in its official report on the Wieland case and State Department security generally, answered the last question, if not the first two. The report declared that Wieland, as Director of the Office of Caribbean and Mexican Affairs could not "escape a share of the responsibility for the Communist capture of Cuba."[11]

Otepka's landmark evaluation of Wieland, completed in August 1961, thoroughly substantiated the Senate subcommittee's charge. Yet Wieland continued to receive promotions and raises in salary *after* the Senate report was issued.

During Otepka's penetrating investigation, SY and the FBI interrogated more than one hundred people who had known Wieland, or who had significant information about him. Seven separate and distinct charges were developed in Otepka's evaluation, any one of which provided ample grounds for firing Wieland under the Foreign Service regulations or Executive Order 10450.

One of the charges centered on Wieland's name. In the original application forms he put his signature to, Wieland failed to list any other name or alias he may have used in the past. Yet for some years in Cuba he went under the surname "Montenegro," using various first names with it—Guillermo, Arturo, their English equivalents, and sometimes a combination of the two.

Strangely, Wieland's true name, and even the actual date of his birth, has never been fully resolved. According to records in the New York County Clerk's office, Wieland was born November 20, 1907, the son of William Arthur and Kathleen Dooley Wieland. The name listed on the birth certificate is William Robert Wieland, but the future State Department policy-maker never used that middle name. Further, he invariably listed November 17, 1907 as his birthday.

When Wieland was four his father died and his mother soon married a native of Venezuela named Manuel Montenegro. The boy and his sister, Dorothea, were apparently treated kindly by their stepfather and, in gratitude, they claim that they later adopted his name as their own. Young Wieland-Montenegro went to grade school in New York, spent a year in a private military academy, and did another brief stint at a private school in Havana. A year at Villanova College outside Philadelphia ended his formal education.

In 1927 he enlisted in the U.S. Cavalry. The name he used on this occasion was "Monty Wieland." Fifteen months later, in December 1928, Wieland bought his way out of the Cavalry and promptly headed for Havana. What he did in Havana during his first four years there, if indeed he remained in Cuba all that time, is still something of a mystery. At least he never listed any employment for this period on his State Department forms. It is known, however, that he was married in Cuba in 1931 to Leona Kukowska, who claimed to be a native of Minnesota. Although he was then generally using the name "Guillermo Montenegro," he supposedly was married under the name William Wieland.

By 1933 Wieland had a job on the old Havana *Post*. The newspaper's offices were in the heart of Havana's lively nightlife district and Guillermo Montenegro won a reputation as a *bon vivant* in the pseudo-artistic milieu of gay, cosmopolitan *Habana*. Inevitably, this milieu attracted a number of revolutionaries, not a few of whom represented the more fanatical elements of the Left.

The most extreme of the extremist groups then attempting to topple the government of Cuban President Gerardo Machado was the ABC Party, an underground terrorist organization which enjoyed Communist support. A number of former *Habaneros* have identified William Wieland, alias Montenegro, as a member of the ABC Party. But in sworn testimony before the Senate subcommittee in 1961 Wieland denied this. He also denied that he had ever known, or even heard of, one Fabio Grobart, alias Aron Sinkowitz, a top Soviet agent in Cuba who helped direct the anti-Machado revolt in 1933.

Tossed out of Cuba in 1950, Grobart-Sinkowitz returned in 1960 as Castro's Minister of State. But Wieland, the State Department's leading expert on Cuban affairs, could not remember, in 1961, ever having known anything at all about this notorious spy. As the Subcommittee Report discreetly put it, Wieland should at least "have known the name and something of the background of Fabio Grobart."[12]

Wieland did admit, however, that he knew Sumner Welles in Havana. Welles, a flagrant homosexual who later became Undersecretary of State, had been sent to Cuba as Franklin Roosevelt's personal representative to mediate a settlement among the multitudinous political factions. Ironically, the result of Welles' wrist-slapping intervention was that the man Welles most opposed, Fulgencio Batista, became Cuba's strong man.

It was Welles who first suggested, in about 1941, that Wieland join the State Department. He "told me it would be a good idea," Wieland recalled years later.[13] In the meantime, Wieland had been fired by the Havana *Post*, another little fact he preferred to conceal on his application at State. The newspaper's owner, Mrs. Clara Park Pessino, had several good reasons for getting rid of Wieland-Montenegro in 1937. The one she decided to use was that he was pirating stories from the Associated Press wire she paid for and peddling them to other papers that did not subscribe to AP.

The Associated Press, as much a victim of Wieland's piracy as Mrs. Pessino's *Post*, inexplicably rewarded him with a job. Working out of New York and Washington for AP, Wieland primarily covered the Latin American scene. In the fall of 1939, during the Hitler-Stalin Pact years, he journeyed to Panama for a diplomatic meeting and was reported on chummy terms with two German newsmen identified as Nazi agents. Submarines of the Third Reich were taking a heavy toll of British ships coming through the Panama Canal into the Caribbean and most newsmen gave the German agents a wide berth. They were also warned to stay clear of Wieland, because he had the reputation of being quite hostile to England during the period of the pact.

In June 1941 Wieland was hustled aboard at the State Department with the blessing of Sumner Welles and another old friend, Lawrence Duggan, later head of State's Latin American bureau.* Wieland's friends were in such a hurry to get him on the payroll that he was actually sworn in several days *before* he got around to filling out an application. Significantly, the form was marked *"Birth Certificate Not Necessary."* It was the lightning-like pace of his being hired, Wieland later testified, that made him forget all those niggling little details he should have listed.

With similar dispatch, Wieland was shipped off to Rio de Janeiro to serve as a press attaché and special assistant to the U.S. Ambassador to Brazil. He managed to survive the war years in Rio, remaining there until November 1946 and returning again for three more years in 1951 despite the fact that he gave at least one Ambassador, William D. Pawley, a decidedly "squirmy feeling."

Wieland's mannerisms alone would have been enough to make any ambassador squirm. A large, husky man with a grenadier guard's moustache and a loud, often booming voice, Wieland alternately affected an

---

* Lawrence Duggan was identified by both Whittaker Chambers and Mrs. Hede Massing as a member of one of the Soviet espionage rings operating in Washington in the 1930's and '40's. Duggan died, rather mysteriously, in a plunge from a Manhattan office building on 45th Street just off Fifth Avenue on the night of December 20, 1948. Supposedly a suicide, Duggan was suspected by some Intelligence men to have been the victim of an assassin. No public disclosures about Duggan's ties to Soviet spy rings had been made prior to his death. However, there were indications he might have been preparing to cooperate with Congressional investigators. Duggan's is only one of a number of dubious "suicide victims" in the sub-rosa world of espionage—"suicides" that continued right through the 1960's when the Soviets were alleged to be "mellowing."

unbearably pompous air and a back-slapping hail-fellow personality. During the war he was an outspoken champion of our ally, the Soviet Union, and he was known to have connections with Brazilian Communists. Asked about these connections by the Senate subcommittee, Wieland claimed it was all in the line of duty. He was merely trying "to find out what the Communists were up to."

In 1946 Wieland was sent to the embassy at Bogota, Colombia. It was there that Fidel Castro first cast his dark shadow across William Wieland's unsteady path.

Castro came to Bogota in the spring of 1948 with scores of other Communist students, among them the Argentine-born terrorist, Che Guevara. Their target was the Ninth International Conference of American States, opening in Bogota on March 30 with U.S. Secretary of State George Marshall in prominent attendance. Before Castro and his fellow students departed they touched off the bloody *Bogotazo*, riots which killed thousands and turned the city into a smoldering ruin.

The spark that ignited the explosion in Bogota was the assassination, on April 9, 1948, of the popular Jorge Eliecer Gaitan, "sole leader" of Colombia's minority Liberal Party. Castro and Rafael del Pino, one of his Cuban companions, were seen in the company of the assassin, a drifter named Juan Roa Sierra, less than two hours before the crime.

Within minutes after Gaitan's death, organized teams appeared on the streets, the leaders carrying lists of buildings earmarked for burning.[14] In less than an hour the mobs were surging into the Parliament Building where the International Conference held its sessions. From there they descended on the Presidential Palace, but Dr. Mariano Ospina Perez, Colombia's chief executive and leader of the Conservative Party, courageously held out with a small band of soldiers against repeated assaults.

Churches were burned, the schools and colleges of the Jesuit Order systematically sacked, public buildings, stores and factories went up in flames. Even the historic home of South America's great liberator, Simon Bolivar, was put to the torch. Corpses littered the streets and the wounded were left to care for themselves or die. For four days the rioting continued unabated, with Castro and his Communist cadres directing the rampaging mobs.

Fidel Castro's role in the *Bogotazo* was no secret. When order was finally restored, the police, newspapers, radio stations, even President Ospina in a public address, all identified Castro and del Pino as among the Communist agents who planned the insurrection.[15] Yet William Wieland, who was in Bogota all during the riots, sent a lengthy report on the uprising to Washington without ever once mentioning Castro or his friends.

In the years following the *Bogotazo* Wieland kept in close touch with the whole Latin American scene while pretending to remain blissfully ignorant of Castro's many links to the Communist conspiracy. From Bogota, he was assigned to El Salvador in July 1949, then back to Rio de Janeiro in August 1951, and from there to Quito, Ecuador, just three years later. In February 1957 he got his big break. Brought to Washington as a State Department public affairs officer, within three months he was Director of the Office of Middle American Affairs. By September of the following year the title was changed to Director, Office of Caribbean-Mexican Affairs, which embraced Cuba, Mexico, Haiti and the Dominican Republic, all the lesser Caribbean islands, and Central America.

In Washington Wieland-Montenegro became one of the two chief State Department apologists for Castro. The other was Roy Rubottom, who was also at the U.S. embassy in Colombia during and after the *Bogotazo*. Rubottom rose to Assistant Secretary of State for Inter-American Affairs and served as Bill Wieland's immediate boss during the critical years when the success or failure of Castro's revolution hung on the question of whether or not the U.S. government considered Fidel a Communist.

Throughout the late 1950's, and even into 1961, the official Wieland-Rubottom position, steadfastly held in the face of numerous Intelligence reports to the contrary, was that Castro had never been a Communist.* On the day before Castro rode victoriously into Havana, Rubottom swore to the Senate Foreign Relations Committee that "there was no evidence of any organized Communist element within the Castro movement or that Señor Castro himself was under Communist influence."[16] Rubottom and Wieland continued to maintain this position long after Castro's communism became perfectly apparent to the whole world.

The Senate Internal Security Subcommittee produced the equivalent of a fat book documenting Wieland's successful efforts to keep the overwhelming evidence of Fidel Castro's communism hidden from his superiors in the Department of State. It would be tedious even to summarize that substantial record here. But Otepka, in working on his landmark evaluation of Wieland, was struck by several incidents that surfaced in the Senate testimony.

* This was their *official* position. However, there is no doubt that Wieland *knew* Castro was a Communist all along. Several friends of Wieland's testified before the subcommittee that Wieland had definitely told them in 1957 and 1958 he knew Castro to be a Communist. One of these friends was Samuel Shaffer, a *Newsweek* correspondent.

Earl E. T. Smith told the subcommittee what happened when he went to Wieland for a briefing when Smith was appointed Ambassador to Cuba in July 1957. Wieland passed Smith on to Herbert Matthews, with the implication that here was a man who had the real dope on Castro and Cuba. Matthews, of course, was the New York *Times* correspondent who had made himself the premier propagandist for Fidel.

Commenting on the "close connection" between Wieland and Matthews, Smith pointed out that Matthews' front-page stories in the *Times* early in 1957 had "served to inflate Castro to world stature." "Until that time," Smith said, "Castro had been just another bandit in the Oriente Mountains of Cuba, with a handful of followers who had terrorized the campesinos . . . . After the Matthews articles, which followed an exclusive interview . . . he was able to get followers and funds in Cuba and in the United States. From that time on, arms, money, and soldiers of fortune abounded. Much of the American press began to picture Castro as a political Robin Hood."[17]

Smith didn't fall for Matthews' fairy tale. He tried repeatedly to alert Washington about what was actually transpiring in Cuba. But his reports had to go through Wieland and Rubottom before they reached the top. Needless to say, neither John Foster Dulles nor Christian Herter ever saw them.

Otepka recalls sending Wieland "hundreds of reports" from the Intelligence community documenting Castro's Communist connections. "Either Wieland did not read them," Otepka testified, "or if he read them he deliberately misinterpreted them."

Robert C. Hill, Ambassador to Mexico from May 1957 to January 1961, told the Senate subcommittee how Wieland belligerently blocked an effort made in August 1959 to penetrate the protective cocoon shielding President Eisenhower from hard knowledge of Castro's true colors. Hill tried to get the word to the President via his brother, Dr. Milton Eisenhower, who was acting as a White House advisor on Latin America. The effort was made on an airplane trip from Mexico City to Mazatlan. With Ambassador Hill and Dr. Eisenhower on this flight were Raymond Leddy, political affairs counselor at the Mexico City embassy; Colonel Benoid Glawe, embassy air attaché, and the erudite chief of the Caribbean-Mexican desk, the Honorable Mr. Wieland.

Hill asked Leddy to show Milton Eisenhower some of the voluminous evidence on the real predilections of Castro, whose government was then under active consideration for substantial American aid. Ambassador Hill vividly recalled the debate that followed:

Each time Mr. Leddy would say, "This is Communist-dominated" or "This is a Communist" he was met with Mr. Wieland saying "It is not true. . . ."

But when Mr. Leddy attempted to project the actual documents into the picture, an argument ensued [Wieland actually accused Leddy of lying!] . . . . Colonel Glawe referred to Mr. Wieland as either a damn fool or a Communist and, of course, it caused tempers to flare and Dr. Eisenhower said he did not want to hear any more about the situation.[18]

Milton Eisenhower should have pursued the subject, but there is no evidence he ever did. The result was that Castro was able to consolidate his rule without fear of American interference. Twenty-one months later, when the signal was finally given for the Bay of Pigs invasion, it was long since too late to dislodge Fidel short of all-out intervention, which the Kennedy Administration had no stomach for. By the mid-1960's Cuba was a bristling fortress, with armed forces second in size and fire-power only to the United States in the Western Hemisphere though its total population was less than that of the City of New York.

The critical decisions that paved the way for Castro's victory centered on the withholding of U.S. arms to the Batista forces. The Senate sub-committee record makes it plain that these decisions were engineered by William Wieland and Roy Rubottom.

Tragically for Cuba, and for America, the arms shipments were with-held at Wieland's behest at the worst possible time. As Senator Roman L. Hruska of Nebraska noted in a postscript to the 1962 subcommittee report, "If we had preserved the situation in Cuba for just two months and brought about a peaceful transition to the already-elected government of Rivero-Aguero, it should have been possible to go on from there and develop a government truly responsive to the will of the people of Cuba. But instead of attempting this, we notified Rivero-Aguero we would not support him; our Ambassador, under instructions, told Batista the United States had lost confidence in him, and he had better go. . . ."[20]

It seemed to Senator Hruska "that something more than bad timing was involved in all this." In fact, he said, "the plain truth is that the U.S. Department of State was the principal collaborator in creating the vacuum into which Fidel Castro stepped."[21]

There was yet another side to the tarnished Cuban coin, however. Wieland's old boss, former Ambassador Pawley, described it to the Sub-committee in 1960. Pawley said Wieland "was the one, no question about it, who came up with the idea of not selling arms to either side in Cuba. But here is an interesting thing: while they were doing this, I lived in Miami, and this is a fact—more than 10,000 men were armed for Castro out of Dade County with all of the officials closing their eyes to Castro receiving their arms in spite of the neutrality law. And the minute Castro came in, the Justice Department sent down 250 special agents [who are] there today to prevent anyone from hurting our friend Castro."[22]

Gangster elements in the United States, including Cosa Nostra "couriers" who have found it pays to do business with Communists, were deeply involved in the brisk gun-running trade with Castro's well-heeled agents. They can justifiably claim a share of the credit, with the State Department, for Fidel Castro's success.

When Otepka first interrogated Wieland in January 1961 he showed him "quite a number of these reports [on Castro's Communist ties] which I had sent him, and he had the greatest case of amnesia I ever saw. He didn't remember anything. Apparently," Otepka concluded, "he didn't want to remember, because he was always writing to the top echelon saying there is no proof, there is no hard evidence that Castro is a Communist."

William Pawley, who first felt "squirmy" about Wieland way back in Rio, stated it more bluntly than Otepka. Pawley told the Senate subcommittee that when he found out Wieland had been placed in charge of Caribbean affairs he tried to alert the State Department that it was in for serious trouble. He met with Douglas Dillon, then at State and later President Kennedy's Secretary of the Treasury. But Dillon ignored Pawley's warning and an underling made it plain that the Department resented Pawley's "pressure."

Jay Sourwine asked Pawley straight out if he thought Wieland was a Communist. Pawley replied: "No, I don't have any reason to believe that. I only know that many of these men, that get involved in this type of thing over the years . . . are serving the cause of our enemies, that is all."

"You think he is doing this wittingly, intentionally?" Sourwine inquired.

"I have got to say," Pawley frowned, "that he is either one of the most stupid men living or he is doing it intentionally."

Otepka, in his evaluation, officially found that there was no hard evidence that Wieland was a Communist. But he recommended that Wieland be fired on the grounds of unsuitability. Nonetheless, Roger Jones later swore to the subcommittee that Otepka and the Office of Security never made any "adverse" findings on Wieland. "They threw up the facts for us at the higher level to decide," Jones testified.[23]

At the time, Wieland had just been promoted to Foreign Service officer, Class 1, no doubt for his brilliant performance in Cuban affairs. On top of that, he was slated for yet another promotion as Consul General to Bremen in West Germany.

Otepka completed his evaluation in August 1961 after interrogating Wieland for a second time in July. The full report ran to 844 pages but he boiled this down to a 136-page digest containing the most pertinent facts. Herman Pollack then asked him to send copies of the digest to Abram Chayes, the Department's Legal Advisor, and to John Siegenthaler, a special assistant to Bobby Kennedy in the Justice Department. A third copy went upstairs to Roger Jones.

In mid-September an initialed note from Jones' aide, Hugh Appling, floated down to SY. It tersely stated that *"Mr. Jones, having studied digest of Wieland case, approved Wieland's assignment as Consul General, Bremen."* No mention was made of Secretary Rusk having reviewed the case, as was later alleged.

Three days later, on September 18, Boswell sent Otepka a brief memo with Appling's note attached. Boswell said that Jones' action "will, of course, be reaffirmation of his (Wieland's) E.O. 10450 security clearance." Otepka protested immediately. He informed Boswell that his evaluation called for "specific recommendations . . . and that this memorandum was not responsive to those recommendations because I discussed the man's suitability and security, and I expected a full and complete answer on both counts."[24] In short, Otepka refused to give Wieland a clearance.

Boswell, uncharacteristically, let it go at that. Wieland's clearance was still unresolved on the day Jack Kennedy administered his unprecedented tongue-lashing to Sarah McClendon. Then, on the following day, after Boswell and Jones had put their nervous heads together, Otepka received another memorandum. In two short paragraphs, Boswell stated that Jones had confirmed "that no action against the employee (Wieland) is warranted or advisable in the interest of national security" and that "no further action need be taken regarding Mr. Wieland."

Once again, Otepka was forced to bow to the unreasoning orders of his superiors.

Somewhat later the Senate subcommittee suggested that the Justice Department might want to consider prosecuting William Wieland for perjury. The record of his testimony, and the conflicting statements of other witnesses, was made available to Justice. Wieland had splattered the record with blatant lies, but Bobby Kennedy's department simply ignored them. It refused to prosecute.

There was one little lie, however, that Otepka decided no one should ignore. Wieland had told Otepka that he had met Fidel Castro only once in his entire life, though he had intimated to others that he knew Fidel "personally." A few weeks after President Kennedy's public defense of Wieland, Otepka happened to spot a newspaper photograph that showed Wieland chatting amiably with Castro.[25] Something about the picture vaguely troubled Otepka. Wieland had sworn to him that his sole meeting with Castro, a most casual one, had been at a luncheon former Secretary of State Herter tendered Castro during his visit to Washington in April 1959. There were thirty other guests present. Wieland said he had no chance to talk with Castro except within this rather large group. Yet the photo showed them with only one other person.

Otepka put his men on the trail. They quickly verified that the picture had been taken in the library of the National Press Club four days *after* Secretary Herter's luncheon party. Before the SY team was done they discovered Wieland had been with Castro at least six times during Fidel's Washington sojourn. On one of these occasions, just before a reception at the Cuban embassy the evening of April 17, 1959, Castro had been observed slipping off into a private room with his arm wrapped affectionately around Bill Wieland's shoulders. They remained in the room, just the two of them, for more than an hour.

On the basis of this information, Otepka managed to extract a promise from his superiors that the Wieland case would be reopened. The assignment to Bremen was held up again. Chancellor Konrad Adenauer's government had learned about Wieland's record in Cuba by then, and Bonn apparently wanted no part of him anyway. Wieland was kept in Washington for the time being. Later, he was foisted off on Australia, becoming Consul General at Melbourne.

Otto Otepka, meanwhile, had his hands full with other problems. Dean Rusk and his minions had grudgingly put him back in charge of SY's critical Evaluations Division just three days before Jack Kennedy tangled with Sarah McClendon. Ironically, Otepka's superiors let it be known that the principal reason they demoted him to this post was because he had spent entirely too much time during 1961 on evaluations, particularly on the case of William Arthur Wieland.

CHAPTER XII

Back on the Beat

IN DEMOTING OTTO OTEPKA TO THE EVALUATIONS DIVISION THE POW-
ers that be in the Department of State undoubtedly believed they had
trimmed his sails sufficiently to insure against his causing any serious
difficulty in the future. But they very soon found that they had made a
bad miscalculation. By putting him back on the beat, however hemmed
in and closely watched, they had created for themselves a far more
dangerous situation than had hitherto existed with Otepka moored fast
to the special project.

Even with Evaluations stripped of so much of its personnel and
denuded of many of its old duties, Otepka came back to this division,
which he had built and headed years before, with a strong, firm hand.
Perversely, the special project had enabled him to create probably the
best security team that had ever watched over the murky scene on Foggy
Bottom. Somehow, he was able to keep it intact when he was shifted into
Evaluations.

The two original members of the Otepka team, Harry M. Hite and
Billy N. Hughes, had been trained as evaluators under him during the
1950's. Previously, both of them had rather extensive experience as
government investigators in other agencies. They knew the security field
very well indeed, and Boswell was only too happy to let Otepka take

them for the special project when it was just getting started early in 1961.

Four other seasoned security experts were carefully selected by Otepka later on when he got formal approval for the project. Two of them, John R. Norpel, Jr. and Francis V. Gardner, were veteran FBI agents. Norpel, who was then 35, had joined the FBI in 1951 after studying law at Temple University in Philadelphia. He had become a specialist in counter-espionage and had been personally commended by J. Edgar Hoover no less than nine times for outstanding performance, once receiving a special award for supervising cases involving Soviet bloc spies operating out of Washington embassies and the United Nations.

Gardner, a 38-year-old former Marine, was a native of Washington and had practically grown up in the ceaseless battle against subversion. From 1948 until he signed on at the State Department in July 1961, he had been in the FBI and, like Norpel, had distinguished himself in the hazardous counterspy field.

Another member of the team was Edwin A. Burkhardt, also 38. He originally hailed from Wilkes Barre, Pennsylvania, and had been awarded the Purple Heart in World War II for wounds received when his bomber was shot down over enemy territory in central Europe. He had wandered for months behind the German lines, hiding from patrols by day and walking by night, until he was rescued near the war's end. Burkhardt had served for six years in the Civil Service Commission as an investigator and in 1954 had followed Otepka to the State Department. He had been in Evaluations ever since, working with Otepka on many cases, including the interminable riddle of John Stewart Service.

The last and oldest member of Otepka's special project squad was Raymond A. Loughton, then 45. Born in Utah, he had come east to work for the Justice Department in 1938 and, like Otepka, had studied for his law degree at Columbus University in Washington. Admitted to the District of Columbia Bar in 1941, he became an investigator at Justice and, with two years out for wartime service as a Navy officer, he remained there until 1948 when he became a hearing examiner for the Civil Service Commission. In 1951 Loughton joined the old Civil Defense Administration as Security Officer. Later, during the entire eight Eisenhower years, he was Assistant Director of Security in the Department of Defense, which in effect made him Otto Otepka's counterpart at the Pentagon.

After observing what was developing under Robert Strange McNamara and Adam Yarmolinsky at DOD, where internal security deteriorated as swiftly as at State with the advent of the New Frontier,

Loughton apparently decided he would be better off with Otepka, though when he crossed the Potomac from the Pentagon to C Street he must have sensed he was leaping from the frying pan into the open fire.

Loughton, Norpel and Gardner all joined Otepka's Special Project in July, and were technically attached to the Evaluations Division. They had hardly begun to get organized, with Loughton as the senior supervisor under Otepka, when the reduction-in-force disrupted the whole Office of Security. As the newest members of SY's staff their jobs were clearly in jeopardy. But with Otepka's help they managed to weather the ensuing storm and sailed with him into the dismembered Evaluations office on January 21, 1962.

Until then Otepka and his team had taken no part in the day-to-day review of Presidential appointees and other lesser lights twinkling onto the scene. Beginning in December 1960, right after his conference with Dean Rusk and Bobby Kennedy, all "sensitive" cases were routed clear around Otepka, traveling circuitously from Evaluations to Boswell.

In mid-summer, Otepka was booted out of his old office in SY's executive suite and moved from the third to the fourth floor just to make certain he didn't accidentally discover what was going on in Boswell's busy little shop. He politely protested this shift, but Boswell, a fat little man with thinning black hair, removed his horn-rimmed glasses and shook his head. "You'll just have to move," he said bluntly, nervously reaching for another of the cigarettes he smoked in an endless chain.

Otepka went, quietly as always, taking his team with him up to the floor above and bringing it back down again when he was moved back to the third floor, but not into the old executive suite, in January. Once resettled with the Evaluations Division on three, Otepka started picking up the thread of what had transpired during the whole of 1961. Before long, he and his men uncovered what Otepka calls "gross irregularities in the handling of security clearances." This is, to say the least, an understatement of the most magnanimous kind.

Dean Rusk, in the fourteen months Otepka had been kept on the shelf, had personally signed no less than 152 security "waivers" for Presidential and other political appointees in order to get them on the State Department payroll without first subjecting them to an annoying background investigation by the FBI. Rusk and his loyal yes men were to defend these actions as necessary to bring talented people into State and to put them to work as quickly as possible. But in the entire eight years of the previous Eisenhower Administration only five such "emergency" waivers had been signed by the Secretary of State. When two of the five backfired, Foster Dulles had wisely discontinued the practice.

Rusk's wholesale issuance of security waivers was done with the certain knowledge that once you get an official on board in any government agency it is exceedingly difficult to make him walk the plank and get rid of him. Cursory national agency checks are all that are needed to qualify for a waiver. The full field investigations that follow are conducted after the fact and the information they uncover can easily be edited or ignored.

Otepka found, however, that even the once-over-lightly national agency checks had turned up serious derogatory information against some of the 152 officials, including possible Communist sympathies and associations.[1] On top of that, a number of officials had been appointed by Rusk without his notifying the Office of Security at all. And just to confuse the situation further, some of the waivers Rusk signed had been backdated to make it appear that they were issued *after* the agency checks or background investigations had been made.

There was more to come. Otepka and his team found that there had been a flagrant abuse of the "blanket waiver" under which scores of lesser jobs were filled. By mid-May 1962 they had identified more than 600 individuals who had crawled into the State Department under this generous blanket since January 1961. All of these clerks, stenographers, secretaries and what-have-you were cleared to work on classified material if necessary.[2] Many were on the payroll for months, and some for more than a year, before any investigation into their past was conducted.

Towards the end of February, Otepka went to Boswell's office to give him a preliminary report on some of these discoveries. He specifically told Boswell that he had found several instances of backdated waivers and his men believed there were a whole lot more. Boswell archly observed that the cases were being handled "according to the prerogatives of management" and made it plain that Otepka was not to interfere.

When they testified before the Senate Internal Security Subcommittee a few weeks later, on March 8, 1962, Boswell and Roger Jones denied any knowledge whatever of the backdating. "I do not recall any case in which it has been done," Jones swore in reply to a direct question from Sourwine. Boswell, of course, followed Jones' lead:

SOURWINE: Do you know of any single case?
BOSWELL: No, sir.
SOURWINE: In which a security clearance was backdated?
BOSWELL: No, sir.[3]

Reluctantly, Jones conceded that the Secretary of State might occasionally issue a security waiver "if there is urgent need for an individual's services." But, he added, "I do not happen to remember any such cases at the present time." (Much later it was established that *all* of the 152 waiver cases had gone up to Rusk via Jones' office.) If there were any such cases, though, Jones admitted the individuals "would have access to classified information" during the ninety-day period the waiver was in effect.[4]

Boswell and Jones were badly shaken by Sourwine's questions. Very quickly, they moved to paint an innocent face on the messy waiver picture. Audaciously, Boswell tried to enlist Otepka's aid in this endeavor. On March 17, 1962, he instructed Otepka to undertake a thorough study of each of the 152 officials who had been granted emergency clearances since January 1961. The ostensible purpose was to determine how many of the clearances had been backdated.

Otepka wisely acknowledged Boswell's order in a written memorandum the very same day. In it, he reminded Boswell that he and his men had already identified a "large number" of backdating cases, although two years later Boswell was still vehemently denying under oath that he had any prior knowledge of this practice.

Otepka also stated in this memo that he was "unalterably opposed" to backdating clearances and "would resist any attempt" to persuade him to approve them. Further, he emphasized that backdated clearances, which made it appear that State Department officials had been properly cleared for access to classified information when, in fact, they had not, were in "clear violation of the regulations."

In short order, Otepka supplied Boswell with a list of thirty-two individuals, including Assistant Secretary of State Harlan Cleveland, whose clearances had been backdated. Eventually, the list grew to some forty-four, with cases antedated as much as 135 days. But the State Department continued to pooh-pooh the significance of this illegal practice, invariably claiming that all the people who came in on waivers were eventually cleared anyway so what difference did it make? For one thing, of course, there was a great deal of difference in *who* was issuing the clearances, as Otepka's initial exile on the special project had now so dramatically demonstrated. But there was much, much more to it than that.

Otepka's memorandum of March 17 served notice on his superiors that he did not intend to sit idly by while they continued to populate the State Department with people who could never pass the reasonable doubt strictures of Executive Order 10450. Boswell conferred with Jones on Otepka's challenge and it would hardly stretch one's imagination to conclude that the problem was discussed at much higher echelons as well. What resulted was a very clever ploy designed to lift Otepka and his team out of the backdating controversy completely.

A few days after Otepka sent Boswell the memo, the nervous little Director of SY informed him that the backdating investigation would be conducted by the Foreign Service Inspection Corps. He ordered Otepka to turn in all his files on the backdated cases. The message, which Otepka heard loud and clear, was that he was to keep hands off from there on in.

Roger Jones promptly notified the Senate subcommittee that he had learned of some backdating cases after all, and he piously assured the Senators that he had already ordered an investigation. The subcommittee, however, was not entirely satisfied. Otepka was ordered to appear in Room 2300 on April 12. This time, Jones personally briefed Otepka in advance. He advised him to "cooperate" with the subcommittee, but stressed that if there was any sensitive information they wanted, Otepka was to tell the Senators to request it in writing from the Department. Otepka fully understood. He was no stranger to the "executive privilege" gambit which government agencies have increasingly invoked to keep information from the Congress.

At the hearing, Otepka, who had not seen a transcript of the Jones-Boswell testimony of March 8, was questioned by Sourwine about the waivers and backdating. The conflict between his truthful answers and the devious replies of his bosses was, of course, immediately apparent. Unknowingly, Otepka had plunged deeper into the hot water that already boiled all around him.

The glaring "inconsistencies" in his superiors' sworn testimony which Otepka had innocently exposed very quickly caused them to hatch another shabby little plot to get rid of him. Pending this, though, they kept pecking away at what remained of Otepka's authority, obviously hoping he could be made to submit his resignation and save them further embarrassment.

Testifying before the Senate subcommittee, Jones and Boswell jointly attempted to cast doubt on Otepka's abilities. When pressed by Sourwine, however, Jones backed off and wisely decided to attack Otepka's job rather than the man. Bluntly, he called Otepka's old Deputy Director's post a "phony." But his only complaint about Otepka, Jones said, was that he was just too "thorough." So thorough, in fact, that Jones found Otepka's evaluations caused "frustrations to those who had to review his work."

The mounting hostility towards Otepka manifested itself in many other ways. Boswell and his friends no longer attempted to hide it, even at purely social gatherings. That spring, just before Boswell left for Cairo to become Deputy Chief of the U.S. Mission there, his colleagues at the State Department gave him a farewell cocktail party. It was a typical Department affair, held in one of the party rooms reserved for such functions.

Several officials got more than politely smashed. One of them, a Boswell partisan in SY, staggered up to Otepka and began berating him for his "bullheadedness." In the midst of his tirade, the official lurched forward and spilled a brimming martini all over his former boss. Hardly bothering to apologize, he snatched another cocktail from a passing tray and wandered off on unsteady legs. Later in the evening he had to be literally carried out of the party. It was not an unusual performance for this individual, for Otepka had noticed him drunk on the job more than once. But, as Otepka later remarked, "it didn't seem to impede his progress in the Office of Security."

This was the very last State Department party Otepka was ever invited to attend.* He had found them amusing, often revealing. But Boswell's successor was not the kind of man who bothered with amenities, unless it suited his purpose, so Otepka was summarily cut out of State's crowded social calendar.

In the meantime, the first of a series of news leaks on the notorious Rostow Papers began to give Otepka a much more understandable picture of why the high-ranking officials on the seventh floor were so anxious to force him out of the State Department. The initial story was broken by Thomas Ross of the Chicago *Sun-Times.* It appeared, coincidently, within two days after Otepka made his April trek up to Capitol Hill to answer the Senate subcommittee's second call. By the weekend, newspapers across the country were carrying it. As usual, the New York *Times* led off, on Page One, with the Administration's official alibi.

Beneath a two-column headline, "New Master Strategy Plan Under White House Study," the *Times* consoled its readers with the misinformation that the policy paper drafted under Rostow's aegis had not yet been "officially adopted." Moreover, the *Times* said, it really "offers no sweeping new policies."[5] This latter was at least partly correct, inasmuch

---

* There was a slight slip in 1964 and the office of Protocol invited Otepka to a $100-per-person fund-raising party for President Johnson, but he did not accept the invitation.

as most of the policies outlined had been in effect all during 1961 without the public being aware of them. But the fact remains that the Rostow Papers represented nothing less than a sweeping revolution in U.S. foreign policy.

Rostow's rationalizations for the wholesale unilateral disarmament of the United States were masterpieces of a kind. For example, according to reporter Ross, "Rostow's plan recommends a revamping of the nation's arsenal to eliminate first-strike weapons—bombers and missiles that are vulnerable to sneak attack and, therefore, reliable only for striking the first atomic blow. . . . However, *the Rostow plan flatly rejects the concept of a preemptive attack—hitting an enemy first on intelligence reports that he is about to hit you.*"[6]

Having thus set up America and its population as sitting ducks for a Soviet nuclear attack, Rostow then proceeded to show the way towards building bridges to the East in order to make our eventual surrender relatively painless. Very little of this latter got out at first. Perhaps because America's scuttling of a first-strike policy seemed like old hat, having been announced by President Kennedy not long after Rostow's return from Moscow more than a year earlier, the first little squall over the Rostow Papers soon subsided. It was not until two months later that the real storm finally broke.

Tom Ross had done a superb job in his April scoop on Rostow's grand plan, but it remained for Willard Edwards, the veteran Washington correspondent of the Chicago *Tribune*, to unveil the plan in more comprehensive form. On June 17 and 18 the *Tribune* ran two Edwards' articles which spelled out many embarrassing details of the Rostow strategy. To the chagrin of the State Department, it was obvious that Edwards had somehow got hold of the volatile 278-page document. The Department, which slaps a classified label on anything it wants to conceal from the American people, had intended that this particular document, above all, was "to remain secret," as the New York *Times* correctly phrased it.

In 1968 the Rostow Papers were still being kept on classified ice at State. But it is now possible to grasp the Grand Design in all its majesty and splendor, and to reveal the following summary of what it proposed—and, more important, what it has accomplished in "converging" East and West. The informed reader will immediately perceive that most of Rostow's schemes have long since gone into effect. But there are still a few, like the China offshore island caper, yet awaiting official action.*

* All quotes in this summary are taken verbatim from the Rostow Papers.

- Heart and soul of the Rostow strategy is the disarmament program. The scuttling of America's first-strike forces was merely the initial step towards Rostow's "disarmed world." Ultimately, the program "would involve the reduction and eventual elimination" of all armed forces— "except those required for maintaining internal order and for an international police force."* The Rostow Papers discreetly avoid the critical question, *who will control the "police force"—and therefore the "disarmed world"—the U.S. or the USSR?*

- Disarmament must be fed to the American public in imperceptible doses, lest the voters discover Washington intends to surrender their national sovereignty. "The problem," Rostow & Company frankly admit, "is one of devising programs which could attract sufficient public support."

- Keep the true intent of the government in this sphere hidden at all times. "New approaches to this problem should be studied intensively" since any overt "action to achieve the objective . . . would require difficult political decisions for the people of both the United States and its allies."

- The prescribed first dose for the unsuspecting citizenry of the U.S. was a "limited" test ban treaty. By the summer of 1963 the American public had swallowed this pill whole, without realizing that it may well prove lethal since it handed the Soviets a tremendous technological advantage over the United States.

- The next big step was to be a "non-proliferation" treaty to freeze all other free nations out of the nuclear club. It took five years to get agreement on this, and when it came many other nations refused to swallow it. The U.S. Senate finally gulped it down in 1969. Meanwhile, several other big peace moves were concocted, including the Nuclear Space Ban Treaty, which granted the USSR yet another long lead since Russia already had space weapons with a nuclear capability by 1967 and the United States did not.

- "General purpose forces" were to be strengthened in order to de-emphasize nuclear deterrence as America's primary defense policy. Beefed up infantry, artillery, etc., could then "frustrate without using nuclear weapons" any aggression by "Sino-Soviet forces."** This

* Students of U.S. disarmament policy will recognize this as an almost verbatim precursor of the official "U.S. Program for General and Complete Disarmament in a Peaceful World" (State Department Publication 7277) issued one year later.

** This slip—"Sino-Soviet forces"—carries much more significance than first meets the eye. For a decade Rostow had been preaching the importance of the Moscow-Peiping split. In the 1960's, the split, along with disarmament, became the foundation stone upon which policy, successfully pushed by Rostow in 1961, had resulted in more than 200,000 American casualties in Vietnam by early 1969. By any yardstick it had proved a tragic failure. But Presidential Assistant Rostow was still cheerfully promoting it from his White House office as the casualties continued to mount.

• "Creation of some facility [for] direct communication between national military command centers" in order to "minimize the need for hasty military responses." After the Cuban missile crisis of 1962, this proposal was adopted when a "hot line" was installed between the White House and the Kremlin. Appropriately, Rostow was the first man to use it, on behalf of President Johnson, during the 1967 Mideast crisis.

• Go easy on Moscow's satellites at all times. "We cannot," the Rostow Revelations claim, "as experience with Hungary has shown, hope to expand our . . . penetration into a satellite country while simultaneously castigating its government."

• Discourage uprisings behind the Iron Curtain. In fact, if revolts do erupt, the U.S. should join with the Soviet Union to smother them as quickly as possible. Above all, America should "avoid being moved" by the "importunities of our allies or of our own public to prolong and expand the crises in an effort to inflict a dramatic humiliation on the Communists." The results of this particular policy were tragically evident in America's official silence during the Soviet invasion of Czechoslovakia in 1968.

• Build bridges to Eastern Europe through increased trade. In short, surrender our once avowed policy of liberation for the captive nations and consign the Czechs, Poles, Hungarians, et al., to everlasting slavery while we strengthen their Communist overseers with transfusions of American capital via "expanded economic contacts."

• Covertly condition the Germans to accept the hard fact that their country will remain split in two forevermore. ("To indicate [openly] that we regard the division of Germany as permanent would be to shake West German confidence in the West.") In order to help the conditioning process along, "we should encourage the West Germans . . . to expand rather than contract their own [trade] contacts with the East Germans."

---

the new U.S. foreign policy was built. Therefore, "Sino-Soviet" should never be hyphenated when used with the word "forces," since this indicates they are joint forces, and hints that Rostow did not place as much credence in the "split" as he steadfastly claimed he did.

• "Leave ajar possibilities for expanding commercial, cultural and other contacts with Communist China. We should make clear that there is no final bar to the entrance of Communists China into more normal relations with the U.S."

• Persuade the Nationalist Chinese regime to remove their forces from the "offshore islands" of Quemoy, Matsu, etc., in order to "disengage U.S. prestige from the Formosa Straits." (Later deleted from the Rostow Papers, this particular ploy was to be effected *before* Communist China detonated its first nuclear bomb, still thought to be a gleam in Mao's eye in 1961.)

• Forging the "northern nations of the world" (including the USSR and the U.S.) into "an effective military and economic coalition" that could then minister to the poor "underdeveloped southern half."

Through all this strained and labored verbiage, one theme runs true, now muted, now fortissimo, sounding much like the fading *Marseillaise* in Tschaikovsky's "1812 Overture" as it records the retreat of another Western force before the onslaught of Muscovy. That theme, of course, is Rostow's nationless world—"a world effectively organized for peace."

To most Americans, including Otto Otepka, it sounds much like the opening bars of a symphony dedicated to the peace of the slaves. And for a fleeting week or two in the early summer of 1962 it sounded exactly like that to the trained ear of Senator Everett McKinley Dirksen. The day after Willard Edwards' second Chicago *Tribune* article had thoroughly raised the alarm in Illinois, the venerable Minority Leader rose on the floor of the United States Senate to alert the nation.

"The core of Mr. Rostow's proposal," said Dirksen, "is an assumption that the Soviet Union and its Communist masters are 'mellowing'; that Russia is becoming a mature state; that if we are only nice to the Soviets they will drop all their suspicions of the free world and peace will finally bloom." The American people, Dirksen declared, are entitled to know—"perhaps through questioning by appropriate Senate committees"—"what intelligence information Mr. Rostow has to support his basic assumption."

A week later Rostow was hailed before the Senate Foreign Relations Committee and questioned for three hours. He slithered up and down the scale of his soothing piano, lulling his inquisitors with hawk-like ballads that sounded downright patriotic to many of them. But both Maestro Rostow and Undersecretary George Ball politely refused to let the Senators take a peep at the original score as composed in the Rostow Papers, claiming that the Great Policy Symphony was subject to executive privilege.

Actually, Rostow and Ball had adroitly managed a nice diversion. As it turned out, Rostow was not questioned about the Rostow Papers at all, but, as Senator Barry Goldwater put it, the discussion covered "the whole range of world affairs." For once, Goldwater found himself in agreement with Senator Fulbright, the dovish Democrat chairman of the Foreign Relations Committee. Fulbright admitted the document in question had not been discussed. The closest they came to it, apparently, was listening to George Ball claim that the Willard Edwards articles "were so distorted one couldn't tell whether the reporter had seen the paper, talked to somebody, or written thoughts he himself may have had."[7]*

When it was all over, Fulbright and some other Democrat members of the Committee gave Rostow what one reporter called "a clean bill of health." Indeed, they went beyond that "and paid him glowing tributes."[8] But Everett Dirksen was "not wholly satisfied." "I still have some concern," he told newsmen as he left the hearing room.

Rostow, having talked for the better part of three hours, was uncharacteristically reticent when he came away. A reporter asked whether he had anything to say to the press. "Not a thing," he replied, breezing bruskly down a corridor and out a side entrance of the Capitol.

That was on Tuesday, June 26. One week later a group of Congressmen, dissatisfied like Dirksen, laid down a booming barrage in the House of Representatives in a futile attempt to shell Walt W. Rostow out of his impregnable State Department bomb shelter.[9] Congressman Robert T. Stafford of Vermont led off with a penetrating analysis of what was then known of the Rostow Papers and described them as charting "the road to disaster."

Stafford decried the fact that the policy guide was kept secret from the Congress and the American people although it was a safe assumption that the "significant parts" of it which had appeared in print were already "under study by the Soviet Union." He was followed by Durwood Hall of Missouri, who questioned whether a man who claimed in his writings that America was nothing more than "a continental island off the greater land mass of Eurasia" should be in such a powerful position to influence U.S. policy.

Congressman Alphonzo Bell of California said that Rostow's policies were designed to hasten the day when "Lenin's proclaimed 'encirclement

---

* This reporter, who *has* seen the Rostow Papers, will vouch without reservation for the accuracy of Edwards' paraphrased accounts.

of the capitalist world by socialism' will become a reality."

Garner Shriver of Kansas declared that Rostow and his colleagues were engaged in a "massive governmental effort to brainwash all of us." And James Battin of Montana charged that Rostow's policies "would lead to the destruction, devastation and demoralization of what we today know as the United States."

Seldom, if ever, in modern history had any official of the federal government been the target of such a withering attack on the floor of Congress. Granted, the attack had been mounted by members of the minority party. But their words were obviously spoken not so much out of any partisan political interest, as out of sincere and deep concern for the future of their country. They had conclusively indicted Walt Rostow as a non-American striving to consign millions of innocent people to eternal slavery under communism while endangering the security of the United States and the lives of its inhabitants.

Yet somehow Dr. Rostow emerged from the battle more secure than ever in his position of power. If anything, his prestige had been enhanced, rather than tarnished. President Kennedy defended him vigorously in a press conference that same week and other prominent Democrats rushed to his aid. Influential segments of the press championed Rostow's cause. Even the Communist *People's World* openly rallied to Rostow's banner, praising his attempts to find "specific alternatives" to U.S. foreign policy and heaping scorn on his critics.

Although he was later to become Lyndon Johnson's alter ego on foreign policy, Rostow was at this time serving as Bobby Kennedy's personal tutor. He was unofficial dean of faculty at Hickory Hill U., the cozy little running seminar conducted at Bobby's home in McLean, Virginia, for the New Frontier "in group."

During recreation periods there was fun-and-games in the swimming pool. Rostow's fellow Hickory Hill professor, Arthur Schlesinger, was once dropped, fully clothed, into Bobby's pool. (A member of the Harvard Board of Overseers later remarked to this writer that it didn't surprise him that former Harvard historian Schlesinger had been pushed into the pool, but he "couldn't understand, for the life of me, why anyone bothered to fish him out.")

In between the high jinks, Rostow deftly molded Robert Kennedy's mind. Bobby had become increasingly active in shaping Administration foreign policy after the Bay of Pigs disaster and, on occasion, he acted in effect as America's Secretary of State. It was Bobby who sent New York lawyer James B. Donovan to East Berlin to negotiate the release of Francis Gary Powers, the U-2 pilot captured by the Russians when his spy plane went down over the USSR. The Soviets, as usual, got the best of the bargain. In exchange for Powers and an American student held by the East Germans, the Russians received Colonel Rudolf Abel, the master spy who had operated a vast Soviet espionage network in the United States during the 1950's and who resumed direction of Communist penetration of our society when he returned to Moscow.

Under Rostow's tutelage, Bobby Kennedy blossomed forth as the Clan Kennedy's resident expert on world affairs. In February 1962, while Otepka and his team were probing the waiver scandal in Dean Rusk's State Department, Bobby, accompanied by his wife, Ethel, was touring the globe, meeting with world leaders and making secret commitments right and left. It was on this junket that Bobby gratuitously gave Indonesia's Sukarno Dutch New Guinea and seriously shook Charles deGaulle's confidence in the United States.

Bobby returned from his world tour ready, willing, and (so he thought) eminently able to tackle the State Department's internal difficulties with the troublesome Otepka. Dean Rusk's Foreign Service boys had fumbled the ball. It was time for the Kennedys to send in a trusted quarterback. Luckily, they just happened to have one available in the person of one John Francis Reilly.

CHAPTER **XIII**

Reilly

JOHN FRANCIS REILLY, AN OBSCURE JUSTICE DEPARTMENT ATTORNEY who had been temporarily farmed out to the Federal Communications Commission, thought he had the world in his hip pocket when he stepped from the FCC to the State Department on April 16, 1962. As a Massachusetts Irishman, he could rejoice in the knowledge that "one of his own" reigned in the White House. Moreover, no less a personage than the President's brother seemed to be taking an active interest in his career, which had been floundering a bit of late.

Reilly, a tallish, florid-faced man with close-cropped black hair just running to gray around the temples, knew that he must have won the confidence of the men "higher up" to be given such an important assignment at State. For at 41 he was taking over the Department's embattled Office of Security from William O. Boswell, who had made such an embarrassing hash of the whole business in recent months.

The account of how Reilly came to step into Boswell's mincing shoes is best described by Reilly himself. Under questioning by defense attorney Roger Robb on June 29, 1967, during the State Department hearings in the Otepka case, Reilly carelessly revealed the identity of his mentor in the following manner:

ROBB: How did you happen to transfer to the State Department?
REILLY: I was asked if I would accept the job.
ROBB: Who asked you?
REILLY: Mr. Roger Jones. . . .He was then Deputy Undersecretary of State for Administration.
ROBB: Had you known Mr. Jones before?
REILLY: No, I had not.
ROBB: Do you know how he happened to hear about you?
REILLY: Yes. I understand that a longtime acquaintance, Mr. Andy Oehmann, recommended me.
ROBB: Who is Mr. Oehmann? Or who was he?
REILLY: At that particular time I believe he was Executive Assistant to the Attorney General. I had known Mr. Oehmann since my early days in the Department of Justice.
ROBB: Who was the Attorney General?
REILLY: Mr. Robert F. Kennedy.

It would stretch one's imagination to the breaking point to assume that Andy Oehmann, Bobby's executive assistant, did not at least clear Reilly's appointment to State with his boss, who was then taking an increasingly active interest in Dean Rusk's department. More likely, though, Oehmann was merely the go-between. The decision to dispatch Reilly to State to handle the tempestuous crisis created by Otepka's stubborn presence was made at a more exalted level. Reilly's high-handed, even brutal, actions in his subsequent dealings with Otepka are eloquent evidence of his confidence that he had the full backing of the Kennedys.

Reilly, after a frustrating year of attempting to rid the State Department of the unbudgeable Otepka, once remarked grimly to Jack Norpel, "I was sent over here to do a job, and by God I'm going to do it."

Exactly who sent him, and what kind of a job he was expected to do, was a source of abiding interest to the Senate Internal Security Subcommittee at the height of the furor over Otepka's firing in the fall of 1963.[1]

Reilly, however, knew how to play the game. He went to considerable pains to protect Bobby Kennedy—and Dean Rusk. In the highest tradition of a bureaucratic underling taking the rap for his superiors, he assumed full responsibility for the purge of Otepka. Nonetheless, he slipped very badly on one occasion in his testimony before the subcommittee.

On November 15, 1963, under Jay Sourwine's relentless questioning, Reilly admitted that "one of my assignments was to find out if there had been people furnishing information" to the subcommittee.[2] But when

Sourwine tried to learn who had given him this "assignment," Reilly refused to put the finger on anyone higher than his predecessor, William Boswell:

SOURWINE: You knew there had been for some time prior to your entry into the Department an effort to get Otepka out, is that correct? You knew that from Mr. Boswell?

REILLY: That is correct.

SOURWINE: And it is true that you were led to believe, and did believe, that this was entirely on Mr. Boswell's own responsibility?

REILLY: That is my understanding, sir.

SOURWINE: When you continued the effort to get Mr. Otepka out, were you doing it entirely on your own responsibility?

REILLY: Yes, sir.

On its very face, this was ludicrous. Can one really picture John Reilly, a government official for fifteen years, stepping into a new job and taking his cue from a nervous little Foreign Service officer who was leaving for a remote post in far off Egypt? Yet Reilly swore under oath that this was so. But then, to Reilly an oath meant no more than it did to a number of other officials in the Department of State, which is to say it meant nothing at all.

It could not always have been like that. Earlier in his life, Reilly had undoubtedly been taught to have a proper regard for the truth, and for the other more homely virtues that once were considered suitable standards of conduct. Born in Springfield, Massachusetts, Reilly grew up in nearby Longmeadow, graduated from Springfield's Classical High School and went on to Holy Cross College in Worcester. A tall, graceful and rather handsome youth with dark hair and blue eyes, he showed a predilection for such "intellectual" subjects as literature, philosophy and history. He did quite well at "The Cross," and shortly after receiving his Bachelor of Arts degree in June 1941 he moved to Washington where he signed on as a clerk with the War Production Board.

Somehow Jack Reilly escaped service in World War II and while still employed by the federal government he enrolled in 1943 in Georgetown University's Law School. The year before his graduation he was admitted to the District of Columbia Bar, became law clerk to Judge Brice Clagett of the local Court of Appeals, and was elevated to associate editor of the *Georgetown Law Journal.* Thus, he already seemed to have a long head start in his chosen profession when he took his law degree in June 1947, emerging second in his class. That fall, at 27, he confidently opened his own law office in downtown Washington. For John F. Reilly, attorney, the future looked very bright indeed.

Less than four years later, in the spring of 1951, Reilly decided to give up his private practice and enter the Department of Justice. He began as a trial lawyer in the Anti-Trust Division, and soon switched to the Criminal Division, specializing in internal security cases. Though he had been taken on during a Democrat administration, Reilly easily survived the mild Eisenhower reformation and continued to progress up through the ranks, becoming Special Assistant to the Republican Attorney General in July 1956. In this capacity he worked closely for a time with the old Operations Coordinating Board of the National Security Council.

When the Kennedy Administration collapsed the OCB early in 1961, Reilly was temporarily shunted back to the Criminal Division. As a Truman Administration appointee who had continued to rise during the Eisenhower years he may have been suspect in New Frontier circles and probably had to prove his loyalty to the Democrat Party all over again. In May 1961 he was moved over to the Federal Communications Commission. After a year, in which his loyalty was tested and obviously proved, Reilly was sent over to the State Department to head up the critical Office of Security.

When Boswell briefed Reilly on the tense situation in SY he was terribly upset about "leaks of information" to the Senate Internal Security Subcommittee. Boswell and Roger Jones had just had a most trying session with the Senators during which they had been closely questioned about security clearance waivers signed by Secretary Rusk and, most particularly, about the backdating of those waivers. Boswell was convinced that inside information had been given to the subcommittee, and that Otepka was the man responsible.

This, in itself, is indicative of both the curious perspective and the nagging paranoia that prevails in the Department of State. Otepka maintains he had nothing to do with these leaks. In fact, it was to be a long year before he provided the subcommittee with any private information on the internal operations of SY. But Boswell's wish was father to Reilly's thought, and the chances are both they and their superiors *did* believe Otepka was the culprit responsible for embarrassing the Department. If the disclosures of State's crumbling security program continued, the whole Rostowian revolution in American foreign policy would be endangered. One way or another, Otepka had to be gotten rid of. That, of course, was Reilly's primary job.

At the outset it must have seemed to Reilly that the job would be accomplished easily enough. When he assumed control of SY from the harried Mr. Boswell he did not step into a hostile environment. There were a number of people already in SY who were in sympathy with the Rusk-Rostow axis. There were more who were merely political hacks to be manipulated at will. And there was a hard core of Kennedy men on board who could be counted on to do Reilly's bidding.

Among the latter was Joseph E. Rosetti, a Boston boy who had worked in Jack Kennedy's congressional office before joining State in 1951, and Robert J. McCarthy, another Massachusetts loyalist who boasted *ad nauseam* of his connections with the Clan Kennedy. A third member of the Massachusetts Mafia in SY was Charles W. Lyons, who was serving as Otepka's deputy in the Evaluations Division. Before long they were joined by still another Old Bay State hand, David I. Belisle. Belisle became Reilly's "special assistant," in effect inheriting Otepka's abolished job as Deputy Director of SY. All four of these men from Massachusetts were to play important roles in the new plot to oust Otepka.

Once in the pilot's seat at SY, Reilly wasted little time zeroing in on his priority target. It must be said that he tried the gentle approach with Otepka before he really got rough. For openers, he attempted to con Otepka with a liberal application of Boston blarney.

A few weeks after his arrival, Reilly invited Otepka to his office. Smiling broadly, he asked, "Where's your rabbit's foot?" Mystified, Otepka raised his eyebrows in question. Reilly laughed and, maintaining his air of benevolent affability, he explained that Otepka had just been selected to attend the National War College. This was an honor usually reserved for Foreign Service officers marked for higher things. Being human, Otepka was naturally pleased. Reilly seemed genuinely delighted that such good fortune had befallen a member of his staff and for just a moment Otepka was taken in. He accepted the appointment with thanks, and perhaps with a sense of relief that he could escape, at least temporarily, from the strained atmosphere that prevailed in SY. Reilly shrewdly asked him to put his acceptance in writing.

That same day, May 7, Otepka wrote Reilly a memorandum formally expressing his willingness to attend the War College for ten months beginning in August. However, he could not resist adding, tongue in cheek, that the appointment had come as something of a surprise to him because the State Department had repeatedly assured him, the Congress, and the public that he would be kept in a responsible position in the Office of Security. Reilly returned this memo with the request that Otepka delete his comments on the Department's promises. Otepka complied.

Reilly lost no time putting the seal on Otepka's acceptance. He fired off a memo to Michel Cieplinski, Acting Administrator of the Bureau of Security and Consular Affairs, in which he rhapsodized about Otepka's "very real and substantial contribution to the Office of Security and hence to the national security." Laying it on thick for Otepka's benefit, Reilly added:

Selection for the National War College is a high honor for a career officer and offers almost unlimited opportunity for career development. Therefore, although releasing Mr. Otepka will work a hardship on the Office of Security, it is my feeling that I should not stand in Mr. Otepka's way, and accordingly, I recommend that he be released as he has requested."

The slushy tone of this epistle made Otepka a little uneasy. He decided to make some quiet inquiries about his appointment. Soon he learned that the regular nominations to the War College had been made months before and that his was in the nature of a last-minute emergency appointment.

Otepka went to Reilly and asked whether he would be able to return to SY when his stint at the War College was completed. Reilly frowned and said he would "have to fill in behind" Otepka when he departed. He admitted he had no plans for bringing Otepka back to SY.* In that case, Otepka said, he would like to withdraw his acceptance. Reilly's former affability fell from him like an irritating plastic mask. His red face turned dangerously purple, but he held his tongue. With a shrug and a peremptory wave of his hand he dismissed Otepka.

Coincidentally, the day before this meeting Senator Karl Mundt got wind of Otepka's appointment to the War College and dispatched a letter to Roger Jones. In it, he questioned whether the assignment was wise, particularly at this time when "a new man" (Reilly) was just "breaking in." Mundt, whose knowledge of the inner workings of the State Department dated back to the time he helped Richard Nixon expose Alger Hiss, reminded Jones of "the critical role which Mr. Otepka plays in the security program at State." He also recalled the then recent conviction of Irving Scarbeck, who had been caught spying for the Communists while working at the American embassy in Warsaw. In view of this continuing Soviet penetration of the State Department, Mundt said, "we can ill afford to take a veteran security officer like Mr. Otepka off the firing line."

---

* Reilly later repeatedly denied, under oath, that he had informed Otepka that he could not return to the Office of Security.

Two days later Jones, flanked by Department lawyers Abram Chayes and Andreas Lowenfeld, was confronted with a copy of Senator Mundt's letter when he reappeared before the Senate subcommittee. Jones, informed the subcommittee that Otepka's War College appointment had just been canceled at his own request. But Sourwine still insisted on finding out why the appointment had been offered in the first place. Jones again went into his soft-shoe routine about the "great stress" Otepka had been working under. And he claimed that the appointment was designed "primarily to give him a break and rest."[3] With a perfectly straight face, Jones denied that the War College ploy had been an effort to axe Otepka from SY.

The Senate subcommittee's obvious annoyance at the Department's ill-concealed second attempt to force Otepka out of SY probably saved him from another direct assault, at least for the time being. Reilly now realized that blarney wouldn't work. He next decided on a more stealthy approach and began by surrounding Otepka with a whole network of his spies.

Less than a week after Otepka turned down the War College appointment Reilly placed his first spy in Otepka's office. Without consulting him at all, Reilly named one Frederick W. Traband as Otepka's assistant. Traband had previously been one of SY's experts on homosexuals, hardly a broad enough background for holding down the sensitive post of assistant chief of Evaluations.

However, Traband had endeared himself to the new breed at State by endorsing a "report" prepared by Charles Lyons severely castigating the "ultra-conservatives" in SY left over from the Eisenhower Administration and calling for more realism in granting security clearances to keep the Office of Security in step with the times. A tall, cadaverous man with a pale, drawn face, Traband later joined the swelling ranks of the State Department's "truth squad" by denying under oath that he had ever taken part in any surveillance of Otepka.[4]

Reilly's next move was to bring in David Belisle from the National Security Agency. Belisle, whose subsequent perjury before the Senate subcommittee was almost as blatant as Reilly's, had been Deputy Director of Security at NSA for nine years. It was during those years that NSA became riddled with homosexuals and security risks. The odorous case of William Martin and Bernon Mitchell, the two NSA boyfriends who defected to the Soviet Union in 1960, was merely the visible tip of an iceberg that ran down through all levels of NSA's structure, even reaching into its Office of Security.

Belisle escaped from NSA and found sanctuary at State in July 1962, just one month before the House Committee on Un-American Activities released its chilling report on that super-sensitive agency. The National Security Agency had been set up under Defense Department jurisdiction a decade earlier to handle "certain very highly classified functions of the government vital to the national security." It was so super-secret that its specific duties—as the House Committee report noted—"are carefully guarded, not only from the public, but from other government agencies as well."[5] Yet as a result of the Congressional investigation, 40-odd officials of NSA were fired, 26 of them for what the Committee delicately termed "indications of sexual deviations."[6]

Among those swept out in the NSA housecleaning was the Director of Personnel, a former Army major who, among other fabrications, had manufactured an LL.B. degree from Harvard on his own application form and had covered up damaging reports on a whole battalion of fellow NSA officials. In addition, NSA's Director of Security and two other employees in its Office of Security were ordered to resign for misconduct.[7]

All this had gone on right under David I. Belisle's nose for nine years. But Belisle kept quiet until the Martin-Mitchell escapade threatened to blow the lid clear off NSA's thoroughly rotten security setup. Then, to save his own neck, he quietly spilled the beans to a House committee investigator. That made his position at NSA untenable, of course, so his Massachusetts political friends sent him over to State to give Jack Reilly a hand.

With Reilly's approval, Belisle quickly set about establishing the same security procedures at State which had resulted in the wholesale scandal at NSA. The first of these was the so-called "short form report," which eliminated a whole flock of those irritating questions concerning one's background that New Frontier people found so awfully embarrassing.

The short form report was simplicity itself. Reilly and Belisle merely ordered SY's field investigators to eliminate all the lengthy findings they had unearthed on an individual and substitute instead a brief comment that no derogatory information had been turned up, or, if it had, to summarize it as briefly as possible. Many of the investigators were, of course, fledglings in the security field and were not really qualified to judge whether a given piece of intelligence was derogatory or not. That was the job of the Evaluations Division. But, as Otepka later observed, the Reilly-Belisle system "made the investigator an evaluator."

By way of illustration, Otepka said that a field investigator "might be interviewing a witness who could be a prominent member of a Commu-

nist organization . . . but the investigator-evaluator could give no significance to the record of that person, but simply list him as a witness
without including any comment that the witness was a wheel in some
Communist activity." It is not difficult to visualize the sins of omission
that were soon being committed under the guise of efficiency with David
Belisle's NSA practices now in effect at State.

Belisle, by nature a rather belligerent man, was in SY only a few weeks
when he locked horns with Otepka. The clash came over the matter of
issuing a security clearance for Matthew McCloskey, the powerful Philadelphia financial angel of the Democrat Party who had been nominated
by President Kennedy as Ambassador to Ireland. Otepka's right-hand
man in Evaluations, Raymond Loughton, had handled the case and
found that there were extremely serious questions regarding McCloskey's suitability which Loughton felt needed further investigation. These
questions centered around numerous alleged fraudulent deals in McCloskey's conduct of his construction business.

Otepka endorsed Loughton's evaluation of the McCloskey case, but
Reilly and Belisle insisted the derogatory information be edited out of
McCloskey's file. In addition, Reilly absolutely refused to order a further
investigation. Belisle sent Loughton several nasty notes roundly criticiz-
ing him for having the temerity to raise questions about a man like Matt
McCloskey.

In the end, of course, Reilly overrode the strong objections of Otepka
and Loughton and simply ordered McCloskey's clearance out of hand.
Dean Rusk upheld him, and the burly McCloskey, after receiving the
approval of an uninformed Senate, sailed happily off for Ireland. Some
months later his mysterious role in the multi-million dollar Rayburn
Building boondoggle on Capitol Hill finally came to light, but by then
McCloskey was home free in Dublin.

The McCloskey case was but the first of many in which Reilly and his
Massachusetts Mafia rode roughshod over Otepka and the Evaluations
Division. Before long it became standard practice in the Office of
Security to issue tailor-made clearances carefully cut to the specifications
desired by Dean Rusk's Seventh Floor, Bobby Kennedy's Justice Department, and Brother Jack's White House. Unfortunately, most of these
clearances were bestowed upon people with much more questionable
backgrounds than Matt McCloskey.

One example of SY's supine desire to accommodate the every wish of
Reilly's revered "higher ups" was the malodorous case of Frank Montero. A Negro described in a press dispatch as "a dynamic specialist in

African affairs," Montero was named to Adlai Stevenson's staff at the United Nations in August 1963.[8] The same dispatch, from the Chicago Daily News Service, succinctly related how Montero got his job:

> The Montero appointment, it was learned, was approved by Stevenson last spring, but had been tied up in red tape, including the Portuguese objections. Attorney General Robert Kennedy, a political friend of Montero, heard about the delay and acted to speed the appointment.[9]

The "Portuguese objections" were based on Montero's activities in Angola, where he had traveled early in 1961 as an official of the American Committee on Africa. Otepka and his staff were unaware of the Portuguese position in the matter, and would not have been influenced by it if they had been. What they were aware of, and what the news story failed to mention, was Montero's alleged role in helping run arms through the Republic of the Congo to the inhuman terrorists who were murdering blacks and whites indiscriminately in Angola. Among the many playful pastimes these terrorists had engaged in was feeding the bodies, both living and dead, of a group of villagers at Luvo through a sawmill in order to mutilate them more efficiently.*

Otepka insisted that an additional investigation was required to determine the extent of Montero's reported part in aiding the Angolan terrorists, most of whom were based in the Republic of the Congo where they were largely supported by Communist elements. But Reilly and Belisle kept pressuring him to put through Montero's clearance. The pressure was not confined within SY, however. An assistant to Harlan Cleveland, Assistant Secretary of State for International Organizations, quietly advised Otepka to issue Montero's clearance because Robert Kennedy wanted it. Even Reilly later admitted, without naming Bobby, that "we were endeavoring to expedite it." But he laid responsibility for the actual approval of the clearance on David Belisle.[10]

The lengths to which John Francis Reilly was willing to go to please Robert Kennedy and mollify Dean Rusk are nowhere better seen, however, than in his support of Harlan Cleveland's attempt to resurrect and beatify the ghost of Alger Hiss. Once again Reilly found, like Boswell before him, that the man blocking the way was Otto Otepka.

---

* For the best documented account of the terrorism in Angola the writer recommends Bernardo Teixeira's *The Fabric of Terror*, Devin-Adair, New York, 1965.

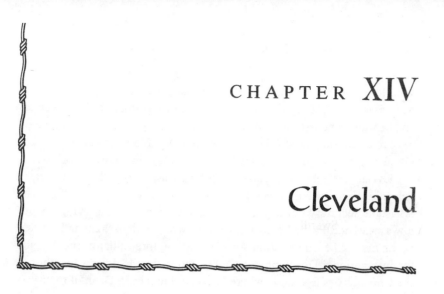

CHAPTER XIV

Cleveland

THE SUMMER OF 1962 BROUGHT A SUDDEN SURGE OF CONFIDENCE TO the New Frontier. Despite a near-disastrous stock market dip in May, continued Soviet nuclear tests, and ominous rumbles from Cuba, the Administration of John Fitzgerald Kennedy seemed to be coming into its own. Newspapers and magazines spoke glowingly of the Kennedy "style" and of his promising steps towards peace. Towards the end of June the President finally got Laos "neutralized" and went off on a triumphal tour of Mexico. He returned in time to deliver a July 4th address calling for a "declaration of *inter*dependence" that would join "the new union now merging in Europe and the old American Union."

Behind the scenes on Foggy Bottom, however, there was a growing uneasiness. Otto Otepka was making it increasingly difficult for Bobby Kennedy, keeper of the patronage keys, to unlock more security doors. During 1961, with Otepka nailed down on his special project, there had been no real problems. The State Department had been thoroughly overhauled and repopulated at the policy level. Rostow's revolution was proceeding almost according to plan. But now it seemed excruciatingly difficult to get additional members of the new breed aboard.

On a sultry day in July, John Reilly called Otepka into his office. Harlan Cleveland, the Assistant Secretary of State for International Organization Affairs, was complaining about the delay in securing a clearance for his good friend, Irving Swerdlow. Reilly knew Swerdlow had been fired as a security risk in 1953 by the old Mutual Security Agency and he wanted no part of the case. In a different atmosphere, Reilly would have rejected Swerdlow's clearance out of hand. Now, however, he asked Otepka to confer with Cleveland and see what they could work out.

Cleveland, a tall, distinguished looking man with a broad forehead below his thinning hair, received Otepka in his Seventh Floor office. The Assistant Secretary politely inquired about the holdup on Irving Swerdlow's clearance. He had known Swerdlow when both of them had worked in the Economic Cooperation Administration, forerunner of the Agency for International Development (AID). Later they had been together at the University of Syracuse, where Cleveland had been Dean of the Maxwell Graduate School of Citizenship and Public Affairs before coming into State in 1961. He could see no reason why Swerdlow should not be permitted to join the State Department too, and right away.

Calmly, with his unfailing patience, Otepka explained that the background investigation of Swerdlow, required by law, would have to be completed first. Then the evaluation would have to be done. He could foresee no early completion of the case.

Cleveland's heavy brows knitted in a worried frown. He asked what Otepka thought the outcome might be.

Based on what he knew of Swerdlow's record, Otepka said he doubted a clearance would be forthcoming at all. He reminded Cleveland that Swerdlow had been discharged as a security risk only eight years earlier. Very few people had ever actually been fired by the government on those grounds. Otepka knew of no case where any had been put back on the payroll.

Cleveland, obviously annoyed, shifted in the comfortable chair behind his big desk. Harold Stassen, Eisenhower's AID chief, had fired Swerdlow, Cleveland pointed out. And everyone knew that Stassen had very "extreme views" on security, Cleveland charged.

Otepka was somewhat surprised to hear Harold Stassen characterized as an extremist. For twenty years the former governor of Minnesota had been the perennial presidential candidate for a tiny, quite Leftist group within the Republican Party. But Otepka didn't argue. He merely said that Mr. Stassen's security policies didn't enter into his judgment of Irving Swerdlow.

Harlan Cleveland's frown deepened. He seemed to be thinking of something else now. At last he spoke.

"What are the chances of getting Alger Hiss back into the Government?" he asked.

Otepka, case-hardened as he was after a year-and-a-half of dealing with New Frontiersmen, was frankly shocked. If almost anyone but Cleveland had asked that question, he would have been sure he was joking. But Harlan Cleveland was not one to joke about such serious matters. Otepka, hoping his shock did not show, managed to reply in his usual matter-of-fact tone.

"I don't think there would be any hope of bringing Alger Hiss back in," he said evenly. "He was convicted of perjury, which is a felony, in a case involving the national security. The law prohibits the rehiring of anyone convicted of a serious offense like that. I would say Alger Hiss wouldn't stand a chance of getting back into the federal government."

Cleveland merely nodded. Then he rose to indicate the interview had terminated. Otepka departed. When he got back downstairs to SY he reported the conversation to Reilly. Even Reilly shook his head. But he offered no comment. A year later, after he drummed Otepka out of the Evaluations Division, Reilly approved Irving Swerdlow's clearance. And although Alger Hiss did not return to government, a number of his closest friends were brought back in, through Reilly's acquiescence and Cleveland's intercession.

Otepka's meeting with Harlan Cleveland made him decide to take a closer look at Cleveland's own security file. Cleveland had been brought into the State Department on a security waiver signed by Dean Rusk, and a backdated waiver at that. Moreover, Otepka knew that his predecessor as chief of the Evaluations Division, Emery Adams, had been under strong pressure to rush through Cleveland's clearance before an up-to-date FBI investigation could be completed. Adams had protested to Boswell, but to no avail.

As Otepka picked up additional bits and pieces to add to Cleveland's file, he began to get a fairly clear picture of the Assistant Secretary's past. The picture was still somewhat murky in places. But Otepka had enough data by the time he was exiled from SY to convince him that he would never, under any circumstances, have approved a security clearance for Cleveland to even the least sensitive post in the Department of State.

James Harlan Cleveland, the man who later presided over the piecemeal demolition of NATO as U.S. Ambassador to that alliance, is a classic example of the patrician converted to collectivism. His father was the Episcopal chaplain at Princeton. His mother, Marian Phelps Van Buren, could trace her ancestry to the Republic's eighth President, and she had once been Dean of Women at Rollins College in Florida.

Cleveland was born in New York City on January 19, 1918, but spent most of his childhood in Madison, Wisconsin, where his father then served as chaplain at the state university. When he reached prep school age, young Harlan went east to Phillips Academy in Andover, Massachusetts. Graduated *cum laude* at 16, he entered Princeton that fall and soon plunged into the radical political activities that were to become his chief preoccupation for life.

Long before the word was coined, Harlan Cleveland was a peacenik. He was president of the campus Anti-War Society at Princeton and fought bitterly against the entrenched ROTC program. In his sophomore year he became one of the founders of the American Student Union, which was cited by a congressional committee as a Communist front. Cleveland claims he later disowned the ASU. He preferred, in those days, to style himself as a "socialist."[1]

Peacenik Cleveland was a big man on the Princeton campus. Many of his professors thought him "brilliant," if rather a bit erratic in his extracurricular activities. He was editor of a publication called *Bulletin*, which delighted in bombarding the University's administration with protests. The *Guardian*, a more stable Princeton paper, once named him "Man of the Week" and described him as "the leading campus leader to the leftward."[2] His Anti-War Society also won the plaudits of another magazine, *Champion of Youth*, official organ of the Young Communist League.

During the 1937 summer vacation, Cleveland and a group of his friends traveled to China and Japan on a "study tour." They were shepherded by Professor Robert Reischauer of Princeton, then an editor of the Soviet-Red Chinese propaganda and espionage vehicle, *Amerasia*. Dr. Reischauer was killed during a Japanese air raid on Shanghai, but luckily his student charges escaped injury. This incident must have solidified Harlan Cleveland's abhorrence of war. He never served in the armed forces during World War II, preferring to remain in civilian jobs throughout.

Picking up a Phi Beta Kappa key en route to his A.B., Cleveland graduated from Princeton in 1938 with high honors in political science. He had won a Rhodes scholarship too, and went off to Oxford hard on the heels of Walt Rostow, who was finishing up at Balliol that year. One of Cleveland's tutors was Harold Wilson, who later presided over Britain's final retreat from the stage of world power as Labor Prime Minister in the 1960's. The summer after Cleveland's arrival at Oxford, war broke out in Europe and, he says, "they told us all to go home." If it occurred to him to stay and help the British fight the Nazis, the thought was quickly smothered by his peacenik proclivities.

Back in the States, Cleveland acquired an "internship" in Senator LaFollette's Leftist-ridden office on Capitol Hill, courtesy of the National Institute of Public Affairs. By 1940 he had landed a job as a writer with the old Farm Security Administration, which was equally laden with members of the Far Left. His immediate supervisor was Jack H. Bryan, devoted member of several Communist fronts. Cleveland must have got on well with Bryan because he later recommended his old boss for a job in the Economic Cooperation Administration.

Bryan, however, was only one of a dozen or more security risks Cleveland personally sponsored at ECA when he became an executive there in the late 1940's and early '50's. One of Cleveland's proteges had been fired because he was reliably reported to be a member of the Communist Party, but the future Assistant Secretary of State pushed his reemployment anyway. He said the charges were baseless, and he vigorously defended other ECA friends dismissed or forced out on security grounds.

In July 1941, while working at the Farm Security Administration in Washington, Cleveland married the former Lois Burton. (They later became the parents of three children, two girls and a boy.) The following year he began his long romance with foreign aid as a staff member of the Board of Economic Warfare, great-granddaddy of ECA, AID, et al. The board was one of the five wartime agencies whose mass merger with the State Department inundated State with subversives in 1945. Cleveland stayed with the board through its first name change—to Foreign Economic Administration. Then, in 1944, after the Germans evacuated Rome, he was sent there as executive director, economic section, Allied Control Commission.

Although the Germans were eventually driven out of Italy entirely, that country remained the crucible of a bitter struggle that had raged all during the war years between Communist-led partisans and more democratic elements in the resistance. Cleveland's office supplied both sides indiscriminately, though there are some who claim the Communists got the lion's share of U.S. aid while he was in charge.

Cleveland remained in Rome until May 1947, serving the last year there as deputy chief of the UNRRA mission.* At that time, the UNRRA boss in Italy was Harold Glasser, a Harvard product later identified as a Soviet agent. A member of the Victor Perlo espionage ring

* United Nations Relief & Rehabilitation Agency.

in Washington, Glasser helped load UNRRA with countless Communist spies, including Henry Julien Wadleigh and David Weintraub. This group channeled hundreds of millions of dollars in American aid through UNRRA to Communist governments in Eastern Europe. They were also involved in the forced repatriation to the Soviet bloc of an estimated 2,500,000 refugees, many of whom were systematically murdered when they were shoved behind the Iron Curtain. Hundreds more, among them a large group of valiant Poles who had fought with Allied forces against the Germans in Italy, committed suicide rather than return to the unspeakable tortures that awaited them in their captive homelands.

When his work in Italy was done, the 29-year-old Cleveland journeyed to China to head up the UNRRA operations there. In Shanghai, he found his UNRRA office brimming over with Communists. If he felt uncomfortable with them, he never let on. At any rate, Cleveland strongly sympathized with their benevolent view of agrarian reformer Mao Tse-tung. And he unfailingly fought the Nationalists' attempts to keep UNRRA supplies, virtually all paid for by American taxpayers, from the Chinese Communists. Once he went so far as publicly to charge Chiang's government with a villainous "conspiracy" against the lives and property of Mao's legions.[4] But Mao's own Kremlin-supported conspiracy never seemed to trouble Harlan Cleveland.

When he returned to Washington for a visit, he testified before the House Foreign Affairs Committee. He was only mildly critical of the Kuomintang's efforts to keep UNRRA supplies from the Communist-controlled areas. For the moment, he adopted a "plague on both their houses" approach.

Helen Gahagan Douglas, the Congresswoman from California who was shortly to lose a Senate election to Richard Nixon, led Cleveland into a discussion of where the UNRRA aid went:

MRS. DOUGLAS: Were not some UNRRA supplies allowed to reach the military?

CLEVELAND: Some supplies and equipment from UNRRA were diverted to military purposes. We tried to stop that at every turn, and in some considerable measure we were successful. . . .

The same tendency was also evident in sending material into the Communist areas. The Communist relief organization had just as much difficulty fending off their military as the Chinese government relief organization had in dealing with their Nationalist military. If it were not for the terrible sufferings of the Chinese people under communism, and the millions of lives sacrificed to the kind of thinking Harlan Cleveland represents, this seeming naivete would be laughable in the extreme. How Cleveland thought he could keep the Chinese Communists from using his UNRRA supplies for war purposes, if indeed he thought it could be done at all, must stand as the epitome of ignorance, to put the most generous possible light on his actions.

Cleveland, at this same House Foreign Affairs Committee session, came forward with some other very strange views of the China struggle. He accused the Chiang regime of spurring inflation by spending "eighty percent of their national budget on civil war," and therefore for "nonproductive purposes." Minnesota's Walter Judd, who had served as a medical missionary in China and knew the true situation there probably better than any other member of the Congress, was somewhat startled by Cleveland's ideas.

JUDD: You believe that the only way to combat or overcome inflation would be to decrease the military expenditures

CLEVELAND: Yes.

JUDD: There are only two ways for them to decrease their military expenditures. One is to submit to Communist demands, the other is to carry on until they win, which will require assistance.

CLEVELAND: I think there is an intermediate path—to reduce the size of the Army, part of which is not fighting and contributing little or nothing to the war against the Communists, and make it a much more streamlined and much more efficient force.

Cleveland had managed to slide out of that one, though he did not explain how Chiang's embattled forces could be "streamlined" overnight while waging all-out war against a Soviet-backed horde that was soon to push them into the sea.

Cleveland managed to get out of China before Shanghai fell. Because he had done such a splendid job of getting UNRRA supplies to both sides, he was rewarded with a post in Washington as Director of the Economic Cooperation Administration's China program. In the capital, where aid programs had become a major State Department industry, Cleveland took up the torch for his many Far Left friends who were already being shoved out by the Truman Administration. Between times, he supervised U.S. aid to China, though it must be said that this was really being run from the Treasury Department, where Soviet spy Harry Dexter White and his crew were bravely calling the shots that killed off Nationalist China. When there was no more Chinese Republic to aid, except for the tattered remnant on Formosa, Cleveland once again shifted his attention to Europe, becoming Assistant Director for European aid in ECA's successor, the Mutual Security Agency.

In that same year, 1952, Cleveland's friend, Irving Swerdlow, was placed under charges as a security risk when he refused to resign decently. Despite Cleveland's later accusation that it was Harold Stassen, with his "extreme views" on security, who was responsible for Swerdlow's dismissal, the fact is that the charges were filed while Truman was still President and before Stassen took over under Dwight Eisenhower.

While helping ECA dispense Marshall Plan largesse to Europe (it was offered to the Soviet bloc too, but the Kremlin foolishly turned it down), Cleveland is credited with coining the now shopworn slogan, "revolution of rising expectations." However, the Republican election victory in November 1952 represented a revolution of temporarily shattered hopes for Harlan and hordes of his co-ideologues. Those of them who did not have Foreign Service status or Civil Service protection were swept from office, leaving behind privileged cadres who continued to nibble, termite-like, at the more firm foundations of U.S. policy. Cleveland had no difficulty finding a good job on the "outside." He wound up as executive editor, and later publisher, of *The Reporter*, an earnest fortnightly of respectable liberalism.

Almost as prolific as Walt Whitman Rostow, Cleveland concocted scores of articles and wrote, edited, or co-authored a half-dozen books over the next decade. Writing had always been his second love after politics. While still quite young he wrote for the pro-Mao *Far Eastern Survey*, a kept publication of the tainted Institute of Pacific Relations. *The Reporter* was at least several good cuts above IPR's propaganda organ, and after Cleveland left it in 1956 it showed an occasional tendency towards independence, at least insofar as international questions were concerned.

Cleveland's next way-stop was Syracuse University, where his old friend Irving Swerdlow also found shelter during the Eisenhower years. As Dean of the Maxwell School, Cleveland had jurisdiction over a broad range of graduate study programs, from anthropology to political science. From this lofty Ivory Tower he was able to propagate his peculiar beliefs, not only among impressionable students, but among more adult audiences in the world at large.

He had early been a champion of a world socialist state, and of the United Nations. Now, in articles with such titles as "Petty Americans" he attempted more subtly to subjugate the trivial concept of nationhood to the far more sublime ideals of one-worldism.⁵ Frequently, in a speech or article, he would attack that dangerous old devil, internal security.

Thus, with the arrival of the New Frontier, Harlan Cleveland was a logical candidate for an important post in the Department of State. Adlai Stevenson naturally wanted a compatible companion on Foggy Bottom to look after his U.N. interests, and he backed Cleveland for Assistant Secretary in charge of International Organization Affairs. True, the United States is officially a member of no less than fifty-one international organizations, and contributes substantially to twenty-two more. But the U.N. is top dog and Cleveland became, in effect, its Washington commissar.

As Arthur Schlesinger admiringly described his duties, Cleveland was "indispensable not just in working out our U.N. policy but in preserving communication and confidence within the eternal triangle of the State Department, the United States Mission in New York (U.N.), and the White House."⁶

Cleveland also developed into one of the Kennedy Administration's most verbose spokesmen on world affairs generally. He was a favorite on television panel shows and on the filet mignon circuit. Urbane, articulate, always ready with an answer to any question, he could be counted on to captivate uninformed audiences. Only occasionally did the old arrogance, noted by so many of his associates, flash through.

One of Cleveland's favorite themes (taken straight from Rostow) was the withering away of communism's totalitarian tendencies. As he put it, "We see new leaders of communism facing with realism the fact that their old dream of a Communist one-world is an obsolete and perilous delusion."⁷ This being the case, he advised Americans to shed "the illusion that foreign policy issues are comfortably two-sided."⁸

To help Americans rid themselves of *that* dangerous "illusion," Assistant Secretary Cleveland decided to set up an "Advisory Committee on International Organizations" under the all-forgiving aegis of the State Department. One avowed purpose of this group was to get more American citizens into jobs at the U.N. and the fifty lesser international bodies revolving, sometimes erratically, around that glimmering star. Another was to help channel more U.S. tax money into foreign aid programs administered by the U.N.

In his memorandum to Undersecretary George Ball, formally proposing the Advisory Committee, Cleveland took an interesting tack. He said it was necessary to staff U.N. posts with Americans in order to combat effectively Soviet subversive designs on U.N. agencies.[9] No one could quarrel with that. But, as we shall see, Cleveland really had a quite different goal in mind.

Not long after Otto Otepka's eerie interview with Harlan Cleveland on Irving Swerdlow and Alger Hiss, SY received a request for security clearances for members of the proposed Advisory Committee. Otepka was not surprised to find several old friends and supporters of Hiss on the committee. But since the objectives of the group coincided with the new policies of the Kennedy Administration, there wasn't much he could do at the outset.

Reluctantly, Otepka approved limited clearances for Cleveland's committee. First, however, he extracted a written pledge from the Assistant Secretary's office that the information handled by the group would be carefully controlled. Moreover, the committee was to serve in a purely non-paid consultant capacity and its members were not to become employees of the State Department. The clearances were good for just the first meeting of the committee. Members were not to receive building passes or have access to additional classified data until they had been fully investigated and cleared.

Before long Otepka learned that the committee's top order of business was to devise an end run around the State Department's security regulations in order to put more Left-leaning Americans to work at the United Nations. To do this, Cleveland and his team would have to reinstitute the procedures originally introduced by that great architect of the U.N., Alger Hiss.

Few Americans are aware of it, but Hiss was primarily responsible not only for drafting the U.N. charter, but for the massive infiltration of the U.N. by U.S. Communists. As we have already seen in the testimony of Carlisle Humelsine, Dean Rusk maintained Hiss's policy when he succeeded Hiss at the State Department in 1947. This policy actually encouraged the hiring of American citizens by the U.N. without any pre-appointment investigations by the U.S. government. It is estimated that Hiss and his brother Donald personally recruited more than two hundred people for U.N. jobs.

The Hiss-Rusk policy was scrapped by the Truman Administration only after a New York Federal Grand Jury and the Senate Internal Security Subcommittee disclosed the shocking colonizing of the U.N. by home-grown Communists and their flagrant collaboration with Soviet espionage agents. The subcommittee found, among other things, that there was "no safeguard whatever" against U.N. employment of Americans who were spying for Moscow in New York and elsewhere under the U.N.'s aegis.[10]

President Truman, and later Eisenhower, both issued executive orders forbidding the State Department to approve the U.N. employment of any citizen who had not first had a thorough background investigation and security clearance. An International Employees Loyalty Review Board was set up under the U.S. Civil Service Commission to handle the investigations with FBI help.

Trygve Lie, then Secretary General of the U.N., was as shocked as anyone by the Grand Jury disclosures, though he had long had his private suspicions about many of the Americans recommended for U.N. jobs by the Department of State. Lie made an agreement with the U.S. government, which was binding on his successors, not to hire any Americans who failed to receive Washington's approval. It was no more than the U.N. was doing, and would continue to do, for all other member states. One could hardly picture the United Nations taking on, for instance, a Soviet citizen, who did not have the full blessing of his government.

Senator Pat McCarran of Nevada, then chairman of the Internal Security Subcommittee, introduced a bill to add more legal weight to the agreement with the U.N. However, the State Department rushed to head off McCarran at the gap by solemnly assuring him and the Congress that the executive orders and the new International Loyalty Board would be more than sufficient to take care of the problem.

But in 1962 Harlan Cleveland's handpicked Advisory Committee decided to abrogate the Truman-Eisenhower policy and put Alger Hiss's back into effect. Otepka, after studying the composition of the committee, sensed what was coming. Once again his radar was functioning right on target.

CHAPTER **XV**

Alger's Friends

THE CLEVELAND ADVISORY COMMITTEE ON INTERNATIONAL ORGANIZATIONS held its initial meeting on July 25, 1962. Five days later, on July 30, a curious letter to the editor appeared on the editorial page of the New York *Times*. The letter suggested a solution to the very problem which so troubled the new Committee. It was signed by one Leonard Boudin, a lawyer for the American Civil Liberties Union who had fought many a legal battle for accused Communists. One of them was Judith Coplon, Justice Department "G-Girl," convicted, but never imprisoned, for trying to deliver government secrets to Valentin Gubitchev, the first in a long line of Soviet agents caught operating out of the U.N.'s skyscraper headquarters in New York. Boudin had also represented some of the forty security risks fired or suspended by the U.N. in the 1950's.

In his letter to the *Times*, Boudin blamed the "McCarran Internal Security Subcommittee" for the persecution of the dismissed U.N. employees. He argued that eleven of them who fought their firings had not been guilty of disloyalty to the United States. All they had done, Boudin said, was to decline to answer questions put to them by the Senate subcommittee, claiming their rights "under the First and Fifth Amendments." Boudin did not, of course, bother to mention that many of the

178

questions pertained to alleged membership in the Communist Party and espionage activities on behalf of the Soviet Union.

Sounding a timeworn refrain, Boudin questioned the "validity" of the subcommittee's authority. Moreover, he blasted both Presidents Truman and Eisenhower for having the audacity to issue executive orders "which screen, on political grounds, American employees of the United Nations and other international organizations." "Such screening," claimed Boudin, "is inconsistent with the (U.N.) charter's principle."

"The present administration [of John Fitzgerald Kennedy] would now score a major achievement," Boudin advised, "if it were to . . . eliminate its so-called loyalty program in the international field."

The day after Boudin's recommendations appeared in the *Times*, someone in Bobby Kennedy's Justice Department sent John Reilly a clipped copy with a scribbled note, "Jack, this is of possible interest to you." Reilly forwarded the clipping, with the note, to Otepka.

Reilly later swore—up, down and sideways—that Otepka had sent *him* the clipping. Apparently, he did not want the Senate subcommittee to know that it had come over from Justice and that both he and the Justice Department had been privy to the link between Boudin's suggestions and those that were soon to emerge from Harlan Cleveland's Advisory Committee.

For one thing, Leonard Boudin was no stranger to security people. Even Reilly admitted that he had known about him "for a long period of time." Otepka, for his part, was aware of the lawyer's connections with several members of Cleveland committee. Indeed, Boudin had mentiond one of them, Andrew Cordier, in his letter to the *Times*.

The close proximity in time of the committee's first meeting and Boudin's letter may have been a coincidence, of course. But Otepka thought it a rather strange one, particularly when he learned that the committee was going all out to implement Boudin's ideas.

However, before Cleveland and his committee could start repopulating the U.N. a la Boudin, they first had to obtain security clearances for the committee members themselves. This, in itself, was no small order. But Harlan Cleveland thought for a while he had the answer to that little problem. It would be a simple matter, he suggested through an aide, just to bring the whole kit and caboodle in on security waivers.

When Otepka got wind of this plan he moved quickly to stop it. He protested that the State Department had just recently decided not to issue any more waivers except in urgent situations. The decision had been made in the wake of Otepka's testimony and other Senate subcommittee findings on Secretary Rusk's wholesale abuse of the waiver system during his first year in office.

For once, Reilly supported Otepka, if only temporarily. In a memorandum to George M. Czayo, the Cleveland aide who had requested the waivers, Reilly flatly rejected by-passing regular security channels. Further, he noted that five of the people on Cleveland's committee "have data in their files developed by prior investigation that is not entirely favorable."[1]

At this point, in mid-September 1962, full clearances had been issued for only two of the Advisory Committee's ten non-government members —Francis O. Wilcox and Arthur Larson. A month later Otepka approved clearance for Sol Linowitz, chairman of the Xerox Corporation and a leading businessman-booster of the U.N. In November, a fourth committee member, Lawrence Finkelstein, was cleared. Although he had worked for the Institute of Pacific Relations into the 1950's Finklestein had won a modicum of recognition in recent years as a disarmament expert while laboring in Alger Hiss's old vineyard at the Carnegie Endowment for International Peace.

The other six members, all of whom merely held limited, one-time-only clearances for the July meeting, continued to function as full-fledged consultants on Harlan Cleveland's advisory team. It seems superfluous to mention that this ran directly contra to the written pledge Cleveland's office had made when the committee was formed. It is equally superfluous, as it was futile for Otepka, to point out that participation of the uncleared members was a brazen violation of State Department security regulations.

Cleveland ran no risk in ignoring regulations, however. He was confident that eventually he would get clearances for all the members of his consultant team. By then, of course, no one would remember that they had not been cleared all along.

Cleveland's confidence ultimately was justified. One by one his crew was smuggled aboard, much as he had been brought on board himself as a security stowaway at State in 1961. But some of them had to await Otto Otepka's final departure from SY before they received official sanction.

Because of the Senate subcommittee's curiosity about Cleveland's committee, several members did not receive final clearance for quite a long time. Marshall D. Shulman, associate director of Harvard's Russian Research Center and an academic thinker in the Rostow line, picked up interim approval in 1963 but waited until June 1965 for SY's full approval. Two others, Harding Bancroft of the New York *Times* and Andrew Cordier of Columbia University, similarly rode on temporary clearances until the final blessing was handed down in the summer of 1966.

Most of these people had been wheeling and dealing in international affairs for years. Bancroft, for instance, had been in the State Department until 1953 when he left to work for the International Labor Organization at Geneva. A few years later someone tried to bring him back into State. But when it became known that SY was judging him under the "reasonable doubt" strictures of Executive Order 10450, Bancroft's application was withdrawn and he subsequently wound up as executive vice president of the *Times*.

An admirer of Alger Hiss, Bancroft had frequently demonstrated his deep sympathy for Hiss's views. Loy Henderson, hardly an extremist in security matters, had once described Bancroft as "pro-Soviet" because, among other things, Bancroft strove desperately to have Soviet troops left in Iran after World War II.

Andrew Cordier, a short, stumpy bull of a man with a hawk-like nose and alert, ever-shifting eyes, was another old internationalist hand. An obscure professor at tiny Manchester College in Indiana until Alger Hiss tapped him for a job in the State Department, Cordier quickly blossomed into an expert on "international security." He and Hiss toured the country together, selling community groups on the desirability of a new and stronger international organization to replace the hapless old League of Nations. In 1945 Cordier worked with Hiss at the United Nations' founding meeting, over which Hiss presided in San Francisco. From there on his rise was spectacular. In short order he became Executive Assistant to the Secretary General of the U.N., in effect the great world body's No. 2 man. In the cool marble halls at the foot of 42nd Street, Andrew Wellington Cordier was known as Dag Hammarskjold's "left-hand man."[2] After Hammarskjold's death, he left the U.N. to become dean of Columbia University's school of international affairs. When the student riots at Columbia forced Grayson Kirk to resign in 1968, Cordier succeeded him as "acting" president.

Working hand in glove with Cordier on a number of U.N. projects was a New York lawyer named Ernest Gross. Like Cordier, Gross was selected by Harlan Cleveland to serve on his Advisory Committee on International Organizations.

Attorney Gross was well known in the more respectable Leftist circles. A leading Protestant layman, he was one of the key delegates to the World Order Study Conference of the National Council of Churches in Cleveland, Ohio, which first signaled the really massive movement to converge organized Christianity and Communism beginning in the late 1950's.

A lawyer for the National Labor Relations Board in its palmier days under FDR, Gross had become the State Department's legal advisor during the era of its most notorious earlier Communist infiltration. In 1949 President Truman named him Assistant Secretary of State for Congressional relations. The following year he became U.S. Ambassador to Korea, which in view of Gross's decidedly noncombatant personality may have encouraged the Communists to try their invasion in June of that year almost as much as Dean Acheson's notorious invitation. Later, Gross served as an alternate U.S. delegate to the United Nations until the Eisenhower Administration put him on ice in May 1953.

Retirement to private life did not, however, inhibit Gross's evangelistic efforts on behalf of the Left. From his paneled Wall Street law office he continued to work diligently for such causes as U.S. recognition of Communist China and a more polite approach to Soviet Russia. Through negotiation, Gross told an Arden House Conference at Harriman, New York, in the autumn of 1956, "we might induce in the Communist leaders a will to modify their present lawless course of behavior."[3] This prayerful plea was made less than two weeks *after* the Russians moved back into Budapest to crush the Hungarian rebellion. And it was accompanied by a strong recommendation from Mr. Gross for the government to stop "inflaming the public on the matter of possible recognition of Communist China."

One of the reasons Otepka cited for refusing to clear Cordier and Gross without full background investigations was their allegedly close friendship with Alger Hiss. Another was the tandem role they played in the Bang-Jensen affair.

Povl Bang-Jensen was the Danish diplomat driven from his U.N. post for refusing to turn over the names of more than 80 refugees who had testified secretly before the U.N. commission investigating the Hungarian revolution. Bang-Jensen maintained, in the face of excruciating pressures from Andrew Cordier's office, that to identify these people to the U.N. Secretariat would inevitably bring reprisals against their families in Hungary.

When the Dane did not yield to Cordier's bludgeoning, Cordier picked Ernest Gross to head up the committee that gave a transparently thin legal veneer to Bang-Jensen's dismissal. Not content with building merely a legal case, the Gross Committee openly branded Bang-Jensen as deranged.

J. Anthony Panuch, the former State Department security director who served for a time as Bang-Jensen's attorney, has summed up the Cordier-Gross juggernaut against the Dane in the most damning terms. "In my long years of government service," wrote Panuch, "I have never seen anything to approach the Gross Committee 'report' as a scurrilous and cowardly attack on one official of an international agency by his supposedly reputable colleagues, aided and abetted by an outsider [Gross]."[4]

On Thanksgiving Day 1959 Bang-Jensen's body was found in a Long Island park with a bullet through his head. Two years later the Senate Internal Security Subcommittee issued a report seriously questioning the New York Police Department's official verdict of suicide. The report made clear that it was not beyond the realm of possibility that Bang-Jensen had been murdered by Soviet agents. The motive? Mrs. Bang-Jensen, a widow struggling to raise five children, provided a clue in her subcommittee testimony:

He (Bang-Jensen) told me that there were several (Soviet) members of the United Nations Secretariat who would like to defect. They were unwilling to do it through the normal channels . . . *they told my husband that there was infiltration in the security agencies of the U.S. Government, in the CIA and in the State Department. . . . They asked my husband if he would take this information for them to the President.*[5]

Mrs. Bang-Jensen also said that the potential defectors offered to provide evidence of this infiltration at State and CIA. In addition, they intended to supply "evidence of some control of the 38th floor, which is the administrative offices of the United Nations, by Russians. . . ."[6]

Bang-Jensen never got an audience with the President. But before he died, he made a report to the FBI and also talked with Allen Dulles, Director of CIA. How much he told them is still unknown. But it *is* known that the intended defectors did not receive asylum and their evidence of Soviet control of the U.N. Secretariat was never delivered.

In 1963, the Cleveland Advisory Committee, carefully packed with such men as Andrew Cordier and Ernest Gross, predictably produced a report calling for a return to Alger Hiss's old policy of placing Americans in U.N. jobs without first subjecting them to those irksome field investigations by the FBI. The rationale underlying this recommendation was contained in a wordy foreword to the committee's report, sounding the old Rostowian theme, or a softly muted version thereof:

President Kennedy has set forth our primary objective of international organizations as the development of "a world community of independent [actually he had preferred the word *interdependent*] nations living together in free association and at peace with each other".....

It is against this background of strong U.S. support of international organizations as a basic tenet of foreign policy . . . that the Advisory Committee . . . makes this report on the staffing of international organizations.[7]

Harlan Cleveland's end run around the battered line of America's internal security structure almost came off. Almost, but not quite. The Assistant Secretary was tackled just short of the goal by linebacker Otepka. And when it was discovered that Cleveland was carrying Alger Hiss's deflated old ball under his sweatshirt, he promptly tried to bury the matter in full view of a mystified audience comprised of members of the United States Senate.

On Tuesday morning, March 19, 1963, the Senate subcommittee's wary scorekeeper, Jay Sourwine, started questioning Otepka about the Cleveland Advisory Committee's fast-charging tactics. With Senator Hruska presiding in Room 2300, Otepka explained that SY had not had jurisdiction over American employees at the U.N. since 1953, when President Eisenhower set up the International Employees Loyalty Review Board under the Civil Service Commission. However, Otepka said that he was "frequently consulted" on such matters.

Sourwine remarked that he wanted to "find out if Mr. Boudin's demand is having any effect." He asked Otepka if he knew "of any efforts to eliminate the clearance procedure for American nationals at the United Nations." Otepka conceded that he did. Under further questioning he said that he had come across a "formal document" (the Cleveland committee's original report) which recommended doing away with pre-appointment investigations for U.S. citizens being hired by the U.N.[8] He added that he had drafted a protest for Reilly's signature only a few days earlier.

The revelation that the Cleveland committee had officially recommended resurrecting Alger Hiss's old policy, which had riddled the U.N. with American subversives years before, sent the Senators into high dudgeon. The telephone lines between Capitol Hill and Foggy Bottom very nearly burned up that week. For a change, the State Department was forced to retreat.

By the time Otepka's boss, John Reilly, was hailed before the subcommittee a month later, Cleveland's Advisory Committee had performed some major surgery on its report. The offensive passages on doing away with pre-appointment investigations for Americans entering U.N. service had been delicately cut out. Reilly was almost proud to present a copy of the revised report to the Senators, giving them the courtesy of looking it over before it was officially released the following Monday, April 29. However, Reilly felt compelled to lie on at least a half-dozen different points pertaining to the report and to the Advisory Committee.[9]

In his eagerness to cover up the participation of Bobby Kennedy's Justice Department in the affair, Reilly stumbled all over himself. "I was not," he swore, "familiar with the position taken by Mr. Boudin in the New York *Times* letter until Mr. Otepka brought that article to my attention."[10] Unfortunately, he had forgotten that he routed the Justice Department note to Otepka along with the Boudin clipping.

There was more of the same. A lot more. But by now the Senators were getting a fairly good gauge of Mr. Reilly's veracity. If he had not attempted to smear Otepka as an incompetent and a hot-eyed zealot, the subcommittee might have let it go. The Senators had become a bit jaded listening to State Department fabrications over the past few years.

The original Cleveland committee report, which had precipitated much of Reilly's perjury, was a classic of sorts. The changing of the security rules was only one of the interesting tidbits it contained.

Demanding that the United States "alter its attitude toward the staffing of international organizations," the committee strongly urged that the business of "directing the execution of a single U.S. recruiting policy" be placed under Harlan Cleveland's office. Moreover, hiring czar Cleveland was to recruit "foreign nationals" as well as Americans "for service in international organizations."[11]

Further, the report demanded more "recognition" for Americans "contributing to international amity through service in international organizations." Translated, that particular passage could have cost American taxpayers, already shoveling out more than $300 million annually to the U.N. alone, additional millions in higher salaries and more liberal expense allowances for the internationalist bureaucracy. But the drain on the U.S. Treasury was not intended to stop there. The Cleveland committee also urged the U.S. to sponsor pay hikes "for all U.N. agency personnel," especially those working in aid programs.

The security overhaul was the part upon which all else hinged. When the Senators finally got a good look at it, they could hardly believe their eyes. The report went far beyond the elimination of field investigations. It recommended doing away entirely with clearances for federal employees transferring to the U.N. And on top of that, it would have thrown out the International Employees Loyalty Review Board, as per Leonard Boudin's suggestion. Moreover, it would have placed "all such [security] checks and investigations" under the State Department, which would then be "permitted to use any investigative agency it chooses"—thereby cutting the FBI out of the action too!

All this Otto Otepka had thwarted with his timely disclosure of Harlan Cleveland's master plan. The paragraph on security was exorcised *in toto* from the revised report the State Department finally released.

This was, however, the very last time Otepka was able to defeat the cabal bent on the destruction of effective internal security in the Department of State and all other government agencies. For by the time the Cleveland committee temporarily retrenched to avoid the wrath of Congress, Washington was already far into that sunny spring of 1963, and Otto Otepka's days in SY were fading faster than the blooms on the Japanese cherry trees around the Tidal Basin.

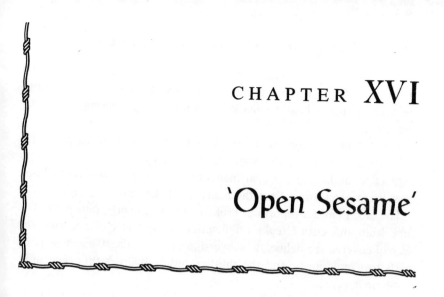

CHAPTER XVI

'Open Sesame'

IT IS, PERHAPS, ONE OF THE CROWNING IRONIES OF THE LONG STRUGGLE between totalitarianism and democracy that a group of United States senators sought to alert the nation to its rapidly deteriorating internal security at almost the precise moment that America was faced with its most critical public confrontation with the Soviet Union in the 1960's.

In October 1962, the Senate Internal Security Subcommittee, after nearly two years of exhaustive hearings, approved the release of its first report on the Otepka case and State Department security. Almost at once the report was smothered under the avalanche of alarming news erupting from Cuba.

The man who first sounded the alarm on the Soviet missile buildup on Cuba was Senator Kenneth B. Keating of New York. Two years later Keating was to be defeated in his campaign for reelection by Robert F. Kennedy. But in that autumn of 1962 the silver-haired Senator withstood the withering scorn heaped upon him by the Kennedy Administration and turned it into his finest hour, an hour which unfortunately his constituents soon forgot.

On the very last page of the subcommittee's 202-page report, Senator Keating referred in a special statement to the "breakdown" in the transmission of "vital intelligence to top echelon State Department officials" that caused the policy failure which permitted Fidel Castro's ascension to power. With an obvious eye on the massive Soviet attempt to transform Cuba into a bristling nuclear-weapons base, Keating regretfully remarked:

> There is no evidence that any steps have been taken to close this intelligence gap. On the contrary, the highly questionable security practices of the [State] Department described in the report suggest that we have not learned from the mistakes of the past.

The subcommittee report was broken into three overlapping parts. The first dealt with Otto Otepka's difficulties in the Office of Security; the second covered the deliberate subversion of law in the issuance of passports to Communists, and the third traced William Arthur Wieland's mysterious career.

State Department officials were sharply criticized for their handling of the Wieland matter, although Senator Dodd, loyal Democrat always, strained hard in that election year to exonerate President Kennedy and Secretary Rusk for their coverup of Señor Montenegro. However, even Dodd was almost rough on Rusk in a few places.

In a highly unusual move, the subcommittee demanded that Otepka be put back in command of the twilight war against subversives in the State Department, a war that had been suspended by tacit truce since Dean Rusk's elevation to Secretary of State. The report said: "The committee urges that, as a minimum, Mr. Otepka be restored to his former position of Deputy Director of the Office of Security, where his expertise, born of many years of highly responsible experience as a security officer, will be of inestimable value to the Department of State, and, not less importantly, to the security of this country."

Significantly, the report was unanimously signed by all nine members of the Senate subcommittee, five Democrats and four Republicans. Except for Dodd, all the Democrats were from the South—Chairman Eastland of Mississippi, Olin Johnston of South Carolina, Sam Ervin of North Carolina and John McClellan of Arkansas. But the Republicans represented a broad cross section of their party. In addition to conservatives Everett Dirksen, the minority leader, and Nebraska's Roman Hruska, there was the New York moderate, Ken Keating, and Hugh Scott, a Pennsylvanian increasingly identified with the most Liberal fringe of the GOP.

The Senators were particularly upset about Secretary Rusk's manipulation of security waivers. Rather pointedly, they singled out Harlan Cleveland's entry into State on a backdated waiver without even a rudimentary name check with the FBI or other agencies. However, the Senators revealed nothing of Cleveland's interest in "getting Alger Hiss back into government." Nor did they delve, even superficially, into the Assistant Secretary's many other attempts to protect and promote security risks.

The subcommittee was deeply disturbed, as it should have been, about a State Department effort to "monitor all contacts" employees had with the people's elected representatives on Capitol Hill. In a clumsy memorandum, Jack Kennedy's former White House aide, Frederick Dutton, had ordered that Department officials report "any meeting, telephone call, or social contact they have with members of the Congress or Congressional staffs."[1]

Dutton had issued the order in February 1962. But the subcommittee found out about it, and the State Department, at that time still somewhat sensitive to Congressional criticism, promptly rescinded the order when the Senators protested. (It was put back into effect at a later date.)

The Senate report reserved some of its most blistering criticism for the State Department's successful attempt to set itself above the law, the Congress, and even the Supreme Court in helping known Communists travel on U.S. passports. As knowledgeable Intelligence people had warned, this bit of arrogance actually made the United States an exporter of Communist revolution, especially to Asia, Africa, and Latin America.

Frances Knight, the petite but iron-willed Director of the Passport Office, played much the same role on this front that Otepka did in personnel security. And for her pains in striving to uphold the law she was harassed and buffeted about almost as callously as the man in SY.

Miss Knight had taken charge of the Passport Office in 1955. It had long been in a state of hopeless confusion, but Frances Knight, with the help of the Office's able general counsel, Robert Johnson, had introduced modern management methods, and in short order the shop was operating with surprising efficiency. The waiting time for most passports was cut from as much as a month, and sometimes more, to a few days.

Equally important, Miss Knight insisted on observing the law and regulations which forbade passports for members of the Communist conspiracy. Two Secretaries of State, Dean Acheson and Foster Dulles, had issued bans against the worldwide wanderings of American subversives. Moreover, the 1950 Internal Security Act was quite explicit in making it a *criminal* offense for any State Department official to issue passports to individuals who they had reason to believe were involved in Communist activities.

The Supreme Court, which has done its part in undermining internal security laws, complicated the passport ban with typically tortured rulings. In a 1958 decision it held that the right to travel was a basic American liberty which could not be denied without due process of law. Then, on October 10, 1961, it partially reversed itself by upholding the Subversive Activities Control Board order requiring the Communist Party to register as a subversive organization.

The Court's decision made it, among other things, immediately unlawful, under Section 6 (b) of the Internal Security Act, for a Communist to use a U.S. passport.[2] Any Communist could still sue through the courts for a passport, but in doing so he would necessarily expose his own and his comrades' underground activities. "At long last," the subcommittee report said, "it appeared the United States had a litigation-tested statute providing a method by which travel of Communist Party members could be curtailed."[3]

Amazingly, the Supreme Court decision was soon subverted, not by the Communist Party, but by a small group of State and Justice Department lawyers headed by Abram Chayes, Andreas Lowenfeld, Abba Schwartz, Nicholas Katzenbach, and Walter Yeagley. Personally approved by Dean Rusk on January 9, 1962, a new set of passport regulations drafted by this group gave Communists the right to "confront" the individuals who identified them as party members.

This had the effect, as the Senate report noted, of "nullifying the law and facing the U.S. government with the problem of either permitting the Communists and their attorneys virtually free access to the confidential files of the FBI, the CIA, and other investigative agencies, or issuing passports to Communists notwithstanding the prohibition now in effect."[4]

Frances Knight and the Passport Office were placed in the impossible position of being forced to grant passports to Communists even though she and her staff knew they were violating the law and could be subjected to criminal prosecution. When Miss Knight and Bob Johnson testified before the Senate subcommittee to this effect, their boss, Abba Schwartz, the new Administrator of the Bureau of Security & Consular Affairs, began a long campaign of harassment designed to drive them from their posts.

To cover the legal niceties, Chayes, Lowenfeld, et al., got Rusk to set up a new Board of Passport Appeals. The board was comprised of senior State Department officials who were under order to remain deliberately ignorant of the cases they were to pass on. In weighing each case, they were expressly forbidden to use FBI and other Intelligence files. All they could consider was the "public record"—newspaper stories and the like.

The board's intentional ignorance did not help Frances Knight out of her predicament. Whether she liked it or not, she had acquired considerable familiarity with the secret records of hundreds of undercover Communists. Now, however, she was compelled to *forget* her knowledge.

"As the issuing officer," Miss Knight told the subcommittee, "I am supposed to tailor my 'reason to believe that the applicant is a member of a Communist organization' to data which can be made public regardless of how much classified information is produced by the FBI or other agencies of government to the effect that the individual is a dangerous Communist. . . .

"I maintain that no one can do this in good conscience," Miss Knight went on. "This places me in a difficult position between the law and the government's expert legal advisors who interpret the law.

"*It is a fact that under the present regulations, the more treacherous and vicious and destructive the individual may be, the less likely it is that he will be denied a passport.*"[5]

Both Bobby Kennedy's Justice Department and Dean Rusk's Foggy Bottom brigade had implied through news leaks that the State Department was going to crack down on Communist travel. But Miss Knight charged in her Senate testimony that the public was being deliberately "misled." "There appears to be no realization," she said, "that the few (Communist) functionaries who may be caught in this very ineffective net are relatively unimportant."[6] As the subcommittee report pointed out, the really dangerous espionage agents have no public records which could be judged by Secretary Rusk's monastic board.

Abram Chayes thought Miss Knight was worrying herself needlessly about her dilemma. All she had to do, he contended, was to brainwash herself of her prior knowledge about Communist spies and saboteurs. "Brainwash" was not the word Chayes used. In fact he objected to it vigorously. But Roger Jones openly admitted it was possible to "brainwash" a person through "administrative order," and Jones, Chayes, and other State Department officials made it abundantly plain that is just what they wanted Miss Knight to do to herself.

Chayes maintained that "*a person who had acted under orders of a legitimate superior would not be committing a crime.*"[7] This, of course, was exactly the same rationale employed by Nazi underlings when they herded thousands of prisoners into the gas ovens at Dachau and Buchenwald. But the similarity didn't trouble Mr. Chayes, a former professor at Harvard Law School who had undoubtedly drilled his students in the same kind of amoral legal convolutions.

Besides, Chayes contended, it was the Secretary of State who was ultimately responsible for the new passport regulations, and if anyone was to be charged with violating the law, it would be he.[8] This was reassuring. No one really expected the Justice Department, which had to be the prosecuting agency, to bring criminal charges against Dean Rusk.

Although the Senate subcommittee didn't know it at the time, the man who had pushed most strenuously for by-passing the law via the ersatz passport regulations was the Attorney General, Robert F. Kennedy. Not only did he go all-out for bestowing U.S. passports on American Communists, Bobby also made it possible for foreign comrades to travel at will within the United States.

An admiring Arthur Schlesinger revealed Bobby's role in considerable detail in *A Thousand Days*. Bobby, Schlesinger says, was "active on questions of visas and travel restrictions. The basic immigration law excluded politically suspect aliens from the country unless a waiver could be secured from the Department of Justice. . . . *Robert Kennedy thought the system injurious to the national interest, granted waivers whenever the State Department asked for them and, if the Department hesitated, often spurred it on to make the application.*"[9]

Schlesinger adds that "the Attorney General also strongly supported the move within the executive branch to remove restrictions on American travel to China, Albania and other forbidden lands."[10] The people who first recommended lifting the passport limitations, according to Schlesinger, were Averell Harriman and George Ball, though they discreetly decided it would be wise to keep Cuba on the proscribed list for the time being.

But Bobby Kennedy "went even further than the internal State Department proposal and favored lifting restrictions on travel to Cuba as well," Schlesinger says. "It seemed to him preposterous to prosecute students who had a desire to see the Castro regime in action. 'Why shouldn't they go?' he once said. 'If I were twenty-one years old, that's what I would like to do this summer'."[11]

Though the late President Kennedy's ardent admirers might find it difficult to believe, Jack was just as strong as brother Bobby for the new open-door visa policy. As Schlesinger puts it, the President "was vigorously of the same mind." Jack told Abba Schwartz that he was "tired of the impression of the United States as a sort of police state, obsessed with security. . . . It continued to enrage him to read in the newspapers that a distinguished foreigner invited to the United States had been turned down by a minor consular official."[12] The White House, like State and Justice, invariably took steps to overrule the men in the consulates who were trying to uphold the law.

Jack Kennedy apparently preferred not to see that his position was analogous to inviting the termites to come on in and chew the house down, while at the same time loosing our own home-grown termites on the houses of all our neighbors in Latin America and elsewhere.

The effect of the Kennedy brothers' passport and visa policies was quickly felt in every country in the Free World and in the colonies and newly emerging semi-states of Africa as well. Terrorists like Holden Roberto, who with the alleged aid of Bobby Kennedy's friend Frank Montero had touched off the slaughter in Angola, were invited to use the United States as a base for their deadly activities. Lionized by American diplomats at cocktail parties in New York and Washington when he returned from his inhuman work in Africa, Roberto sought, and found, financial support in the U.S. for continuing his Angolan "war of independence" which in one day alone had butchered and maimed more than a thousand men, women and children, both black and white.[13]

American Communists were now free to reestablish fully their direct lines of communication with the Kremlin and with KGB-MVD agents all over the world. Admittedly, the passport restrictions had not always thwarted them, since they could keep in touch with Moscow via the Soviet bloc embassies in Washington, the various Communist delegations at the U.N. in New York, plus numerous other contacts in the underground. However, these diplomatic and netherworld contacts were frequently dangerous for espionage agents, since they subjected them to the possibility of surveillance by the FBI, the one U.S. agency they still feared. The FBI does not operate overseas except in the most cursory manner. Thus the Kennedys, under the influence of Abram Chayes, Abba Schwartz and the rest, helped make life a lot simpler for the growing army of domestic spies, saboteurs, and professional agitators dedicated to the destruction of the American society.

It would be impossible to calculate the mischief done by the relaxation of passport and visa restrictions in the 1960's. Only a fool would deny that this move did not give the Communists far better opportunities to plan, organize, and execute their multitudinous plots. Ostrich-like, the Justice Department insisted on obscuring the role of trained Communist guerrillas in the race riots that have to date afflicted some two hundred American cities, and have resulted in the sacking of large areas of Detroit, Newark, Los Angeles, and Washington. Similarly, American revolutionaries have traveled to Hanoi with impunity to plan "anti-war" activity and sedition on U.S. campuses.

True, riots may explode without Communist direction. But lacking expert organization, they certainly would not be nearly so devastating. Black Power gangs, some set up and financed by the Communists, proliferated, and it is no coincidence that this occurred after the lifting of passport and visa restrictions.

When Jack Kennedy waved his magic White House wand and murmured "Open Sesame" on visas to known Communist agents, he made it possible for them to swarm in from Latin America, Africa, and Asia to instruct their American comrades and countless dupes in the niceties of planned insurrection. Conversely, the subversion of the passport law made it relatively easy for unknown numbers of Americans to receive guerrilla warfare training in Cuba, Russia, and the Eastern European satellites. By mid-1968 Intelligence reports estimated that there were at least several hundred Black Power terrorists in training in Cuba, many of them members of the Peiping-backed Black Panther movement.

The public, hopelessly deluded by managed news from Washington, would believe that poverty alone was responsible for the riots. Honest Negroes know better. And so do the police and firemen caught in the expert crossfire of trained snipers shooting from rooftops and melting into the darkness when their hiding places are brought under return fire.

The immediate effect of the sabotaging of the passport law was that a goodly number of the 547 passports held by American Communists as of January 1, 1962, were to be given a new lease on legality, however dubious. Most of these passports had been issued initially after June 16, 1958, when the Supreme Court first reopened the door, in its Kent-Briehl decision, that it later slammed shut again.* The regulations drawn up by Andreas Lowenfeld, with the blessing of Abram Chayes and Abba Schwartz, and the collaboration of Bobby Kennedy and Nicholas Katzenbach in the Justice Department, stirred up a new wave of Communist applications for passports.

Frances Knight was now unable to revoke or halt the issuance of

* One of the litigants in this case was Rockwell Kent, the aging American artist who championed Communist causes for nearly a half-century, most recently the cause of the Viet Cong in the Vietnam War.

passports even to the most notorious Communist Party functionaries. When Miss Knight, acting under the authority she clearly had from the Supreme Court in its 1961 reversal, tried to lift the passport of that obese old Party *maman*, Elizabeth Gurley Flynn, Legal Advisor Chayes promptly overruled her. It was an act of plain humanity, you see. Miss Flynn was then in Moscow, making her last pilgrimage to the sacred shrine of Lenin. She died soon after, and was buried in the Kremlin wall with other heroes of the glorious revolution.

Meanwhile the United States was slowly discovering that it had left itself wide open to a sneak nuclear attack from the new Muscovite province ninety miles off the Florida coast. Not that Jack Kennedy *wanted* to acknowledge the threat, mind you. He would have much preferred to pretend it wasn't there, even after CIA chief John McCone told him in September that the Russians were up to something very dangerous in Cuba. But Senators Keating, Thurmond, Goldwater, and a handful of other alert members of the Congress were insistent that a missile threat did exist in Cuba, and it was getting more difficult every day for the White House to ignore them in that election season of 1962.

On October 14 McGeorge Bundy, the President's special assistant for national security, stated flatly that he knew, beyond the shadow of any doubt, that "there is no present evidence" and "no present likelihood" that the Cubans and the Soviets "would in combination attempt to install a major offensive capability " on Cuba. "So far," said Bundy, "everything that has been delivered in Cuba falls within the categories of aid which the Soviet Union has provided, for example, to neutral states like Egypt and Indonesia."

Yet five days before Bundy delivered his statement, U.S. Intelligence had provided the White House with photographs of Soviet IL-28 nuclear bombers parked menacingly on Cuban air bases. Moreover, a U-2 plane had earlier that day, October 14, snapped photos of a formidable complex of missile sites ringing the San Cristobal area of Cuba.

The public knew nothing of these Intelligence reports, of course. But they instinctively sensed something was wrong, and the pundits were predicting a Republican sweep in the November Congressional elections. All at once, Jack Kennedy reversed field. A full week after he first saw the U-2 photos of the missile bases, he interrupted a campaign swing through the Midwest and, pleading a cold, flew back to Washington.

The Russian Ambassador had been by to see Bobby Kennedy in September and had delivered a personal message from Premier Khrushchev for the President. Schlesinger tells us that 'tthe Soviet leader pledged in effect that he would stir up no incidents before the Congressional elections in November."[14] Now the Soviets came forward with more solemn assurances that they would never, never try to install nuclear weapons on Cuba.

Finally, on the night of October 22, the President went on television and in effect admitted that he had been dangerously misleading America for months. But now he was ready to make amends. He revealed that he had ordered an air-sea "quarantine" on Cuba. If nuclear missiles were launched from Cuba against any nation in the Western Hemisphere the United States would, he declared, make "a full retaliatory response upon the Soviet Union."

Everything ended happily, or so it seemed at the time. The Soviets were reported to have withdrawn their missiles, the Democrats retained control of both houses of the Congress, and John Fitzgerald Kennedy emerged as the strong, forceful young leader who had rescued his country and saved the world from a nuclear Armageddon.

Today, we know more exactly what happened. In 1967 both Nikita Khrushchev and Fidel Castro boasted that they had made a pretty darn good deal in the missile crisis. They got Kennedy secretly to declare Cuba a privileged sanctuary. And Khrushchev was delighted to accept the President's offer to remove U.S. Thor and Jupiter missiles from England, Italy, and Turkey in payment of a Russian missile withdrawal from Cuba, which to this day is still in doubt.

Jack Kennedy backed down on his demand for on-site inspection to make certain the missiles had been taken out of Cuba. He appeared satisfied that those monstrous objects, covered with tarpaulins, which were seen aboard the Soviet ships sailing back across the Atlantic were, in fact, missiles. But in May 1963, the Senate Preparedness Subcommittee, dominated by Democrats, reported that U.S. Intelligence officials "readily admit that in terms of absolutes, it is quite possible that offensive weapons remain on the island concealed in caves or otherwise." The Intelligence community could *not* guarantee that the missiles had ever been removed, the Senators said.

Chances are that some if not all of the 1962 missiles were removed. But there is strong evidence that they were later replaced—by more lethal types.* In August 1964, for example, Juanita Castro, disenchanted sister of Fidel, defected to Brazil where she told newsmen that "In Cuba there are long-range ballistic missiles which are well camouflaged." But

* A recently published book, *The Losers* by Paul Bethel (Arlington House, New Rochelle, N.Y.), covers the whole missile crisis.

Lyndon Johnson followed the Kennedy lead in deliberately blinding himself to these reports, though his Intelligence people, who had to feed their information to the President through Walt W. Rostow, *knew the reports to be true.*

Who stayed Jack Kennedy's hand at that critical moment in American history in October 1962? There were many people hovering over him, cautioning against precipitous action—Dean Rusk, Walt Rostow, Douglas Dillon, Adlai Stevenson, McGeorge Bundy, George Ball, a host of others. Robert Strange McNamara was the one who first seriously advanced the idea for a "quarantine" of Cuba rather than more drastic action. But according to Arthur Schlesinger it was Bobby Kennedy who ultimately won his brother over to this more "reasonable" approach:

> The blockade, the Attorney General concluded, would demonstrate the seriousness of our determination to get the missiles out of Cuba* and at the same time allow Moscow time and room to pull back from its position of peril. . . .
>
> In retrospect most participants regarded Robert Kennedy's speech as the turning point. . . . Someone observed that the United States would have to pay a price to get them out; perhaps we should throw in our now obsolescent and vulnerable Jupiter missile bases in Italy and Turkey. . . .[15]

Those "obsolescent" missile bases had only recently been installed at a cost of many millions of dollars to American taxpayers. They had been placed in Italy and Turkey—and England too—in direct response to yet another missile threat from the Soviet Union, which still has upward of 750 similarly "obsolescent" intermediate-range missiles aimed at England, Western Europe, and Mideast-Mediterranean targets. But the Kennedys were willing to scrap our Thors and Jupiters even *before* the Russians made any such demand. And the people around the Kennedys, many of whom could never have received a bona fide security clearance a few years before, were only too happy to "throw in" our IRBM bases as part of a bad bargain.

More than missiles were thrown in to appease the Soviets, though President Kennedy undoubtedly would have been shocked if he had known. It was not until September 1966 that the role played in the Cuban missile crisis by the courageous Russian colonel, Oleg Penkovskiy, was finally disclosed to the public.[16]

Penkovskiy, an MVD officer who "moved at the very peak of the

---

* A blockade, as Dean Acheson points out, does not serve to *remove* anything, but rather to prevent entry of troops or arms into a country.

Soviet power structure," was tormented by the knowledge that the Kremlin was building its nuclear forces for a possible first strike against the United States.[17] He realized that the American response would destroy a good deal of his own country too, and in 1961 he decided to warn the West of the Soviet's plans. Eventually, he made contact with British Intelligence through an English businessman, Greville Wynne, who traveled frequently to Moscow.

Colonel Penkovskiy tried to convince Britain and the United States that the only way they could save the world was to keep their strategic defenses strong. Ironically, his warnings came at the very time Rostow, Wiesner, and the rest were persuading the President to take America's first giant steps toward disarmament. Thus, the alarm he sounded went unheeded, if indeed it ever reached Jack Kennedy in unadulterated form.

Early in October 1962 when Kennedy at last decided to verify the Soviet's intentions in placing missiles in Cuba, he asked his Intelligence people if they could find out what the Kremlin was really up to. Through cut-outs, CIA contacted Penkovskiy in Moscow. According to *This Week* magazine, "Thirty-two hours later the answer came back: *Soviet nuclear forces not in a state of war readiness.*" On the basis of this information, the President made his move to "quarantine" Cuba, though it is plain that he could safely have taken much more positive action.

What the magazine could not know when it reported this incident in 1966 was that Oleg Penkovskiy sealed his own fate with this single Intelligence exercise. When CIA moved to contact him, two men in the agency, men who had not previously been privy to Penkovskiy's identity, got hold of his name. On October 22, the same day President Kennedy made his televised speech announcing the Cuban "quarantine," Penkovskiy was arrested by the KGB in Moscow and ten days later Greville Wynne was kidnaped in Budapest and whisked off to Lubianka Prison. They were tried the following May in Moscow, and Wynne, who has since been released, is convinced Penkovskiy was executed.

This tragic espisode lends a great deal of credibility to the fears expressed by many about Soviet penetration of the CIA and other U.S. Intelligence agencies. Frank Gibney, the editor of *The Penkovskiy Papers*, makes it clear that Penkovskiy had reason to believe he was under surveillance by the KGB before the Cuban missile crisis.[18] But Gibney apparently had no way of knowing that Penkovskiy's cover was in all likelihood blown by people within the CIA. Nor is this the only incident of its kind on, or more precisely off, the record.

With the Cuban missile crisis, the United States may well have lost its ultimum opportunity to turn the tide against communism short of nuclear war. Lyndon Johnson, Walt Rostow, Dean Rusk, Robert McNamara, and all the others kept telling us into 1968 that Vietnam was the place where America could reverse the "last" (to use Rostow's word) great onslaught of totalitarianism. But Oleg Penkovskiy, who gave his life in an effort to save mankind, knew where the last great battle would really be fought, if he knew not when. Otto Otepka, who knew very well where all the interim preparatory wars were being waged, was moved to bow his head in respect for the courage of yet another casualty sacrificed on the bloody altar of political expediency—an expediency that refuses to recognize where the Soviets are pushing in this climactic era of what they openly refer to in the USSR as the "final phase" of the world struggle.

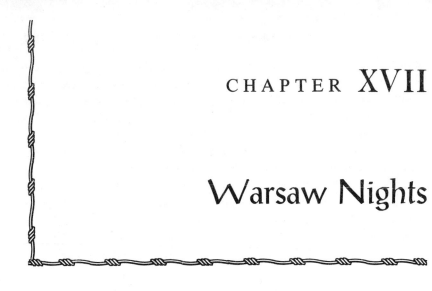

CHAPTER **XVII**

Warsaw Nights

On a brisk morning early in March 1963 a bewildered little man with sandy hair and frank brown eyes appeared in Otto Otepka's office at the State Department and introduced himself. He was George Pasquale, an electronics engineer who until a few weeks before had specialized in ferreting out wire tap devices placed by the Communists in American embassies in Europe.

Although he had only worked for the State Department for fourteen months, Pasquale had a rich background in electronics stretching back to his boyhood in Kansas City. As a youth he worked in North American Aviation's test flight division and during World War II he had flown all over the world as a communications expert with the Air Transport Command. For fifteen years after the war he had been a flight radio officer for Trans World Airlines, chalking up more than four million miles in the air, mostly on TWA's cross-Atlantic runs to Europe.

Five years earlier Pasquale had left TWA to start his own radio-electronics shop in Silver Spring, Maryland, a suburb of Washington. His business had thrived and he soon moved it to a larger store in Wheaton near Otepka's home, although until that March morning the two men had never met.

In 1961, taking John Kennedy's advice literally, George Pasquale asked himself what he could do for his country. By October of that first year of the New Frontier, Pasquale finally found an answer. He turned over his business to a partner, taking care to keep a share for himself against a rainy day, and accepted a job with the State Department at the Office of Security's post in Frankfurt, Germany.

Pasquale's work for SY was more than satifactory. Even John Reilly gave him a complimentary pat on the back during a visit to Frankfurt in the autumn of 1962. Now, less than six months later, Pasquale was out of a job, summarily fired for mysterious reasons never fully explained to him. It was the first time in his life that he had been dismissed from any position, and it troubled him deeply. He couldn't help but feel that it was all connected somehow with that trip he had made to Warsaw the previous spring.

As Otepka listened, Pasquale unburdened himself of a strange story about one of the weirdest characters ever to prowl the precincts of Foggy Bottom—Elmer Dewey Hill. In January 1962, Hill had joined the Department of State as an electronics expert. Within a matter of months, he had been elevated into a lofty position as chief of SY's worldwide wire tapping (and counter-wire tapping) operation, the euphemistically named Division of Technical Services.

When Pasquale came to see him, Otepka had no inkling that Elmer Hill would shortly play a major role in his life. His interest in Elmer at that time was purely professional, not personal. As the official still nominally charged with primary responsibility for the issuance of security clearances to State Department personnel, Otepka found Pasquale's tale quite fascinating.

There were certain details about Elmer Hill's meteoric rise in SY that intrigued Otepka even before Pasquale popped into his office. Hill had been an obscure research assistant at Stanford University before he arrived on the State Department scene. He had been described to Otepka as a bona fide beatnik, and this seemed to be no exaggeration. When he first came to the Department, Hill delighted in slopping around in old sneakers, sans socks, and his blue jeans looked as though he had slept in them for months. He sported a wispy beard, of which he was inordinately proud, and he shaved his head shiny clean. Everyone thought he was emulating Yul Brynner with the shaved-head bit, but Pasquale discovered in Warsaw that Hill had someone else in mind.

Hill's bald beatnik act did not, however, retard his progress in the once staid old Department of State. His security clearance was "expedited" by the private little extra-legal evaluations group William Boswell had set up in his office. When Jack Reilly came to SY he took an almost paternal interest in Elmer's career and kept part of Hill's security file under lock and key in a drawer of his desk.

Just before his rapid promotion, Elmer Hill flew to Europe on a memorable junket, and that is where George Pasquale first encountered him. Hill arrived in Frankfurt on Holy Thursday, April 19,1962. That night, the chief of SY's post in Frankfurt, Frederick Sullivan York, tossed a cocktail party in Hill's honor. Pasquale escaped this Continental debut of his future boss, but York and his parents, who were visiting in their son's home, later described it to him in vivid detail.

According to Pasquale, the Yorks told him that Hill got rather more than politely gassed at the party. As the evening wore on, they said he stripped down to trousers and tee-shirt, started screaming obscenities at the other guests, and finally passed out on a couch. He disappeared sometime during the night after the Yorks had gone to bed. At noon the next day he called the SY post in Frankfurt and asked directions on how to get there.[1]

Good Friday passed without recorded incident, but the following day Hill and Pasquale flew to Warsaw on a "technical inspection." The U.S. embassy security officer, Victor Dikeos, threw another party for Elmer that night, and the guest of honor graced the gathering with a repeat performance of his Frankfurt floor show, with some additional embellishments, including an inebriated lecture on the glories of socialism and the saintly qualities of Nikolai Lenin.[2]

A few nights later, Hill dined with Pasquale at a Warsaw nightclub appropriately called the *Krokodil.* Pasquale claims that Elmer had polished off a bottle of sherry in his hotel room and was already wobbly when they were seated at their table on the edge of the *Krokodil's* dance floor. More wine flowed at dinner and Hill, by Pasquale's sober estimate, also got through half a bottle of cognac.

At one point, when the orchestra took a break, Hill summoned the *maitre de* and got permission to put on a little recital. Pasquale says his bearded companion, shaved head glistening in the spotlights, sat down at the piano and held his hands aloft until an expectant hush fell over the whole room. Having captured the attention of his audience, Elmer then proceeded to pound the piano unmercifully, without even an attempt to coax out a tune. The unmelodic, but undeniably deafening, pounding continued for what seemed to Pasquale like fifteen minutes, though his embarrassment may have made time slow to an uncomfortable crawl. A large party at the next table from the British embassy looked as embarrassed as George felt, and several of them cast discreetly pitying glances in his direction.[3]

When maestro Hill had finished his hammer and anvil concerto he rose unsteadily, bowed elaborately, and staggered back to the table. No one applauded, but that did not deter Elmer from going on with his act. Minutes later, after the orchestra returned, he barged in on a party of Poles seated nearby, fetched a blonde woman from her escort's side, dragged her to the dance floor and attempted a stumbling polka. The dance ended, and they made it back to the woman's table. An altercation followed between the blonde and a Polish male who had wandered in, and the management obligingly tossed the man out on his ear.[4]

Pasquale finally managed to get Hill out of the *Krokodil* and back to the hotel. But the following night there was more of the same when they dined at the Dikeos' apartment with several other Americans, including Frederick Galvin, a security engineer just arrived from Frankfurt.

The worst, however, was yet to come.

One morning toward the end of his soggy stay in Warsaw, Hill left the hotel with Pasquale to walk the few blocks to the embassy. The Communist regime was preparing for the upcoming May Day celebration, and banners and bunting had begun to appear along the streets. Near one large intersection a gigantic portrait poster of Lenin had been hoisted. When Hill spotted it he stopped abruptly. Pasquale went on a half-dozen steps before he missed him. Turning, he was surprised to see Hill standing reverently under the poster, gazing in adoration at Lenin's portrait, and fondly stroking his own beloved beard.

Within a few minutes, a curious little crowd gathered around Hill. Most of them could tell from his clothing that he was an American, and they were plainly stunned by his behavior. Several shook their heads in open disgust. But most of them just looked on in stoic silence. Pasquale edged his way to Hill's side and quietly tried to persuade him to leave. Hill shook his head. Although he maintained a solemn expression, he was obviously enjoying himself immensely. Out of the corner of his mouth he told Pasquale, with ill-concealed pride: *"They are all staring at me because I look so much like Lenin."*

Pasquale, a mild-mannered man with a usually inexhaustible sense of humor, almost lost his patience. His first inclination was to stalk off and leave Elmer basking in his fool's glory. But he felt a certain responsibility for the unpredictable Mr. Hill and he was naturally shamed to see a fellow American making such a spectacle of himself. Then, too, he could not help but pity the poor Poles. He knew that the great majority of them secretly hated their Communist oppressors and looked to America for their ultimate deliverance. What, he thought, must these people be thinking? The crowd was ominously silent, but Pasquale heard a few people muttering under their breath, and several were beginning to glower dangerously at the Yankee Lenin.

At last, Pasquale prevailed upon Hill to end his fatuous pantomime. With a show of reluctance, Elmer permitted himself to be led away, though not before pointing several times at the Lenin poster and at his own shaved head and beard, just to make certain no one missed the resemblance.

In between Hill's binges, Pasquale tried to get him to bear down on their job, which was to probe for hidden wire taps, both in the old U.S. embassy and in the new one then under construction at 31 Ujazdowska Street. Pasquale maintained that the only way to find concealed transmitters was to search behind the walls. But Hill insisted that the new electronics detection gear he had brought from Washington could ferret out any taps without going to all that trouble. Adamantly, he refused to probe the walls. Later, on this same tour, Hill conducted a similar "inspection" of the American embassy in Moscow.

As the world now knows, both the Warsaw and Moscow embassies were subsequently found to be literally wired for sound, from the basements to the roofs. A team of Seabees was forced to tear apart some thirty rooms in the new Warsaw embassy in 1964. They unearthed more than forty microphones in the walls, some inserted in hollowed concrete blocks imported from our Marxist "ally," Yugoslavia. The wiring had evidently been installed at a very early stage of construction, before Hill came to Warsaw.

The Moscow embassy, an older building rented from the Soviets, had hidden microphones everywhere, even in the great seal of the United States which hangs in the ambassador's office. The State Department admitted that the taps had been put in place when the structure was renovated by Russian workers before our diplomats moved into it in 1953. Thus, for more than a decade the KGB had direct lines into America's most sensitive embassy abroad.[5]

William Crockett, Deputy Undersecretary of State, testified before the House Appropriations Committee in 1965 that "there is always the obvious question . . . whether we got all" the microphones.[6] In the era of détente, there remained, however, a more serious question, namely, what difference did it make? The conversations the KGB tuned in on at our Moscow and Warsaw embassies probably didn't provide information anywhere near as important as the Kremlin received through extra-diplomatic channels straight from Washington.

Then, too, without resorting to wire taps the Communists are in an excellent position to pick up intelligence in all U.S. embassies behind the Iron Curtain. More than half the people employed in those embassies are "locals"—Russians, Poles, Czechs, and other indigenous individuals—hired right off the street with the blessing of the secret police. In Moscow, for example, the American embassy telephone operator during the 1960's was a Russian woman who jealously guarded her little cubicle. She strongly resented it when Americans occasionally poked their heads in to pass the time of day.

Thus, if Elmer Hill had taken George Pasquale's advice that Easter week of 1962, by no means all the security leaks in our Warsaw embassy would have been plugged up. There were other kinds of leaks, too—leaks of a much more serious nature than electronic listening devices or the occasional pilferage of information by "locals," as we shall soon see.

A few days after Elmer's public impersonation of Lenin, Pasquale was relieved to learn that Hill had decided to leave Warsaw. Happily, Pasquale was working on the installation of a "secure room" at the embassy and was obliged to stay behind.

But instead of continuing on to Moscow, as mapped out in his official itinerary, Hill announced that he was going to backtrack to Prague. No one at the embassy thought he could get a visa to Czechoslovakia for at least several weeks, however, and for a time Pasquale thought he was going to be stuck with Hill indefinitely. At that time, unless visas to specific Communist Bloc countries were obtained before one left the States or another point of origin, it could take as much as a month to get one behind the Iron Curtain. Miraculously, Elmer Hill got *his* visa almost overnight from the Czech embassy. Pasquale bid him goodbye, politely, but with an exhilarating sense of release.

When Pasquale returned to Frankfurt with Fred Galvin the first week in May, their boss, Fred York, asked them to write reports on Hill's exotic behavior in Warsaw. York, still smarting from the memory of the party at his home, told them he was filing a full report on Hill with Washington. Pasquale and Galvin were a bit dubious. They had picked up scuttlebutt that Hill was about to be promoted to head SY's Division of Technical Services and they raised the question about what would happen to them if Hill became the big boss and got hold of their reports.

But York was insistent. He instructed them to write their reports in informal out-of-official-channel letters, and he sent them off to Washington.[7]

Ten days later York showed Pasquale and Galvin a letter from headquarters demanding more information. Acting under York's orders, they sat down and drafted new letters giving more details on Hill's escapades. After that, the whole thing subsided into silence. Two months went by. Then, early in the summer, Elmer Hill was elevated to chief of the State Department's worldwide "electronics" operations.[8]

In Frankfurt, Fred York was incredulous when he heard the news. He expressed amazement that Reilly could have approved Hill's promotion. But he soon made the bureaucrat's typical adjustment to unforeseen situations.

When Reilly visited Europe that October with SY's Raymond Laugel in attendance as his aide, York and his co-chief of the Frankfurt post, Edwin Hiller, feted them at a gala reception in the "Blue Room" of a local casino. It was quite an affair. SY people from all over the Continent converged on Frankfurt to pay homage to their overlord from Washington. One, the security officer from an American embassy in the Balkans, showed up with his fiancée, a lovely Yugoslav suspected of being an agent for the Communist apparat.

York waited for a chance to mention the reports on Elmer Hill to Reilly. He didn't get to it at the Blue Room party but he raised the matter in a private conversation at his apartment. Mrs. York later told Pasquale that Reilly just shook his head and replied: "I cannot have anything happen to that man. I will have to disregard the reports completely."[9]

Pasquale had a private chat with Reilly too, but he did not bring up Elmer Hill. They simply talked about Pasquale's work, which Reilly said was perfectly fine. A few weeks later George received a raise. In mid-December, however, he heard that Edwin Hiller had filed a derogatory efficiency report, complaining that his work was unsatisfactory. Hiller did not actually *write* the report. His wife did. But it undoubtedly reflected Hiller's, or rather Hill's, desire to get George Pasquale out of the way. At a cocktail party (one begins to wonder what *else* they do in Frankfurt!) Mrs. Hiller openly boasted about what fun she had doing the efficiency reports on the people who worked for her husband.[10]

Seeing the axe coming down on his exposed neck, Pasquale flew to Washington at his own expense late in December to head off his impending dismissal. He tried to see Reilly but was shunted off to David Belisle. Pasquale told Belisle and Joe Rossetti, Jack Kennedy's former aide, about

Elmer Hill's excursion to Warsaw and they pretended that it was all brand-new news to them.[11]

Receiving assurances at SY that he had nothing to worry about, Pasquale took a plane to Frankfurt and went back to work. Less than six weeks later he received the official notice that he was being fired. He made the mistake of signing a "resignation" when Peter Szluk, a State Department personnel officer, suggested it would be easier for him that way. It was made clear that he would be blackballed with future employers if he didn't sign.[12]

Pasquale, having been on the Foreign Service reserve payroll less than a year-and-a-half, had no appeal rights, which is probably why he was singled out for reprisal for having reported Elmer Hill. Fred York had tenure and, as a long-time Foreign Service officer, he also had friends. Galvin may have been considered just an innocent and harmless bystander. So Pasquale took the rap. It was to be nearly five years before he again found regular employment, as a radio officer on cargo ships carrying arms to Vietnam.

In January 1968 when the Senate subcommittee got around to releasing its long-delayed second report on the Otepka case, it told why Pasquale had been fired. The subcommittee said that "the key factors" in Pasquale's separation "point in one direction: to the use of State Department machinery and personnel to get rid of him because he had reported on the misconduct of Elmer Hill."

Otto Otepka was interested in Pasquale's tale for a number of reasons. The Elmer Hill business was only one. Otepka had been having trouble with the security situation at the U.S. embassy in Warsaw for several years, and he questioned Pasquale closely about some of the American personnel there. Irving Scarbeck, an embassy official, had been convicted only four months earlier for delivering information to the Communists through his Polish mistress. But Otepka knew that Scarbeck was merely one of a half-dozen State Department security risks laboring in Warsaw. The others had never been exposed.

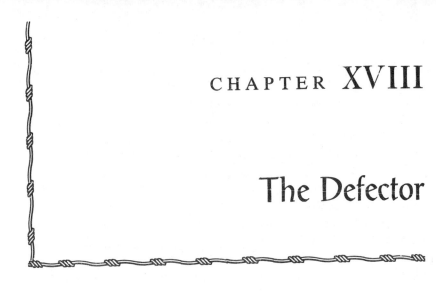

CHAPTER **XVIII**

The Defector

ALL DURING THE 1960's WARSAW WAS THE SITE OF CONTINUING "INformal" talks between American and Communist Chinese diplomats. Thus, the U.S. embassy there was rated second in importance only to Moscow among all State Department missions abroad. It was a natural high-priority target for Communist penetration, and no doubt the Soviets and Chinese, always eager to cooperate closely in espionage enterprises, long ago entered into a lively competition to see which could poke the biggest holes in the naive Americans' security screen. As usual, the Russians got there firstest with the mostest.

As early as 1959 Otepka began to get a pretty clear picture of what was going on in Warsaw. His first reliable evidence that the embassy, then under the aegis of a career ambassador named Jacob D. Beam, had been seriously penetrated came one day that summer when he was invited to the office of Loy Henderson, the Acting Secretary of State. With Henderson were two ranking officials of "the Agency," alias CIA.

The CIA men unraveled an intricate story that plainly stunned Loy Henderson and came very close to shocking the unshockable Otepka. They reported that an anonymous "defector-in-place" within the Communist secret police had identified several key American officials at our Warsaw embassy as Soviet agents. Henderson and Otepka were warned not to move against these officials for fear of endangering the informant. The agency hoped to get more intelligence from "our man in Warsaw." The data already received had been checked out and proved accurate. During the meeting in Loy Henderson's office the CIA men handed Otepka a top-secret document listing the names of those involved, emphasizing again that no action was to be taken unless CIA gave him the green light.

The agency's request was scrupulously honored. Otepka kept his promise not to investigate the men named until he heard further from CIA (which he never did), and the officials were permitted to complete their normal tour of duty in Warsaw. By that time the Kennedy Administration had taken over and Otepka was powerless to act. One of the diplomats exposed by the defector was reported to have been an agent of the KGB for eighteen years. When he returned to the States from Warsaw he was assigned to the U.S. Information Agency, which he had actually worked for all along, his State Department affiliation being merely a cover. Otepka informed the USIA security officer of the accusations against the man (CIA had never bothered to tell USIA), and he is said to have been interrogated at some length. Not long after this he was allowed quietly to resign.

A second Warsaw embassy official identified by the mysterious defector as a long-time Soviet agent was later claimed by the CIA as "one of our own." Neither of the high-ranking agency officials who talked with Otepka and Henderson indicated anything of the kind, and it is likely that they would have under the circumstances. But with CIA's protection this man continued to receive promotions in the State Department while allegedly working for the agency. In the late 1960's he was serving as U.S. consul in a large Canadian city.

There was a third official at the embassy in Warsaw who was initially identified as having cooperated with Soviet Intelligence. This case turned out to be similar to the second in that CIA claimed this official too, although in this instance he was actually known to be an agency man.*

Another American official in Warsaw was not known to be working for the Soviets, though the defector said he might as well have been. He was the security officer at the embassy and although nominally under SY's jurisdiction he was, like all overseas security men, a member of the

---

* The confusion in whether a given official is actually on State's payroll or CIA's derives from the common practice of giving CIA people a State Department cover when they work out of embassies abroad. The cover is often transparent, but the fiction has to be maintained, although a casual perusal of the State Department "Biographic Register" makes it child's play to pick out the agency men because the background information on them is almost always so scanty.

Foreign Service Corps. Way back in 1956 Otepka had tried to get this man removed when he admitted homosexual acts. But Otepka was overruled by the Department's Legal Advisor, who held that such acts did not constitute misconduct. The man continued to move up the ladder at State and by 1968 occupied an important post in the Orient.

It was during this man's tour as security officer in Warsaw that our embassy was thoroughly penetrated. The CIA people told Henderson and Otepka that three American code clerks had been compromised by Polish girls working for the Communists, and there was a good chance our code had been broken.

On top of that, ten of the Marine guards stationed at the embassy had been implicated. Not that their loyalty was in question. They had simply proved easy prey for the girls, all prostitutes on the secret police payroll, who made the embassy their headquarters, coming and going virtually at will. The defector reported that the girls had turned over valuable embassy documents to their Communist masters.

One case disclosed by the defector was particularly tragic. It is almost a parable of our time in that it reveals the evil lengths to which the Soviets will go to achieve their goals. It seems that the wife of a perfectly loyal American diplomat in Warsaw had an affair with a Russian agent on a visit to Moscow. The KGB made tape recordings and photographs of the tryst and then deposited a large sum of money in a Swiss bank in the husband's name.

When these complicated arrangements had been completed, the KGB contacted the husband and threatened to identify him as a Soviet spy unless he went to work for them. They informed him that they would reveal the existence of the bank account and send the lurid photographs and recordings of his wife's Moscow escapade to his superiors if he refused to cooperate. In this case, the Soviets miscalculated the strength of their target. The diplomat apparently never wavered. He went to the American ambassador and laid out the whole sordid plot. But one must wonder how often the KGB has attempted similar blackmail on weaker subjects.

The "Polish defector," as he was called in Intelligence circles, claimed after his escape to the West that the Irving Scarbeck case was a deliberate diversion created by the Soviets to take the heat off more serious security risks in our Warsaw embassy. The defector did not identify Scarbeck. He says the Soviets did that.* If so, it would not be the first time the KGB

* The defector later claimed he never said this, but this retraction was made in 1968, by which time he was embroiled, as we shall see, in a many-sided battle either to discredit himself or completely confuse U.S. Intelligence.

has "surfaced" one of its people to distract attention from more important operations. Moreover, it is exceedingly strange that Scarbeck's bewitching Polish mistress, Urszula Maria Discher, was gratuitously produced by her Communist employers to serve as the chief witness against her lover at his trial in Washington.

The individual identified to Otto Otepka and Loy Henderson in 1959 as "our man in Warsaw" turned out to be Colonel Michal Goleniewski, perhaps the most mysterious product of the never-ending struggle between East and West. More than a year before Otepka learned of Goleniewski's existence, a strange figure made contact with U.S. Intelligence under the cover name *Heckenschuetze*, "protector of little fowl." Still later he was to change it to "Hercules."

The first contact was effected early in 1958 when a packet of letters was tossed over the wall of the U.S. embassy in Berne, Switzerland. Delivered to Ambassador Henry J. Taylor, the packet was found to contain a sealed envelope addressed personally to J. Edgar Hoover. Goleniewski later said he singled out Hoover because the FBI was the only American agency the Soviets had not been able to penetrate. He failed to reckon, however, with the rigid protocol of the American bureaucracy. Since the matter of *Heckenschuetze* was clearly outside the geographical limits of the United States, Ambassador Taylor was forced to turn the whole thing over to CIA, ironically the agency this informant feared most.

Making his future contacts through a complicated system of "cutouts," over the next thirty-three months Goleniewski provided America and its Allies with information far more important than the revelations about the diplomatic love nests in Warsaw. In all, he is said to have "identified several hundred KGB operatives in Europe, the United Kingdom and the United States."[1] It is claimed that his tips led to the arrests and convictions of members of at least two important espionage nets in England, the spy ring that had penetrated the Admiralty and another within British Intelligence. These and other similar claims attributed to Goleniewski are in all likelihood vastly exaggerated. However, the cases credited to him are, in themselves, all authentic and it is interesting to review them briefly as examples of the far-reaching activities of Moscow's *apparatchiks*.

The spies caught in Britain, for example, included the classic case of the "sleeper" agent cited by Otepka in his Senate testimony—George Blake, the M16 double agent whose own wife remained blithely oblivious to his dual role. According to Dame Rebecca West, Blake was really a

Dutch national named Behar and the descendant of a wealthy family of Sephardic Jewish bankers long settled in Egypt.[2]

The Admiralty ring was comprised of as motley a crew of misfits as ever slithered down treason's trail. One of them, Harry Houghton, had worked in the British embassy in Warsaw until his carousing proved too much for even the tolerant Britons and he was posted home. Promoted upon his return to a much more important job in the Admiralty's Underwater Weapons Establishment at Portland, Houghton took up with a spinsterish fellow employee named Winifred Gee, who was only too happy to help him spy for the Communists. Another couple, legitimately married, were outside couriers for the Admiralty ring. They were Peter John Kroger and his wife, Helen, who were known to the FBI as Morris and Longa Cohen, formerly of New York. The Kroger-Cohens had been hiding out in Britain and other way-stops since their precipitous flight from America, where they had done yeoman service for the Rosenberg-Greenglass team that stole so many of our atomic secrets during the 1940's.

Presiding over this cosmopolitan assemblage as the KGB's resident chairman of the board was one Gordon Arnold Lonsdale, alias Molody. The son of a Soviet scientist, Lonsdale-Molody had lived with an aunt in California as a boy, attending school in Berkeley where he acquired the easy fluency with the English language which was to hoodwink dozens of British and American businessmen and Armed Forces personnel in the years to come.

Lonsdale labored in the bountiful espionage vineyards in America for five years, ending in 1955. A decade later he boasted of this interlude to a Western newsman: *"If I were in a position to divulge the contents of some of the data we obtained, I am certain there would be an agonizing inquest at the United States State Department."*[3]

The British, however, were widely, and unfairly, blamed for Lonsdale's many coups. He slipped into the United Kingdom after he left the U.S., posing as a Canadian businessman leasing jukeboxes and peddling, of all things, bubble-gum machines. His jaunty predilection for all things American even extended to his place of residence, an apartment building on London's Albany Street known as the White House.

Lonsdale and his friends were tried in Old Bailey in the spring of 1961, convicted, and sentenced to long terms in prison. However, Lonsdale was returned to Russia on April 22, 1964, in a swap for Greville Wynne, the doughty English businessman who had been Oleg Penkovskiy's prime contact. By now Lonsdale, under some other name, may be selling magazines door-to-door near American missile bases in the Golden West. And, alas, George Blake may be with him. The former M16 agent escaped over the wall of the Wormwood Scrubs Gaol in October of 1966 after serving only five-and-a-half years of his forty-two year sentence.

The explosive chain reaction set off by Colonel Goleniewski's disclosures is also said to have led to the arrest and conviction in the fall of 1962 of W.J.C. Vassall, a 38-year-old Admiralty clerk with an effeminate manner and an unhappy penchant for collecting Naval secrets for his Russian boyfriends. The son of an Anglican clergyman, Vassal had been recruited by KGB homosexuals while serving at the British embassy in Moscow in the mid-1950's. After several years in the Soviet capital he returned to London by a devious route which took him through the United States and Scandinavia. Among the documents he supplied to the Soviets was said to be highly technical data on U.S. Polaris missiles.

Goleniewski's information is also credited with the bagging of Colonel Stig Wennerstroem, the peripatetic Swedish Air Force attaché in Washington who roamed at will among America's industrial plants and military installations in the 1950's, lifting blueprints and plans for the Soviets.[4]

Another notorious agent picked up in the wake of Goleniewski's disclosures was Dr. Israel Beer, close friend and confidant of former Israeli Prime Minister, David Ben-Gurion. Beer held the rank of lieutenant colonel in the Israeli army, which he served as official historian. He had also run *Haganah*, the underground Zionist organization, for ten years, and his arrest in 1961 drew an agonized cry from old Ben-Gurion, who reportedly exclaimed, "I am surrounded by treachery!"[5]

The ramifications of Goleniewski's defection were also felt in West Germany, where a large and very able Soviet spy ring, or rather a number of concentric rings, was blown clear out of the water via the surfacing of George Blake in England.*

Strangely, however, not one of the many Americans named by Goleniewski has ever been prosecuted. To Otepka's great disgust, the veteran KGB man the defector fingered in our Warsaw embassy was allowed to resign, even though the State Department later publicly admitted that he had engaged in espionage for the Soviet Union. Similar action may have been quietly taken against one other individual in the State Department. But a number of alleged Soviet agents at high policy-making levels of the

---

* In this, as in the other cases cited, it is possible that Goleniewski's role in the apprehension of Soviet agents in England, Israel, Sweden, and Germany may have been deliberately exaggerated. We have only Goleniewski's word for all of it, as transmitted to author Guy Richards and others.

United States government whom Goleniewski claims to have identified to CIA were never molested.

Goleniewski obviously was not operating alone behind the Iron Curtain. When he came out through Berlin in January 1961, he brought ten other people with him, including an East German woman, Irmgard Margareta Kampf, whom he has since married. More recently he has made extravagant claims about the existence of a "Secret Circle" which is supposed to have carried on an uninterrupted struggle with the Communists for many years. However, almost anything Goleniewski says these days is subject to grave doubt. For reasons that have been open to all sorts of speculation he has deliberately discredited himself. He did this by claiming to be no less a personage than the Grand Duke Alexei Nicholaevich Romanov, the Czarevich of Russia and heir to the vanished Imperial throne.

One difficulty with Goleniewski's tale is that the Grand Duke Alexei, his father, Czar Nicholas, and all the other five members of their immediate family were reported murdered by the Bolsheviks at Ekaterinburg, now Sverdlovsk, Siberia, in July 1918. Alexei was then 12 years old, which would make him 16 years older than Goleniewski's Polish papers claim him to be.

Through the years there have been recurrent rumors that one or more of the Romanovs escaped execution. Several alleged daughters turned up in Europe and the United States, at least two claiming to be Princess Anastasia. Goleniewski maintains that the whole family was permitted to emigrate to Poland on the pledge that they would never reveal their true identities. On its face this story is transparently fictitious. It would have been impossible to keep the lips of so many Romanovs sealed for more than forty years while they lived outside Russia in a country that was independent for twenty-one of those years.

Goleniewski's claim seems all the more astounding in light of the acknowledged authenticity of the intelligence which he fed to the West from the Soviet Bloc for nearly three years before he fled Poland. However, it is well to remember that, so far as is known, no one from Western Intelligence agencies ever laid eyes on Goleniewski until he crossed over into West Berlin. Thereafter, the CIA kept him hidden from the world, and for that matter, from the rest of the Intelligence community, for more than three years, first in Germany, then in two CIA "safe houses" in northern Virginia, and finally in a New York apartment.

Goleniewski, a tall, powerful man with piercing blue eyes and a commanding presence, charges that British Intelligence has confirmed that he is indeed the czarevich and that the CIA knows his claim is true. He says that Allen Dulles, when still Director of CIA, told him, "You would look exactly like your father (Czar Nicholas), if you would have a beard and moustache like your father."[6] Dulles, of course, may merely have been humoring him.

Although Goleniewski had become a subject of widespread gossip in Washington months before, it was not until early 1964 that his existence was revealed to the public. Guy Richards, city editor of the New York *Journal-American,* broke the story in the Hearst newspapers on March 6. From there on the CIA, with substantial help from certain members of Congress, including House Republican minority whip Leslie Arends of Illinois, pulled out all the stops to discredit not only Goleniewski, but the admittedly invaluable intelligence he had furnished. Largely because of this campaign, the man who is widely regarded as the most important defector ever to come over to the West has to this day never testified before a Congressional investigating committee. The only glimpse any Congressmen got of him was in the summer of 1963 when the CIA produced him for a brief inspection by the House Immigration Subcommittee headed by Michael A. Feighan of Ohio.

The occasion for this guarded unveiling of Goleniewski was a special bill the Immigration subcommittee had under consideration to grant him full U.S. citizenship. In requesting the subcommittee's approval, CIA had nothing but the highest praise for the defector. The agency cited his "truly significant" contributions "to the security of the United States." It also acknowledged that "he has collaborated with the government in an outstanding manner and under circumstances which have involved grave personal risk."[7]

Only the sketchiest bits of background on Goleniewski were supplied by CIA. It said he had been born in Nieswiez, Poland, on August 16, 1922, had "completed three years of law at the University of Poznan, and in 1956 he received a master's degree in political science from the University of Warsaw." He was said to have joined the Polish Army in 1945 and the Communist Party in 1946.The date of his initial defection-in-place was given as April 1958.[8]

There was not so much as a faint hint about Goleniewski's claims to the Russian throne. Nor did he allude to them when he appeared before the four members of the Immigration subcommittee. He did try to assume the Romanov mantle when Congressman Feighan later visited him with two subcommittee staff members, Dr. Edward O'Connor and Colonel Philip J. Corso. However, Corso, a veteran Army Intelligence man who once served with Dr. O'Connor on the National Security Council OCB staff, quickly halted Goleniewski's flight of fancy.

When they got down to business, Goleniewski named a score of influential Americans who he claimed were agents for the KGB. More than a dozen were in the Department of State. Four were in CIA. Three others were outstanding scientists who have had a telling impact upon national policy. The scientists, all of whom have access to highly classified information, were described by Goleniewski as brilliant men whose "humanitarian" ideals and one-world outlook preconditioned them to the Klaus Fuchs-Robert Oppenheimer thesis that all scientists are morally bound to share their laboratory findings regardless of narrow "nationalistic" considerations.

Feighan, Corso and O'Connor spent several informative hours with Goleniewski. After this first interview, Colonel Corso returned at a later date to question the defector again. On this trip he was armed with the State Department "Biographic Register" and other public records. Goleniewski verified the names of the alleged traitors he had identified before. The names were made available to the proper authorities and Congressman Feighan took the matter up personally with John McCone, Allan Dulles' successor at CIA. No action was ever taken against any of the people on Goleniewski's list, though McCone may have decided that the "Grand Duke Alexei" hardly made a credible informant.

There is, in fact, a current theory that Goleniewski is not Goleniewski at all, let alone the Grand Duke Alexei. The real Goleniewski, this theory runs, was seized by the KGB and an imposter substituted in his place before the "defection" to West Berlin.

One might postulate that if Goleniewski is in fact an imposter sent over to stir up confusion and plant seeds of suspicion within our society, it is just as well that the people he named have not been bothered. There is only one large difficulty with that line of reasoning. Most of the individuals named already had substantial amounts of questionable information in their security files long before anyone ever heard of Michal Goleniewski. Several had previously been identified as possible Soviet agents by other more ostensibly reliable sources. At least two of the scientists have openly espoused Communist causes or policies that have served the USSR's purposes. Moreover, it is impossible to overlook the indisputable evidence that a good deal of the information Goleniewski allegedly provided about Soviet spies in other countries proved correct.

Nonetheless, the nagging question remains: Why did Goleniewski claim the ephemeral crown of the Romanovs? It has shattered his credibility. It is doubtful it could really save his life if the Soviets were bent on revenge. It probably scared off J. Edgar Hoover, the one man in all the world he claimed he most wanted to see. And it forestalled the appearance he said he so badly wanted to make before the Senate Internal Security Subcommittee. In this latter connection it should be noted that Goleniewski was twice served with subpoenas by the subcommittee to testify in secret session. This was prior to Guy Richards' news break on the case and the startling public disclosures of Goleniewski's Romanov routine. Yet both times Goleniewski found reasons for not testifying.

The Goleniewski business became the subject of caustic debate during the Senate subcommittee's hearings in the Otepka case. It developed that not only Otepka, but one of his old special project team, Jack Norpel, had early information on the Polish army officer who had penetrated the Soviet's dread KGB.* Norpel had learned of the defector when he was still in the FBI's counter-espionage section. He said the story was widely known in the FBI.[9]

For some odd reason, the State Department tried to pin responsibility for the mishandling of the Goleniewski case on Otepka. In a voluminous memorandum sent to Senator Eastland on March 10, 1964, Deputy Undersecretary of State William Crockett pointed out that Otepka was Acting Director of the Office of Security when the Department was first notified of the matter by CIA in 1959. (Boswell was away at the time.)

"The case was subsequently controlled in large part by Mr. Otepka and his subordinates," Crockett charged. He added that this "control" over the Goleniewski business was maintained by Otepka after he was shifted back to SY's Evaluations Division.[10] Crockett said that "despite the fact that this case occurred some four years ago, the Department does attach importance to it."

Otepka contradicted Crockett. He submitted a statement to the subcommittee denying that he had been "permitted at any time to have control over a large part of the Goleniewski case." He said he passed the CIA information on to William Boswell when Boswell returned from his trip in 1959. Boswell took over from there, and neither he nor the CIA ever notified Otepka when the defector finally came in from the cold.

"If anyone in the Office of Security controlled a large part of the Goleniewski case," Otepka charged, "it was Boswell. By late 1960 he saw fit to divest me and other division chiefs of our personal involvement in matters normally within our operational jurisdiction, which he himself

---

* Goleniewski claims he was chief of the "Independent Scientific and Technical Intelligence" branch of the Polish government, but he obviously had lines into the KGB too.

wished to control." He said Boswell wouldn't even let him touch the Scarbeck case and even refused to let him see the file when he tried to "determine the extent of the implication of other State Department employees in the Scarbeck affair."[11]

Among the officials Boswell briefed on the Polish defector was the U.S. Ambassador to Poland, Jacob Beam. In January 1968, *The Government Employees Exchange*, a weekly newspaper published in Washington, publicly linked Beam with a mysterious Polish woman spy.[12] The woman turned out to be Madam Jerzy Michalowski, alleged "wife" of the Polish Ambassador to the United States.

Madam Michalowski, nee Myra Zandel, lived in America in the 1940's when she was married to Professor Ignace Zlotowski, a member of the faculty at Vassar College. The professor and his wife were later identified by another Polish defector, General Izyador Modelski, as Communist agents. Zlotowski, the General said, was a member of a special atomic espionage unit.[13] Myra, meanwhile, was working for the U.S. government in the old Office of War Information. There she took up with one Stefan Arski, the notorious "Black Stefan" who defected from OWI to Poland after the war. His principal assignment in both Washington and Warsaw was to suppress reports of the Soviet murders of 15,000 Polish officers and soldiers in the infamous Katyn Forest Massacre. Myra Zandel, who was reportedly his wife, helped out on this assignment in OWI and the story remained buried for eight long years.[14]

As of this writing, Jacob Beam had not bothered to deny the story. After his return from Warsaw in November 1961 he was shunted into the semi-autonomous U.S. Arms Control and Disarmament Agency where weightier matters undoubtedly occupied his mind. Early in 1969, much to the amazement of the Intelligence community, President Nixon named Beam as U.S. Ambassador to the Soviet Union.

The Warsaw embassy sex-and-spy scandals erupted during Beam's tenure as ambassador. Many of the people involved kept casting their long shadows across Otto Otepka's path for years afterward and we shall meet a few more of them later on. But before we leave romantic Warsaw, a word on America's policy of "building bridges" to the East European satellites is certainly in order.

The theory of "fragmentation" of the Soviet Bloc predates the Rostow Papers, which merely made it official (if still "secret") policy and lent America's tacit approval to the suppression of uprisings behind the Iron Curtain. But the theory can be traced back to those two great earlier State Department theoreticians, George Kennan and Charles (Chip) Bohlen, who were peddling the "breakup" of monolithic communism almost at the outset of what used to be called the Cold War.

As late as 1967, Kennan was still suavely peddling his old line. "I just don't know what 'Communist' means today precisely, for the reason that there are so many varieties of it," Kennan confessed to the Senate Foreign Relations Committee in testimony supporting President Johnson's bridge-building trade bills.[15]

For years the inner councils of government have echoed with such wishful thinking. Poland, Hungary, Czechoslovakia, Romania, and the other satellites are always seen on the verge of splitting off from Soviet Russia and traveling their own independent roads. The fact that the wish never quite catches up with reality does not deter the Kennans of the world. They go merrily along, forever forecasting the fragmented millennium to come.

The Soviets, as chief beneficiaries of a paralyzed U.S. policy which gave them precious time to build their nuclear might, were happy to encourage America's *idée fixe* that we could somehow woo Warsaw, Prague, Budapest, et al. from their enforced marriage to Moscow. But Warsaw and its ravished sisters knew well that any real attempt at a divorce would cause the Russians to shotgun them down in earnest, as they did to Budapest in 1956.

Any lingering doubts the satellites may have entertained in this regard were erased forever when Prague attempted an amicable, and quite limited, separation in 1968. The more than 600,000 Communist troops that descended on Czechoslovakia revealed Walt Rostow's "fragmentation" theory for what it really was: a myth perpetrated to insure the bondage of the captive peoples for generations to come.

The fact that the Soviets were also able to entwine their chains around the United States embassy in Warsaw certainly encouraged the Kremlin in its belief that the Americans were indeed soft marks. They knew from the information they were able to pick up there, and in many other places, that the U.S. would never come to the aid of the oppressed millions of Eastern Europe, at least as long as the Rostows and Rusks and Kennans ruled the Department of State.

CHAPTER **XIX**

Shillelagh

IN HIS MEANDERING SHORT STORY, "IVY DAY IN THE COMMITTEE Room," James Joyce causes Mr. O'Connor, one of his political characters, to cry out against "a certain little nobleman with a cock-eye," who, while masquerading as a Sinn Feiner, was probably in the employ of the British who ruled from Dublin Castle: "O, the heart's blood of a patriot! That's a fellow now that'd sell his country for fourpence—ay—and go down on his bended knees and thank the Almighty Christ he had a country to sell."

Every country in every era of history has had such men. Not traitors, really. Opportunists is a kinder word, and more accurate. But they serve the traitor's purpose well. He could buy them for a farthing in any Dublin gutter once upon a time. Today, with inflation and prosperity, the price has risen considerably. The opportunist now demands, and gets, rich rewards indeed. If he plays his cards carefully, he can rise to a cabinet post or beyond. At a minimum, he can easily wind up with a lifetime job carrying a fat pension for those golden years of retirement. The devil of it is that in nine cases out of ten he hasn't the faintest idea of what he has done. His conscience, if he ever had one, becomes so benumbed as he moves up in government that his only thought is how best he can

220

maintain himself and reach that next rung on the ladder. In August 1962, after only four months in the State Department, John Francis Reilly climbed another rung. He was promoted to Deputy Assistant Secretary of State for Security, a brand-new title created especially for him, in recognition, no doubt, of his having successfully kept Otto Otepka off the sensitive backs of the people on the Department's seventh floor.

Reilly took his elevation as a signal to strip off the kid gloves, which fitted him rather badly anyway, and fetch up the shillelagh with which he now intended to bludgeon Otepka clear out of the Department of State. He almost succeeded, too. For whatever his limitations, this big, florid-faced man did not hesitate to use power when it was handed to him, even if it meant knocking over a few laws here and there. He had the nerve for anything, and the Kennedys always admired that quality in a man—as long as he was on their side.

Reilly's other attribute was that he had the knack of winning strong allies. When the name of the game was con, Reilly, the master of blarney, could play it very well. In the beginning, he completely disarmed Senator Thomas J. Dodd. At this time Dodd was virtually running the Senate Internal Security Subcommittee. For some reason the actual chairman, James O. Eastland of Mississippi, seemed content to ride in the back seat and let Vice Chairman Dodd take the bows from behind the wheel. Forever the loyal party man, Dodd went out of his way not only to exonerate Jack Kennedy and Dean Rusk for their handling of the Wieland affair, but to give Jack Reilly an undeserved pat on the back.

Dodd took some of the sting out of the 1962 subcommittee report on State Department security by noting in his addendum that "there have been several notable improvements" at State. Chief among these, Dodd thought, was Reilly's appointment and subsequent promotion. At the time, he viewed this as a "most salutary development."[1]

Otepka was understandably discouraged by Dodd's view. Forced to live with Reilly's decisions in SY, he could see that the new Deputy Assistant Secretary of State was systematically destroying sound security and shattering the morale of all sincere security officers. For this, and other services rendered in muffling Otepka, Reilly was elevated by Dean Rusk, probably with a nod from the watchful overseer of patronage, Robert Kennedy.

Reilly celebrated his promotion by spending a sizable chunk of the taxpayers' money on an extensive and lavish refurbishing of his office.

Partitions were knocked down to double the space. Wall-to-wall carpeting, leather-upholstered lounges, ceiling-to-floor draperies, and other expensive status symbols were installed.

These changes did much to puff up the pride of Marie Catucci, the secretary Reilly had inherited from William Boswell and a long line of other predecessors. An SY newsletter published in March 1966 featured a profile on Mrs. Catucci. It trumpeted that she had been "close to nearly every major decision of importance in SY for over twenty years."* She also made no secret of her antipathy for Otepka.

On one occasion when Otepka asked her for some information she did not wish to give him, La Catucci flew into one of her frequent rages. In the presence of several others, she snatched things from her desk and hurled them vehemently about the office. Screaming curses, she started to tear her hair and ended by throwing herself on a couch, kicking wildly at the upholstery. Otepka reported her unseemly conduct to Boswell. But Boswell merely shrugged and mumbled that it was Otepka's problem. Reilly, shrewdly seeing in Marie Catucci a valuable instrument for his plans, took much the same view.

Now that her latest boss held the exalted title of Deputy Assistant Secretary, Mrs. Catucci became even more unbearable. She treated Otepka with queenly disdain, though sometimes his unruffled calm got the better of her and she reverted to screams and curses. When she saw that her tirades had no effect on Otepka she began to harass his secretary, Mrs. Eunice Powers, bombarding her with viciously critical notes.

Reilly enlisted David Belisle as his chief-of-staff in the spreading campaign of harassment against Otepka and all those in SY who demonstrated any sympathy whatever for the principles Otepka stood for. The members of Otepka's special project, who were now with him in the Evaluations Division, were singled out as ripe targets. Raymond Loughton, having given up the job of Assistant Director of Security in the Pentagon to join the State Department, was bluntly informed by Belisle that there was no future for him in SY. Belisle openly described former FBI man Francis Gardner as "puerile" because he included some sala-

* The introduction of the newsletter, "People, Places, Things," after Otepka was forced out of SY is indicative of the inanity to which security had descended in the Age of Détente. Published as a personnel "morale booster," it contained a good deal of information on the personal lives of SY's staff. Although this information would be innocuous if provided by most government offices, when it is gratuitously supplied by the Office of Security it must make for interesting reading each month in the Soviet and satellite embassies, which are busy building dossiers on anyone even remotely connected with the U.S. Intelligence community.

cious, albeit relevant, information in a security evaluation. Those two veteran evaluators, Harry Hite and Billy Hughes, were repeatedly reprimanded by Belisle because their reports were much more thorough than required by the "short form" résumés he had brought with him from the National Security Agency. Eunice Powers was once reduced to tears by Belisle's heavy-handed cross-examination of her about Otepka's activities.

Immune from criticism were all those in the Evaluations Division who cooperated with Reilly and Belisle. Chief among these were Frederick Traband, Joseph Sabin and Carl Bock, "progressive" evaluators who had realistically adjusted to the changing times.

Suitable rewards were soon forthcoming for SY people who joined the New Order. When Elmer Hipsley accepted voluntary exile to Switzerland in the fall of 1962, he was replaced by Joseph Rosetti, the former aide to Jack Kennedy who had notably failed to distinguish himself during his years in SY. Others were similarly promoted or jumped in grade. The classic case, of course, was that of the beatnik, Elmer Hill, who became Chief of the Technical Services Division. But there were many with equally dubious abilities, if less flamboyant personalities, who moved up in SY under Reilly and Belisle simply because they knew how to "get along."

According to Otepka, Belisle himself was "abysmally ignorant" of the law and of all security regulations. Time after time, Otepka was forced to explain to him in primer form the most rudimentary provisions of Executive Order 10450 and other rules. Yet with Reilly's blessing Belisle kept a special evaluations team directly under him to "expedite" clearances they didn't want Otepka and his staff to handle.

In addition, Belisle's introduction of the short-form reports, that same little device which had enabled the Communists to penetrate NSA so efficiently, removed from Otepka's vision most of the "raw material" he had previously received from the FBI and other agencies. With SY investigators, many of them neophytes in security, now acting as evaluators, much of the background information on applicants was weeded out before it reached Otepka's desk.

Reilly went so far as to relegate the issuance of security clearances to SY's file room. John Noonan, the cooperative supervisor of the files, was instructed to issue emergency clearances to clerical applicants if Noonan deemed that the preliminary security checks had failed to turn up any derogatory information.

When Otepka protested these measures, Reilly and Belisle literally sneered at him, reminding him that they were his superiors and he was to do as they said. Ironically, Reilly instituted most of the revolutionary changes in SY's procedures at about the time Senator Dodd was waxing enthusiastic about Reilly in the Senate subcommittee report.

Knowing Jack and Bobby Kennedy's keen interest in the Wieland case as well as Dean Rusk's, Reilly was especially careful in the handling of this matter. A promise had been made during Boswell's tenure to reopen the case after Otepka and his men unearthed evidence that Wieland had lied about his associations with Fidel Castro. But the promise had not been kept. For several months in the autumn of 1962 Otepka tried to get Reilly to lift the lid that had been firmly clamped on the Wieland affair. Reilly consistently refused. Then, in December of the same year, the Civil Service Commission sent SY a transcript of the Senate subcommittee's hearings with the admonition that it contained data on Wieland that the State Department had not considered when Secretary Rusk ordered Wieland cleared. Legally, this made it mandatory for SY to reopen the case. Otepka promptly notified Reilly of the commission's action. Otepka recommended that Harry Hite, who had worked with him on the Wieland business from the outset, be named as the primary evaluator. When Hite had finished the job, Otepka said he would review the findings himself. Reilly agreed, or at least pretended to agree.

A few months later Reilly repeatedly swore to the Senate subcommittee that Otepka had disqualified himself from further handling of the Wieland case. Obviously, this wasn't so, but the whole thing had by then become purely academic. Even before consulting Otepka, Reilly had turned over the Wieland file to Robert McCarthy. The fact that McCarthy was an investigator, and not a qualified evaluator, didn't bother Reilly. He told Otepka that he wanted someone to "take a fresh look" at the case. From Reilly's standpoint, McCarthy was certainly an ideal man for that. He took six months to give the Montenegro-Wieland file a "fresh look" before he finally surrendered it to Harry Hite. No one ever found out what he did with it during that period, except to keep it out of sight while Reilly stalled for time.

Otepka discovered that McCarthy was a past master at burying security information. In June 1963 Otepka upheld the finding of Ray Loughton that a high-ranking Foreign Service Officer, who had just completed a course in "counter-insurgency" at the Foreign Service Institute, be dismissed as a security risk.

Otepka had kept a weather eye on this particular diplomat for some time. Several years before, he had been bounced out of Mexico City when he became passionately involved in an affair with the wife of an ambassador from a NATO nation. Although he denied the affair at first, he later boasted about it to SY's investigators. Moreover, he also defended homosexuality among Foreign Service men, claiming that there were times when it came in handy to have the "boys" around on diplomatic missions.

Transferred to Caracas after a mild reprimand and a two-week suspension, the romantic diplomat continued to indulge openly in his favorite extracurricular activities. He did not, however, neglect his purely professional chores. In fact, Otepka received complaints in Washington that he was attempting to help secure U.S. visas for a number of Venezuelan Communists. An investigation was ordered, but the results were something less than satisfactory. It just so happened that Robert McCarthy was a security officer at the Caracas embassy at the time, and he had become quite friendly with the man in question. There was good reason to believe that McCarthy helped to bury the whole matter of the illegal visas.

Otepka, however, refused to let the case stay buried. He kept after Robert Berry, the chief of SY's Investigations Division, to follow through. Toward the end of 1962 yet another report on the diplomatic Don Juan came in from Caracas, although by then he had been called back to Washington. The security officer in Venezuela cautioned that the case "might prove embarrassing if followed through too thoroughly." Otepka demanded to know what he meant by that. McCarthy's name was injected, and although he had apparently not been involved in any personal misconduct himself, he had certainly countenanced his friend's peccadillos.*

Otepka decided to find out more about Robert McCarthy, who by now was sitting firmly on the Wieland case. Digging into the files he kept in a special safe in his office, Otepka came up with a report on an incident in Caracas which had caused the United States considerable difficulty in 1961. On June 14 of that year Teodoro Moscoso, the U.S. Ambassador to Venezuela, visited the Central University in Caracas. He left his limousine in the care of his chauffeur, a Venezuelan "local." In the limousine was his briefcase. And in the briefcase were some highly classified State Department documents.

Moscoso's carelessness is somewhat surprising, in view of the fact that

* "Don Juan" was still on the State Department payroll in 1968, having enjoyed several promotions since Otepka's exile.

roving bands of Communist terrorists made no secret that their head-quarters was at the University. Everyone in Caracas knew this. And anyone could have predicted what happened next: a crowd of students on a rioting rampage attacked the limousine and set it afire, being careful first to remove the Ambassador's briefcase.

Two months later, at the Inter-American conference in Puenta del Este, Uruguay, Che Guevara publicly produced copies of the classified documents stolen from Moscoso's car. In Guevara's eyes, and perhaps in those of many a non-Communist Latin American at Puenta del Este, the official papers were conclusive proof that the *Yanquis* were plotting to deprive Latin nations of their sovereignty. The Fidelistas got a lot of mileage out of this "evidence," and they continued to use it in their propaganda offensive long after the conference adjourned.

Otepka's files showed that the man who had investigated the incident of the Ambassador's stolen briefcase was none other than Robert McCarthy. Going over McCarthy's report again now, he saw that it was a complete whitewash of Moscoso's carelessness. McCarthy had been at pains to leave out a number of pertinent facts. Among them was an approach the thieves made through an American in Venezuela to sell back the briefcase and its volatile contents to the Ambassador. Moscoso, perhaps rightly, had refused to negotiate, probably on the theory that copies of the documents had been made anyway. But McCarthy's deliberate omission of this and other information raised additional questions about his professional standards as an investigator.

Otepka's annoying persistence began to get on John Reilly's nerves. When he revealed to Jack Norpel that he had been sent over to State "to do a job" and vowed that he would do it, Reilly told Norpel: "Otepka is a nut!" This was not to be the only time that Reilly was to question Otepka's sanity.

Day by day, Reilly escalated the harassment of Otepka and his evaluations staff. Reilly's chief-of-staff, Belisle, was named to head the management survey team that was again looking into SY's functions. The result of Belisle's survey was a further effort to strip Otepka of the necessary tools of his trade. Among other things, Belisle arbitrarily removed a valuable card-index file on all questionable personnel cases that Otepka kept as a ready reference for his evaluators. Without these cards, they were now forced to spend hours searching for material, and they could never be sure that they hadn't missed some vital piece of information.

For ten years Otepka had served as the State Department's representative on an intra-governmental committee charged with improving ways to protect classified data. But in January 1963 he was replaced by Joe Rosetti of SY's Massachusetts Mob. Rosetti confided to Otepka that he hadn't the faintest idea what he was supposed to do on this important committee. In fact, he was so frightened at the prospect of serving on it that he eventually begged off and had himself renamed as Otepka's alternate. However, the committee came under the control of Bobby Kennedy's Justice Department, and Otepka was never invited to another meeting.

In this same month, Reilly erased Otepka's name from the list of SY officials who could be contacted by the FBI and other agencies after-hours and on weekends and holidays. Otepka's assistant, Fred Traband, was put on the list in his place. When Otepka asked why this had been done, Reilly unctuously explained that Traband was an expert on homosexuals and most of the after-hours calls involved reports on State Department perverts who had been picked up by Washington's Metropolitan Police Department. Otepka wryly observed that the homo business must be pretty good these days since there had been a considerable increase in their acknowledged numbers at State during the past year.

Despite his quip, Otepka realized that his removal from the after-hours calling list was a further diminution of his authority. Many of the homosexuals caught by the Washington police were high-ranking Foreign Service officers and it was obvious that Reilly did not want their names to come to Otepka's attention any longer. Their identities would be much safer in the discreet hands of Frederick Traband.

Although never a laughing boy, Otepka had a quiet sense of humor and it did not desert him as Reilly and his gang tightened the screws on his Evaluations Division. Nor was he above retaliating with a sly injection of the needle in Reilly's thick hide. Early in 1963 SY was asked to list its noteworthy achievements for the previous year. Tongue in cheek, Otepka suggested to Reilly that the list contain the uncovering of the one hundred-and-fifty-two security waivers signed by Secretary Rusk, plus the backdating, that Otepka and his men had unearthed. Certainly, Otepka observed, this was a noteworthy accomplishment. But Reilly accused him of seeking the new SY regime's endorsement for the "jogging" Otepka had given Boswell and Roger Jones.

The slipshod security practices that Reilly and Belisle introduced into the State Department were fast winning State a malodorous reputation throughout government. The Civil Service Commission complained that the Department's reports left a great deal to be desired. The Atomic Energy Commission, whose own highly touted "Q-Clearance" program was itself being slowly watered down, repeatedly rejected Belisles's new short-form clearances for State Department officials working on AEC projects.

In some instances, it was like the pot calling the kettle black, since internal security was swiftly going up in smoke throughout the federal government. Nonetheless, the New Order was moving much more quickly at State than in many of the other agencies. The dedicated security people at the AEC and elsewhere were doing their best to fight a rear-guard action. But they now found the pace of the wholesale retreat from sanity being set by the State Department Hisses much too swift for even the most fleet-footed bureaucrats among them.

Otepka, forced to struggle every inch of the way in his own rear-guard battle, was beginning to despair. The Senate subcommittee's report had had no impact whatever on the State Department. On the contrary, Reilly was outdoing Boswell in the demolition of State's security structure. The procedures introduced in recent months, most of which by-passed the law, had left the clearance system in a shambles.

After first having pretended to side with Otepka on the matter of Harlan Cleveland's advisory committee, Reilly was now cooperating fully with Cleveland's scheme to restore Alger Hiss's old rules for getting Americans onto the United Nations staff. Otepka saw that all reason was being tossed to the winds in Reilly's efforts to placate his masters. His head figuratively bloodied, Otepka stood amidst the ruins of his once proud and competent Office of Security. He continued to do battle to protect his country's interests. But he was almost ready to bow.

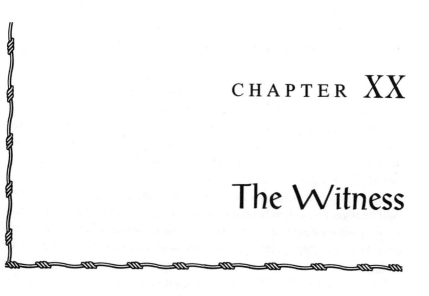

CHAPTER **XX**

The Witness

As winter slipped almost imperceptibly into spring in that final year of John Fitzgerald Kennedy's brief reign, the pressure on Otto Otepka to resign from the State Department's Office of Security mounted inexorably. Robert McCarthy, the bully-boy from Massachusetts who boasted everywhere of his "connections" with the Kennedys, passed the word that he would "fix up" Otepka with any job he wanted, even an ambassadorship, if he would only step quietly out of SY.

When Otepka laughed off this offer McCarthy complained to John Norpel, the veteran FBI agent Otepka had brought into SY. "Why is Otepka fighting?" the incredulous McCarthy asked. "What *is* his price to quit? Every man has a price."

Norpel ventured the opinion that Otepka could not be bought. The only thing he was interested in, Norpel pointed out, was the restoration of a real security program at State. McCarthy shook his head in wonderment. It was quite beyond his comprehension.

Unknown to McCarthy and Norpel, however, Otepka *had* considered quitting, though it never crossed his mind to sell out and accept a promotion. Otepka reached his crossroads late in 1962. He saw that there were only two paths left for him to take. One would carry him right out of the Department of State and away from government. The other was obscured by a dense fog, though he strongly suspected that it might send him careening into a stone wall that would shatter his career.

Otepka later swore that this was the only time he ever so much as thought of resigning until the very end of 1967. He did so because it was obvious to him that Dean Rusk had not the slightest intention of implementing any of the recommendations made by the Senate Internal Security Subcommittee in its blistering 1962 report. He felt that if a group of powerful senators, acting officially and in unanimous concert, could not get through to Secretary Rusk, there was little likelihood a man in his position could do anything at all to influence a return to sound security in the Department of State. He was, however, persuaded not to resign.

The man who talked Otepka out of quitting was Jay Sourwine. In the final analysis, the State Department's whole case against Otepka was to rest on the relationship between Otepka and this veteran Chief Counsel of the Senate Internal Security Subcommittee. One might suppose from this that Sourwine was thought to be some sort of subversive, perhaps (dread the thought!) a Soviet agent. But in the eerily surrealistic atmosphere of the Kennedy-Johnson Era, Otepka's—and Sourwine's—crime was far more serious than that: they were both dedicated to the proposition that the internal security laws of the United States should be upheld. On the New Frontier, and later in the Great Society, there was apparently no greater sin than this.

All the traditional crimes, especially if perpetrated on a mass scale, could readily be forgiven by the beneficent psycho-sociologists masquerading as politicians in Washington. Murder, arson, looting, rape, even a little dab of treason as exemplified in the Peacenik protests, were eligible for absolution.*But not the "crime" that Otepka committed through his association with Sourwine.

Before his original Senate subcommittee appearance in the autumn of 1961, Otepka had met Sourwine just once, briefly and casually years before. But toward the end of 1962 they took to lunching together once or twice a month. Both men were conscious that they could not for a moment shed their official mantles even in purely social meetings. Sourwine maintained that he *always* wore the cloak of the Senate subcommittee's chief counsel. Otepka certainly never forgot his own position.

Otepka was aware that the State Department frowned on his new-

* Hubert Humphrey, speaking in Chicago on November 1, 1968, hailed the "brave men who led the dissent" over the Vietnam war during the Democratic national convention two months earlier. He said that these "Yippies" had "made their mark on policy [and] helped the search for peace."

found friendship. But he reasoned that if the Department, and even the White House, could encourage officials to socialize with representatives of the Soviet Union and other Communist countries, there should be no ethical objection to his having an occasional lunch with the counsel of a committee of the United States Senate.*

Weeks after the senators' 1962 report had time to penetrate the consciousness of the State Department's seventh floor, Otepka confided to Sourwine that he was seriously considering handing in his resignation. His brother Rudy was expanding a highly successful printing machinery business in Chicago. Rudy needed an executive vice president to help with the rapidly multiplying responsibilities. If Otto would join the company, the financial rewards would far surpass any salary he could ever hope to earn in government. It was a tempting offer. But much more tempting than the money was the prospect of escaping from the insane atmosphere that now prevailed in the Department of State and its Office of Security.

Sourwine protested vigorously. He told Otepka his departure from State would be an irreparable loss to the whole internal security program throughout government. Other sincere security officials would certainly take note of the fact that he had been forced out. Many of them were already demoralized. If Otepka quit, whatever hope they still harbored for holding the security line would quickly crumble. Sourwine emphasized that it was Otepka's duty to stay and fight for sound security.

Otepka said he didn't see *how* he could fight any longer. He had already been stripped of most of his authority. It ran through his mind that there was very little real security left at State to fight for.

Then, bit by bit, Sourwine opened a door. He was confident that the Senate subcommittee would want to know whether its recommendations were being carried out. If Otepka would testify again, he could enlighten the senators on that score.

Otepka shook his head. He had been over that route before and his only reward for testifying truthfully had been an endless campaign of harassment.

Sourwine frowned. If honest public officials resorted to silence, he said, because they feared reprisals for telling the truth, then the enemies of effective security will have scored a smashing victory. Otepka was forced to agree with that. But the legal position still perplexed him. The question

---

* In *A Thousand Days*, Arthur Schlesinger refers several times to his luncheons and other contacts with "my friend," Georgi Kornienko, counselor of the Soviet embassy. (Op. cit., pages 263, 378, 385.) At the time, Schlesinger was on the President's official staff at the White House.

of whether government officials had the right to testify about sensitive matters before Congressional committees had been cast under a cloud of increasing doubt in recent years. The Truman directive of 1948 forbidding officials to disclose classified information had complicated the point immensely. Otepka said he had no intention of violating the Truman order.

Nonetheless, Sourwine saw that he had forced Otepka to stay his hand. There was no more talk of resigning. Over the next half-dozen weeks both men studied the legal questions thoroughly. They found many precedents for what Sourwine wanted Otepka to do. As far back as 1924, Felix Frankfurter, then a Harvard professor and later Franklin Roosevelt's favorite Supreme Court Justice, had written on the problem in connection with the efforts to hush up the Teapot Dome scandal.

"The question," Frankfurter had declared, "is not whether people's feelings here and there may be hurt, or names dragged through the mud, as it is called. The real issue is whether the danger of the abuses and the actual harm done are so clear and substantial that the grave risks of fettering free Congressional inquiry are to be incurred by artificial and technical limitations upon inquiry."

Otepka also recalled another relevant message of much more recent vintage. He went back to President Kennedy's first State of the Union address and found strong additional support for the veiled invitation he had received from Sourwine and the subcommittee. The President had said that his administration recognized the value of "daring and dissent" by federal employees, and that it greeted healthy controversy as the "hallmark of a healthy change."[1]

Otepka was not so naive that he failed to realize that Jack Kennedy had quite a different brand of dissent in mind. But he rationalized that men must live by their words, as well as their deeds. If the President had meant what he said, surely Otepka's dissent would give him a chance to prove it.

The one thing Otepka feared most was that he might be branded a "McCarthyite." "But," he mused years later, "I thought my whole record would prove that I was *not* a McCarthyite, I had never approved of Senator McCarthy's tactics. Everyone in the security field knew that."

Having considered all aspects of the situation, and knowing full well that he stood in real danger of bringing the awesome wrath of the White House down on his head, Otepka finally reached his decision. He informed Sourwine that he would testify on any matter the subcommittee wished to question him about. But he again emphasized that he would have to adhere strictly to the 1948 Truman directive and he insisted that the subcommittee formally request his appearance through the proper channels. He would not testify unless his superiors granted him official permission.

Sourwine saw no difficulty in this. For the State Department to refuse Otepka permission to testify would be tantamount to an open confession that the Administration had an awful lot to hide. The Senate would never stand for that, or so he thought. It was a safe bet that the seventh floor, having weighed the risks both ways, would give Otepka permission, however grudgingly.

In mid-February 1963 Otepka received notice from the office of the Assistant Secretary for Congressional Relations that he was to appear before the Senate subcommittee on the 21st of that month. During February and March, Otepka testified before the subcommittee on four separate occasions. It was all quite proper. Everyone observed established protocol. As Sourwine had foreseen, the State Department invariably, if reluctantly, gave Otepka formal permission to appear. He was always accompanied by a Department attorney, John S. Leahy, Jr., a middle-aged Missourian who had been around Washington for many years. The hearings were held in secret executive session beyond the reach of reporters and television cameras. No one issued press releases. Otepka answered only the questions asked of him. He never volunteered information. Where possible, he avoided mentioning names.

At the very first of these hearings, with Senator Dirksen presiding, Sourwine got right down to business. He asked Otepka if he had been "subjected to any reprisals" for having testified before. The reply Sourwine got was not quite what he expected.

"Reprisals?" Otepka frowned. "I don't—that seems like a rather strong term, Mr. Sourwine." It was apparent that Otepka intended to play the game with his typical caution. Sourwine was forced to rephrase the question several times before Otepka finally admitted that his authority had been reduced.[2]

Gradually, then, and with care not to make any direct accusations against his superiors, Otepka unraveled the sorry story of the past year. He told of how the Evaluations Division had been stripped of the vital Intelligence reporting function. He told of the ten evaluators taken from him, of the removal of the initial national agency checks his division had traditionally made on all applicants at State, of how the Wieland case had been shifted out of his control, of the introduction of Belisle's short forms, and of many other changes within SY.[3]

Senator Dirksen was plainly shocked. More than once he shook his head in wonderment. In questioning Otepka about the short-form report he showed that he understood the implications of this very well, including the fact that it cut the FBI almost completely out of the security act at State.[4] He asked with obvious incredulity whether Otepka really meant that SY's investigators were now forced to "interpret their own findings." When Otepka replied that the Senator had "stated it correctly," Dirksen's bushy brows rose in something approaching alarm.

At the hearing on Wednesday afternoon, March 6, 1963, Jay Sourwine handed Otepka an excerpt from testimony given some months earlier by the State Department's Chief Legal Advisor, Abram Chayes. It concerned the formation of a new departmental Advisory Committee on the Arts which was being set up under the aegis of the Bureau of Cultural Affairs.

In the prior questioning of Chayes, Sourwine had unexpectedly dropped a small bombshell sprinkled with star-studded names from a bygone era. "Mr. Chayes," Sourwine asked, "isn't it true that efforts are being made right now to circumvent the provisions of the law I cited to you, and to secure without pre-investigation for security, appointments to the U.S. Advisory Commission [sic] on the Arts of, among others, Archibald MacLeish, Melvyn Douglas, Agnes DeMille and George Seaton?"[5]

Chayes replied that he didn't know, "except I think one of those names was the one on which we consulted, and for which we said that a full field [investigation] would be required." There was a lot more to it than that, as Attorney Chayes well knew, and now Counsel Sourwine intended to wring it out of Otto Otepka. It wasn't easy. Otepka, still the studiously correct government servant, seemed bent on shielding his superiors if at all possible.

"I don't feel," Otepka said, "that anyone in the Department was trying to circumvent a law." He was giving the Department the benefit of an extremely large doubt here, as we shall see. But he was loath to point a direct finger at Dean Rusk & Company and baldly cry *J'accuse* when there was a question of deliberate violation of the law involved.

Sourwine, however, was not about to let either Otepka or the State Department off the hook. He went at the question again, more obliquely this time. He asked Otepka whether there had been any effort "to get individuals cleared" for the Arts Committee without their having filled out the Department's application or security forms. (This *is* required by law, but Sourwine refrained from alluding to that.)

Otepka conceded that such an effort had been made "initially." When Sourwine tried to find out just who had made it, Otepka told him bluntly "I don't want to mention names of any specific individuals in this." But Sourwine was not to be denied. He kept hammering away, trying to bludgeon the names of the responsible officials out of Otepka, finally asking whether the witness was refusing to supply names "to save your own skin."[6]

With a glance at the nervously noncommittal Mr. Leahy, Otepka asked to go off the record. Although the testimony was always taken in secret session, Otepka was aware that it might be released to the public some day, as his previous testimony had been when the Senators issued their report that past October. When they got back on the record again, Otepka at last admitted that he had "initial conversations" about the investigation of Melvyn Douglas and the others "with a Mr. Max Isenbergh."[7] Isenbergh, it developed, was an aide to Philip Coombs, who had recently stepped down as Assistant Secretary of State for Cultural Affairs. Sourwine then demanded to know whether Otepka had "gone along with" the suggestion that the Committee members be cleared without the required investigations. Otepka said he "had no choice but to insist that there be full compliance with the law."[8] As a result, the formation of the Committee on the Arts had been delayed for more than a year. And thereby hangs a tale which was told only partially in the Senate hearings.

When the delicate matter of the Advisory Committee on the Arts first came up, ten persons were suggested as possible members. Besides Agnes DeMille, Melvyn Douglas, Archibald MacLeish and George Seaton, a half-dozen other reasonably prominent devotees or practitioners of the arts were nominated. They included singer Marian Anderson; Roy E. Larsen, Chairman of the Executive Committee of Time, Inc.; Peter Mennin, composer and President of the Juilliard School of Music; and Warner Lawson, Dean of Music at Howard University.

Otepka promptly cleared the way for the appointments of Miss Anderson, Roy Larsen and Peter Mennin, who were already serving on President Kennedy's White House Commission on International Educational and Cultural Affairs. George Seaton, a movie writer and producer whose films included "Country Girl" and "The Bridges of Toko-Ri," was issued a clearance after he satisfactorily explained some dubious former associations, and Howard University's Dean Lawson received his clearance without any difficulty at all. Agnes DeMille, the choreographic daughter of the late great producer, Cecil B. DeMille, had flirted with some Communist fronts back when fronts were fashionable, but had long since recanted. Following an investigation she too was cleared.

However, both poet MacLeish and actor Douglas refused to fill out and submit the State Department's standard employment form and security questionnaire. This was understandable. The employment application, Standard Form 57, contained two questions which these gentlemen rather strongly resented, to wit: (1) *"Are you now or have you ever been a member of the Communist Party, or* (2) *of any Communist organization?"* The questionnaire required them to list any Communist, Fascist or other subversive organizations to which they may have belonged.

It was all too embarrassing. Melvyn Douglas had a number of fronts to his credit. More to the point, he had been identified in the House Committee on Un-American Activities hearings on the motion picture industry as once having been a member of the Communist Party U.S.A. along with his wife, Helen Gahagan Douglas, the former Congresswoman who had lost to Richard Nixon in the 1950 California race for the United State Senate. As far as Otepka was concerned, and for that matter the security-intelligence community generally, these allegations against the Douglases had never been entirely cleared up. Otepka felt that if Melvyn Douglas had nothing to hide he should not object so strenuously to filling out a few forms and letting the FBI run a thorough investigation on him. Indeed, Otepka reasoned, it might even clear Douglas' name once and for all. The trouble was that the aging Hollywood idol didn't see it quite that way.

As for Archibald MacLeish, he would have quickly run out of space on the security questionnaire if he had attempted to list half the Communist fronts he had joined over the years. MacLeish, the venerable Bard of Harvard Yard who never let the world forget those halcyon days when he was Franklin Roosevelt's speech writer, had signed on with no less than twenty-six fronts at last count. There may be more. But the Attorney General stopped issuing his list of subversive organizations a decade ago and technically no Communist fronts have been created since then.*

When the ticklish matter of the Advisory Committee on the Arts was first referred to SY, John Reilly devised a clever end run designed to sidestep full field investigations by the FBI. He asked the Bureau to run a very special kind of an investigation on MacLeish, Douglas and two of

---

* Once upon a time, during those "witchhunting" days of Senator McCarthy, Archie MacLeish had denounced Walter Lippmann in print as an enemy of civil liberties. Writer Russell Kirk later observed: "The fact that Mr. Lippmann had sternly criticized Senator McCarthy only made matters worse, MacLeish reasoned. It was simply a clever dodge by that columnist to conceal his own innate McCarthyism."

the others Otepka recommended for investigations. Without the necessary employment forms and questionnaires, the FBI was forced to fall back on such unilluminating sources as *Who's Who in America*, which could hardly be expected to require its clients to list Communist front affiliations. Armed with the results of this ersatz FBI investigation, Reilly then demanded that Otepka issue security clearances.

At this point, Otepka balked. He sent Reilly a blunt memorandum stating that "we cannot accept the blandishments that the intellectual brilliance of distinguished exponents of the arts, letters, and sciences goes hand in hand with non-conformity and therefore (a) their conduct needs no explanation and (b) they need not fill out government forms (especially *before* employment), sign loyalty oaths, etc." He said he was "dutybound to comply with the existing law" and if "the present security rules are to be tempered to suit individuals . . . then I think someone in authority should change the rules."

Reilly knew as well as Otepka that only Congress, or conceivably the Supreme Court, could "change the rules." But he decided to set himself above those two august bodies. Through his Massachusetts handyman, David Belisle, he ordered Otepka to issue clearances for MacLeish and Douglas, even though no employment or security forms had been received from either one of them.

Otepka was forced to bow once again to Reilly's shillelagh-wielding tactics. He had not, however, spent a decade in the Department of State without learning that there was more than one way to skin a cat. When he sent the clearances for MacLeish and Douglas to the Personnel Office he sent their files along too, and the required forms were rather conspicuous by their absence. Personnel made yet another attempt to extract the despised forms from the Bard and the Thespian. They refused again to fill them out. The Personnel Office felt it had no alternative but to drop both of them from the vaunted Advisory Committee on the Arts. Although Otepka won this round he was promptly ordered by Belisle not to send security files to Personnel in the future. Thus, yet another door was blocked against him.

On the last of his four appearances before the Senate subcommittee the morning of March 19, Otepka testified on two extremely sensitive matters. One touched on Dean Rusk's assembly-line production of security waivers to bring more people sympathetic with the New Order into the State Department. The practice had supposedly been stopped after Otepka's disclosures to the subcommittee the previous spring. But Sourwine insisted on knowing whether any new waivers had been issued in recent months. Otepka admitted that he knew of one "at the officer level," but he would not supply the name.*

However, he revealed that *no less than three hundred and ninety-eight waivers had been manufactured for clerical and secretarial personnel between the publication of the subcommittee's report and mid-March of 1963, a period of less than five months!* [9] It was apparent, then, that the Department of State had stepped up its wholesale production of "emergency clearances" in direct defiance of the Senators' warnings.

As everyone connected with the Intelligence community knows, spies are not always particular about what kind of job they get in a government they have been ordered to penetrate. For one thing, a good espionage agent posing as a file clerk stands to make more than the Secretary of State if he does a good job for his moonlight employers at the Soviet embassy or wherever. Moreover, it is often easier for an obscure clerk or a trusted secretary to waltz off the premises with a top-secret document than it would be for an official at the policy-making level who is afraid he is being watched.

The State Department's open-door hiring policy under Dean Rusk created a potentially dangerous situation. One can only hope that the Communists have come to view the low-level spy as superfluous and therefore have not taken full advantage of Rusk's waivers. But if they did, Richard Nixon and his successors in Washington will be forced to live with a problem they can never hope to correct. It is much easier for a new administration to clean house on the upper echelons where a good many officials are political appointees than to get rid of clerks who have built up years of Civil Service seniority.

The other matter Otepka testified about on March 19 proved even more volatile than the resurrection of the waiver scandal. Under Jay Sourwine's dogged questioning, Otepka acknowledged the existence of the original report Harlan Cleveland's advisory committee had just slipped under Rusk's door in the attempt quietly to reestablish Alger Hiss' old system for getting Americans into United Nations posts.** He

---

* The State Department later supplied the names of two officer-level people who had come in on waivers signed by Dean Rusk after the Senate report was issued. They were Robert E. Asher and Jacob Blaustein. Both came in as "consultants."(Senate Internal Security Subcommittee, Otepka Hearings, 1963-65; Part 13, page 962.) However, Secretary Rusk personally told the subcommittee on October 21, 1963, that there had been "six such cases since the subcommittee's report was issued last year." (Otepka Hearings; Part 5, page 270.) Rusk did not name any of the six officers whose waivers he had signed during that period.
**See Chapter XV, "Alger's Friends."

did not name any of the dubious cast of characters Cleveland had assembled for this job. In fact, he did not even mention Cleveland, nor did he so much as allude to the running battle he had been waging over clearances for the advisory committee. All this came much later, after Otepka was exiled. The only person identified in any way in this segment of his testimony was Reilly, but only in passing, and not in a manner which did any damage at all to the Deputy Assistant Secretary for Security.[10]

In retrospect, Otepka's restraint is amazing. He had gone through four lengthy sessions in Room 2300 without ever opening up on any of his superiors. Jay Sourwine was plainly disappointed. Not only had Otepka adhered religiously to the outworn Truman directive, which was meant to apply merely to the disclosure of material in personnel security files, he had also refused for the most part to identify the officials responsible for scuttling the security lifeboat of the Department of State. Small wonder, then, that Sourwine was moved at one point to complain that "it gets like pulling teeth" to extract information from him because he "is doing his best to protect the Department."

Nonetheless, he had answered every question truthfully. When Sourwine had asked the right questions, which Otepka felt he could answer without violating the Truman directive, his replies were almost always forthright. Moreover, the total picture he had painted for the subcommittee, under the severe restrictions he had placed upon himself, was of a security system that was fast slipping down the drain.

In another era, when Americans were more concerned for their freedom, Otepka's calm disclosures would have rocked the State Department to its marshmallow foundations. But in 1963 they created hardly a ripple on the placid pond that camouflaged the mysterious birth of America's détente with Soviet communism.

With the notable exceptions of Everett Dirksen and Roman Hruska, it is doubtful whether any of the other Senators who heard or read his testimony fully understood its implications. The subcommittee as a whole tended to view the problem as a complex bureaucratic wrangle. In part, at least, this was Otepka's fault. He had insisted upon playing the game strictly according to the rules. In doing so he allowed himself to be drawn into interminable discussions on minute legal points. His precise explanations, which never infringed on conjecture, were undeniably tedious. He refused to draw conclusions. He stuck determinably to the facts. But the facts never quite seemed to zero in on the target. Indeed, some of the Senators must have wondered just what the target was.

Initially, the only ostensible purpose served by Otepka's lonely marches up to Capitol Hill was to spur a more ferocious assault by Jack Reilly and the shillelagh brigade. They were more determined than ever to beat Otepka to his knees and they meant to use whatever weapons they could find. The bitter behind-the-scenes war that had been waged against Otepka for more than two years was now about to shift into a new and far more vicious phase.

CHAPTER XXI

Under Surveillance

IN WAS SHORTLY AFTER THE THIRD OF HIS FOUR LATEST APPEARANCES on Capitol Hill that Otto Otepka first began to have difficulty with his telephone. His secretary, Mrs. Powers, noticed the trouble too. Frequently when they dialed a number there would be dead silence on the line. Sometimes Otepka had the sensation that he was talking into an empty iron barrel which echoed his voice in an odd and booming fashion. Clattering noises interrupted his conversations. Occasionally there were strange voices on his extensions when he picked up the phone.

All these mysterious phenomena would today be written off as electronic accidents or, worse, evidence of Otepka's paranoia, if the Senate Internal Security Subcommittee had not come up with conclusive proof that Otepka's telephone had actually been tapped, not by enemy agents, but by his superiors in the Department of State.

The evidence was so irrefutable, and the circumstances such a flagrant invasion of Otepka's privacy, that even the American Civil Liberties Union was moved to protest in his behalf. Nonetheless, although admissions of guilt were finally wrung from at least two of the officials responsible for the illegal tapping, the Justice Department of Robert F. Kennedy refused to prosecute.

It was the Massachusetts mob in SY, headed by John Reilly, who implemented the wire taps and other surveillance techniques used on Otepka. As a lawyer, Reilly must have been acutely conscious that he was breaking the law as well as a State Department directive specifically banning electronic taps except where there was good reason to believe the national security was being compromised. But Reilly also was confident that he had *carte blanche* to get Otepka and he did not hesitate to use whatever weapons came to hand.

No suspected Communist agent in the State Department was ever subjected to a more thorough surveillance than Otepka. Not content with the telephone tap, his superiors bugged his office so they could listen in on *all* conversations he had with his staff or with visitors. Like scavengers, they carefully hoarded the discarded papers he threw in his waste basket and in "burn bags" reserved for carrying unwanted duplicates of classified material to the incinerator. There is evidence that they hired a private detective agency to mount all-night watches on his home. And they secretly drilled open the safe where he kept his private papers and the more damaging material about various State Department officials he was keeping tabs on in his line of duty.

For nearly a year Otepka had been surrounded by bumbling spies in his Evaluations Division. But the intensified and systematic watch on his activities was first mounted on March 14, 1963—a week after Otepka confirmed the State Department's attempts to circumvent the law in the delicate matter of Melvyn Douglas and Archibald MacLeish. The "crime" his superiors later claimed triggered their decision to place him under close surveillance was his suspected cooperation with the Senate subcommittee, and especially with Chief Counsel Sourwine.

From Sourwine's groping questions, and from his frustration with Otepka's answers, it was apparent that Otepka had thus far lived up to his pledge not to supply classified information, even in sworn testimony. But even if he had, this would not have constituted an attempt to compromise national security. Sourwine was fully authorized to receive classified data, not merely from the State Department, but from the far more sensitive Atomic Energy Commission and from the Department of Defense.

Setting aside the legal niceties, however, the simple fact that the hierarchy at the Department of State felt compelled surreptitiously to tune in on Otepka and Sourwine at all shows how touchy the seventh floor was to the possibility that the Congress, and through it the American people, might discover how the internal security program was being deliberately destroyed.

Did the hierarchy know what was going on? Reilly, at least, thought he had their blessing, though he did his best to shield them from direct involvement in the illegal wiretapping. After discussing the matter with David Belisle on March 13, he went to William Orrick, who had taken Roger Jones' place as the overlord of administration in the Department. He told Orrick that he suspected Otepka of feeding information to Sourwine and the subcommittee. Orrick's only admonition was that Reilly "make sure of his facts." Orrick, of course, was in close and almost daily contact with Dean Rusk.

Otepka soon felt the net tightening about him. He often worked late at night, sometimes going out for dinner and returning afterwards. On the night of March 24, 1963, he came back to his office, Room 3333, shortly after 10 o'clock. About twenty minutes later David Belisle cautiously entered with Terence Shea, a fellow New Englander who had worked with him in the National Security Agency.

The two intruders were obviously taken aback to find Otepka at his desk. Belisle blurted out that they had just seen a cleaning woman come into Room 3333 and they had decided to check on her. Otepka trained a steely eye on the nervous Belisle. "I've been here for some time," he said evenly. *"No one just entered—or left."*

Flustered, Belisle and his crony beat a guilty retreat. A few weeks later, Otepka learned that the Massachusetts Mafia had obtained the combination to his top-secret safe some time before this incident. In mid-March, Reilly had ordered Joe Rosetti to get SY's safe-and-lock expert, Russell Waller, to crack Otepka's safe. They waited until a night when they were certain Otepka had gone home. Then they pulled the job. Waller removed the metal ring around the tumbler, drilled a small hole, inserted a tiny dental magnifying mirror called a pharyngoscope, and in this manner observed the numbers on which the tumbler fell. When he had the combination, Waller ran a test to make sure it worked. After opening the safe, he locked it up again, taking care to replace the metal ring so Otepka wouldn't spot the drilled hole. Then the combination was delivered to Reilly.*

Jack Kennedy's old aide, Joe Rosetti, was also the leader of the waste basket and burn-bag brigade which carefully sorted out Otepka's discarded trash in search of evidence that he was cooperating with the Senate subcommittee. Acting under Reilly's order, Rosetti, Belisle, Terry Shea, Robert McCarthy, and Fred Traband all joined the Great Scaven-

* Rosetti, in sworn testimony before the Senate subcommittee, at first denied that safes were ever cracked by his Division of Domestic Operations. Later, he admitted the whole story.[1]

ger Hunt. Everyone of these men knew that Otepka was not a subversive. Yet they all willingly, even gleefully, took part in rummaging through his trash. Worse, they prevailed upon a young girl to help them.

When Otepka's secretary, Eunice Powers, took ill late in March, Reilly and his crew planted Joyce Schmelzer, an attractive young bride, in Otepka's office. Much later, Mrs. Schmelzer broke down in tears and protested that she had not wanted to participate in the undercover spying on a man she knew to be completely loyal to his country. But, she said, Reilly's gang had forced her to be their "courier."

To Joyce Schmelzer fell the untidy job of gathering up the burn-bag trash, marking it with a big red 'X' and delivering it to SY's mail room. Traband, Otepka's assistant chief of the Evaluations Division, would alert Rosetti by phone that the trash was on the way. Rosetti would retrieve the trash from the mail room and deliver it to Reilly, Belisle, McCarthy or Shea.

It must have been a pretty spectacle—the exalted Deputy Assistant Secretary of State for Security and his well-paid minions poring over the crumpled scraps of paper, piecing them together, searching for "evidence" that Otto Otepka was cooperating with a committee of the Congress of the United States.

The scavenger hunt, wiretapping, safecracking, and other surveillance techniques apparently failed to produce conclusive evidence against Otepka. So in the end Reilly and his gang resorted to a heavy-handed frame-up which, as we shall see, was to place Otepka under "criminal charges."

Ironically, the only real crimes committed had been perpetrated by the State Department itself in attempting to frame Otepka and in tapping his telephone. Given the level of bureaucratic efficiency that prevails on Foggy Bottom, it is not surprising that the Department bungled both these jobs, though not nearly as badly as it later pretended.

After righteously and repeatedly denying under oath that any electronics eavesdropping had been attempted, Reilly and one of his henchmen later confessed that they had tried it, but that it turned out to be a comedy of errors. There is no reason to believe that they told the whole truth. But their account is interesting nonetheless.

According to Reilly, it was March 18 before he got around to asking Elmer Hill, the *bon-vivant* of Warsaw, to look into the possibility of tapping Otepka's telephone. Reilly said he didn't actually *authorize* the tap at this time, but Hill certainly thought that he had. Hill promptly rounded up an electronics man on Reilly's staff, Clarence Schneider, to give him a hand.

Working late at night, Hill and Schneider used some of the expensive new gear the State Department was busily acquiring. With it they linked Otepka's two phone extensions to a tape recorder hidden in Hill's laboratory. However, these two high-priced experts claimed that the interference on the taps was so bad that their recorder could hardly hear what Otepka was saying. At first, this probably was true.

The day after the tap was planted, Clarence Schneider complained to Stanley Holden, the deposed chief of SY's electronics unit, that he had been unable to clear up a humming noise on a line he had just tapped. He asked Holden's help, but Holden guessed whose phone was being compromised and he declined.

The following day, March 20, Reilly allegedly changed his mind about the whole tapping business when Hill informed him of what had been done. That same night Reilly says he stood guard with Schneider outside the door to Otepka's office while Hill disconnected the illegal wires. Reilly and Hill later swore that no conversations had been recorded. But the State Department made the mistake of admitting that it had several tapes stashed away.

The improbable tale concocted by Reilly and Hill might be a bit more credible if it were not for the fact that Otepka continued to have trouble with his phone long after the tap was allegedly disconnected. Early in April Otepka invited Russell Waller to his office. After listening to the strange noises still emanating from both of Otepka's extensions, Waller stated flatly, "Your phone is bugged."

Waller was not a member of the new inner circle in SY. He had cracked Otepka's safe apparently under the impression that Reilly and Rosetti needed the combination for legitimate reasons and were entitled to have it. In his innocence, he now went to Rosetti and reported that Otepka's telephone was acting oddly. Rosetti, of course, told Reilly. And Reilly dropped by to see Otepka.

Almost cheerfully, Reilly remarked that he had "heard" that Otepka was having trouble with his phone lines. He pretended that he had had some difficulty with his own telephone. But it had been checked out, he said, and nothing was found wrong. The implication was that nothing was wrong with Otepka's phone either.

George Pasquale, the unwilling Warsaw companion of Elmer Hill, was the first to confirm Otepka's growing suspicions about the wiretapping.

In May, Pasquale told Otepka that his former boss, Stanley Holden, had informed him that Otepka's phone was definitely bugged. Not long after this when Holden came by Room 3333, Otepka started to ask him some questions. But Holden silently signaled him to stop, pointing at the phone and at the ceiling to indicate that even non-telephonic conversations were being picked up.

Otepka knew that there was a device that could be placed in a phone which would transmit all audible sounds even when the telephone was in its cradle. He waited for another opportunity to question Holden elsewhere. Holden hinted that a listening device had been installed in the walls or ceiling of Otepka's office. He said that Rosetti was clued in on the operation and that Belisle and Shea were in charge of the physical surveillance of Otepka outside the building as well as within it. Later, Holden refused to tell him more, clearly implying that he feared reprisals. His fears were realized too. Reilly and Hill tapped Holden's telephone a little later—just before Holden suffered a mysterious accident.

On April 25, six weeks after the surveillance of Otepka was escalated to the status of a television spy drama, John Reilly was hailed before the Senate subcommittee. Senator Dodd, who had not attended any of the four sessions in which Otepka testified, was at first quite favorably inclined toward Reilly. "I want to say, at the very beginning, that I have a very high opinion of Mr. Reilly," Dodd beamed by way of welcome. "I have never met him until this meeting, but I have heard a lot about him and I am very happy that he is on the job."

It is doubtful whether Dodd had yet had a chance to go over Otepka's revelations when he extended this praiseworthy greeting, just after Reilly took the oath. At any rate, Dodd's initial magnanimity changed quickly to ill-concealed suspicion as Reilly began to spin his evasive tales.

Reilly wasted little time teeing off on Otepka. He described the "backlog" of cases that had built up in the Evaluations Division and, in answer to a Sourwine question, he branded Otepka "the bottleneck of bottlenecks." Among other things, Reilly said, Otepka insisted on reviewing cases "four or five times."[2]

Asked if the State Department had taken any action on the recommendations in the subcommittee's report, Reilly brazenly pretended that he had implemented some of the suggestions. In fact, he swore that he had put them into effect *before* the report was issued. "Our minds ran in parallel channels," he unctuously added. However, when Sourwine and Dodd pressed him for particulars, Reilly conveniently had a lapse of memory. He did not, he said, have the information "at my fingertips."[3]

Sourwine inquired about the status of the Wieland case. Reilly tried to slither around that one by stating that it was "presently pending in the Department of Justice." Both Dodd and Sourwine wanted to know why that precluded the State Department from taking action. Reilly at last admitted that it didn't, and swore that Justice's decision "would not make a difference" to State.*

When Sourwine wanted to know who was handling the case in SY, Reilly said that Harry Hite was. (Hite had not yet received the Wieland file from Robert McCarthy.) He claimed that Otepka had voluntarily "disqualified" himself because he did not want again to "sit in judgment" on a case about which he had testified before the Senate subcommittee.[4]

Dodd's wind was really up now. He was beginning to see through Reilly's evasions and in the Wieland thing he smelled something worse. A minute later he lost patience entirely.

Reilly had just handed over the press release the State Department was about to issue on Harlan Cleveland's advisory committee. The Cleveland committee's initial report had been thoroughly revised and scrubbed since Otepka's disclosure before the subcommittee a month earlier. But Dodd was plainly stunned by the composition of the committee itself. He shook his head and murmured, "This is some board, I might say."[5]

At this point Sourwine suggested they all go off the record. The matter of Cleveland's attempt to restore the old Alger Hiss method to the U.N.'s hiring of Americans was covered at some length. By the time they got back on the record Dodd was thoroughly exasperated. "I must say," he frowned, "that I am surprised at this testimony; I am shocked by it."[6]

Reilly left the hearing room somewhat shaken himself. As soon as he got back to the State Department he went to Otepka's office. His usually florid complexion had taken on a paler hue and his hand trembled noticeably as he stroked his five o'clock shadow. Behind the closed door of Room 3333, Reilly confessed to Otepka that Senator Dodd had given him a "bad time." He said that Dodd had questioned him closely about Otepka's "voluntary" withdrawal from the Wieland case.

To Otepka's amazement, Reilly then asked Otepka if he would get him off the hook. Specifically, he wanted Otepka to tell Dodd that he had in fact "disqualified" himself from the Wieland matter.

Otepka regarded Reilly with calm dark eyes that contained no hint of his feelings. Characteristically, he decided against engaging Reilly in a debate or a name-calling contest. Instead, he quietly informed him that

* Reilly's chief-of-staff, Belisle, later ordered Wieland cleared on the grounds the Justice Department had decided not to prosecute for the manifest perjury Wieland had committed before the subcommittee.

he did not know Senator Dodd personally. If he was called as a witness, however, he said that he would testify precisely about the conversation they had had on the Wieland case.

That night, Ben Mandel, the aging research director of the Senate subcommittee, telephoned Otepka at his home. Mandel had sat in on Reilly's testimony that day and for some reason he thought Senator Dodd had been unnecessarily hard on Reilly. He asked Otepka to contact Dodd and "clarify" the little business of his having "disqualified" himself from the Wieland case. Otepka told Mandel he had no intention of rescuing Reilly from any situation he had knowingly gotten himself into. He intended to tell the truth, period.

When Mandel hung up, Otepka called Sourwine. He told him about Mandel's plea, adding that he thought Ben had acted in good faith. He asked Sourwine if he could have additional information about what Reilly had told the subcommittee since it involved him directly. Several days later Sourwine gave Otepka a transcript of Reilly's testimony. He pointed out that there were some obvious conflicts between Reilly's statements and his own, but he thought Senator Dodd, at least, saw that Reilly was the one who was lying.

On Monday, April 30, Reilly again appeared before the subcommittee. Dodd immediately went after him on the Wieland matter and this time Reilly forsook whatever chance there may have been that he had previously misunderstood Otepka's intentions. He said that he had talked with Otepka after his last appearance and that Otepka had "again stated" that he did "not want to involve himself in a full-time evaluation of the case."[7]

Before he was done that morning, Reilly dotted the whole record with lies. There seemed to be nothing he could bring himself to tell the truth about. Some of his fabrications appear entirely unnecessary, except in the light that he was willing to do anything to defend the State Department's actions. At one point, he even went so far as to defend the Cleveland committee's motives in trying to revive the old Hiss-U.N. hiring formula.[8]

However, Reilly did pull in his horns—slightly and temporarily—on his previous charge that Otepka was a "bottleneck." Amazingly, he admitted that most of the 150-odd applications and promotions Otepka had held up in recent months were "Communist cases." Moreover, he further agreed with Sourwine that they were cases which involved "serious derogatory information."[9]* But he still complained because Otepka

---

* Virtually all of these "Communist cases," as Reilly called them, were given security clearances by the State Department after Otepka's ouster two months later.

had refused to help him "expedite" cases for which the seventh floor had requested quick clearances! Following Reilly's magnificent encore, Sourwine contacted Otepka and suggested that they get together. When they met, Sourwine reported that Reilly had persisted in his previous testimony regarding the Wieland business and other matters. The gaps between Reilly's and Otepka's stories had widened considerably. The subcommittee was growing more disturbed by the conflicts and Otepka knew that sooner or later he would be expected to resolve them.

CHAPTER **XXII**

Decision

THE ATMOSPHERE IN THE HEARING ROOM WAS NOTICEABLY CHARGED when the Senate subcommittee called John Reilly back to Capitol Hill toward the end of May. The Senators were beginning to grasp that something was dangerously wrong in the Department of State. They had not quite put a firm finger on the real trouble, but it was obvious that the Office of Security was, at the very least, being badly mishandled.

Senators Dodd, Dirksen and Scott alternated as chairmen and observers at Reilly's three latest command performances. Sourwine once again conducted the interrogation, with Ben Mandel and Frank Schroeder, the subcommittee's chief investigator, sitting watchfully by. At the very first session, Reilly revealed his growing sense of desperation.

Lashing out viciously at Otepka, Reilly claimed that the former security chief "had a great tendency to dwell in the past" and had taken his demotion too hard. "He seems emotionally overwrought on that topic," Reilly observed. "He does not strike me as being a balanced individual."[1]

Over the years, Sourwine had seen many people who tried to defend their country against communism branded as insane or emotionally unbalanced. He was not surprised that Otepka should be so branded now.

"I have been wondering if this was coming." Sourwine nodded his leonine head judiciously. "This the first suggestion we have heard from anybody that Mr. Otepka was mentally unbalanced. But I have been wondering if that wasn't about due."

The irony was completely wasted on Reilly. A second later, Sourwine asked, "How long have you noticed this mental unbalance?" and Reilly answered in all seriousness: "I noticed that shortly after I arrived [at State] when I had a session with him that lasted, oh, almost four hours."

Reilly also questioned whether Otepka was being "honest" with him, and he further suggested that "he is misleading one or the other of us," meaning himself or the Senate subcommittee.[2] Moreover, he called David Belisle "a stronger man" than Otepka, offering this as the reason he had slipped Belisle in over his evaluations chief.[3]

When they got down to specifics, Reilly rattled off a long list of grievances against Otepka. He tried to create the impression that Otepka had cleared all but one of the members of Cleveland's advisory committee without raising any questions at all. "There was only one case, Mr. Sourwine, that was brought to my attention," he maintained.[4] He similarly pretended that there had been no real difficulty over the Advisory Committee on the Arts, nor over the matter of a special clearance for Abba Schwartz, the Administrator of the Bureau of Security and Consular Affairs.

The lies went on, *ad nauseam* for three days. Reilly, having overruled Otepka any number of times in the last year, swore that he had only "overruled him on one or two occasions." But, he added, "I can't for the moment bring any particular cases to mind." He denied that Otepka had been subjected to reprisals. He denied that the War College appointment had been a ploy to get Otepka out of SY. He denied that the removal of the Intelligence reporting function had hurt the Evaluations Division. He denied, in fact, everything that would cast any doubt whatever on his own administration in SY, and anything that might confirm that Otepka had told the subcommittee the truth about the existing situation.

After Reilly was done on Thursday afternoon, May 23, Sourwine phoned Otepka and said that he had better come see him. It was well past 5 o'clock when Otepka arrived. The two men sat alone at the far end of Sourwine's long, dimly lit office on the third floor of the New Senate Office Building. Sourwine told Otepka that the conflicts between his and Reilly's sworn testimony now loomed larger than ever. In fact, there were dozens of statements that were totally irreconcilable. Otepka asked to see the transcripts of Reilly's testimony. A few days later Sourwine supplied them.

Pouring over the transcripts, Otepka saw clearly that the Senator must now believe that one or the other, either he or Reilly, had to be lying. He took note of Reilly's charge that he had been misleading the subcommittee. He was dismayed, though not surprised, to see that his honesty, and even his sanity, had been questioned by the Deputy Assistant Secretary of State for Security.

Up to now, Otepka had done his best to keep personalities out of his own testimony before the subcommittee. He had tried hard to focus the debate on issues and procedures. He had bent over backward to refrain from making direct accusations against his superiors. But he saw now that his efforts had gone for naught. His own name had been dragged through the mud and his motives cast under the muddiest and most damaging cloud of all—the question of whether he was entirely sane. There were only two courses open to Otepka at this juncture: either he told the Senate subcommittee the whole story, or he had to go through channels in the Department of State to demand retractions from John Reilly. He had seen enough of the New Order to know how far he would get with the latter course. In a very real sense, that door had been barred to him since his meeting with Dean Rusk and Bobby Kennedy way back in December 1960.

For a fleeting moment he wondered just where he might stand now if he had not taken such a firm position on the matter of Walt W. Rostow. He knew that he had gotten off on the wrong foot with the new Administration right at the start. He saw that his present difficulties stemmed directly from that inauspicious beginning. But he also saw that the course of events would have been inevitable in any event. Something more than a clash of personalities was involved. Two very different philosophies lay at the heart of the matter. And the one that Otepka so firmly opposed had always believed that the end justifies the means.

Otepka reflected at length on the situation in the Department of State. He knew that the Department had on its rolls many men who had been defended and retained after it was clearly established that they had deliberately concealed material facts about their past, such as former membership in the Communist Party. He knew of many others, similarly protected, who had committed fraud, engaged in sexual perversion, lied on their application forms, leaked information to known Communists, or supplied classified papers to people who neither had security clearance nor were in any way connected with the federal government.

He knew that William Wieland was not the only American diplomat who had undermined the leaders of friendly foreign governments in order to supplant them with people more sympathetic to their own views. There were countless cases he could name where the highest officials of the State Department had spilled U.S. plans and military policies to the press simply because they had personally opposed those policies.

"The concern I had—and have—about the conduct of these and other State Department officials," Otepka told this writer in 1968, "has in many respects a parallel in the cases of Alger Hiss and so many of the others who were unmasked as Communist agents in the 1940's and '50's. It also has a parallel in a number of cases in England. The disclosures about the career of 'Kim' Philby should be a lesson to all of us, if we think the lessons of our own experiences here in America are in some way 'outdated.'

"Philby rose steadily, even mercurially, through the Foreign Office and British Intelligence although he now boasts, from his home in Moscow, that he was a Soviet agent for some thirty years. To rise like this, despite obvious aberrations in his character, he most certainly had to have protection. Whether it was provided innocently or with deliberate malice the result was exactly the same. This is the same kind of protection that scores of questionable officials have received for years in our State Department.

"Even during my tenure as Deputy Director of the Office of Security there was really very little I could do at my level to get these people out, though an honest effort was made to keep more of them from coming in," Otepka remarked. "After 1961, all the barriers were torn down. All that remained was a shabby pretense that the State Department was upholding the internal security laws."

Otepka said that there was never any question in his mind back in 1963 about resigning in the face of John Reilly's charges. To have quit under the dark cloud that Reilly had spewed forth would have left his name besmirched forever. But more important, he sensed that his resignation would be the final death knell for internal security, not just in the State Department but, as Sourwine had pointed out, throughout the federal government.

Otepka recalled sitting one night in the solitude of his basement study at home, browsing through some excerpts he had noted down over the years from the words of outstanding men he admired. One in particular reinforced him in the decision he was about to make in May of 1963. Otepka, knowing that his career of twenty years as a security officer was rapidly drawing to a close, took comfort from the words of Daniel Webster:

What is the individual man, with all the good or evil that may betide him, in comparison with the good or evil which may befall a great country, and in the midst of great transactions which concern that country's fate? Let the consequences be what they will. . . . No man can suffer too much . . . in the defense of the liberties and constitution of his country.

It was with Webster's words in mind that Otepka at last made his fateful decision. He informed Jay Sourwine that he would open up completely with the Senate subcommittee He realized full well that it would mean breaking the Truman directive. But there now was no other way to clear his name and strike a blow for sound security. To others, who do not see this archaic order as carrying the full force of a law passed by Congress, this might not seem like such a bold step. But no one will probably ever know what it cost Otto Otepka to take it.

Sourwine suggested that the best way to refute Reilly's testimony would be for Otepka to isolate each point of conflict and prepare his rebuttal item by item. At Otepka's discretion, he said, it would be wise to support each of his points with documented evidence. Without such proof, the subcommittee would be in the position of judging one man's word against the other's. Even though the Senators seemed inclined to believe Otepka rather than Reilly, they might be forced to declare the whole mattter at an impasse unless Otepka could substantiate his claims.

Over the next ten days, Otepka painstakingly prepared his case. On Monday morning, May 27, he began dictating his "brief " to Mrs. Powers in Room 3333. He was entirely aware that he was being watched, and he knew that his every word was probably being recorded in Elmer Hill's laboratory. But it was typical of him that he decided not to hide. His conscience was clear. He had no intention of sneaking around corners to deliver information to a Congressional committee, as David Belisle had done a few years before to save his neck from the NSA guillotine.

On Wednesday, Mrs. Powers finished transcribing Otepka's brief. It ran to thirty-nine pages, double-spaced, and it was carefully keyed to each point in Reilly's testimony. During the following week Otepka appended to the brief, or resumé as he prefered to call it, a total of thirty-six documents to support his own statements and to refute Reilly's. Twenty-five of the documents were unclassified; six were labeled, "Official Use Only"; three were marked, "Limited Official Use." Two bore the unmistakable red stamp, "Confidential."

"I read the contents of each document carefully," Otepka later said, "to be certain that I was not giving any information which would be prejudicial to the national security or the national defense if it were to be published by the Senate subcommittee. The two papers marked 'Confidential' were only transmittal memorandums that referred to certain attachments. *I did not give those attachments to Mr. Sourwine.* The memos themselves contained information which had already been published by Congressional committees about certain individuals. It was obvious that these two papers were overclassified."

Ironically, Otepka had himself assigned the various classifications to most of the documents he delivered to Sourwine. The resumé he handed over ran the whole gamut of Reilly's exhaustive list of lies, bowling them over one by one. Within two weeks after Otepka gave the subcommittee this explosive package, four members of the Massachusetts mob—McCarthy, Rosetti, Shea and Traband—were hailed into Room 2300 to answer Sourwine's probing questions.

By then Otepka knew he had reached the end of the line. The surveillance net that had been thrown around him in March was tightening inexorably. For some weeks his suburban home had been watched almost every night by a strange man sitting in a parked car. Otepka regarded the stranger's presence as just another manifestation of the systematic harassment he was now being subjected to daily at the State Department. He was inclined to shrug it off. But when the stranger took to parking directly across the street from the Otepka home and peering at it through binoculars, Edith Otepka had had enough. She complained to Otto and he called the local police department. A squad car swooped down on the inquisitive stranger and demanded identification. The police found that the man, one Eric Steinberg, was employed by a private detective agency. Otepka knew it was not unusual for the government to hire private eyes for special jobs and he planned to have a chat with Steinberg the following night. Unfortunately, Steinberg never showed up again.

It was during this same period that John F. Kennedy formally stamped the Presidential seal of approval on the Rostowian policy of convergence and détente. Up to this point the administration had been feeding it to the public in small, cautious doses, as Dr. Rostow had prescribed. Now, less than eight months after his dramatic disclosure that the Soviets were busy installing nuclear missiles on Cuba, the President decided it was time for a massive injection to pave the way for the long-sought test ban treaty. At American University on June 10 he unveiled his formula "not merely [for] peace in our time, but peace for all time."

Speaking of the Soviet Union, he declared that "no government or social system is so evil that its people must be considered as lacking in virtue. . . . we must reexamine our own attitude—as indivuduals and as a Nation—for our attitude is as essential as theirs . . . every citizen should begin by looking inward—by examining his own attitude toward the possibilities of peace, toward the Soviet Union."

The President warned Americans "not to see only a distorted and desperate view of the other side, not to see conflict as inevitable, accommodation as impossible." Instead, he urged, we should "direct our attention to our common interests and to the means by which those differences [sic] can be resolved." He called upon the United States to "help make the world safe for diversity." This was a far, far cry from the Wilsonian promise to "make the world safe for democracy" for which thousands of Americans had died in France a generation before. It was also a long, long way from the principles of the Atlantic Charter for which thousands more gave their lives in World War II. But the ideals of a great nation can shrivel dramatically in a matter of decades.

"Let us reexamine our attitude toward the Soviet Union," Mr Kennedy reiterated. The move toward peace "would require," he said, "increased understanding between the Soviets and ourselves . . . increased contact and communication." He then announced that talks would soon begin in Moscow "looking toward early agreement on a comprehensive test ban treaty."

Nikita Khrushchev was ecstatic. He later told Averell Harriman, the chief U.S. test ban negotiator, that it was "the greatest speech by any American President since Roosevelt."

Reading the newspaper accounts of President Kennedy's remarks Otto Otepka understood a little better why Dean Rusk and Bobby Kennedy so desperately wanted him purged from the Department of State. And through his experiences since he had been placed under surveillance by their hired hands, he understood, too, what the President and his advisors really meant by "convergence" with the Soviet Union.

CHAPTER **XXIII**

Strange Interludes

ALL DURING THE PERIOD THAT OTEPKA WAS UNDER CLOSE SURVEIL-
ance he managed somehow to get on with his work at the Department
f State. Sensing that his every move was being watched, knowing that
very word he uttered in his office was monitored, he nonetheless kept
rying to fulfill his duties. The long hours he was forced to take out to
estify before the Senate subcommittee he made up at night and on
veekends at his desk in SY. Even the preparation of his voluminous
ebuttal of John Reilly's false testimony failed to divert him from his
rimary task. Although he realized that he might be removed from his
ob any day, he never once relaxed his vigilance.

About the time President Kennedy was gearing up for his historic
American University address, Otepka made a number of chilling discov-
ries. Each one provided additional evidence as to how far the United
tates had already moved down the path toward convergence with the
Soviet Union. The first of these discoveries convinced Otepka that the
Administration no longer intended to maintain even the empty pretenses
f past policies.

Earlier that spring, Reilly approved a proposed change in regulations
o permit the rehiring of former State Department officials who had
reviously been dismissed on security grounds. Leo Harris, an attorney

257

in Abram Chayes' office, told Otepka that one of the principal reasons for the recommended change was to give John Paton Davies a chance to return to State.

Politely, Otepka put Harris on notice that he would oppose any move to bring Davies back. He had handled the Davies case himself years before. There was incontrovertible evidence that Davies had delivered secret U.S. documents to Communist agents in the days when the China cabal was fanatically working to help Mao Tse-tung to power.

Otepka reminded Harris that a Department hearing board had unanimously voted that Davies be fired as a security risk. He pointed out that Secretary Dulles had upheld the dismissal. Otepka suggested that Davies take his case to the courts if he felt he had been dealt with unjustly, instead of having his friends at State tailor security regulations to suit him.*

Otepka was cognizant that Davies, who was now running a furniture business in Peru, had been flying back to Washington off and on since the advent of the New Frontier.** It was known that the exiled diplomat was privately advising the Administration on the Alliance for Progress and other matters. Now the old pro-Mao cabal, with patron Dean Rusk occupying the office of Secretary of State, obviously intended to complete the rehabilitation of John Paton Davies, much as it had attempted the resurrection of Alger Hiss.

Through this nightmare world, Otepka continued to move with his customary calm. Almost every week that spring he was confronted with efforts to reinstate old security risks like Davies or bring in new ones. Sometimes he was able to block their appointments. More often he was not.

With the strong backing of Bobby Kennedy, Frank Montero, friend of the Angolan terrorists, was subsequently named, over Otepka's objections, to Adlai Stevenson's staff at the U.N. Fred Traband, who was soon to succeed Otepka as working head of the Evaluations Division, recommended Montero's clearance. Otepka, in exile by then, read about it in the newspapers. Traband also issued the clearance for another individual, this one with known Communist connections, whom Otepka had turned

* Among many other things, Davies had lied under oath before the Senate Internal Security Subcommittee during the Institute of Pacific Relations hearings in 1951-52. The 1968 Subcommittee Report on the Otepka Case (Part IV, p. 31) recalled that the subcommittee found that "John Paton Davies, Jr., testified falsely . . . in denying that he recommended the Central Intelligence Agency employ, utilize, and rely upon certain individuals having Communist associations and connections."
** The furniture business Davies operated in Peru was reliably reported to be a "cover operation" supported by CIA.

down on security grounds. This man was then appointed to the staff of William Crockett, the Deputy Undersecretary for Administration, a staff which supervises all personnel and security functions in the State Department.

When Otepka opposed clearance for a man with a notorious pattern of personal misbehavior, including embezzlement of funds from his church, Traband lectured him on the necessity of yielding to "reality" when applicants like this had hefty political backing. Otepka rejected the clearance anyway, although Traband later issued it. However, this individual's record was so bad on its very face that the Personnel Office decided to turn him down rather than risk the chance that his hiring might become public knowledge.

Otepka lost the next round, though, when Mrs. Patricia Glover Barnett was appointed to the Bureau of Intelligence and Research as a specialist in Far Eastern Affairs. Her husband, Robert Warren Barnett, had recently been named Deputy Assistant Secretary of State for Far Eastern economic affairs. Years before Otepka had recommended that Barnett be suspended in the interest of national security. Now he refused to clear Mrs. Barnett, under the State Department's security standard.

"I was not in any way influenced by the fact that Senator McCarthy once charged that Robert Barnett and his wife had close and constant contacts with known Soviet agents," Otepka later insisted in answer to a question. "My judgment of the Barnetts was based solely upon the record."

In this instance, the record is very interesting indeed. Born in China of missionary parents, Robert Barnett was already listing to the left during his student days at the University of North Carolina in the 1930's and as a Rhodes scholar at Oxford. Later, he belonged to such flagrant Communist fronts as the old American League for Peace and Democracy and was an official of the Washington office of the Institute of Pacific Relations. He contributed articles to publications like *Amerasia*, which was edited by the Soviet agent Philip Jaffe, and *China Today*, official organ of the Communist-controlled American Friends of the Chinese People. Along the way, Barnett acquired an impressive list of influential friends and associates, including Alger Hiss, Harry Dexter White, Virginius Coe, Lauchlin Currie, Frederick Vanderbilt Field, and a host of other members of the old espionage clubs.

Mrs. Barnett's record closely paralleled her husband's. It was only natural that they should have the same friends and interests. She had worked for the State Department before, and had quietly departed when the word got around that charges might be brought against her. Robert Barnett brazened it out and kept right on moving up the promotion ladder. It is quite possible that Senator McCarthy saved him. By naming Barnett publicly he created a vast reservoir of sympathy for him in the State Department, and powerful friends rushed to his aid when Otepka and Scott McLeod recommended his suspension.[1] One of them was Dean Rusk, who got into the act even before Otepka moved to State. During the 1952 Congressional hearings on tax-exempt foundations, Rusk went out of his way to defend Barnett. On December 5 he testified as president of the Rockefeller Foundation, which had given four separate grants to Barnett, one of them through the Institute of Pacific Relations for a trip to China in 1940.

"I happen to know Mr. Barnett because he served under me while I was Assistant Secretary of State for Far Eastern Affairs," Rusk said. He added that if there was "any possible question or doubt" about the loyalty of anyone under him, he would have known about it. What he would have *done* about it is another question, but no one asked him that. However, Rusk's sweeping absolution apparently was sufficient to remove all doubts about Barnett, at least in his own mind. "I have no reason myself to regret this relationship," Rusk declared. "He has done a fine job of public service as I have observed it directly."[2]

Now, with Otepka overruled on both the husband and the wife, the Barnetts were both happily ensconced in the State Department, where "togetherness" has many meanings.

Considerable pressure was exerted on Otepka that spring to issue an especially sensitive type clearance to Abba Schwartz, czar of the Bureau of Security & Consular Affairs and a protégé of Adlai Stevenson. Involved were top-secret documents that Schwartz had no real need for in his job but to which he wanted access anyway. Unfortunately, Schwartz's security file was liberally sprinkled with a number of dubious connections. It is a matter of public record that he was active in the vividly tainted National Lawyers Guild, whose members have devoted themselves unstintingly to defending Communists and Communist causes.[3] Moreover he had first come into the government, back in the Hiss era, on the recommendation of a suspected Soviet agent.

Schwartz had worked in London during the postwar era for the Intergovernmental Committee on Refugees (ICR), which was heavily infiltrated at the time.* From London he flitted to Geneva in 1947 as an

---

* Among the ICR's more illustrious alumni was Harry Collins, genial host of several Washington-based espionage rings and friend of Whittaker Chambers during the latter's service as a Soviet courier.

official of the U.N.'s International Refugee Organization (IRO), another favorite nesting place for questionable characters. While laboring in behalf of the poor refugees, Schwartz liberally feathered his own financial nest. In fact, his law firm, Landis, Cohen, Rubin and Schwartz, collected fees totaling $130,000 from IRO's successor agency, the Intergovernmental Committee on European Migration (ICEM) during the 1950's when Schwartz was its special counsel.*

Schwartz's more recent record in helping Abram Chayes, Nicholas Katzenbach, and Bobby Kennedy subvert the law with regard to issuing passports to Communist agents also troubled Otepka. He knew too that Schwartz was striving to get $25 million in federal funds to scatter around the Free World thousands of unscreened Russian refugees who were suddenly turning up in Hong Kong, Turkey and other unlikely places. And he was aware of the role played by Schwartz's bureau in the recent Cuban prisoner ransom. (Schwartz later admitted to a Congressional committee that Fidel Castro picked half the refugees who entered the U.S. on this deal. Although the public was led to believe that only victims of the Bay of Pigs invasion and their families were involved, the *émigrés* included three hundred and thirty-three non-Cubans, including natives of the Soviet Union, China, Poland and Hungary.)

On balance, Otepka thought it would be a good idea to hold up the special clearance for Abba Schwartz. This particular clearance would give him access to Intelligence reports obtained by intercepting the coded communications of other governments, including Communist states. Such clearances had always been decided on a genuine "need-to-know" basis. They had been handled with delicate discretion and Otepka had a firm understanding with the U.S. Intelligence Board that he would not issue them unless the "need-to-know" could be provided. Not only could this not be proved in Schwartz's case, but Schwartz himself was clearly not eligible for the clearance because of certain sensitive information in his security file. Otepka had sat in with the Intelligence Board when the regulations governing these clearances were first drawn up for the National Security Council, and he was on solid legal ground in denying Schwartz access to the decoded reports.

David Belisle was nevertheless determined that Schwartz should have

---

* The Landis of this firm was James M. Landis, confidant of the Kennedy family, who was convicted for failing even to trouble himself with filing income tax returns for some years. Landis was found dead at the bottom of his swimming pool in 1964. He was fully clothed, but his demise was officially termed "accidental."

his way. Although the authority to issue these supersecret clearances had been delegated to Otepka for nearly a decade, Belisle simply took it away from him and vested it in himself. He not only handed Schwartz his special clearance, but he and Reilly later appropriated the safe where Otepka had long kept his files on all State Department personnel who had been cleared to receive this sensitive decoded information.

Such chores as this must have earned Belisle a special place in the hearts of the Kennedys. He could not have been unaware that Abba Schwartz had contributed a substantial sum to Jack Kennedy's Presidential campaign.* Moreover, before the 1960 election Abba had worked hard to bring about a rapprochement between Jack and Mrs. Eleanor Roosevelt, an old friend of his.

For these and other services rendered the Kennedys, Schwartz was rewarded with Scotty McLeod's old job in the Department of State. Dean Rusk had to split off SY from the jurisdiction of the Bureau of Security and Consular Affairs before Abba could step in, however. Everyone knew that the Senate might kick up its heels if Schwartz had been made overlord of SY too. As it was there was enough trouble getting the Senate to advise and consent to his nomination in 1962. On the floor of the Senate, Strom Thurmund of South Carolina raised a number of embarrassing questions about Abba's past activities, including the question of whether Schwartz had violated the Foreign Agents Registration Act.**⁶

Otepka's battle with Belisle over the special clearance for Abba Schwartz reached its unseemly climax in May 1963. During this same month Otepka learned through one of his contacts in the Treasury Department of interesting information about Deputy Assistant Secretary of State Herbert K. May who had succeeded Richard Goodwin, a Kennedy protégé, as second in command of the Bureau of Inter-American Affairs. It seems that May was under investigation because he had failed to file any income tax returns for the years 1953 through 1961. Otepka reported the matter to Reilly, noting that Department regulations provided for the immediate dismissal of any employee or official who had wilfully failed to submit federal tax returns. Reilly's reaction was typical. He sent one of his investigators to grill Otepka about his liaison with the Treasury Department.

---

* $17,000 to be exact.
** In replying to Senator Thurmond's questions, Senator John Sparkman of Alabama, vice chairman of the Foreign Relations Committee, spoke of Schwartz's law firm helping the Netherlands get loans from the U.S. However, Thurmond may have had another country in mind. Schwartz was known to have close ties with the Intelligence service of Israel.

Later the State Department was forced to drop Herbert May from its payroll when Senator John J. Williams of Delaware publicly exposed May's tax delinquency. But May was allowed to resign without prejudice and he was never prosecuted. In fact, he was given a $25,000-a-year job with the Communications Satellite Corporation, a virtual subsidiary of the government he had been cheating for so many years.

One incident piled atop another, each adding fresh evidence of the true meaning of convergence. Probing constantly behind the paper curtains of official reports Reilly and his crew did their best to keep from his view, Otepka made several more frightening discoveries.

Perhaps the last person in SY one would expect to find involved in the once delicate business of issuing security clearances was the bearded toast of Warsaw, Elmer Hill. Yet there Hill was, happily poaching on Otepka's old domain.

For some months Hill had been negotiating contracts with private companies for the development and manufacture of wiretapping and detection equipment. In working on these contracts employees of the companies could have access to classified information that might be quite helpful to the Soviets.

Under the State Department's security regulations, the companies and their employees were supposed to be cleared by SY's Evaluations Division. But Hill had gone ahead and let the contracts without ever consulting Otepka. In effect, Hill had taken it upon himself to issue blanket clearances to the companies and their employees. When Otepka protested, Hill merely pleaded ignorance of the regulations. Needless to say, no one ever reprimanded him.

In the month of May, Otepka uncovered the most damning evidence to date of the Administration's anti-security campaign. He found that David Belisle had started clearing State Department applicants without so much as going through the formality of ordering the required background investigations at all. Moreover, Belisle wasn't even bothering to get security waivers from the Secretary of State for some of the new people the seventh floor hierarchy was putting on the payroll.

Otepka's revelation about Secretary Rusk's wholesale issuance of waivers in 1961-62 had proved too irritating. It had now been decided to avoid a repetition of the waiver scandal by the simple expedient of scuttling the security regulations entirely. Obviously, this decision had to be made at a very high level. Veteran bureaucrats like Reilly and Belisle would never run such a risk on their own.

Thus, the last vestige of the State Department's security program had now been dumped overboard, and with it the laws so painstakingly passed by the Congress, signed by previous Presidents, and upheld by the Supreme Court.

While Otepka kept focused on his job, Reilly and his stooges in SY stayed focused on Otepka. They were spending thousands of man-hours and tens of thousands of tax dollars to railroad Otepka out of the State Department. Otepka, by nature a frugal man, occasionally bridled at all the waste. During May and June his assistant, Fred Traband, was devoting more and more of his time to secret conferences with Reilly, Belisle, Rosetti, and other members of the Massachusetts Mafia. Clarence Schneider, Elmer Hill's listening device "expert," spent hours huddled with Traband in the office next to Otepka's.

When Otepka chided Traband for giving too much time to these activities and asked him point blank whether he was spying for Reilly and Belisle, Traband flared up. Pounding his fist on Otepka's desk, the tall, cadaverous security officer vehemently denied reporting on Otepka. "You have no reason to distrust me!" he shouted in righteous indignation. It was a good act, but not very convincing. Traband went back to his desk to keep his eye on Otepka's burn bag so he could make the next call to Joe Rosetti.

In June, the tempo of harassment picked up. Reilly and Belisle bombarded Otepka with snide notes, reprimanding him for the most ridiculous things. On June 18 Reilly sent him a memo saying that his secretary, Marie Catucci, had noted from her records that Otepka had taken no closing action on Harlan Cleveland's security clearance. Reilly, apparently trying to build a specious case for Otepka's "inefficiency," charged that he had not responded to a Belisle inquiry on the Cleveland matter way back in January.

Otepka replied, in moderate tone, that he had answered the Belisle query within seven days and attached a copy of his memo to prove it. He also reminded Reilly that Cleveland had been cleared by Secretary Rusk on August 11, 1961 (he refrained from mentioning that it was on a back-dated waiver), and no further clearance was now called for. He said he would be happy to explain why he had kept Cleveland's security file. But Reilly never asked him. Instead, he curtly demanded that Otepka surrender the Cleveland file to him.

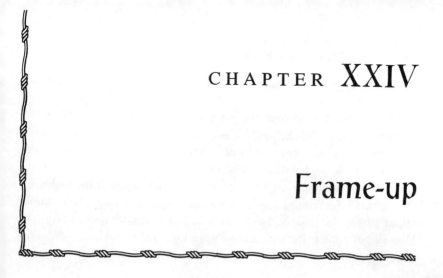

CHAPTER **XXIV**

Frame-up

THE SAME DAY REILLY ISSUED HIS BUMBLING REPRIMAND OF OTEPKA for the "nonclearance" of Harlan Cleveland, there culminated a strange series of incidents that were later to figure prominently in the official charges against the deposed security chief.

Many months earlier, President Kennedy had asked the State Department to look into a report that Latin American Communists had infiltrated the Organization of American States and other international agencies maintaining offices in Washington. The department played hide-and-seek with the President's request for weeks on end. Finally, in late April, a meeting was called by State's Bureau of Inter-American Affairs to discuss the next step. The Office of Security was represented by John Noonan, major domo of the file room.

No one bothered to notify Otepka of this meeting, but early in May, Belisle gave him a copy of Noonan's report. Otepka discovered that Noonan had committed him and the Evaluations Division to conduct the investigation, which, as we shall see in a later chapter, was merely an empty make-work assignment.

Attached to the Noonan report were three other documents. One was a confidential memorandum to White House aide McGeorge Bundy. It had been prepared by George N. Monsma in Inter-American Affairs and

265

was signed by one J.T. Rogers for William H. Brubeck, an aide to Dean Rusk.

When Belisle turned over the material to him, Otepka placed one of his evaluators, Joseph Sabin, in charge of the project. He also directed Raymond Levy, another evaluator, to prepare a memo for Belisle describing the planned *modus operandi*.

Xerox or Thermofax copies of all the pertinent documents, including the memo to the White House, were made for the guidance of SY people taking part in the inquiry. Levy, Sabin and an evaluator named Norman Doe all got copies, for which they were held accountable. So did Traband, Ray Loughton and Carl Bock, three supervisors serving under Otepka.

The second week in June, Joe Sabin complained to Otepka's secretary, Mrs. Eunice Powers, that his copies were illegible and asked for substitutes. Mrs. Powers called Monsma in Inter-American Affairs and he personally brought her his copies to be reproduced for Sabin.

At this point, the burn-bag brigade's accomplice, Joyce Schmelzer, came into the picture. Cheerfully, she volunteered to make copies from Monsma's memo. When the machine copies still turned out indistinct, she graciously offered to type the whole set. On Monday, June 17, Joyce gave Mrs. Powers the typed pages she had finished. But she still had more to do.

The next morning, June 18, Mrs. Powers came to work limping badly. She had twisted her ankle and by noon her whole foot was painfully swollen. Otepka sent her to the State Department dispensary where a nurse advised her to have the foot X-rayed immediately. At 2:30 p.m. Otepka and Jack Norpel got a wheelchair from the dispensary, took Mrs. Powers down to the garage under the building, and drove her to Sibley Hospital.

Before leaving the office, however, the conscientious Mrs. Powers asked Joyce Schmelzer to return the Bundy memo and other material to Monsma as soon as she had finished typing it. When the X-rays taken at the hospital revealed a fractured bone in Mrs. Powers' foot, she was taken home and did not return to work until the following Monday, June 24.

While Mrs. Powers was gone, Mrs. Schmelzer had free access to Otepka's office and to the safe where he stored his current work. This safe contained the illegible copies of the Latin American project material she had duplicated earlier. Identical copies later turned up in the exhibits accompanying the statement of charges against Otepka. They had allegedly been found—with their classified labels neatly clipped off—in a burn bag Reilly's scavengers produced. Otepka later charged (and the State Department never refuted him) that these documents had been planted in his burn bag as part of a deliberate frame-up.

Significantly, eight of the thirteen official charges accused Otepka of "de-classifying" these particular documents on June 18—the day he drove Mrs. Powers to the hospital. But no mention was made of who delivered them to the burn-bag bag surveillance team, although Joyce Schmelzer was specifically identified with several other deliveries.

Coincidentally, the very next day after the "mutilated" documents mysteriously popped up in Otepka's burn bag, four members of Reilly's shillelagh squad trooped up to Capitol Hill to answer an urgent summons from the Senate Internal Security Subcommittee. They were Joe Rosetti, Robert McCarthy, Terence Shea and Fred Traband. Elmer Hill was supposed to go too, but as John Leahy, the State Department attorney who accompanied them, explained, "Mr. Hill is out of town and out of the country."[1] The boys had already guessed that the subcommittee wanted to quiz them on the surveillance of Otepka, which by then was a matter of common knowledge in Washington, though the details were still obscure.

Senator Edward Moore Kennedy, a member of the parent Judiciary Committee but not of the subcommittee, was on hand to provide a little moral protection for his Massachusetts constitutents, especially for brother Jack's old aide Rosetti. It was an unusual but revealing appearance, and the only time Ted Kennedy ever showed up at any of the Otepka case hearings.

Traband was the first on the stand, and the first to perjure himself. A minute or two after taking the solemn oath, he denied having any part in the "physical surveillance" of Otepka. At this point, Counsel Sourwine detonated his biggest bombshell to date. *"Do you have any knowledge of any electronic surveillance of Mr. Otepka or of his office, or his telephone calls?"* Sourwine asked. "No, sir," replied the surprised Traband, "Absolutely not."

This was the first hint that the subcommittee was on to the State Department's illegal wiretapping game. It must have come as quite a shock. In fact, the revelation shook Traband so badly that a moment later he was spilling the beans, or a few of them at least, about the burn-bag brigade. However, he said he had "no knowledge of what was found" in the one burn bag he admitted reporting to Reilly's other henchmen, and he couldn't rightly say "who examined it."*

Terry Shea took his cue from Traband. He too admitted a role in the burn-bag detail. When Sourwine pressed him, Shea said Reilly had given him to understand that he was to look "for anything transmitting information in connection with this committee."² Another yelping cat was now out of the bag and the handsome Teddy Kennedy, sitting placidly next to Senator Dodd, must have inwardly squirmed.

Shea couldn't recall any other instance where a State Department official's burn bag had been seached since he had shifted over from NSA nearly a year before. Otepka, obviously, was the only man in the Department under suspicion for leaking information, although a cursory scanning of the New York *Times* in any given week would have revealed one or more such leaks, leaks that were often injurious to the national security.

Before he was done, Shea let another little kitten escape from the State Department's bag of tricks. He denied ever searching Otepka's office after hours, but he did admit that he knew Reilly had personally searched Otepka's files and safe. On the whole, Shea's testimony had been refreshingly straightforward.

Joe Rosetti was next. He was so upset that when Sourwine asked him what he knew about tapping telephones in SY he pleaded, "Excuse me. I am a little nervous." Dodd, conscious of the Kennedy presence, hastened to reassure him: "Don't be nervous. This is not a hostile hearing."³

Rosetti was not so nervous that he couldn't lie, however. He solemnly swore that SY never broke into its employees' safes under any circumstances. And with a pious shaking of his head he told the subcommittee: "We do not condone any monitoring of phones or anything of that nature."

Sourwine kept boring in on the safecracking job. Rosetti had already established the fact that he was Chief of the Domestic Security Division, but Sourwine was curious if he knew what responsibilities went with the job.

Incredibly, Ted Kennedy interrupted to ask: "Does he have the competency to know that? I just did not know whether the witness understands the full responsibilities of the Division Chief. Maybe he

---

* Traband's much more extensive role in the burn-bag surveillance was later admitted by the State Department. The statement of charges filed against Otepka three months hence was to detail Traband's part and the fact that he was present when the contents of the bag were examined.

does, but I just want to know that, if he does know and understand what those responsibilities are or not."[4]

"Yes, sir," Sourwine nodded. Then, turning to Rosetti again he asked: "You are a Division Chief?" Rosetti repeated that he was. Then he went on with more denials about any knowledge of the taps on Otepka's telephone.

Robert McCarthy's testimony centered on his relationship with Elmer Hill in letting contracts for electronics research and on the Wieland case. McCarthy had the gall to say that after reading Otepka's evaluation of Wieland and the Senate subcommittee hearings he could not see where Wieland had "slanted" any of his reports on Fidel Castro.[5]

For a troupe of amateurs, it was quite a virtuoso performance. Had the four actors concealed their obvious stage fright a bit better, it might even have been a convincing one.

However, if the subcommittee hoped to frighten Dean Rusk from taking further action against Otepka by revealing that it was aware of the State Department's illegal wiretapping, the Senators grossly underestimated their man. Rusk was fully prepared to defy the subcommittee and the whole United States Senate if necessary. John Reilly must have known this, or sensed it. If he had not been entirely confident that he had the backing of Rusk, and behind Rusk the shadowy power of Bobby Kennedy, he never would have flown in the face of the Senate subcommittee as he did just eight days later.

Otepka sensed, too, that the drama was building to a climax. On the afternoon of June 25 he stopped by the desk of Joseph Sabin to see how Sabin was coming with the Latin American project. Otepka spotted a file on Sabin's desk that had nothing to do with that job. It was the security file of one Seymour Janow, a file which Reilly had insisted Otepka surrender to him a week earlier.

Seymour Judson Janow was one of the officials Otepka had been watching for some time. He was assistant administrator of AID for the Far East and as such supervised the expenditure of hundreds of millions of dollars in U.S. funds in the Orient. Janow had been under investigation for a possible conflict-of-interest case allegedly involving a consulting company he had controlled in Japan just prior to joining AID. He had ostensibly divested himself of his holdings in the company, United States Consultants, Inc., because it was already doing contract work for AID. He took care, however, to keep the holdings in the family by selling out to a brother-in-law.

Born in New York, Janow had moved to California with his family when he was 12 and had attended the University of California, both at Berkeley and Los Angeles. There were allegations that he had been active in Communist youth organizations on both campuses, but Janow later denied this under oath.[6] During World War II Janow wound up in China as a civilian consultant to General Claire Chennault, commander of the famed 14th Air Force "Flying Tigers." His job included certain Intelligence chores and he spent the last few months of the war in Chungking where the State Department's China cabal was busy slitting Chiang Kai-shek's political throat. It was in China that Janow first met Fowler Hamilton, who in the 1960's became the head of AID.

After the war, Janow drifted to Japan where he worked, still as a civilian, for the Supreme Allied Command Pacific (SCAP). He resigned from SCAP early in 1949 while under investigation by Army Intelligence but he swore in 1963 that he had not known until then that an Army inquiry board had declared him a security risk.* He said that at the time he had asked his attorney in New York, Fowler Hamilton, to find out why he was being investigated, but Hamilton replied that he was unable to determine the basis for the case.

Janow spent the next dozen years in Tokyo, eventually getting control of the consulting firm he joined in 1949. The rewards, for Janow at least, were handsome. He wound up paying himself a salary of $85,000 a year while the Japanese engineers and other native help made do with mere pittances.

It was a tough decision to give up his lucrative Tokyo company when Fowler Hamilton, who had been doing legal chores for his firm, asked Janow to join AID right after the 1960 election. But Seymour Janow's patriotism got the better of him, and he agreed to sign on the government payroll at what can only be described as a great personal and financial sacrifice. Unfortunately, the State Department's Office of Security, which had jurisdiction over AID presidential appointees who had to be confirmed by the Senate, did not at first show the proper gratitude. In fact, Otepka obdurately refused to issue Janow a clearance.

The old allegations, which had prompted the Army inquiry board to decide Janow was a security risk, were but one of the skeletons in Janow's background that Otepka felt uneasy about. There was a much more recent record he was anxious to get. It seems the U.S. Army had another investigation pending on Seymour Janow just then. It had nothing to do

---

* The Army inquiry board was overruled by the Secretary of the Army on July 13, 1949, after Janow had left SCAP.

with security, but it did concern the possible involvement of Janow's company in an alleged illegal business venture. Otepka insisted that the Army investigation be completed before Janow's name was submitted to the Senate. More than a year went by and the Army investigation was still going on. Janow and Fowler Hamilton became impatient. Hamilton took it upon himself to "clear" his old client and sent his endorsement over to the White House. Ralph Dungan, a special assistant to President Kennedy, seconded Hamilton's "clearance" and the Senate, under the misapprehension that Seymour Janow had been cleared through normal SY channels, confirmed his appointment.[7]

Otepka knew that the FBI had reported that it had not been able to complete the Janow investigation because no report had as yet come in from the Army. This, in itself, made Janow's "clearance" illegal. Moreover, the State Department's certification to the Senate that the investigation was complete was patently fraudulent. There wasn't much Otepka could do about it, but he kept the Janow file locked up in his safe, hoping that he could still get the missing information from the Army in Japan so the case could be reopened.

Late in May a newspaper story hinted that a "high official" of AID was under investigation in a conflict-of-interest case. It also mentioned that the unnamed official was "a leading advocate" of shipping America's surplus food stocks to Communist China.[8] Reilly apparently put two and two together and came up with five. He correctly recognized the anonymous official as Seymour Janow; but from there his addition went haywire: he deduced that Otepka had given the story to the press. Ironically, Otepka did not even know any newsmen very well at the time, and he had never been responsible for leaking information to them.

When Otepka discovered Joseph Sabin working on the Janow file instead of his assigned chore, he naturally asked what he was doing. Sabin replied that Reilly had personally instructed him to evaluate the case. Otepka, used to being bypassed by Reilly, merely nodded and went on about his business. However, the next day he paused again at Sabin's desk and this time he saw that Sabin was inserting some new papers in the Janow file that referred to him. Mystified, Otepka inquired as to exactly what Sabin was supposed to be evaluating in the Janow case. Sabin's answer was that he did not know. It struck Otepka that this was a pretty fishy reply from an intelligent security officer and he told Sabin that he was going to have a look at the new papers himself.

Back in his own office Otepka glanced over the document and immediately saw that Sabin had been working on a chronology of his handling of the case. The chronology made it appear that Otepka had been dilatory, if not delinquent, in his duty. One item that purported to prove this was entirely fraudulent, and Otepka understood at once that Reilly was attempting to trump up a case against him. He handed the document to Mrs. Powers and asked her to run off a copy on the Thermofax machine.

Otepka was still at his desk when a moment later Reilly pushed by Mrs. Powers and burst into his office. His face was livid with rage and his hand trembled as he pointed an accusing finger at Otepka. In a voice croaking with anger, Reilly shouted: "When I assign a case to a member of your staff I do not expect you to interfere!"

Otepka, having become accustomed to Reilly's mercurial temperament, simply replied, "Yes, sir." Then Reilly accused him of taking the chronology from Sabin. "You took it!" he almost screamed. "Where is it? Do you have it in your possession?"

Otepka acknowledged that he had the document. "Give it to me!" Reilly yelled. "I demand that you turn it over at once."

Rounding his desk, Otepka started for the outer office to retrieve the papers from Mrs. Powers. Reilly, almost as big a man as Otepka but clearly no match for him physically, stopped him. For one fleeting second Otepka thought that the Deputy Assistant Secretary of State for Security was going to strike him. But Reilly, for once deciding that discretion might be the better part of valor, only demanded in a somewhat more subdued voice if Otepka had made any copies of the chronology. Coolly, Otepka said he did not think copies had been made as yet though he intended that they should be. He then went out and got the papers back from Mrs. Powers.

As Otepka stepped back into his office, Reilly snatched the document from him and stormed off without another word. Hoping to get an explanation, Otepka went in search of Sabin. The evaluator was not at his desk, but a second later he came in the door. Otepka inquired if he was just getting back from Reilly's office. Sabin shrugged and admitted that he had been there. But when asked if he had told Reilly that Otepka had taken the chronology, Sabin denied it. Otepka shook his head and returned to his own office.

If Sabin had told the truth, he concluded, it could only mean that the listening device Stanley Holden had warned him about six weeks earlier was still in operation. Someone may have overheard him ask Mrs. Powers to make a copy of the fraudulent chronology. If so, that meant Reilly and his minions were no longer relying solely on a tape recorder to pick up his conversations; they had to be manning their electronic listening post at all times, as Stanley Holden had indicated.

Before another hour was out, George Warren, a Foreign Service officer on Reilly's staff, showed up in the Evaluations Division with a veteran SY messenger. Otepka and his people looked on in astonishment as they disconnected the Thermofax machine and carted it off. Warren mentioned, *en passant*, that the machine was being removed on Reilly's orders.

Several people on Otepka's staff, and a few from outside his division, commiserated with him that afternoon. Invariably, they tried to tell him that they were disheartened by the behavior of Reilly and his henchmen and by the disruptive atmosphere that had prevailed now for two-and-a-half years. But Otepka cut them short. He still had no intention of encouraging the people under him to complain about his superiors, realizing that this could only destroy what little was left of their morale. Moreover, he did not want to see them get themselves in trouble by airing their complaints in the confines of an office where even the walls had ears.

At the end of the day, Otepka took the elevator to the underground garage under the State Department building. He couldn't be certain, but as he drove his white Buick Le Sabre home through the rush-hour traffic he felt that this might very possibly have been the last day he would be permitted to function as the chief of SY's all-important Evaluations Division. Unfortunately, his hunch proved correct. The incident of the Janow file was but a prelude to the final showdown that was to take place on the morrow.

CHAPTER **XXV**

High Noon

It was just fifteen minutes before noon on Thursday, June 27, 1963 when the telephone rang in Otto Otepka's office. The voice of Marie Catucci curtly notified him that "Mr. Reilly wants to see you *immediately.*" La Catucci's almost triumphant emphasis of the last word hinted that momentous developments might be in the offing. With an aching sense of weariness, Otepka lifted his heavy frame from his chair and started toward the office of the Deputy Assistant Secretary of State for Security.

In the reception room, Mrs. Catucci, a prim smile on her thick lips, motioned Otepka to Reilly's private office with an eloquent jerk of her head. Inside, the florid-faced Reilly sat expectantly behind his big, broad desk. David Belisle was lounging in a chair nearby. Neither of them rose when Otepka entered.

"I've got something for you," Reilly remarked with a pompous sneer. He handed Otepka a brief, two-paragraph memorandum. It was dated that day and addressed to Otepka from Reilly. A playful smile flitted about the corners of Reilly's mouth as he suggested that Otepka read it. It took Otepka about a dozen seconds to take in the first paragraph:

Effective immediately, I am temporarily detailing you to devote your full time and attention to preparing guidelines for evaluators and developing recommendations for me relative to updating and reviewing the Office of Security handbook. During the course of this temporary detail you are relieved of your present official responsibilities. You will, for the duration of this assignment, occupy Room 38-A05. Such stenographic and/or typing assistance as you will require to carry out these assignments will be made available as you make such needs known to Mrs. Catucci. . . .

The second and last paragraph noted that Otepka had planned to take his vacation at the end of July and into August. Magnanimously, Reilly granted him permission to take the annual leave guaranteed him by Civil Service. Orally, Reilly asked if Otepka had any "comments." Glancing at his watch, Otepka said that since it was so close to lunch he would prefer to return and discuss it afterward.

"Okay," snapped Reilly, rising briskly from behind his desk. "Let's go."

With Reilly and Belisle flanking him like two guards, Otepka was marched down the corridors to Room 3333. As they went, curious faces of other SY personnel peered out of open doorways. The few people they encountered in the hall stepped aside and stared openly when they swept by. Everyone seemed to realize they were witnessing the long-awaited expulsion of Otto Otepka.

En route, Reilly told Otepka that he wanted the combinations to all the safes and file cabinets under his care. Ushered into his outer office, Otepka asked a startled Mrs. Powers to give Reilly the combinations. The words were hardly out of his mouth when five security officers burst into the office. Joe Rosetti was at their head and the others included Robert McCarthy, Russell Waller, Joseph McNulty and Frank Macak. Working swiftly under an obviously prearranged plan, they began changing the combinations to the dozen safes and cabinets in the reception area.

Without a word of protest, Otepka went into his private office and sat down behind his desk. Reilly followed him as far as the door, where he stationed himself, alternately eyeing Otepka and supervising the activity outside. He frowned menacingly when Otepka glanced at the two safes beside the desk. It was in these that Otepka kept his private files and the most sensitive cases he was handling. Otepka knew that if he made a move toward these files Reilly and the others were prepared to pounce on him. It ran through Otepka's mind that this was precisely what Reilly wanted most, to provide him with "evidence" of Otepka's "emotional unbalance." Otepka decided not to oblige. He made no move to take anything from his safes.

Reilly, seeing that Otepka was not to be provoked, stood guard at the door only a few more minutes. Then, abruptly, he ordered Joe Rosetti to relieve him and stalked off toward his own office. Russ Waller, plainly irked by the distasteful task he was required to do, came in. Under Rosetti's watchful eye, he began changing the combinations on the two small safes by Otepka's desk.

Stoically, Otepka looked on, realizing that the work of two decades was being wrested from him and impounded by the New Order. "The files in those safes, and in the dozen cabinets outside my door, were the key to all persons in the State Department who had ever been accused of being Communists or Communist sympathizers," he later recalled. "They contained the original material of the more than twelve thousand employees of wartime agencies that were merged with State in 1945 at the very beginning of what has been termed the 'massive infiltration' of the Department.

"Those files included vital material on the *Amerasia* case, on the original FBI investigation of the Department in 1945, on the critical Congressional investigation in 1947, when the Taber Committee was given access to the files and came up with one-hundred-and-eight serious subversion cases. There were in those files the records of some seven hundred-and-seventy-five cases processed by the old Loyalty Security Board through 1952. There were all the reports and the actual cases presented to the Civil Service Commission and the unpublished reports of various House and Senate committees. There was all the back-up material on the eight-hundred-and-fifty-eight cases I sifted out for special attention in 1956 when I completed the survey which came to be called the 'McLeod List.'

"Much of this may seem like ancient history," he mused. "But literally hundreds of those reports pertained to people who are today in high policy-making positions in the State Department. Many of them had been recommended for dismissal but had been kept on because the Office of Security had been overruled by higher authorities who, I'm sorry to say, simply did not understand the significance of our evaluations or of the background material in the files.

"Moreover, I kept in those two safes in my office the security files or other data on scores of officials who had come into the Department since 1961. It was my duty to watch over these cases even though the individuals had received clearances. I could not permit myself to forget that more than one-hundred-and-fifty of these officials had been brought in on security waivers signed by Secretary Rusk."

It was ten minutes past twelve when Russell Waller finished his work. In grim silence, Otepka rose from his desk and walked out of his office. Returning from lunch an hour later, he found the third floor of the State Department building buzzing with gossip. Several people furtively stopped him in the corridors and said the news had spread that he had been arrested on criminal charges. One of them silently handed him a copy of a memorandum from Reilly addressed to all SY headquarters personnel. Circulated during the noon hour, the memo put everyone on notice that Otepka had been "relieved of his duties as the Chief of the Division of Evaluations." It added that his duties would henceforth be "performed by Mr. David I. Belisle." At the bottom of the memo was a single underlined word: *"Unclassified."* Reilly wanted the world to know immediately what he had done.

Back in his office, Otepka found Mrs. Powers sitting at her desk in tears. Reilly had summoned her right after Otepka had left for lunch and presented her with a memo officially transferring her to SY's Washington field office, which was located in another building. With obvious relish, Reilly had informed her that she would no longer be doing secretarial work. Instead, she would be put to work transcribing dictaphone cylinders.

Otepka learned that two of his best evaluators, Jack Norpel and Billy Hughes, had been similarly transferred to the field office and demoted. The combinations to the safes in their offices had been changed by Reilly's shillelagh brigade immediately after the invasion of Room 3333.

Four more top evaluators—Raymond Loughton, Harry Hite, Francis Gardner and Edwin Burkhardt—were soon to follow Otepka and the others into exile. All of them had worked with him on the now defunct special project and were apparently suspect for that reason. In addition, Howard T. Shea, a veteran SY investigator, was purged too, simply because he had made the mistake of expressing sympathy for Otepka. Thus, nine people in all were summarily railroaded out of their chosen profession by John Reilly, a blatant perjurer acting under the orders of men determined to complete the hidden revolution in U.S. foreign policy.

There had never been a purge comparable to this in the Department of State. Even suspected Soviet agents had always been treated with courtesy and consideration. But Dean Rusk, who had railed against "guilt by association" as forcefully as any a few years before, was perfectly willing to approve the removal of eight government servants simply because they were thought to be friendly or sympathetic to Otto Otepka.

At two o'clock that Thursday afternoon, Otepka called on Reilly. Belisle, apparently on double duty as bodyguard and witness, was again present. Otepka asked Reilly for an explanation of the events that had transpired that noon. At first, Reilly refused to offer one. He stared at the wall and shook his head, saying that he did not want to enter into a discussion. But Otepka persisted, and Reilly finally swung his swivel chair around to face him. Scornfully, he shook his finger at Otepka, his red face turning dangerously purple.

"When I first came on board here," Reilly barked, "I emphasized to you the need for institutional loyalty."

"I will never," replied Otepka firmly, "subordinate loyalty to principle and to my country to loyalty to an institution."

Knowing the futility of debating Reilly on these grounds, Otepka changed the subject. He asked Reilly to clarify the new duties he had been assigned and how he was expected to go about them. Specifically, he wanted to know if he would continue to have access to classified material.

"The nature of your job won't require it," Reilly answered.

"Then you are, in effect, terminating my security clearance?"

"No, no, no, no, no, no," Reilly staccatoed, shaking his head wildly. He had apparently just recalled that it would take a formal declaration that Otepka was a security risk to lift his top-secret clearances.

Insisting that he had not violated any law or code of conduct, Otepka asked Reilly what his future status would be in the Office of Security.

"We shall see," snorted Reilly.

Otepka never once shed his calm. He outlined the material he thought he would need to write the guidelines for evaluators and revise the SY handbook. He pointed out that much of the material was in the files from which he was now obviously barred. He would have to have it, he said, if he were to fulfill his new duties properly.

Reilly, worn down by Otepka's persistence and baffled by his calm manner, unexpectedly capitulated. He said he would let Otepka sort through the files. Then, turning to Belisle, he instructed him to watch Otepka closely during the sorting.

With Belisle mounting guard on him, Otepka returned to Room 3333 and began sifting the files. Methodically, Belisle examined each document Otepka set aside. As the afternoon wore on, he repeatedly urged Otepka to "work faster." Otepka, in a last despairing effort to salvage something out of the wreckage for the future of SY, tried to impress on Belisle the importance of maintaining these files in an orderly fashion. Knowing that Belisle was taking over the Evaluations Division, he attempted to brief him on the significance of some of the projects that had been undertaken in the past. Belisle evinced no interest whatever, only impatience at what he apparently construed as Otepka's deliberate delays.

The following morning Belisle resumed his surveillance. But he soon tired of watching Otepka sort patiently and painstakingly through the files. Belisle finally summoned Raymond Laugel, the new Chief of SY's Foreign Operations Division, to relieve him. Before he left, Belisle mentioned that Reilly was leaving on vacation and would be gone the entire month of July. "It was like a hit-and-run driver fleeing the scene of an accident," Otepka remarked in 1968.

Otepka spent all day Friday and the following Monday under Laugel's guard. Mrs. Powers was given a temporary reprieve to assist him. On Monday morning, however, Belisle showed up and with a surly jerk of his thumb ordered Mrs. Powers to "pick up your things and get out." When Laugel notified him that the project was done, Belisle, filling in as Acting Director of SY while Reilly was vacationing, rudely ordered Otepka to take up his new assignment. Otepka was notified later that he was forbidden to enter either the Evaluations Division or the Central File Room. All files were barred to him, and his former colleagues were instructed to keep away from their old boss.

On Tuesday, Otepka moved into Room 38-A05, an isolated cubbyhole just across the hall from Elmer Hill's electronics laboratories. George Warren, the Foreign Service officer who had supervised the removal of the Thermofax machine a week earlier, arrived with a porter to deliver the material Otepka had been permitted to keep. The files were dumped on the floor in two cardboard cartons. Warren, embarrassed by the tasks he had been forced to perform, stood by the door and remarked wryly, "The things I don't have to do for my country." Many a truth is spoken in jest, as the old saying has it. George Warren's brave little joke was an apt paraphrase of John F. Kennedy's challenge to his countrymen. It was also the last civil word Otepka ever had from anyone on John Reilly's staff.

Entering the lonely exile which was to continue for more than five years, Otto Otepka made a private vow that he would never surrender.

He found a full-page newspaper photograph of Winston Churchill, one of the men he most admired, and tacked it up just inside the door to Room 38-A05 where anyone entering or leaving would be certain to see it. Under his black homburg, Churchill's eyes were alight with a grim but determined smile, and his stubby fingers flashed the famous V for Victory sign. Inscribed in big print below was an excerpt from a speech the Prime Minister had delivered to the boys at Harrow, his old school, in the darkest days of 1941. These were the words Otto Otepka resolved to live by:

> Never give in. Never, never, never, never! Never yield in any way, great or small, large or petty, except to convictions of honor and good sense. Never yield to force and the apparently overwhelming might of the enemy.

The hanging of Churchill's photograph was not a gesture of defiance. It was Otepka's quiet way of informing his superiors, all the way up to Secretary of State Dean Rusk, that he intended to continue his fight for sound security. Dimly at first, but with increasing clarity, he came to understand that other security officers regarded him as a symbol of sanity in a world turned upside down.

Otto Otepka knew too well that the security program in the Department of State was already in shambles long before June 27, 1963. Reluctantly, he later admitted that the events of that day were the final *coup de grâce* of the once proud Office of Security. For in the short space of twenty-five minutes that noon hour, Dean Rusk, acting through John Reilly, had smashed it completely. With one blow, the tottering security program was simply obliterated. The force of that blow was felt throughout the United States government.

If any citizen believes that even a remnant of real security was left after Otepka's exile, he is sadly and tragically deluding himself. All that remained was an empty shell, a group of offices on Foggy Bottom manned by frightened bureaucrats going through the motions of approving clearances for officials handpicked by revolutionaries in business suits who would continue to guide the destiny of America in Walt Rostow's chaotic world arena.

BOOK THREE

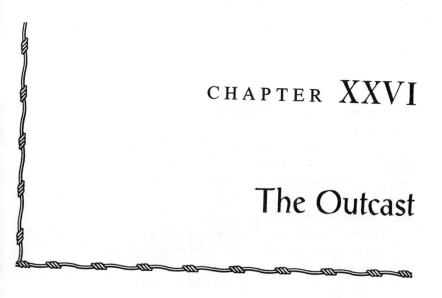

CHAPTER XXVI

The Outcast

ALL THROUGH THE SWELTERING SUMMER OF 1963 AND ON INTO THE early autumn the world at large remained blissfully unaware of the purge of Otto Otepka and his associates from the State Department's critical Office of Security. Not that the world would have been concerned if it had known; it was absorbed then, as always, with more mundane matters, though there was one that seemed more pressing in that season of the sun. The great statesmen were struggling once again with the everlasting problem of salvation—or rather the illusion of salvation as revealed by the Rostowian prophets in the tantalizing garb of the Nuclear Test Ban Treaty.

Even among the handful of people privy to Otepka's fate there were not more than a few who understood fully the connection between the Treaty of Moscow and what had happened to the man in SY. President Kennedy never grasped it, nor his brother Bobby. Dean Rusk knew, of course, and certainly Walt Rostow. But their chief concern at the moment was to keep Otepka's ouster quiet and get the Senate to consent to the treaty, lest the slumbering nation awake to the intimate relationship between the two.

Thus cloaked in anonymity, Otepka stoically settled into the routine that was to become the pattern of his life for the next four years. It was a routine often punctuated by crises. For the most part, however, one day followed another with a dreary sameness. Otepka's workaday world at the Department of State had shrunk to the dimensions of a solitary confinement cell.

The sentence invoked upon him by Dean Rusk began right after he was drummed out of SY. Much later, Dom Bonafede, Washington correspondent of the now defunct New York *Herald Tribune,* movingly described the tempo of Otepka's days, a tempo that was to persist during the entire period of his long exile:

Five days a week a well-built man with pleasant features and close-cropped hair drives into the basement of the State Department to the section reserved for top-echelon officials. He parks, enters an elevator and rides to the third floor, where he walks to Room 38-A05. . . .

Ordinarily this daily ritual would seem little different from the pattern habitually followed by tens of thousands of government employees in Washington.

There is a vital difference, however, which is eerie, almost unbelievable, not unlike an ancient Greek drama: no one speaks to the man and he speaks to no one.

When he enters the elevator the conversation fades to a painful silence. In the corridors one or two people nod in mute recognition, but quickly lower their eyes.

Inside Room 38-A05 he sits behind his bare desk to face another morning in solitude. . . . There are no departmental instructions or reports or communiqués waiting for him. There is no mail. There is a telephone but it is more ornamental than functional since it never rings.

The sole occupant of the room is, for all intents and purposes, nameless. There is no nameplate on the door, as is customary with all high-ranking State Department officials.

Around the corner a nameplate outside Room 3333 reads, "Otto F. Otepka." But if you were to go inside to find Otepka you would not find him there. He is the man in 38-A05. . . .

Otepka is a human island, ostracized by all other State Department workers.[1]

Bonafede went on to tell of several incidents connected with Otepka's confinement. "On one occasion," he wrote, "a fellow employee visited Otepka in his office. When the associate returned to his own office he was immediately summoned by his chief and ordered not to call on Otepka again." As Bonafede pointed out, this man, like many others "who silently sympathize with Otepka," shunned him after that "rather than damage his career."

The two security officers initially purged with Otepka were isolated even more effectively. Otepka at least still had an office in the State Department building. But Jack Norpel was pounding the bricks out of SY's Washington field office, assigned to the kind of routine cases he had handled years before as a novice breaking in with the FBI. Billy Hughes was banished from the capital entirely. On July 10 he was ordered to New Orleans as an investigator, eventually winding up in Memphis for a long and very lonely stretch.

At first, Otepka had no inkling of what the Secretary of State intended to do with him. In his anomalous position he tried to feel his way, cautiously as always. He took a week's vacation in the middle of July and returned to 38-A05 on Monday, the 23rd. The following morning he walked into his old office to have a look around. He was there only a few minutes, but someone tipped David Belisle by telephone. When he stepped into the corridor Belisle swooped down on him. Frowning sternly, he admonished Otepka in his harsh, belligerent voice: "You are not to have access to the space occupied by the Division of Evaluations."

Mildly, Otepka made the point that he was not under any charges and therefore should be free to maintain purely personal contacts with his co-workers. Parrot-like, Belisle simply repeated his command. The next day Otepka received an official memorandum confirming the order.

During this same week Edith Otepka naively tried to reach her husband by telephone at his office. Joyce Schmelzer answered the call and informed Edith that "Mr. Otepka is no longer here." It was apparent that Mrs. Schmelzer had orders to give this standard reply to all callers inquiring for Otepka. The unmistakable implication was that he had already been fired.

The phone in 38-A05 was rigged so that Otepka could take no incoming calls himself. There was no buzzer on the instrument, which was merely a silent extension of the telephone in the adjoining office. The secretaries and clerks there had to knock on his door and tell him to pick up his phone when a call came in. They could easily have listened in on his conversations on their own extension, of course. But that probably wasn't necessary. Elmer Hill's wiretap lab was right across the hall from Otepka's new office.

The last week of July Otepka learned that he was under investigation by the FBI for alleged violation of the Espionage Act. His former secretary, Mrs. Eunice Powers, and six of his erstwhile associates—Norpel, Hughes, Edwin Burkhardt, Francis Gardner, Harry Hite and Raymond Loughton—were herded one-by-one before two FBI agents and interrogated at length about Otepka's activities.

Mrs. Powers was subjected to the most exhaustive questioning. Hour after hour she was confronted with official State Department documents and memorandums, many of which she knew Otepka had kept in the private safe that had been seized by Reilly and his crew on June 27. With a splendid show of spirit, Mrs. Powers finally informed the FBI men that it was John Reilly they should be investigating, not Otepka. She said it was perfectly obvious to her and to everyone else that her former boss was being framed. Nonetheless, the interrogation continued, relentlessly, on and on. At last she was excused, only to be called back later by the FBI agents to sign a brief statement regarding her knowledge of Otepka's association with Jay Sourwine. When she was recalled a third time, the two agents started to ask the same questions all over again. Mrs. Powers steadfastly maintained that she had already told them everything she knew. Reluctantly, they let her go.

Joyce Schmelzer was also interrogated by the same two FBI men. Otepka never learned what they asked her, or what she told them. He only knew that Mrs. Schmelzer returned to her office in tears.

At half-past 10 o'clock on Wednesday morning, August 14, Otepka was himself summoned for questioning by the FBI. He was asked to appear at 1 p.m. at the Washington field office of the Bureau, located in the old Post Office Building on Pennsylvania Avenue. This gray-stone edifice, with its tall tower and medieval battlements, was just one block from the old Farm Credit Administration where Otepka had begun his government career twenty-seven years before.

A few minutes before the appointed hour, Otepka walked through the doors of the aging structure and took an elevator to the seventh floor. The interrogation room, one of a dozen cubicles ranged around the rim of an ancient auditorium, was stifling in the mid-August heat. An old-fashioned electric fan rotated laconically from a hollow pole in the ceiling, half-heartedly stirring the sultry air.

The two FBI agents, Robert Byrnes and Carl Graham, were cordial and courteous. Rather apologetically, they explained that they were conducting the investigation on him at the request of "higher authority" in the Department of Justice. Otepka took this to mean the Attorney General, Robert Kennedy, rather than J. Edgar Hoover, who is always identified with the Bureau, not with the parent department.*

Otepka was invited to sit down at a small wooden table near the center of the barren room. The FBI men took chairs a little to one side and he had to twist his large frame to face them. They were at pains to assure him that the room was not bugged. "It doesn't make any difference to me," Otepka replied. "I have nothing to hide."

The interrogation, which was to continue for three long, hot days, began. In response to the probing questions posed by Byrnes and Graham, Otepka freely admitted his association with Jay Sourwine. He told them about the memo he had written for Sourwine, and why. He described the documents he had transmitted with the memo, and explained why they were necessary to prove that he had been telling the truth to the Senate subcommittee.

Otepka reviewed an endless parade of official documents. He recognized many that had been taken from his confiscated safe. Reilly had obviously supplied them to the FBI in the hope of proving that Otepka was a spy. That he was accused of espionage for a committee of the United States Senate rather than for a foreign power must have seemed somewhat strange to the two FBI agents. But they had no alternative except to get on with their job.

Without hesitation, Otepka identified the documents as having once been in his possession. Most of them, however, he had never considered delivering to the subcommittee. He began to get the drift of the Reilly-Rusk plan when the agents confronted him with certain papers from which the classified labels had been clipped. He had no knowledge of who had clipped them and he said so. "At no time," he told the FBI men, "did I clip any document or instruct anyone else to do it in order to provide the remaining portions of the document to any unauthorized person."

Otepka realized that clipping the labels off any classified paper for this purpose was a criminal act. At the time, however, he still could not bring himself to believe that his superiors were attempting anything so crude as a deliberate frame-up. He credited the seventh floor with more finesse than that. But he was shortly to find that the hierarchy's methods were no more polished than Reilly's, which indeed they condoned.

On the second day of the FBI's studiously polite grilling, Otepka was given a chance to dictate a lengthy statement. In it he refuted the charge

* It was nearly two years later before the Senate Internal Security Subcommittee extracted the information from the State Department that the FBI investigation of Otepka had been requested by the Secretary of State in a message to the Department of Justice.² John Reilly had hand-carried Dean Rusk's request to Justice.

that he had delivered any classified information to an "unauthorized person." He cited the law establishing the right of all Civil Service personnel "to furnish information to either house of Congress or to any Committee or member thereof." The law pointedly states that this right "shall not be denied or interfered with."³

Without mincing words, Otepka defended his right, under this law, to provide information to the Senate subcommittee, particularly in secret executive session. All information "was given only in direct relationship to my testimony," he maintained. "The whole record of my statements was classified by the committee as 'Confidential.' I have not in any sense ignored that classification. I am at a loss to understand, therefore . . . who is the 'unauthorized person.' I would find it incredible to believe that the Chief Counsel of the United States Senate Committee on the Judiciary is such a person within the purview of some law I am alleged to have violated."

"To me," Otepka said in his statement, "loyalty to . . . my country is paramount. . . . I sincerely always have believed that he who has truth on his side is a fool and coward if he fails to own it because of other men's opinions."

When he came back for this third session with the FBI on Friday morning, Otepka was given a transcript of the statement. He read it over carefully and signed it. About half-past twelve, Agent Byrnes told him that Sourwine had been attempting to locate him. He called the subcommittee office and Sourwine informed him that the Senators wanted him to resume his testimony at one o'clock. Excusing himself, he hurried from the FBI office to Capitol Hill.

Without knowing it, Otepka was breaking a brand-new State Department rule in going up to the Hill this time. He had testified before the subcommittee the previous Monday with the Department's permission and was scheduled to appear again the following day. However, he was notified that the second hearing had been postponed until further notice. Since he had been tied up with the FBI for the better part of the next three days it was not until the following Monday that he returned to 38-A05 to find two memos on his desk. Both were from Reilly and addressed to all personnel in the Office of Security. They expressly forbade SY people to testify or have any further contacts with the Senate subcommittee or its staff without advance permission from William Crockett, the Deputy Undersecretary of State for Administration.

This "gag rule" as the subcommittee correctly called it, had gone into effect on August 14, the day after Secretary Rusk personally ordered it.⁴

It was primarily aimed at Otepka, who had disclosed in his August 12 testimony what had transpired when Reilly tossed him out of the Evaluations Division. But because of his enforced isolation and the lengthy FBI interrogation, the rule did not catch up with him until August 19 after he had testified a second time. By then Otepka had read into the subcommittee record a small mountain of revealing information, including the 39-page memo he had prepared for Sourwine, along with the attachments.

Although only spasmodically effective, the gag rule was to remain in effect for the next two years. Every State Department witness summoned by the subcommittee was strictly instructed by Department officials to refrain from discussing the merits of the Otepka case. Those few brave souls who failed to follow these orders were promptly subjected to reprisal.

Despite Rusk's gag on his subordinates, the Internal Security Subcommittee decided to push ahead with its investigation of the Otepka case. There were at least three State Department officials whom the Senators had no intention of letting off the hook, no matter how strenuously Dean Rusk and the White House might wriggle and squirm. This "lying trio," as the subcommittee later branded them, was comprised of John Reilly, Elmer Hill and David Belisle.

Hill had ensnared himself in a tangled web of lies about the wiretap on Otepka's phone when he had testified before the subcommittee on July 9. He denied, under oath, any knowledge whatever of the tap. Three weeks later Belisle followed suit, and on August 6 Reilly made the perjury unanimous.[7]

The subcommittee now had three medium-sized Foggy Bottom sharks all caught up on one very sharp hook. Instead of reeling them in, however, the Senators decided to play out their line in total secrecy. Quite obviously, they hoped that Dean Rusk would get the message and promptly restore Otepka to the Evaluations Division. Once again they underestimated the Secretary of State.

For six more weeks the case remained in a state of suspended inanimation. Otepka, still confident in the powers of the Congress, shared the subcommittee's optimism. He had heard that the FBI investigation into the Department's allegations that he had violated the Espionage Act had collapsed of its own unwieldy weight. More and more he tended to regard his exile as merely temporary and he looked forward to getting back to work. The atmosphere in SY, he believed, would certainly be cleansed by the Senate probe.

CHAPTER **XXVII**

Under Charges

WHEN THE FBI INVESTIGATION OF OTEPKA FAILED TO DEVELOP EVI-
dence that could sustain a Grand Jury indictment against him under the
Espionage Act, the Senate subcommittee hoped Dean Rusk and Bobby
Kennedy would relent and begin a search for a suitable solution. Otepka,
as much as anyone, shared this hope. During the next month his optimism steadily grew.

In mid-September Otepka took another week of his vacation to drive
his daughter Joanne to Saint Louis, where she had enrolled as a freshman
at Washington University. He had never discussed his office problems
with Joanne and he did not do so now. Like any other teenager going off
to college for the first time, she was filled with a mixture of anticipation
and excitement. Her father had no desire to cast a pall over her initial
adventure with higher education by burdening his only child with his
own professional difficulties.

Otepka was glad to get away from Washington for a few days. Driving
over the Alleghenies and out into the broad Midwestern farmlands
beyond, he feasted on the sights of a bountiful land in the fullness of yet
another harvest. It was, he reminded himself, a country worth preserving.
More than once he asked himself if the people would wake up before
their freedom had been stolen from them entirely. But he did not see it

as his mission to awaken them. He had faith that the democratic system, with its free press, would fulfill that responsibility.

Stopping off in Chicago for a few days he visited his parents and his brother's family. Ferdinand and Johanna Otepka welcomed him with beaming smiles. They had grown old during the years he had worked in Washington but they wore their age with grace. They knew nothing of their son's present troubles and he did not enlighten them. He did confide in his brother Rudy, expressing confidence that everything would work itself out. There was no reason, he said, to expect any further reprisals from the State Department. His chief accuser, Reilly, had perjured himself before the Senate subcommittee, along with two, and very probably more, of his henchmen. It was difficult to see how the Department could take more action against him based on the accusations of perjurers. From Chicago he drove to Saint Louis. With conflicting feelings of pride and regret, he deposited his daughter at the university and drove back to Washington.

His optimism still intact, Otepka returned to his cell at the State Department on Monday, September 22. The following morning, at about 10:30, one of the secretaries in the adjoining listening post knocked nervously on his door to inform him that he had a telephone call. He picked up the mute extension on his desk. On the line was John Drew, an old friend in the Office of Personnel who had recently been designated as a Department disciplinary officer. Drew asked him to come immediately to his office on the second floor.

To save time, Otepka bypassed the elevators and walked down the dimly lit steel and concrete stairs. Drew, a former bank clerk who had spent the last fifteen of his 39 years rising slowly to a middle-echelon position in government, was waiting for him in a private office. "I have a letter for you," he said, handing Otepka a sealed envelope. "You might want to read it now. If you have any questions, I'll try to answer them."

Opening the envelope, Otepka found a long letter signed by John Ordway, Chief of the Personnel Operations Division at State. One glance at the first page shattered all the hopes he had quixotically nurtured for the past month. The second paragraph began: *"You are hereby notified that it is proposed to remove you from your appointment with the Department of State. . . ."**

In silence, but with mounting incredulity, Otepka read through the thirteen separate charges leveled against him. Unbelievably, three of them were based on the voluntary statement he had given the FBI. The

* The full text of the Statement of Charges appears in Appendix A.

other ten rested upon the scavenger hunt conducted over a period of three months by the burn-bag brigade, all of whom were identified by name—Reilly, Belisle, Fred Traband, Joe Rosetti, Terence Shea, Robert McCarthy, and their unwilling blonde accomplice, Joyce Schmelzer.

The first three charges brazenly accused Otepka of conduct "unbecoming an officer of the Department of State." Rooted in his statement to the FBI, the charges covered alleged violations of the vague 1948 Truman directive which sought to sweep the Alger Hiss "red herring" under a White House rug. Incredible as it may have seemed to Otepka when the FBI took his statement, the Chief Counsel of the Senate subcommittee was indeed deemed to be an "unauthorized person." All three counts openly named Jay Sourwine as the illegal recipient of three official documents, two of them classified.

One document was laboriously described as "a classified memorandum entitled 'Francis O. Wilcox, Arthur Larson, Lawrence Finkelstein, Marshall D. Shulman, Andrew Cordier, Ernest Gross, Harding Bancroft, Sol Linowitz.' " All these people were, of course, members of Harlan Cleveland's select Advisory Committee on International Organizations. The second classified memo cited in the charges also dealt with the Cleveland committee. Otepka had placed both of them in the Senate subcommittee record during his last appearance on Capitol Hil on August 16 right after he left the FBI field office. As he had told the FBI agents, he had previously given these papers to the subcommittee through Sourwine to refute Reilly's lies.

The documents underlying the third charge was an unclassified investigative report on an applicant for a State Department job, Joan Mae Foglantz. The 1968 subcommittee report on the Otepka case noted that this report revealed "the extent to which an adversary proceeding can go—when you want to get rid of some subordinate." The subcommittee emphasized that the document "was included only as an example of the short-form investigation report as against the traditional long form."

There was no derogatory information on Miss Foglantz. On the contrary, the report on her was quite favorable. Otepka introduced it, as the subcommittee pointed out, merely to show how "Mr. Reilly had lied about the short form in various ways."[1]

Two of the remaining ten charges also accused Otepka of "unbecoming" conduct. These focused on garbled transcripts made from a one-time-typewriter ribbon and carbon paper Mrs. Powers had discarded in the burn bag when she was typing Otepka's lengthy memo to Sourwine in May.

The other eight counts charged that Otepka was "responsible" for the "mutilation" or "declassification" of four official papers, all of them allegedly taken from his burn bag on June 18, the day he and Norpel drove Mrs. Powers to the hospital to have her broken foot X-rayed. Every one of these four documents was being retyped by Joyce Schmelzer that day. All four concerned the highly hush-hush investigation of Latin American Communists operating out of the Washington offices of various international organizations.

Chief among those classified papers was the memo to McGeorge Bundy at the White House, signed for William Brubeck, a special assistant to Dean Rusk who bore the title "Executive Secretary" of the Department of State. The other three included file chief John Noonan's report on how he had committed Otepka to the Latin American project; a memo that evaluator Ray Levy had prepared with Fred Traband on how SY would handle the investigation; another memo drafted by one J.M. Barta in Inter-American Affairs.

Under four of these eight counts Otepka now faced a total of twenty-four years in federal prison and up to $16,000 in fines. Yet he later swore that he had "absolutely nothing to do with clipping the classified labels from the documents that formed the basis for these criminal charges."

"I was not particularly disturbed by the charges regarding my association with Jay Sourwine or the data I'd furnished him for the subcommittee," Otepka later recalled. "But I was shocked and angered to find that the State Department had resorted to a cheap, gangland frame-up to place me under charges for crimes it knew I had never committed."

The fact that the frame-up had been perpetrated by acknowledged perjurers did not for a moment trouble Abram Chayes, the Department legal advisor whose office reviewed the charges against Otepka. Nor did it tweak the conscience of Secretary Rusk when he approved them. Both Rusk and Chayes were perfectly willing to place an innocent man under criminal charges if it served their long-range purpose.

In John Drew's office that September morning, Otepka once again demonstrated his magnificent self-control. When he finished reading the long list of charges, he calmly asked Drew what alternatives were open to him. "Well," drawled Drew, "you *could* resign."

In spite of himself, Otepka smiled. He shook his head slowly. He had been given ten days to answer the charges and the dismissal would not go into effect until twenty days after that. He told Drew that he intended to get a lawyer. They chatted for some minutes about the regulations covering dismissal notices. Otepka knew them as well or better than

Drew, but, typically, he made doubly sure of his ground before he left. The meeting had lasted less than a half-hour.

Otepka climbed the stairs to the third floor and went back to 38-A05. He sat down at his desk and started to pick up the phone. Then he thought better of it. (Just a week later the former wiretap chief, Stanley Holden, told him his phone in the little office had been fixed to pick up all conversations, on or off the telephone line. Elmer Hill had a tape recorder twirling in his lab across the hall to monitor every word.)

There was no place he could go in the State Department to seek advice. There was no one there he could talk to without endangering the person's position. Alone in his solitary cubicle, he pondered his next step. It was not yet noon in Washington. But the hour was late, much later than even Otepka realized. . . .

At that very hour, a long march away on Capitol Hill, the Senate of the United States was in the final throes of its bitter debate on the Nuclear Test Ban Treaty. The debate had raged, off the floor more savagely than on it, for two bewildering months. Never in the history of the Senate had so many arms been twisted so painfully behind so many locked doors. Hitherto courageous men, knowing that the future of their country and of all mankind was at stake, nonetheless broke, one by one, under the excruciating pressure of the relentless psychological rack that operated day and night through those fateful weeks.

Whispers of blackmail filled the corridors of the Capitol. Senators who had taken solemn oaths never to approve a test ban that did not insure adequate inspection rights within the Soviet Union suddenly reversed themselves and plumped eloquently for ratification of a treaty that guaranteed no on-site inspection at all.

It was the supreme masterpiece of the Kennedy Administration. Directed by the White House, aided and abetted by the State and Defense Departments, drawing where necessary on the esoteric talents of CIA, the campaign to force the reluctant Senate to ratify the Treaty of Moscow was ruthlessly coordinated by Robert Kennedy from the Department of Justice. Revealing dossiers were allegedly built upon the most secret FBI and CIA files. If political pressure failed to break a recalcitrant opponent of the treaty, Bobby knew there were other ways to make a man "come around."

The treaty itself had been initialed in the Kremlin on July 25 by the U.S. representative, Averell Harriman, and by Nikita Khrushchev. Ten days later Dean Rusk flew to Moscow with a gay little party that included

Adlai Stevenson and Senator Hubert Humphrey. At the formal signing on August 5, news photographs flashed around the world showing the joyful American delegation toasting the treaty with Khrushchev and his beaming commissars.

For the Communists, the treaty was the culmination of an all-out propaganda war waged for nearly two decades. It had begun at Hiroshima and had gained great impetus when America tested the world's first hydrogen bomb over the Eniwetok Atoll in 1952. In every country "peace" groups took up the torch to blaze the trail. By 1958 their unrelenting pressure had caused the Eisenhower Administration to agree to a test ban "moratorium"—a unilateral move that required nothing more than a sly nod of approval from the Kremlin.

"We wished so hard for a test ban that we based our control system on hopelessly inadequate science," wrote Earl Voss in his revealing 1963 book, *Nuclear Ambush*.[2] A Washington *Star* reporter and former president of the State Department Correspondents Club, Voss understood very well the rationale of the moratorium, the identical rationale used five years later to sell the Treaty of Moscow to a thoroughly befuddled American public.

"Deep fears always give rise to wishful thinking," Voss observed. "Deep fears of nuclear weapons gave rise to wishful thinking that a nuclear test ban could somehow send the threat of nuclear war away. . . . Soviet psychology took skillful advantage of the wishful thinkers."[3]

The moratorium was, however, merely the first tentative dipping of America's toes into more chilling waters. For five invaluable years it kept our technology in a deep freeze while the Soviets soared from behind to overtake and surpass U.S. science in this most critical of all arenas of power. Having achieved dramatic technological breakthroughs via their massive 1961-62 nuclear tests, the Soviets were naturally eager for a treaty that would prohibit the United States from duplicating their achievements. On December 19, 1962, less than two months after the Cuban missile crisis, Khrushchev wrote President Kennedy: "It seems to me, Mr. President, that [the] time has come now to put an end once and for all to nuclear tests, to draw a line through such tests."[4]

Kennedy rose to the Pavlovian bait. After all, he had been pleading with Khrushchev from the very outset of his administration for just such a move. Further, he had devoted a major part of his considerable energies to conditioning the American people to accept it. He in turn had permitted himself to be conditioned by the platoons of ultra-Leftists and wishful thinkers strategically deployed in the White House, the Department of

Defense, and, over Otto Otepka's strenuous objections, in the State Department.

As yet, however, there was no hint that the United States would even consider a test ban treaty without some kind of on-site inspection within the borders of the USSR. Even Nikita Khrushchev had promised in his December letter to meet the U.S. "halfway" on the inspection issue.[5] But through the winter and spring the number of inspections the U.S. was willing to accept was steadily whittled down—from ten, to eight, to five, and ultimately to zero.

"This has become an exercise not in negotiation, but in give-away," Senator Dirksen caustically remarked at one point. In February, when the number of inspections was still publicly pegged at a half-dozen, Senator Dodd declared that far too many concessions had already been made. He said he would oppose the comprehensive test ban that would have prohibited underground as well as atmospheric tests because it would halt development of a neutron bomb and of anti-missile missiles. Dodd, although an outspoken anti-Communist, was still a widely respected Northern Liberal. He was expected to lead the opposition to ratification of the treaty in the Senate.

A few months later Dodd almost singlehandedly pulled the rug right out from under the opposition he was to have led. As Schlesinger tactfully puts it, "the Connecticut Senator had the grace to change his mind."[6] Towards the end of May, Dodd linked arms with Hubert Humphrey and thirty-two other senators in introducing a resolution calling for a limited test ban. It was "the sense of the Senate," the resolution declared, that the U.S. should "pursue it with vigor, seeking the widest possible international support," even if the USSR proved reluctant.

Dodd's surprising about-face ended all meaningful opposition to the Treaty of Moscow two months before it was signed. It was no trick after that for the Soviets to cut the number of on-site inspections to none. Averell Harriman, a warm friend of the Soviet Union since his youth, cheerfully cooperated. "I am always right when I *know* I am right," Harriman archly announced upon his return.[7]

The advice and consent of the Senate was now the only remaining hurdle. Skillfully, the State Department propaganda machine was pressed into high gear. Ad hoc committees were formed Left *and* Right to support the treaty. Newspaper advertisements blossomed forth bearing the ancient message of hope, "peace on earth." One mighty two-page ad which appeared in the New York *Times* on August 15 was signed by some of the most prestigious leaders of American industry and finance.

Among them was Winthrop Aldrich, uncle of the Rockefeller boys and former chairman of the Chase Bank. For "name-recognition" value there was a Cabot (Thomas B.), a Baker (G.Y.), and a Roosevelt (John). Others included Sol Linowitz, Xerox Corporation chairman and Cleveland committee member; Thomas B. McCabe, Scott Paper Company chairman; Sydney J. Weinberg of Goldman Sachs; Charles B. Mortimer, chairman of General Foods; J. Wilson Newman, the managing head of Dun & Bradstreet.

In executive session the Senate Preparedness Subcommittee listened attentively to a parade of witnesses testifying pro and con. But with each passing day there were fewer and fewer men who dared stand against the grand illusion of peace. The Joint Chiefs of Staff, who only months before had steadfastly declared that even six inspections annually would be unacceptable to them, were suddenly willing to accept none. An old friend who saw General Curtis LeMay, the Air Force member of the Joint Chiefs, emerge from the subcommittee hearing room described LeMay to this writer as "a beaten man."

Valiantly, a dwindling band of opponents fought on. They were led by Dr. Edward Teller and a corporal's guard of retired military men. Prominent among them were three ex-admirals—Lewis Strauss, Arleigh Burke, and Arthur Radford. General Thomas Power, still chief of the Strategic Air Command, was the only leading active-duty officer to oppose the treaty publicly, though many argued against it in private. By doing so, Power knew he was forfeiting his expected promotion to the Joint Chiefs. But he never wavered.

Bluntly, Dr. Teller told the Senators: "If you ratify this treaty . . . you will have given away the future safety of this country." Admiral Radford put it just as strongly. "The decision of the Senate of the United States in connection with this treaty will," he said, "change the course of world history."

When the treaty came to the floor for open debate, an estimated thirty Senators were still aligned against it. Day by day the number dwindled. Strom Thurmond of South Carolina rallied the rear guard with incisive arguments that cut through the heavily emotional support of the treaty and exposed it for what it was—a blueprint for disaster. Thurmond was joined by Barry Goldwater; Richard Russell of Georgia, chairman of the Armed Services Committee; John Stennis of Mississippi, Preparedness Subcommittee chairman; and Frank Lausche of Ohio, the only Northern Democrat who stood firm against the administration juggernaut.

Significantly, in the two weeks of debate every Senator who *supported* the treaty confessed the fear that he might be tragically wrong. But political and other considerations outweighed their fears. The final vote came on September 24, the day after Otto Otepka's as yet unnoticed dismissal. Only 19 Senators were recorded against the treaty; 80 voted for it.

Jack Kennedy rightly claimed his greatest victory—a victory which he had been warned could one day spell ultimate defeat for his country. Arthur Schlesinger justifiably crowed: "The absence of major criticism [to the test ban], whether in Congress or the press, showed the transformation which, despite Berlin and despite Cuba, the President had wrought in the mind of the nation."[8]

Otto Otepka, now under criminal charges and threatened with imprisonment, knew far better than either Kennedy or Schlesinger exactly how this miraculous transformation had been wrought. For he knew, as no other man in Washington, the security pedigrees of the men who had ushered in the New Order. Alone, abandoned by all but a handful of friends, he saw through the ghostly charade of the Nuclear Test Ban Treaty, and silently vowed to continue his struggle against those seemingly mysterious forces which had brought it about.

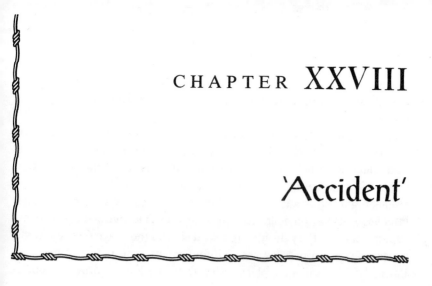

CHAPTER **XXVIII**

'Accident'

THE NIGHT OTEPKA RECEIVED HIS DISMISSAL NOTICE FROM THE STATE
Department he had a long talk with his wife, Edith. They sat in the large
paneled basement room he had installed himself a few years before as a
combination family room and art gallery. Edith's own paintings were
ranged around the walls, each glowing softly under the subdued light of
individual bulbs concealed by a wooden valance that ringed the ceiling.

Although he had kept Edith apprised of the main events of recent
months, until now he had avoided going into great detail. However, since
he had been placed under criminal charges that morning he felt his wife
deserved to understand more clearly just what was at stake. Not that
there was any need to draw diagrams for her; Edith had long ago grasped
the central issues of the bitter drama in which her husband found himself
the principal character. But Otepka wanted her to see the full dimensions
of that drama so she could better assess, as he had already done, the
strength of the forces arrayed against him.

It was no longer a contest between himself and the Department of
State. He was now engaged, with the Senate subcommittee as a tentative
ally, in a struggle against the whole executive branch of the United States
government. In approving the charges against Otepka, Dean Rusk knew
that he was openly defying not only a powerful group of senators but the

constitutional prerogatives of the Congress itself. This was a step no Cabinet officer would dare take without the full backing of the White House.

At the time, Otepka still had faith in the Congress and in the ultimate impartiality of American justice. Nonetheless, he knew that justice could come dear. He would have to retain an attorney, and competent attorneys were expensive.

That night, Edith and Otto toted up their savings. With their daughter in college, it was obvious that the sum they had put aside would not stretch very far. They decided to take a second mortgage on their home, if necessary, to hire a lawyer. Without mentioning it to her husband, Edith also began making plans to return to teaching in order to supplement their income.

The next day the financial picture seemed to brighten. Otepka received private assurances that the Senate subcommittee would find some way to cover his legal costs. After all, it was the subcommittee's fight as much or more, than his.*

Otepka discussed possible attorneys with Jay Sourwine and several other friends. One of them suggested Edward Bennett Williams, the flamboyant criminal lawyer. In the end, he settled on Roger Robb, who had more familiarity with internal security by virtue of his handling of the Oppenheimer case for the Atomic Energy Commission. An outstanding Washington lawyer, Robb was highly respected in legal circles nationally.

It was several days before the press got wind of Otepka's dismissal. Dean Rusk was later to deny that the State Department released the charges. "Nor has it issued any statement discussing the substance of them," Rusk told the Senate subcommittee four weeks afterward. However, the subcommittee wrung an admission from the Department that one of its press officers, Richard I. Phillips, had in fact "confirmed" the charges when queried by the Associated Press and United Press International on Thursday afternoon, September 26.[1]

If the AP and UPI extracted the details of the charges from Phillips, neither wire service let its clients in on the secret. Twenty-four hours passed before the full story finally broke. Otepka came home on Friday evening to find Edith waiting with a question on her lips. She had just heard a radio newscast which disclosed his firing and actually quoted

* The subcommittee never came through on its promise.

om the statement of charges. Dr. Robert Morris, the former Chief
Counsel of the Senate subcommittee had released the charges in Texas
where he was then serving as president of the University of Dallas. How,
Edith wanted to know, did Dr. Morris get hold of the charges?
Otepka was momentarily puzzled. He had not been in contact with
Morris and no one had warned him that the charges were about to be
released. However, he realized that Morris still had good friends on the
subcommittee. Otepka had, of course, given a copy of the dismissal
notice to the subcommittee since its present Chief Counsel was openly
named.

That weekend the first spate of newspaper stories on Otepka's firing
were sprinkled inobtrusively on back pages across the country. Very few
newspapers gave it any prominence. The Chicago *Tribune*, in Otepka's
home town, was one of the few exceptions. Willard Edwards, *Tribune*
Washington correspondent, zeroed in on the story immediately. That
Sunday his initial article covered nearly two full columns. Edwards
quoted one of the Senators on the subcommittee who described Otepka's
still secret testimony as "political dynamite."[2]

"The State Department was reportedly alarmed lest the Senate subcommittee's disclosures should be made public before or during Senate
debate on the Treaty of Moscow," Edwards wrote. He described the
charges against Otepka in accurate detail, and predicted a "head-on
clash" between the State Department and the Senators over the dismissal. Edwards quoted subcommittee Chairman Eastland as saying:
"The powers of Congress are at stake, and I intend to protect Mr. Otepka
by every means at my command."[3]

A few days later Eastland and the other members of the subcommittee
indicated that this was to be no empty challenge. For three months they
had been trying unsuccessfully to get Secretary Rusk to come before
them to answer their accumulated questions. Their first invitation had
been issued the day after Otepka's ouster from the Evaluations Division.
Thus far, Rusk had adroitly sidestepped the subcommittee. Now, however, the Senators were determined to confront him.

The parent Judiciary Committee unanimously approved a blistering
ten-page memorandum to Rusk, vigorously protesting Otepka's dismissal
and demanding that the Secretary appear before them. It was perhaps the
most scathing communication ever addressed by a committee of the
Congress to a Cabinet officer. The memo raked Rusk over a wide field
of hot coals, ranging from the breakdown in SY to the illegal practices

forced on Frances Knight in the Passport Office. It charged Rusk's de
partment with a coverup and accused his sycophant subordinates of lyin
under oath.

The memorandum put Rusk on notice that the Senators knew "wh
ordered" the tapping of Otepka's telephone and "who did the work, wha
mistake was made in the initial effort to connect an electronic device . .
who asked for help to correct the error—the whole story." But it did no
inform the Secretary of how the subcommittee had come by this knowl
edge.

The Senators itemized the security collapse in unmistakable detail
pointing accusingly to the continued use of waivers, the improper han
dling of Intelligence information flowing into the State Department, the
granting of security clearances without sound evaluation of pertinen
data, the deliberate coverup of security risks, the practice of permitting
these risks to continue in important postitions.

The Senators also heatedly criticized the State Department for subject
ing Otepka to "humiliating" treatment when he was removed from the
Evaluations Division in June. However, the committee members could
not yet bring themselves to believe that Rusk had personal knowledge
of the vendetta, and they took some of the sting out of their indictmen
by noting that they were not accusing him of "anything improper."

In a highly unusual move, the Judiciary Committee directed that the
urgent memorandum be hand-carried to the Secretary of State. On
Wednesday, October 2, Senator Dodd flew to New York with Jay Sourwine to deliver the summons personally. Dodd forced the reluctant Rusk
to tear himself away from some vital chores the Secretary was taking care
of at the United Nations, which was readying itself for the "next step"
toward Walt Rostow's dream of a disarmed world—a resolution co-
sponsored by the United States and the USSR to ban orbiting nuclear
weapons in space.

His famous "cool" ostensibly unruffled, the imperturbable Mr. Rusk
blandly accepted the memorandum from an obviously agitated Senator
Dodd. Whatever words were exchanged between them were unfortunately not recorded for posterity. But it is apparent on the record that
Rusk's powerfully reassuring personality quickly smothered Dodd's
long-smoldering anger, at least temporarily.

It is also apparent that Dodd bore down hard on the fact that the
subcommittee had the goods on Rusk's boys for the illegal wiretap on
Otepka's phone, and this bit of information immediately touched off a
mysterious sequence of events. Rusk was determined to find out just how

uch the subcommittee knew about the electronic surveillance and
here the information had originated.

Actually, the subcommittee's source was George Pasquale, who had
estified in secret session on September 10. Since Pasquale was no longer
n the State Department payroll, the Senators were under no compulsion
o send a transcript of his testimony to Secretary Rusk. The Secretary
sked for it, of course, but he was turned down flat. Thus, he could not
e sure just how much the subcommittee knew.

Pasquale had informed the Senators that Stanley Holden had told him
f the plot to bug Otepka's office. Holden, via Pasquale, had implicated
Reilly and Clarence (Jerry) Schneider, Elmer Hill's inept assistant.
Schneider had since been shipped off to London, where he was to suffer
he first of several reported "nervous breakdowns."

Subsequently, on September 30, Otepka had a private talk with Holden
and Russell Waller, the safecracking expert. Holden once again warned
Otepka that all conversations in his new office, on or off the phone, were
being monitored. He said his own phone had been bugged, as well as
hose of several other people in SY.* Holden also mentioned that there
was a good possibility Otepka's home phone had been tapped.

A few days later Russ Waller was rushed to the hospital with what was
thought to be a heart attack. But Waller later told Otepka that what he
had really suffered was a nervous breakdown, brought on by the strain
of working in the Orwellian atmosphere that pervaded the Office of
Security.

On the same day, October 3—the day after Dodd confronted Rusk in
New York—Stanley Holden suffered a mysterious "accident." Like
Otepka, Holden had been under surveillance for some time. He was
known to be friendly with Otepka and that was more than enough to
make him suspect in John Reilly's eyes. In September, when Holden
discovered that both his office telephone extensions had been tapped, he
traced the bugged lines to a closet just outside Elmer Hill's office.[4]

Holden took the matter to Joe Rosetti and together they went to
Reilly's office. Reilly pretended that he knew nothing at all about the tap.
Then he called in Hill, who also feigned innocence.[5]

Whether through the tap, or via some other form of surveillance, or
because Dodd let Holden's name slip out in his talk with Rusk, Reilly
knew for certain on October 3 that Holden had been feeding information
to Otepka. It was at this point that Holden had his "accident." George

* The subcommittee later found that one of the other bugged phones belonged to Raymond
Loughton, Otepka's deputy on the defunct special project.

Pasquale happened to call Holden's home that Thursday afternoon. Mr. Holden told him that Stan had suffered a severe face injury at the office His face and tongue had been badly cut and stitches had been require to sew up the wounds. Mrs. Holden refused to give Pasquale any informa tion on how it happened.

There were reports that Holden had been beaten up by the shillelag brigade. Later, Holden told Otepka that he was working on an apparatu in his lab at SY when a heavy spring came loose and struck him in th face. It was an unlikely accident, but Otepka didn't press him for details Holden obviously didn't want to talk to him any more. Whatever hap pened, he had been taken out of the game, as his subsequent testimon before the subcommittee demonstrated.

While Holden was recuperating at home, Reilly sent Joe Rosetti an Robert McCarthy to question him. As Rosetti ingenuously put it in hi testimony several months later: "I think Senator Dodd submitted a lette to the Secretary of State setting forth some facts that Mr. Otepka's phon had been tapped and that you [the subcommittee] had positive proof o this nature, and Mr. Reilly wanted to ascertain how the committee go this information. . . ."[6]

Rusk obviously thought Dodd was bluffing in New York. But h couldn't be completely certain. It is apparent from Rosetti's testimony that Rusk ordered Reilly to find out just how much "proof" the subcom mittee had. The very next day Holden met with his "accident" and Rus Waller was shipped off to the hospital. With his tongue painfully lac erated, Holden was in no condition to talk that day. But when Rosett and McCarthy dropped by his home a few days later he apparently could make himself understood.

McCarthy belted down several shots of whisky on the patio in Hol den's back yard and went to work. He started grilling Holden about his relationship with Otepka. He demanded to know exactly what Holden had revealed about the wiretaps. How much had he told Pasquale? Had he involved Reilly? Hill? Rosetti?

When Holden balked, McCarthy became more belligerent. (He later confessed to the subcommittee that he was "loud and abusive.") As he consumed more whisky, McCarthy acquired more courage.

"Where is your loyalty?" he screamed. "Don't you have any loyalty at all? Don't you think you owe Joe Rosetti any loyalty?"

Several of Holden's neighbors came out into their yards to see what the ruckus was all about. At last, Stan Holden had had enough. He asked McCarthy and Rosetti to leave.

"I'll get you for this!" McCarthy vowed at the top of his lungs. As he
eparted, he turned on Holden once more. Still yelling for all the neigh-
orhood to hear, he threatened to have Holden fired if it turned out he
ad been responsible for giving Pasquale and Otepka the information
hat had put Dean Rusk on the spot.

CHAPTER **XXIX**

Rusk's Defiance

WHEN DEAN RUSK GOT BACK TO WASHINGTON AFTER HIS TALK IN NEW York with Senator Dodd, he asked Undersecretary of State George Ball to give him a hand with the reply he would have to make to the Senate subcommittee. Ball in turn passed part of the buck to an obscure attorney in Abram Chayes' office, Thomas Ehrlich. It took them the better part of three weeks to construct a reply, but when they were done Rusk and his legal advisors had created a classic piece of sophism.

In the meantime, Rusk had one more try at avoiding an appearance before the Senate subcommittee. Suspecting a trap had been set for him with the wiretap evidence, he fired off a letter to the parent Judiciary Committee, which Senator Eastland also headed, saying that he would refuse to appear until he was given access to all the information in the subcommittee's possession. One senator described the tone of the letter as "arrogant."[1] What Rusk still wanted, of course, was a copy of Pasquale's testimony.

Before the Senators could reject this presumptuous bid, President Kennedy was cornered on the Otepka case during his October 9 press conference. Asked by a reporter what he intended to do about the matter, Kennedy quickly decided that the potato had become too hot to handle.

Apparently on the spur of the moment, he tossed it to Dean Rusk. The Secretary, he said, would be happy to tell his story to the Senate subcommittee. Kennedy was certain that Rusk stood ready to explain the entire case, including the action against Otepka. It would then be reviewed by the State Department, the Civil Service Commission, and eventually by the courts, he said. The President added that he would review the matter personally along the way, though he failed to specify just where. The Senators were pleasantly surprised by this seeming reversal. It was obvious that the President had decided to force Rusk to face them. Rusk might still be reluctant to appear, but for the moment he had no choice.

On October 21, nearly four months after the subcommittee first invited him to come before it, Dean Rusk finally made his appearance. Seven of the nine members of the subcommittee were present, with Dodd presiding in Chairman Eastland's absence. As usual, Dodd went out of his way to pour oil on the Democrats' troubled waters. He hastened to assure Rusk that "our letter was not a letter of charges in any way," although that is precisely what it was. "We do not want you here to answer any charges," Dodd emphasized. "There is no such thing in our mind."²

Rusk thanked the Senators for their kindness and launched forthwith into his lengthy prepared statement. Unctuously, but with just that right touch of seeming firmness that conned two generations of Americans from Korea to Vietnam, Dean Rusk declared that "both the Department and the subcommittee had a common goal, protection of our national security, and it seems to me clear that we should work together to this end."*

With words worthy of the late Joseph McCarthy, the redoubtable Rusk conceded that "the Department of State, like any foreign office in any important country, has real security problems. These are never ending and require constant vigilance. The most serious are those resulting from the attempts of other governments to penetrate the Department both physically and through personnel. . . .both those seeking employment and *those already on our rolls.*"**

"I give the combination of these problems a considerable amount of personal attention and am in regular touch with the various agencies who assist us in dealing with them," he assured the Senators.

Having set the stage, as he was always wont to do, with a seemingly hawk-like stand, Rusk hastened "to try to clear away the underbrush of

All quotes from Secretary Rusk's appearance before the Senate subcommittee are taken from Part 5 of the subcommittee's 1963-65 Otepka Hearings.
*Emphasis added throughout.

misunderstanding and suspicion on a number of specific issues which, think, has [sic] brought us to the difficult situation we are now in." H listed four "principal issues" which had been covered by the Senator bristling memorandum: the charges against Otepka, the new passpoı regulations, the reorganization of Abba Schwartz's Bureau of Securit and Consular Affairs, and "certain aspects of the security practices withı the Department."

Tackling the Otepka case first, Rusk immediately trapped himself i several glaring "inconsistencies."* Fortunately for him, however, he wa not under oath, since Cabinet officers are traditionally absolved from th necessity of being sworn in before Congressional committees.

After muddying the record with highly dubious tales of how and whe he first came to take an interest in the Otepka matter, Rusk piousl announced: *"I can assure you, however, that the charges were not brougł in retaliation for Mr. Otepka's testimony before the subcommittee, nor d they mark any attempt by the Department to interfere with the work ₑ the subcommittee."*

With nary a blink, he went on from there to summarize the charge against Otepka, which, of course, made it perfectly plain that the Depart ment had filed the charges as a reprisal.

A little later in the game, the Secretary of State compounded Johı Reilly's barefaced lie that the Department was taking action to imple ment the changes recommended by the subcommittee's 1962 report. Fo one thing, he emphasized, "we have eliminated 90-day waivers for De partment officers except in very rare cases." He said there had been "onl; six" such waivers in the year since the subcommittee report was released This was still one more than the five issued in the entire eight years o the Eisenhower Administration, but by comparison with the 152 Rusł had signed in the first year of the New Frontier, one must admit it wa an improvement.

Rusk glossed over the potentially dangerous practice of issuing blanke waivers to clerical personnel. He wisely refrained from mentioning tha 398 such waivers had been wholesaled in the five months followinᵢ publication of the subcommittee report.

The other "specific actions" he claimed his Department had taken oı the Senators' 1962 recommendations were equally dubious. In fact, sev eral he simply invented. Worse, he took instances of bad security prac tices cited by Otepka and turned them around to make them appear a

* See Chapter VI.

definite improvements. One was the Intelligence reporting function which had been removed from Otepka's reach by J. Clayton Miller's management survey.

"Previously," Rusk said, "the Office of Security received all FBI reports and those CIA reports dealing with counter-Intelligence. Now, these are sent directly to the Bureau of Intelligence Research unless they concern physical or personnel security. This eliminates one step in the process of transmission and helps assure that important items of information in these reports reach the top levels in the Department on a continuing priority basis."

Like so many of Rusk's statements during his long tenure as Secretary, this *sounded* perfectly plausible. On closer scrutiny, however, the facts failed to bear him out, as Otepka had already made clear on this particular item. Among other things, it blocked SY's view of the U.S. officials named in Intelligence reports.

There was a portion of Rusk's tall tale to the subcommittee that one is tempted to suspect he inserted for comic relief. He went into some detail about how he had "improved" security in U.S. embassies and consulates abroad, particularly through the development of "highly sophisticated technical instruments" for "seeking out listening devices in our oversea posts." This was, he said, "a function to which I devote a good deal of personal time and interest" and he boasted that "we now employ a select corps of professional security engineers."

Rusk was aware, of course, that the head of his "select corps" was Elmer Dewey Hill, whose Warsaw escapades had been so vividly described to the subcommittee by George Pasquale six weeks earlier. This may explain John Reilly's touchiness about Hill, who shared with Rusk this "personal interest" in the fine art of wiretapping. Luckily for both Rusk and Hill, the Soviet taps in the Warsaw and Moscow embassies had not as yet been revealed. If they had, the Secretary's apparent pat on the back for Elmer would have looked even more ludicrous than it did.

With more admirable *savoir faire*, Rusk glided lightly over the gag rule he had imposed on State Department witnesses the Senators had wanted to question about the Otepka case. Then, going on the offensive, he audaciously laid down the laws he wanted the subcommittee to observe in conducting its hearings.

"Before beginning a subcommittee investigation relating to the Department," declared Rusk, "the chairman . . . should send to the Department a statement of the scope and nature of the inquiry." He was refreshingly honest about why he was making this particular demand: It would, he said, give the Department witnesses a better chance to "be prepared."

"This will also permit me to know the nature of the problems in which the subcommittee is interested," he added. If the matters at hand had not been so filled with potential tragedy for the future of the country, Dean Rusk's demand would have been laughable in the extreme. Here he was, the Secretary of State, asking the Senate for prior revelations of its plans while audaciously defending his right, as a purely appointive official, to control all witnesses and any information the Senate might receive from his Department. As if this were not enough, he then demanded that the subcommittee grant him full powers of censorship over whatever it might release on the Department of State.

"Before publication of the testimony of any Department witness who appears before the committee, I should have the opportunity to review it for security purposes," he said.

In the next breath, he defended his right to put an unbreakable seal on the lips of all his subordinates. Citing the 1948 Truman directive, he stated: "Neither I nor any of my subordinates should be asked to violate that directive." Further, he lifted Otepka's argument that the law gave Civil Service personnel the right "to furnish information to either House of Congress," and tossed it right in the Senators' faces.

"Nothing in these guidelines [the demands he had just laid down], or any other action by me or my subordinates is in conflict with that statute," Rusk asserted.

From there he moved to a thinly veiled threat. Knowing how sensitive every Senator, or for that matter every man in American public life, would normally be to the Great Lesson of Joe McCarthy, Dean Rusk closed by pointedly citing the "censure charges against the late Senator McCarthy."

With commendable patience, the subcommittee had sat silent through the Secretary's undeniably brilliant performance. They had put up with the "inconsistencies," the half-truths, the demands, and finally the threats. Now they were ready to ask their questions.

Crusty old Senator McClellan bridled just a bit. "I do not see any reason why there is such a great secrecy between the executive branch and this committee in working out these problems," he said. "I have no axe to grind in it. I am opposed to some arbitrary attitudes in the executive branch. . . . As I find them, I will press my opposition to them."

But Rusk refused to give an inch. Suavely, he turned McClellan's

gument aside and defended his actions in forbidding State Department
ople to testify in the Otepka business.

McClellan didn't let him get away with it entirely, however. Slyly, he
ked if Otepka was "in danger of losing his job because he testified
fore this committee." Rusk never batted an eye. "His testimony before
is committee had nothing to do with it, Senator," he replied evenly.
Senator Hruska managed to set the record straight. He squeezed an
dmission from Rusk that the charges were in fact based on information
ven to the subcommittee's staff. McClellan said that's what he meant
the first place: "I regard the committee's staff in the pursuit of its duties
you would regard somebody under you." Counsel Sourwine's dealings
ith Otepka were, he insisted, a "committee action."

Hruska called it a "perverted idea of loyalty" to expect a man like
tepka to put the State Department above the country. He said he was
not prepared to concede" that the Secretary of State could "prescribe
nder what conditions we shall be able to call witnesses from the State
department or any other department."

Rusk backed off just a little. He claimed that he was "not trying to
ictate to the committee," though the record was clear that his demands
mounted to just that. Then, a minute later, he took the offensive again,
ashing irrelevantly at a newspaper story "that indicated that Harlan
leveland . . . had recommended that the Department of State rehire
lger Hiss."

Such tactics threw the Senators off balance, though several of them
ept trying to keep the Secretary pinned down to the Otepka case. "That
the most pressing [thing]," said McClellan.

Dodd seemed more concerned, however, about what Rusk and the
enators were going to tell the little knot of newsmen waiting outside the
earing room. "We are going to be bombarded," he said. It was decided
hat the reporters should be told that it had been "a very amicable
iscussion" and that "some progress was made toward an understand-
ng."

No progress had been made at all, of course. Rusk had succeeded in
eflecting the Senators from their main target, which was to get the
harges against Otepka quashed. Moreover, he had not budged a bit on
is insistence that he would continue to control the testimony of his
ubordinates.

Otepka was still in no man's land. Just a week before Rusk's polite duel
vith the subcommittee, he had filed his formal answers to the thirteen
harges. With Roger Robb's help, he had prepared a stunning reply. He

had stuck staunchly by his guns, insisting that he gave information to th subcommittee through Sourwine because "I had not only the right, b the duty to defend myself, to correct the committee's record, and t support my oral testimony."

"It is a familiar rule that regulations, like statutes, must be interprete with common sense," his reply stated. Pointedly, he cited an ancient la enacted in the reign of Edward II. It held "that a prisoner who break prison shall be guilty of a felony." But, Otepka emphasized, the gre jurist Plowden ruled that this did not "extend to a prisoner who break out of prison when the prison is on fire 'for he is not to be hanged becaus he would not stay to be burnt.' "[3]

Otepka noted that the Department had refused to let him and hi lawyer see the original documents which formed the basis for the crim nal charges except under strict supervision. He found this "puzzling" an reminded the Department that it had permitted John Stewart Service "t examine all documents and papers . . . which might be material to hi defense." He refrained from underlining the obvious double standar involved in this contrast.

In conclusion, he submitted that "the charges against me are withou foundation and should be dismissed." He knew, of course, that he wa whistling in the wind. His only hope lay with the Senate subcommittee On October 31, exactly ten days after Rusk's appearance, a brief lette signed by every member of the subcommittee was dispatched to th Secretary of State by Senator Eastland. Although polite in tone, it backe Otepka to the hilt.

Insisting on the right of a Senate committee to receive testimony fron "any official or employee of our government," the letter stated that suc witnesses should not be "penalized or disciplined in any way" for testify ing truthfully.

"Mr. Otepka's testimony has been a valuable contribution to the Inter nal Security Subcommittee's current investigation of security in the Stat Department, and we feel he had performed a substantial service for hi country," the Senators said. "We would consider it a great tragedy if th services of this exceptionally able and experienced security officer wer lost to the United States government on the basis of alleged technica violations growing out of his cooperation with the Senate Interna Security Subcommittee."

Five days later Rusk again thumbed his nose at the Senators. O November 5, 1963, Otepka was handed his "final" dismissal. Personnel' John Ordway, acting on Rusk's orders, upheld all the charges agains im. In his letter, Ordway said Otepka had ten days to appeal and noted at the President "will review the matter" if Otepka decided to take his ppeal to the Civil Service Commission.

Dean Rusk, with the support of the Kennedy brothers, had thrown own the final gauntlet. In upholding Otepka's dismissal, they served otice on the Congress that the executive branch would do what it leased. It would bend the internal security laws any way it wished. It ould hire security risks whenever it felt like and fire loyal security fficers who objected. It would push for further convergence with communism. It would sacrifice whoever needed to be sacrificed in the construction of the Rostowian dream.

CHAPTER XXX

Challenge

SHORTLY BEFORE NOON ON TUESDAY, NOVEMBER 5, SENATOR DODD received word that Otepka just got his final walking papers from the Department of State. Dodd could hardly believe his ears. Since June he had been maneuvering behind the scenes to keep the case from breaking into the open. With the other members of the Senate subcommittee, he had given Dean Rusk the benefit of many large doubts, hopeful that in the end the Secretary of State would find a way to resolve this irritating business.

The presidential election was only a year away. Dodd had no desire to embarrass his party as it moved toward what promised to be a tough campaign. He would be up for reelection himself in Connecticut, but that really didn't enter into it. Dodd's seat was considered safe. President Kennedy's chances were far more uncertain, and growing more so every day.

There was little love lost between Tom Dodd and the Kennedys. About all they had in common was their Irish ancestry and a party label. But that label meant something to Dodd. It had kept him in the Congress for eleven years, five of them in the Senate. Unlike some of his more independent Southern colleagues, he could ill afford to take on the

Kennedys. Despite their declining national popularity, they could still make trouble for him in Connecticut.

It must be said for Dodd that, whatever his failings, he never once hesitated to do what he had to do on that November day. The Southerners on the subcommittee, and the Republicans too, could not then have commanded the attention that he did as a Northern Liberal. It was up to him to carry the ball, and he did. Putting all political considerations aside for the moment, he strode onto the floor of the Senate that afternoon and bravely picked up the gauntlet Rusk and the Kennedys had thrown down.

"I consider the dismissal of Mr. Otto Otepka by the Department of State a serious challenge to responsible government and to the system of checks and balances on which it is based," Dodd declared to an unusually full Senate chamber. Bluntly, he described the action as "an affront to the Senate" and a "denial of its powers."

Dodd cited the law that gave civil servants the right "to furnish information to either house of Congress or to any committee or member thereof." But, he said, "the State Department, by its action in the Otepka case, has, in effect, nullified this statute and issued a warning to all [government] employees that cooperation with the established committees of the Senate . . . is a crime punishable by dismissal."

"The significance of the Otepka case cannot be overstated," Dodd thundered. "No one suspected of espionage or disloyalty has to my knowledge been subjected to such surveillance and humiliation.

"In the topsy-turvy attitude it has displayed in the Otepka case, the State Department has been chasing the policeman instead of the culprit. . . . The words 'security violation' have come to mean not the act of turning over information to an alien power, but the act of giving information to a committee of the Senate of the United States."

For the first time publicly, Dodd revealed that a tap had been placed on Otepka's telephone. "Although a State Department official has denied under oath that this was done," Dodd said, "the subcommittee . . . has proof that the tap was installed."

Neither Rusk nor the Kennedys apparently believed Dodd would reveal *that*. It is quite possible they still thought the subcommittee was bluffing on the wiretap evidence, since Reilly's mob had been unable to extract any information from Stanley Holden. This was a serious miscalculation, and the Administration saw at once that it was in for trouble. "Wiretap" had become the nastiest phrase in Washington's lexicon. It was the one thing calculated to fire up the Congress.

With all the other more damaging implications of the Otepka case, the importance attached to the telephone taps may seem rather exaggerated. But the climate in Washington in the early 1960's had become highly charged with suspicion. During Bobby Kennedy's reign in the Justice Department, many congressmen felt that no one's home or office was safe from electronic snoopers.

These often vague suspicions were verified a few years later when an electronics expert named Bernard B. Spindel told a Massachusetts state commission that "a Justice Department agency" had a permanent tap into a main telephone line in Washington. "This line laid open every congressman on Capitol Hill to the possibility of listening devices," Spindel claimed.[1] The taps were not confined to Congressional offices, however. One member of the House Armed Forces Committee came home unexpectedly from Texas, picked up his phone, and overheard snoopers from *two* different agencies which had tapped in on his house line.

Stories of the all-out tapping that allegedly went on during the Test Ban Treaty debate were still rife in Washington when the Otepka case reached its boiling point that fall. Thus, the Senate was more than usually sensitive about electronic eavesdropping. Tom Dodd had struck a raw nerve that was bound to generate a great wave of sympathy for Otepka. Equally important, it brought to the surface a widespread feeling of resentment against the Administration that was shared by many Democrat lawmakers as well as by most Republicans.

The pace of events accelerated swiftly after Dodd's speech on the Senate floor. That night there was a series of worried conferences at the State Department. A temporarily chastened Dean Rusk ordered that Reilly, Hill and Belisle sign letters to the subcommittee "amplifying" their false testimony about the wiretap. George Ball and Thomas Ehrlich were rushed into action to help prepare the statements. Ehrlich and the three trapped SY officials worked on them until well after midnight and again the next morning. When they were done, Rusk reviewed the letters and approved them.

Everyone involved in this emergency operation, including the Secretary of State, now became a party to yet more perjury. As the 1965 subcommittee report tactfully phrased it, the amplification letters "added new knots to the tangle." It took the Senators days of hearings, the report said, "to strip away the technical dodges, the half-truths and plain lies to lay bare the facts."[2]

Dripping with transparent falsehoods, the three letters were sent, with Rusk's personal blessing, to the subcommittee the very next day. The Senators were dumbfounded. Although they should have known better by then, they were shocked that the Secretary of State would permit himself to become an open accomplice in the steady stream of lies flowing from Foggy Bottom.

Reilly's letter was a gem of duplicity. He swore that his previous answers to the subcommittee were "accurate." When he first talked to Elmer Hill about a tap, Reilly said he wanted Hill to study only its "feasibility." "I made it clear to Mr. Hill that I was not authorizing the actual interception of any conversations," he wrote. Moreover, he asked the Senators to believe that "no conversations were intercepted."[3]

Hill also swore that his earlier testimony was "correct." But although he had denied the tap before, he now admitted it. Like Reilly, he claimed the tap was "unsuccessful."[4]

Belisle had testified, under oath, that he knew nothing whatever about any tap on Otepka's phone. Now he changed this to "no first-hand information" about the tap. On November 14, when the subcommittee hauled Belisle up for another session, he confessed that Reilly had "mentioned" the tap to him, but he classified this as "hearsay" and insisted that his previous answers had been truthful.[5]

Reilly came before the subcommittee the following day and ensnared himself further in the spreading web of State Department fabrications. His utter disregard for the truth finally enraged old Senator McClellan, who questioned him closely about the reason for tuning in on Otepka's telephone:

McCLELLAN: The idea was to get the man. If you could not get him out of the trash can, get him out of a telephone conversation, a tapped, compromised telephone. The idea was to get him.

REILLY: The idea was not to get him. The idea, sir, was to find out whether or not these things I had reason to believe were true or not true—not to get a man. . . .

McCLELLAN: Why don't you just come clean and tell the whole story? Why don't you do that? Anybody reading this record knows . . . that you didn't give truthful answers to the questions that were asked you. Everybody knows that. Why don't you come clean here and just shell down the corn, and state what you were after, and what you did do to try to get it?[6]

Clinging frantically to the last tattered shred of the tall tale he had concocted with the connivance of Dean Rusk, George Ball, and the legal advisors, Reilly stubbornly continued to insist that he had been telling the truth, or at least part of it, all along. No one believed him, of course. His credibility had become about as negotiable as a Confederate dollar the day after Appomattox.

Three days later, on November 18, Elmer Hill compromised Reilly's testimony further. Hill finally admitted that Otepka's telephone conversations had been intercepted and that the tapes had been given to "some stranger" at Reilly's behest. He couldn't refrain, though, from yet another little lie: the tapes, he said, had been erased. Nonetheless, Elmer's testimony was perhaps the most candid yet given by any State Department official, including Secretary Rusk. When Sourwine reminded him that he had previously sworn that he had "never engaged" in tapping a fellow employee's phone, Hill said that he had lied because "this was my obligation to the Department."[7]

"Mr. Reilly did not care what means were used," Hill stated. "He was concerned with the results." As for his own falsehoods, Hill said he was only "trying to tell the truth but skirt the fact."[8]

Hill could afford to be at least partially honest with the subcommittee on that occasion. He had just been forced to submit his resignation to the State Department. So had John Reilly, though he was to be kept on the payroll for four more months. Both of them were permitted to resign "without prejudice." No black marks appear on their government employment records. They were both free to return to Federal Service, and in less than a year Reilly was smuggled back into the FCC.

David Belisle got off scot-free. As the subcommittee noted in its 1968 report, "Lying under oath before a Congressional committee can hardly be classed as casual fibbing. If the Department of Justice had chosen to prosecute, the charge would have been perjury—a felony."[9] Needless to say, Bobby Kennedy's department never so much as considered bringing action against any member of what the Senators called "the lying trio." But Belisle's retention by the State Department outdid even Bobby's sin of omission. It was yet another piece of evidence showing how lightly Dean Rusk regarded the Congress.

William Crockett, who was forced to take the rap for much of Rusk's insouciant defiance of the people's elected representatives, later explained how the Department came to make a distinction between Reilly and Hill, on the one hand, and Belisle on the other. Reilly and Hill, said Crockett, had "lost the confidence of top departmental officials because of their conduct under oath before the committee."[10] (Not, mind you, because of their conduct with regard to Otepka and his associates.) But

Belisle, Crockett rationalized, was only fibbing about "hearsay" and, in the Department's view at least, this was "different" than fibbing about things one knew at "first-hand."[11]

Although the full extent of the perjury of Reilly and his henchmen was not immediately made known to the public, enough of the story got out to make the Otepka case an overnight sensation, particularly in Washington. Some of the staunchest Liberals in the Senate were momentarily forced to sit up and take notice. In the wake of the letters submitted by the three prevaricators with Rusk's collusion, Hugh Scott of Pennsylvania demanded a full-scale investigation of all aspects of the Otepka case. The dismissal of Otepka, said Scott, indicated that something must be seriously wrong in the Department of State.[12]

Quite suddenly, even some of the most Leftward-leaning elements of the press were also temporarily horrified. A perceptive handful of newspapers had been playing the story faithfully ever since Dr. Robert Morris unveiled the statement of charges in Texas. Willard Edwards, Clark Mollenhoff, David Sentner and a corporal's guard of other reporters had caught the significance of the case from the outset, though most of their colleagues in the Washington press corps studiously ignored it. Now, however, everyone was getting into the act.

The New York *Times* front-paged Otepka's dismissal as if it were completely fresh news the morning after Dodd's November 5 speech. It also ran a rather laudatory sketch on Otepka in its daily biographical column inside. This story quoted an anonymous State Department official who charged that the crux of the present controversy was simply that Otepka was "out of step with the times." "We have no security risks, and he knows it," the faceless official added.

The Washington *Post* was predictably the last to hold out. "What Otto F. Otepka did was not only unlawful but unconscionable as well," the *Post* trumpeted in an editorial as late as November 10. However, two days later even the *Post* nibbled a little crow. It didn't exactly take back what it had said before, but a November 12 editorial showed that it had belatedly become aware that Gestapo-like tactics had been used against Otepka:

> The Department of State must be a delightful place to work these days. The atmosphere of affectionate camaraderie and warm mutual confidence prevailing there has probably not been matched since the heyday of the Medicis. . . .
>
> This kind of bugging and spying and tattling produces no kind of security at all. It produces nothing but an atmosphere of crippling and

suffocating suspicion. Decent men should not be asked and cannot be expected to work in such an atmosphere. The foreign affairs of a free people should not be conducted in so malign and miasmic a climate.

The American Civil Liberties Union, traditional champion of unlimited rights for the Left, issued a special press release on November 20 taking its friends in the State Department to task for the Otepka wiretap. The ACLU professed that it was "shocked" by this development. The Department "has no business invading personal privacy in this manner," the ACLU said in a statement released by its executive director, John de J. Pemberton, Jr.

Earl Voss of the Washington *Star* reported that ACLU lawyers "may file a brief on Mr. Otepka's behalf asking that no evidence obtained by wiretapping be used "in the departmental proceedings against him." As Voss pointed out, the tap was a clear violation of Section 605 of the Federal Communications Act.[13] Therefore, Reilly and his boys had not only committed flagrant perjury, the root of that perjury lay in their knowledge that they had been caught violating another law, in addition to all those they had shattered within SY.

To the Administration's mounting uneasiness, the Otepka story kept exploding right on through those early weeks of November. It bounced back onto the front pages with each new development. On November 9 the subcommittee released the Reilly gang's earlier testimony along with the "clarifying" letters. The same day, Rusk decided it was time to dump Reilly and Hill, though at first it was understood to be merely a temporary measure. The next morning the New York *Times* headlined the story on page one: "Otepka Accusers Placed On Leave."

"The indications were," wrote the *Times'* Max Frankel, "that Secretary of State Dean Rusk would reluctantly ask both, and perhaps all three to resign."[14]

Columnists and editorial writers hinted darkly that much more important developments were in the offing. "There had been a housecleaning of personnel security officials in the Kennedy Administration to remove the last traces of the tougher policies of previous administrations," wrote the highly respected columnist, Richard Wilson.[15] Arthur Krock of the New York *Times* cited the "deceitful and worse" actions of the Department of State as an instance of the "insensitive ethical attitude of public officials."[16]

David Lawrence, editor of *U.S. News & World Report*, wrote in one of his daily newspaper columns that the Otepka matter "is more important than the alleged scandals that are being investigated on Capitol Hill in domestic affairs."* He aptly recalled that "there have been too many instances in which employees in the executive branch of the government have been given security clearance and later turned out to be indiscreet in passing out to friends and acquaintances information which eventually reached the Communist side."[17]

Henry J. Taylor, drawing on his own inside knowledge of State Department security gleaned during his tenure as Ambassador to Switzerland in the 1950's, reminded his readers that the "destruction of the then unknown Otepka" in 1961 was the "key" that unlocked the door to the reinfiltration of the State Department by security risks.

"Make no mistake about it," wrote the intrepid Mr. Taylor. "We remain on the road back to the days of Alger Hiss."[18]

In a subsequent column on November 18, Taylor cut incisively through all the sound and fury surrounding the wiretap flap and the obfuscating issue of perjury and got right to the heart of the whole matter: "The State Department security section, which Otto F. Otepka headed after serving under every administration for nineteen years, had been knocked into utter shambles by a Left-wing element that moved into the State Department when the New Frontier took over." Then he went on:

The prize—and priceless—information needed by any enemy nation is: What are America's intentions and capabilities? This requires continuously tapping into our top-secret circles of decision, if possible—penetration at the highest policy level. Soviet agents deal in two commodities, information and people. And they deal in these here [in Washington] on the largest scale of anywhere in the world.

Because the United States is the only country Russia fears, it is impossible to overstate the skill, cunning and patience, the resources and ruthlessness of this attack on us. Yet where are the bulwarks against this in the State Department today?

In the Otepka case, columnist Holmes Alexander also detected disquieting echoes of an earlier era. He remembered that "the State Department behaved this way toward its officials who suspected Alger Hiss and toward Senate committees which investigated the strange doings of Owen Lattimore." He recalled, too, that "another Democratic President and his Secretary of State bore some bruises from a fracas of this sort." It was Harry Truman "who called the original Hiss investigation a 'red herring' and Secretary Acheson who vowed he'd 'never turn my back on Alger Hiss,' " Alexander reminded a slowly reawakening public.[19]

"Will the Otepka case blow up to something the size of Hiss-Lat-

---

* The allusion here was to the notorious cases of Bobby Baker and Billy Sol Estes.

timore?" Holmes Alexander asked. "Unless Secretary Rusk backs down
. . . this new story could follow the same lines and assume the same
proportions as the older ones."[20]

This is precisely what the Kennedy Administration most feared at this
juncture. As November wore on without any let-up in the hue and cry,
Rusk relented just a bit and threw the Senate subcommittee a rather dry
bone by "accepting" the resignations of Reilly and Hill. It was apparent,
however, that this had come too late to satisfy either the Senators or the
public.

The day after the subcommittee was privately notified that Reilly and
Hill were on their way out, Tom Dodd again carried the battle to the
Senate floor. "I am certain that when the facts are made public," Dodd
said, "they will shock every member of the Congress and every American
citizen, as they have already shocked members of the Senate Subcommittee on Internal Security."

"I am confident," Dodd declared, "that the subcommittee will relentlessly pursue the investigation on which it has now embarked. No one,
regardless of how high or how low his job, will be exempt or excused in
the course of this investigation."

It took courage for Dodd to throw out this challenge to the White
House and the State Department. For no man knew better than he just
how vulnerable his own affairs were. Even then, a full year before the
"testimonial" dinners that were to enrich and ensnare him, Dodd had
long since succumbed to the blandishments of the lobbyists. Like many
before him, this white-maned lawmaker had fallen, a victim to the "good
life" and a perverted American dream. In so doing he must certainly have
realized that he had moved into a very fragile glass house. Yet he dared
throw stones at the most powerful men in America.

Otepka, meanwhile, had filed a formal appeal from his dismissal, requesting a State Department hearing as the first step. Columnist Richard
Wilson assessed this move in the Washington *Star*. It would be "a transparently meaningless process," said Wilson, because "Mr. Rusk and
President Kennedy will pass on their own decisions."[21]

On Tuesday, November 19, the subcommittee resumed its hearings a
few hours before Dodd issued his last challenge. Senator Eastland presided and Roman Hruska and Hugh Scott sat attentively on either side
of him. Across the big mahogany table the witness, Abba Schwartz, eyed
the Senators warily. Scott wanted to know if Schwartz had anything to
do with the charges filed against Otepka. Abba hastened to assure the
Senator that he had "no connection whatsoever with the Otepka case or

any matters dealing with personnel or physical security."[22]

Scott vowed that he would vigorously press through the subcommittee, or on his own if necessary, to urge Secretary Rusk "to review the Otepka case" in light of recent developments. "In the interest of justice," said Scott, "I feel that the case should be reopened *de novo* and the charges brought up again and disposed of."[23]

There was an excellent chance that Tuesday that Hugh Scott would soon have his wish, and more. Dean Rusk was fast becoming a major political liability to the Administration, one that a political realist like Jack Kennedy could ill afford to carry into his second Presidential campaign. Rusk had torn the Democratic Party asunder within its highest visible council, the United States Senate.

Kennedy had never really understood his Secretary of State. "You never know what he is thinking," the President complained of the man with the "Buddha-like face and half-smile,"[24] Rusk was the only member of the Cabinet Kennedy did not call by his first name. No doubt he would be loath to dump Dean Rusk. As Schlesinger observed, the "dismissal of his Secretary of State would constitute too severe a comment on his own original judgment."[25] But Kennedy's pragmatism almost certainly would have won out well before the next year's election.

Tuesday, Wednesday, Thursday . . . the November storm over Otepka's firing was still building, far more fiercely behind the scenes than on public view. Dean Rusk's days at the helm of the Department of State were dwindling down to a precious few. Then, on Friday morning, John Fitzgerald Kennedy flew to Dallas for his final rendezvous with history. In the numbing aftermath of that fateful day, Otto Otepka was soon forgotten.

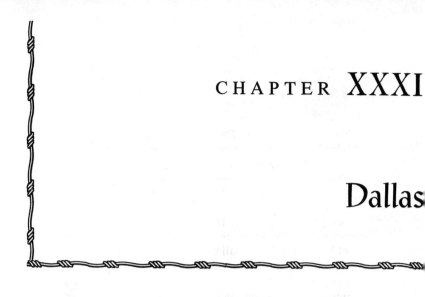

CHAPTER XXXI

Dallas

SOME TIME PRIOR TO HIS EXILE FROM THE OFFICE OF SECURITY OTEPKA started work on a study of Americans who had defected to the Soviet Union and other Communist countries. One of the names on his list was that of Lee Harvey Oswald. Before Otepka and his staff got very far with the study, SY was thrown into a state of almost total disruption and Otepka was subsequently banished.

It may be too much to hope that even if he had been permitted to complete the study on Oswald and the other defectors, Otepka could have prevented the assassination of President Kennedy. Nonetheless, given his customary thoroughness, which so irked his superiors from 1961 on, it is not inconceivable that he could have raised a red flag in Oswald's security files which would have caused the authorities at least to take a closer look at that strange young man.

For example, Otepka almost certainly would have delved very deeply into the curious circumstances surrounding the expeditious granting of a visa to Oswald to enter the Soviet Union from Finland in October 1959. Although the State Department told the Warren Commission that in 1959 it "usually took an American tourist in Helsinki one to two weeks to obtain a visa," Oswald got his within two days after he applied.[1]*

* The State Department misled the Commission. Actually, visas to enter the USSR had

Then too, Otepka would have demanded to know what Oswald did during the two years and eight months that he lived in Russia. The Warren Commission admitted that "Oswald's life in Minsk [where he reportedly resided from January 1960 until June 1962] is the portion of his life concerning which the least is known." The commission conceded that "Oswald was given considerable benefits which ordinary Soviet citizens . . . did not have." It even revealed that Oswald himself had "frankly stated" the relatively munificent sums paid to him "had come from the 'MVD.' "[2]

Otepka would hardly have been as easily satisfied as the Warren Commission with the vague explanations of Oswald's membership in a Soviet "hunting club."* If he had still had his full former authority as the working chief of SY, he doubtless would have ordered his investigators to seek out Oswald and question him closely about the reasons for his belonging to such a club.

Otepka's expert eye could not have failed to note the highly unusual handling of Marina Oswald's departure from the Soviet Union with her American husband. Marina's exit was expedited almost as efficiently as Oswald's entry. Even the CIA later reported that a spot survey it conducted of eleven Russian wives of American citizens who tried to leave the USSR disclosed that they "had to wait from five months to a year to obtain exit visas."[3] Moreover, it is just possible that Otepka's investigators would have unearthed some information to show that Marina Oswald came from a *Chekist*, or secret police, family. If they had, Otepka surely would not have covered it up as the Warren Commission later did.**

Without doubt, Otepka would have required much more information about Oswald's own curious departure from Russia. He would have wanted to know why the Soviets gave the future assassin an exit visa a month and a half in advance of his leaving when, if they wanted to get rid of him as they later claimed, all they had to do was hand him his walking papers and send him on his way, pronto.

It would not have been difficult for Otepka to discover that Oswald had planned his return to the United States nearly a year ahead of time. The defector and his wife turned up at the U.S. embassy in Moscow as early

to be processed then through a central file in Moscow. This usually required at least 30 days, and more often, 60 to 90 days.
* The commission accepted the CIA's dubious report that hunting clubs are "very popular" in the Soviet Union and that anyone can own a shotgun, if not a rifle. The CIA claimed there was nothing at all untoward about Oswald's membership in such a club.
**At least two of Marina's uncles, including the one she lived with in Minsk when she met Oswald, were high-ranking officers in the MVD.

as July 1961 to pave the way for their leisurely "flight" from the workers' paradise; they did not arrive in the U.S. until June 1962.

Otepka would have insisted on knowing why Oswald was handed back the passport he had turned in at the embassy when he renounced his American citizenship upon his arrival in Russia. He would have demanded to know who authorized the payment of $435.71 in State Department funds to finance Oswald's return to the country he had denounced and rejected.

The Otepka study would have traced Lee Harvey Oswald's background to his childhood. It would have determined who influenced him to become a fanatical Marxist. It would have unearthed early evidence of his mental instability. It would, in short, have marked Oswald as a man well worth keeping a wary eye on because all this, and more, was within the scope of the study as Otepka planned it.

Finally, if Otepka had not been under the Rusk-Reilly gun, if he had been operating in a sane atmosphere, he would have found out that in June 1963, the same month he was marched into exile, Oswald received a passport to return to Russia on the approval of Abba Schwartz. The new passport regulations, fostered by the Chayes-Katzenbach-Schwartz clique with Bobby Kennedy's backing, would have prevented Otepka from having the passport voided. But he would have vigorously protested the fact that Schwartz had approved Oswald's passport on one day's notice without undertaking the customary name check. Even the minor flap that this confrontation most certainly would have caused might have been sufficient to reopen Oswald's file independent of Otepka's study on defectors.

Too much to hope? Not if one studies Otepka's record carefully. Prior to 1961, at least, this is the way he could and did operate. Moreover, we have seen that he persisted in proceeding in the same painstaking, careful manner against insurmountable obstacles right down to the day he was ousted from the Evaluations Division less than four months before President Kennedy went to Dallas.

However, there was one thing Otepka could not have controlled: the permissive climate that prevailed during the period of the Grand Détente, which of itself gave Lee Harvey Oswald the ability to roam unmolested in and out of the country as he planned his heinous crime. In this climate, most closely analogous to that of an asylum where the criminally insane are given free run of the wards and grounds, Otepka could not have prevented Oswald's journeying to Mexico City to confer at the Soviet embassy with a man identified as one of the top KGB operatives in the Western hemisphere. Nor could he have stopped Oswald from returning to Texas after this visit some weeks before the assassination.

Going back just a bit further, the creation of this climate was to a very large degree the work of the men who had come stampeding into the State Department in 1961 when Otepka was strapped to the special project. One former Intelligence official summed it up this way: "These men, most of whom came in the back door on security waivers signed by Dean Rusk, are in a very real sense accomplices before the fact of the President's murder. They caused the whole country to relax its guard. A whole regiment of Oswalds could operate freely in the atmosphere that prevailed then, and, I'm sorry to say, still prevails in 1968."*

Chief Justice Earl Warren, even after the surprising discovery that a self-professed Marxist had committed the crime, blamed it on the "climate of hate" that allegedly gripped the country that autumn. Given this predisposition, it was predictable that the commission Warren headed should exonerate the Communist conspiracy of any complicity.

All this is not to say that *only* Communists are capable of plotting political assassinations, which are, after all, the oldest method known to man for ridding a government of its leader. In fact, just three weeks before Jack Kennedy's untimely death the world was treated to the astonishing spectacle of an American government involved in the coup that led to the murder of the president of Vietnam, Ngo Dinh Diem.

In his sentimental reminiscences of Jack Kennedy's career, Theodore Sorensen claims that the coup on November 1 and 2, 1963, "received no help from the United States. Neither the timing nor the scale of this one was known in the United States . . . much less to Kennedy."

It might not have been known to Sorensen, but, as the late Marguerite Higgins substantiated, the plan for Diem's overthrow (if not his assassination) was well known to John Kennedy. The President certainly knew of the secret cable sent from Washington on August 24 which set the wheels of revolt in motion in Saigon. Moreover, the mysterious Colonel Conein of the U.S. embassy was, according to Miss Higgins, "given the essentials of the revolt plan by General Tran Van Don, the mastermind of it all."[4] Conein "participated in every meeting during the overthrow" and was at the "rebel command post the whole day and night" of the furious bloodletting. The colonel kept Ambassador Henry Cabot Lodge closely informed of developments, and CIA's John McCone apprised the President of every important move, before and during the uprising.

*Ironically, this realistic assessment was made a month before Senator Robert F. Kennedy's assassination in June 1968.

In its November 8, 1963, issue, *Time* looked back with understandable distaste upon the assassination of Diem, his brother, and other members of their family. "There could be no question," *Time* said, "that the U.S. . . . had effectively encouraged the overthrow of the Diem regime." The magazine reminded its readers that "only a few weeks ago" President Kennedy, during a CBS television interview with Walter Cronkite, "argued that the winning of the war against the Communist Viet Cong would probably require 'changes in policy, and perhaps in personnel' in the Diem government."[4]

The Diem assassination, culminating as it did the long series of foreign policy disasters that began with the Bay of Pigs and the Berlin Wall, undoubtedly contributed to the growing uneasiness in America that Jack Kennedy encountered everywhere he went that fall.

The leaders of his party cautioned Kennedy that he was in for serious trouble in the 1964 campaign. Many had already written off the Deep South. Lyndon Johnson warned him that Texas might be lost too, and urged him to start stumping the state now in an effort to rebuild the crumbling Democrat political fences.

Concurrent with the decline in Kennedy's popularity, the country was witnessing an amazing rise in support for Barry Goldwater, the Senate's foremost conservative. The Goldwater phenomenon was visible proof that the grassroots were beginning to stir.

By and large, the voters knew little about the massive Leftist re-population of the State Department. But they had begun to detect signs of disquieting changes in Washington and more and more of them looked with favor upon Senator Goldwater, who only six months before had not been given a chance to come within range of the Republican nomination, let alone election.

In October, *Time* published the results of a nationwide survey by its correspondents. The Test Ban Treaty had just been steamrolled through the Senate, and although some polls purported to show that this had increased Kennedy's popularity, the *Time* survey found little evidence of it. Not long before, *Time* noted, most political prophets figured Kennedy could win in a walk against any Republican in 1964. "Now," it said, "many are changing their minds." The *Time* survey showed that at least one Republican, Barry Goldwater, "could give Kennedy a breathlessly close race," though "Kennedy could easily beat any other GOP candidate."

In a September speech delivered in the Mormon Tabernacle in Salt Lake City, the President let loose his first volley against Goldwater.

Although he did not mention the Senator by name, the Associated Press reported that, "Without question, Kennedy in this speech went further than ever before toward challenging Goldwater."

By mid-November Jack Kennedy had also decided to dump Lyndon Johnson. In her 1968 book, *Kennedy and Johnson*, the President's personal secretary, Evelyn Lincoln, revealed a conversation she had with her boss on November 19, 1963:

"Who is your choice as a running mate?" Mrs. Lincoln asked Kennedy. She said the President "looked straight ahead, and without hesitating he replied:

"At this time I am thinking about Governor Terry Sanford of North Carolina. *But it will not be Lyndon.*"

Jack Kennedy no doubt had many reasons for arriving at this decision. It is doubtful if the Otepka case entered into it in any major way. Still, Lyndon Johnson's primary assignment as Vice President had been to keep the Congress from stepping out of line, and most particularly his former colleagues in the Senate.

One of Johnson's closest friends in the Senate was Tom Dodd, and the same day that Kennedy disclosed his plans to Mrs. Lincoln, Dodd had run off the reservation again by challenging the Administration on the Senate floor and promising a no-holds-barred investigation of the Otepka matter.

Johnson had failed to quell Dodd, if indeed he had bothered to try. But he had failed to quell the Congress on other things too, and in Jack Kennedy's pragmatic eye Lyndon's usefulness had dwindled to zero.

At his last press conference before taking off on two flying trips to Florida and Texas, Kennedy betrayed his frustration with the mounting rebellion against him in the Democrat-dominated Congress. Angrily, he lashed out at the Congress for its refusal to act on his tax-cut and civil rights bills.

The President was also stung by Congress' stubborn refusal to pass on his proposal to sell 150 million bushels of wheat to the Soviet Union on long-term credits. In one speech that fall he argued that if the U.S. turned down the wheat deal it would only convince the Russians "that we are either too hostile or too timid to take further steps toward peace . . . and that the logical course for them to follow is a renewal of the Cold War."

Jack Kennedy, as he flew to Dallas the morning of November 22, had obviously made up his mind that the Cold War was over, at least between the United States and the USSR. In Tampa and Miami a few days before, the crowds along his announced routes had been sparse and unresponsive. That morning, however, the Texans turned out to give him and his wife a resounding welcome. It was the first time in many months that Jacqueline Kennedy had traveled with her husband. She had lost a new-born son the previous summer and taken a prolonged vacation in Greece. Now her presence seemed to buoy up the President—and the crowds. The Presidential motorcade left the airport and sped toward downtown Dallas. Entering Dealey Plaza, the open Kennedy limousine headed north on Houston Street, then turned left down Elm, passing under the Texas School Depository Building. From a sixth-story window, a man took aim through the telescopic sight of his rifle and fired. At least two shots rang out, echoing, it seemed, after the young President fell lifeless, his head cradled in his wife's lap. In the seat in front of them, the wounded Governor of Texas, John Connally, thought he heard a third shot, giving rise to endless speculation that more than one assassin had been involved.

It is not within the scope of this book to explore all the blurred facets of the Kennedy assassination. By now, so much has been written about it, so many theories and counter-theories offered, that it becomes more impossible each year to unravel the intricate threads of the story and separate truth from fiction.

The Warren Commission decided that Oswald was the murderer. It also decided that he acted entirely on his own. Because so much doubt has been cast upon the second part of this decision, many have come to question the validity of the first. Yet logic, and the evidence, dictate that the one might well be true without the other: Oswald could have slain Kennedy, not on his own, but as a member of a conspiracy.

There was probably more hard evidence against Lee Harvey Oswald than against half of the criminals who have been executed for murder in the United States in the preceding century. The rifle he left on the stairwell of the Book Depository, the fingerprints smeared on the rifle, the threads from his shirt caught in the stock, the precipitous flight from the building, the murder of Policeman J.D. Tippit who tried to apprehend him—all this (and there was much more) would have been enough to convict Oswald in a court of law.

William Manchester, selected by the Kennedys as the "official" historian of the assassination, states that "the evidence pointing to his [Oswald's] guilt is far more incriminating than that against [John Wilkes] Booth, let alone Judas Iscariot. He is the right man; there is nothing provisional about it. The mark of Cain was upon him."[5]

In accepting the Warren Commission's pronouncement of Oswald's guilt, Manchester also accepted the Commission's opinion that Oswald was a free-lance assassin. In short, both the Commission and Mr. Manchester refused to believe that there could have been a conspiracy, and most especially a Communist conspiracy.

Manchester was free to decide otherwise, of course, though his ideological predilections prevented him from admitting the possibility of a conspiracy. But it would not have made much difference in 1967 if a lone author voted for a verdict of guilty, and branded the Communists as the perpetrators of the crime, four years after it was committed.

However, if the Warren Commission had judged the Communists guilty a scant ten months after the assassination when it issued its report, *that* decision would have been pregnant with danger. It might not have brought on nuclear war, but it would have collapsed all the carefully constructed bridges to the East and shattered all the delightful illusions so painstakingly concocted by the State Department and the White House. The Commission could not, as a matter of national policy, find the Communists guilty.

Yet the doubts persist. Oswald was a Marxist. He defected to Russia and lived there, under MVD protection, for more than two-and-a-half years. He shot and killed the President of the United States barely seventeen months after his return to America and only a few weeks after he traveled to Mexico to confer with a top KGB agent. He was planning to return to Russia again and had obtained a passport for that purpose.

All that is missing is the motive. Why, one asks, would the Soviets want to kill John Fitzgerald Kennedy? He was doing his utmost as President to cement the détente he had unilaterally declared. He was proving America's good faith by quietly canceling and shelving nuclear weapons and delivery systems. He had just rammed an inspectionless Test Ban Treaty through the Senate and had approved the U.N. ban on nuclear weapons in space. He was trying to get a reluctant Congress to let him send tons and tons of wheat to Russia. More and bigger "steps toward peace" were in the hopper kept by Walt Rostow's Policy Planning Council at State.

On the surface, there seems to be no logical reason for the Soviets to dispose of President Kennedy, though some have argued that Castro, suspecting a Kennedy-Khrushchev plot to oust him, may have had a motive.

It might never be known *why* Kennedy was killed. However, among the 20,000-plus documents that the Warren Commission deposited with the National Archives in Washington, there is a curious report to which the Commission obviously gave no credence. It is File No. 3106, containing a handwritten statement (in Russian) left at the U.S. embassy in Moscow by a Soviet citizen who risked his life to deliver it.

Six months after the assassination this anonymous informant came to the embassy, slipped past the Soviet police stationed outside, and presented himself to an unnamed American official. Although the statement he wrote was extensively censored by the State Department (with the Warren Commission's blessing), enough of it survives today in the National Archives to detect the main import of the man's message.

The informant said he knew the Oswalds in Gorky, where he claimed they lived for several months. He identified Marina as a KGB agent and verified her identity when shown a photograph. He said her sister, whom he also knew, belonged to the KGB too. Moreover, he said Oswald himself was connected with the KGB.

Oswald once asked him what he thought "would happen if the President of the United States was assassinated." Oswald said he knew Communist Party people in America "who could carry this out." When the Russian asked what would be the purpose of such an act, the future assassin replied that it would "prove a reaction against the *besheny* [right-wing 'wild men'] in the United States."

Most startling of all, the informant said that Oswald claimed to know a man named Jack Ruby, whom he called "an old friend."

The embassy official who interviewed this man attached a covering letter, now expurgated, with the file he sent to Washington. In the letter the official said: "We agree these are incredible statements. . . but he [the informant] stuck to his story and never contradicted himself."

Unless he were deranged, it is inconceivable that the Russian would invent such a story. For in giving this statement he laid himself open to the terrorizing revenge of the KGB, even if the tale were pure fiction. He may not have known enough about American Intelligence to realize that his accusations would one day wind up on public view in the National Archives. But he must have been aware that the tentacles of the KGB octopus reach into the innermost councils of every government in the world, and his chances of staying alive after delivering his story were very slim indeed.

Like the courageous Colonel Penkovskiy, this man may have felt a compelling need to tell the Free World the truth in the vain hope that it would heed yet another warning. Either that, or he was insane, though the official who interviewed him gave no hint that there were any signs of mental instability.

From File No. 3106, it is plain that this faceless Russian believed firmly that President Kennedy was the victim of a *Soviet* conspiracy which had used Lee Harvey Oswald as a willing instrument. However, he had no substantiating evidence beyond his alleged knowledge of the Oswalds and the conversations he claimed to have had with them in Gorky.

A credible Soviet motive for slaying Kennedy is still missing. It is difficult to see them disposing of a friendly President merely to ignite a purge of the *besheny* in America, as Oswald is said to have claimed. True, the conservatives were growing stronger by the day in the U.S. that autumn. On November 22 the Houston *Chronicle* carried the results of a statewide straw vote which showed Barry Goldwater leading Jack Kennedy in Texas by 52 to 48 percent. But Kennedy's popularity had not sunk sufficiently for the Russians to take such a drastic step, or so it seems to our Western minds at least.

One eminently knowledgeable American Intelligence expert told Otto Otepka early in 1965 that he thought there was a more plausible motive for Soviet complicity in the crime. By way of evidence, he referred to a Stewart Alsop column in the *Saturday Evening Post.*[6]

"Shortly before he died," Alsop related, "President Kennedy called one of the government's leading experts on the Far East into his office for a talk. The conversation concerned a subject which . . . troubled the late President more deeply than any other—the developing Chinese nuclear capability. He asked if there was any chance for 'accommodation' with the Chinese Communists. When the Far East expert said no, the President appeared to agree. He asked the expert what should be done."

"I've given a lot of thought to that question," the expert replied. "It should be technically possible at this stage in their nuclear development to destroy the Chinese nuclear plants in such a way that it will seem an atomic accident.

"The thing could be done as a surgical operation, without nuclear weapons, using high explosives," the official continued. "We could have plans for you, with various operational means for taking out the plants, in the near future."

The official told Alsop that Kennedy pointed at him meaningfully and said: *"You do that."*

This was an order, a Presidential directive to start the intricate machinery of the U.S. government rolling on a plan to "take out" China's nuclear capability. Unfortunately, it was not a very closely held secret. In fact, Stewart Alsop recalled in his *Post* column that he had written "about the time this conversation took place . . . that the President had decided 'in principle that China must be prevented, by whatever means, from becoming a nuclear power.' At a press conference a few weeks earlier, President Kennedy had hinted very strongly at this decision-in-principle."

In discussing the Alsop revelation with Otepka, the Intelligence expert said he had known of Kennedy's decision too. But until Alsop's published column appeared he had not felt free to talk about it because, despite the late President's press conference hint, it was highly classified information.

"How does this indicate Soviet involvement in the assassination?" Otepka inquired.

The man frowned thoughtfully before replying. The answer he finally gave is given here *in toto*, not verbatim, of course, but in its essence.

"As you know," he said, "I am one of the few people who have never completely bought the Sino-Soviet split. I am willing to concede that there are differences between Peiping and Moscow, personality clashes and occasional policy disputes. You might even liken the 'split' to the schism that divided Christianity into the Roman and Byzantine camps. There were often serious differences between Rome and Constantinople, but for a thousand years they continued to cooperate on many things. During the Crusades, which were initiated by Rome, the Byzantines frequently [and sometimes literally] cut the Crusaders' throats. Other times they helped them.

"We know that the Soviets and the Chicoms continue to work closely together on espionage and subversive activities in many places. Cuba and South America are but one area; Africa is another. We also know that they are teamed up against us in Vietnam. The Soviets supply most of the arms for the Communist forces in a country which Peiping wants to dominate and eventually absorb.

"Now, let's look at the Chinese nuclear capability, which rightly worried President Kennedy. No matter what the propagandists might tell you, this could be a Russian capability—*not* Chinese.

"The Russians would never *give* a neighboring nation, particularly China, a plant to produce nuclear weapons. Those plants in North China may be owned by Russia, operated by Russians, protected by Russians, with some help from reliable Russsophile Chinese, of course.

"I will not deny that the Chinese have the technical know-how to produce a hydrogen bomb, as they have done. They are very intelligent people and their scientists, some of them trained right here in America, are top-notch.

"What China does *not* have, and could not possibly have either now or in 1964 when they exploded their first atomic bomb, is the industrial base to build not only the bombs, but the highly sophisticated electronic guidance systems that go into the nuclear missiles we now know they also have. The metallurgical problems alone are far beyond China's industrial capacity. As late as the early 1960's they had to abort their 'great leap forward' when their backyard steel furnaces started blowing up all over the place.

"Yet our State Department asks us to believe that the Chinese could manufacture atomic and hydrogen bombs, along with guidance systems and missiles, in the mid-1960's, a bare fifteen years after Mao took over an industrially primitive country which had been devastated by nearly thirty years of continuous rebellions and warfare.

"Even the French, who invented atomic energy with the Curies, have not been able to develop a nuclear capability comparable to what we are told the Chinese now have. And France is a highly developed industrial nation.*

"What does all this have to do with Jack Kennedy's asassination? Let me write you the script which Suslov and his boys wrote ten years ago, with Mao's approval then, though he may have changed his mind since.

"Certain Americans had been predicting a Sino-Soviet split for some years. Rusk was telling us in 1949, before the Korean War, that the Chicoms were completely independent of the Russians. Rostow peddled the same line out of MIT. It worked pretty well right through the Korean War. It kept us focused on the Chinese and the North Koreans, who would have collapsed in a month if the Russians hadn't kept feeding them arms. Eventually, our whole foreign policy came to be based on the theory of the 'split.' So Suslov says, they want a split, we'll give it to them—but good.

"The Russians then proceed to build their nuclear plants in North China and Inner Mongolia, close enough to Siberia so they can shuttle their scientists back and forth to their nuclear science center near Novosibirsk. [In 1967 it was learned that Bruno Pontecarvo, the Italian-born defector from the British nuclear laboratories, *was* shuttling between these installations.—Editors Note.]

"The Russians can't make it look as though China has just inherited

* In 1966 the French were testing atomic—not hydrogen—bombs in the South Pacific by dropping them from balloons. But by the end of 1968 the Red Chinese had exploded a hydrogen bomb of at least three megatons, many times more powerful than the French, and were known to have between 70 and 100 such bombs, in addition to missile delivery systems.

a nuclear capability overnight. So they build it up gradually, slow enough so the West won't get suspicious, but fast enough for their own purposes.

"Now, here is the final act of Suslov's scenario: At some point in the future, missiles launched in China strike the United States, or possibly some nation we are committed to defend, like Vietnam or Japan or any one of the others.

"Whom does the United States 'second strike' force respond against? Russia? Why, Russia isn't involved at all. We think China hit us, so we hit China back. They can afford to lose a few hundred million people. Communists have never hesitated to sacrifice people. What industry exists can be sacrificed too, because the great Communist industrial base—Russia—gets off without a scratch.

"After the nuclear exchange, the Russians will probably cast themselves in the role of the Great Peacemakers. The Soviet Union simply steps in and picks up the pieces. They get what they've been clawing and scratching for since 1917—One World, ruled by Russia, or, more to the point, the small clique that controls Russia."

The Intelligence expert paused at this point in his narrative. His eyes narrowed and he looked hard at Otepka.

"When Jack Kennedy gave the order to plan the destruction of those nuclear plants in China in the fall of 1963, he signed his death warrant right there. He didn't know it, but he was striking right at the heart of the Soviet's grand strategy for the final subjugation of the world."

Otepka didn't necessarily buy this story, though he admitted that he had long entertained grave doubts about the validity of the Sino-Soviet split. He had seen too many pro-Soviets in the State Department peddling the split to credit it out of hand. In common with most Americans, he had his own private ideas about the assassination of President Kennedy. But he felt the results more permanently and personally than most citizens—and he felt them immediately.

"On November 22 the assassination blotted out nearly everything else," William Manchester wrote.[7]

Among many other things, it blotted out Barry Goldwater's chances for election in 1964. It blotted out the short memories of millions of Americans who had been leaning away from the Democratic Party. And it blotted out the Otepka case at the very moment that it threatened to blow up Dean Rusk's Department of State.

Not for five long years would the plight of Otto Otepka surface again around the receding rims of the public conscience, and even then it would not penetrate so deeply as it had in that momentous November of 1963. The bullets that snuffed out Jack Kennedy's life in Dallas, simultaneously extinguished the flame of hope that had begun to illuminate Otepka's cause.

The Senate subcommittee continued its hearings, though with dwindling enthusiasm, behind closed doors. After Lyndon Johnson's ascension to the White House, those doors remained more tightly shut than ever before.

Five days after the assassination, Congressman John M. Ashbrook of Ohio made a valiant attempt to pry open the Otepka case in both the House and Senate, wisely tying it to the climate that permitted Lee Harvey Oswald to commit his crime.

Introducing a resolution to authorize a joint Congressional investigation of the State Department and the Otepka purge, Ashbrook took note of the Department's role in financing Oswald's return to America from Russia.

"This is but one of scores of examples of the State Department's policies which show mismanagement, bad judgment, and even subversion," Ashbrook charged on the floor of the House. He pointed out that Otepka's dismissal had "signaled the end of effective security" in the Department.

In that speech, Ashbrook came publicly closer than any other member of Congress to the central issue of the Otepka case, though many had voiced similar fears in private.

"Personnel of the State Department" he said, "have played a major role in engineering a series of miniature Munichs, including nuclear agreements, grain deals, [and] over 25 percent unilateral disarmament . . . in evolving a policy of peace through appeasement."

Unfortunately, neither the Congress nor the people heeded John Ashbrook's warning. Communism feeds on confusion, and in those black November days following the death of the President, confusion reigned supreme across a numbed and frightened land.

CHAPTER **XXXII**

Lyndon

THE NEW PRESIDENT OF THE UNITED STATES WAS A MAN WHO BE-
lieved in action. Where John Kennedy had been wont to turn a thing over
and over in his mind before reaching a decision, Lyndon Baines Johnson
would walk around it once, size it up, draw a figurative six-shooter, and
empty all six shots into his target. Many of his bullets were blanks and
thus the problems didn't always stay dead after he plugged them. But just
the act of taking aim and squeezing the trigger did wonders for him. It
seemed to release all that nervous energy, if only for the moment.

As everyone knows, President Johnson preferred to gun down his
targets in the back room, which was sound-proofed to keep all the shoot-
in' and screamin' from being heard up front in the bar of public opinion.
You could also deal better back there. People were more apt to listen,
to "reason together," when they knew the world wasn't tuned in on them.

The Johnson style, so different from Jack Kennedy's, called for real
honest-to-goodness deals where the other fellow got something nice if he
did what you wanted him to do. If he didn't, there were other ways of
handling him. Most of the time, anyway.

That Otepka business was only one of a hundred problems crowding
in on Lyndon Johnson as he moved into the White House. He realized

hat the assassination had removed it from the crisis file. Yet characteris-
ically he wasted no time trying to settle it.

A month after the tragedy in Dallas, newspaper stories began to hint
it Johnson's intervention in the Otepka case. One claimed that the
'resident had proposed a compromise. Under this first of several LBJ
ormulas for settlement the State Department would drop the dismissal
:harges and reinstate Otepka, "but in another job at his previous pay."[1]

Otepka would never agree to this, though the President couldn't un-
lerstand why. It seemed eminently fair to him. People were always more
interested in money than most anything else. Sometimes they had to save
ace too, but didn't the dropping of the charges and the reinstatement
:ake care of that?

Lyndon Johnson was totally unequipped to fathom what Otepka stood
for. In his book, internal security was just another one of those irksome
little issues that kept popping up to plague people in public life, though
fortunately not very often in recent years.

He had known a lot of suspected Communists and Communist-front-
ers in his time. A few of them were pretty wild, but most of them seemed
reasonable enough. Why, as a young fellow when he headed the National
Youth Administration in Texas, Lyndon's boss in Washington, Aubrey
Williams, had been tagged as a member of some Communist fronts, and
old Aubrey was downright level-headed. In fact, Lyndon still regarded
him as a friend.

In the beginning, Johnson entertained no doubts that he would hit on
a workable formula to settle the Otepka matter. Fortunately, his old
friends Jim Eastland and Tom Dodd were in charge of the Senate committee that had been kicking up such a ruckus just before Dallas. He
could count on Jim and Tom to cooperate, especially with an election
coming up. Neither of them would do anything to embarrass him. More,
they would do their best to help him fix things right.

Fixing things right had always been a Johnson speciality. That and
riding the right coattails. Way back in 1931 he had combined the two to
land his first job in Washington.

Lyndon was helping out Richard M. Kleberg, owner of the King
Ranch, in Kleberg's race for a vacated Congressional seat that year. The
tall, lanky 22-year-old ran a lot of errands for Kleberg during the campaign. One of them turned out to be pretty important.

The Mexican wards in San Antonio weren't about to go for a wealthy
gringo like Kleberg. But Lyndon took care of that. He acted as Kleberg's

liaison with the man who controlled the Mexican wards, Don Quill. After Kleberg was elected, Quill became Postmaster of San Antonio. In Washington, as Congressman Kleberg's assistant, Lyndon learned fast. He found another coattail too, and this one belonged to a man with a powerful political future, Sam Rayburn. In 1935 Mister Sam helped make him chief of the NYA in Texas.

A year earlier Lyndon had latched onto a sturdy apron string. It belonged to a winsome brunette named Claudia Taylor, whom he rechristened Lady Bird so they could have the same initials. Much has been written about how Lady Bird's money was the foundation of Lyndon's fortune, but that's really not fair. For one thing, Claudia Taylor's inheritance totaled a piddling $69,000, which of itself could hardly be parlayed into the million-dollar-a-year income Johnson was allegedly reaping after he became Senate majority leader in 1955.

By 1937 the Texas NYA chieftain had grabbed the biggest coattail in the land—Franklin Delano Roosevelt's. Running in a field of ten candidates for a Congressional seat left vacant by a death, Lyndon seized the Supreme Court issue and defended FDR's right to pack it. He was the only one of the ten candidates to champion this unpopular cause, which had the salubrious effect of focusing the district's Liberal minority on Johnson when they trooped to the polls. With the conservative Democrat votes diffused among his nine opponents, LBJ won the primary, which was, as they used to say in the South, tantamount to election. President Roosevelt congratulated him personally, and after he moved back to Washington a photographer took a picture of them together in front of the White House.

When Pearl Harbor plunged America into World War II, Lyndon got himself a commission as a lieutenant commander in the Navy. On an inspection tour of New Zealand and Australia, he flew as an observer on a Naval bombing run over New Guinea. The squadron was intercepted near the target area by eight Japanese fighters, but luckily the plane LBJ was in had to turn back because of mechanical trouble. For this "gallant action" Lieutenant Commander Johnson was awarded the Silver Star, a grateful nation's third-highest military medal. Neither the pilot nor any of the crew members was cited for this mission, but Lyndon had a ribbon which he wore proudly in his lapel ever after.

In 1948, with Harry Truman up for election as President, Congressman Johnson decided to take his second crack at the Senate.* Of all the things

* He lost the first in 1941.

BJ fixed in his life, the primary election in Texas that year was certainly
or him the most important.

Johnson ran against the popular governor of Texas, Coke Stevenson,
nd several others. When the returns were in, Stevenson had 71,500
nore votes than Johnson but he lacked a majority in the crowded field,
o the primary was forced into a runoff. Again, Stevenson came out
head—or so everyone thought.

Down in Jim Wells County in South Texas there was a recount next
lay in Precinct 13 in the town of Alice. Precinct 13 had already produced
‹25 votes though only 600 ballots were distributed at the polling place.
Now George Parr, the notorious "Duke of Duval" and Democrat boss
of all the surrounding counties, manufactured 203 more votes in the
precinct—202 of them for LBJ.

"It was not quite up to the loaves and fishes of scripture," wrote
reporter James Lucier years later. "But half a loaf is better than none, and
the whole thing *was* pretty fishy."

Fletcher Knebel of *Look* tells another little parable about Lyndon's
first Senate victory:

Pedro, why are you crying?

It is because of my poor dead father, *Señor*.

But Pedro, your father died ten years ago!

That's just it. Yesterday my father came back to vote for Lyndon
Johnson, but he no come to see me!

Despite the tombstone votes, it took a lot more fixing before Johnson
could claim his Senate seat. Governor Stevenson sued for redress in a
Federal District Court. After hearing all the arguments, Judge T. Whit-
field Davidson was moved to remark: "There has not one word of evidence been submitted to disprove this plaintiff's claim he has been
robbed of a seat in the United States Senate."

However, before Judge Davidson could rule on the case, Johnson got
his good friend Abe Fortas to rouse U.S. Supreme Court Justice Hugo
Black, the former Ku Klux Klansman who distinguished himself as a
faithful advocate of Leftists during his long years in the nation's highest
court. Justice Black simply signed a court order, in effect validating
Lyndon Johnson's election to the Senate, and that was that.

Wheeling and dealing in the Senate, Lyndon quickly won a place for
himself in the highest councils of his party. Within a half-dozen years he
was majority leader in the Senate. His old friend, Sam Rayburn, was
Speaker of the House by then and between the two of them they got just

about anything they wanted in the Congress. Old Sam helped Lyndon make a strong bid for the Presidential nomination at the Los Angeles Democrat convention in 1960. When the bid failed, Jack Kennedy offered him the second slot on the national ticket and Johnson eagerly grabbed the Kennedy coattail.

After the 1960 election, however, Lyndon felt a little left out of things as Vice President. By the fall of 1963 it was an open secret around Washington that Kennedy planned to leave Lyndon out in the cold completely in 1964.

Several of Lyndon's deals as Senate majority leader had come back to haunt him. Bobby Kennedy, with the help of the FBI, had built at least two big fat files on LBJ. One was labeled Bobby Baker; the other Billy Sol Estes.

The Baker business was bad enough. It smelled redolently of call girls and fast money—really big money mysteriously made and distributed. And although the President disclaimed Bobby as his protégé, everyone knew that the slippery young secretary to the Senate Democratic Majority was Lyndon's boy. Some Senators, old Alan Bible of Nevada among them, openly called Bobby Baker "Lyndon Junior."

The Billy Sol Estes business was, however, much worse. There was not only more money involved; there was at least one, and possibly two murders. One of Billy Sol's accountants had been found dead in an automobile in El Paso. The body was so badly decomposed no one could, or would, tell what had happened to him.

The man who first blew the whistle on Billy Sol, an Agriculture Department official in Texas named Henry Marshall, had been buried as a suicide. When the body was exhumed the pathologist, Dr. Joseph Jachimczyk, found that Marshall had been shot five times with a bolt-action rifle, once in the back.

The Agriculture Department attorney in charge of the Estes file, N. Battle Hales, was whisked out of his Washington office and into a safer station. His secretary, Mary Jones, tried to preserve his files. She was dragged bodily from her office and slapped in a mental ward at a Washington hospital. Twelve days later some uncooperative psychiatrists declared her perfectly sane and got her released. But in the meantime the controversial file had been placed in more "reliable" hands.

Both the Billy Sol Estes and Bobby Baker cases were pending before Senate committees as Lyndon Johnson stepped briskly into the White House. The new President had a much greater personal interest in each f these than in the Otepka case. Yet oddly enough he had more success eeping the fix on the Otepka matter than he did on the other two. Ultimately, Estes and Baker were expendable; Dean Rusk and the tate Department were not. Besides, the electorate had repeatedly shown hat it would countenance ordinary run-of-the-mine corruption in high laces. But it had not yet been conclusively proved whether it would put ip with revolutionaries in business suits intent upon converging them vith communism. For this reason, it was much more important to keep hat damn Otepka thing under wraps, at least until after the 1964 election.

In that campaign year, Johnson also saw that it was vital to reassure he Liberal community, which had long distrusted him, though down deep he felt he had belonged to them ever since his NYA days. A revival of the Hiss era atmosphere via a reopening of the Otepka case would have made all the Liberals jumpy about the President's ability to manage such painful problems.

At the start, Lyndon was determined to placate as many groups as he could, clear across the political spectrum. But he understood, as Kennedy had before him, that the most important single group, to a man who wanted to reach or hold the White House, was the Liberals. Their Svengali-like hold on so much of the opinion-forming ganglia of our society had given them virtual veto power over the highest office in the nation.

After accompanying the Kennedy casket to Bethesda Naval Hospital upon the return of Air Force One to Washington the evening of November 22, Johnson climbed into a helicopter for the short flight to the White House lawn. With him were Robert McNamara, McGeorge Bundy, and George Ball, who was filling in for Dean Rusk, still en route back from a conference in Hawaii.

"I need you all," the brand-new President told them. "I need you more than he needed you." As Stewart Alsop later observed, those words "were to become a Johnsonian theme song throughout the great transition."

"From the very first," Alsop wrote, "and in contrast to every previous Vice President who has succeeded to the presidency—Lyndon Johnson made an extraordinary effort to retain the whole of John F. Kennedy's Cabinet and White House staff intact."[2]

What Alsop called Johnson's "herculean effort" to keep the Kennedy team playing on his side, did not succeed entirely. Before long Ted Sorensen left; then Arthur Schlesinger and Pierre Salinger. But these were mere messenger boys, though their public identity with the Whit House was important as a confidence-building factor among Liberal generally.

The really key men stayed on: Rusk at State, with Rostow and the res of the New Breed; McNamara in the Pentagon, with Yarmolinsky and the other disarmament boys and computer kids; McGeorge Bundy in the White House; Orville Freeman over in Agriculture, where that Billy Sc Estes file was buried; Stewart Udall at Interior, to help maintain the image of youthful vigor in the new Administration; Sargent Shriver, to run the popular Youth Corps, lay the groundwork for the war on poverty and keep the Kennedy family's imprimatur tentatively stamped on the Johnson era.

Bobby Kennedy could have had the Justice Department as long as he wanted it, though in various subtle little ways he was made to understand that it would be best if he moved on. Bobby was out of things now, no longer a part of the inner council that really counted. There was a good deal of talk about his being chosen as the next vice presidential candidate Lyndon was content to let the talk get about, but he never entertained the slightest idea of elevating Bobby. They despised each other, and not at all cordially.

Dean Rusk would prove the most durable of them all, though before President Kennedy's assassination his position was easily the shakiest, next to Johnson's. "Lyndon Johnson does in fact need Dean Rusk more than Kennedy needed him," Stewart Alsop wrote three months after Dallas.[3] It was never made clear why, but the President obviously believed this too. Thus, the Otepka case per se might not have been high on the Johnson agenda, but protecting Dean Rusk was.

"I have had some conversations with Secretary Rusk concerning that [the Otepka] case and I have complete confidence in the manner in which he will handle it," became Johnson's stock reply when asked about the matter.[4] At first, however, it looked as though Rusk might be a difficult man for even the President to protect.

CHAPTER **XXXIII**

Quietus

ALTHOUGH LYNDON JOHNSON'S INITIAL EFFORTS TO "SETTLE" THE Otepka case failed miserably, the White House and State Department attempts to keep the matter under wraps proved, on the whole, quite successful. In the beginning, however, there were a number of irritating news leaks that caused passing embarrassment to the new Administration.

Less than a month after the assassination of John Kennedy, Congressman William Cramer, a Florida Republican, put the finger of blame for Otepka's ouster firmly on Dean Rusk. Even when it had been most exercised about the security chief's dismissal, the Senate subcommittee had refrained from accusing Rusk publicly. Indeed, Senator Dodd had gone to considerable lengths to conceal Rusk's personal involvement in the case. But Congressman Cramer had the goods on the Secretary of State.

In a brief speech on the floor of the House, Cramer produced a "confidential memorandum" which he inserted in the *Congressional Record*. This document, Cramer charged, proved "the probability that Secretary Rusk has previously called the signals covering past actions against Otepka and is admittedly still the quarterback."

The memorandum in question dealt with two meetings held in Washington on November 19, the day of the last important public detonation over Otepka's firing. The first meeting was presided over by Deput Undersecretary William Crockett at the State Department. The other, few hours later, was held in the Washington Field Office of SY's Investi gations Division at 515 22nd Street Northwest. This second meetin substantially verified what transpired at the first.

Crockett, according to the memo, lectured the SY division heads an branch chiefs at the first meeting about the need for "loyalty," and th message was passed to the Field Office personnel at the second. Crocket was quoted as saying that "Secretary Rusk was very disturbed about th Otepka case" and its related events.

During a *tête à tête* meeting he had just had with Rusk, Crockett wa said to have reported that the Secretary intended to insist upon th highest loyalty of all personnel. In Rusk's view, that meant loyalty to th Secretary of State, and not to any of those ancient abstractions lik conscience and country.

"These men went out of bounds," Rusk told Crockett, referring t Otepka and his associates. "When that happens, you cure the situation."

Crockett told the SY chieftains that the Secretary promised that th Otepka case would be "vigorously pursued." And he allegedly said tha Rusk pledged "other persons in the State Department who are disloya to the Secretary will be identified and ousted" when Otepka and hi friends had been squashed.

"We will sweep the place clean," Rusk reportedly vowed.

A month earlier public disclosure of this memorandum might have been sufficient to sweep Dean Rusk himself clean out of the State Depart ment. Now, however, Washington was still reeling from the shock o Dallas and the country was so numb it wasn't reacting to anything Besides, the Cramer revelations got very little coverage in the mas media, so most people were not even made aware of their import.

The Otepka case did not fade from public view completely, however In January 1964 there was a spate of news stories when the Senate subcommittee released the perjurious wiretap testimony of Reilly, Hil and Belisle right after the New Year. William Moore of the Chicag *Tribune's* Washington bureau turned out a withering series on "the lying trio." But that was the last real news to come from the subcommittee fo the next twenty months.

In February and March, Willard Edwards of the *Tribune* and Guy

* All quotes are taken from the "confidential memorandum" introduced in the *Congressional Record* of December 19, 1963, by Congressman Cramer. According to this source they are attributable to Crockett, who was quoting Rusk.

Richards of the New York *Journal-American* pried loose the story on the mysterious "McLeod list." Both papers front-paged the fact that most of the 850-plus security and suitability risks on the list were still in the State Department. "The list is very much alive," wrote Richards. "Death and attrition have exacted only a small toll."[1]

The subcommittee refused to comment, and the State Department simply ignored the stories. As the months wore on, Otepka began to perceive that he was gradually being imprisoned behind a silken curtain of silence. The White House-engineered quietus was working.

Roger Robb and Otepka rightly insisted that they be provided with all the Senate subcommittee testimony in the case before Otepka was brought to trial in his departmental hearing. The charges had sprung from Otepka's dealings with the subcommittee. If he were to show why he had been forced to deal directly with its chief counsel, he needed to have all the testimony. The small portion the Senators had released on the wiretap business would be of little help to him. It constituted only an infinitesimal part of the total record, which had already run to more than a million words.

Lyndon Johnson had no intention of letting that damning record get out in that election year. Soon his cronies in the Senate concocted an excuse for suppressing it: they were still conducting hearings and they could not release any more of the testimony until the last word was in the record. Interminably, the Senate hearings dragged on. Three times during 1964 Robb and Otepka were forced to ask for postponements of the pending "trial." Otepka's right to a "speedy trial" was being stalled, not by the State Department, but by the Senate Internal Security Subcommittee.

Virtually all of the damaging testimony was in the subcommittee record before the assassination. The hearings conducted thereafter contributed little or nothing. The "relentless investigation" promised by Senator Dodd on November 19 was conveniently forgotten. To keep up appearances the committee went through the motions, leisurely summoning witnesses from time to time, cluttering the record with secondary or inconsequential testimony, always getting further and further away from the really important issue.

With each little flurry of activity on Capitol Hill, Otepka's hopes would rise, only to be dashed again and again. In January 1964 the subcommittee called a total of five witnesses—William Crockett, Abram Chayes, Robert McCarthy, Jack Norpel, and Victor Dikeos of the Warsaw embassy. In February, there was only one, William O. Boswell, home on leave from Cairo. During the first week in March, Harry Hite testified and so did Harris Huston, back for a visit from his exile in Curaçao. Those were the last hearings for nearly five months. Then, toward the end of July, the subcommittee suddenly hailed up a score of State Department officials. For three weeks they were questioned, one by one, mostly about relatively trifling details that shed no new light though many of the officials were caught in flagrant contradictions.

By this writer's count, at least sixteen State Department officials committed outright perjury or played fast and loose with the truth in their sworn testimony during 1963 and 1964. In the end, the Senate subcommittee identified only three of them—the same three everyone knew about: Reilly, Hill and Belisle. The Senators' 1968 report did make it plain that others had lied too, but it refrained from naming names.

This was perjury on the grand scale. Yet when it finally did surface via the Senate report, the news media had become so conditioned to the credibility gap in government that it passed virtually unnoticed, although it should have been obvious that even the State Department would not have indulged in perjury of this magnitude unless it had a good deal to conceal.

A whole year lapsed between Otepka's appearances before the subcommittee. When he finally was called again, on August 17, 1964, Roman Hruska of Nebraska was the only Senator present.

Since he was technically on the State Department payroll, Otepka had to get permission from Crockett to testify. Before he went up to the Hill, he was briefed again on the ground rules by two of Abram Chayes' assistants, Richard Frank and Lawrence Hoover. Attorney Frank warned him not to discuss "the merits" of his case, a warning which had become standard for all Department witnesses.

For the most part, Otepka was questioned by the subcommittee about routine matters or ancient history—the Cleveland committee, the McLeod list, his dismissal, and his new assignment. On April 30, Crockett had taken him off the security-guidebook job and put him on another make-work task. He was ordered to make a "comprehensive review" of the *Congressional Record* and other material published by the Congress. The purpose, Crockett's order said, was to give the State Department "an insight into Congressional attitudes, ideas, and thinking on security problems."[2]

If there was any real purpose to this assignment, it was to get Otepka to help cut his own throat by providing his superiors with "insights" into how they might defeat the subcommittee. More likely, however, Rusk just wanted to needle the Senators a little to see how much further he could go in making a mockery of their solemn pledges to restore Otepka to his old job.

Some weeks before his final subcommittee encore, Otepka had received an invitation to appear before the Republican platform committee at the San Francisco convention. Stating that he was also willing to appear before the Democrat platform committee in Atlantic City, Otepka requested permission from the Department to appear. The Department, of course, turned him down. Needless to say, the Democrats never invited him to Atlantic City.

The Democrat convention, which as author Theodore White wrote, "was staged and produced entirely by Lyndon Johnson," turned out to be a lachrymose spectacle liberally laced with mushy Pedernales corn pone. Ten days after Otepka's last solitary trek up to Capitol Hill, the boardwalk convention was in full swing on the Jersey shore. But the President still had not revealed his running mate. Since his own nomination was a foregone conclusion, his only chance to squeeze any drama at all out of the dull proceedings in Atlantic City was to keep the world guessing about his choice for Vice President. As usual, Lyndon overplayed his hand.

Johnson had ruled out Bobby Kennedy some weeks earlier with an announcement that he would not select anyone from his Cabinet. Then, on Wednesday, August 26, he led a small army of newsmen on a grueling hike round and round the White House lawn. Talking expansively every step of the way, the President paced off fifteen quarter-mile laps. At the end of the trail, he left the correspondents sweating and exhausted in the 90-degree heat, but with his secret still untold. It was, said Teddy White, "a public circus that perhaps has never been equaled before anywhere."[3]

The press guessed, nonetheless, that the choice was between two Senators, Thomas Dodd and Hubert Humphrey. The smart money was on Hubert, despite the fact that Dodd apparently deluded himself to the very last that he was in the running. A few hours after the President conducted his peripatetic guessing game, Humphrey and Dodd turned up at the White House. Leading them inside past the throng of reporters, Lyndon played cat and mouse for several more hours.

Finally, at six o'clock, he released Dodd. The pompous little man from Connecticut had had his moment of basking in the Presidential sun. It was over now, but he appeared quite satisfied. He had enjoyed his ultimate recognition, granted by a beneficent President for many services rendered, not the least of which was Dodd's dampening the fuse on the explosive Otepka affair.

Meanwhile, back inside the ranch house on Pennsylvania Avenue Johnson was bestowing the vice presidency on a temporarily humble Hubert Humphrey. Dean Rusk, Robert McNamara and McGeorge Bundy were hastily summoned to the informal coronation in the great Oval Office. In their presence, Johnson told Hubert that both Rusk and McNamara had been pushing for him. "This Georgian here," drawled the President, signifying the Secretary of State, "has been carrying on a one-man campaign for you."[4]

It was already dusk, and light rain was falling outside when Lyndon led Hubert before the assembled newsmen and introduced him as "Mr. Vice President." There followed two more sprightly laps around the lawn with the reporters tagging after both men like a fatigued retinue of the Sun King at Versailles. Together, then, Johnson and Humphrey flew off into the night to the festival at Atlantic City.

The campaign that followed was probably the most bitter in America's history. The Republican candidate, Barry Goldwater, was branded as an inhuman warmonger, willing to sacrifice little children to a nuclear holocaust. The Democrats had already received substantial aid from certain Republicans in thus labeling Senator Goldwater. In his book, *The Making of the President—1964*, Theodore White cast the drama of that acrimonious campaign in iridescent perspective:

> Never in any campaign had I seen a candidate so heckled, so provoked by opposition demonstration [sic] . . . so cruelly bill-boarded and tagged. . . . For the fact was that Goldwater was running not so much against Johnson as against himself—or the Barry Goldwater the image makers had created. Rockefeller and Scranton had drawn up the indictment. Lyndon Johnson was the prosecutor. Goldwater was cast as defendant. He was like a dog with a can tied to his tail—the faster he ran, the more the can clattered.[5]

Thus pressed, Goldwater could never seem to establish a theme for his campaign. He was on the defensive from the outset, and neither he nor his advisors were able to do more than throw up improvised fortifications against the relentless attack. Several times toward the end, the GOP candidate injected the Otepka case into his speeches. But he was never able to make it a central issue, which is what the case needed if the people were to be made to understand its true meaning.

However, even if Barry Goldwater *had* succeeded in getting the gut message of the Otepka controversy across, the American people would not have elected him President. In that autumn of 1964 the overwhelming majority of them had but one thought—to save their own hides. Lyndon Johnson, avoiding real issues as though they were contaminated, presented himself to the voters as their savior, and they rushed en masse to prostrate themselves before him at the polls.

If the illusion had any validity, if by voting for Johnson they were in fact saving their hides, the electorate might have been justified. Unfortunately, the illusion proved the most dangerous America had ever embraced, for the Soviet Union wisely used the next four years to gain nuclear parity, and perhaps superiority, over the once unchallenged strategic forces of the United States.

Lyndon Johnson was not entirely insensitive to those elements in his own party that insisted upon maintaining America's defenses and a sound internal security program. It was reliably reported that he promised certain Democrat members of the Senate subcommittee that there would be a thorough housecleaning at the State Department after the election.[6] In return, the Senators promised not to issue a report on the Otepka case until after the campaign was over.

On the first anniversary of Otepka's dismissal it was disclosed that the President's closest and most trusted aide, Walter Jenkins, had just sent out a White House memorandum asking all federal department heads and bureau chiefs to be careful not to get caught with any security problems that fall.

"We have been somewhat concerned about our procedures in requesting security name checks . . . for appointees to the federal service," Jenkins said. He urged that the checks be made "prior to serious consideration being given to an individual and most certainly before a firm commitment is made."[7]

"These procedures," the White House memo stated, "can prevent considerable embarrassment both to the government and to the potential employee himself." With the Johnson campaign in full swing, the message was plain: all "embarrassing" appointments should be avoided, at least until after the election. The avidity of the Presidential appetite for votes dictated caution.

"Apparently the Administration feels it is more important to protect political security than national security," caustically remarked Congressman August E. Johansen of Michigan, ranking Republican on the virtually defunct House Committee on Un-American Activities.

Ironically, the man who wrote the White House warning to avoid embarrassing appointments was soon to become the President's greatest embarrassment of 1964. In October, it was revealed that Walter Jenkins had been arrested by the Washington police department while engaged in a homosexual act in the men's room of the downtown YMCA.

It was not the first time Jenkins had been caught. The police had picked him up during a similar episode several years before. At that time, the then Senate majority leader, Lyndon Johnson, had sent down the money to bail Jenkins out. Lyndon's all-pervasive influence had also managed to keep that earlier escapade of his confidential aide out of the public eye. Abe Fortas and Clark Clifford, later Supreme Court justice and Secretary of Defense respectively, very nearly succeeded in getting the Washington news corps to ignore Jenkins' second arrest.

When the 1964 arrest did break, an alibi was quickly concocted for Jenkins. It was found that he was suffering from a modern malady, "White House fatigue." FBI Director J. Edgar Hoover helped soothe him during his recovery by sending flowers and a warm personal note. This gesture helped greatly to mollify the public.

Walter Jenkins' vulnerability to blackmail raised the question as to whether he might ever have compromised the national security. But Edgar Hoover took care of that problem too. He sent the results of an "extensive investigation" by the FBI to Nicholas Katzenbach, the acting Attorney General. The investigation, Hoover, said, "disclosed no information that Mr. Jenkins has compromised the security or interests of the United States in any manner."

Otto Otepka and other experienced Intelligence people wondered at the speed of the FBI investigation. How even the efficient FBI could have delved into all facets of Walter Jenkins' background in a matter of days remained something of a mystery. But Director Hoover's report was produced a good two weeks before the election and it read like a commendation. It claimed that "a favorable appraisal of Mr. Jenkins' loyalty and dedication to the United States was given the FBI by more than 300 of his associates, both business and social. . . ."[8]

The Jenkins affair washed right over the benumbed public conscience. There was no more shock value in the discovery of perverts in high places than in the continuing hints of security risks formulating U.S. foreign policy. Internal security, of any kind, was simply not an election issue.

Early in the campaign it had been revealed that the State Department had ordered the destruction, by burning, of the security files maintained by the SY field offices in fifteen major cities. Several senators and congressmen protested, but their protests, like the original story, were confined to a few paragraphs on the back pages of most newspapers, where they were carried at all. The State Department claimed that the burning of the files was an efficiency and economizing measure, to save both personnel and office space. Besides, it said, the files were merely duplicates of information stored by the Office of Security at its Washington headquarters.

On this and all other non-issues of the 1964 campaign, the public overwhelmingly accepted the slick patent medicines doled out by the bureaucracy in Washington. Some of the pills were a bit hard to swallow, but President Johnson's soothing presence somehow made them go down.

When the returns were in on November 3, Lyndon Baines Johnson was elected to his first and last full term as President by the largest popular-vote majority in history. He had gathered in 43,126,506 votes—nearly 16,000,000 more than the 27,176,799 cast for his opponent, Barry Goldwater. Thus, America delivered itself up overwhelmingly to the nostrums of the Great Society.

The morning after the election Otto Otepka walked through the dismal corridors of the State Department building en route to his solitary cell. Passing his old office, he noticed that the gray card that still bore his name had been turned around in its metal holder. Printed on the blank side in heavy black letters was the "R.I.P."

CHAPTER **XXXIV**

Dodd

HAVING EUCHRED THE SENATE SUBCOMMITTEE INTO HOLDING UP RE-
lease of the Otepka testimony until after the 1964 election, Lyndon
Johnson soon found yet another excuse to delay its publication. Immediately following his stunning victory at the polls, the President asked the
Democrat leaders in Congress for "ninety days of harmony" while he
launched his Great Society. High up on the President's harmony agenda
was further suppression of the Otepka matter.

The man Johnson picked to take care of this particular chore was his
old Senate friend, Tom Dodd. From the administration's standpoint,
Dodd was the ideal choice. The myth of Dodd's unwavering anti-communism placed him above suspicion. Even the most staunch conservatives would find it difficult to believe that Senator Dodd could have any
but the purest motives for delaying public action on an issue he had done
so much to force out in the open. But sometimes, as Shakespeare once
observed, "delays have dangerous ends."

To many, the abrupt change in Dodd's approach to the Otepka controversy still seems inexplicable. Yet the explanation is not at all difficult to
fathom.

Whether because of a perverse Irish jealousy, or because he really
could not stomach their policies as he so often demonstrated, Dodd

distrusted the Kennedys. Lyndon Johnson, on the other hand, he held in high regard.

In 1960, Dodd had defied the Kennedy steamroller at Los Angeles to place Johnson's name in nomination for President. The Kennedys never forgave him, and when Jack entered the White House the doors were all but barred to Tom Dodd.

After Dallas, with Johnson's ascension to the Presidency, the doors quickly opened and Dodd was led to believe that he was one of Lyndon's closest confidants. Visions of the Vice Presidency danced before Dodd's ambitious eyes through much of 1964, and even when the vision proved hallucinatory Dodd still deluded himself that he would remain in the role of trusted lieutenant. Nowhere did he play this role better than in his mishandling of the Otepka case, which he managed to stall for almost four years.

The State Department was delighted to play along with Dodd's delay. Dean Rusk knew that the longer the case dragged out the safer he would be. If he could keep Otepka in solitary confinement indefinitely while he scattered the other conscientious security men to the four winds, he would not only maintain total control over those troublesome clearances originating in SY, he would also avoid another embarrassing battle with the Congress when he finally marched Otepka to the chopping block.

Dodd's invariable alibi, when asked about the delay in releasing the testimony, was that "we still have some testimony to take to wind it up." As it developed, the subcommittee summoned exactly one solitary witness after the hearings held in July and August 1964.

Amazingly, the State Department official whose testimony was deemed so important that it could hold up the whole show for nearly a year turned out to be none other than William Crockett. At the tail end of the August hearings, the esteemed Deputy Undersecretary of State for Administration had been the last witness called. He showed up again one month later, on September 16. Then Dodd gave him a free ride all the way into May of the following year.

The whispered rationale for patiently waiting on Mr. Crockett was that there were "certain conflicts" in his testimony that had to be resolved. That there *were* conflicts is abundantly apparent on the record. However, by no stretch of the imagination were the conflicts so serious as to warrant postponing publication of testimony in a case on which hinged the whole internal security program of the United States government.

"Cool it," was Dean Rusk's strategy throughout. And Thomas J. Dodd was only too happy to keep the case on ice for him, or more precisely, for Lyndon.

As early as the summer of 1964 there were reliable reports that the Senate subcommittee had already voted, at least informally, to release the testimony taken over a period of twenty months. Then the word leaked out: Vice Chairman Dodd had slapped a stop order on it until after the November election.

Otepka accepted the delay in silence, never betraying his deep disappointment. He received reports that the subcommittee had agreed to the postponement because the Senators had allegedly been promised that he would be vindicated and restored to SY as soon as the campaign was over. The key that was to open the door to this happy ending was the threat of publication of the testimony and the subcommittee report that was to follow soon after. If all went well and Otepka was taken back, there might be no need to release either one.

Just before the election this writer received solemn assurances from a subcommittee source that the release of the testimony would begin no later than December. But as Christmas neared Willard Edwards revealed in the Chicago *Tribune* that Dodd had "again ordered publication held up."[1] The reason given was Lyndon Johnson's request for a period of "harmony."

Otepka was baffled. Dodd's renewed censorship forced him and Roger Robb to request a fourth postponement of his State Department hearing. He refused to believe, though, that Dodd had deserted him.

Nonetheless, it was soon evident that Dodd had quietly executed another of his famed acrobatic flips. Just as he had reversed field on the Test Ban Treaty in 1963, he now turned completely around on Otepka. From thundering threats of a full-scale investigation, he had retreated to a more prudent position which called for nothing less than Otepka's surrender. Eventually, he moved on to public attacks against the man he had once so vigorously defended.

Otepka began to detect the change in Dodd's attitude early in 1965. Although he had no direct contact with the Senator, one of Dodd's aides took him to lunch to sound him out. There were delicate hints of a compromise, though at the time Otepka preferred to think that the hints had originated with the aide rather than with Dodd.

Otepka made it quite clear that he would never settle for a compromise. He wanted his old job back and he wanted to be able to work at it in such a way that he could help protect the national security. If he were restored even to his downgraded position as chief of the Evaluations Division, he would insist on observance of the internal security laws and regulations.

Dodd, like Johnson, could not believe anyone could be so downright stubborn. Everyone had a price, and both Tom and Lyndon believed Otepka's could be found. Through intermediaries, who sometimes discreetly disclaimed that they were acting for the Senator, the price kept going up. But Otepka proved as unbudgeable as Gibraltar. He refused to be moved one inch.

The first piece of public evidence that Senator Dodd was prepared to sell out Otepka came during a television-radio discussion on Sunday, March 14, 1965. On the program, "Opinion in the Capital," Dodd was interviewed by Jack Bell of the Associated Press and Mark Evans of Metromedia. Evans brought up Otepka first:

Evans: The country is pretty much interested in the Otepka case which seems to fall below the horizon occasionally. I know you have been a strong advocate of this man's rights. Where does it stand now?

Dodd: The hearing for Otepka in the Department of State, which he requested, has been postponed several times, *at his request.* I wish they would get on with it and get it done.

My own view is that it's a mistake on all sides here. This matter ought to be resolved and it can be very simple. Otepka has a lot of ability. He ought to be taken back. *I don't say on this or that job,* but he ought to be brought back into the Department and put to work.

The thing got off on the wrong foot. *I think Otepka probably got a little touchy about things that were not of consequence,* encouraged by well-meaning friends; the Department got its back up [and] can't be made to appear as backing down.

It's all nonsense to me. Let them both back down and let us get on with the business of getting the job done.*

Anyone listening to this program, which was carried in eight cities from New York to Los Angeles and on the Armed Forces Network, could not fail to get the impression that Otto Otepka was just an obdurate sorehead, a hypersensitive nit-picker concerned with *"things that were not of consequence."*

Moreover, Dodd deliberately created the impression that Otepka was responsible for the repeated delays in the State Department hearing when he knew, better than anyone, that the one man most responsible

* All emphasis added.

for those delays was Tom Dodd himself. By refusing to release the subcommittee's testimony, Dodd was denying Otepka the right to use his most telling arguments in the pending hearing.

It was plain that Dodd was getting exceedingly impatient with Otepka's refusal to compromise. And not long after this telecast Otepka learned of yet another public display of the Senator's impatience. At a press conference sponsored by the *Reader's Digest* at the Beverly Hilton Hotel in Los Angeles, Dodd went on the offensive against Otepka. He called him a "prima donna" and charged that he had "exaggerated his martyrdom."

"I think Otepka can bend a little," Dodd said, adding that up to then all he had done was to have "made himself more difficult."

Not content with castigating Otepka, Dodd did his best to whitewash the State Department. "It isn't that bad," he said, referring to the source of the feud between Otepka and Rusk. "They've both made mistakes." At still another point he emphasized that "this is not all one-sided."

Pressed for the identity of remaining subcommittee witnesses, Dodd came up with one name—Crockett. "How soon will Secretary Rusk release Crockett?" he was asked. Stammering with anger, the Senator replied: "Mr. Rusk has *not* been holding up Crockett. . . he's a busy fellow. I don't think there has been any deliberate attempt to avoid the session. . . . I don't think there has been any resistance."

This outright defense of Rusk and the State Department contrasted sharply with the stormy threats and brave promises Dodd had made on the Senate floor a little more than a year earlier. Instead of the thoroughgoing investigation of the Department that he had pledged then, Dodd now publicly emphasized his new strategy: "I think we can get this thing settled," he said. "We ought to be able to settle it . . . *reasonably.*"

Otepka was not merely dismayed when someone in Los Angeles sent him a transcript of Dodd's attack on him. He felt like a prizefighter down for the count who suddenly opens his eyes to find he is being kicked in the stomach by the referee.

Until then, Otepka had shared the same high regard for Dodd that so many of the Senator's colleagues in the Congress had. No one knew then that there were two Tom Dodds.

It has become a cliché in certain circles that Senator Dodd would never have been "persecuted" if it had not been for his forthright stand against communism. There may be an element of truth in this, but it overlooks many things, not the least of which is that Dodd left himself wide open to "persecution." His was not an innocent slip; nor was it but one slip.

Unfortunately, the slips had become a familiar pattern.

On balance, there is very little to choose between Tom Dodd, the intrepid crusader against communism, and the Senator who could, and did, fix most anything. The crusade may have been something more than mere rhetoric, but not much more. His curious behavior in the Otepka case is proof enough of that. But his role in paving the way for the Senate's overwhelming approval of the Test Ban Treaty, an issue in which he knew the future of his country was clearly at stake, offers conclusive substantiation that Dodd stood ready at all times to abandon his principles.

One might legitimately ask, of course, what were Dodd's principles? He supplied part of the answer, at least, during the Beverly Hilton press conference when he revealed that his political philosophy was not so very far removed from that of the people pushing most hard for the sacred millennium.

"You know," he said, "I'm a World Government guy. I'm as bad as you can get. And I always have been and still am. I see nothing contradictory in that. I hope it comes in my time, your time, the time of our children."

Where Dodd first became infected with this virus is somewhat difficult to detect. For one thing, he had once served briefly in the FBI, and it is doubtful that he caught it there. Nor is it likely that he learned it at his father's knee. Tom Dodd, Sr. was a hard-working Irish-American contractor in Norwich, Connecticut, in an era when most sons of Erin were inordinately proud of their patriotism. His mother was an O'Sullivan, and it is reasonably certain that she never planted any one-world notions in her son's formative mind.

Devout Roman Catholics, the Dodds sent their son to Catholic Providence College in nearby Rhode Island. From there young Tom proceeded to Yale Law School. This was long before the reign of Dean Eugene Rostow, brother of Walt, though it is possible that the seeds of world governmentism took root there. If so, the roots were never ostensibly strong enough to shove aside his Catholicism or his patriotism, which he bravely paraded throughout his political career.

Taking his law degree from Yale in 1933, Dodd married the former Grace Murphy of Westerley, Rhode Island, the following year. Though he was to use his FBI service as an effective vote-catcher years later, Dodd served only a short time with the Bureau during this early period. He left it for, of all things, the National Youth Administration, which was, as every security officer knows, riddled with Reds.

It is possible, of course, that Dodd reported on some of the more questionable NYA characters to his erstwhile colleagues in the FBI. But it is just as possible that he first picked up his one-worldism from the same people. If they couldn't convert you to communism, they settled, then as now, for implanting the Grand Illusion. It should be noted, however, that many "World Government guys," as Dodd styled himself, were never neutralized in their patriotism. They were simply confused.

Dodd stayed three years with NYA, a year longer than Lyndon Johnson at approximately the same period, and, like Lyndon, he also became a state NYA chieftain. In 1938 he left Connecticut for Washington, where he served as a special assistant to a succession of Attorney Generals, beginning with the bitter anti-capitalist crusader, Homer S. Cummings. Another of them, Robert H. Jackson, later plucked Dodd out of the Justice Department and carried him off to the Nuremberg trials. Jackson, a Supreme Court Justice by then, was the chief prosecutor at Nuremberg, and Dodd served as his executive trial counsel and occasional stand-in.

When he returned from Nuremberg, Dodd joined a Hartford law firm and in 1952 made his first successful race for Congress. Two terms in the House launched him into the Democrat Senatorial nomination in 1956, but he was defeated by incumbent Prescott Bush in the general election. By 1958, however, his political muscle had developed to the point where he was able to knock off both Chester Bowles and William Benton in the primary and go on to whip Republican Senator William A. Purtell in November.

Once in the Senate, Dodd very quickly won a reputation as a two-fisted fighter, though a few people at ringside early noted that the gentleman from Connecticut had a tendency to pull his punches in the more critical clinches. Nonetheless, his forthright manner of speaking, and the often blunt words he hurled about the Senate chamber made it appear that he was cloaked in an armored suit of impregnable integrity. No man in the whole Congress could come down harder on both sides of the same issue than Tom Dodd. As one semi-official biography tactfully put it, "his strong stand against extremism of both the Left and the Right has won him wide acclaim."[2]

Dodd wasted no time getting himself appointed to a clutch of key Senate committees—Foreign Relations, Judiciary, Aeronautical and Space Sciences. His FBI background, built up out of all proportion to the reality, helped project him into the vice chairmanship of the Judiciary's Subcommittee on Internal Security, which Chairman Eastland was content, for the most part, to let Dodd do with as he pleased. There was a practical political consideration involved in this too; Dodd's Northern Liberalism made his anti-communism more palatable than Jim Eastland's Mississippi drawl.

To give Dodd his due, he handled the subcommittee very well—until his friendship for Lyndon Johnson caused him to turn his back on Otepka. The subcommittee was very active during the years he operated it in tandem with Senator Eastland. It conducted a good many hearings and released dozens of volumes of telling testimony. The only difficulty was that it produced virtually nothing in the way of meaningful legislation.

A similar pattern is seen in Dodd's chairmanship of another Subcommittee, the publicity-producing tribunal on juvenile delinquency. In 1961 Dodd opened up, with great fanfare, on the television industry for feeding so much crime and violence into the nation's homes. The Delinquency Subcommittee staff zeroed in on the NBC network, and particularly its president, Robert Kintner, as the principal fountainhead of the stomp 'em, knife 'em, shoot-'em-up productions flooding the airwaves. But an incisive report on the NBC-Kintner role in peddling crime, sex and violence to young television audiences was quietly killed by Dodd. Later, another network, Metromedia, got into the act and Dodd nipped a new investigation into this company's programming.

James Boyd, ringleader of the four former aides who stole the files which led to Dodd's downfall, later claimed that Dodd had accepted lavish gifts from Metromedia, whose executives practically adopted the Senator as a house pet, feeding him with campaign contributions and caviar parties.[3]

Boyd may be a dubious source, but there is no denying that he did waltz off with all those files, and furthermore he made his charges stick. If Boyd is to be believed (and without condoning his theft, one must grant him an excellent track record), the $130,000 diverted from campaign dinners to the Senator's personal account was the least of Dodd's sins.

The suppression of the Juvenile Delinquency Subcommittee probes certainly will have far more damaging effect upon generations now approaching adulthood than the easy money Tom Dodd turned at the expense of willing contributors. All the same, it would have been nice if the Senator had reported the loot on his income tax returns. Nor were these lucrative dinners the only financial feasts Dodd partook of in the Senate.

A virtual collector of Senate committees, in 1961 Dodd wangled the chairmanship of a special investigating unit within the Anti-Trust and Monopoly Subcommittee. One of the main assignments of this unit was to probe widespread abuses within the insurance industry.

According to Boyd, the records he lifted "showed that Dodd received more than $24,000 in testimonial gifts, honorariums, fees and favors from sources within the insurance industry."⁴ On top of that, the distinguished Senator from Connecticut declared himself a little bonus in the form of insurance premiums which he never bothered to pay. By Boyd's estimate, the free premiums totaled $3,500 through 1965, which meant that they kept in force several hundreds of thousands of dollars in insurance on Tom Dodd.

Although he did conduct inquiries into the dubious activities of foreign insurance companies and domestic fly-by-nights, Dodd never let a real investigation of the big firms get off the ground. In fact, he held a series of "cooperation meetings" for insurance executives with a view towards increasing their business with the federal government.

This, then, was the Dodd nobody knew. When his colleagues in the Senate were finally introduced to him early in 1966, most of them refused at first to recognize that he existed. It took them nearly a year and a half to acknowledge formally that he did. The censure motion drawn up by Mississippi's John Stennis and his Ethics Committee was finally brought to the floor of the Senate in mid-1967. There followed one of the most mawkish displays ever witnessed in the Capitol. Defending himself during the debate, Dodd cried out:

How many times do you want to hang me? If you want to do it, be done with it—be done with it! Do away with me and that will be the end!

But in the twilight of my life—and how many years are left to me? Probably few, probably few—I ask you to search your souls about these facts, in the knowledge that every Senator has about others in this body.

The threat, and all the weeping and gnashing of teeth, failed to move the Senate. On June 23, 1967, by a vote of 92-to-5, it censured Thomas Dodd, holding that his conduct "is contrary to accepted morals, derogates from the public trust expected of a Senator, and tends to bring the Senate into dishonor and disrepute."

Afterward, there was a good deal of talk, in both Liberal and conservative circles, that Dodd was merely the victim of a system that countenanced flagrant chicanery. This may be true, but it still does not exonerate Senator Dodd. Moreover, it casts a slur upon the heads of all senators and congressmen, the honorable as well as the fixers. For although it may be difficult for many to believe, there *are* honorable men in the Congress, Dodd's innuendoes notwithstanding.

Ironically, the censure vote on Dodd was taken at the very hour that Otto Otepka was nearing the end of the State Department hearing that Dodd had done so much to delay.

Less than a month before, co-columnists Drew Pearson and Jack Anderson, the eager recipients of more than 4,000 duplicated private papers filched from Dodd's office, had ludicrously tried to blacken Otepka's name with the stolen tar they had been using on the Senator. The closest they could come to tying Otepka to Dodd's untidy tail was a memorandum-of-record the Senator had dictated after his last private meeting with Lyndon Johnson at the White House in 1965. By then, Dodd and Johnson had been discussing the Otepka case for nearly two years. Usually Dodd brought up the subject. But this time the President took the initiative. The Dodd memorandum quoted in the Pearson-Anderson column said:

> He [LBJ] then started to talk about Otepka. He said he wanted to get a message to Otepka through a third party that he wanted to straighten this matter out. He [Johnson] said, "I want Otepka to step out of the Department and we will do something good for him."[5]

"Something good," in Lyndon's limited view, turned out to be the creation of a new post for Otepka as Chief of Personnel Security at the White House. At least this was the way it filtered through to Otepka. Knowing that he would merely bear an empty title in a job that removed him from the crucial battlefield where foreign policy was concocted, Otepka simply shook his head. He was a man singularly unsuited for surrender.

It was just as well for Otepka that he rejected this offer which, like all the others, was served to him in discreet hints. A few months later, in April 1966, President Johnson brought Walt Whitman Rostow back to the White House from the State Department and installed his brother, Eugene Victor Debs Rostow, as the Number 3 man on Foggy Bottom. Otepka would never have issued Walt Rostow a security clearance at the White House, having turned him down three times at State. One of them would have had to go, and it is interesting to speculate which one Lyndon Johnson would have selected.

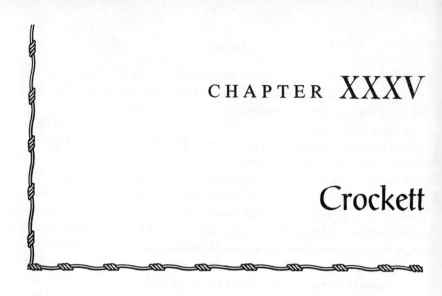

CHAPTER **XXXV**

Crockett

SENATOR DODD'S FAVORITE WITNESS, WILLIAM JAMES CROCKETT, WAS perfectly cast in his role as Dean Rusk's leading front man. Sometimes it seemed that Crockett almost relished the punishment he absorbed in the Otepka case. His primary duty, as he saw it, was to protect the Secretary of State, and one must grant that he fulfilled this duty unselfishly well—up to a point.

A heavy-set man with aggressive manners, Bill Crockett could have been a balding twin of John Reilly, except that he was just slightly more polished. And although he was not above twisting the truth, he seldom got caught in an outright lie.

Thus, when finally faced with a choice between seriously damaging his own career and putting the finger on Secretary Rusk as the Number 1 villain in the Otepka affair, Crockett decided that his duty to Crockett came first.

The ostentatiously debonair Deputy Undersecretary of State for Administration initially identified Rusk as the mastermind of the Otepka purge in August 1964. As mentioned earlier, he was up for promotion to the rank of career minister at the time. He sang, as they so quaintly put it in underworld circles, "to clear his own record" when the Senate Foreign Relations Committee quizzed him about Otepka.[1]

Rusk let that one pass. But when Sourwine cornered Crockett before the Internal Security Subcommittee on May 4, 1965, he again fingered the Secretary by agreeing that Rusk was "substantially in charge of the Otepka case." Of course, he qualified this by adding, "insofar as the final determination is concerned."[2] But Dean Rusk got the message. There was hardly anyone he could trust around the State Department anymore.

On the whole, however, Crockett did a fine job as Rusk's chief cover-up man. He not only managed to sweep almost everything under the rug, he managed to keep it all there without too many revealing mounds and lumps and suspicious wrinkles showing on the surface. When Rusk's vacuum cleaner had "swept the place clean" in SY, Crockett helped the Secretary lay new wall-to-wall carpeting, carefully nailed down at the edges to prevent any unsuspected survivors of the purge from crawling out into the open. Moreover, Crockett's nails were made of pretty sturdy steel, forged in CIA.

After the Department reluctantly dumped Reilly, Rusk and Crockett brought in a man from the Agency to take his place. His name was G. Marvin Gentile and he originally hailed from South Dakota. Fortunately, he had spent a half-dozen years with the FBI before beginning his career with CIA in 1952. This was calculated to reassure the Senate subcommittee, and it succeeded, at least in part.

In Otepka's old job as chief of the Evaluations Division, they inserted another CIA alumnus, Henri G. Grignon. A New Englander, Grignon had attended Tom Dodd's alma mater, Providence College, which may have helped the Senator feel a bit more comfortable, though even Dodd must have looked askance at Grignon's almost total lack of qualifications for the critical post he now held. The 1968 Senate subcommittee report caustically commented:

> Mr. Grignon conceded that his only experience as an evaluator was for a period of about four months in 1952. . . . He did not write any evaluations. He does agree, however, that it takes "substantial experience and training to make a good evaluator, a competent evaluator."[3]

Although Henri Grignon had spent thirteen years in CIA's equivalent of SY, the subcommittee discovered that he was virtually ignorant of the Eisenhower Executive Order 10450 and other regulations and laws upon which Otepka had attempted to build a sound security program at State. While granting that Grignon "should be excellently qualified in some areas of Intelligence and security work," the subcommittee was moved to comment that "the consequences of such ignorance can be disastrous."[4]*Actually, however, the importation of CIA "ignorance" into SY was only a small part of the disquieting picture.

With the security screen obliterated by the Otepka purge, Rusk and Crockett hastened to paint in a surrealistic masterpiece consisting of one very large controllable hole. A "personnel panel" was set up under Crockett to review all security cases. There was not, however, one security officer on the panel, unless we count David Belisle, who served as the group's "executive director" until a more comfortable post was found for him abroad. The subcommittee held that the panel gave SY an excuse for "consciously avoiding its responsibilities."[5]

One of the things this panel was supposed to do was review the McLeod list. Otepka had testified that "a substantial number" of the 858 security and suitability risks on this ancient list remained in the Department. Out of the sublist of 258 officials in policy posts a decade before, he estimated that "at least 150" were still around.[6]

Although Crockett denied that the McLeod list existed, he later reversed himself. In line with his policy of telling the truth when there was no other way out, he eventually confirmed Otepka's estimate, and even upped it, placing the current residue from the smaller and more sensitive sublist at 166.[7]**

Crockett said he didn't think the McLeod list was important, being comprised, as he claimed, of drunks and homosexuals and cases of mistaken identity. Yet somehow it was important enough for him and Rusk to refuse absolutely to surrender it to the Senate subcommittee. Still, Abram Chayes, the State Department's Legal Advisor, continued to insist that State had "nothing to hide."[8]

There were times, though, when Rusk wished that he could hide Bill Crockett. It was not merely Crockett's annoying habit of popping off at untimely moments. That was bad enough. But the man's total lack of *savoir faire* must have offended the Secretary's Oxford-trained instincts. For despite Crockett's pretensions, rough edges still showed beneath the thin veneer of diplomacy.

It was too bad, really, that Crockett ever entered government. He may have made a more substantial contribution to his country if he had remained in his native Midwest. Born in Cimarron, Kansas, in 1914 he went to work in a bank in Hastings, Nebraska, right out of high school. In World War II he served in the Army, emerging as a captain. Afterward

* The Senators were referring, of course, to the State Department's personnel security program, but one is forced to wonder what kind of similar program existed at CIA all during the years that Grignon labored in that shadowy jungle.
** Raymond Loughton counted 175 still in the Department from the policy-making list. Otepka, of course, had been denied access to SY files and this is why he was able merely to give an estimate.

he completed work toward his B.S. degree at the University of Nebraska. Then he headed for Naples, Italy, where he joined the U.S. Maritime Commission.

A year in Naples apparently spoiled Crockett for the mundane world of business. He wanted to get back into it, but it just didn't work. First he tried his hand at running the Hi-Way Signs Company in Denver. One year of that sent him back to the bank in Hastings, where he became an assistant vice president. By 1951, however, he was seeking more venturesome pastures. With a little political help, he found them in the Department of State.

Assigned initially to Beirut, Lebanon, Crockett moved from there to Karachi, and finally to Rome, where he spent four years as an attaché. In Italy he met a nervous little fellow Foreign Service officer named William O. Boswell and they became, according to Boswell, "close friends." They came into Washington about the same time, in 1958, and after Boswell was given the title of Director of the Office of Security, Crockett was named Deputy Assistant Secretary of State for budget and finance. In 1963 he ascended to the lofty perch of overseer of administration in the Department with jurisdiction over personnel, security and myriad other domains. As Dean Rusk once testified, he was in almost daily contact with Bill Crockett. For a while, at least, they made a great team.

No matter how repugnant Rusk's more sensitive sensibilities may have found Crockett, the Secretary seemed to regard him as almost indispensable. Rusk was disappointed when Crockett identified him as the man who controlled the Otepka case. But he could shrug that off, though the second time it must have gotten a bit sticky.

It would never do, of course, for Rusk to make it appear that he wanted to get rid of Crockett because of anything connected with the Otepka matter. That would have been tantamount to an admission that the solid ranks on the Seventh Floor were beginning to break. But a couple of things happened in the early part of 1966 which gave the Secretary sufficient cause to ease out Crockett and at the same time chalk up a few points with the Liberals, who were becoming increasingly critical of Rusk's public stand on the Vietnam war.

First, there was the messy flap over the firing of Abba Schwartz. With Bobby Kennedy out of the executive branch, Abba had lost his principal protector. But he continued to operate with his customary boldness, overriding Frances Knight at every turn.

Schwartz had also been one of the chief authors of a new immigration bill which was described by one Intelligence expert as "the biggest Trojan horse in history." If Abba had had his way, several million alleged refugees from Russia and other Iron Curtain countries would have flooded into America, selected of course by the KGB. The bill was revised in the Congress and most, though not all, of Schwartz's plans were jettisoned.

Abba's role in attempting to force his own peculiar immigration philosophy on the country brought heavy Congressional pressure on President Johnson to fire him. But the President correctly anticipated a barrage of powerful criticism if he did. Caught between two strong hands, Johnson held his cards close to his vest and waited for Abba to deal another one from the bottom of the deck. As might be expected, he did not have long to wait.

In January 1966, three months after the President signed the new immigration law, Schwartz brazenly approved a passport for one Joseph North to attend a Communist conference in Havana. North did not fall into the category of hidden Communists who could be protected by the new passport regulations; he was a columnist for the Party's official organ, *The Worker*, and as such could be denied a passport even under the hopelessly ineffective new rules.

The issuance of the passport to North was a flagrant violation of the Supreme Court ruling, and although Schwartz had been getting away with similar violations for several years, this time the President flashed the signal to axe Abba. A Presidential aide, W. Marvin Watson, sought out Crockett, who allegedly suggested a replay of the old "reduction-in-force" gambit which had been used to cut down Otepka the first time around in 1961. The decision was made simply to abolish Schwartz's job as Administrator of the Bureau of Security and Consular Affairs. As in Otepka's initial demotion, it would be called "an economy measure."

The screams of outrage from the Liberal community resounded in Washington for weeks. Columnists Rowland Evans and Robert Novak hinted darkly of "deep White House involvement" in the forced resignation of Schwartz.[9] Like many others, they exempted Dean Rusk, claiming he "knew only the barest outlines of what was happening." Instead, they zeroed in on William Crockett.

Lyndon Johnson felt the lash too, and no doubt it taught him a lesson or two. Speaking ruefully of the "great public-relations job" in behalf of Schwartz, a White House source was quoted as admitting: "It has hurt us more than anything in years."[10] Practically pleading for a let-up in the flogging his boss was taking daily in the Liberal press, White House aide William Moyers insisted that the President planned "no change" in the

ncreasingly wide-open immigration, travel and refugee policies ad-
ocated by Abba.[11]

The stark contrast in the outcry over Schwartz's ouster and the treatment Otepka received from these same elements of the press is indicative
of the double standard that is tragically imposed by so much of the
Fourth Estate. The attack on William Crockett is, in this instance, further
evidence of the hysterical outbursts which the Liberals periodically indulge in when one of their own is hurt. There was such a hue and cry
raised against Crockett that it offended the conscience of at least one
Liberal, the Negro columnist Carl Rowan. He accused "some newspapers and a host of Liberals" of jumping "off the deep end over the firing
of Abba Schwartz."

"If Crockett is a reactionary," wrote Rowan, "then I'm the grand
dragon of the Ku Klux Klan." He went on to cite Crockett's role in saving
William Wieland from what he called "the McCarthyites" and then
added:

The irony of the conservative tag being pinned on Crockett is all the
more obvious to anyone who knows the abuse he has taken from
conservatives because of his handling of the Otepka case.[12]

Rowan, formerly chief of the U.S. Information Service, devoted a
lengthy column to an eloquent plea for mercy for Crockett. But he might
as well have saved his strength. Abba Schwartz's friends had something
they had been saving for Bill Crockett and now they let him have it—
right between the eyes.

The Washington *Post* opened up on Crockett in a crusading front-page
article that went on for forty-odd blistering paragraphs. It must be said
that the writer stuck religiously to the facts, but unluckily for Mr. Crockett each fact was more damning than the last. We will approach this story
here in somewhat different sequence than was reported in the *Post,* going
back a full year before the curtain rises in the newspaper account. . . .

In May 1964 a State Department messenger brought Otepka one of
the rare pieces of mail that found its way to his solitary cell in Room
38-A05. It contained a white card captioned "Salute to President Johnson," and although no message accompanied the card, it was self-
explanatory. Otepka could reserve seats, at $100 each, for the "salute"
to Lyndon at the Washington Armory. Checks were to be made payable
to the Democratic National Committee.

It was a violation of the law for State Department personnel to make
political solicitations on government property, but Otepka knew it would
be futile to protest so he simply ignored it. However, a few days later he

got a call from Mrs. Daisy Johnson, a member of the staff of Angie
Biddle Duke, the Department's wealthy Chief of Protocol. Apparently
Otepka's status as an exile had not penetrated to Protocol, which i
concerned with the lighter side of State Department life. At any rate
Mrs. Johnson graciously invited him to a buffet supper that would pre
cede the salute to LBJ. All he had to do to get in was come across with
at least $100 for the Armory show.

The hosts of this exclusive affair, Mrs. Johnson said, were to be Mr
Duke and Mr. Crockett. Otepka declined, with thanks, and the gala wen
on without him. Several hundred Department officials showed up
though, and the press overheard some of them grumbling about the
political contributions they had been forced to pay.

A year later Crockett threw another cocktail party for Department
officials who kicked in with another minimum $100 for still another
salute to the President at the Armory, this time a Congressional tribute.
Otepka did not receive an invitation to this party, but it is at this point
that the Washington *Post* story begins.

Crockett asked a close friend, Norman K. Winston, to foot the bill for
the party. Winston, a real estate developer with offices in New York, was
serving as Crockett's official consultant on State Department realty problems in Paris and Mexico City. But Winston had just been dunned for
$1,000 to attend the Armory affair, bringing his total contributions to
Democrat causes since 1960 to $25,000. All he would come up with for
Crockett's party was a paltry $300.

Faced with the prospect of being stuck with the biggest chunk of the
party bill, Crockett assigned two of his staff, Kenneth Strawberry and Ben
Weiner, to seek other sources of support. As the *Post* put it:

> They decided to use the party to display American foods and wines
> which manufacturers and trade associations would be happy to con-
> tribute. "We only asked for token contributions," said Strawberry—
> wines, bourbon, cheeses, packaged meat, and things to nibble on.[13]

As an inducement, Crockett's men promised that the companies which
came through would be permitted to display and serve similar American
products at U.S. embassies in an overseas sales promotion program—that
is, if the wine and goodies washed down well at the party.

The bash cost Crockett $227.50 in out-of-pocket expenses, but he
figured that he got off cheap. Several thousands of dollars of "free" food
and drink were consumed. A few weeks later he journeyed to New York
to thank his friend Winston for helping out. Winston reciprocated by
giving Crockett a hot tip on some stock in Daltona, a Winston firm

ecializing in Florida real estate sales to government employees. Crock-
t was a little pressed for cash, but Winston sent him 70 shares of
altona stock, plus a box of expensive neckties, as a token of his esteem.
More than a month later Crockett paid for the stock with a $630 check
rawn on his old bank in Hastings, Nebraska. Four more months passed
efore Winston cashed the check. By then it was almost time to toss
nother party.

The next Crockett fete was a $100-a-plate testimonial dinner for Con-
ressman Thomas Morgan of Pennsylvania, Chairman of the House For-
ign Affairs Committee. Once again, the long-suffering State Department
ontributors were hit, along with some others. But it was worth it. Mor-
an's committee had favorably reported on Crockett's pet piece of legis-
ation, the Hays Bill, somewhat earlier and the least the Department
ould do was show its appreciation.

Under the Hays Bill, Crockett would have become high commissar
ver a vast Foreign Service domain with power to liquidate the jobs of
ny and all Otepka adherents or other heretics who might be hiding in
he woodwork at State. Instead of the complicated hearing procedure he
nd Rusk had been forced to offer Otepka, he could simply draft all Civil
ervice personnel into the Foreign Service Reserve where they could be
selected out" with no appeal rights. The bill failed, but Crockett could
ardly hold that against Tom Morgan. There was always the next Con-
ressional session and the Hays Bill might fare better another year.

Unfortunately for Crockett, there wouldn't be any more full years at
State. The Washington *Post* revelations, coming on top of the Abba
Schwartz fandango and the repeated squealing on Dean Rusk in the
Otepka business, finished him off. He did his best to wriggle out of the
most damaging item in the *Post* indictment, his relationship with Nor-
man Winston. But it didn't wash.

On May 9, 1966, Crockett claimed through his aides that "no official
of the State Department had any financial dealings with Winston." Two
days later he thought better of this flat denial and admitted the stock deal.
"I did nothing wrong," he said, "but I think I was stupid because of the
way it might look from the outside."[14]

"There is a political world here," Crockett sighed resignedly, "and one
has to learn to live in it." It was too bad that just when he had learned
to live in it so well, he was booted out.

Before he went, though, Crockett took a few more lumps. The Senate
subcommittee had finally started releasing the testimony in the Otepka
case, and with virtually each new volume the worthy Deputy Under-

secretary absorbed yet another jab. Part 19 was particularly rough o
him. His own words underlined his role in the 1964 burning of the S
field office files and the tightening-up of control over the activities of th
investigative staff.

Economy was the well-worn excuse once again, but the testimon
made it apparent that this was not the real motive. Senators Eastland an
Dirksen had vigorously protested the burning of SY's files in fifteen citie
but Crockett, after giving the subcommittee a lot of double talk, wer
right ahead and had them burned anyway, right down to the index fi
cards the SY investigators kept on suspicious characters in their area.

The files included records on potential assassins who might be tempte
to take a pot shot at the President or other dignitaries. Crockett's excus
was that the records were merely duplicates of papers already stored a
headquarters in Washington, but that would be small consolation for
visiting ambassador or what have you if a local hothead or trained Com
munist decided to slay him in Portland or Podunk. One example of th
tragic stupidity, or worse, in the file-burning order is the fact that the Lo
Angeles office of SY should have had a line on one Sirhan Sirhan befor
he gunned down Robert Kennedy in June 1968.

Two Republican members of the House Committee on Un-America
Activities, Congressmen August E. Johansen of Michigan and James B
Utt of California, subsequently disclosed that Crockett had not told th
full story about the files. An investigation they conducted, which in
cluded questioning of the new SY chief, G. Marvin Gentile, convinced
them that originals of the destroyed material were not all stored in
Washington. They said Gentile and other State Department witnesses
before their committee had given deceptive testimony about the files.
"Gentile gave us gravely misleading answers to our inquiries," they
charged. The material that was burned included, in their view, "vital and
absolutely indispensable data."[15]

The file-burning was, however, only one part of a two-pronged offensive against the field offices. Their number was reduced from nineteen to
seven, and although resident agents were left in most of the cities their
authority was seriously undermined.

In questioning Crockett, Jay Sourwine accurately observed: "It appears these men . . . are going to lose all control over the work they do
. . . over the reports they file, even to the point of checking whether they
were properly transcribed. They are going to lose all office equipment
except dictating machines, and including typewriters. . . . Does the

epartment mean to have these men work out of their homes . . . out
f their hats, so to speak?"

Crockett said he wasn't sure. "We might," he replied. "I don't see
nything wrong with it. . . . It might save some money."[16]

Crockett had also tried to save some money by keeping the guards in
ne State Department headquarters building to a minimum. But a rash
f rapes and assaults in the halls, stairways, elevators, and even in the
ffices, revealed the fallacy of his economy. A woman in the Passport
)ivision was pounced upon in an enclosed stairway between floors and
sexually molested." Another woman was reportedly raped in a ladies'
oom. Both of these incidents occurred within one week in the summer
f 1965, but the assaults continued long after that. The Passport Division
ad to order its women employees to work after hours only in teams and
hey had to be escorted in and out of the building by guards or male
fficials.[17]

The little crime wave on Foggy Bottom was not reflected in the testi-
nony released by the subcommittee, of course. But so much other da-
naging information was disclosed that it is quickly apparent why Lyndon
ohnson and Tom Dodd struggled so hard to suppress it. One sample will
uffice here. In a memorandum dated February 1, 1965, Otepka had at
ast stated the heart of his case in blunt terms:

It is a fact that I found much data indicating that so-called errors in
foreign policy were motivated by persons with dubious backgrounds
who occupied critical positions in the [State] Department, giving them
the opportunity to influence or pervert policy.

Unfortunately . . . my findings laid the foundation for future action
against me because I have trod in hallowed places where no other
security officer in the Department had dared enter.

At long last, Otepka had placed his cards on the table, though he
characteristically refrained from turning them face up so they could be
identified. Nonetheless, Dean Rusk and William J. Crockett could guess
what the faces looked like, which explains their unusual determination
to keep Otepka from ever again returning to SY. His files there had been
rifled, as Otepka discovered when he was given a quick peek at them in
1964. But there was always the danger that despite the burnings in the
field offices and the rifling of the files at headquarters, he might put some
of the pieces back together again.

CHAPTER XXXV

The Unwanted

LOST SOMEWHERE IN THE INTERMITTENT AND EVER MORE FEEBLE OUT cries surrounding Otepka's dismissal and exile was the fate of the seven other unwanted men who were purged with him from the Office of Security. Yet the story behind what happened to these top-notch security officers is in many ways equally as revealing as what befell Otepka.

In the beginning, only two were exiled with Otepka—Billy Hughes and John Norpel. Before long, however, five others were to join them. As the 1968 Senate subcommittee report pointedly put it, "There was no slip of the hand from the weapon" that had cut down Otepka when it was turned against his suspected supporters.[1]

After smashing the Office of Security in June 1963, Dean Rusk proceeded to pick up the few remaining sturdy pieces and hurl them headlong into obscurity. Anyone even remotely suspected of harboring sympathy for Otepka and what he was fighting for was banished from SY.

To maintain the flimsy façade that these men were still engaged in security work, Rusk created a very special Siberia for them. Like the project to which he had happily let Boswell strap Otepka in 1961, this particular piece of *verboten* territory had already been staked out. And thereby hangs another tale. . . .

On a state visit to Washington early in the New Frontier, President

rge Alessandri of Chile had taken Jack Kennedy aside at the White
ouse. The Chilean's Intelligence people had reported that the United
:ates was being penetrated by Latin American Communists, many of
lem accomplished Soviet spies. Alessandri felt it was his duty to warn
resident Kennedy.

President Alessandri told Kennedy that several dozen suspected Com-
lunist agents, most of whom were working right in Washington, had
ttached themselves to the Organization of American States, the Pan-
.merican Union, Pan-American Health Organization and other interna-
onal agencies. Several had wormed their way into key policy positions
'ith OAS. Others were involved in helping to find suitable channels for
1e *Allianza de Progresso* largesse which was about to pump hundreds of
1illions of American tax dollars into Latin America.

Alessandri was understandably alarmed. He could see that U.S. funds
vould be used to finance further Communist subversion and terrorism in
,outh America. The people and governments of the Latin countries were
1aving a difficult enough time combatting the Communist agents de-
cending on them like locusts from the Soviet base on Cuba. To have
inlimited transfusions of *Yanqui* dollars strengthening the terrorist and
)ropagandistic activities of these agents was indeed a frightening pros-
)ect.

The President of Chile never suspected, of course, that the New Breed
n the State Department was busily laboring to make America a leading
:xporter of revolution. He could not have guessed then that these face-
.ess functionaries would soon enlist Bobby and Jack Kennedy in their
:ause. Before long, however, many Latins were jolted by a Kennedy
offensive which strangely echoed the same arguments used by the *agents*
vrovocateurs swarming down on them from Cuba.

"Each year," Arthur Schlesinger reminds us, "he [President Kennedy]
made a Latin American trip, with the democratic revolution his constant
theme."[2] During one incendiary speech in Costa Rica, Kennedy had
shaken his hosts by urging a student audience to struggle for "land for
the landless" and a speedy end of "ancient institutions which perpetuate
privilege," both favorite Communist themes in all Latin countries.[3]

Nonetheless, President Alessandri's warning struck a mildly responsive chord in Kennedy's Celtic soul. Some dimly remembered memory
from the days when he had harbored the same suspicions as Joe
McCarthy caused him to bestir himself, if only just a little. It was one
thing to advocate the destruction of "ancient institutions" in Latin
America; it was quite another to countenance openly their too speedy

demolition in the United States. Or perhaps he merely wanted to alla
Alessandri's fears.

Whatever his motivation, Kennedy actually did initiate an inquiry int
Alessandri's allegations. In due time, a memorandum traveled from th
White House to the State Department requesting an investigation. Man
months later the reply went back, conspicuously addressed to McGeorg
Bundy. As we have seen, this reply became a principal part of the frame
up of Otepka. However, the references to it in the dismissal charges wer
carefully cloaked in ambiguity. No one was supposed to know about th
project to which the Bundy memo referred. It bore a top-secret label.

The project floundered aimlessly around the State Department unti
mid-March 1964. At that point a half-dozen of the most suspiciou
characters thought to be siding with Otepka were rounded up and reas
signed en masse to the Bureau of Inter-American Affairs to work on th
superclassified problem of President Alessandri's charges.

Only Billy Hughes, still languishing in the Memphis field office, escaped this sentence. Of the others, four were plucked right out of th
Evaluations Division—Edwin Burkhardt, Francis Gardner, Harry Hite,
and Raymond Loughton. A fifth, Howard Shea, was lifted from SY's
Investigations Division. The sixth was Jack Norpel, who was resurrected
from the Washington field office and returned to Evaluations a month
earlier, just in time to join the exodus to the "secret" project in Inter-
American Affairs.

New quarters were found for the exiles in the gleaming new Foggy
Bottom headquarters, but they might as well have been several thousand
miles away. In fact, it probably would have been easier for the men to
communicate with their superiors from far off Irkutsk or Outer Mongolia.

Very little mail came into their office, and none of it was in any way
connected with personnel security in the Department of State. Norpel
and the others were told that they had to deal with the Department
through Colonel George W. French, Jr., a retired Army officer roped into
SY to give a reassuring military bearing to the dismembered security
program. The colonel was polite, but singularly uncommunicative.

The assignment that the exiles had been handed was a masterpiece of
State Department double-think. They were told to check into Alessandri's allegations, but they were given few tools to work with. As a matter
of fact, their security officer credentials were eventually taken from them
to make certain they could not conduct a meaningful investigation.

However, even if they had been given *carte blanche* to do the job, little
or nothing could have been accomplished. They were supposed to be

ecking on foreign nationals, but unless they had free access to the most cret Intelligence files of a score of countries abroad, preferably includ- g Russia's, there was virtually no way of pinning down precise back- ound information on the suspects. Many had been shifting about from he country to another for years, probably changing their names and over at each new stop.

Some of the people Alessandri identified had been working in America or a decade or more. But the privileged sanctuaries they occupied in the ntouchable international organizations made it extremely difficult to heck on their activities.

More to the point, though, all six of the ousted security officers knew hat the whole project was a farce, designed purely and simply to remove hem from SY. If by some miracle Norpel and his co-workers *had* got the oods on the men Alessandri named, they realized that the State Depart- ent would do exactly nothing about it. For the truth is that many of hese same alleged agents had been identified years before by other eliable sources. Yet they had been permitted to reside, and presumably ly their esoteric trade, in Washington, New York, Miami and other way tops along the courier routes to Moscow, Havana and Peiping.

The fatuousness of the project is demonstrated by the fact that it had een proposed, explored and rejected by the Office of Security more than decade before. Moreover, as Otepka had repeatedly pointed out, there was a very simple solution to the whole problem. All the State Depart- ent had to do was to lift the visas and resident permits of the suspected Communist agents and evict them from the United States. Of course, the Department would never consider such rude action, and Otepka's rec- ommendation was rejected out of hand.

By clamping a "top secret" classification on the entire project, the State Department hoped to keep it from public view. Like so many projects similarly classified in the Kennedy-Johnson era and, for that matter, before, the "secret" stamp was applied solely to hide information from the American people and its duly elected representatives.

Despite this precaution, the story eventually did get out. On Septem- ber 28, 1964, the American Security Council's *Washington Report* car- ried a description of the project by this writer, pieced together from various sources.[4] Its significance was lost in the sound and fury of the Presidential campaign, and there was little reaction—except from the State Department. Jack Norpel was ordered to investigate the "leak" and he was forced to interrogate me for several hours. Needless to say, the sources were not revealed.

The sensitivity of the Department to the disclosure of the Latin sp project is rather puzzling. For when Kennedy tossed the ball to the Sta Department he might as well have broadcast President Alessandri charges to the world.

One of the first things the Department did was to send a circular all U.S. embassies in Latin America describing the President's inquii and asking for information on "this general subject." Thus, all Foreig Service officers south of the Rio Grande, among whom, we can safe presume, was at least one blabbermouth, or worse, were alerted to th "top secret" project.

The list of suspected spies eventually grew to several score name some supplied by Chile and some from other sources, including th ancient information the U.S. had been sitting on since the early 1950'.

Interestingly, many of the more recent arrivals among the accuse espionage artists were Cubans, and not a few had actually served in Fid Castro's government. Several were known to have been in touch with th Soviet embassy on 16th Street. Some had close friends in the Departmer of State, with whom they were often seen bending fraternal elbows in th capital's bistros and sidewalk cafes.

A whole clutch of Cubans were laboring in the Pan-American Unior assiduously drawing up economic aid projects for American taxpayers t finance. Another Cuban clique was operating inside the Pan-America Health Organization, planning additional surgery on the U.S. Treasury

One of the "economic experts" in the Pan-American Union, an inti mate friend of William Wieland, had actually been registered as a foreig agent in Washington during the late 1950's. His name was Ernest Betancourt y Hernandez and he had represented Castro's "26th of July" revolutionary movement. The day Castro moved into Havana, Betan court and a gun-toting gang of other Cubans seized the Cuban embass in Washington on behalf of Fidel. He was rewarded with an importan post in Havana, as managing director of the Cuban Bank of Foreig Trade, but within a year he had lost his job. When he returned to Wash ington he was promptly hired by the Pan-American Union.

There was no proof that Betancourt was a Communist, but his activi ties on behalf of the "26th of July" gunmen should have been enough t rule out his employment by an organization devoted to inter-American amity and largely supported by U.S. taxpayers. Betancourt, however, wa but one of dozens with similar backgrounds and he is mentioned here only as an example of the overall problem.

Isolated in the Bureau of Inter-American Affairs, where they had good reason to suspect their offices were wired for sound, Otepka's former associates understood too well that their individual careers had been ruined.

Each one of these men had devoted the best part of his working life to the essentially thankless job of trying to help protect his country against subversion by a ruthless enemy bent on America's destruction. They had all accepted the anonymity of their profession as a necessary part of the game and they knew that the financial rewards, while adequate, would never make them wealthy.

Any one of them could have done far better in business or industry if he had started early enough. Now, however, they were all fortyish or over and one was in his fifties. It would have been difficult for them to launch new careers, though that was not the primary reason why they hung on at State. They all knew that they had become symbols, with Otepka, of the cause of sound security.

Not content with exiling and isolating these men, the State Department exerted other pressures on them in the obvious hope that they would resign or give up. The Department tried to get two of the castoffs to submit to psychiatric examinations and a third, Edwin Burkhardt, was actually accused, in effect, of having flipped his lid.

The Senate subcommittee saw this as another piece of the familiar pattern it had observed earlier in Reilly's accusations against Otepka. The Senators found that an adverse efficiency report on Burkhardt was based on remarks he had made when the perjury of Reilly & Company was revealed in the fall of 1963. On that occasion Burkhardt had been indiscreet enough to say that "I would hate to have to interview applicants today, questioning their integrity, with the headlines that are in the newspapers this morning."[5] For this mild remark he had been cited for his "emotional displays of temper"!

When summoned by the subcommittee in 1964, four of the outcasts gave testimony which supported Otepka's position. Their accounts of what had transpired in SY during the reign of the Rusk-Kennedy puppets thoroughly substantiated many of the points made by Otepka in the subdued picture he had drawn of the deliberate destruction of SY.

Further reprisals for this were soon forthcoming. One by one the six men were picked off. Their little group was broken up and its members scattered. Ray Loughton was the first to go. In January 1965 he accepted assignment to the Foreign Service Institute and then to the consulate at Guadalajara, Mexico, where his long years of security experience in the Justice, Defense and State Departments were sure to be wasted.

In March of 1965 Jack Norpel and Howard Shea were notified that they too were to be banished from Washington. Norpel was assigned to the SY office in El Paso and Shea to Denver. Both men decided to fight the transfers and they were dismissed without pay. A year passed before the dismissal charges against them were dropped. On the advice of their attorneys, who saw that the two men were merely bloodying their heads against a stone wall, Norpel and Shea agreed to submit their resignations. They collected their back pay and were sent packing.

Shea went to the Internal Revenue Service, relieved to be free of the funny house on Foggy Bottom. Norpel weathered several lean years, determined to find work in the security field. Although former FBI agents are usually in demand both in government and industry, Norpel discovered that there were no jobs available to him in the Washington area. Finally, however, he was given a post on the staff of the Senate Internal Security Subcommittee, and in late 1967, when Ben Mandel retired as research director, Jack Norpel took his place.

Francis Gardner, the other ex-FBI man Otepka had hired for his special project staff in 1961, saw that the indifference of the public and the Congress had doomed the internal security business and he decided to get out of it entirely. In the summer of 1965 he accepted a transfer from the Latin American spy project to a management analyst post. From there he was assigned, in late 1965, to Juarez, a Mexican post suitably insulated from the countersubversion field to which he had devoted seventeen years.

Only Harry Hite and Ed Burkhardt were left in Rusk's Siberia. Both of them had appealed their original transfers to the Civil Service Commission, as had Norpel. But the commission, supposedly set up to protect the rights of government employees, discreetly decided it had no jurisdiction in their cases.

After Gardner left in 1965, Hite and Burkhardt were shipped off to a State Department annex, a filthy old building about to be condemned. When all the other tenants on their floor moved out they were still there, occupying a small suite of offices with a lone secretary. Appropriately, the windows of their office were laced with heavy-gauge wire, giving it the look, as well as the feel, of a prison. Across a narrow alley they could see Otepka in his solitary cell in 38-A05. It was as though Hite and Burkhardt had been placed on private exhibition in a cage as a constant reminder to their ex-boss that he was responsible for their incarceration.

After a while the Department decided it was safe to drop even the shabby pretense of the Latin American spy project and Hite and Burk-

ardt were "reassigned," though to what task they could never determine. Week after week they sent memorandums to their superiors asking
what they were supposed to be doing. Virtually all of their communications were simply ignored.

Roaches and other vermin abounded in the deserted annex. In moving
out, the other State Department personnel left mountains of trash, and,
since the cleaning people no longer came, the trash remained. It attracted
a swarm of rats and mice who took possession of the building, ignoring
the chain stretched across the main entrance.

In between writing memos to their superiors and keeping abreast of the
news, Hite and Burkhardt played chess. To amuse themselves, they
arranged a display of plastic cockroaches on the office wall under an
improvised sign which read: "This place is bugged."

Looking back, Hite later said: "We could take everything—the ostracism, the turning away of heads of fellow employees, the incarceration
in a rat-infested building—but the strain of idleness was beginning to
wear on us toward the end of 1967. At home, I spent most of the time
trying to think of an answer to my nine-year-old son's constant questions
about what I did for a living.

"We came to realize the probable purpose of the treatment was to
break us down mentally until we started shouting at each other," recalled
the mild-mannered, soft-spoken Virginian. "It didn't work out that way,
but we don't know whether it might not have, eventually."

Ed Burkhardt smiled in agreement. "It was a matter of principle with
us," he said. "We weren't going to resign. But we would have lost our
sanity if we hadn't maintained our sense of humor."

Ultimately, the conditions in the abandoned annex proved too much
for the secretary who innocently shared their exile. One morning early
in February 1968 she was at her desk when a mouse climbed out of her
wastebasket and ambled off on its daily rounds. Something in the noncha-
lant, insouciant manner of the mouse touched a tender nerve. The poor
girl broke into tears. Bidding goodbye to Hite and Burkhardt, she departed, never to return.

Sometimes it is the small, seemingly insignificant incidents that have
the greatest impact. In this case, the appearance of the mouse led to the
rescue of Messrs. Burkhardt and Hite. When Harry mentioned it to his
wife that evening, Janet Hite resolved that the time had come for her to
intervene.

The next day Mrs. Hite went up to Capitol Hill to call on her Congressman and other members of the House and Senate. None of them was

much interested, but someone suggested that Janet contact Willard Ed
wards. Although he was one of the few members of the Washington pres:
corps familiar with the details of the Otepka case, Edwards admitted he
was "disinclined at first to believe that government employees could be
subjected to such treatment as Mrs. Hite described."[6]

A visit to the annex and an interview with Hite and Burkhard
"confirmed the shocking reality of her report," Edwards said. The story
he wrote describing the conditions they had coped with for so long wa:
front-paged by the Chicago *Tribune* on February 3, 1968.

Seldom has a single news story brought such immediate results. Tha:
same afternoon John J. Williams of Delaware, the Senate's most re
spected investigator, visited the annex building with Congressman H. R
Gross, an Iowa Republican who had long been interested in the Otepka
controversy. They wandered through the deserted eight-story structure
searching for Hite and Burkhardt, appalled at the rubbish and the filth
At last they found the two men and verified Edwards' report that neither
of them had been able to get the State Department to give them even
make-believe work for a year and a half.

In an impassioned speech to the Senate, Williams said he was "shocked
and dismayed to find that the State Department is operating a special
isolation ward or cooler for employees whose only crime is telling the
truth to a Senate committee." Hite and Burkhardt were being penalized
solely because of their role in the Otepka case, he charged.

Williams delivered an ultimatum to the Department of State, giving it
exactly seventy-two hours to get the two men out of the annex and back
to work. If it failed to act, he promised to introduce a Senate resolution
to fire whoever was responsible for what he called this "incredible outrage."

In the House, Congressman Gross said he would introduce a companion resolution. "Heads should roll," he thundered, "and the first man to
go should be Secretary Rusk himself."

For once, the jaded press galleries sat up and took notice. Williams had
invited the press "to visit this junk-filled, deserted building," and within
an hour reporters, radio commentators and television cameramen were
converging on the annex. The resulting media blitz greatly strengthened
the position taken by Williams and Gross. Other members of the Congress began to fall in line.

The heat became so intense that Dean Rusk at last decided a tactical
retreat was in order. He instructed Idar Rimestad, Crockett's successor
as Deputy Undersecretary for Administration, to quell the uprising. Wil-

iam B. Macomber, Jr., the Assistant Secretary in charge of Congressional relations, paid a visit to Hite and Burkhardt, looked around a bit,
and exclaimed in mock horror, "What an awful place!" Then he fled.

By mid-afternoon, the two outcasts were summoned to Personnel.
They were told that their old jobs as security officers had been abolished
and would not be available, but they were offered new positions.

Rusk might retreat, but he had no intention of surrendering. To place
Hite and Burkhardt back in SY, the dauntless Dean knew he would run
the supreme risk that they would discover many more security risks who
had doubtless received clearances in the five years since he cleaned
house. He had managed to keep all those he had brought in prior to June
1963 hidden, but he might not be so lucky again.

Rusk, however, was past master of the fine art of "crisis management."
By getting Hite and Burkhardt out of the abandoned annex, he satisfied
most of the media and successfully put down another threatening Congressional revolt. To be sure, a number of Senators, Everett Dirksen
among them, were taking a cue from Williams and Gross by demanding
Otepka's full reinstatement too, but the Secretary could ignore that. It
was old stuff, and the greater part of the press wouldn't buy that as easily
as the colorful story of the two discarded men in a condemned rat-
infested building.

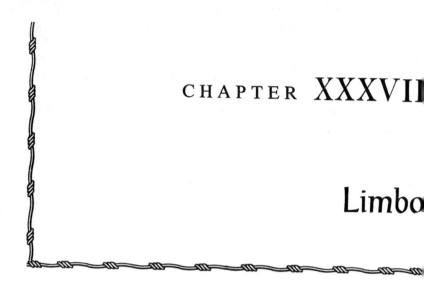

CHAPTER XXXVII

Limbo

POWERLESS TO HELP THE MEN WHO STOOD BY HIM IN THE UNSEEN BAT-
tle for a sane security program, Otto Otepka never failed to give them
what moral support he could. Hardly a day went by that he didn't call
or visit or lunch with one or more of his former associates.

Deprived with him of their right to work in SY, the little band of
former security officers made Otepka's home their real working headquarters. Evenings, weekends, and holidays were devoted to exploring
the various possibilities for legal redress. Plans were carefully laid for
each barrage of memorandums before it was fired off at the Seventh
Floor. Appeals to the Civil Service Commission were studied and prepared. Although idleness was forced upon them during working hours,
at all other times they were never idle.

At lunch in the Washington restaurant where they were least likely to
be seen by other Department officials or CIA snoops, Otepka and his
friends exchanged the latest intelligence on security risks they knew were
setting national policies. World events that increasingly confused the
American people were often crystal-clear to them. They were familiar
with the backgrounds of the people who were pulling the strings behind
the managed news screen of the Johnson Administration, and they real-

ized that many of the most disastrous foreign-policy failures were not entirely accidental.

Anyone who dined or lunched with these men was immediately struck by their warm, though subdued, camaraderie. Their sense of humor never deserted them, no matter how hopeless their cause appeared. Bitter disappointments that would have crushed most men were passed off with a smile or a quip.

After Hughes, Loughton, Gardner and Shea had been scattered to Memphis and Mexico and into the Internal Revenue Service, the circle shrank to three survivors—Otepka, Burkhardt and Hite. But Jack Norpel, all during the long period of his enforced unemployment, also remained a full-fledged member of the beleaguered band. Like the other three, he was determined to keep his knowledge of the security field current. None of them ever considered giving up his profession.

There were times of deep discouragement, of course. They were reminded every waking moment of what was being done to their country by the reality of their own exile. And periodically that knowledge was driven home more forcibly when the Johnson Administration heaped rewards and honors on their antagonists.

Several days after the 1964 election the word got out that John Reilly had been rehired by the Federal Communications Commission. Although he "resigned" in November 1963 from State, he had been carried on the payroll until the following spring; and now he had a $17,000-a-year post at the FCC. Except for a few months, he had continued to receive his federal pay checks regularly. Periodic raises soon brought his salary up to the $20,000 level.

David Belisle was similarly rewarded for his perjury. In December 1963 he was promoted out of SY and into the office of the Deputy Undersecretary of State for Administration as a special assistant to William Crockett. The Senate subcommittee later found that this new position, in which he served as executive director of Crockett's personnel panel, gave Belisle the power to make "initial decisions about the review of security cases."[1] In August 1964 he was promoted again, to a Class 2 officer in the Foreign Service Reserve, and appointed to a plush post at the U.S. embassy in Bonn.

William Wieland, his long-delayed clearance finally approved despite the fact that the last honest evaluation in SY had declared him a security risk, was named counselor of the embassy in Canberra in July 1965 and consul general at Melbourne a short time later. When he first went to

Australia he received a pay raise of $4,000, bringing his salary to $24,000 a year, and other increases were forthcoming after that.

Harlan Cleveland had bestowed upon him the magnificent title of Ambassador Extraordinary and Plenipotentiary when the President appointed him as the permanent U.S. representative to the NATO Council on September 9, 1965. It may have been a coincidence, but this was the very day Charles de Gaulle called a press conference in Paris and announced that he was pulling France out of the NATO military alliance.

Robert McCarthy was named security officer at Brussels, where the NATO headquarters was subsequently relocated, and he was given a special citation, appropriately, by Harlan Cleveland.

Month after month Otepka was obliged to witness the elevation of many other questionable officials while he waited interminably for his State Department hearing. Early in 1967 Senator Sam Ervin, genuinely puzzled by the seemingly unending delays, remarked sadly to this writer, "Justice certainly is traveling on leaden feet."

Unfortunately, neither Senator Ervin nor most of the other members of the Subcommittee on Internal Security realized that a large part of the lead that had slowed justice to a snail's pace had been molded by the subcommittee itself, or more precisely by Senator Dodd.

Busy with many seemingly more pressing matters, most of the Senators never really understood the reason for the repeated postponement of Otepka's hearing. If they had, a majority of them, Sam Ervin included, would surely have voted to overrule Dodd's stop orders.

When William Crockett finally testified for the last time in May 1965 four more months were permitted to elapse before the subcommittee began issuing the published testimony in the Otepka case. There are those who doubt that it would have been released even then if it had not been for a sudden, although limited, public awakening.

In Illinois and California, where a few newspapers had done a much better job than elsewhere in reporting the case, groups of outraged citizens organized a massive letter-writing campaign on Otepka's behalf. The campaign received a strong boost in mid-summer when the *Reader's Digest* published the only story on Otepka's ordeal that ever appeared in a major national magazine. The outpouring of written protest that followed nearly inundated the State Department and the subcommittee. Thousands of letters descended on Washington, and in August Senator Dodd was finally forced to lift the ban he had singlehandedly imposed.

"Dodd would have dragged out the publication of the testimony until doomsday had it not been for the public pressure," said James M. Stewart, the Chicago-area salesman who organized the campaign in the Mid-west.

As it was, publication was stretched out over a period of fourteen months, beginning in August 1965. Because it was released piecemeal, one volume at a time, without any clarifying explanation from the sub-committee, its impact was sadly muffled. Only the handful of newsmen who had taken the trouble to understand the significance of the case were able to enlighten their readers. Outside the circulation areas served by their papers, the country at large remained almost totally ignorant of the full impact of the story.

Far worse than the failure of much of the Fourth Estate to grasp the true meaning of the Otepka case were the deliberate distortions. At times it seemed that the Associated Press, which serves the majority of the nation's daily newspapers and radio-TV stations, was conducting a vicious vendetta against Otepka.

With the release of the fourth volume of testimony, AP fed out a story on its wires which uncritically highlighted Reilly's effort to brand Otepka as mentally unstable. As an example of slanted news, the lead on this AP dispatch, datelined Washington, August 19, 1966, stands as a classic:

> Otto F. Otepka, dismissed chief security evaluator of the State De-partment, was described two years ago by his former superior as "emo-tionally over-wrought," a man who "does not strike me as being a balanced individual."

Six full paragraphs of this relatively short item were devoted to Reilly's testimony on this point. But nowhere did the story mention that the man who gave this testimony had proved to be a perjurer. The AP alluded to the fact that "Reilly himself resigned in November 1963" but it gave no hint whatever as to the reason for his resignation. Nor did it quote the Reilly testimony in the context of Sourwine's questions, which would at least have shown that the subcommittee had been expecting this accusa-tion to emerge. Further, it simply ignored William Crockett's rebuttal of this particular piece of Reilly testimony, for even Crockett had denied that he, or anyone in the State Department except Reilly, had ever considered Otepka "unbalanced."

Instead, the AP story emphasized that although Otepka had been dismissed nearly two years earlier he "is still on the Department's pay-roll." And it reported that Otepka's hearing had been "postponed five times on request of Otepka's attorney." The reason for the delay was not given.

Six months later the AP was still at it. From another volume of the hearings, issued on February 3, 1966, the Washington bureau plucked out Crockett's specious charge that Otepka's files were "a rat's nest." It pinned the lead and follow-up paragraphs on this accusation, once again without giving Otepka's side of the story.

Yet Otepka had provided a detailed answer to the charge in which it was evident that the "rat's nest" had been created *after* the files had been seized by Reilly's shillelagh brigade. Given a chance to examine the files briefly in January 1964, Otepka said he had found "an unrecognizable mess." More than that, he had pointed out that these were working files on pending cases and he thought it "incredible" that they had been permitted to remain in such a disordered state without any action having been taken on them.

The real story here, of course, was the fact that Otepka's files had been rifled when they were taken from him and that pending cases had been permitted to lie dormant. But the Associated Press writer gave no hint of this, and millions of people who read this story were left with the impression that Otepka was an untidy incompetent who deserved to be fired by the State Department.*

Apparently various AP reporters did stories on the Otepka case testimony as it was doled out by the subcommittee a bit at a time, for the AP file was not all uniformly in this same vein. But enough of it was to raise very serious questions about the quality of the "news" being fed out of Washington by the nation's largest wire service.

Fortunately, United Press International did a far better job overall on the Otepka story. But UPI still does not serve as many clients as AP, on which the largest number of newspapers depend almost exclusively for world and national news. When one examines the AP coverage of the Otepka case, the reason for the public's indifference and confusion becomes more clear.

Part of the confusion can also be traced to the manner in which the testimony was issued. No doubt most of the members of the subcommittee were well motivated in ordering the twenty volumes to be released separately. It would only have increased the confusion if the vast torrent of testimony had been dumped all at once into the public domain. However, the clarifying report that was to have followed on the heels of publication of the raw testimony was not issued for another two-and-a-half years, finally appearing in four more separate volumes in January 1968.

* It would be interesting for the client newspapers and other media served by the Associated Press to request an investigation of why these stories were written as they were.

The last volume of the testimony itself, the controversial Part 20, was almost entirely suppressed. In this instance, however, it was not Dodd nor the other Senators who were at fault. It was the State Department, which surreptitiously tried to slap a "classified" label on this portion of the testimony, particularly the segment dealing with Harlan Cleveland's Advisory Committee on International Organizations. In its 1968 report, the subcommittee disclosed a small piece of what had transpired:

High-level State Department officials waged a protracted contest— so determined as to make many wonder why—to suppress great chunks of what proved to be Part 20. . . .

The argument over what the subcommittee should suppress or be allowed to print stalled release of Part 20 for months.[2]

Originally planned for release as Part 10, this particular volume contained, in addition to the enlightening information on the Cleveland committee, the lengthy memorandum Otepka had prepared for Jay Sourwine and the other documents he delivered to the subcommittee. Frightened that the public might possibly see in this material how the internal security program had been wiped out, the State Department didn't hesitate to throw all of its power into the threatening breach.

At the end of May 1966, all nine members of the Senate subcommittee received letters from Undersecretary George Ball demanding that the Cleveland committee and other information be excluded. Each letter was portentously stamped "Secret," thereby forbidding the Senators from disclosing its contents.

The letters were followed by personal visits to each Senator from the current Assistant Secretary for Congressional Relations, Douglas MacArthur II. This misnamed nephew of the late General strongly urged the Senators to suppress the Otepka testimony on the pain of breaking the holy classified seal which supposedly protects the national security.

The magic word "classified" had become such a sacred cow in Washington that the Senators were loathe to shoot it down. As a result the subcommittee was thrown into confusion. Behind closed doors all through the middle months of 1966 the great question was debated—to release, or not release. Each time the subcommittee appeared on the verge of deciding in the affirmative it was confronted with fresh objections from the State Department.

In late August, William Crockett, acting as usual for Dean Rusk, added the Secretary's considerable weight to the protest. He reminded the Senators, in a particularly brazen letter, of an old Truman directive prohibiting dissemination of security clearance material without White

House consent. The State Department, which had not quailed at placing Otepka under framed criminal charges and wrecking the careers of seven other innocent men, claimed that publication of the information on Andrew Cordier, Ernest Gross, et al. "could cause (them) undue embarrassment and distress."[3]

Autumn arrived before the Senators finally asserted themselves and overrode the State Department's heated objections. On October 2, a Sunday, the *verboten* Part 20 was let loose at last.

The contortions of influential segments of the press, horrified that the subcommittee would name names in internal security cases, were something to behold. The Milwaukee *Journal,* for example, roundly spanked the Senators for "typical irresponsibility." In an editorial titled "Smearing Loyal Americans," the *Journal* pronounced the subcommittee "guilty of unfair and unjust conduct" and assailed it for having the temerity to release the testimony "in the face of bitter protests by the State Department."[4]

Once again, outright distortions crept into many news stories. The Washington *Post* falsely claimed that "all ten" members of Cleveland's advisory committee "ultimately were given a clean bill of health by Otepka himself."[5] For the most part, however, the press played the story straight, albeit without enthusiasm or understanding. Even the Associated Press correctly predicted that the release of Volume 20 had cleared the way for Otepka's departmental hearing. The AP also confirmed reports that Dean Rusk had "agreed to delay the hearing," at the subcommittee's request, until this "last volume was made public."[6]

The New York *Times* buried the story back on Page 80, though its coverage was fairly lengthy. A dozen paragraphs were devoted to the feeble rebuttals of a few of the people named in the Cleveland committee scrap. But this was as it should be. Interestingly, Harding Bancroft, the executive vice president of the *Times* and a member of the controversial committee, told his own newspaper: "I don't want to comment at all."[7]

Ernest Gross was much more loquacious. He termed it "outrageous that this sort of irresponsible action should be taken so long after the death of McCarthy." Claiming that he had been "repeatedly cleared for some of the highest positions in government," Gross asserted that he had "never been accused of anything which could be remotely regarded as subversive or disloyal." Further, he denied that he had ever had "any connection with Alger Hiss in any official matter," though he acknowledged that "I knew him, as did many others, for a short time. Our service in the State Department overlapped and I've never myself voiced any doubt as to his guilt."

LIMBO

Andrew Cordier, describing Andrew Cordier as "an anti-Communist," exonerated Andrew Cordier for his handling of the Povl Bang-Jensen affair at the United Nations. Incredibly, he claimed that he was a "friend" of Bang-Jensen, and tried to put the blame for the Danish diplomat's fatal dismissal on the late U.N. Secretary General, Dag Hammarskjold. Unfortunately, Hammarskjold was not alive to defend himself, but there were enough people still around who were familiar with the Bang-Jensen ouster to see through Cordier's patent hypocrisy.

Tragically, the release of the twentieth and last volume of testimony had been made to appear as an anti-climax. After reading the news stories many people wondered why the State Department had so fiercely fought its publication. Taken out of the context of the other nineteen volumes, and forced to stand alone without any explanatory background report from the subcommittee, it was, to put it bluntly, a dud.

The press was not entirely responsible for this, nor was the subcommittee. Otepka's own restraint, his infuriating habit of refusing to call a spade by its proper name, was equally at fault. But there was yet another factor in the failure of the Otepka case to stir public concern.

Fed a steady diet of intrigue and violence via their TV screens and daily newspapers, most Americans regarded the Otepka matter as pretty pallid stuff. In the age of James Bond, Otto Otepka seemed a plodding bureaucrat. He was not a swinger. He had never made love to a beautiful Russian on a night train from Istanbul. He had no opportunity to practice karate on Smersh agents. He had never confronted a Goldfinger on a trans-Atlantic jet or matched wits with a Le Chiffre at Casino Royale. The people he had struggled against might be more dangerous than Doctor No, but they were decidedly less colorful.

The truth is the American public had become satiated with espionage, to a point where it no longer registered. During the fourteen months that the subcommittee testimony was being issued, the news abounded with real-life spy stories.

In August 1965 a top sergeant with an Army Intelligence unit in Germany disappeared without a trace. A month later a warrant officer went over the hill after delivering secret material to "a depot in New York State." In Kansas City, George John Gessner, an Army nuclear weapons specialist, was freed when a Federal Circuit Court ruled that he had confessed "involuntarily" to stealing atomic secrets for Russian agents.

On the floor of the Canadian House of Commons in Ottawa a bitter debate broke out in March 1966 over the amorous relationships of several former cabinet members with an alleged Mata Hari.

This same spring, while the State Department fought the issuance of Part 20 of the Otepka hearings, two Czech diplomats were caught in a plot to place electronic bugs in the building on Foggy Bottom.

In July 1966 Lieutenant Colonel William Henry Whalen, who had once served in the office of the Joint Chiefs of Staff, was arrested for conspiring to steal strategic weaponry information for two Soviet embassy officials. In September another member of the USSR embassy's staff, Valentin A. Revin, was expelled when the FBI caught him trying to buy space and missile secrets from an industrialist who turned him in.

The defection to Russia of a Roman Catholic priest from Chicago, Father Harold M. Koch, was also disclosed in September. He had worked for a time in 1964 for Radio Liberty, a CIA operation headquartered in Munich. In October, when Part 20 was finally released, George Blake escaped from prison in England, and a U.S. Air Force sergeant, Herbert W. Boeckenhaupt, was picked up by the FBI in California for allegedly handing over top-secret military information to yet another Soviet embassy spy, Aleksey R. Malinin.

Espionage had, in fact, become so commonplace that Americans were more apt to joke about it than take it seriously. TV's Maxwell Smart was a true product of his time. However, the jokes failed to conceal the hopeless naïveté of most citizens regarding the dangers of the all-out espionage offensive against their country and its allies.

Laboring for a sophisticated lead that would match the current climate, one *Time* writer succeeded only in revealing his ignorance in reporting on the arrest of Colonel Whalen and the bugs that failed to get planted in the State Department. "The Communist spy, who doubtless regards the East-West *détente* as a conspiracy, has yet to come in from the cold war," the *Time* man smirked.[8] Obviously, the writer regarded the *détente* as reality and the conspiracy as merely an antique that had no more than curiosity value, and very little of that.

Of course, as Otepka and his friends so well knew, the spy stories that made the headlines were for the most part pure trivia. The top agents who wheel and deal at the policy level, where the truly critical decisions are made, seldom get caught.

CHAPTER **XXXVIII**

The Long Wait

WHEN THE TWENTIETH AND LAST VOLUME OF THE SENATE SUBCOMMIT-
tee testimony was released in October 1966, three years and three
months had passed since the day Reilly and Belisle had marched Otto
Otepka down the corridors and into exile.

The days piled drearily one atop another: 1,199 days in all, and some
four hundred more would come and go before Dean Rusk would hand
down the decision that was to remove Otepka formally and physically
from SY and his cell in Room 38-A05.

The tiny office across from the wiretap laboratories became smaller
each day, its interior space literally shrinking. Inch by inch the ostracized
prisoner was robbed of arm room as the *Congressional Records* and fat
Federal Registers were brought in every day and stacked up—on the
desk, on the floor, on top of the bookcases around the wall, covering the
radiator shields, overflowing from the single extra chair.

As a concession to the subcommittee and public pressure, the Department permitted Otepka's loyal secretary, Eunice Powers, to return to
duty in his office. She kept the small mountains of paper under control
for a time, but eventually the silence, the meaningless tasks, the abiding
sense of always being watched, became too much for her. Otepka gave
Mrs. Powers permission to transfer to Frances Knight's Passport Divi-

393

sion, and he was once again entirely alone in the dingy little room.

A visitor stopping by 38-A05 about this time would have found Otepka behind his scarred old desk leafing through a copy of the *Congressional Record*, looking for material that would give his superiors a better idea of Congress's attitude toward internal security, as his make-work assignment dictated. His back would be to the dusty windows that looked out on D Street, the view across the narrow thoroughfare looking out on the barred windows of the annex where Harry Hite and Ed Burkhardt were confined on the Latin American project.

On the wall just inside the door the big newspaper photograph of Winston Churchill still hung, the Prime Minister's grim smile and famed victory sign continuing to defy the forces of darkness. From where he sat Otepka faced the doughty old warrior. He got in the habit of reading Churchill's words beneath the picture every day: "Never give in. Never, never, never. . . ."

Eight large bookcases closed in around the solitary occupant of 38-A05. They contained printed copies of Congressional hearings and reports on internal security going back twenty years and more. Collectively, they comprised the basic guide for all good security officers.

At the very start of every investigation on an applicant or incumbent official, the master indexes of these hearings were once checked as a matter of course. Not infrequently, the subject's name would be found, his membership in Communist fronts established or refuted. Quite often these volumes provided invaluable leads that opened up avenues of investigation that would otherwise have remained totally unknown. They were the primer, the kickoff point, the indispensable tool used to pry open the first door.

This material had once resided in a handy central location in SY. But long ago it had been gratefully dumped in Otepka's little office. It was the only full set of these volumes in the whole State Department building, but the New Order was happy to be rid of them.

"They have no use for them any more," Otepka remarked with a tight smile that belied the import of his words. "Once in the last three years a security officer came by and asked if he could check something in the Congressional indexes. That was the only time SY has bothered with them, to my knowledge. They're no longer interested in this sort of thing."

Depriving security officers of this fundamental source in the Congressional hearings was tantamount to asking an astronaut to fly to the moon in a space ship that had no fuel to get it off the launching pad. As a yardstick to measure what was left of the internal security program in the State Department, this is as good as any: simply put, the program no longer existed.

While Otepka still carried the title of Chief, Evaluations Division, there was, of course, nothing for him to evaluate. The visitor might notice that there was also none of the accouterments of a real office in 38-A05 —no typewriter, no dictating machine, no "In" and "Out" box.

At about 11:30 a.m. a young stenographer from the Foreign Operations Division next door would come in and deposit another copy of the *Congressional Record* on Otepka's desk. This and the other printed material he was assigned to "study" were virtually the only mail he received from one month to the next.

If the visitor were to ask Otepka a sensitive question, he might smile and point to the ceiling or the walls. In view of his experience one would know that his suspicions were well grounded. But there was often fresh evidence for their basis in reality.

Earlier that same year, Joseph Alsop had written a column that painted an accurate picture of the atmosphere in Washington during the 1960's. He pinned his tale to the White House, and wrote it in the context of what was being done on the managed news front, but it applied, as Alsop mentioned, to the Defense and State Departments too:

A part of the curious espionage system to which members of the White House staff are subjected has been rudely brought into the open. All staff members' telephone calls are noted. All places they visit outside the White House are reported by government chauffeurs. And these lists of contacts are nightly studied, for symptoms of dangerous associations. . . .

Yet it is, of course, an open secret that the telephone and limousine checks are only parts of a much wider system of surveillance that now covers most of the city of Washington. It is informal, but it works very efficiently.[1]

The purpose of the surveillance, as Alsop pointed out, was to keep facts from the American people, or, better yet, cast them into the category of "un-facts." He said the President wanted "the freedom to decide whether facts are indeed facts. . . . if they are just not mentioned, then they remain un-facts."[2]

Lyndon Johnson, with Tom Dodd's help, did his best to keep Otto Otepka classified as an un-fact. The difficulty was that Otepka was a living, walking, and eminently knowledgeable real fact who kept bobbing up to remind people, a few people at least, that something must still be wrong in the State Department.

Walking through the Department corridors with Otepka in that autumn of 1966, one began to get the feel of the climate. On the way to 38-A05 from the elevator, Otepka and a companion might pass as many as twenty people. The people all knew him, of course, but no one so much as passed the time of day. Going out to lunch, or returning, or leaving for home in the late afternoon it would be the same. Guilty eyes would suddenly shift away when the familiar big, dark-haired figure appeared. Occasionally, a brave soul might nod or attempt a surreptitious smile. No one ever was caught stopping him to engage in open conversation.

In these corridors of the Office of Security it was impressed on the transient observer that something new was creeping into the once friendly and outgoing character of the American people. One did not encounter it only here, of course. Bureaucracies, governmental and corporate, were molding new personalities everywhere, and the increasing press of population in the urban centers was deepening the anonymity of millions. But here in SY even the superficial civility that varnishes the personalities of people thrown together in the workaday world was completely lacking, at least for Otto Otepka.

He had learned to live with it, of course. But the ostracism by people who had formerly been so amiable when he was their boss still rankled. Otepka had never been a gregarious man, though he had been unfailingly polite and usually considerate of persons working under him. He had always tried to preserve the amenities. Now his former subordinates didn't even bother to do that. He did not condemn them for it, however, for he knew why they behaved as they did.

Once, a security officer returned on leave from a post abroad. He poked his head into 38-A05 and smiled mischievously: "Otto, I've come to say hello despite the fact that I was instructed not to."

"Who gave you that instruction?" Otepka inquired.

"Mrs. Catucci."

"What did she say?"

The security officer wrinkled up his nose and squinted in mock disdain: "She said, 'Stay away from Otepka.'"

There were others who came to him too, less openly, outside the State Department. But there were not many who risked being seen with him off the premises because there was the general feeling that he was still being closely watched. Except in his office, however, he went about his business with seeming unconcern. He chose not to play hide-and-seek, knowing that he had nothing to hide.

In the summer of 1965 he purchased a small outboard motorboat and took up fishing. Almost every weekend for the next few seasons he could be found on Chesapeake Bay or in one of the countless inlets and rivers punctuating its shores. Sometimes one of his friends went along; George Pasquale, still unemployed since being forced out of State, was a frequent companion.

Boating with Otepka and Pasquale over the gentle swells of the beautiful bay on a short sail to Annapolis or one of the other little ports, it was difficult to believe that these men still stood in the center of a vicious controversy upon which the future course of their country might yet hang. The conversation was always of fish and currents and shifting winds, almost never of the fate that had befallen them or of the threatening storms that even then were beginning to engulf America.

Otepka was a good sailor. He took no chances with the weather and he steered clear of the faster craft, large and small, that darted up and down and across the bay. Once, however, he got lost. Following a school of striped bass southward, night closed in and caught him in unfamiliar waters. Typically, he waited out the darkness, keeping his warning lights operating through the night. When dawn came he headed for his home port.

On this occasion his wife called the Coast Guard to look for him. She was not so much afraid of an accident; Otto was not apt to collide carelessly with another boat or run afoul of a jutting rock. There were other things that worried Edith, though she never let her husband know.

To a man so professionally isolated as Otepka the new friendships he formed during his exile took on a dimension one suspects did not exist at an earlier time. He had been so totally absorbed in his work for so many years that virtually all his social contacts had been extensions of his duties in the Department of State. There were exceptions, of course: the usual run of family relationships, old friends, suburban neighbors. But to an extraordinarily large degree the people he knew best and associated with most were men in the security and Intelligence community.

When the State Department placed him under criminal charges, it automatically cut him off from these people, though here too there were important exceptions. They did not so much shun him, as did the frightened residue in SY; he just did not seek them out any longer because he was aware that his status as an outcast might place them in jeopardy within their own agencies.

The new friends he made fell into several categories. The smallest of these were the newsmen who took an interest in his case, a half-dozen "regulars" who called him each time there was a new development, and a like number of irregulars who contacted him only occasionally.

There was a much larger group, too, that Otepka came to know and respect, a conglomerate comprised of people who might loosely be called his nonprofessional supporters. They resided in almost every state, with the heaviest concentrations in California and Illinois, and they came, quite literally, from every walk of American life. Most of them he never met. But they wrote him encouraging letters, bombarded the State Department, the Congress, and the White House with protests, and contributed to the fund set up to help offset his heavy legal expenses.

The man most responsible for this effort was James M. Stewart, a young sales executive in Wood Dale, Illinois, a suburb of Chicago. On his own hook, Stewart formed the American Defense Fund to raise money for Otepka's ever-mounting legal fees. By early 1968 nearly 2,500 people had contributed a total of some $25,000, mostly in small sums of under $10. Part of the money went to pay the lawyers retained by Jack Norpel and Howard Shea.

Stewart operated the fund out of his home, with his wife and children helping with the clerical work. In 1966 an investigator from a federal agency called on his boss, and a short time later Stewart was out of a job. No reason was given for his dismissal, though the boss told him, rather regretfully, "I hope I'm doing the right thing."

After losing his job, Stewart managed to reestablish himself in a home-appliance sales business of his own and continued to run the American Defense Fund. However, he and his family were subjected to various petty harassments, including what he called "nut telephone calls" that on one occasion went on all through the night at regular intervals.

Stewart's major difficulty, however, was not the cranks, but the U.S. Post Office Department. On three occasions Stewart had to ask the postal authorities to investigate apparent pilferage of his mail. A postal inspector agreed that one large manila envelope had been intentionally opened and clumsily resealed, but Stewart was never given a report on the result of the investigation. In the summer of 1967, a postal inspector did call on Otepka's attorney, Roger Robb. But he was not investigating Stewart's complaints. Rather, he was investigating Stewart!

Despite these aggravations, Jim Stewart and his wife kept right on with their work in behalf of Otepka. And Otepka was frank to admit that he probably could not have carried on his fight without their selfless help.

"I would have been in the poorhouse long ago if it had not been for Jim and his wife and all those people they rounded up to help pay the legal bills," he said in early 1968. At the time Otepka had just been forced to borrow $8,800 to pay the latest bill. But the Stewarts once again got to work and raised enough money to help pay the legal fees.

There was one other man who steadfastly gave Otepka encouragement throughout his long ordeal. He was Strom Thurmond, the senior Senator from South Carolina. Although Thurmond was not yet a member of the Subcommittee on Internal Security when the case first broke, he took an active interest in it from the start. He did more than lend words in support of Otepka on the Senate floor. He gave him a place of refuge.

Trapped in the diminishing confines of 38-A05 where his every word may have been recorded, his every move watched, Otepka needed more than anything a place where he could breathe and work freely. He could never be certain of his home, which had obviously been under surveillance once and where his phone continued to behave strangely for years. But through Senator Thurmond he found sanctuary.

The door to Senator Thurmond's own suite in the New Senate Office Building was always opened to Otepka. And the Senator's able staff never failed to make him welcome.

Moreover, the secretaries in Senator Thurmond's office also lent Otepka much valuable assistance. With no secretary of his own, he was often hard pressed to keep up his burgeoning correspondence. But Miss Dee Workman, the daughter of a South Carolina newspaper editor, and the other girls on the Senator's staff often stayed after working hours to do his typing.

"If it hadn't been for Senator Thurmond and his staff," Otepka confessed, "there were times when I may have been tempted to call the whole thing quits. But they never let me get to that point. You just don't think of quitting when you have people like Strom Thurmond behind you. I was often angered by the calcified image of the Senator projected by the press. I suspect the people writing those stories didn't know him very well. Strom Thurmond can be tough when there is a point of principle involved, but he is the most gracious, considerate human being I have ever met."

During the long wait for his State Department hearing, Otepka never missed an opportunity to add to his knowledge of the security situation in the government. In August 1966 his experienced eye was caught by a series of stories in the *Government Employees Exchange* describing the plight of Stephen A. Koczak, a Foreign Service officer who had been "selected out" several years earlier. The stories had a familiar ring, and before long he got the whole picture from Koczak himself.

A native of Trenton, New Jersey, Koczak had graduated cum laude from Harvard in 1942. Entering the Army, he served on General Eisenhower's staff during and after the war and stayed on as an officer in the military government in Germany. Koczak joined the State Department in 1946, and three years later he was expelled by the Communists from Hungary because he allegedly tried to help Cardinal Mindszenty.

Other assignments followed, both in Washington and abroad. Well known for his opposition to communism, Koczak could not expect quick advancement at State but he moved slowly up the ladder nonetheless. His work was so thorough that his superiors were hard-pressed to find fault. Never once did he receive a really bad efficiency report, and in 1960 he was commended for his "brilliant work" in Israel.

In September of that same year, Koczak was transferred to Berlin as deputy chief of Eastern Affairs at the U.S. Mission. In this capacity, he specialized in intelligence research on the Communist bloc. Soon, he found himself at odds with his immediate boss, Thomas A. Donovan, who had recently been eased out of the Warsaw embassy in the wake of the Goleniewski disclosures. One of the causes of their differences was that Donovan was continually playing host to numbers of visiting Poles, sometimes slipping into East Berlin to meet them secretly or to call a Polish girl friend he had left behind in Warsaw. On at least one occasion, Donovan made an unauthorized trip to Warsaw, ostensibly to see his Polish friends.

Donovan failed to report these contacts to security officials, as required by State Department regulations, and when they continued Koczak became more and more concerned. He was caught between two fires: if he reported Donovan he would be branded a stoolpigeon; if he maintained silence he would in effect be Donovan's accomplice.

Early in 1961 Koczak took up the matter with Howard Trivers, deputy to the assistant chief of the U.S. Mission in Berlin, Edwin Allan Lightner. From that moment on Koczak was marked for expulsion from the Department of State. Trivers and Lightner, who had been old classmates at Princeton many years before, teamed up with Donovan to doctor the efficiency reports on Koczak, and in 1963 they finally got him selected out of the Foreign Service. With seventeen years of faithful service to the State Department behind him, Koczak was out on his ear without any rights of appeal.

Moving to Washington, Koczak repeatedly tried to get the State Department to reconsider his enforced "retirement." One of the people he saw was Jules Bassin, chief of the Functional Personnel program division at State. Bassin warned Koczak that if he took his case to the press or to Congress he would only become "another Otepka."

Referring to Otepka as a "damned fool," Bassin held him up as an object lesson for Koczak and all other government servants who failed to "bend with the wind." Bassin told Koczak that Otepka was merely "sitting up there in his little room doing nothing, wasting his life." He said that Otepka "could have made a deal with us a long time ago . . . he could be a Consul General by now."

Instead, Bassin pointed out, Otepka insisted on carrying on a "petulant fight" which he couldn't possibly win. Otepka, he said, was "just a biological being" and eventually his liver would give out, his heart would give out, but the State Department as an institution would go on because it could not be destroyed.

Bassin referred to the late President Kennedy's book, *Profiles in Courage*, as so much hogwash. The television version, he said, was just something manufactured "for all those suckers out there to look at."

If Koczak followed Otepka's course, Bassin warned, he would meet the same fate. Moreover, he could not expect the State Department to give him a recommendation for another job. "If you're not reasonable and don't reconcile yourself to the facts of life," Koczak quoted Bassin as saying, "we can't really say you're very sober and you're very good."

In spite of this friendly warning, Koczak did decide to follow Otepka's course. In April 1966 he submitted a statement to a subcommittee of the Senate Foreign Relations Committee which was studying the Hays Bill, designed, as we have seen, to extend the "selection out" process to all employees of the State Department. Koczak vigorously opposed the bill, citing his own case as an example of what could happen on a much broader scale if it became law.

Later, in interviews with Sidney Goldberg, the crusading publisher of the *Government Employees Exchange*, Koczak went further in describing "the web of intrigue" which manipulated and altered personnel records in the State Department and suppressed vital information intended for the President.

The Koczak case added new impetus to Congressional demands for revitalization of the State Department's desiccated security program. Senator Eastland, backed by Dirksen, Hruska and Dodd, introduced the first of several bills designed to overhaul SY. Although Otepka was not mentioned by name, of course, the bill pointedly stated that the Office of Security "shall be headed by a director, who. . . . shall be chosen from individuals specially qualified by training and experience. . . ."[3] Moreover, it specifically barred Foreign Service officers from the job. Unfortunately, the bill died an untimely death in that second session of Lyndon Johnson's Great Society Congress.

Meanwhile, Otepka was moving slowly, but inexorably, towards the long-awaited State Department hearing. In the fall of 1965 the Department named a retired federal judge, E. Barrett Prettyman, as hearing officer. But after the release of the final volume of the subcommittee testimony in the Otepka case, Judge Prettyman bowed out.

Before retiring into the wings, Prettyman made several efforts to get the case settled. He held a series of meetings with Robb and two Justice Department attorneys assigned as prosecutors for the hearing, Irving Jaffe and Isaac Benkin. At the last of these on Thursday, October 27, Otepka and the lawyers were all present in Prettyman's chambers at the U.S. District Court in Washington.

After a lengthy conference, Otepka said he would agree to a settlement only if he was restored to his post and disciplinary action was taken against the people responsible for declassifying and mutilating the documents cited in the criminal charges. This would have been the equivalent of the Department's confessing its attempted frame-up, and everyone in the room knew that Dean Rusk would never permit such a confession.

As Otepka and Robb were preparing to leave, Judge Prettyman told them that if the case went to a hearing "somebody is going to get hurt."

Robb observed that he didn't see how his client could be hurt any more than he had been already. The old Judge looked Robb square in the eye and said in a slow, deliberate voice: *"Oh yes he can."*

Seven more months passed before Otepka got his hearing. The interval was marked by further behind-the-scenes attempts to squelch the case. Nicholas Katzenbach, Bobby Kennedy's successor as Attorney General, had moved into the State Department as Undersecretary, and was said to be in charge of the new efforts at compromise. Reliable reports had it that President Johnson gave Katzenbach firm instructions to settle the matter before it went any further.

In the spring of 1967 more tentative feelers were put out. Otepka heard that the State Department would agree to let him retire on a full pension that would bring him a reasonably good income for life, or it would help him find a job at increased pay in another government agency. He was given to understand that this would be absolutely the final offer. For the last time he said no.

The machinery for his hearing was finally set in motion. Robb and Otepka made one last effort to get an independent hearing officer to preside, naming several former outstanding jurists, including ex-Supreme Court Justice Charles Whittaker, as possibilities. The State Department ignored them and summarily appointed a Foreign Service officer with some legal background, Edward A. Dragon.

Otepka demanded an open hearing to which the press would have free access, but the Department insisted that it would be closed. Thus, after nearly four years under charges, Otto Otepka was finally brought to trial behind locked doors before a "judge" handpicked by the Department of State.

CHAPTER **XXXIX**

Star Chamber

IT WAS A LOVELY SOFT SUMMER MORNING. ONLY A FEW WHITE WISPS of cloud sailed the blue sky overhead as Otepka left his home in suburban Wheaton. He steered his aging Buick through the gracefully curving back streets to Connecticut Avenue and headed south toward the District line. At long last, Otepka was on his way toward his oft-delayed confrontation with the Department of State.

As he swung around Chevy Chase circle and crossed into the city of Washington, the 9 o'clock news served up the latest developments of the Arab-Israeli war which had erupted at dawn the day before. Israeli armored columns had hammered deep into the Sinai desert. They were reported within seventy-five miles of Suez. There was no mention, of course, about the Otepka hearing that was to begin at 10 a.m. On June 6, 1967, the Mideast crisis had blotted out virtually all other news.

Senator Eastland and a group of his colleagues had planned one last thundering salvo in support of Otepka on the Senate floor the previous afternoon. But when the Mideast exploded they decided to hold their fire. Nothing could possibly compete with the new war. The old one, in Vietnam, was wiped from the front pages and crowded off the airwaves. Otepka was to be tried in oblivion.

Turning left off Connecticut to get out of the heavy inbound traffic, he drove down along the beautiful Rock Creek Parkway. As he emerged onto Constitution Avenue the brooding statue of Lincoln looked out from the shadows of the imposing memorial a block away. At the other end of the mall, the soaring Washington Monument glistened in the morning sunlight. In this quarter, at least, the city had never seemed more majestic, more peaceful.

Promptly at 9:15 a.m. Otepka entered the State Department garage, stopping at the bottom of the ramp to show his official pass to the polite Negro guard. He found a parking place near the elevators and unloaded four large leather bags crammed with the material he had been storing up for forty-four months.

On the first floor several television crews guarded the main entrance, waiting hopefully for Secretary of State Rusk or some other Department dignitary to enlighten the country on the confusing situation in the Mideast. None of the TV men seemed to recognize Otepka as he came out of the elevators carrying his bags.

Near the entrance to Room 1410, the suite where President Kennedy had primped for his press conferences, only one reporter was waiting. In a clipped, rather British accent he introduced himself as Nick Danoloff of UPI. Regretfully, Otepka said he could not answer any questions. Danoloff expressed the wish that he could attend the hearings. "I wish you could too," Otepka smiled. They both shook their heads.

Otepka and Roger Robb had continued to protest the closing of the hearing to the press right down to the eleventh hour. Some newspapers, and even the American Civil Liberties Union, made the protest public. But the Department stood firm. Nothing could raise Rusk's iron curtain.

In the reception area of 1410 the door to the hearing room opened and the "judge" burst through, breezily shaking the defendant's hand. Hearing Officer Edward Dragon looked, at 38, like a model bureaucrat. Heavy spectacles hid part of his large, bland face under a sloping forehead and receding dark hair. A native of Rhode Island, he was a product of Tom Dodd's alma mater, Providence College, of Georgetown Law School, and of CIA, where he had worked as an "intelligence analyst."

Dragon exchanged pleasantries with the man he was to help Dean Rusk judge and, since it was still quite early, Otepka deposited his bags and went to the little automatic commissary at the lower end of the main lobby for coffee. It is an impressive lobby, with the flags of all the United Nations hanging above the glass façade that gives onto a large courtyard opposite the main entrance. At the other end of the long lobby stands a handsome statue presented to the United States in 1965 by the government of Greece. It is a replica of an original found at Piraeus, the port of Athens, and is believed to be a likeness of Melpomene, the Muse of tragedy.

From her marble eyes, Melpomene, or whoever, stared blankly at the tall dark man waiting patiently for the curtain to rise on the latest act of a drama that rivaled the tragedies in her ancient repertoire. Soon the other players began to appear. At 9:43 the prosecutor, Irving Jaffe, strode purposefully across the lobby, a grim little man with wavy gray hair and a determined look in his eye. Trailing a step or two behind came his young assistant, Isaac Benkin, weighed down with bulging briefcases. Exactly one minute later Roger Robb arrived. Smiling encouragingly, he walked with Otepka to the hearing room. The door shut behind them, barring the proceedings from the public eye and ear. Otepka's long ordeal had begun its final phase.

The State Department hearing into the dismissal charges leveled against Otepka was to last four weeks, all through the remaining part of June. The record came to fill some two thousand typed pages, each one supposedly secret. For Prosecutor Jaffe's first act, after withdrawing the ten criminal charges that had blackened Otepka's name for nearly four years, was to request that the entire proceedings be branded "Classified."

Roger Robb vigorously protested this move. He pointed out that not even the Oppenheimer hearings before the Atomic Energy Commission's Gray Board had been classified in toto. Only those sections dealing with technical information on atomic weapons had been withheld. The rest of the Oppenheimer transcript had actually been published.

The Otepka hearing could not possibly disclose information that would in any way be damaging to the national security. It was certain, however, to prove damaging to the Johnson Administration and the State Department, and that, of course, was reason enough for Jaffe's request to keep the record secret, and for the earlier decision to bar the press.

The basis for the request was utterly ridiculous. It was rooted in the fact that the three remaining charges against Otepka dealt with certain classified documents. But these same documents had already been published by the Senate Internal Security Subcommittee and they had been widely reported in the press.

Nonetheless, "Judge" Dragon granted the prosecution's request. The record was classified and the pattern thereby set for a show trial that bore a curious resemblance to those charades that pass for trials in Moscow and Peiping. Indeed, the resemblance is so strong as to make them virtually identical, one with the other. For judgment had already been pronounced on Otepka just as surely as it had been passed on the trio of Russian intellectuals who were to stand trial in Moscow some months later. The only difference is that even in Moscow such trials are conducted more or less in the open of late, while in the Department of State the whole proceeding from beginning to end was conducted in the utmost secrecy.

A few trickles of information did leak out, however. Stories appeared in the press that the ten criminal charges against Otepka had been dropped and that the hearing record had been classified. This prompted the State Department to threaten the defense. On Friday, the fourth day of the hearing, Jaffe said his "client" had noted the leaks.

"I have been requested to apprise the attorney for Mr. Otepka of executive orders safeguarding official information in the interests and safety of the United States," Jaffe stated.

"Who requested this admonition?" demanded Robb.

"It's not an admonition, but an *instruction,*" replied Jaffe with a meaningful nod.

"Tell your client, the State Department, I shall give it the consideration to which it is entitled," said Robb, refusing to bow before the threat.

Fortunately, however, the State Department was operating at its usual high level of efficiency. Having gone to such extremes in keeping the record secret, it completely forgot to place the official stamp "Classified" on the transcripts delivered to the parties concerned. Therefore, it will be no crime to summarize briefly that astounding record here.

Only three witnesses testified during the entire four weeks—Otepka, Sourwine and, most reluctantly, Reilly. Robb and Otepka purposely refrained from calling all the other members of the shillelagh brigade, and perhaps Dean Rusk, and other high officials, deciding to save them against the day when the case might get into a proper courtroom.

Otepka took the stand first, and was seated at the conference table occupied by Jaffe and Benkin. Immediately, Jaffe attempted to lay the basis for Otepka's alleged violation of the Truman directive of March 13, 1948, on which the whole case now rested. He asked Otepka if he had read Secretary Rusk's "testimony" before the Senate subcommittee where Rusk had quoted the Truman order and stated that "Neither I nor any of my subordinates should be asked to violate that directive."

Isn't that part of the policy of the State Department, Jaffe inquired? Otepka owned that "the Secretary has quoted correctly from the Presidential directive." But he refused to "accept any inference in there that

I violated any provisions of that directive." He made the point that all of the material he had given Sourwine on Andrew Cordier and the rest had already been in the public domain.* Moreover, he showed that Dean Rusk had himself waived the old Truman order when it suited him.

Thus, the duel began. It very quickly became obvious that Irving Jaffe was not only outmatched but rather woefully unprepared. Strange as it may seem, much of the State Department's case hinged on the published record of the Senate Subcommittee. But there were whole broad expanses of that record where Jaffe simply drew a blank. It was apparent that he had been primed, but not really informed, by Department officials whose dirty linen he was being forced to launder.

For example, in a futile attempt to show that Otepka had been dilatory in the handling of security cases, Jaffe brought up the name of one Philip Raine. He asked Otepka what the Raine case was about and drew a succinct reply.

Otepka said that the Raine business centered on alleged Communist activity. Raine was a friend of Robert T. Miller III, who had been dismissed from the State Department on security grounds. Miller had run a Leftist publication called *The Hemisphere,* and Raine had worked with him on it.**

After a half-dozen more questions on Raine, Otepka was moved to remark: "I don't know what you have in mind in bringing up this subject."

"Frankly, Mr. Otepka," Jaffe frowned in bewilderment, *"I don't know what it means either. . . ."*

Jaffe was equally at sea in dealing with the intricacies of the internal security laws and regulations, but that is entirely understandable. One really has to live with them for years, as Otepka did, to plumb their murky depths. Frequently the defendant took pity on the prosecutor and tried to help him by patiently explaining the law.

More puzzling, however, was the unbelievable weakness of the central *raison d'être* of the prosecution's case. Jaffe built his argument on the specious contention that Otepka's *only* duty was to obey the orders of his superiors. Just one of many instances of the essential frailty of this thesis is seen in Jaffe's questioning of Otepka about his protests against

---

* There was one exception, as Jaffe noted. The document on Harlan Cleveland's advisory committee contained information about one of the members, Lawrence Finklestein, that was not a matter of public record. During World War II Finklestein had been declared ineligible for military service because of "psychiatric" reasons. The subcommittee had subsequently deleted this information from the published record of its Otepka hearings.
**Philip Raine was named a Consul General in 1963, posted to Rio de Janeiro in August 1965, and made a Minister on March 17, 1966.

he clearance Bobby Kennedy had rammed through for Frank Montero:

Jaffe: Was not your responsibility and obligation fully discharged, Mr. Otepka, when you expressed your opinion . . . that the background investigation did not resolve the information that appeared in the file, and submitted that to your superiors? Didn't that discharge your responsibility?

Otepka: No sir, not my responsibility as chief evaluator, and as a person sworn to uphold and defend all the laws of the United States. . . . I do not think I am fulfilling my obligation by permitting a case to be buried without derogatory security factors being amply resolved.

Jaffe seemed incapable of understanding this line of reasoning. To him there was no higher law than the wishes of one's boss, or so he tried to make the "court" believe.

Roger Robb did a brilliant job in his opening statement on June 7, flinging wide many doors of argument for the defense that might otherwise have been shut. He contended that the papers Otepka gave Sourwine and the Senate subcommittee were "not within the scope" of the Truman directive "construed in the circumstances of this case."

"The papers contained . . . not loyalty or security information in the proper sense of that term," Robb said. "There was no loyalty case pending or contemplated against any of the persons involved." The classification of those documents was, he stressed, immaterial in this instance "since Mr. Sourwine in his official capacity and the members of the (Senate) committee were authorized to receive such documents."

He argued persuasively that it was Otepka's duty to produce these documents for the subcommittee, "a duty that was imposed by his oath to tell the truth." If Otepka had failed to take this action, Robb pointed out, he would have condoned and shielded John Reilly's perjury.

For Otepka to have sought redress through his superiors in the Department of State would have been a "vain and futile thing" when those same superiors had been out "to destroy or get Otepka by fair means or foul," Robb declared.

Against the charge that Otepka had conducted himself "in a manner unbecoming an officer of the Department of State," Robb promised to produce evidence that the conduct of many other Department officials was truly notorious and dangerous, yet they had been promoted, not dismissed.

More than that, he stated, "the evidence will show that these charges (against Otepka) were the culmination of a conspiracy, beginning as early as 1960, to get rid of Otepka by a relentless campaign of harassment and reprisal, by surrounding him with unfriendly and disloyal associates, by wiretapping, by clandestine surveillance . . . and finally on the part of his immediate superiors, by perjury."

Robb said "the proof will show" that the motivation behind the plot to oust Otepka was simply that he had "consistently and resolutely insisted that sound and proper security practices he observed by the Department of State" and that he worked constantly to "discover and eliminate employees in the Department who were security risks and to prevent the appointment of persons who might become security risks."

In contrast, Robb went on, the evidence would prove that his superiors—"Reilly and Belisle and those above them"—"constantly endeavored to relax or bypass security restrictions or standards. . . ."

"The result of all this for Otepka was inevitable," Robb concluded. "When he refused to submit passively, while the security system for which he was responsible was being destroyed—when he testified about the situation frankly and honestly before the Congressional committee—his superiors determined that he himself must be destroyed."

When Robb had finished, Jay Sourwine lumbered to the witness chair. He described how the discrepancies had developed between the sworn statements of Reilly and Otepka. "I have seldom seen such sharp conflict between the testimony of two people working in the same shop," he said.

Sourwine told how he had made it clear to Otepka that it was "up to him to put up or shut up." "His boss, in effect, had called him a liar, and if he had any evidence to support what he told us, I wanted him to bring the evidence in and put it in the record."

Jaffe tried hard to trip Sourwine. But he made the mistake of attempting to set his snares with Reilly's testimony, which, as Sourwine said, were "full of evasions, dodging, half-truths and plain lies." At first the subcommittee chief counsel declined to speculate on Reilly's motivation, but finally he offered the opinion that "Mr. Reilly was trapped in a sense by his own ego. He would frequently pull answers out of thin air which I knew . . . were not the truth, or at best only a half-truth. And then he would begin hedging and seek to justify them as much as he could. . . ."

Sourwine wound up his testimony on the third afternoon of the hearing. The following morning, a Friday, Otepka went back on the stand, there to stay for the next three weeks with time out only for the weekends and for one or two other recesses. It was the culmination of his long ordeal. But it soon became apparent that it was much, much more than that.

CHAPTER XL

The Nation on Trial

THE TESTIMONY OF OTTO OTEPKA AT HIS JUNE 1967 TRIAL, RANGING
as it did over more than two decades of the ineffectual struggle against
Communist subversion, must stand as one of the most remarkable *tours
de force* in the long legal history of the English-speaking world. Hour
after hour, day after day he built his case. Before the inexorable march
of his evidence and the incisive slashes of his ruthless logic, the specious
arguments of the Department of State withered and fell, like shrunken
leaves fluttering down from a dead and rotted tree.

Even the men who were forced to serve as his prosecutors must soon
have realized that it was not the defendant Otepka who was on trial; it
was the Department of State and, in reality, the Government of the
United States.

The primary reason, indeed the sole rational justification, for the existence of any government is the protection of the people under its care
from enemies within and without. But in the testimony of Otto Otepka
it became crystal-clear that the American government had failed and was
continuing to fail in this primary responsibility.

Against the onslaught of a system irretrievably dedicated to the destruction of America, the government had for thirty years and more
wavered and dallied, compromised and cooperated. Brave men had died

in dozens of battles and anonymous skirmishes from Korea to Vietnam to protect their country against the ever-encroaching juggernaut, while behind their backs the weak and depraved had sold their sacrifices piece-meal, and sometimes in carload lots.

By refusing to stand against subversion, by retreating before the hys-terical criticisms of a conditioned minority, by forever seeking accommo-dation with an enemy that could never be accommodated, the politicians had permitted the few rotten apples to contaminate the whole barrel. They had winked at the perversion of their own policies, and blanched at every confrontation with reality. They had courted the zombies who sought to destroy them, and cut down the people like Otepka who tried to defend them and their country. They had curried favor with the enemy, while the enemy stole America's military secrets and adapted them to the building of a mighty war machine.

Otepka did not actually *say* any of these things, of course. But they are all implicit in the record. Beginning with his exposure of the policies that had promoted John Stewart Service for aiding in the fall of China to the coddling of William Wieland for abetting the Communist capture of Cuba, Otepka laid bare the skeletons that rattled in every State Depart-ment closet and haunted every major policy failure.

He told of his meeting in December 1960 with Bobby Kennedy and Dean Rusk, and for the first time identified Walt W. Rostow as the principal subject of discussion. He did not disclose all the reasons why Rostow had been deemed a security risk by Air Force Intelligence and twice denied a clearance by the State Department. But he revealed just enough to call into serious question the judgment of the men who had elevated Rostow both at the White House and at State, the same men who based the fundamental U.S. foreign policy of the 1960's on Rostow's theories of a "nationless" world.

In dealing with the security waivers that suddenly mushroomed under Dean Rusk, Otepka showed how the cancerous cells that had retreated to obscure corners of the body politic during the Eisenhower Administra-tion had burst forth from their hiding places to join the new invasion. He told how Harlan Cleveland had been brought in despite the recommen-dation of Emery Adams, former chief of the Evaluations Division, that Cleveland be denied a security clearance. He disclosed how Irving Swerdlow, fired once as a security risk, had returned under Cleveland's protection. He revealed why Reilly had become so incensed over his handling of the Seymour Janow file, and why Abba Schwartz had been given a highly sensitive clearance he had no business holding.

Otepka disclosed how the FBI had been shunted aside so investigations could be conducted by the more malleable Office of Security. One such case involved a Foreign Service officer named John L. Topping, who had espoused the Wieland line during Castro's rise to power. Without an FBI investigation, Topping was cleared with William Boswell's connivance and later appointed as the alternate U.S. representative to the Council of the Organization of American States.

Otepka explained why he had opposed the transfer of the Intelligence reporting function from his office to the Bureau of Intelligence and Research. A probe into the backgrounds of that bureau's personnel had revealed, he said, "a large concentration of persons evaluating intelligence information who had records of activities and associations with Communists."

To refute the charge that he had conducted himself in a manner unbecoming an officer of the State Department, Otepka ticked off a long list of officials who had set the tone for truly reprehensible conduct in the Department. He said that his act of giving information to the Senate should, in fairness, be judged against the standards set by these people, many of whom had been rewarded with promotions while had had been dismissed. He did not often name names, but it is worth reviewing a few of the cases he cited:

• • • A Foreign Service officer who admitted that he engaged in homosexual acts. The Department's medical officers declared him unfit to serve abroad again because his homosexual tendencies made him a potential security risk. Yet he was given an assignment in a critical post behind the Iron Curtain.

• • • Another Foreign Service officer whose past membership in the Young Communist League and the Communist Party was proved beyond doubt though he had concealed this information on his application form. Yet, he was still employed in the State Department.

• • • A security officer stationed in Moscow who permitted himself to be enticed by a woman agent into a tryst which was photographed by her KGB employers. Although he had exposed himself to the most elemental recruitment tactics known to the greenest novice, he was never disciplined.

• • • Another security officer in an Eastern European country who lectured his associates on avoiding personal relationships with foreign nationals while openly maintaining a mistress reported to be a Communist agent. When he divorced his wife, the Department gave him permission to marry his mistress and he continued to serve as a security officer.

• • • A Foreign Service officer who borrowed money from the Department credit union by forging the endorsement of a woman employee to his application for the loan. When he admitted the forgery, he was rewarded with an important assignment in the White House.

• • • A Foreign Service officer who sexually violated his own daughter but was never disciplined. In fact he was later designated as a part-time security officer at a post which did not have a full-time professional, giving him, in effect, the right to pass judgment on his colleagues.

All of these cases had come to Otepka's attention in recent years. He listed a score of them and admitted that he was "familiar with scores and scores of other cases" of people who had flouted the most elementary rules of honesty, discretion and normal behavior.

"I did not hold that these persons . . . were security risks in the terms of the definition of Executive Order 10450," Otepka said. "But management, with due regard for maintaining high standards, could have at least prevented the majority of these individuals from obtaining key positions where their motivations and weaknesses would not have been prejudicial to the conduct of our foreign policy."

In the light of these revelations, the Department's charge that Otepka had failed to live up to its standards was ludicrous on its face.

By way of answering the related charge that Otepka had fed out classified information to "unauthorized" persons, Robb led his client into a brief review of cases where secret material had been handed over by State Department officials to people who did not have clearances like Jay Sourwine and the members of the Senate subcommittee. The most notorious recipient of classified documents was, of course, Drew Pearson, the Left's muckraking hatchetman. Otepka testified that the Office of Security had "at least two file cabinets full of material consisting of investigations relating to leaks of information to Drew Pearson."

This, of course, is the same Drew Pearson who railed for years against Congressman and Senators attempting to expose Communists and other Leftist subversives in the federal government and who castigated Otepka for giving information to the Senate subcommittee. To Otepka's knowledge, no State Department official had ever been reprimanded for secretly feeding classified material to Pearson, a man whom three Presidents had branded a liar.

Cross-examining Otepka on June 19, Jaffe made a feeble attempt at showing that the defendant had a persecution complex. He kept asking him to identify the people who were out to get rid of him. Referring to the Senate subcommittee's record, Otepka first named Boswell and Roger Jones. Then the following exchange took place:

Jaffe: Who (else) entered into your mind?

Otepka: A high official of another government agency.

Jaffe: Would you identify him please?

Otepka: . . . It had to enter my mind in the sequence of events as they were developing. The person was Robert Kennedy.

Not surprisingly, Jaffe quickly steered the testimony away from his former Justice Department boss. But he then made the mistake of similarly forcing Otepka to name Dean Rusk. "What has Secretary of State Rusk said or done," Jaffe asked, "to make you believe that he is at all interested in removing you from the Office of Security?"

"In that respect," replied Otepka, "I will rely on his own testimony and on the testimony of Mr. Reilly and Mr. Hill and Mr. Belisle as to what he has done."

Once again, Jaffe was caught short. He tried to cover his mistake by quoting excerpts from Rusk's statement before the Senate subcommittee and asked Otepka if that was what he was referring to. It was one of the very few times during the whole hearing that Otepka chose to fire back in anger.

"Now let me talk about what you just read," Otepka said. "He [Rusk] said, 'this evidence [against Otepka], if true, seemed to me on its face to present some serious questions of security in the Department.' *What kind of security is he talking about?* Is the inference there that I violated the national security by testifying truthfully to the United States Congress?

" . . . I am considering the innuendoes which are implicit in those remarks, which subsequently were repeated over and over and over again in the hundreds and hundreds of press releases issued by the State Department, and letters sent by the State Department to committees of Congress, to individual Congressmen and Senators, and to the general public—always repeating exactly what Mr. Rusk said: that Mr. Otepka, in effect, violated the national security."

Jaffe tried to back-pedal by pointing out that Rusk had said "questions of security—not national security." But Otepka refused to separate the two. "He was talking, sir, about *security,*" he retorted. "Security, as we understand it in our security community, means practices relating to the national security."

The prosecution retired in obvious disorder and abruptly dropped the sensitive subject of security. But Otepka wouldn't let Rusk off that easy. He raked the Secretary and the State Department over some more exceedingly hot coals, especially the attempted burn-bag frame-up. Jaffe wanted no part of that one either, but Otepka wasn't done. He documented Dean Rusk's deep involvement in the vendetta against him every step of the way. In addition, he proved that Rusk had personally approved the compounded perjury of Reilly, Hill and Belisle by instigating and okaying their lying letters of "clarification" to the subcommittee.

Completely routed, Jaffe abandoned the field after having innocently helped to prove Dean Rusk's complicity. He valiantly tried to salvage what, if anything, was left of the Secretary's credibility by weakly suggesting that Rusk had no prior knowledge of the wiretaps, but Otepka refused to leave him even that.

All that Jaffe had accomplished in trying to nail the defendant as a paranoiac was to substantiate further the facts of the conspiracy that had cast Otepka out of the Office of Security.

At times it was apparent that the hearing was primarily a fishing expedition, conducted in secrecy to find out just how much Otepka knew. Sensing this, Otepka refused to nibble at the bait. He did not tell a hundredth part of what he knew, though he told enough to convict Dean Rusk and his hired hands for conspiracy in any impartial court of law.

Otepka spent the fourth anniversary of his banishment from SY under cross-examination for the fifth day. Jaffe was fishing again, trying to get Otepka to reveal how much he remembered from the files that had been wrested from him on June 27, 1963. The prosecutor insisted that Otepka had been dilatory in his duty, that he had sat on cases assigned to him. This had become the latest line of argument, plagiarized directly from Reilly's testimony before the subcommittee. Jaffe couldn't make it stick, any more than Reilly had, but he gave it the old college try, only to get thrown for another loss.

The prosecution absorbed yet one more setback two days later when Reilly himself finally appeared. He had not made up his mind until a few days before whether he would grace the hearing with his presence. When

Robb asked him about the delay in his reaching a decision Reilly said he feared "further harassment."

Reilly sat heavily in the witness chair, his stomach protruding over his belt when he opened his coat jacket. The ruddy face was beginning to show traces of purple veins and the close-cropped dark hair had more gray in it now. Squinting nervously, he asked "Judge" Dragon if he might chew mints while he testified. Permission was granted and within a few hours he had polished off a pack.

Robb began by establishing just how Reilly had come to join the State Department in 1962. His appointment to head SY was swiftly traced to Bobby Kennedy's office at Justice. Reilly admitted that he had told the Senate subcommittee that "one of my assignments was to find out if there had been people furnishing information" to others outside the Department. But he could "give no details on it."

Reilly had, in fact, suffered a monumental loss of memory about most everything. "My memory for detail going back to those days is not at all precise," he confessed repeatedly. Robb was gentle with him, nevertheless. He had dealt with legal amnesia victims before, and at least with this one there was the damning record already made before the Senate subcommittee. By and large, Robb was content to rest on that, though Reilly would have much preferred not to, of course.

Not surprisingly, Reilly did recall with perfect clarity the position he had taken before the subcommittee on the wiretap business, and he clung to it tenaciously. Still, he was fuzzy about the names of the people on the Seventh Floor with whom he had discussed his surveillance of Otepka in March of 1963. When Robb asked him if he had discussed his suspicions about Otepka with anyone outside SY, Reilly squinted hard and then replied: "I honestly can't say that I did. I just don't have any.... I don't have any recollection of anything along that line."

It suddenly came to him, however, that he had admitted to the subcommittee that he *had* talked with William Orrick, Crockett's predecessor. But he caught himself just in time and swore that he had not informed Orrick that he intended to mount a watch on Otepka.

He slipped once rather badly, though. Robb trapped him into admitting that he actually planned to intercept *all* "conversations going on in [Otepka's] office", not merely telephone chats. This escalated Reilly's surveillance from the status of a phone tap to a "bug"—a listening device that could pick up every word. There was nothing new in this, of course, aside from Reilly's admission.

There was nothing new, either, in the fact that Reilly continued to commit flagrant perjury. He swore over and over that he could not remember whether any of Otepka's private conversations had been intercepted and refused to name the mysterious "stranger" Elmer Hill had admitted delivering the tapes to on Reilly's order.

The State Department had already confessed the existence of the tapes, though when Robb demanded them for the present hearing it took the Department more than a week to discover that the tapes had been "erased." (In 1968 it was charged that the tapes had been turned over to an aide of Bobby Kennedy.)

Reilly didn't seem to care anymore whether people believed him or not. He wore his "amnesia" with noticeable weariness, claiming that it had afflicted him as early as the fall of 1963 when he sat down with Undersecretary of State George Ball and Department attorney Thomas Ehrlich to discuss Senator Dodd's charges about the wiretap.

Robb did get Reilly to admit that he had been informed rather promptly about the letter Dodd took to Rusk in New York. But he clung to the long-established State Department line that Stanley Holden had been injured in an accident right after the letter was delivered. "The spring just released and caught him by surprise," Reilly claimed. His memory was quite clear on that.

Jaffe and Dragon tried to come to Reilly's rescue several times but Robb did not oppose them too strenuously. "I understand," he said sadly. "I think the witness' answers speak for themselves." One Reilly answer that spoke quite eloquently for itself was his assertion that he had "no knowledge one way or the other" as to who actually mutilated the documents found in Otepka's burn bag.

For some odd reason Reilly claimed that he was not involved in referring the Otepka case to the FBI and the Justice Department in the summer of 1963. *"I understand that was done up at least Crockett's level,"* he said. It was the closest Reilly came to pointing a finger at Dean Rusk. Crockett, by the Secretary's own admission, was in daily contact with him on the situation in SY throughout this period. Thus there is a very strong indication here that it was Rusk's idea to enlist the FBI in the attempt to have charges placed against Otepka for violation of the Espionage Act. If the idea did not originate with him, he certainly had to approve it, and this of itself is rather revealing evidence of Dean Rusk's personal philosophy.

Despite this temporary lapse, Reilly played all the rest of the game that day strictly according to the bureaucratic code. He continued to protect all high officials as much as possible; his job at the Federal Communications Commission was at stake, and this was all poor Reilly had left to him.

It was a dismal performance throughout. Irving Jaffe barely roused himself in an attempt to refute one or two small points Robb had made during his questioning. Then he let Reilly go. Jaffe was obviously glad to be rid of him.

Once again, Reilly comes close to evoking pity. Otepka admits he almost felt sorry for him on that June day. He had to remind himself of the terrible issues involved to get Reilly back in proper focus.

The reel had run out. Otepka's hearing was at an end. Technically it was kept open to give counsel for both sides time to file their briefs. But the defendant's day in court was over. The proceedings had been conducted in a star chamber, but he had managed to illuminate many dark corners. The American people were not permitted to glimpse the curious people and policies that his testimony revealed and Otepka wisely disclosed no more than he had to. But the record is there for posterity. Generations to come might look to that record, if they can find it, for an insight into the bewildering events of the 1960's. They might also discover another clue in the secret talks that were held at Glassboro, New Jersey, over the last weekend in June 1967.

The Otepka hearing was in its final recess when Lyndon Johnson met with Soviet Premier Aleksei Kosygin at Glassboro State College. With the President was his chief advisor on national security, Walt Rostow, and a handful of other American officials. The summit conference was ostensibly prompted by the Mideast crisis but it ranged over a wide field. It was accompanied by much mawkish talk about grandfathers, a club Johnson had just recently joined.

"He has been a grandfather longer than I have," the President said, referring to Kosygin. "He and I agreed that we wanted a world of peace for our grandchildren."

Kosygin disclosed just how much that kind of talk meant to him when he returned to the United Nations on Monday to resume his attack on U.S. "aggression" in Vietnam and elsewhere. The summit had left him and Johnson far apart, Kosygin clearly indicated.[1]

It was a rude slap at the President, who had offered the Soviet Union all kinds of goodies if it would just let the United States off the hook in Vietnam. Although the public was never informed, Johnson magnanimously promised the equivalent of billions of dollars in trade and aid to the USSR if Kosygin would help find a formula to save America's face in the Far East. Kosygin was willing to take whatever Johnson would give him, of course, but he had no intention of giving anything in return.

At the U.N. he did present some gratuitous advice, however. It was a line he had stolen from the American "doves." Unless the arms race ceased, Kosygin said, it would siphon off even greater funds that all nations should be investing in "the improvement of the living standard of the people."

While the Soviet Premier talked in New York, Russia was engaged in doubling its intercontinental missile force during 1967, greatly increasing its supply of nuclear-grade weapons materials, producing more and bigger space weapons, frantically building an anti-ballistic missile system, and in general strengthening its already awesome armed might. Despite Kosygin's pious advice about living standards, all this was being accomplished at the expense of the Russian people. For in the Soviet Union consumer production is deliberately kept at a low level to divert all available resources into the maw of the Central Committee's war machine.*

Although relatively few Americans realized it, their government was already substantially aiding the Soviet buildup when Johnson pledged additional help at Glassboro. In 1966 the President had taken the initiative in opening wider trade channels to Russia. U.S. shipments to the Soviet Bloc included such "innocent" items as petroleum cracking plants, copper scrap, electronic parts, computers, chemicals, steel processing plants and a host of other matériel that could be used either directly in the Soviet military buildup, or indirectly by permitting Soviet production to devote more and more of its tremendous effort to armament.

As early as 1965 David Dubinsky, president of the International Ladies Garment Workers Union, expressed deep concern about this policy. Communist governments "are working overtime to hurt and destroy us," Dubinsky declared. "Where is the sense in making a few dollars in profits one day and then facing the danger of losing your country, your business and even your very life the next day?"[2]

Dubinsky blamed the business community, and no doubt it must share some of the blame. But in the late 1960's it was becoming increasingly difficult for business to resist policies imposed upon it by Washington,

* This Soviet policy was documented by the Senate Internal Security Subcommittee as early as 1964 in its penetrating report, "The Many Crises of the Soviet Economy." "The Soviet military establishment is indeed impressively equipped and it would be foolish to underestimate it," the Senate report said. "The industry which feeds this establishment has been built up, without regard to cost, by ruthlessly starving virtually every other sector of the Soviet economy."

especially when a determined President pushes them so hard.

Many of the men who promulgated these policies of building trade bridges to the East had been named in other contexts by Otto Otepka during his secret hearing. It was not such an arduous task for him to understand why America was sending millions of dollars in goods to the Soviet Bloc, though most other citizens were as baffled by this policy as David Dubinsky. Tragically, the American forces in Vietnam suffered most from it. For the country was slowly becoming aware that the overwhelming bulk of the weapons being used against its men in that far-off war was coming in a steady stream from Russia and its captive satellites in Eastern Europe.

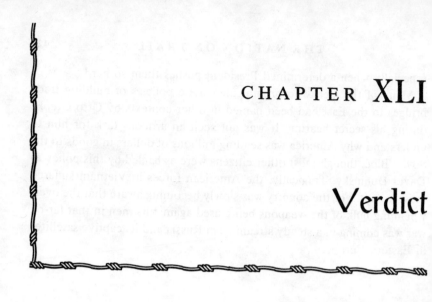

CHAPTER XLI

Verdict

NEARLY SIX MORE MONTHS DRAGGED BY AFTER OTEPKA'S STATE DE-
partment hearing before Secretary of State Rusk handed down his decision toward the very end of 1967. The world continued to spin dizzily
onward, but it was during these same months that many people belatedly
awakened to the fact that their planet had changed, perhaps irrevocably.
America, once so supremely self-confident, seemed to be losing its sense
of direction, at home as well as abroad.

The war in Vietnam bogged down in more death and bloodshed. Peace
protests swelled and grew more ugly, with demonstrators attacking the
Pentagon, draft offices, and every public hall where Administration
spokesmen tried to air their uncertain views. In Stockholm, President
Johnson was tried as a "war criminal" by Bertrand Russell's Tribunal of
the Left. Devaluation of the British pound in the fall brought heavy
pressure on the dollar, and doubts were openly expressed about the basic
soundness of the U.S. economy. On the fiftieth anniversary of the Bolshevik revolution, the Soviets unveiled more terrifying weapons of mass
destruction for their "final phase." And in the streets of America's once
proud cities the watchword that summer was "Burn, baby, burn."

As Otepka waited for his preordained fate to be formally announced,
full-scale rioting erupted in Newark and Detroit and scores of other

communities, large and small. The Administration continued to play down the role of militant Leftists in the mounting disorders, both on the "civil rights" front and in the anti-Vietnam demonstrations now firmly merged with the Negro protest movement. But many Police Departments knew, or sensed, that the rioters were better organized, and certainly better armed that summer. The lengthening list of casualties was testimony to that.

The Newark and Detroit uprisings brought the casualty toll in Negro riots since 1965 to 130 dead and 3,623 wounded. Of the wounded, 1,199 were policemen. Nearly 29,000 arrests had been made, but less than 20 percent resulted in convictions. Whole sections of cities were burned out; the Senate's McClellan subcommittee counted 7,985 separate cases of arson in 101 major riots over the two-year period. Property losses were now totaled in hundreds of millions.[1]

"It is apparent that a new philosophy has flourished in recent years," said Senator McClellan. It has "as its central theme the theory that we are no longer a nation of laws."[2]

Otepka had discovered that in 1961, and he knew full well that Dean Rusk would prove it again in 1967. The internal security laws may have been among the first to go, but there were many other laws that had become largely meaningless in the new climate. There was a new one, too, that summer, a law which quickly became perhaps the most cynically used of them all. It was the "Freedom of Information Act" which President Johnson had signed the year before but which did not go into effect until July 4, 1967. It was supposed to guarantee the press and the public access to all but the most highly classified secrets of the United States government.

The very first test of this law came in connection with the Otepka case. The State Department had barely opened its brand-new "freedom of information" office when in walked James M. Stewart of Wood Dale, Illinois. He formally requested all the records on the Otepka matter, including the transcript of the hearing that had just ended. As director of the American Defense Fund which was assisting Otepka with his legal expenses, Stewart reasoned that the several thousand citizens on his mailing list had a valid right to this information under the law. Donald J. Simon, chief of the Department's records service division, solemnly promised Stewart "as much information as is possible under State's regulations."

"Seventy-six days later, after repeated rebuffs," wrote Willard Edwards in mid-September, "Stewart has been forced to the conclusion that 'the State Department either reads this law differently than I do or various responsible officials have not read it at all.' "[3]

Much the same conclusion was reached by the Freedom of Information Committee of Sigma Delta Chi, the national journalism professional society. In an incisive report documenting dozens of breakdowns in the law, and in the spirit of the law before it formally went into effect, the committee cited the State Department for its "outrageous pattern of deception" in the Otepka case.

"The State Department secrecy in this instance was an obvious effort to hide a record that is embarrassing to Secretary of State Dean Rusk and other high officials," the journalists held. " . . . A study of this entire case makes it obvious that the State Department was misusing a claim of national security for purposes of hiding or obscuring the record."*

Individual Senators and Congressmen continued to take up the cudgel for Otepka, although they knew they were fighting for a lost cause. In late September Senator Roman Hruska of Nebraska placed an editorial from the Omaha *World-Herald* in the *Congressional Record*, prefacing it with a brief but penetrating statement.

"It will do the Administration little good to try to sweep the Otepka case under the rug or to wish it into oblivion," said Hruska. "Many of us in government and many private citizens will recall often the shameful treatment accorded Mr. Otepka by the State Department. The indefensible way the Department tried to eliminate a conscientious security officer has been etched indelibly in our minds."[4]

Hruska correctly observed that Otepka's fate had also been etched into the minds of all security people. "It will take exceptional courage for these security experts to oppose their superiors, even in cases of clear danger to the nation," he concluded. "It is here that America will pay most heavily for what has happened to Otto Otepka."

The Omaha paper's editorial similarly zeroed in on some sacrosanct targets. "The affair will leave a black mark forever on the record of the State Department," the *World-Herald* said. "In the minds of many Americans, it will cast doubt as to whether the conduct of their country's foreign affairs is in completely trustworthy hands."

Tracing Otepka's trouble back to 1955, the editorial said it all began when he rejected clearance for "a prominent figure—as yet unidentified." Then it added: "Twice more in five years, the same name came up and both times Mr. Otepka produced the same evaluation."[5]

Washington had been buzzing for days about the possible identity of

---

* See Appendix B for full text of the Sigma Delta Chi report.

this "prominent figure." On Tuesday, October 3, Clark Mollenhoff revealed who it was. In a story written for the Cowles newspapers in Des Moines and Minneapolis, Mollenhoff disclosed that "Walt Whitman Rostow, now a special assistant to the President on national security affairs, was rejected three times by the Eisenhower Administration as a possible security risk."[6]

The source of Mollenhoff's information was the brief filed by Roger Robb with the State Department hearing officer the day before. In this 97-page document, Robb gave a short account of the meeting Otepka had in December 1960 with Dean Rusk and Bobby Kennedy. He referred to Otepka's response to Rusk's questions about what kind of security problems might be involved in obtaining a clearance for Rostow, and he quoted Kennedy as calling the Air Force Intelligence people "a bunch of jerks."*

Ten days after Mollenhoff's disclosure, Rostow found a friendly Associated Press reporter and fed out a half-truth which most newspapers promptly swallowed whole. "From 1951 onward," said Rostow, "I had continuous security clearance from various agencies of the federal government."[7]

Associated Press also unearthed an anonymous source who claimed that "the rejections of Rostow for certain assignments . . . were not based on security reasons but because Rostow's particular talents did not meet the requirements."[8] This lie was printed without refutation by hundreds of newspapers across the country.

Strangely, Rostow's statement, and the false explanation of AP's anonymous informant, seemed to satisfy almost everyone, perhaps because they *wanted* so strongly to believe it was true. Certainly it did seem too monstrous that the man Lyndon Johnson credited with holding "the most important job in the White House, aside from the President," should turn out to be a security risk. It was enough to numb the imagination. The whole affair had about it an eerie, unreal quality, and this may account for, though not excuse, the failure of the press to look beyond Walt Rostow's own comforting words.

The meaning of disclosures in the Otepka brief was soon bypassed by a major public relations campaign in Rostow's behalf. Somewhat earlier in 1967, a number of newspapers and magazines had begun to focus on the erstwhile oracle of Cambridge as a key man in the formulation of U.S. policy in Vietnam. As early as May he had been identified as a charter member of President Johnson's "Tuesday luncheon club," which met

* See Chapter I.

each week at the White House to discuss future steps in the war. Rostow, Rusk and McNamara were the three most important regulars in this club, which only occasionally played host to General Earle G. Wheeler, Chairman of the Joint Chiefs of Staff, and virtually never to the other military chiefs.

"Decisions made at the Tuesday lunch vetoed one JCS request after another," *U.S. News & World Report* said in June. The magazine quoted one nameless insider as saying: "The Tuesday lunch is like an iceberg. There is much more to it than meets the eye."[10]

Down below the surface, in the basement of the White House, Rostow had built himself a powerful empire. He had trained the remnant of the National Security Council staff, which he headed, to jump through all the proper hoops like performing seals. He ruled the Situation Room, the President's private communications center, with a firm hand. He presided over the "hot line" that linked the White House with the Kremlin. No one else in "Sit Room," as it is appropriately named, dared alert the President about any crisis before Rostow gave the word.

"I'm the first person ever to call the President and tell him the hot line from Moscow is up," boasted Rostow that autumn when he seemed so eager to establish his credentials.[11] Ironically, this incident had occurred on June 5, the day before Otepka's State Department hearing began. At 2:38 a.m. a teletype in Sit Room clattered out the news that the Arab-Israeli conflict had started. Rostow was notified at his home immediately and was on the scene within the hour. But he waited until 4:35 a.m., two hours after the first flash, before he called the President sleeping upstairs.

Just before 8 a.m. the hot-line teletype hookup with the Kremlin clicked out a message that Kosygin wanted to communicate with Johnson. Rostow relayed this to his boss with commendable alacrity. A reply went out within the hour, and twenty messages were exchanged during the Mideast crisis, each side assuring the other it had no intention of getting involved. The "best use of the hot line" came when American planes scrambled, belatedly, to assist the U.S.S. *Liberty*, which had been attacked by the Israelis. It was vital that the Soviets know that the planes were not going after the Russian fleet that had plowed through the Dardenelles into the Mediterranean.

The success of the hot line, which had been Rostow's idea originally, pleased him immensely. Of course, the Soviets managed to use the Mideast crisis to jump with both feet into a region where they had been only tentatively dipping their toes before. But that did not dawn on many Americans until months later.

Rostow's role as maestro of the hot line did not become generally known until the really big public relations buildup for him started after the Otepka brief broke. But back in May the Washington *Post* did a splendid spread on the Great Society's ruling Triumvirate—Rostow, Rusk and McNamara—in which it correctly noted that "Many Administration figures say a major reason for Rostow's White House success is his role as a creator of what amounts to an improvised Johnsonian Grand Design."[12]

Laudatory biographical sketches on Rostow were run in both *Look* and *Life* in early December. Both articles bolstered his growing reputation as a "hard liner" who was really an old softy at heart. *Life* ignored the explosive information in the Otepka brief entirely, confining itself to such rhapsodizing as "Rostow's mind is a sharp, fast, flowing political instrument."[13] *Look* kissed off the Otepka revelations way down in its story with one paragraph:

> Recently, Rostow's name made headlines when a dismissed State Department security officer was reported as blaming his discharge on his refusal to clear Rostow at the beginning of JFK's term without a field investigation. (McGeorge) Bundy says, "I read that file in 1961, and *there was nothing in it that raised any questions at all about Walt's loyalty, security or other qualifications.*" He says he accepted Rostow with "three cheers."[14] [Emphasis added.]

Otepka's name was never mentioned. Nonetheless, the *Look* and *Life* stories were unwittingly among the most damaging articles that had ever been printed on Walt Rostow. For in attempting to reinforce his acknowledged position as the Administration's leading great thinker, they proved conclusively how tight a grip Rostow had on the President's mind and on U.S. foreign policy.

His thought, said *Look*, "supplies the understructure on which are raised the President's policies. . . ." Rostow's "biggest fan is LBJ, who says, '*His detractors raise him in my estimation every day.*'"

Look brought up the Tuesday luncheons at the White House. "There," it said, "the question repeatedly comes: 'What do you think, Walt?' And Rostow usually knows precisely what he thinks; he has a thought-out vision of the world and America's place in it. U.S. foreign policy parallels that vision surprisingly."

If two of the most influential mass-circulation periodicals in the country were so obviously complacent about Walt Rostow, there were others which were not. Capitol Hill still hummed with worried conjecture about the information on Rostow in the Otepka brief.

The astounding disclosure that Otepka, with his wide reputation as a fair and careful evaluator, had repeatedly rejected clearances for Rostow rudely shook many Congressmen and Senators. The fact that Otepka's recommendations had twice been upheld by high officials in the State Department during the Eisenhower Administration, including Undersecretary of State Herbert Hoover, Jr., added to their concern.

The Air Force Intelligence finding that Rostow was a security risk and CIA's action in dropping him from a sensitive contract contributed further to the fears felt behind many doors in the Senate and House office buildings. That these fears were seldom voiced openly is merely additional evidence of a deeper and more pervasive fear: there were very few in the Congress who could risk being burned with the ugly brand of McCarthyism.

In late November, the Administration finally concocted another alibi for Walt Rostow. Seven full weeks after Clark Mollenhoff's original story, the White House belatedly let it out that President Johnson had insisted that the FBI run a full field investigation on Rostow before he was brought back to the Presidential staff from State in April 1966. It is possible that this *was* done, but the implication that the FBI had "cleared" Rostow is woefully misleading. The FBI has no power to issue a clearance for officials in other government agencies. Nor did the FBI necessarily have access to the same information that Otepka had when he first evaluated Rostow. Otepka was aware of files on numerous officials that the FBI to this day does not know existed.*

In this instance, moreover, it is a safe bet that the file on Rostow which Otepka accumulated in the late 1950's no longer bore any resemblance to the original. Nearly three years passed between the time Otepka's files were confiscated by the New Order and the return of Rostow to the White House from State. When Otepka was permitted a glimpse of those files six months after his ouster from SY, he saw at once that they had been rifled. No one will ever know how many sensitive personnel security records disappeared or went up in smoke in the State Department incinerator.

The largely underground sensation touched off by Mollenhoff's stories on the Otepka brief was exacerbated by another series of articles published in England at about the same time. Seizing on Harold (Kim) Philby's boast from Moscow that he had been a member of the Commu-

---

* Under the so-called "third agency rule," information acquired by, for example, the State Department from CIA or Air Force Intelligence can be refused to any other agency requesting it. If the FBI asked for certain documents (even assuming it knew they existed), the State Department or any other agency does not have to provide them.

nist espionage network for more than thirty years, the London *Sunday Times* ran a month-long exposé on the activities of this master spy, the mysterious "third man" who tipped Burgess and Maclean that British Intelligence was closing in on them.

A clever "sleeper" agent who posed as a hard-line anti-Communist, Philby was even decorated by Francisco Franco in Spain during the Spanish Civil War, which he covered as a correspondent. In the British Foreign Office, Kim Philby's impeccable old school ties assured his rapid rise. His Cambridge chum, Donald Maclean, and many others pushed Philby up the ladder in much the same fashion as Otepka had observed certain individuals at State being elevated. (A prerequisite for such elevations is always the development of a reputation for "brilliance.")

Switching to British Intelligence, Philby enjoyed the same preferential treatment. By 1944 he was in charge of a new Intelligence department specifically designed to penetrate the Soviet apparat. ("You can imagine what kind of information I was able to send to Moscow," he told a team of *Izvestia* reporters in December 1967.) Three years later he was sent to Washington to help the American novices set up their new Central Intelligence Agency. His friend Maclean was working out of the British embassy at the same time, feeding Moscow vital material he got from Philby and other sources.*

The London *Sunday Times* said that a 1956 State Department report (which, incidentally, Otepka was privy to) made it clear that "Donald Maclean had access to every crucial Anglo-American policy decision at the height of the Cold War." Tragically, many of these decisions pertained to U.S. strategy in the Korean conflict.

Philby's superiors displayed the same curious blindness on security matters that Otepka had so often noted among his own superiors at State. Even Prime Minister Macmillan dismissed reports that Philby was a spy with the remark that there was "no reason to conclude that Mr. Philby had at any time betrayed the interests of this country." The British, too, had been afflicted with a pathological dread of being tarred with the dread brush of McCarthyism.

On November 22, 1967, the fourth anniversary of Jack Kennedy's assassination, John Ashbrook of Ohio painted a vivid analogy between the Philby disclosures and the fate of Otto Otepka. He introduced a brief review of the Philby-Burgess-Maclean case in the *Congressional Record*

* Maclean was First Secretary of the British embassy in Washington and later head of the American department in the Foreign Office. He escaped to Moscow with his homosexual boyfriend Burgess when Philby tipped them in 1951. Maclean reportedly divorced his wife in 1967 and Mrs. Maclean is said to have become the fourth Mrs. Philby.

to "provide a background against which our own security problems at State should be evaluated." Then he went on to trace a few of the actions taken against both Otepka and Stephen Koczak.

Congressman Ashbrook was careful not to draw a comparison between Kim Philby and Walt Rostow on the basis of the scant information available in the Otepka hearing brief. But he cited the Rostow business as "another case which has a direct bearing on security matters" and he scored the Administration for the steady stream of untruths it had poured out to cover up the clearance rejections.[15]

Although the President continued to stand firmly by Rostow, in late November he was at last forced to dump the man primarily responsible for the implementation of Rostow's policies—Robert Strange McNamara. There were many others who had helped translate the central thesis of the Rostow Papers into action—Paul Nitze and Adam Yarmolinsky in the Pentagon, Dean Rusk, George Ball, Harlan Cleveland at State, to name just a few. But it was McNamara's iron will that had imposed the Rostowian vision on America's defense establishment.

In pursuit of Rostow's dream, McNamara had scuttled many major weapons systems, held back the Defense Department's critical research and development programs, pushed for "gradual escalation" of the Vietnam War in lieu of victory. On Capitol Hill, McNamara's credibility had sunk precipitately and his annual "posture statements" were viewed by many lawmakers as blueprints for national suicide.

In July 1967 Congressional concern deepened to alarm when a high-level special committee of the American Security Council, a private organization, published a landmark report in cooperation with the House Armed Services Committee. The private committee was headed by General Bernard A. Schriever, the man primarily responsible for the Air Force's missile development from its inception. It also included a blue-ribbon group of sixteen other retired military commanders, scientists and scholars.

Point by point, this committee built an iron-clad case to support its thesis that the Soviet Union "is driving hard toward a goal of overwhelming superiority in the decisive field of nuclear weapons."[16] Moreover, it demonstrated how close the Soviet was to achieving this goal in certain areas such as space weapons at a time when the U.S. was cutting back on many of its strategic forces.

At last, McNamara's computerized estimates were shown up for what they were—the rationalizations of a man intent upon justifying the Rostowian policy of disarmament. The position of the Secretary of Defense had become untenable. President Johnson had no alternative but to fire him. There were other contributing factors, of course. Vietnam was one. But the Congress' realization that the United States was fast heading for second place in strategic weaponry was the primary reason for McNamara's exile to the World Bank.

From the sidelines, Otto Otepka watched these developments with mounting interest. In the rapid erosion of America's strategic superiority, he could see the fulfillment of the policies laid out by Walt Rostow and others whose security clearances he had steadfastly opposed. He knew that McNamara, the Kennedys, and even Lyndon Johnson had permitted themselves to be used as pliant tools by people who could never pass the acid test of Eisenhower's Executive Order 10450.

More dramatic evidence of how badly they had been used was supplied by the weapons paraded in Moscow in November 1967 on the occasion of the fiftieth anniversary of the Bolshevik Revolution. McNamara, in a futile effort to take some of the surprise element out of the Soviet's new arsenal, admitted a few days beforehand that Russia had what he called a Fractional Orbital Bombardment System (FOBS). But he added that he was "not concerned."*

Dean Rusk obviously wasn't concerned either. He was photographed toasting Soviet Ambassador Anatoly Dobrynin at the golden anniversary party in the Soviet embassy on November 7. Asked why he violated his standing rule against attending such cocktail parties, Rusk explained merrily: "Well, for the fiftieth anniversary, I make an exception."

The spectacle of a U.S. Secretary of State congratulating the Soviet Union on its fifty years of oppression caused deep dismay among many Americans, particularly at a time when thousands of U.S. servicemen were being killed and maimed by Soviet weapons in Vietnam. But there were others in the world who had even greater cause for dismay, especially the millions forced to live under communism.

In his monumental book, *Workers' Paradise Lost,* Eugene Lyons assessed "the fearsome costs to the Russian peoples and the rest of mankind" of the half-century of Soviet history to which Dean Rusk paid honor:

> It is a price paid in the coin of terror, forcible collectivization, man-made famine, slave-labor camps, blood-purges, thought control, brutal exploitation of workers and farmers, persecution of religion, political oppressions, genocidal massacres and deportations. This does

---

* Like virtually all of McNamara's announcements about Soviet strategic capabilities, the FOBS disclosures came long after the Intelligence community had first reported it.

not exhaust the melancholy inventory, for it must embrace other costs that cannot be reduced to figures.[17]

Lyons reviewed the various estimates of the actual death toll taken by communism. He pointed out that one British journalist, D. G. Stewart-Smith, had placed it as high as eighty-three million, more than all the fatalities in both World Wars. Equally horrible, Lyons said, was the fact that "millions of the victims, in the torture chambers and in the slave camps, were denied the solace of quick and easy death."[18] Nor was the terror confined to the Stalinist era in Russia and the Mao period in China. It continues, as Lyons and others have shown, down to the present, abating only when it serves some Communist purpose.

In the dehumanized milieu of high diplomacy, Secretary Rusk's toast was condoned rather than condemned. It was considered symbolic of the great "improvement" in Soviet-American relations that had taken place over the preceding seven years. To a world focused more on symbols than on reality it was a comforting gesture.

Not long after the glasses clinked in Washington and the mammoth space missiles rumbled through the streets of Moscow, Rusk received the findings of his handpicked judge for the Otepka hearing, Edward Dragon. The State Department brief prepared by Irving Jaffe accused Otepka of "disloyalty" to his country. Dragon did not dare go quite that far, but his findings went far enough to satisfy Rusk.

The Secretary delayed making the decision known until the second week in December when Congress was embroiled in its annual rush for adjournment. Shortly after 7 p.m. on December 11, 1967, a Foreign Service officer named Donald Woodward rang the doorbell of Otepka's home in Wheaton. He handed him an imposing document bearing the seal of the Department of State and festooned with red ribbons from top to bottom. The seal had been affixed by Undersecretary Nicholas De B. Katzenbach and the document, No. 67/11019, conveying "Greetings" from the Department, was signed by Dean Rusk, Secretary of State.

"I have considered the entire record of Mr. Otepka's appeal," Rusk began. He said he accepted Dragon's finding that "there are no extenuating circumstances that would justify or excuse" Otepka's action in delivering documents "outside the Department of State." (Reilly's perjury was not mentioned.)

"His action," Rusk went on, " . . . was incompatible with his responsibilities to the Government from which he held appointment."

"It is my conclusion on review of this case," said Rusk, "that the grounds urged by Mr. Otepka in his appeal are without merit." The

ecretary proclaimed that he upheld the hearing officer's findings that the
defendant had indulged in "conduct unbecoming an officer of the Department of State," as charged.

"I therefore decide that disciplinary action is required in this case and
hereby direct that the following actions be taken with respect to Mr. Otto
F. Otepka:

    (a) That he be severely reprimanded.

    (b) That he be reduced in grade from GS-15 to GS-14, step one.

    (c) That he be transferred to duties in the Department of State
which are within his qualifications but which do not involve the administration of personnel security functions."

The last act had been played out. After four-and-a-half years sentence
had finally been pronounced: Otepka was formally removed from the
Office of Security and stripped of the title, Chief, Evaluations Divi-
sion/SY. He could remain in the State Department, if he so chose. But
he would have to accept still another demotion, this one to a nebulous
position as an analyst in the Office of Management. His salary was cut
by more than $5,000 or about 25 percent—from $20,585 a year to
$15,106.

Dean Rusk's decision was a half-measure to keep Otepka's supporters
in the Congress from rising up *en masse* in protest, yet strong enough to
drive home the lesson the Secretary did not want the security community
to forget. The decision bore the stamp of the schoolmaster, rapping an
errant pupil's knuckles in front of the class. It was superfluous in that
sense, though, for the security people in the State Department had long
since learned their lesson well.

There was about the whole thing a musty aura of anti-climax, as
Senator Hruska had foreseen months earlier. "Unfortunately," Hruska
had predicted, "the outcome of this hearing makes no material difference
to Mr. Otepka because his career already has been ruined. Perhaps more
important, it makes little difference to the security of the United States.
The damage has been done; in large measure it cannot be repaired."

CHAPTER XLII

Whirlwind Reaped

THE KALEIDOSCOPIC EVENTS THAT ROCKED THE NATION AND THE world in the year 1968 left neither the public nor the Congress time to ponder the implications of Dean Rusk's decision in the Otepka case. By mid-summer, when a massive Soviet invasion smashed the "peaceful revolution" in Czechoslovakia, America was staggering like a punch-drunk old champion, groping in befuddlement for the ropes, instinctively trying to stay on its feet until the bell sounded for Election Day and hoped-for relief.

In the first week of January the Senate Internal Security Subcommittee finally issued its long-awaited official report on the Otepka matter. Released in four separate volumes over an eight-day span, the report was virtually ignored by large segments of the Fourth Estate. An Associated Press dispatch, carried on page 41 of the New York *Times* voluminous Sunday edition of January 7, highlighted the defense of Otepka by Senators Thurmond, Eastland and Dodd—a neat little device which ignored the fact that the report had been approved by a preponderant majority of the ten-man subcommittee.

The AP story, as printed in the *Times*, did mention (in paragraph fifteen) that the report rapped officials of the State Department for "deliberate falsehoods." But the names of the officials were not disclosed. Nor did the published account allude to the subcommittee's pertinent observation that "tactics used by certain witnesses strongly suggest that the Department had something to hide" and that "an abundance of other evidence of the weakness of State Department security . . . freely imputes vulnerability of the Department's security procedures."[1]

This was pretty strong language for a Senate committee to direct against an important agency of the government, particularly in time of war. But the AP, which serves literally thousands of newspapers, TV and radio stations, blatantly claimed that the statements of the three Senators were "the only new material" in the first volume of the report.*

Barely a week after the fourth and last volume was released, the country was stunned by the first in a long series of traumatic crises. On January 23 the U.S. Navy's intelligence ship *Pueblo* was captured off North Korea and its 83-man crew consigned to the tender mercies of the commissars. Walt Rostow came back briefly into the news in connection with this incident; the report of the *Pueblo's* seizure had reached Dr. Rostow's command post in the White House basement quickly enough, but did not deign to notify the President for several hours, or until the ship had reached the Communist port of Wonsan. Robert Strange McNamara, in one of his last public appearances as Secretary of Defense, told a "Meet the Press" television audience on February 4 that the United States made no attempt to protect or rescue the *Pueblo* because it would have been interpreted by the Communists as "a provocative act." Thus had the options of the world's mightiest nation shriveled under Dr. Rostow's theory of "crisis management."

At the end of January, on the first day of a mutually agreed upon truce for the Tet lunar new year holiday, the Communist forces in Vietnam opened a series of ferocious attacks on Saigon and thirty provincial centers. Thousands of civilians were killed and maimed and nearly a half-million people left homeless. American casualties in the first week of the Tet offensive reached a new record of nearly 3,200 killed and wounded and South Vietnamese military losses were equally severe. The

---

* This was but one example of the incredible press treatment of the Otepka story that same week. At a press conference held by Secretary of State Rusk on January 4, 1968, Clark Mollenhoff asked Rusk a series of a dozen questions pertaining to the wiretapping aspects of the Otepka case. These questions—and the Secretary's unbelievably evasive answers— were deliberately omitted from what purported to be the full text of Rusk's press conference in both the New York *Times* and the Washington *Post*. The sharp exchanges between Mollenhoff and Rusk were carried by the Baltimore *Sun* which made them all the more conspicuous by their absence in the *Times* and the *Post*.

press in America found a scapegoat in General William C. Westmore-land. Within a few months he was recalled from Vietnam and booted upstairs to Army Chief of Staff.

The protests against the Vietnam War gained new momentum with the Presidential candidacy of Senator Eugene McCarthy. When McCarthy won the New Hampshire primary, Bobby Kennedy promptly grabbed the steering wheel of the peacenik bandwagon. The two Senators vied with each other for the growing peace vote, promising surrender at almost any price. Harking to an echo of what had happened to his command in Vietnam fourteen years earlier, General Henri Navarre of France observed with sadness: "Every speech by Robert Kennedy does more good for the Viet Cong than if they take a base."

Less than two weeks after Bobby entered the reace for the Democratic nomination, Lyndon Johnson decided he had had enough. On Sunday night, March 31, the President announced on television that he was throwing in the towel. The man who had swept the 1964 election with the greatest majority in history had, within less than three-and-a-half years, seen his dream of the Great Society crumble to dust in the bitter caldron of war and rising internal strife.

Now, virtually begging the Communists to consent to peace talks, President Johnson declared a halt to the bombing of all North Vietnam except a small strip above the Demilitarized Zone (DMZ). Six weeks earlier he had offered to let Ho Chi Minh "write the agenda" if Ho would just come to the table "to reason and talk."[2] The Communists had re-sponded, as always, with stepped-up terrorism and military action.

A little more than a month after the President's withdrawal, Martin Luther King was murdered in Memphis. Violence followed in the wake of the death of the apostle of "nonviolence," much as it had followed every step he had taken in life. Negro riots erupted in one hundred and twenty-five cities, including the nation's capital. More than 2,600 sepa-rate fires were set by arsonists; at least forty-six persons were killed; more than 2,500 were injured, many seriously; well over 21,000 arrests were made by police and the 55,000 Army and National Guard troops called out to quell the uprisings.

The rioting had hardly subsided when late in April the Civil Service Commission issued a ruling upholding Secretary of State Rusk's repri-mand and demotion of Otepka. From the Administration's standpoint the timing was perfect: the public mind was obsessed with civil disorders and the Commission's decision passed virtually unnoticed.

Actually, the Commission's ruling on Otepka's appeal had been ready for more than a month. It was deliberately held up to facilitate the Senate's confirmation of George Ball as Arthur Goldberg's successor in the position of U.S. Ambassador to the United Nations. On March 7, at a closed hearing, Otepka had reinforced his charges that Ball had joined with Rusk in covering up for John Reilly and ten others he named as active members of the conspiracy to purge him from the Department of State.*

Fearing that release of Otepka's testimony would create difficulties for Ball, the Administration moved to squelch it. As a matter of courtesy Otepka was to have received a transcript of the hearing. But his repeated requests for the transcript were ignored and the Commission handed down its decision without ever sending him a copy.

Meanwhile, George Ball was quietly installed at the United Nations. Two Senators were primed to question his role in the Otepka case. But Senator William Fulbright, Chairman of the Foreign Relations Committee, simply held the hearing on Ball's confirmation without notifying his two colleagues. It was a flagrant violation of senatorial courtesy, but Fulbright got by with it and Ball sailed safely into the U.N. post without a ruffle of protest.

There now began a particularly difficult period for Otepka. With the costs for his legal defense steadily mounting, and a second appeal to the Civil Service Commission already in the works, he nevertheless elected for total suspension of his State Department salary. Since December he had been on official leave, with his pay continued for accumulated annual vacations. But rather than accept the nebulous "management" position to which Rusk had demoted him, in mid-April Otepka applied for leave without pay. He preferred to struggle along on what remained of his savings. The alternative, as he saw it, was abject submission to Rusk's decision banning him from the Office of Security.

Otepka realized, of course, that his only hope for ultimate vindication lay in a change of Administration. Despite the continuing, if ineffective, support of a group of Democrat Senators, he knew that he could expect no justice as long as the Democrats retained control of the White House. The events of the past seven years had proved conclusively that a Democrat Administration would never restore sound security practices to the Department of State. If this were true under Lyndon Johnson, it would

* See Appendix C for Otepka's full indictment of Messrs. Rusk, Ball, and the Department of State.

be at least equally true under any of the three frontrunners for the Democratic Presidential nomination—Hubert Humphrey, Robert Kennedy or Eugene McCarthy. Yet Otepka resisted all attempts to enlist his public support for any opposition candidate.

During the period of Bobby Kennedy's brief open candidacy, Otepka never once succumbed to what must have been a mighty temptation to point out that Senator Kennedy had played a prominent role in the destruction of internal security laws and related passport-visa regulations designed to protect the country from subversion. Some of his supporters, particularly in California, urged him to let loose at least one salvo against Kennedy. But Otepka insisted upon maintaining silence.

When Robert Kennedy was put down by the assassin's bullets in Los Angeles during a celebration of his victory in the California primary, Otto Otepka was as stunned as any other citizen. He understood, of course, the tragic irony of the Senator's murder better than most. Like Jack Kennedy before him, Bobby had fallen victim to an apparently deranged youth with Marxist leanings. Sirhan Sirhan's Marxism might not have been quite as undiluted as Lee Harvey Oswald's but it was certainly a factor in creating a cast of mind that prompted desperate action.

Not surprisingly, when Mayor Samuel W. Yorty of Los Angeles disclosed on June 6 that Sirhan's diary contained abundant evidence of "Communist sympathies," the Mayor was bitterly censured by the American Civil Liberties Union. In the eyes of the Liberals and Leftists it was a mortal sin to reveal to the American people that Senator Kennedy had been slain by an extremist of the Left. Sirhan was painted as a virulent anti-Israel Arab, which no doubt he was. But to pretend that an Arab could not be pro-Communist in an era when millions of Arabs were following in the footsteps of Egypt's Gamal Abdel Nasser was idiocy of a very peculiar brand.

The evidence, carefully muted before, during and after Sirhan's lengthy trial, is that the youthful fanatic was at least influenced by the destructive dialectics of Marxism. In shooting down Robert Kennedy, he was, whether he realized it or not, following Lenin's ancient dogma that assassination "is no murder."[3] Like Oswald, Sirhan viewed political assassination as a heroic act.

Otto Otepka, perhaps more acutely than any other man, understood the central tragedy of the deaths of John and Robert Kennedy. Both brothers had devoted themselves to placating and to reaching a détente with the modern disciples of Marx. And both had been sacrificed by the orces they had attempted to placate. This is not to say that the murder of either brother necessarily had to be *ordered* by the Kremlin, but there is no denying that the assassins of both Kennedys were, in varying degrees, *conditioned* by the Kremlin's inflexible doctrines of hate.

The summer of 1968 was Otepka's sixth in exile from SY. On every hand there was growing evidence of the general breakdown of internal security. Earlier the Supreme Court had continued its sustained assault on the nation's internal security laws with a ruling that in effect prohibited defense industries from firing known Communists. In a decision written by Chief Justice Earl Warren, the Court held that the 1950 law banning Communists from employment in defense plants was a violation of workers' rights to freedom of association under the First Amendment to the Constitution.[4]

As if anticipating the Supreme Court's decision, the Department of Defense had a few months before this upheld its right to issue a security clearance to one Robert Arthur Niemann, a research assistant at the University of California at Los Angeles. Niemann had been an active member of the W.E.B. DuBois Clubs, cited by FBI Director J. Edgar Hoover as "Communist- controlled." Yet the Defense Department had cleared him to work on an Air Force defense contract.

Niemann freely admitted that his involvement in far-Left causes had not been limited to membership in the extremist DuBois Clubs. Even while employed on the Air Force contract, he continued to work devotedly for a variety of New Left causes and took a leading part in anti-Vietnam War demonstrations, including a violent clash with police outside the Century Plaza Hotel in Los Angeles on June 23, 1967, when President Johnson was addressing a Democrat dinner.

The Niemann case was by no means an isolated one. It is cited here merely as one example of the complete collapse of internal security throughout the government by mid-1968. Literally hundreds of old and young activists, with records as bad or worse than Niemann's, were deployed in sensitive positions in federal departments, including State and Defense. Moreover, whole platoons of known subversives and individuals with long criminal records were virtually running the Office of Economic Opportunity (OEO) and other Great Society programs.

It remained, however, for the President personally to indulge in the most flagrant flaunting to date of the nation's internal security laws. Lyndon Johnson had served in the House and the Senate when most of these laws were framed. He knew as well as any man that it was the intent of Congress to bar any individual who had ever played footsy with

Communist causes from federal employment, no matter how lowly the job. Yet President Johnson defiantly nominated Abe Fortas to be Chief Justice of the United States.

Onetime close friend of Alger Hiss and Harry Dexter White, Fortas had a long history of affiliation with known Communists and their pet fronts. Inexplicably, very little of this surfaced during the interminable hearings on Fortas' nomination before the Senate Judiciary Committee in the summer of 1968.

Otto Otepka and other veteran security officers were familiar with Attorney Fortas' role in defending subversives and security risks. Indeed, Fortas had been one of the founders of the International Juridical Association, a cited Communist front which devoted itself to the legal defense of party members who ran afoul of the law.* Fortas served prominently on the National Committee of this organization and was an active member of the National Lawyers Guild, also cited by a Congressional committee as Communist controlled.

Other fronts with which Abe Fortas was identified included the Washington Committee for Democratic Action, which was listed by Attorney General Tom C. Clark, a Democrat, as a subversive organization, and the American Law Students' Association, on which he served as a "faculty advisory board" member. He was also listed as a supporter of the Southern Conference for Human Welfare in 1947—a full three years *after* this notorious front was cited by a Senate committee for "serving the Soviet Union and its subservient Communist party in the United States."

The list of people Fortas was closest to in Washington during the 1930's and '40's reads like a *Who's Who* in the Soviet espionage rings that flourished in the capital during that period. Arthur Schlesinger, in his book *The Coming of the New Deal,* identified Fortas as one of the "brilliant young men" who came into government in Franklin Roosevelt's first term. Among the others similarly identified by Schlesinger were Alger Hiss, Lee Pressman, John Abt, and Nathan Witt.

Fortas rose rapidly in the federal hierarchy of FDR's reign and at age 32 he was elevated to Undersecretary of the Interior. This was in 1942, about the time he mysteriously ducked out of war-time service with the Navy. During the war years Fortas was a member of a select group assembled by Soviet spy Harry Dexter White to formulate long-range policy for the United States. Other members of this tight little band included Lauchlin Currie and David Niles, special assistants to the Presi-

Guide to Subversive Organizations and Publications (Page 88, Revised Edition, Dec. 1, 1961), stated that the International Juridical Association was a "Communist front" which "actively defended Communists and consistently followed the Communist Party line."

dent who were later identied in sworn testimony before Congressional committees as Communist agents.

Named as an advisor to the U.S. delegation attending the founding conference of the United Nations at San Francisco in 1945, Fortas is said to have helped Alger Hiss and Harry White draft the U.N. charter that gave the Soviet Union three votes to one for the U.S. and stacked the secretariat with officials from the USSR.

Aside from Lyndon Johnson, Abe Fortas' best known client was probably Owen Lattimore, the Institute of Pacific Relations agent whom John F. Kennedy once identified as a chief architect of China's delivery to communism. Fortas served as Lattimore's attorney during the IPR hearings before the Internal Security Subcommittee. Lawyer and client were in close consultation throughout, and Fortas was often seen whispering suggested replies into Lattimore's ear. Subsequently a grand jury indicted Lattimore on six separate counts of perjury for this particular testimony. Still later, Fortas helped Lattimore write his apologia, *Ordeal by Slander*, a smear-filled diatribe against the Senate Subcommittee and virtually everyone else who had the temerity to question the old China hand's patriotism and loyalty.

Outweighing all of Abe Fortas' dedication to Communist causes, at least in Lyndon Johnson's Presidential view, was Abe Fortas's equally dedicated devotion to Lyndon Johnson. Fortas, was the attorney who euchred Supreme Court Justice Hugo Black into signing the order validating LBJ's dubious first election to the United States Senate. Thereafter old Abe was always on hand to help out when Lyndon needed him. In 1964–65 Attorney Fortas represented Bobby Baker in the law suit which opened the door on "Lyndon Junior's" shadowy manipulations. During the 1964 election it was Fortas who joined Clark Clifford in attempting to convince the Washington newspapers that they should scuttle the story on the morals arrest of Presidential aide Walter Jenkins.

Fortas' reward for services rendered to LBJ was a seat on the Supreme Court as associate justice in 1965. Few would have dreamed then, however, that the President would attempt to elevate his old crony to Chief Justice. And fewer still could have predicted that that Senate Judiciary Committee would actually vote to confirm Fortas in that powerful and exalted position. Fortunately, before the full Senate could ballot on the Committee's recommendation, Everett Dirksen had an abrupt change of heart. The Republican minority leader withdrew his support for the nomination of the President's old crony, and Fortas' dream of ultimate glory went aglimmering.

Months later, in May 1969, *Life* magazine broke the story on Abe Fortas' financial links to convicted stock manipulator Louis Wolfson. It seems Fortas had accepted $20,000 from the Wolfson Family Foundation while the Securities and Exchange Commission was looking into Wolfson's tangled financial affairs. Although the money was returned about a year later, after Wolfson's indictment by a federal grand jury, the Justice Department—now under Attorney General John Mitchell—let it be known that it had "far more serious" information on Fortas' private dealings.[5] It was later revealed that the deal was for $20,000 a year for life, with the payments continuing to Mrs. Fortas in the event of her husband's death.

In the midst of the new hue and cry over Fortas, Senator Robert P. Griffin, the Michigan Republican who had led the fight against Fortas' nomination as Chief Justice, revealed that his life had been threatened. "The threat relates to my position on the Fortas matter," Griffin admitted.[6] Significantly, the threat was made only a short time after the Senator disclosed that "more incriminating information might come out" on Fortas than had thus far been brought to light.

It was pure coincidence, but this same week Otto Otepka appeared to be nearing the end of his interminable ordeal, as the Senate of the United States moved to take final action on his appointment to a position to which he had been named by President Richard M. Nixon.

CHAPTER **XLIII**

Pledge

DURING THE 1968 PRESIDENTIAL CAMPAIGN, THE ENTRENCHED BU-
reaucracy that presided over the endless procession of America's foreign
policy failures from Yalta to Vietnam was plunged into temporary
trauma. The occasion for their shock was a brace of solemn pledges made
by Richard Milhouse Nixon.

In mid-October Nixon vowed that, if elected, he would cleanup the
accumulated mess in the Department of State. There was no equivocation in this promise. "I want a Secretary of State who will join me in
cleaning house in the State Department," he firmly declared in a Dallas
television interview. "We are going to clean house there. It has never
been done . . . it wasn't even done during the Eisenhower Administration."[1]

This statement, and its frank acknowledgement of past failures, was
uttered barely ten days after the publication of another earnest, and
intimately related, commitment by the Republican candidate. Along the
campaign trail, Nixon had been asked, in a private interview with Willard
Edwards of the Chicago *Tribune*, what he planned to do about Otto
Otepka. Several times over the preceding two years Nixon had said he
was entirely familiar with this matter. Now, he answered Edwards without hesitation.

Speaking with obvious respect for Otepka, Richard Nixon promised that as President he would see that *"justice is accorded this man who served his country so long and so well."* [2]

For Otepka, after nearly eight years in a Kafka-like nightmare, Nixon's words provided the first really substantial hope for deliverance and vindication. There had, however, been some prior indications that the election of Dick Nixon would bring about Otepka's release from the bureaucratic netherworld in which he had been wandering. In fact, once he had received a significant signal from Nixon himself.

In February 1966 Edith and Otto Otepka were invited to a dinner at the Sheraton Park Hotel in Washington. Richard Nixon was the guest of honor, and before the banquet there was a small private reception for him which the Otepkas attended as guests of Phil Guarino, a well known capital restaurateur and an old friend. When Guarino introduced them to Nixon, the future President's face lit up in recognition.

"I know all about you and your case," Nixon said, grasping Otepka's hand warmly. "I hope you'll stay in there and fight."

Otepka nodded and replied with a smile: "I only hope, Mr. Nixon, that I can show the same fortitude that you demonstrated in your battle over Alger Hiss."

Nixon, apparently stirred by bitter memories of that earlier era, frowned deeply and looked Otepka right in the eye. "You hang in there," he repeated meaningfully. "Some day the worm will turn."

It was a slender thread, but Otepka, though he kept Nixon's words to himself for nearly two years, clung to it when all other hopes were dashed. He knew, of course, that Richard Nixon had a long, long way to go to get the Republican nomination and win the White House. Moreover, he was conscious of the fact that he could do little to help him. As long as he remained on the State Department rolls, even without pay, Otepka would insist on observing the law—so widely and flagrantly ignored by thousands of others—that constrains civil servants from active political campaigning while on the job.

Although he took no active part in the pre-convention and general election campaigns of 1968, it was only natural, however, that Otepka should watch the unfolding of events on the political scene with deep interest. After Nixon's unbroken succession of primary victories, Otepka was rather surprised to see the vigorous moves to block the former Vice President at the Republican convention in Miami.

There were a fleeting few hours when Ronald Reagan, working in loose cooperation with Nelson Rockefeller, nearly succeeded in stopping

Nixon before the balloting began on the convention floor. Due mainly to the efforts of Strom Thurmond, and his two former aides, South Carolina Republican chairman Harry Dent and attorney Fred Buzhardt, Reagan's bid to capture the Southern delegations fell short by a narrow margin. Across the country, Senator Thurmond was recognized by the press as the real "kingmaker" of the Miami convention. Although Thurmond exacted no firm commitments on the future fate of Otepka, there can be no doubt that he would never have entertained any serious consideration of supporting Richard Nixon unless he felt certain that Nixon would take action to right the many wrongs done Otepka and restore the sound internal security program that Otepka symbolized.

Three weeks after Nixon's nomination in Miami a querelous and confused Democrat convention opened in Chicago. The events of the convention itself were very nearly drowned out by the din of the rioting in Grant Park and along Michigan Boulevard where well organized gangs of Vietnam War protesters took up their battle stations. The Chicago police, acting under orders from Mayor Richard J. Daley, were castigated by much of the press, including the nation's top television commentators, for their "brutal" treatment of the rioters. Apparently the police were expected to stand docilely by while the rampaging "Yippies" disrupted the convention and hoisted Viet Cong flags from historic monuments in the park.

A true measure of the actual support for the Yippies' sullied cause came during the balloting on the convention floor. Their champion, Senator Eugene McCarthy, received barely 600 delegate votes to more than 1,760 for Vice President Hubert Humphrey. Yet the Yippies could rightfully claim a victory, for a humbled Humphrey eventually praised them as heroes and patriots.

The clamorous events in Chicago followed within days of the Soviet invasion of Czechoslovakia. Nonetheless, there was very little oratory at the convention on the truly brutal oppression of the Czech and Slovak peoples. The Rostow Papers' policy, which first called for America's cooperation with the Soviet in quelling uprisings behind the Iron Curtain, was working very well indeed, as the strange official silence of the United States government during the invasion so amply demonstrated. America had, to use the words of Rostow's 1961 blueprint, avoided "being moved" by the "importunities . . . of our own public to prolong and expand the crises. . . ."

More tragic was the fact that there had been virtually no "importunities" on the part of the American public seriously to protest the Soviet juggernaut's move against Czechoslovakia. Americans, buffeted by a bloody succession of crises at home and by the rising casualty toll in Vietnam, were unable to focus on the fate of a small country in central Europe.

Incredibly, the Liberals, taking their line on this occasion from former Supreme Court Justice Arthur Goldberg, hailed the invasion of Czechoslovakia as a "defeat" for the Soviets—a view that must have caused a good deal of merriment in the Kremlin.

The Soviets had additional cause to laugh up their sleeves at the inanities of the West that summer. While President Johnson's envoys begged and pleaded with the Communist delegation at the Paris talks to give just some slight sign that they wanted to settle the Vietnam conflict, the Viet Cong and North Vietnamese stepped up their terrorism and military operations from the DMZ to the Mekong Delta. During the week of the Democrat convention in Chicago, 108 Americans were killed in Vietnam and nearly 2,000 wounded. By the end of August, total U.S. casualties in the war were nearing 200,000, including 27,508 boys who had been sent home in military coffins while the legions of the unwashed romped on university campuses across the nation, literally under the banner of the Communist troops and terrorists who were killing their fellow citizens.

Otto Otepka, familiar as he was with the backgrounds of many of the professors who incited the youthful demonstrators, was moved to wonder how long America would permit its young to be converted into zombies. Not a few of these professors had moved in and out of the Department of State over the years, some in the same kind of consultant capacity that Dr. Rostow had used to such good advantage in the 1950's when he was setting the stage for the future conflict in Vietnam by cutting that country in two at the 17th Parallel. Once Otepka had been able to block the entry of a good many academic brainwashers into the State Department because of their known Communist Party and Communist front affiliations. Now all the bars were down, and the professors could lead a campus anti-Vietnam "teach-in" one day and be formulating war policy on Foggy Bottom the next.

Like most other citizens, Otepka observed the election race in the autumn of 1968 with mounting suspense. Although months earlier Senator Everett Dirksen had found the voters in Illinois "all hopped up about the Otepka case,"[3] Otepka was not surprised when it again failed to become a major issue. He was frank to agree that Richard Nixon would have been foolish to attempt to inject the internal security issue too strongly into the campaign, given the climate that prevailed.

Nevertheless, Nixon's stand on the Otepka case was anything but ambiguous, though there was an apparent attempt to make it so. The candidate's brother, Edward Nixon, was given the chore of answering inquiries about certain issues from the campaign headquarters in New York. One of these issues was the Otepka controversy. The stock reply that went out over Edward's signature was that his brother would not comment on the case since it was still in the process of appeal. Whether this was Edward's idea, or some faceless functionary's at headquarters, was never determined. But when Dick Nixon was asked about it, he appeared to be quite upset. "That isn't my position," he replied with candor. "I didn't give him authority to write those letters."

Moreover, there was no equivocation in Nixon's reply to Willard Edwards' question. The twin pledges of "justice" for Otepka and a "house-cleaning" at the State Department could only mean one thing— or so it seemed at the time. In politics, however, pledges have a curious habit of being forgotten after elections, and although the pledge to Otepka was not exactly forgotten, it was not fulfilled in the way everyone, including Strom Thurmond, thought it would be. . . .

Perhaps because voters got the impression that Richard Milhouse Nixon was not meeting the issues squarely enough in the fall of 1968, he came very close to losing. President Johnson's unilateral cessation of all bombing attacks on North Vietnam five days before the election was also a major factor. The Administration's move once again raised false hopes for peace, and a large body of "undecided" voters who had been leaning towards Nixon quite suddenly swung over to Hubert Humphrey. The action was so patently political that most observers thought the people would quickly see through the bombing-halt ploy and it would have no effect. But the American people, confused as perhaps never before, were taken in by the thousands.

The callous cynicism of the Administration's eleventh-hour "step toward peace" did not become fully apparent until some days after the polls had closed. By then it was obvious that the President had declared a halt to the bombing in the southern portion of North Vietnam without receiving any assurance whatever that the Communists would respond in kind.

Hanoi, Haiphong, and other major areas of the north had been removed from the always tightly restricted list of American targets when Lyndon Johnson announced his withdrawal from the Presidential race at the end of March. In spite of this, by October the Air Force, Navy, and Marine air arms had very nearly succeeded in cutting off the flow of

Soviet arms to the Communist forces below the DMZ. In the spring of 1969, during a tour of Vietnam, this writer talked to a number of combat pilots and other military personnel about the effect of Johnson's pre-election bombing halt. Almost to a man they admitted that it had had a very serious adverse effect upon the progress of the war.

"Many of us thought we had just about succeeded in accomplishing our mission," one young Phantom jet pilot said. "We had interdicted most of the main Communist supply lines from the North. Whole regiments of the North Vietnamese Army were retreating piece-meal back across the DMZ and into Laos and Cambodia because they no longer had arms and ammunition to fight with. Then came the bombing halt. You know the rest. The Communists resumed their buildup and every day they are getting stronger."

Although the 1969 Tet offensive did not inflict nearly as much damage on our forces and upon the civilian populace as had the previous year's sustained assault, some thousands of Americans and South Vietnamese were killed in the renewed attacks. U. S. casualties soared in early March, and in one night alone the Communists shelled fifty cities, towns, and military camps with rockets and mortar shells brought into the country from the privileged sanctuary to the north. The attacks did not work as much destruction as the headlines in the States and elsewhere would lead one to believe. But the Communists were more interested in the headlines, which they knew would have their paralyzing effect upon American public opinion, then, as always, the primary Communist target.

"We've won this war a half-dozen times out here," one grizzled Marine veteran remarked to me in Da Nang in April 1969. "But each time we win it those bastards back in Washington take the victory away from us."

The Marine may have been overstating the case somewhat, but he came closer to the truth than probably even he knew at the time. Moreover, the overwhelming majority of the American people, forced to grope their way in the dark night of managed news, obviously sensed on November 5, 1968, that the time had come to change the guard.

Despite the fact that thousands were hoodwinked by the Administration's bombing halt, Richard Nixon managed to squeak through to victory. He garnered nearly three million fewer votes than he had won against Jack Kennedy in 1960, but he beat Hubert Humphrey by more than 300,000 nonetheless, and that was enough to give him 302 electoral votes, barely 32 more than he needed to win.

Even most of the Liberal press pointed out that Nixon's 31,300,000 popular votes, when added to the nearly 10,000,000 cast for George

Wallace, showed that the country had gone decidedly "conservative." Great changes were thought to be in the offing in Washington, and Nixon's campaign pledges made it seem that the State Department would be in for the most drastic change of all. But there were a few people in the capital who early foresaw that the changes would not be quite what the preponderant majority of the people had voted for, or, if they were, they would not come nearly as fast as expected.

The appointment of Henry Kissinger, a Harvard professor and former advisor to Nelson Rockefeller, to replace Walt Rostow as major domo of the National Security Council staff in the White House was the first ostensible sign that more ameliorating forces were at work. When William P. Rogers, a former Attorney General with no visible knowledge of foreign affairs, was named Secretary of State, it became perfectly obvious that the "housecleaning" in the Department of State would be delayed, perhaps indefinitely.

Strom Thurmond and a group of other Senators and Congressmen had moved right after the election to have Otto Otepka named Deputy Undersecretary of State for Administration, the job that Roger Jones and William Crockett had held during the destruction of the Department's internal security program. Thurmond and the others reasoned that Otepka was the man best qualified for this critical post, which has overall supervision of all personnel and security functions. However, the incoming Administration announced that it would retain Idar Rimestad in this key slot, although he was publicly known to be Dean Rusk's chief hatchet man and the latter-day grand inquisitor on the Otepka case.

Patiently, as always, Otepka bided his time. The Civil Service Commission had turned down his second and final appeal in October, and if he was not given a job in security by the Nixon Administration he would have to begin the long, tortuous trek that would ultimately take him before the Supreme Court.

Now, however, there was further indication that there was to be no dramatic shift in the direction of the miasmic breezes wafting up from Foggy Bottom. Just five days before Nixon's inauguration, Undersecretary of State Nicholas Katzenbach, the ferocious bald eagle who once figuratively threatened to devour George Wallace on the steps of a University of Alabama administration building, issued a memorandum summarily restoring a security clearance to John Paton Davies, the old China cabalist who for fifteen years had been classified as a security risk. The purpose of the "pardon" for Davies, venerable friend of Chou En-lai and other Chinese Communists, was to pave the way for his appointment as a consultant to the Arms Control and Disarmament Agency in formulating a new U.S. policy on China.

It was common knowledge in Washington that the restoration of Davies had been accomplished with the consent of the incoming Secretary of State. Whatever Rogers' motives were in vindicating John Paton Davies, within a week it became apparent that he had no intention of vindicating Otto Otepka.

CHAPTER **XLIV**

Vindication

THE DAY AFTER RICHARD M. NIXON'S INAUGURATION AS THE THIRTY-seventh President of the United States, the new Secretary of State, William P. Rogers, conferred with Otto Otepka's attorney, Roger Robb. The Secretary bluntly informed Robb that under no circumstances would he give Otepka back his old job, or any job in security at State. In fact, Rogers said, he did not want Otepka in the State Department at all.

For some reason, Robb withheld the latter part of this injunction when he communicated Rogers' position to Otepka. Robb simply said that the incoming Secretary would not restore Otepka to SY and had asked for Otepka's terms of settlement.

Otepka, wearied beyond human endurance by years of constant struggle, reluctantly decided that the time had come to seek a truce. If the new Administration, after all the pontifical campaign promises, did not want to take him back, then there was no point in continuing the fight. At 54 he thought he should be using the years remaining to him in some pursuit that would prove more productive than tilting at White House windmills. For some time he had been carefully planning a campaign to alert the American people to what was happening to them and to their country. As long as he remained in government, his lips were sealed. Once outside, he would at least be free to speak.

451

Within two days after receiving William Rogers' message, as given to him by Attorney Robb, Otepka submitted his minimum terms of settlement, terms that he had been pondering for some weeks as the strange silence that had settled upon the Nixon camp right after election continued to prevail. All that Otepka asked was that Secretary Rogers overturn Dean Rusk's decision, reinstate him nominally, and only momentarily, as Chief of the Evaluations Division in the Office of Security, and declare the framed-up charges that the State Department had leveled against him (and then dropped) as false and untrue. If this were done, Otepka said, he would immediately retire from government. In effect, he offered to take Rogers and the Nixon Administration off the hook.

On February 21, to everyone's amazement, Secretary of State Rogers notified Otepka that his offer of settlement was rejected. Having upheld Dean Rusk's decision, and by so doing condoning the conspiracy against Otepka and the dismemberment of SY, Rogers took off with the Nixon entourage on the President's first quick tour of Western Europe.

The Senate Internal Security Subcommittee, shocked almost beyond belief by William Rogers' hit-and-run action, at last began to bestir itself. Behind the scenes old Everett Dirksen rolled up his sleeves and went to work. Within forty-eight hours of Nixon's return from Europe, the Senate minority leader had nailed down a compromise: the President would appoint Otepka to the Subversive Activities Control Board (SACB), a mute and dormant governmental body that had been forced to play possum for many years, primarily because the Attorney General's office had persistently refused to refer any cases to it.

When Roger Robb, who was himself awaiting a Presidential appointment to the Federal Court of Appeals, relayed the compromise to the embattled exile, Otepka said no. Secretary Rogers' cynical rejection of his armistice offer had rekindled his old fighting spirit and Otepka was prepared to carry the case to the Supreme Court rather than bow to any "deal."

Realizing that the SACB appointment was the last best hope for Otepka's public vindication, Senator Dirksen invited him to pay a visit to Capitol Hill for a conference. In his most soothing and mellifluous tones, Dirksen explained that membership on the five-man Subversive Activities Control Board would be more than just a hollow gesture. It would, he promised, be a turning point in the long suspended war against subversion. The Senate bill that had failed to get to the floor in the last session was in the hopper again. If it passed, and Senator Dirksen said he was confident that it had a good chance to pass, the bill would elevate the SACB to overall supervision of personnel security in all of the sensitive agencies of government—not only the Department of State, but the Defense Department and several others as well.*

With Otepka's expertise and knowledge of security, Dirksen said, the SACB could be forged into the most useful instrument the government had ever had in the internal security field.

In separate conferences that same day, Barry Goldwater and Strom Thurmond reinforced Dirksen's persuasive arguments. Otepka, knowing that all three of these Senators had his interest at heart, and that all of them had in the past demonstrated their deep concern for the restoration of sound security in government, finally agreed to accept the SACB appointment if the President saw fit to tender it to him.

On March 19, 1969, the White House announced that President Nixon was naming Otto F. Otepka to the Subversive Activities Control Board at a salary of $36,000 a year. But before the Senate could move to confirm the appointment, Otepka was forced to suffer through one last battle, in some ways the most vicious of them all.

In April, the New York *Times* spearheaded an editorial vendetta against Otepka, charging that he had "received $22,000 from a fund with extreme right-wing associations." With a reckless disregard for the facts, the *Times* hinted broadly that Otepka had become a member of the John Birch Society. ("Mr. Otepka had the right to join the Birch Society," was the way the *Times* phrased it.[1])

"After this," fulminated the *Times*, "Senators of conscience cannot vote to confirm Mr. Otepka.... (for) his warped concept of Americanism disqualifies (him) from sitting in judgment on subversion."[2]

Having paraded its own "warped concept of Americanism" before the world, the *Times* not only demanded that the Senate reject Otepka's nomination, but directed the Congress forthwith to "follow up by burying the S.A.C.B., a useless relic of an American era best forgotten."

Predictably, a number of other newspapers and magazines echoed the *Times* line. And, as usual, the editorializing spilled over into the news columns. The worst attacks, however, came from that sterling old Custodian of Truth, Drew Pearson. With his acolyte Jack Anderson, Pearson actually set out to brand both Otepka and his attorney as anti-Semites.

---

* Only the FBI, CIA and AEC personnel security programs were to be exempted from SACB control under the provisions of Senate Bill 12. The proposed legislation was largely based upon the recommendations of the Presidential Commission on Internal Security appointed by Dwight Eisenhower, and upon the revelations aired during the Senate's Otepka hearings.

In one of the most *outré* smears of all time, Pearson and Anderson threw discretion to the winds. They charged that Otepka "got into trouble" with Dean Rusk because "he took classified papers to Senator Thomas Dodd." (Otepka, of course, never took any papers to Dodd, whom he had never met outside a Senate hearing room.)

"The classified papers which Otepka gave Dodd," Pearson-Anderson contended, "pertained to the security clearances of several officials, the most important being Walt Whitman Rostow. . . . There were anti-semitic overtones in Otepka's taking classified papers to Senator Dodd, since Rostow is Jewish."

Of all the ludicrous pieces of reporting that have emanated from Washington in the last half-century, this must certainly take the prize. If Pearson and Anderson had read the Senate hearings on the Otepka case, which obviously they had not, they would have known that Rostow's name was never mentioned—by anyone.* Furthermore, Rostow was not injected into the case until nearly two years after the Senate subcommittee hearings formally ended. Otepka's first allusion to Rostow came in June 1967 during his State Department hearing, and in the brief subsequently filed with the Department by Roger Robb.

Otepka's failure to bring Dr. Rostow into the picture long before he did is additional evidence, if any more is needed, of his reticence and restraint. Otepka knew too well that his troubles stemmed from that initial conference with Dean Rusk and Bobby Kennedy in December 1960 and that the principal subject of that discussion was Walt Rostow. But in the distorted view of Drew Pearson and Jack Anderson, Otepka should never have brought up Rostow's name at all, if for no other reason than "Rostow is Jewish."

Having tried, and failed, to label Otepka as a "McCarthyite," Pearson-Anderson had in desperation attempted to tar him with what they called the "neo-Nazi" brush. Otepka, whose mother and father had come to America from Czechoslovakia, a land which had suffered as much or more than any other under the Nazis, shook his head in disbelieving disgust when he read the first in the long series of smear columns concocted by Drew Pearson and his protégé.

"I wonder why," he later mused, "they never mentioned my defense of Wolf Ladejinsky, who also happened to be Jewish, and the many other Jews I defended and cleared for State Department positions."

* His name was listed, with a half-dozen others, on two memorandums submitted by the State Department to the subcommittee in the earlier hearings in 1961 but these did not place Rostow in an unfavorable light, or, for that matter, really involve him in the Otepka case at all.

Edith Otepka was as stunned by the Pearson attacks as her husband. The Otepkas have lived for years in a predominantly Jewish suburb of Washington and have always been on the very best of terms with their neighbors. "We have worked together on many community projects," Edith recalled. "Why, only two or three years ago I joined a neighbor of mine and a group of her friends who came down from Philadelphia and we picketed the Soviet embassy in protest against the oppression of Jews in the Soviet Union."

Mrs. Myra Finkel wrote a moving piece about her relationship with the Otepkas which she distributed in the community to counter "the vicious attack" on them and Pearson-Anderson's "use of the Hitler tactic of repeating the big lie."

"In my six years of living and working in the Washington suburbs," Mrs. Finkel said, "I can honestly say that I have no truer or better friends than Edith and Otto Otepka. And for the information of Messrs. Pearson and Anderson—I am Jewish, [and an] East Coast moderate Republican. . . . As a member of the Jewish faith, I find this 'anti-semitic' charge by two Gentile columnists most nauseating."

Mrs. Finkel noted that her two young daughters were bewildered by the controversy swirling around Otepka. "They think of the Otepka home . . . as the place where they go for summer barbecues or to spend a pleasant weekend when their Mother goes out of town," she wrote. In conclusion, Mrs. Finkel urged all her neighbors and fellow citizens to support Otepka's confirmation by the Senate because "the vindication of Otto Otepka is not a 'right-wing cause'—it is a cause that is right."

On April 15 the Senate Judiciary Committee conducted a hearing on the President's appointment of Otepka to the SACB and Senator Dirksen volunteered to testify—something he rarely had done in the past.

"I have often thought that maybe James Bond, Agent 007 . . . ought to write this story," said Dirksen as he launched into a review of Otepka's career as a security officer.[3] "I salute Otto Otepka for having stood his ground and for having gone through five years of agony . . . [out of] devotion to the country and to the cause of internal security."

Otepka, with his wife Edith and daughter Joanne sitting nearby, also testified at the Senate hearing, but only briefly. As they were leaving the hearing room he was besieged by reporters and television cameramen. The two reporters who pressed him most severely were Neil Sheehan of the New York *Times* and Tim Wheeler of the *Daily World*, official organ of the Communist Party, U.S.A. As Wheeler put it in his story the next day, they "grilled Otepka on his Birchite connections."[4]

The grilling conducted by Sheehan and Wheeler and their inevitable hangers-on was one of the oddest *auto-de-fés* ever witnessed on Capitol Hill. But Otepka walked through the fire with dignity and did his best to set the record straight: "I certainly am not a member (of the Birch Society)," he replied evenly. "I never have been. . . . I have no intention of joining."

"Why not?" one of the inquisitors asked. "Are you opposed to their goals?"

"I am simply not a joiner," Otepka patiently explained. "I prefer to remain independent of the possible control or domination by any organization." When asked about his stand on the Ku Klux Klan, he reminded his questioners that the Klan had been cited by a Congressional committee for having advocated a policy of depriving Americans of their Constitutional rights. "I am opposed to any organization that seeks to take away rights guaranteed under the Constitution," he said.

Senator Dirksen, during his testimony at the hearing accused the New York *Times*—and by inference the other publications which had followed its lead—of conducting a smear campaign against Otepka. The credibility of the *Times*, once the most powerful and feared news organ in the country, had sunk to such low estate that hardly any knowledgeable citizen paid much attention to it anymore. But Dirksen realized that it had the ability to set the pace for a large circle of satellite publications still clinging, against all reason, to the ancient myth of the New York *Times'* invincibility.

Teddy Kennedy, taking his cue from the *Times* and perhaps from some memory of his brother Bobby, launched a final assault against Otepka during the Judiciary Committee's deliberations. Kennedy and three other Senators, Quentin Burdick of South Dakota, Philip Hart of Michigan, and Joseph Tydings of Maryland, had Otepka recalled to Capitol Hill twice to answer a series of silly questions about his alleged connection with the Birch Society and a group known as the Liberty Lobby. Otepka, as he had already pointed out, had never joined anything except the American Legion and the State Department bowling league, and he had no connection whatever with either of the groups named. He was aware that both organizations had supported him in his long fight, but so had many other groups, including the American Legion which had twice passed resolutions at its national conventions in his behalf.

Otepka was also cognizant of the possibility that some members of the Birch Society may have contributed to the American Defense Fund, which had helped pay his legal bills. But again, so had hundreds of other citizens who were interested in his case. He made the point, too, that he had never received a nickel from the Fund or any other organization, though the *Times* had claimed that he "received $22,000." The money collected by the Fund was paid directly to his lawyer, and only for legal fees.

Otepka was grateful for the Fund's indirect aid, and he was frank to admit that it would have been exceedingly difficult, if not impossible, for him to have carried on his six-year legal fight without that help. But none of the other organizations which in the past rushed to help government employees involved in litigation, including the American Civil Liberties Union, had offered to pay his attorney's fees. Of course, if they had come forward with financial support, they could not have "purchased" Otto Otepka any more than the American Defense Fund could. As he had proved repeatedly when a President of the United States had tried to "buy" him, Otepka was simply not for sale.

Otepka was also forced by Teddy Kennedy and the others to give a detailed accounting of his income, exclusive of his State Department salary, since 1961. One hopes the millionaire Senator might have quailed just a trifle when he reviewed Otepka's modest earnings from interest on savings and stock dividends, which had totaled barely $1,700 in the eight years, 1961-68. That, and his wife's salary as a teacher since the fall of 1965, represented the family's only other income during those years, except for a small ($3,400) bequest from an aunt of Edith Otepka, and $1,954 their daughter Joanne had earned since her graduation from college in June 1968.

(Joanne Otepka had worked as an artist briefly for WTOP-TV, the Washington *Post's* television station, after graduation but was soon dropped from the payroll in a hasty "reorganization" reminiscent of her father's purge by Reilly & Co. She came to the office one morning to find that her desk had been removed and when she asked her boss if they wanted her to resign, he replied sternly, "That's the general idea.")

There were more sinister implications to the questions posed by Senator Kennedy and his followers than those implied by the scanning of Otepka's family income, however. Going beyond the *Times* smear and wading right into the muck concocted by Drew Pearson and Jack Anderson, Ted Kennedy, *et al.*, sought to drag in the "anti-semitic" issue too. They pointedly asked Otepka if he thought that "Nazi" groups might "constitute a threat to domestic security," Otepka replied:

"From my general knowledge of history and [from] twenty-seven years of experience as a security officer, I am acutely aware of the potential dangers to the security of any country from . . . totalitarian organizations and individuals of either the right or the left. I would resist with every resource at my command any attempt to establish in this country a Nazi, or Facist, or Communist government, or any other form of totalitarianism."[5]

That would appear to have been enough to satisfy any reasonable man, but it was not enough to satisfy Edward Moore Kennedy. At a meeting of the full Judiciary Committee on Tuesday, May 13, Kennedy again went after Otepka. "I see that you gave a great deal of detail on your finances," Kennedy observed. "But you didn't give the same detail about the trips you made. . . . Would you please tell us about the trips."

Otepka said that he had made several trips in the past five years, including two to California, as the guest of citizens' organizations interested in his case. "The State Department had placed me at something of a disadvantage, Senator, by using resources which I did not possess," Otepka explained. He pointed out that the Department had flooded the country with letters and press releases which had misled the public about his case, including the emphasis almost invariably placed upon the trumped-up criminal charges lodged against him.

"As a matter of elementary fairness," said Otepka, "I felt the public was entitled to hear my side of the story."

Kennedy sloughed this off and quickly zeroed in on a meeting Otepka had attended as a guest in San Diego in March 1965. He demanded to know with "what organization" the man who invited Otepka was connected."

Otepka replied that the man was "connected with the United Republicans of California."

"Oh, my," came the deep-throated voice of Everett Dirksen from among the thirteen Senators present. "That does sound subversive, doesn't it."

The hearing room erupted in laughter and Teddy Kennedy's face flushed a deep red. Before the morning was out, his fellow Senators were shaking their heads in disbelief at Kennedy's specious attempts to cast doubt on Otepka's judgment and patriotism, and more than once they chuckled openly in ironic amusement.

Kennedy's obvious vindictiveness, and Otepka's calm and reasoned replies, made the outcome of the Judiciary Committee's vote inevitable. The balloting came shortly after Otepka was excused. The Senators present voted 10-to-3 for Otepka's confirmation. Even Quentin Burdick, one of Kennedy's staunchest allies, deserted Teddy and voted for

Otepka. Later, three more Senators who were absent had their votes recorded in support of the confirmation.

Kennedy managed to delay the vote on the Senate floor for seven more weeks. But on June 24, by a vote of 61-to-28, the full Senate of the United States agreed to advise and consent to President Richard Nixon's appointment of Otto F. Otepka to the Subversive Activities Control Board.

Otepka's long ordeal was at an end. Whether the Board on which he now served would be given the authority to do the job that so badly needed doing remained to be seen.

But even if the Congress granted the Board the necessary powers to bring the government's internal security program back to life, there would still remain a far, far more crucial question, a question which Otto Otepka asked himself with deepening concern as the decade of the 1970's neared. . . .

Was there still time?

Appendix A

The Department of State

Mr. Otto F. Otepka
Office of Security
   Department of State
Dear Mr. Otepka:

This is a notice of proposed adverse action in accordance with the regulations of the Civil Service Commission.

You are hereby notified that it is proposed to remove you from your appointment with the Department of State, as Supervisory Personnel Security Specialist, GS-15, in the Office of the Deputy Assistant Secretary for Security, thirty (30) days from the date of this letter.

On August 16, 1963, at Washington, D.C. you executed a voluntary sworn statement, dated August 15, 1963, before Carl E. Graham and Robert C. Byrnes, Special Agents of the Federal Bureau of Investigation. A copy of this statement is attached as Exhibit A. Information contained therein will be referred to specifically in some of the charges listed below.

Furthermore, during the period March 13, 1963, to June 18, 1963, Mr. John F. Reilly, Deputy Assistant Secretary for Security, caused the following procedures to be instituted:

(a) Mrs. Joyce M. Schmelzer, secretary to Mr. Frederick W. Traband, Supervisory Personnel Security Specialist, periodically observed your classified trash bag (hereinafter referred to as "burn bag") which was in possession of your secretary, Mrs. Eunice Powers. Mrs. Schmelzer and Mrs. Powers were located in the same room and across from one another.

(b) When Mrs. Schmelzer saw that your burn bag was full, she would ask Mrs. Powers if she wanted her (Mrs. Schmelzer) to take your burn bag to a Department Mail Room with Mr. Traband's.

(c) When Mrs. Powers accepted Mrs. Schmelzer's offer, Mrs. Schmelzer would inform Mr. Traband of this fact. Mr. Traband would then call Mr. Rosetti, Supervisory Security Specialist, or Mr. Shea, Supervisory General Investigator, if Mr. Rosetti was not available, and inform him that your burn bag was being delivered to the Mail Room.

(d) While carrying your burn bag and Mr. Traband's to the Mail Room, Mrs. Schmelzer would mark your burn bag with a red "x" (with a crayon or pencil mark) and deposit both burn bags in the Mail Room, Room 3437.

(e) Mr. Rosetti or Mr. Shea, and on one occasion Mr. Robert Mc-Carthy, Supervisory Security Specialist, would obtain your burn bag from the Mail Room within five to ten minutes after Mrs. Schmelzer left it there and would turn it over to Mr. Reilly or Mr. Belisle (Special Assistant to the Deputy Assistant Secretary for Security), in their office, Room 3811. (On one occasion when Mrs. Powers herself took your burn bag to the Mail Room, Messrs. Rosetti and Shea picked it up from the Mail Room immediately after Mrs. Powers deposited it there.) Your burn bag was then transferred to Mr. Reilly's brief case.

(f) Mr. Reilly's brief case was then taken by Mr. Shea to Room 1410, 2612A or 3811 for examination of its contents. Your burn bag was inspected by Mr. Shea either alone or with Mr. Belisle and/or Mr. Rosetti.

(g) The contents of your burn bags were carefully examined. All carbon paper or copies were read by turning the carbon side toward the light thus allowing the paper to be read from the back. Torn pieces of paper were grouped together and then pieced together to make readable documents. One-time typewriter ribbons were also read on occasion.

During the course of inspecting the contents of your burn bag on May 29, 1963, a typewriter ribbon was retrieved. This ribbon has been read and the contents are reproduced as Exhibit B. Information contained therein will be referred to specifically in some of the charges listed below:

(1) *You have conducted yourself in a manner unbecoming an officer of the Department of State.*

Specifically: You furnished a copy of a classified memorandum concerning the processing of appointments of members of the Advisory Committee on International Organizations Staffing to a person outside of the Department without authority and in violation of the Presidential Directive of March 13, 1948 (13 Fed. Reg. 1359). This Directive provides:

> ". . . all reports, records, and files relative to the loyalty of employees or prospective employees (including reports of such investigative agencies), shall be maintained in confidence, and shall not be transmitted or disclosed except as required in the efficient conduct of business."

You were reminded of the prohibition contained in this Directive on March 22, 1963, when you received and noted a copy of a letter from

Mr. Dutton, Assistant Secretary of State, to Senator Eastland, Chairman of the Senate Committee on the Judiciary, dated March 20, 1963. A copy of this letter, indicating that you "noted" it, is enclosed as Exhibit C.

In your sworn statement, referred to above and enclosed as Exhibit A, you stated on pages 7 and 8 that you gave a copy of a classified memorandum entitled "Francis O. Wilcox, Arthur Larson, Lawrence Finkelstein, Marshall D. Shulman, Andrew Cordier, Ernest Gross, Harding Bancroft, Sol Linowitz," to Mr. J. G. Sourwine, Chief Counsel, United States Senate Subcommittee to Investigate the Administration of the Internal Security Act and Other Internal Security Laws, of the Committee on the Judiciary. This memorandum concerns "the loyalty of employees or prospective employees" of the Department within the meaning of the Presidential Directive of March 13, 1948.

This is a breach of the standard of conduct expected of an officer of the Department of State.

(2) *You have conducted yourself in a manner unbecoming an officer of the Department of State.*

Specifically: You furnished a copy of a classified memorandum concerning the processing of appointments of members of the Advisory Committee on International Organizations Staffing to a person outside of the Department without authority and in violation of the Presidential Directive of March 13, 1948 (13 Fed. Reg. 1359). This Directive provides:

> ". . . all reports, records, and files relative to the loyalty of employees or prospective employees (including reports of such investigative agencies), shall be maintained in confidence, and shall not be transmitted or disclosed except as required in the efficient conduct of business."

You were reminded of the prohibition contained in this Directive on March 22, 1963, when you received and noted a copy of a letter from Mr. Dutton, to Senator Eastland, dated March 20, 1963. A copy of this letter, indicating that you "noted" it, is enclosed as Exhibit C.

In your sworn statement, referred to above and enclosed as Exhibit A, you stated on page 9 that you gave a copy of a classified memorandum entitled "Processing of Appointments of Members of the Advisory Committee on International Organizations Staffing," to Mr. J. G. Sourwine. This memorandum concerns "the loyalty of employees or prospective employees" of the Department within the meaning of the Presidential Directive of March 13, 1948.

This is a breach of the standard of conduct expected of an officer of the Department of State.

(3) *You have conducted yourself in a manner unbecoming an officer of the Department of State.*

Specifically: You furnished a copy of an investigative report concerning a prospective employee of the Department to a person outside of the Department without authority and in violation of the Presidential Directive of March 13, 1948 (13 Fed. Reg. 1359). This Directive provides:

". . . all reports, records, and files relative to the loyalty of employees or prospective employees (including reports of such investigative agencies), shall be maintained in confidence, and shall not be transmitted or disclosed except as required in the efficient conduct of business."

You were reminded of the prohibition contained in this Directive on March 22, 1963, when you received and noted a copy of a letter from Mr. Dutton, to Senator Eastland, dated March 20, 1963. A copy of this letter, indicating that you "noted" it, is enclosed as Exhibit C.

In your sworn statement, referred to above and enclosed as Exhibit A, you stated on page 10 that you gave a copy of an investigative report dated May 27, 1960, to Mr. J. G. Sourwine, concerning "Joan Mae Fogltanz". This report concerns "the loyalty of employees or prospective employees" of the Department within the meaning of the Presidential Directive of March 13, 1948.

This is a breach of the standard of conduct expected of an office of the Department of State.

(4) *You have been responsible for the declassification of a classified document containing classified information without following the procedures set forth in Volume 5, Section 1970, et seq. of the Department's Foreign Affairs Manual as supplemented by FAMC 102, dated January 30, 1963.* This document, which was classified CONFIDENTIAL, was addressed to Mr. McGeorge Bundy, the White House, and was signed by Mr. William H. Brubeck, Special Assistant to the Secretary and Executive Secretary of the Department.

Specifically: On June 18, 1963, the xeroxed copies of the tops and bottoms of the pages of the aforementioned document were retrieved from your burn bag. This burn bag was obtained from the Mail Room in accordance with the procedure outlined above. These tops and bottoms had been cut from a xeroxed copy of the Brubeck document and have been matched with a complete copy for identification purposes.

The act of cutting the classification indicators from a copy of a document declassified that copy of the document. Exhibit D is a statement from Messrs. Belisle, Rosetti, and Shea, attesting to the fact that they have identified these clippings as having come from the classified document referred to above.

(5) *You have been responsible for the mutilation of a classified document in violation of 18 U.S.C. 2071, which provides:*

> "(a) Whoever willfully and unlawfully conceals, removes, mutilates, obliterates, or destroys, or attempts to do so, or, with intent to do so takes and carries away any record, proceeding, map, book, paper, document, or other thing, filed or deposited with any clerk or officer of any court of the United States, or in any public office, or with any judicial or public officer of the United States, shall be fined not more than $2,000 or imprisoned not more than three years, or both.

> (b) Whoever, having the custody of any such record, proceeding, map, book, document, paper, or other thing, willfully and unlawfully conceals, removes, mutilates, obliterates, falsifies, or destroys the same, shall be fined not more than $2,000 or imprisoned not more than three years, or both; and shall forfeit his office and be disqualified from holding any office under the United States. (June 25, 1948, ch. 645, 62 Stat. 795.)"

This document, which was classified CONFIDENTIAL, was addressed to Mr. McGeorge Bundy, the White House, and was signed by Mr. William H. Brubeck.

Specifically: On June 18, 1963, the xeroxed copies of the tops and bottoms of the pages of the aforementioned document were retrieved from your burn bag. This burn bag was obtained from the Mail Room in accordance with the procedure outlined above. These tops and bottoms had been cut from a xeroxed copy of the Brubeck document and have been matched with a complete copy for identification purposes.

The act of cutting the classification indicators from a document "mutilates" that document within the meaning of 18 U.S.C. 2071. Exhibit D is a statement from Messrs. Belisle, Rosetti and Shea, attesting to the fact that they have identified these clippings as having come from the classified document referred to above.

(6) *You have been responsible for the declassification of a classified document containing classified information without following the procedures set forth in Volume 5, Section 1970, et seq. of the Department's Foreign Affairs Manual as supplemented by FAMC 102, dated January 30, 1963.* This document, which was classified CONFIDENTIAL, was addressed to SY - Mr. Belisle from SY/EX - Mr. John Noonan, Supervisory Security Specialist, and was on the subject "Security Meeting".

Specifically: On June 18, 1963, a thermofaxed copy of the tops and botttoms of the pages of the aforementioned document was retrieved from your burn bag. This burn bag was obtained from the Mail Room in accordance with the procedure outlined above. These tops and bottoms had been cut from a thermofaxed copy for identification purposes.

The act of cutting the classification indicators from a copy of a document declassified that copy of the document. Exhibit D is a statement from Messrs. Shea, Belisle and Rosetti, attesting to the fact that they have identified these clippings as having come from the classified document referred to above.

(7) You have been responsible for the mutilation of a classified document in violation of 18 U.S.C. 2071, which provides:

"(a) Whoever willfully and unlawfully conceals, removes, mutilates, obliterates, or destroys, or attempts to do so, or with intent to do so takes and carries away any record, proceeding, map, book, paper, document, or other thing, filed or deposited with any clerk or officer of any court of the United States, or in any public office, or with any judicial or public officer of the United States, shall be fined not more than $2,000 or imprisoned not more than three years, or both.

(b) Whoever, having the custody of any such record, proceeding, map, book, document, paper, or other thing, willfully and unlawfully conceals, removes, mutilates, obliterates, falsifies, or destroys the same, shall be fined not more than $2,000 or imprisoned not more than three years, or both; and shall forfeit his office and be disqualified from holding any office under the United States. (June 25, 1948, ch. 645, 62 Stat. 795.)"

This document, which was classified CONFIDENTIAL, was addressed to SY - Mr. Belisle from SY/EX - Mr. John Noonan, and was on the subject "Security Meeting".

Specifically: On June 18, 1963, a thermofaxed copy of the tops and bottoms of the pages of the aforementioned document was retrieved from your burn bag. This burn bag was obtained from the Mail Room in accordance with the procedure outlined above. These tops and bottoms had been cut from a thermofaxed copy of the document and they have been matched with a complete copy for identification purposes.

The act of cutting the classification indicators from a document "mutilates" that document within the meaning of 18 U.S.C. 2071. Exhibit D is a statement from Messrs. Shea, Belisle and Rosetti, attesting to the fact that they have identified these clippings as having come from the classified document referred to above.

(8) *You have been responsible for the declassification of a classified document containing classified information without following the procedures set forth in Volume 5, Section 1970, et seq. of the Department's Foreign Affairs Manual as supplemented by FAMC 102, dated January 30, 1963.* This document, which was classified CONFIDENTIAL, was addressed to you from Messrs. Traband and Levy (Supervisory Personnel Security Specialist), and was on the subject "SY Evaluative Service to ARA and OIA".

Specifically: *On June 18, 1963,* a xeroxed copy of the tops and bottoms of the pages of the aforementioned document was retrieved from your burn bag. This burn bag was obtained from the Mail Room in accordance with the procedure outlined above. These tops and bottoms had been cut from a xeroxed copy of the subject document and have been matched with a complete copy for identification purposes.

The act of cutting the classification indicators from a copy of a document, declassified that copy of the document. Exhibit D is a statement from Messrs. Shea, Belisle and Rosetti, attesting to the fact that they have identified these clippings as having come from the classified document referred to above.

(9) *You have been responsible for the mutilation of a classified document in violation of 18 U.S.C. 2071, which provides:*

"(a) Whoever willfully and unlawfully conceals, removes, mutilates, obliterates, or destroys, or attempts to do so, or, with intent to do so takes and carries away any record, proceeding, map, book, paper, document, or other thing, filed or deposited with any clerk or officer of any court of the United States, or in any public office, or with any judicial or public officer of the United States, shall be fined not more than $2,000 or imprisoned not more than three years, or both.

(b) Whoever, having the custody of any such record, proceeding, map, book, document, paper, or other thing, willfully and unlawfully conceals, removes, mutilates, obliterates, falsifies, or destroys the same, shall be fined not more than $2,000 or imprisoned not more than three years, or both; and shall forfeit his office and be disqualified from holding any office under the United States. (June 25, 1948, ch. 645, 62 Stat. 795.)"

This document, which was classified CONFIDENTIAL, was addressed to you from Messrs. Traband and Levy, and was on the subject "SY Evaluative Services to ARA and OIA."

Specifically: *On June 18, 1963,* a xeroxed copy of the tops and bottoms of the pages of the aforementioned document was retrieved from your burn bag. This burn bag was obtained from the Mail Room in accordance with the procedure outlined above. These tops and bottoms had been cut from a xeroxed copy of the subject document and have been matched with a complete copy for identification purposes.

The act of cutting the classification indicators from a document "mutilates" that document within the meaning of 18 U.S.C. 2071. Exhibit D is a statement from Messrs. Shea, Belisle and Rosetti attesting to the fact that they have identified these clippings as having come from the classified document referred to above.

(10) *You have been responsible for the declassification of a classified document containing classified information without following the procedures set forth in volume 5, Section 1970, et seq. of the Department's Foreign Affairs Manual as supplemented by FAMC 102, dated January 30, 1963.* This document, which was classified CONFIDENTIAL, was drafted by ARA/RPA: JMBarta (International Relations Officer), and concerned the procedure for reviewing and disposing of adverse information on employees of International Organizations dealing with Inter-American Affairs.

Specifically: *On June 18, 1963,* a xeroxed copy of the tops and bottoms of the pages of the aforementioned document was retrieved from your burn bag. This burn bag was obtained from the Mail Room in accordance with the procedure outlined above. These tops and bottoms which were cut from a xeroxed copy of the Barta document, have been matched with a complete copy for identification purposes.

The act of cutting the classification indicators from a copy of a document declassified that copy of the document. Exhibit D is a statement from Messrs. Shea, Belisle and Rosetti, attesting to the fact that they have identified these clippings as having come from the classified document referred to above.

(11) *You have been responsible for the mutilation of a classified document in violation of 18 U.S.C. 2071, which provides:*

> "(a) Whoever willfully and unlawfully conceals, removes, mutilates, obliterates, or destroys, or attempts to do so, or with intent to do so takes and carries away any record, proceeding, map, book, paper, document, or other thing, filed or deposited with any clerk or officer of any court of the United States, or in any public office, or with any judicial or public officer of the United States, shall be fined not more than $2,000 or imprisoned not more than three years, or both.

> (b) Whoever, having the custody of any such record, proceeding, map, book, document, paper, or other thing, willfully and unlawfully conceals, removes, mutilates, obliterates, falsifies, or destroys the same, shall be fined not more than $2,000 or imprisoned not more than three years, or both; and shall forfeit his office and be disqualified from holding any office under the United States. (June 25, 1948, ch. 645, 62 Stat. 795.)"

This document, which was classified CONFIDENTIAL was drafted by ARA/RPA: JMBarta, and concerned the procedure for reviewing and disposing of adverse information on employees of *International Organizations dealing with Inter-American Affairs.*

Specifically: *On June 18, 1963,* a xeroxed copy of the tops and bottoms of the pages of the aforementioned document was retrieved from your burn bag. This burn bag was obtained from the Mail Room in accordance with the procedure outlined above. These tops and bottoms which were cut from a xeroxed copy of the Barta document, have been matched with a complete copy for identification purposes.

The act of cutting the classification indicators from a document "mutilates" that document within the meaning of 18 U.S.C. 2071. Exhibit D is a statement from Messrs. Shea, Belisle and Rosetti, attesting to the fact that they have identified these clippings as having come from the classified document referred to above.

(12) *You have conducted yourself in a manner unbecoming an officer of the Department of State.*

Specifically: On March 19, 1963, carbon paper consisting of seven pages was recovered from your burn bag. This burn bag was obtained by Mr. Rosetti from the Mail Room after it had been placed there in accordance with the procedure outlined above. The burn bag was inspected and carbon paper recovered from it by Mr. Shea. Mr. Rosetti's signed statement regarding this incident is enclosed as Exhibit E. Mr. Shea's statement is enclosed as Exhibit F. The carbon paper has been reproduced and copies thereof are attached as Exhibit G. This carbon paper contains questions which you prepared and furnished to a person or persons outside the Department for the use of Mr. J. G. Sourwine, in the interrogation of Mr. Reilly. Mr. Sourwine subsequently asked these questions of Mr. Reilly when he appeared before the United States Senate Subcommitteee to Investigate the Administration of the Internal Security Act and Other Internal Security Laws, of the Committee on the Judiciary. Mr. Reilly's signed statement is enclosed as Exhibit H.

This is a breach of the standard of conduct expected of an officer of the Department of State.

(13) *You have conducted yourself in a manner unbecoming an officer of the Department of State.*

Specifically: On June 10, 1963, a one-time typewriter ribbon was recovered from your burn bag. This burn bag was obtained by Mr. Rosetti from the Mail Room after it had been placed there in accordance with the procedure outlined above. Mr. Rosetti's signed statement regarding this incident is enclosed as Exhibit I. This typewriter ribbon has been read and the contents are reproduced as Exhibit J. The ribbon contained twenty-four questions which you prepared and furnished to a person or persons outside the Department for the use of Mr. J. G. Sourwine in the interrogation of Mr. Belisle. Mr. Sourwine subsequently asked fifteen of these questions of Mr. Belisle when he appeared before the United States Senate Subcommittee to Investigate the Administration of the Internal Security Act and Other Internal Security Laws, of the Committee on the Judiciary. Mr. Belisle's signed statement is enclosed as Exhibit K.

This is a breach of the standard of conduct expected of an officer of the Department of State.

Copies of the memoranda and documents referred to in the charges which are classified and concern "the loyalty of employees or prospective employees" of the Department are available for inspection by you and your attorney upon request to Mr. John W. Drew, Jr., of my staff, in Room 2239.

You are hereby given ten (10) days from the date of this letter to answer these charges. You may reply both personally and in writing if you so desire. Any written reply you wish to make should be addressed to my attention. You may furnish affidavits or other evidence in support of your reply if you so desire. If you wish to make an oral reply you may call Mr. Drew, extension 6251, for an appointment.

As soon as possible, after your answer is received, or after the expiration of the ten (10) day limit, if you do not answer, a written decision will be issued to you.

During the thirty (30) day notice period to which you are entitled, you will remain in an active duty status at your present grade and salary.

Sincerely yours,

John Ordway, Chief
Personnel Operations Division

Encloseures:
See Exhibit Index A through K.

Appendix B

Report of the 1967 Sigma Delta Chi
(National Professional Journalism Society)
Advancement of Freedom of Information Committee

In the first two months after the FOI Act went into effect, the State (Department) received about a dozen formal requests for specific documents and granted them all except three. All three refusals covered transcripts of hearings concerning Otto Otepka, a department official accused of improperly leaking information to congressional committees. The State (Department) classified the transcripts as relating to internal personnel matters, a specific exemption under the law.

The State Department secrecy in this instance was an obvious effort to hide a record that is embarrassing to Secretary of State Dean Rusk and other high officials. The only real justification for secrecy on personnel records is for the protection of the government employee. This could not be used in the Otepka case, for Otepka had asked that the hearings be public so he could get the full story of the "get Otepka" conspiracy before the public.

When the fallacy of the original justification for secrecy was pointed out, the State Department then claimed that it was justified in conducting secret hearings because national security was involved. In this instance it was pointed out that two documents used in the hearings as evidence carried a national security classification.

Under questioning, the State Department lawyer admitted that the two documents with a national security classification had already been published in full in the reports of the Senate Internal Security Subcommittee. Although this publication had taken place with State Department knowledge more than a year prior to the Otepka hearing, the State Department refused to change its position.

A study of this entire case makes it obvious that the State Department was misusing a claim of national security for purposes of hiding or obscuring the record. The record of this case discloses a disgraceful pattern of inaccurate and misleading testimony by high State Department officials. These officials gave inaccurate misleading testimony in connection with security cases. When Otepka gave testimony and produced records proving that superiors had lied under oath, the superiors used unauthorized eavesdropping and wiretapping as well as other police state methods to try to obtain grounds for firing Otepka.

High State Department officials denied they had engaged in eavesdropping and wiretapping when questioned under oath by a congressional committee, and they made the same denials to the press. Later, these officials were forced to admit that there had been the eavesdropping and wiretapping as part of a "get Otepka" move.

For the four years that this case has been pending before the State Department, the Department press office has engaged in a broad pattern of inaccurate and misleading statements to reporters and interested citizens in an effort to smear Otepka. That outrageous pattern of deception has continued at least through August 1967.

Appendix C

I am appearing here today accompanied by my counsel, but without witnesses or additional evidence which I expected to have available to me. I have been denied the opportunity to question witnesses and offer such evidence on matters relating to Charges 4 through 13, which have been withdrawn. I must say that I am unable to understand the Department of State's and the Commission's rulings denying me this opportunity on their theory that evidence tending to destroy me, simply because it may also relate to Charges 4 through 14, is irrelevant to the issues in Charges 1, 2 and 3, the only remaining charges against me.

Notwithstanding these rulings, I assert my right to make the following statement before this appellate body. In support of my claim, I respectfully refer the Commission to its own practices under the provisions of the Veterans Preference Act, enacted by the Congress and signed by the President in 1944. I am not only an honorably discharged veteran of the Armed Forces during World War II who is entitled to the rights and privileges afforded by this Act, but I can speak of my own experience as an employee of the Civil Service Commission for eleven years when I was required to carry out the Commission's implementing practices pursuant to this act.

It has always been the Commission's firm policy to allow a veteran affected by an adverse agency action, to personally appear before a Commission representative, and either orally or in affidavit form, present any grievance which he might have against his employers. The employing agency could not restrict this right, even though the Commission, on appeal, could decide the employee's statement was irrelevant. According to my understanding the same principle is still in effect, for it is clearly enunciated in the Commission publication issued in July 1964, called "Conducting Hearings on Employee Appeals", which states, with respect to both veterans and non-veterans, "The employee has a right to answer adverse actions in person, as well as in writing. . . . . .and to be given an opportunity to say what he will in an effort to secure justice and mercy."

While I had the opportunity to respond affirmatively in writing to all of the Department's charges when they were filed against me in September 1963, and to enter a general denial to all of them, the Department deliberately impeded my efforts to obtain justice by refusing to allow my attorney and me to examine the contents of trash bags purportedly containing material that formed the basis of charges 4 through 11. Under this obstacle, I found it extremely difficult, if not impossible, to develop by independent means necessary evidence to prove that these charges were completely false and contrived solely to destroy me. By the time it became possible for me to obtain a hearing on all of the charges and to cross-examine Department witnesses implicated in the trash bag episode, the Department withdrew the charges and summarily denied me the opportunity to present evidence to show that they were false and vindictive.

In pursuance of the Commission's policy to permit an employee of the classified civil service to state his grievances to a Commission representative in the interest of justice, I offer the following statement. Since I am prevented by the Commission's ruling from presenting evidence in support of this statement, it shall be as brief as possible except where clarity demands necessary detail. I am omitting in this statement any comment on charges 12 and 13, which the Department also has dropped.

1. I accuse the Department of State, and specifically John F. Reilly, David Belisle, and Mrs. Marie Catucci, acting individually and collectively, and aided and abetted by Frederick Traband, Joseph Sabin, Raymond Levy, Robert McCarthy, Joseph Rosetti, Terence Shea, Mrs. Joyce Schmelzer, and William J. Crockett, of concocting a malevolent scheme to obtain my ouster from the Office of Security and the Department of State, through the false impression that I had mutilated government papers in violation of a criminal statute.

2. I did not mutilate the documents in question. I did not ask anyone else to do so. If in fact a mutilation did occur and I had been allowed the opportunity to cross-examine each of the above witnesses, the guilty person would have been identified. The charges were withdrawn by the Department to prevent this identification.

3. I accuse the Department of gross impropriety in approving the preparation and distribution of hundreds of pieces of correspondence to the public and the Congress, beginning in September 1963 and continu-

ing until June 1967, when the charges were withdrawn, alleging that I was responsible for the mutilation, although in fact the Department knew during this time that those charges could not be supported.

4. I request that the Civil Service Commission instruct the Department to furnish me with an official communication addressed to me, similar to the letter of charges filed against me, specifying in detail the reasons for the withdrawal of the mutilation charges. The oral statement made by Department counsel, Irving Jaffe, at my hearing, on June 6, 1967, giving only the reason that the charges did not allege the delivery of the documents in question to anyone, is unclear, unsatisfactory and unfair to me. In brief, I insist I am entitled to a "Not Guilty" letter from the Department of State. As a precedent for such a letter, I refer to another case involving the furnishing of official information by a State Department employee to a person outside the Department. In that case, John Stewart Service admittedly gave 18 highly classified documents, not to a Congressional committee, but to a person established as a Communist and Soviet agent. Service was arrested for his offense by the FBI but a Grand Jury refused prosecution because it was satisfied he did not intend to harm the national security. Although Service clearly breached the Department's security regulation, notwithstanding his acquittal on criminal grounds, the Department termed his acquittal by the Grand Jury as a complete vindication and he was issued two letters signed by the Secretary of State and Under-Secretary of State respectively, congratulating him and restoring him to full duty in the same line of work for which he was best qualified professionally.

5. In contrast to the above case, and despite the fact that I have never violated any security regulation whatsoever, I have been penalized by a demotion in grade and salary and assigned to duties entirely incompatible with my professional experience as a security officer for the past twenty-five years, involving only the preparation of elementary and unclassified phrases for inclusion in a so-called Department Manual of Organization. I have been informed that unlike my work as a security officer, none of these duties require access to sensitive material and none shall be given me connection with the performance of my assignment. In effect this decree, until and unless it is revoked, has ended my government career as a security officer because no other government agency will wish to employ me in my profession.

6. The Department dispatched a special messenger to my home on December 11, 1967. He arrived at 7:10 P.M. to deliver a written verdict of "Guilty" signed by Secretary Rusk, on charges 1, 2 and 3. Included

was another letter signed by Idar Rimestad setting forth his implementation of the Secretary's orders of my punishment. Neither official mentioned my acquittal on charges 4 through 13.

In determining whether the Secretary's action in the circumstances has been reasonable and proper, I respectfully submit that the Commission must carefully consider the following facts.

The full record, and Mr. Reilly's own admission, establishes that Mr. Reilly undertook to tap my telephone only because he suspected that I was furnishing information to the Senate Internal Security Subcommittee. I therefore take exception to the Commission's rulings denying my requests to (a) ascertain the identity of the person to whom the tape recordings of my intercepted conversations were delivered, (b) obtain from the Department affidavits submitted to the Secretary on the wiretapping episode by John F. Reilly, David Belisle, Elmer Hill and Clarence Schneider all of whom were involved in that episode, and (c) obtain from the Department the reports of investigation prepared by George W. French, Jr. and Wilson Flake concerning the tapping of my telephone. I contend that these documents and information are relevant.

The documents on which charges 1, 2 and 3 are predicated were not furnished by me to the Internal Security Subcommittee until June 2, 1963. The events preceding my action are most important.

Mr. Reilly began tapping my telephone in March 1963, if not earlier. By his own admission I had done nothing wrong by that time.

Later in March 1963, he placed my trash bag under surveillance.

In April 1963, Mr. Reilly had my office safe drilled open surreptitiously and its contents photographed. It contained information legitimately in my custody for official purposes.

During April and May 1963, without ever having discussed the matter with me as he should have under Civil Service and Department regulations, Mr. Reilly derogated my performance and accused me of emotional instability before the Internal Security Subcommittee.

By May 23, 1963, the fifth day of his testimony, Mr. Reilly had committed one falsehood after the other and compounded several of these falsehoods repeatedly. His statements concerning me had become so patently untrue that they attracted the special attention of the Acting Chairman and the Chief Counsel of the Subcommittee.

As I had become aware of Reilly's activities through information volunteered to me, I reviewed each incident cumulatively and collectively. By the end of May 1963, I could reach no other conclusion except that the consistency and frequency of his actions could occur only with higher approval. After discreetly exploring the possibility of approaching Secretary Rusk in the matter, I came to the logical conclusion that neither the Secretary nor those in the chain of command through whom I had to apply to seek an audience with him, would welcome my complaints. It became apparent to me that they would block my efforts not only to rebut Mr. Reilly's testimony about me but the need to expose his other wrongdoing. I saw no alternative except to perform my honest duty by telling the Congress the truth when called upon to do so. Subsequent events justified my decision, for in November 1963 it was clearly demonstrated by other witnesses before the Subcommittee that Mr. Rusk and Undersecretary George Ball had fully protected Mr. Reilly in his attempts to escape culpability when he was trapped in his own falsehoods. It was not until Mr. Reilly had become so hopelessly enmeshed in his lies, that Mr. Rusk was forced to dismiss him in order to salvage at least a part of the Department's loss of integrity.

As an experienced Department officer I felt that my recourse to the Congress in the circumstances was entirely proper. I do not regret my course of conduct in any way because I am still confident that through the watchdog responsibilities of the Civil Service Commission and the Congress of the United States, the State Department can achieve completely honest administration at every level of its personnel security operations.

I rest my case on the record before the Commission unless the Commission desires to reconsider its rulings and allows the evidence that I have requested.

Notes

PREFACE

1. *A Treasury of Great Reporting*, edited by Louis L. Snyder and Richard B. Morris, Simon & Schuster, New York, 1949, p. 231.

2. Clark R. Mollenhoff, "Life Line of Democracy," *Nieman Reports*, Sept. 1964, p. 27.

3. "The Ordeal of Otto Otepka," *The Reader's Digest*, Aug. 1965.

4. Rebecca West, *The New Meaning of Treason*, Viking Press, New York, 1964, p. 149.

CHAPTER I

1. New York *Times*, Nov. 6, 1963.

2. Arthur M. Schlesinger, Jr., *A Thousand Days*, Houghton Mifflin Company, Boston, 1965, p. 445.

3. "Scholar Who's No. 2 at the White House," *Business Week*, March 25, 1967.

4. Ibid.

CHAPTER II

1. New York *Times*, Nov. 6, 1963.

2. Whittaker Chambers, *Witness*, Random House, 1952, p. 470.

CHAPTER III

1. Chambers, op. cit., p. 470.

2. Prologue to *McCarthy and His Enemies* by William F. Buckley, Jr. and L. Brent Bozell, Henry Regnery Co., Chicago, 1954, p. xii.

3. Schlesinger, op. cit., p. 132.

CHAPTER IV

1. S.1390, introduced by Senator Richard M. Nixon on April 26, 1951.

2. Hearings, Immigration and Naturalization Subcommittee of the Senate Judiciary Committee on S. 1832, Part 3, p. 193.

3. Press release of the Department of State, Sept. 1, 1948, p. 14.

4. *Time*, Feb. 13, 1950, p. 23.

5. Senate Internal Security Subcommittee Hearings on State Department Security, 1961–63, Part 4, p. 435.

6. Ibid., p. 434.

7. Ibid., p. 435.

8. Ibid., p. 436.

9. New York *York Times*, Nov. 6, 1963.

10. Letter from Daniel H. Clare, Jr., March 25, 1957.

11. Memorandum to E. Tomlin Bailey, April 9, 1957.

12. Theodore C. Sorensen, *Kennedy*, Harper & Row, New York, 1965, Bantom Book edition, 1966, p. 51.

13. Ibid., p. 83.

14. Otepka Hearings, 1963–65, Senate Internal Security Subcommittee: Part 10, p. 695.

15. Ibid., p. 694.

16. Ibid., p. 695.

17. Chambers, op. cit., p. 32.

CHAPTER V

1. Reportof the Committee on Government Operations, 1955 ("Army Signal Corps— Subversion and Espionage") pp. 2 and 32.

2. *Saturday Evening Post*, June 13, 1953.

3. Schlesinger, op. cit., p. 15.

4. Ibid.

5. Ibid.

6. Ibid., p. 16.

7. Ibid.

8. Ibid.

9. Ralph de Toledano, *R.F.K.*, G. P. Putnam's Sons, New York, 1967, p. 134.

CHAPTER VI

1. Clark Mollenhoff, Des Moines *Register*, Aug. 6, 1964.

2. Des Moines *Register*, Dec. 25, 1963.

3. Otepka Hearings, Senate Internal Security Subcommittee, 1963–65, Part 5, pp. 267–268.

4. Ibid., pp. 294–295.

5. Holmes Alexander column, Dec. 10, 1963.

6. "Dean Rusk: Cool Man in a Hot World," *Look*, Sept. 6, 1966.

7. "Quarterback of the Cabinet," *Saturday Evening Post*, July 22, 1961.

8. Graham Wallas, *The Great Society*, the Macmillan Company, New York 1914.

9. Rebecca West, *op. cit., pp. 150–151.*

10. *Saturday Evening Post*, op. cit.

11. Ibid.

CHAPTER VII

1. Senate Internal Security Subcommittee, 1952 Hearings, "U.S. Citizens Employed by the U.N."

2. *Foreign Policy Association Bulletin*, Dec. 1952.

3. Philadelphia *Inquirer*, Jan. 14, 1950, and Philadelphia *Bulletin* of same date.

4. *Time*, Dec. 26, 1960.

5. Douglas MacArthur, *Reminiscences*, McGraw-Hill, 1964, p. 362.

6. Ibid., p. 363.

7. Ibid., p. 365.

8. Harry S. Truman, *Memoirs*, Vol. II, *Years of Trial and Hope*, Doubleday, 1955–1956.

9. MacArthur, op. cit., p. 368.

10. Ibid., p. 369.

11. *Look*, Sept. 6, 1966.

12. Ibid.

13. Senate Internal Security Subcommittee, IPR Hearings, p. 2870.

14. Report on the Institute of Pacific Relations, Senate Internal Security Subcommittee, 1952.

15. Ibid.

16. Chicago *Tribune*. Dec. 16, 1952.

17. Schlesinger, op. cit., p. 141.

18. Washington *Sunday Star*, Jan. 8, 1961.

CHAPTER VIII

1. Jan Myrdal is author of *Chinese Journey, Report from a Chinese Village*, and other sympathetic tracts on Maoist China.

2. Richard Starnes, Scripps-Howard Newspaper Alliance, Oct. 4, 1967.

3. *New Fabian Essays*, F. A. Praeger, New York, 1952.

4. *The Dynamics of Soviet Society*, Norton Co., 1953,

5. Walt W. Rostow, *An American Policy in Asia*, John Wiley & Sons and the MIT Press, 1955.

6. Walt W. Rostow, *The U.S. in the World Arena*, Harper, 1960.

7. Rudolf Flesch, Los Angeles *Times*, review of Rostow's *The Stages of Economic Growth*, April 25, 1960.

8. *Business Week*, op. cit.

CHAPTER IX

1. *Business Week*, op. cit.

2. Schlesinger, op. cit., p. 332.

3. Ibid.

4. Ibid.

5. *Business Week*, op. cit., p. 130.

6. *U.S. News & World Report*, Jan. 30, 1967.

7. "The Dangerous World of Walt Rostow," *Look*, Dec. 12, 1967, p. 30.

8. Ibid., p. 27.

9. M. Stanton Evans, *The Politics of Surrender*, Devin-Adair, New York, 1966, p. 262.

10. Ibid., p. 252.

11. Ibid., p. 250

12. Schlesinger, op. cit., p. 488.

13. Ibid.

14. Theodore H. White, *The Making of the President 1964*, Atheneum Publishers, New York, 1965, p. 20.

15. Rostow on a roundtable discussion of the 1960 Pugwash Conference, WGBH-TV, Jan. 3, 1961.

16. New York *Times*, April 16, 1962, p. 1.

17. *Life*, Dec. 1, 1967, p. 87.

18. Schlesinger, op. cit., p. 394.

19. Ibid., p. 445.

20. Ibid.

CHAPTER X

1. David Sentner, New York *Journal-American*, Nov. 9, 1961.

2. Transcript of State Department Press Conference, Nov. 9, 1961.

3. Henry J. Taylor, New York *World-Telegram and Sun*, Nov. 17, 1961.

4. Ibid., Nov. 20, 1961.

5. Report, Senate Internal Security Subcommittee, Oct. 4, 1962, pp. 9–10.

6. "Cato" in *National Review*, Dec. 2, 1961.

CHAPTER XI

1. New York *Times* text of President Kennedy's press conference, Jan. 25, 1962.

2. New York *Times*, Jan. 25, 1962, p. 1.

3. New York *Herald-Tribune*, Jan. 25, 1962.

4. New York *Times,* op. cit.

5. Ibid.

6. Ibid.

7. Ibid.

8. Ibid.

9. Report, Senate Internal Security Subcommittee, 1962, pp. 197–198.

10. New York *Times,* op. cit.

11. Report, Senate Internal Security Subcommittee, 1962, p. 2.

12. Ibid., p. 104.

13. Ibid., p. 98.

14. Willard L. Beaulac, *Career Ambassador*, Macmillan, New York, 1951, p. 255.

15. Nathaniel Weyl, *Red Star Over Cuba*, Devin-Adair Co., New York, 1960, p. 35.

16. New York *Times,* Jan. 1, 1959.

17. Report, Senate Internal Security Subcommittee, 1962, op. cit., p. 160.

18. Ibid., pp. 120–121.

19. Ibid., p. 139.

20. Ibid., p. 200.

21. Ibid.

22. Ibid., p. 140.

23. Ibid., p. 128.

24. Ibid., p. 128.

25. *Washington World*, February 14, 1962.

CHAPTER XII

1. Frank J. Johnson, "The Case of Otto Otepka," *Nation's Security,* American Security Council, Dec. 30, 1963, p. 3.

2. Report, Senate Internal Security Subcommittee, 1962, p. 27.

3. 1962 Series, Part 4, Senate Internal Security Subcommittee Hearings on State Department Security, p. 387.

4. Ibid., pp. 384–385.

5. New York *Times*, April 16, 1962, p. 1.

6. Chicago *Sun-Times*, April 14, 1962.

7. Chicago *Sun-Times*, June 27, 1962.

8. Ibid.

9. *Congressional Record*, July 2, 1962.

CHAPTER XIII

1. Senate Internal Security Subcommittee Hearings, 1963–1965, Part 12, pp. 897–904.

2. Ibid. p. 897.

3. Ibid., Part 2, pp. 222–223.

4. Ibid., Part 3, p. 74.

5. Report by the Committee on Un-American Activities, 87th Congress, Aug. 13, 1962, pp. 3 and 4.

6. Ibid., p. 18.

7. Ibid.

8. Chicago Daily News Service, printed in the Washington *Post*, Aug. 13, 1963.

9. Ibid.

10. Senate Internal Security Subcommittee Hearings, 1963–1965, Part 6, p. 346.

CHAPTER XIV

1. Princeton University Year Book, 1938.

2. Princeton Guardian, May 9, 1937.

3. New York *Times*, April 1, 1965.

4. New York *Times*, Feb. 17, 1947.

5. *Harper's*, March 1959.

6. Schlesinger, op. cit., p. 462.

7. "What's Wrong With the State Department," pamphlet based on series of articles in the New Bedford (Massachusetts) *Standard-Times*, June 1962, p. 4.

8. Ibid.

9. Senate Internal Security Subcommittee, Otepka Hearings, 1963–65, Vol. 20, p. 1722.

10. Report, Senate Internal Security Subcommittee, 1952–53 Hearings on American Personnel in the U.N.

CHAPTER XV

1. Senate Internal Security Subcommittee, Otepka Hearings, 1963–65, Part 20, p. 1722.

2. DeWitt Copp and Marshall Peck, *Betrayal at the UN*, Devin-Adair, New York, 1963, p. 181.

3. New York *Times*, Nov. 18, 1956.

4. Copp and Peck, op. cit., p. 218.

5. Report, "The Bang-Jensen Case," Senate Internal Security Subcommittee, Sept. 14, 1961, p. 28.

6. Ibid.

7. Senate Internal Security Subcommittee, Otepka Hearings, 1963–65, Part 15, p. 1153.

8. Ibid., pp. 1149–50.

9. Ibid., pp. 1151–1231.

10. Ibid., p. 1172.

11. Ibid., pp. 1181–84.

CHAPTER XVI

1. Report, Senate Internal Security Subcommittee, Oct. 4, 1962, p. 47.

2. Ibid., p. 49.

3. Ibid.

4. Ibid., p. 57.

5. Ibid., p. 66.

6. Ibid., p. 91.

7. Ibid., p. 77.

8. Ibid.

9. Schlesinger, op. cit. p. 699.

10. Ibid., p. 700.

11. Ibid.

12. Ibid.

13. Jacqueline Hallowell, "Angola and Mozambique," booklet printed by the New Bedford *Standard-Times*, 1962, p. 1.

14. Schlesinger, op. cit., p. 798.

15. Ibid., p. 807.

16. "The Undercover War," *This Week* magazine, Sept. 4, 1966, pp. 12–13.

17. Ibid.

18. Oleg Penkovskiy, *The Penkovskiy Papers*, Doubleday & Co., New York, 1965.

CHAPTER XVII

1. Otepka Case, Senate Internal Security Subcommittee Hearings, 1963–65, Part 14, p. 1090.

2. Ibid., pp. 1091–92.

3. Ibid., pp. 1093–97.

4. Ibid., pp. 1098–99.

5. Ibid., p. 1138.

6. Ibid.

7. Ibid., pp. 1102–4.

8. Ibid., p. 1104.

9. Ibid., p. 1110.

10. Ibid., p. 1070.

11. Ibid., pp. 1111–12.

12. Ibid., p. 1085.

CHAPTER XVIII

1. Guy Richards, *Imperial Agent*, Devin-Adair Co., New York, 1966, p. 136.

2. Rebecca West, op. cit., p. 298.

3. *Chicago Tribune*, March 22, 1965.

4. Richards, op. cit., p. 129.

5. Ibid., p. 128.

6. Ibid., op. cit. p. 185

7. Ibid., p. 15.

8. Ibid.

9. Senate Internal Security Subcommittee, Otepka Hearings, 1963–65, Part 10, p. 621.

10. Ibid., p. 632.

11. Ibid., p. 699.

12. *Government Employees Exchange*, Jan. 10, 1968.

13. Hearings, House Committee on Un-American Activities, April 1, 1949.

14. *Government Employees Exchange*, op. cit.

15. *Wall Street Journal*, Feb. 14, 1967.

CHAPTER XIX

1. Report, Senate Internal Security Subcommittee, 1962, op. cit., p. 198.

CHAPTER XX

1. President Kennedy's State of the Union Address, 1961.

2. Senate Internal Security Subcommittee, Otepka Hearings, 1963–65, Part 4, p. 151.

3. Ibid., Parts 13, 15, 16, and 18.

4. Ibid., p. 161.

5. Ibid., Part 16, p. 1248.

6. Ibid., p. 1250.

7. Ibid., p. 1250.

8. Ibid.

9. Ibid., Part 13, p. 965.

10. Ibid., Part 15, pp. 1143–1151.

CHAPTER XXI

1. Senate Internal Security Subcommittee, Otepka Hearings, 1963–65, Part 3, pp. 80–81 and 125–127.

2. Ibid., Part 4, pp. 250–252.

3. Ibid., p. 215.

4. Ibid., Part 1, pp. 1–7.

5. Ibid., Part 15, p. 1152.

6. Ibid., p. 1167.

7. Ibid., Part 1, p. 8.

8. Ibid., Part 15, p. 1168.

9. Ibid., Part 11, p. 724.

CHAPTER XXII

1. Senate Internal Security Subcommittee, Otepka Hearings, 1963–65, Part 4, pp. 234–235.

2. Ibid., pp. 234 and 236.

3. Ibid., Part 20, p. 1656.

4. Ibid., Part 15, p. 1215.

CHAPTER XXIII

1. Senator McCarthy's comments on the Barnetts may be found in the *Congressional Record* of Aug. 9, 1951, p. 9707.

2. Hearings of Select Committee to Investigate Tax Exempt Foundations, House of Representatives, 82nd Congress, 1952, pp. 541–542.

3. David Sentner, Los Angeles *Herald-Examiner,* July 16, 1962.

4. *Congressional Record*, Sept. 11, 1962, pp. 17966–67.

Chapter XXIV

1. Senate Internal Security Subcommittee, Otepka Hearings, 1963–65, Part 3, p. 73.

2. Ibid., p. 77.

3. Ibid., p. 80.

4. Ibid., p. 81.

5. Ibid., Part 4, p. 166.

6. Senate Internal Security Subcommittee, Testimony of Seymour Janow, July 23, 1963, p. 5.

7. Senate Internal Security Subcommittee, Otepka Hearings, 1963–65, Part 6, p. 338.

8. Robert S. Allen and Paul Scott, Northern Virginia *Sun,* May 31, 1963.

Chapter XXVI

1. Dom Bonafede, New York Herald Tribune news service, as printed in the Los Angeles *Times,* April 19, 1965.

2. Report, Senate Internal Security Subcommittee, Dec. 15, 1967, Part III, p. 11.

3. Section 652, Title 5, United States Code.

4. 1968 Report, Senate Internal Security Subcommittee, Part I, p. 6.

5. Report, Senate Internal Security Subcommittee, Dec. 15, 1967, Part II, pp. 1-63.

Chapter XXVII

1. 1968 Report, Senate Internal Security Subcommittee, (dated Dec. 15,1967, Part IV), pp. 27–28.

2. Earl Voss, *Nuclear Ambush,* Henry Regnery Co., Chicago, 1963, p. 535.

3. Ibid.

4. Schlesinger, op. cit., p. 895.

5. Ibid., p. 896.

6. Ibid., p. 899.

7. Ibid., p. 907.

8. Ibid., p. 913.

Chapter XXVIII

1. 1968 Report, Senate Internal Security Subcommittee, Part I, pp. 33–34.

2. Chicago Tribune, September 29, 1963.

3. Ibid.

4. Senate Internal Security Subcommittee, Otepka Hearings, 1963–65, Part 3, p. 103.

5. Ibid. p. 104.

6. Ibid. p. 125.

Chapter XXIX

1. Chicago *Tribune*, Oct. 10, 1963.

2. Senate Internal Security Subcommittee, Otepka Hearings, 1963–65, Part 5, p. 266.

3. Church of the Holy Trinity v. United States, 143, U.S. 457.

Chapter XXX

1. UPI dispatch, Boston, Sept. 21, 1966.

2. 1968 Report, Senate Internal Security Subcommittee, Part II, p. 35.

3. Otepka Hearings, 1963–65, op. cit., Part 3, pp. 92–93.

4. 1968 Senate Subcommittee Report, op. cit., p. 57.

5. Ibid., pp. 41 and 44.

6. Ibid., pp. 50–51.

7. Ibid., p. 52.

8. Ibid., pp. 52–53.

9. Ibid., p. 59.

10. Ibid., p. 60.

11. Ibid.

12.. Chicago *Tribune*, Nov. 8, 1963.

13. Washington *Star*, Nov. 8, 1963.

14. New York *Times*, Nov. 10, 1963.

15. Richard Wilson column, Washington *Star,* Nov. 13, 1963.

16. Arthur Krock column, New York *Times,* Nov. 14, 1963.

17. David Lawrence column, as printed in Muncie (Indiana) *Evening Press,* Nov. 12, 1963.

18. Henry J. Taylor column, Nov. 15, 1963.

19. Holmes Alexander column, as printed in the *Maryland Monitor,* Oct. 17, 1963.

20. Ibid.

21. Richard Wilson column, Washington *Star,* Nov. 13, 1963.

22. Otepka Hearings, 1963–65, op. cit., Part 8, p. 493.

23. Ibid., p. 494.

24. Schlesinger, op. cit., pp. 435–436.

25. Ibid., p. 436.

CHAPTER XXXI

1. *Warren Commission Report,* Bantam Book edition, New York, 1964, p. 240.

2. Ibid., pp. 250–251.

3. Ibid., p. 258.

4. *Time,* Nov. 8, 1963.

5. William Manchester, *The Death of a President,* Harper & Row, New York, 1967, p. 278.

6. Stewart Alsop, "A Conversation with President Kennedy," *Saturday Evening Post,* Jan. 1, 1966.

7. Manchester, op. cit., p. 277.

CHAPTER XXXII

1. Allen-Scott Report, Chicago *Sunday American,* December 22, 1963.

2. Stewart Alsop, "Johnson Takes Over: The Untold Story," *Saturday Evening Post,* Feb. 15, 1964.

3. Ibid.

4. Chicago *Tribune,* March 14, 1965.

Chapter XXXIII

1. Guy Richards, New York *Journal-American,* March 20, 1964.

2. Senate Internal Security Subcommittee, Otepka Hearings, 1963–65, Part 8, p. 503.

3. Theodore White, op. cit., p. 338.

4. Ibid., p. 345 (paraphrased quotation).

5. Ibid., pp. 328–329.

6. Willard Edwards, Chicago *Tribune,* Nov. 15, 1964.

7. Chicago Tribune, Sept. 29, 1964.

8. Text of J. Edgar Hoover's report on Walter Jenkins, Oct. 23, 1964.

Chapter XXXIV

1. Willard Edwards, Chicago *Tribune,* Dec. 20, 1964.

2. Roger Winship Stuart, *Meet the Senators,* Macfadden-Bartell, New York, 1963, p. 49.

3. James Boyd, "The Tragedy of Thomas Dodd," *Saturday Evening Post,* Feb. 10, 1968.

4. Ibid.

5. Drew Pearson column, New York *Post,* May 26, 1967.

Chapter XXXV

1. Clark Mollenhoff, Des Moines *Register,* Aug. 6, 1964.

2. Senate Internal Security Subcommittee, Otepka Case Hearings, 1963–65, Part 5, pp. 294–95.

3. 1968 Report, Senate Internal Security Subcommittee, Part III, p. 87.

4. Ibid., p. 103.

5. Ibid., p. 107.

6. Ibid., p. 81.

7. Ibid., p. 82.

8. Ibid., Part I, p. 72.

9. Rowland Evans and Robert Novak, New York *Herald Tribune,* March 9, 1966.

10. Barnard. L. Collier, New York *Herald Tribune,* March 13, 1966.

11. New York *Herald Tribune,* March 11, 1966.

12. Carl T. Rowan, Washington *Star,* March 18, 1966.

13. Richard Harwood, Washington *Post,* May 15, 1966.

14. Ibid.

15. Willard Edwards, Chicago *Tribune,* Oct. 2, 1964.

16. Senate Internal Security Subcommittee, Otepka Hearings, 1963–65, Part 19, p. 1580.

17. UPI dispatch, Chicago *Tribune,* Aug. 5, 1965.

CHAPTER XXXVI

1. 1968 Report, Senate Internal Security Subcommittee, Part IV, p. 87.

2. Schlesinger, op. cit., p. 768.

3. Ibid.

4. William J. Gill, "The Strange Case of Otepka's Associates," American Security Council *Washington Report,* September 28, 1964 (WR 64–31).

5. 1968 Report, Senate Internal Security Subcommittee, Part IV, p. 91.

6. Willard Edwards, Chicago *Tribune,* Feb. 15, 1968.

CHAPTER XXXVII

1. 1968 Report, Senate Internal Security Subcommittee, Part II, p. 95.

2. Ibid., Part IV, p. 17.

3. New York *Times,* Oct. 2, 1966.

4. Milwaukee *Journal,* Oct. 5, 1966.

5. Washington *Post,* Oct. 2, 1966.

6. Associated Press story, as published in the Baltimore *Sun,* Oct. 2, 1966.

7. New York *Times,* Oct. 2, 1966.

8. *Time,* July 22, 1966.

Chapter XXXVIII

1. Joseph Alsop, New York *Herald Tribune*, Jan. 17, 1966.

2. Ibid.

3. S3388, introduced by Senator Eastland in the 2nd Session, 89th Congress.

Chapter XL

1. Associated Press dispatch, June 25, 1967.

2. David Dubinsky, speech before the ILGWU's 32nd convention, May 12, 1965.

Chapter XLI

1. UPI dispatch, Washington, Nov. 1, 1967.

2. Ibid.

3. Willard Edwards, Chicago *Tribune*, Sept. 19, 1967.

4. *Congressional Record*, Sept. 28, 1967.

5. Omaha *World-Herald*, Sept. 24, 1967.

6. Clark Mollenhoff, Minneapolis *Tribune*, Oct. 3, 1967.

7. Associated Press dispatch, Washington, Oct. 14, 1967.

8. Ibid.

9. *Congressional Record*, Oct. 19, 1967.

10. *U.S. News & World Report*, June 5, 1967.

11. "The Dangerous World of Walt Rostow," *Look*, Dec. 12, 1967

12. Washington *Post*, May 24, 1967.

13. "The Most Happy Fella in the White House," *Life*, Dec. 1, 1967.

14. *Look*, Dec. 12, 1967., op. cit.

15. *Congressional Record*, Nov. 22, 1967.

16. *The Changing Strategic Military Balance—U.S.A. vs. U.S.S.R.*, American Security Council-House Armed Services Committee, 1967, p. 11.

17. Eugene Lyons, *Workers' Paradise Lost*, Funk & Wagnalls, New York, 1967, Paperback Library Edition, p. 26.

18. Ibid., pp. 354–56.

CHAPTER XLII

1. Part I, "State Department Security 1963–65," Report of the Senate Internal Security Subcommittee released Jan. 7, 1968.

2. Baltimore *Sun*, Feb. 13, 1968.

3. "Background for Assassination," American Security Council *Washington Report*, March 16, 1964.

4. New York *Times*, December 12, 1967, Story on Supreme Court decision in the case of Eugene Frank Robel.

5. Associated Press dispatch, May 11, 1969.

6. United Press International dispatch, May 10, 1969.

7. Ibid.

CHAPTER XLIII

1. Washington *Post*, Oct. 14, 1968. (Report on Nixon television interview of Oct. 13 on WFAA-TV, Dallas.)

2. Willard Edwards column, Chicago *Tribune*, Oct. 5, 1968.

3. Chicago *Tribune*, Feb. 21, 1968.

CHAPTER XLIV

1. New York *Times* editorial, April 8, 1969.

2. Ibid.

3. Hearing on the Nomination of Otto F. Otepka, Subcommittee of the Senate Judiciary Committee, April 15, 1969.

4. Tim Wheeler, *Daily World*, April 16, 1969, p. 9.

5. Hearings on the Nomination of Otto F. Otepka, op. cit., Part 2, p. 125.

Index